INSIDERS' GUIDE® TO
PITTSBURGH

THIRD EDITION

JENN PHILLIPS, LORIANN HOFF OBERLIN, AND EVAN M. PATTAK

INSIDERS' GUIDE®

GUILFORD, CONNECTICUT
AN IMPRINT OF THE GLOBE PEQUOT PRESS

The prices and rates in this guidebook were confirmed at press time. We recommend, however, that you call establishments before traveling to obtain current information.

To buy books in quantity for corporate use or incentives, call **(800) 962–0973, ext. 4551,** or e-mail **premiums@GlobePequot.com.**

INSIDERS' GUIDE ®

Copyright © 2004, 2005 by Morris Book Publishing, LLC
A previous edition of this book was published by Falcon Publishing, Inc. in 2000.

Text design by LeAnna Weller Smith
Maps by XNR Productions, Inc © Morris Book Publishing, LLC

ISSN 1546-3133
ISBN-13: 978-0-7627-3507-5
ISBN-10: 0-7627-3507-4

Manufactured in the United States of America
Third Edition/Second Printing

Pittsburgh skyline. PHOTODISC

[Top] *Pittsburgh Steelers fans.* GREATER PITTSBURGH CONVENTION & VISITORS BUREAU
[Bottom] *Heinz Field, home to the Pittsburgh Steelers.* GREATER PITTSBURGH CONVENTION & VISITORS BUREAU

[Top] *Honus Wagner statue.* GREATER PITTSBURGH CONVENTION & VISITORS BUREAU
[Bottom] *PNC Park, home of the Pittsburgh Pirates.* GREATER PITTSBURGH CONVENTION & VISITORS BUREAU

Aerial view of Pittsburgh skyline. GREATER PITTSBURGH CONVENTION & VISITORS BUREAU

Fort Pitt Bridge. GREATER PITTSBURGH CONVENTION & VISITORS BUREAU

The Carnegie Museum of Art's Hall of Architecture. GREATER PITTSBURGH CONVENTION & VISITORS BUREAU

Phipps Conservatory and Botanical Gardens. GREATER PITTSBURGH CONVENTION & VISITORS BUREAU

Cathedral of Learning. GREATER PITTSBURGH CONVENTION & VISITORS BUREAU

PPG Place in the heart of downtown Pittsburgh. GREATER PITTSBURGH CONVENTION & VISITORS BUREAU

Oxford Center. GREATER PITTSBURGH CONVENTION & VISITORS BUREAU

Seventh Street Bridge. GREATER PITTSBURGH CONVENTION & VISITORS BUREAU

A charming Pittsburgh neighborhood. GREATER PITTSBURGH CONVENTION & VISITORS BUREAU

Agnes Katz Plaza in the cultural district. GREATER PITTSBURGH
CONVENTION & VISITORS BUREAU

Pittsburgh skyline. PHOTODISC

CONTENTS

CONTENTS

Directory of Maps

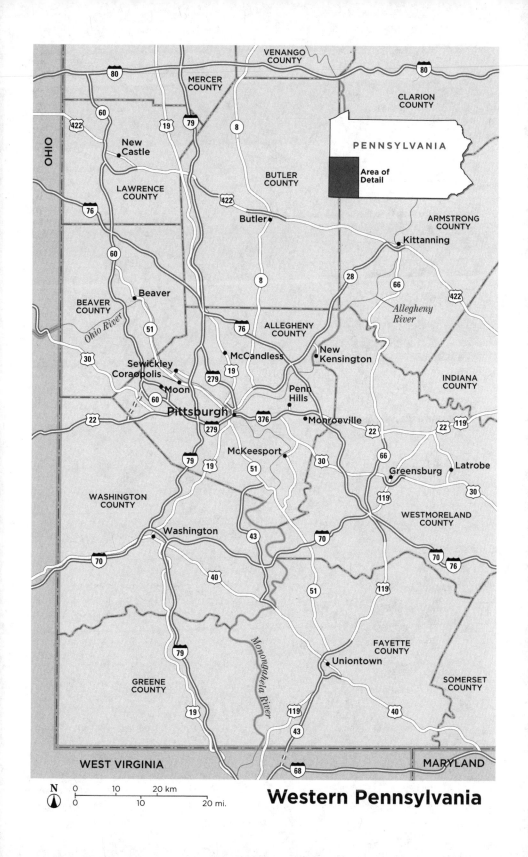

Western Pennsylvania

N

0   10   20 km
0   10   20 mi.

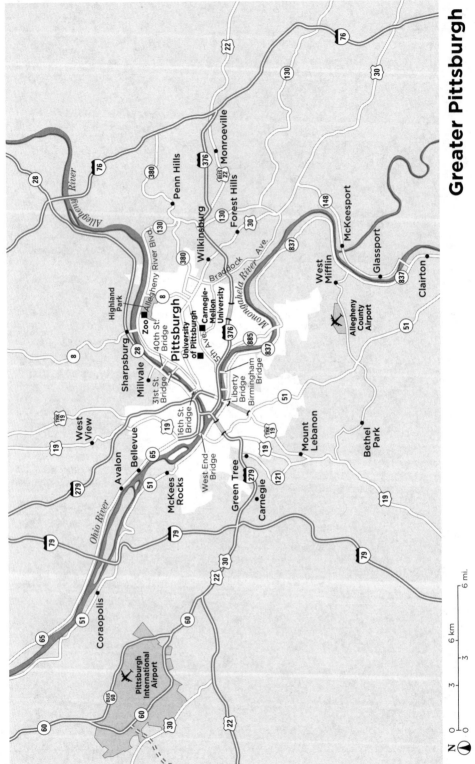

Greater Pittsburgh

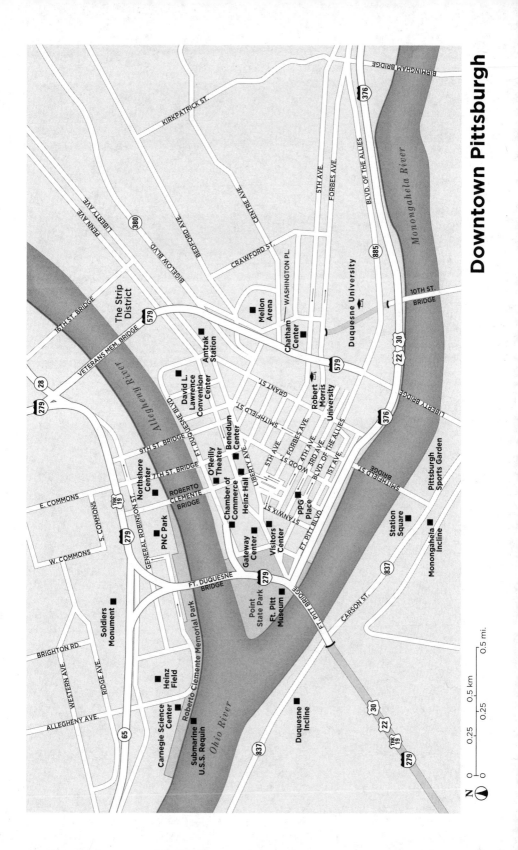

Downtown Pittsburgh

PREFACE

When you arrive in Pittsburgh, what sort of folk will you find here? Southwestern Pennsylvania is diverse enough that generalization about our residents can be tricky. Nevertheless, most people tote around an obsolete image of Pittsburghers that was forged in the furnaces of our steel mills. They envision us as a rough-hewn breed, square-shouldered, lantern-jawed men toughened by backbreaking labor in sweltering mills and subterranean mines.

This hardly dovetails with the reality of modern Pittsburgh, which you'll discover to be a sophisticated, diverse city with an economy driven by service and software industries and, to a lesser extent, manufacturing. Nor does this dated image allow for the increasingly important roles of women and minorities in the local economy and society. It's true that the "old boys" network that ran the mills and mines was a tad slow to provide opportunities for women and minorities. The dominance of steel and coal, however, is part of our history, fuller participation of women and minorities a thing of the present.

Shopworn as that traditional image of our residents may be, as most stereotypes, it still can tell us revealing things about Pittsburghers. First, it speaks of our friendliness, probably our defining characteristic. We are, after all, a people who built America's greatest industrial center, watched it collapse, then rolled up our sleeves and constructed a new, multifaceted economy. In accomplishing all that, we were a cradle of the American labor movement. We're veterans of collective action and the cooperative spirit it requires.

Thus, Pittsburghers are above all a friendly, unpretentious people. Doesn't matter who you are or where you're from. Yinz—our peculiar version of the second person plural—will be accepted here. Nor is there a limit to our friendliness. The spirit of volunteerism is alive and well in Southwestern Pennsylvania, among individuals and corporations. We've developed a far-reaching network of civic and charitable organizations to keep our residents from falling through the cracks. We'll give you the shirts off our backs—skin, too, if that would help.

This uncommon friendliness, however, has its down side—a relentless focus on neighborhoods and the local scene. Our neighborhoods are charming, some even unique, and a considerable strength of our region. We are devoted to them. Allegheny County alone boasts 130 municipalities, while the region is carved into 100 school districts. Think of the duplicative costs for elections, for garbage collection, for street maintenance, for a hundred other services. Whatever its costs, we cherish our parochialism. Pity the poor politician who runs on a platform of municipal consolidation. He'll be tarred with the dreaded "M" word—Metropolitanism—and hooted back to the murky obscurity that produced him.

Those who relocate to this region become keenly sensitive to this duality. They are overwhelmed with Welcome Wagons of friendliness but never quite accepted as natives. Michelle Madoff, a native Canadian who for years was a Pittsburgh city councilwoman and one of our most prominent and high-profile public officials, never ceased to wonder at our attitude. "I've been here for 35 years," she was wont to say, "and I'm still not a Pittsburgher."

Can't be helped, Councilwoman. If you're not from this city, you're not of this city.

This engaging friendliness coupled with a tendency toward the insular marks our culture as well. We are a region of stunning and diverse cultural opportunities. These include Carnegie Museums of Pittsburgh, the Andy Warhol Museum, the Pittsburgh Symphony—world-class institutions each. Our Downtown boasts five halls for the performing arts, including two glittering temples, Heinz Hall and the Benedum Center for the Performing Arts. Our colleges and universities offer community theater, and we boast highly regarded opera and ballet companies. The region is rich in art galleries, well-spaced through many communities.

Nevertheless, the arts community has to put a great deal of effort into reminding us Pittsburghers of the presence of these riches. That's because we're likely to set ourselves on a particular track—one that often involves a path between neighborhood, workplace, and favorite shopping mecca—and forget all else.

Finally, while the typical image of Pittsburghers is accurate in some regards, off the mark in others, perhaps the most glaring omission is that it doesn't begin to acknowledge our rich and ready sense of humor. Yes, we tend to be traditional; our focus tends to be local. We know it, though, and we're comfortable with it. If you want to poke fun at our parochialism and odd turns of phrase, go right ahead—we'll laugh along with you.

ACKNOWLEDGMENTS

It's been a pleasure to have the opportunity to work on the *Insiders' Guide to Pittsburgh,* and I want to thank my editors. I love Pittsburgh, and authoring this guidebook has served to reinforce all the reasons why.

In the early spring in Pittsburgh, especially when we have some unseasonably warm days in February or March, it's common to find the doors of shops and homes propped open and a lot of people standing around outside smiling broadly. Authoring this book involves a significant amount of research, and what I've found in this case—and in my other work as a writer in the Greater Pittsburgh area—is that office doors and hearts here are typically just as open as those we fling wide in early spring.

I would especially like to thank Beth Geisler at the Greater Pittsburgh Convention and Visitors Bureau, as well as Ellen Roth, Ph.D., president of Getting to the Point, a relocation services company. Beth made it very easy for me to feel confident that I'd included all the best attractions in our area, through her comprehensive knowledge of the region and the copious literature she provided. I encourage all visitors to get to the center downtown. The GPCVB really knows its stuff!

Ellen, who was honored by the governor as one the 50 top women in business in the state, was simply delightful to talk with, and she generously spent time on the phone with me, which gave me a very good feel for what it means to relocate to Pittsburgh, especially if one is doing so as a "trailing spouse," without the ready-made community and commitments a new job provides. This new understanding proved very helpful to me as I added material to the book for newcomers to our area.

From another standpoint, I owe thanks and acknowledgment to co-authors on the first edition of this book, Loriann Hoff Oberlin and Evan Pattak. No matter whose names appear on the spine of this book in coming years, the *Insiders' Guide* will always owe much to them. So much of the original research here is theirs—and finely done it is.

On the second edition, my good friend and colleague Tanya Reyes assisted me by making the thousands of phone calls involved in fact checking. And during some difficult life circumstances that occurred while I was completing the book, my colleague David Doorley stepped in with great efficaciousness and helped me add good, new entries to several chapters. Thank you, thank you, David! I was also fortunate to be able to call on another local writer, Michael Dongilli, to write the sidebar in Spectator Sports on our new stadiums, because only a true, blue (or should that be gold?) sports fan could do these terrific new facilities justice.

And finally, I'd like to thank all the people—friends, family, business associates, folks I've just run into—who've expressed enthusiasm about the *Insiders' Guide to Pittsburgh* and my completion of the book you now hold in your hands.

—Jenn Phillips

HOW TO USE THIS BOOK

Many city guides languish on living-room tables. It is our fondest hope that the *Insiders' Guide to Pittsburgh* isn't one of them.

Rather, our purpose in producing this book is to provide you with the most complete, most dependable resource about Pittsburgh. We hope that you consult it often, that it will become your best source of information about the city, its people, and its amenities. While our guide does not strive to be exhaustive—it does not include every restaurant or hotel in the region, for example—we've tried to provide the best and the brightest of Pittsburgh.

We've researched and organized the guide so that it will serve as a valuable resource about Pittsburgh for those newly relocating to the city as well as for tourists and visitors. But we also believe that even longtime residents will find this an indispensable tool. If you're one of those veteran Pittsburghers, don't be embarrassed to refer to this book again and again. As we found out as we wrote this book, there is much more to this town than even natives could know.

This guide includes useful information about restaurants, accommodations, shopping, nightlife, festivals, spectator sports, recreation, attractions, and day trips. We also have compiled key information that should help you navigate the daily course of life. We've included a chapter about elementary and secondary schools, as well as a chapter about Pittsburgh's colleges and universities. A chapter details many of Pittsburgh's most interesting neighborhoods, while others outline services and opportunities for kids and senior citizens.

You'll also find chapters about art, architecture, health care, transportation, golf, media, and worship. In some cases, a Pittsburgh amenity or feature would fit comfortably in more than one chapter. For example, a description of the Pittsburgh Zoo would be at home in both the Kidstuff and Attractions chapters. In such cases, a full write-up is provided in one chapter, with a shorter description—as well as a reference to the primary coverage—in the second chapter.

Any definition of Pittsburgh is bound to be somewhat arbitrary. Most would agree that Pittsburgh does not end with the city's limits, but just what should be included? This guide goes beyond the city and Allegheny County to include Armstrong and Butler Counties to the north, Westmoreland County to the east, parts of Washington County to the south, and Beaver County to the west.

In determining our geographic definition of Pittsburgh, we imagined you asking the question, "what shall we do today?" By including the additional counties, we've tried to provide as many answers to that question as possible.

To help you locate information quickly, we've followed a specific geographic rotation—Downtown, North, East, South, West—in all chapters where such organization is appropriate. In other chapters, material is organized in ways that make the most sense for readers. Where we've strayed from the geographic breakdown, we'll tell you in the chapter introduction.

In the Day Trips chapter, for example, we've transcended the boundaries of Pittsburgh to include destinations within a three-hour drive of the city. In researching Senior Scene, we noticed that many municipal services are restricted to residents of the offering municipalities. Therefore, we have presented those services by county and reverted to standard organization for unrestricted services and opportunities.

In all cases, you can quickly determine if an entity or service is included by checking the comprehensive index in the back of the book.

You'll find several special features that have been developed for your convenience and enjoyment. Frequently called phone numbers and sources of additional information are highlighted in gray boxes. New to town and need a physician? You'll find the phone numbers for physician referral agencies in the Health Care chapter.

We've captured many interesting quick-hitters about Pittsburgh; these "Insiders' Tips" (indicated by ⓘ) are spaced throughout the book. You'll also find "Close-ups"—feature stories about the city, its residents, characteristics, and peculiarities. Both the "Tips" and "Close-ups" will pique your interest in Pittsburgh.

In the Restaurants and Accommodations chapters, each entry includes from one to four dollar signs to give you some idea of the price of a meal or an overnight stay. Prices represent comparisons within the Pittsburgh market only. Thus, a restaurant listed with "$$$$" would be among Pittsburgh's more expensive establishments, but the price should not be compared to those of restaurants in other cities.

Finally, a word about area codes. Phone numbers, of course, are an important feature of this guide, but the challenge of compiling accurate phone numbers was compounded by the introduction of the 724 area code in February 1997 to complement Pittsburgh's 412 area code. Remember that if you're dialing anywhere outside your area code—even if it's only across town—you'll need to dial 1 and the area code before the seven-digit phone number.

We hope you enjoy the *Insiders' Guide to Pittsburgh* and use it often. One of the recurring themes of the guide is the helpfulness and neighborliness of Pittsburgh residents. Being neighborly Pittsburgh residents ourselves, we may drop in on you one day. It's okay if we find this guide on your coffee table . . . so long as the book is well-thumbed.

AREA OVERVIEW

C arved out of hilltops, nestled into valleys, and separated by the rivers, this region we call Greater Pittsburgh is a place people eagerly discover. In years gone by, if you told friends of an upcoming visit to Pittsburgh, they offered their immediate condolences. Images of the steel city translated into perceptions of smoke, soot, grime, and grunge.

The industrial age, sparked by the War of 1812, saw Pittsburgh capitalize on its bituminous coal resources. Mining, coupled with iron, steel, and glass production, flourished, with three convenient rivers to distribute the finished products to the rest of the country. With all that industry, it's no wonder Pittsburgh was called the Smoky City.

Early morning streets were darkened, and building exteriors were blanketed with the filthy remnants of heavy industry. In 1941, Pittsburgh had a higher rate of pneumonia than any other U.S. city. Pittsburgh pride and partnership took exception to the notion that it was simply a dirty city, knowing that if outsiders peered beneath the surface, they'd find a region with deep roots, bursting with life, strong traditions, positive aesthetic properties, and so much potential that it's still being tapped today. Determination to transform the old Pittsburgh into the new paid off in ways even the best urban planners could not have predicted.

The city's first renaissance was initiated in the 1950s, shortly after World War II, as then-mayor David L. Lawrence began a campaign called "Smoke Must Go." Railroad and shipping companies converted from coal-fired to diesel engines, and the steel and coal industries responded in kind with better technologies for eliminating airborne pollutants. Residents even switched from coal furnaces to much cleaner oil, electric, or natural gas.

That was just the first transformation. Renaissance II followed in the 1980s, under the tenure of the late Mayor Richard S. Caliguiri. Old buildings were razed and more modern towering structures were welcomed to the city skyline. This reformation occurred not only in Pittsburgh and in Allegheny County, but also in outlying towns where mills and factories had forged the foundation of many Western Pennsylvania communities. Areas such as Beaver, Butler, Armstrong, Westmoreland, and Washington Counties had their share of coal mines, steel mills, and industrial sites.

When the wrecking ball demolished the last two blast furnaces at the Jones & Laughlin steel mill in the early 1980s, much of the region's industrial strength crumbled with them, as did thousands of jobs. Workers who knew everything about blast furnaces and organized labor knew little of service industries, re-engineering, and how their lives would be affected by Pittsburgh's continuing renaissance.

One thing, however, sets Pittsburgh apart from its counterpart cities—the people who call it home. They are strong, proud, and particularly friendly, even amid adversity.

PITTSBURGH'S PERSONALITY

Pittsburghers stay put. It's not that we think there is no other comfortable place to live, it's just that we value our roots and traditions, our familiar routines, and even our minor frustrations. The occasional complaints about bridge repairs or tunnel traffic along the parkways are understandable, but take away the gorgeous view as we exit the Fort Pitt Tunnel entering the city, and we'd really have something to

Pittsburgh Vital Statistics

Founded: 1758

Incorporated: 1816

Size: 55.5 square miles

Elevation: 1,223 feet

Population:
City of Pittsburgh (2002): 327,898
Allegheny County (2002): 1,261,303

Pittsburgh mayor: Tom Murphy

Pennsylvania governor: Ed Rendell

Airport: Pittsburgh International Airport

Average temperatures:
July: 82.5° F
January: 20.8° F

Average yearly precipitation: 36 inches

Colleges and universities: 29 in Western Pennsylvania, including the University of Pittsburgh, Duquesne University, Carnegie Mellon University, Robert Morris University

Daily newspapers: *Pittsburgh Post-Gazette, Pittsburgh Tribune-Review*

Radio stations: 12 AM, 20 FM

Television stations: 11

Driving laws: Unrestricted driver's license at age 18; junior driver's license (restricted) at 16; maximum speed limit 65 mph; seat belts mandatory for driver and all front-seat passengers.

Famous Pittsburghers: Christina Aguilera, Rachel Carson, Perry Como, Bill Cullen, John Davidson, Scott Glenn, Martha Graham, Lena Horne, Michael Keaton, Gene Kelly, Oscar Levant, Andrew Mellon, Adolphe Menjou, William Powell, Fred Rogers, David O. Selznick, James Simon, Gertrude Stein, Joseph Wambaugh, Andy Warhol, August Wilson.

Important dates in history:
1754: Captain William Trent begins construction of Fort Prince George for Virginia. French and Indians capture the fort soon thereafter.
1758: Brig. Gen. John Forbes in charge of an expedition to reclaim the fort, now known as Fort Duquesne. The French desert the fort, and Forbes names his conquest "Pittsburgh" in honor of British leader William Pitt.
1787: Pennsylvania charters the Pittsburgh Academy, later to become the University of Pittsburgh.
1790: The first U.S. Census shows Pittsburgh with a population of 376, while Allegheny County has 10,309 citizens.
1816: Pittsburgh is incorporated as a city.
1845: The Great Fire destroys 56 acres and 1,000 buildings in the heart of the city. Among the landmarks burned: Monongahela House, Bank of Pittsburgh, Western University, and the Monongahela Bridge.

1848: Andrew Carnegie, age 13, arrives from Scotland.

1856: Pittsburgh hosts the first Republican National Convention.

1858: The Sons of Vulcan, an association of iron puddlers and boilers and a predecessor to labor unions, is formed in Pittsburgh.

1859: Edwin I. Drake strikes oil in Titusville, an hour and a half northeast of Pittsburgh, marking the beginning of the U.S. petroleum industry.

1869: The first H. J. Heinz plant opens in Sharpsburg, just north of Pittsburgh.

1870: Mellon and Sons opens its banking business on Smithfield Street. Also, Monongahela Incline opens.

1880: Immigrants from southeastern Europe begin arriving in large numbers.

1886: George Westinghouse forms the Westinghouse Electric Co. Also formed in Pittsburgh is the Pittsburgh Reduction Co., later to become the Aluminum Company of America or Alcoa.

1892: Pittsburgh's National League baseball team becomes known as the pirates for stealing a player from the Brooklyn Dodgers.

1905: The world's first all-motion picture theater, the Nickelodeon, opens in Pittsburgh.

1910: Robert L. Vann publishes the Pittsburgh Courier, one of the nation's finest black newspapers.

1950s: Renaissance I helps Pittsburgh begin its transformation into a modern city. Among the changes: reclamation of the point downtown.

1953: Jonas Salk announces success with the first polio vaccine.

1974: Point State Park is officially dedicated with the completion of the fountain.

1980s: Renaissance II revitalizes downtown yet again, with a new subway, convention center, and several prominent buildings on the city's skyline.

Greater Pittsburgh Convention & Visitors Bureau:
> Regional Enterprise Tower
> 425 Sixth Avenue, Pittsburgh, PA 15219

Tourism information line: (800) 366-0093

complain about. Sure, some neighborhoods have more parking problems than others, particularly in the winter, but as for the seasons, we revel in all four.

The Pittsburgh climate is not particularly harsh. Some winters we've been hard hit by snow and summers have occasionally been real scorchers, but by national standards, the region doesn't stand out weather-wise. A Pittsburgher's only concern might be springtime flooding and a few too many rainy or overcast days. Such is our weather.

If it's a chilly day, you might see us skating in Schenley Park, and on a cold winter's eve it's a hockey night in Pittsburgh with fans packing the Mellon Arena to watch our Penguins. Spring urges us out among friends, visiting neighborhood parks, taking easy day trips, and, of course, heading to the stadium to root for the Bucs. In summer, the big amusement parks open—Kennywood, Idlewild, and Sandcastle. Office workers take their lunches outdoors and enjoy the Three Rivers Arts Festival in conjunction with their meals. And who could forget Fourth of July fireworks at the Point or the Three Rivers Regatta each August? (See our Annual Events chapter for more detailed descriptions of these popular events.)

As the leaves turn color, it's once again time for those glorious weekend getaways. We'll drive a distance just to pick our own pumpkin out of a patch on an outlying farm. In autumn, we're often back to school, cheering on our Steelers, taking in the fall flower show at Phipps Conservatory, and revisiting and enjoying a vast array of other indoor attractions.

Having such splendid seasons adds to Pittsburgh's appeal. It's no wonder that our pleasant city has often served as the on-screen double for much larger New York City. Film crews have camped out at Pittsburgh landmarks throughout the decades to make such films as *Flashdance* and *Hoffa,* as well as more recent cinema picks such as *Striking Distance, Diabolique, Silence of the Lambs,* and *Inspector Gadget.*

IT'S A 'BURGH THING

Just as the South has its drawl and New England its accent, Pittsburgh has its own dialect (see this chapter's Close-up). Beyond the spoken word, many other items foster familiarity among the locals. You haven't eaten deli fare unless you've actually experienced the fries and slaw inside the sandwich, with Heinz ketchup of course. People all over the world enjoy ham sandwiches, but ours are chipped-chopped. Pittsburghers do take their food seriously. While many ethnic groups enjoy special cuisines and dishes, there's a certain kind of preparation that goes into native pierogies, kielbasa, stuffed cabbages, and Iron City Beer. Ice cream is standard, but Klondike Bars can't be beat. This, friends, is only a sampling of what's on the menu (see the Restaurants chapter to whet your appetite even more).

FAMOUS FACES

If you feel you've already experienced Pittsburgh's personality, it could be a direct result of a famous Pittsburgher. Indeed, this city has served as hometown for more than just Andrew Carnegie and H. J. Heinz, names easily associated with Pittsburgh. Did you know that Arnold Palmer grew up in Latrobe, not far from the origin of Mr. Rogers? The famous golfer still has a car dealership in Westmoreland County.

Other natives include actress Shirley Jones, artist Andy Warhol (whose surname was originally Warhola), playwright August Wilson, composer Stephen Foster, and actor Michael Keaton, who has returned home to make box-office hits such as *Gung Ho.*

Television producer Steven Bochco attended Carnegie Mellon University, and novelist Michael Chabon hit it big with *Mysteries of Pittsburgh,* inspired during his stint as an undergraduate student at the University of Pittsburgh. Chabon went on to write *Wonder Boys,* the movie version of which was filmed here as well.

Although it's technically outside our coverage area, we must point out that Jimmy Stewart was born and raised in Indiana, Pennsylvania, where his father held on to the family hardware store just in case Jimmy's film career didn't pan out. Well, Jimmy didn't need that contingency plan!

Jim Delligatti, a McDonald's franchisee in Western Pennsylvania, introduced the ingredients from his special sauce to a sesame seed bun, creating a sandwich better known today as the Big Mac. Other drive-through chains served double-decker burgers, and Delligatti wanted his creation to be big, so in 1967 the Big Mac was introduced for 49 cents. It took several improvements and lots of fun promotions to get to the Big Mac as we know it today.

In a town known for the industrial strength of men, women have made their marks. Among them are Nellie Bly, the famous newspaper reporter; Rachel Carson, a local biologist who took on the environmental movement; and Mary Cassatt, an artist who later found fame in France as the leading female impressionist painter.

Finally, just as appreciated is Mr. Yuk. That's right; the widely recognized safety symbol used to warn children away from dangerous substances was created at Pittsburgh's Children's Hospital.

ECONOMIC INDICATORS

As we've already mentioned, Pittsburgh's economic infrastructure has been transformed. Some companies and conglomerates, including Mellon Bank, USAirways, Pittsburgh National Bank, the University of Pittsburgh, and the University of Pittsburgh Medical Center (to name only a few)—the powerhouses of the local economy in decades past—continue to provide jobs for area residents. Some companies have, however, reduced their work forces during the years in an effort to stay competitive. U.S. Steel, now known as USX Corporation, may have laid off steel workers, but it continues to be one of the area's major employers as it has moved into oil and gas resources, real estate, transportation, and utility subsidiaries.

Though Westinghouse had its financial struggles throughout the '80s and '90s, becoming CBS and selling off different divisions, the Westinghouse name still exists. The nuclear business remains in Monroeville under American/British ownership that's once again growing the company.

Growth and change bring new partners to the economic front. Innovative players like the former FORE Systems (now known as Marconi Communications), the Pittsburgh Technology Center, and the National Robotics Engineering Consortium add to the region's economic vitality. Small business and entrepreneurship abound here as well. One key word describing the area's employment and economic future would be diversification,

as this region continues to be developed to its full potential.

Already a convenient airport from which business travelers can reach most other U.S. cities with only a two-hour flight, Pittsburgh International is built to accommodate more air carriers adding even more routes, destinations, and accessibility. The newly expanded David L. Lawrence Convention Center opened in fall 2003; 2001 saw the opening of Heinz Field, the city's new football stadium, as well as the opening of PNC Park, which replaced Three Rivers Stadium as the home of the Pittsburgh Pirates. Robert Morris University has announced plans to open a new, 7,000-seat football stadium and athletic facility by September 2005. Several shopping districts and malls in the Pittsburgh area have been opened or renovated since 1999.

According to a recent survey by William M. Mercer, a San Francisco–based consulting firm, Pittsburgh is the 17th cleanest city in the world. The ranking is based on the level of air quality and the efficiency of waste disposal and sewage systems.

NAVIGATING NEIGHBORHOODS

Within the city limits, our neighborhoods have names you'll hear on newscasts and in conversation. Some are easily definable, like Polish Hill, founded by Polish immigrants. From imbibing various beers and tasting the sauerbraten and schnitzel, you'd rightly guess that the influences at the Priory and nearby Penn Brewery on the city's North Side were of German descent. The Mexican War Streets neighborhood, however, doesn't get its name from Mexican Americans who live there— in fact, few do. The streets were named after Mexican battles and generals.

CLOSE-UP

Talkin' Pittsburgh

While traveling, you've probably heard many unique versions of the English language, but if you had a college roommate from Western Pennsylvania, or it you've spent some time here yourself, then you know the version of English to which we refer. For the uninitiated, we call it Pittsburghese.

Indeed, not all inhabitants reflect their Pittsburgh origin when they speak. Many disdain the dialect. Others, however, epitomize the vernacular.

Take the following fictitious conversation, for example:

"Jeet jet?"

"Nah, yunz gonna worsh yer hans?"

"Sure. I was just aht at the Jynt Igl. Brought us some jumbo, chipped-chopped ham, a couple of Klondikes—oh, and I stopped Dahntahn for an Arn."

"Then we better redd off this table. The Stillers game starts at one. Ats what the PG says."

And so it is—Pittsburghese. In our own defense, it's not that we Pittsburghers lack the knowledge of correct speech. It's merely that we're so excited, we can't wait to share what we have to say!

Slurred speech and shortened words aside, Pittsburghese bonds many of us. Above all else, we've learned to laugh at our native dialect. Witness the gift books created: Sam McCool's *New Pittsburghese*, Eric Schuman's *Are You A Real Pittsburgher?*, and *The Tongue-in-Cheek Guide to Pittsburgh*—written as much for our own humor as an out-of-towner's guide.

Here's a sampling of what's in store:

Ahia	state to the west of Pennsylvania that others spell with an O and an o
aht	out
Arn	short for Iron City Beer
Cahr Pahr	Cowher Power (it's a football thing!)
Chipped-chopped ham	our form of lunchmeat or deli ham
crick	creek, as in a small body of water
Cleveland	the butt of many a Pittsburgher's jokes
Dahntahn	Downtown
dill	no, not a pickle, but a deal

You'll soon associate Squirrel Hill with the foundations of Pittsburgh's Jewish community, the Hill District with the African-American community, and Shadyside with either old money or the new and trendy. The South Side (along the flats and slopes) maintains much of its Eastern European heritage, while Bloomfield revels in its Italian traditions. Nearby Lawrenceville is a blend of Italian, Irish, and Polish pride. You'll

dittent	did not
gumbans	elastic fasteners like rubber bands
high hills	not necessarily referring to mountain views, but a description of women's' footwear
in regards to	a wordy expression that sounds a whole lot more impressive than it ever is
jeet jet?	An interrogatory meaning "did you eat yet?"
Jynt Igl	Giant Eagle, as in a supermarket, not a bird
Jumbo	not a synonym for large, but merely bologna
Klondike	popular ice-cream treats savored over the decades
Mon	short for Monongahela (well, hey, would you want to remember that spelling?)
needs	shortened form of "needs to be"
Parkway	trust us, this isn't where you park (unless you're driving at rush hour!)
PG	abbreviated nickname of *The Post-Gazette*
The Point	Point State Park (you know, where the fountain flows)
pop	carbonated beverage most of America calls "soda"
Presby	short for Presbyterian University Hospital
redd up	to clean, tidy, or make better than it is
Sahside	South Side
'Sliberty	East Liberty
spicket	the tap where water flows from
The Strip	no, not exactly a turn on, unless it's a Saturday morning and you're hot after fresh produce
Super Mario	not a video game, but truly our hockey hero who saved the team once by performance, again by owning it
The T	well, of course it follows "S," but in our town, it's the subway
whole 'nother	another whole item
worsh	to wash
Yock	the Youghiogheny river (try spelling that one, too!)
yunz	all of you, or more literally, "you ones"

quickly come to associate Oakland with top universities, but others know it as home. As you'll read in our History chapter, many German families still reside on the city's North Side. And as Pittsburgh has attracted very learned engineers, doctors, and other professionals, many of the surrounding suburbs have become much more multicultural than they were half a century ago.

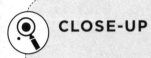

In the Pink

There've been several times since I moved to Pittsburgh in 1989 that I've thought about leaving. Maybe I'd seen all there was to see, maybe it would be easier to meet someone in New York or on the West Coast . . .

Each time I've had these longings, I've found Pittsburgh more than adequate. There's much to see and do here—one certainly never needs to fear boredom. Similarly, Pittsburgh's cultures and subcultures, its professional and social circles are lovely and very layered. The attractive cost of living well draws people from other major cities throughout the country, and our colleges, universities, and certain career opportunities, such as those in medicine, actually attract people from all over the world. And there are some good people who were just plain born here, too.

What those of us who are lesbian, gay, bisexual, or transgendered (LGBT) will find here, then, is diversity, with the opportunity to meet new friends and build relationships with other LGBT people if we actively seek it. It is also quite possible, on the other hand, to remain in the closet in Pittsburgh, or to feel lonely and isolated, if one doesn't know how to go about accessing the culture.

One good place to start getting involved is the GLCC, or Gay and Lesbian Community Center, (412) 422-0114, located at 5808 Forward Avenue in Squirrel Hill, right off the Parkway East exit by that name. The GLCC has operated an all-volunteer, informational hotline since the 1970s, and the center offers a good Web site (www.glccpgh.org) and newsletter, too. Many types of groups meet there, some frankly social in mission, like the Pittsburgh Potluck Womyn, and others oriented around causes or activities, such as the Gertrude Stein Political Club and the Pittsburgh International Lesbian and Gay Film Festival (www.pilgff.org), which celebrates its 20th year in 2005. In addition the GLCC sponsors Pridefest and the Pride Parade annually in June, as well as other cultural and social events throughout the year, including dances and arts events. There's also a nice lending library at the GLCC. You'll find drop-in hours on weeknights and Saturday afternoons, when the phone line is staffed, and the space is cozy enough to feel good in just sitting around reading a book or magazine.

If you can't find something to do when you're browsing the community calendar posted on the GLCC's Web site, or if you need tickets for just about anything, call or drop by A Pleasant Present in Squirrel Hill (412-421-7104 or www.apleasantpresent.com). The owner of this well-stocked card and gift store, Michael, and his staff can tell you what's going on for sure. For more on the presents-to-be at A Pleasant Present, see the entry in our Shopping chapter.

Another good place to start is TNL, Thursday Night Live, (412) 363-5TNL, a networking organization for professionals. TNL events usually revolve around food and drink—dinner at local restaurants, mixers at upscale bars, for example. Recently the group stepped beyond this and partnered with Community College of Allegheny to offer an annual series of noncredit courses taught by and designed for the LGBT community. Some popular topics last year included wine-tasting, ballroom dancing, legal issues, and the basics of buying a home.

Speaking of which, where to live in Pittsburgh? Almost anywhere is the answer. We passed antidiscrimination laws here more than ten years ago that apply to both housing and employment. You'll find rainbow flags flying in all kinds of places. Some especially good bets for friendliness and openness in the city are Shadyside, the Mexican War Streets, Squirrel Hill, Regent Square, and Highland Park.

One volunteer organization, GLENDA, or the Gay and Lesbian Neighborhood Development Association, devotes itself to matching volunteers for a day with other organizations, like the Food Bank, for example. So we help alongside people who might not otherwise interact with LGBT people. Seems a fitting strategy for the town where Fred Rogers' "Won't you be my neighbor?" got its start.

Likewise, in terms of employment, Pittsburgh is also relatively friendly. While employers are not required, for example, to offer same-sex-partner health benefits, some do, and all are required to treat diverse employees equally and respectfully.

You'll also find there are good resources in Pittsburgh. The GLCC puts together a free telephone directory called "Pride Direct" that lists LGBT-owned and friendly businesses and organizations, so you should call and ask for a copy. Some helping organizations

you might want to know about are the Pittsburgh AIDS Task Force (www.patf.org, 412-242-2500); Persad, at 32 years old one of the oldest centers devoted to LGBT mental health in the United States (www.persadcenter.org, 412-441-9786); Shepherd Wellness Community, an HIV/AIDS service organization (www.swconline.org, 412-683-4477); and PAAR (Pittsburgh Action Against Rape), which, like Persad, offers counseling services that are aware of and conversant in issues often affecting LGBT individuals (www.paar.net, 412-431-5665). PAAR also sponsors a 24-hour rape crisis hotline, (866) END-RAPE. Most local colleges sponsor organizations related to LGBT life, among the most notable Safezone/Soho at Carnegie Mellon, which includes faculty and staff who self-identify as "allies"; TransPitt at the University of Pittsburgh, which serves the transgendered/transsexual community; and Sayso at Chatham College, formerly a lesbian-centered group, which has expanded its mission to include all Chatham women and focuses on healthy sexual life, including assertive boundary setting.

Some of these same organizations sponsor fundraisers that offer social and volunteer opportunities as well. For example, each spring, the Task Force sponsors Art for AIDS, a wonderful auction of work by local artists, and in the summer, the AIDS walk. For outright entertainment in Pittsburgh, don't miss the film festival held each fall, featuring the best, new independent films made by LGBT artists (www.pilgff.org). You'll want to know that we were among the first to see *Priscilla, Queen of the Desert; Bound;*

and *Chicago!* You'll also want to make sure to attend performances of the Renaissance City Women's and Men's choirs (www.rccpittsburgh.org), which reach out to our community and the general public in song. All year-round, you'll find certain bars and neighborhood hangouts pleasant. For example, New York New York, (412) 661-5600, in Shadyside is a restaurant, with a bar and a back patio. You'll find our handful of bars and dance clubs listed in the Nightlife chapter, and there are also a couple of coffee shops in the city that are particularly LGBT-friendly, among them Enrico's Tazza D'Oro in Highland Park, (412) 362-3676, and, for the funkier crowd, Quiet Storm in Lawrenceville, (412) 661-9355.

Despite neighborhoods that are composed of a certain folk, there's a good racial and ethnic mix in many areas. While you will find wealthy communities, the per capita income in 2000 (the most current year reported) was $30,644, slightly above the national average of $25,288. And according to the U.S. Census Report, the median family income as of 2000 was $38,795.

Allegheny County is the most populated of the Western Pennsylvania counties. It's interesting to note that this territory, which includes the city of Pittsburgh, encompasses the gamut of urban settings, as well as hundreds of outlying farms, many golf courses, and smaller neighborhoods that seem like little villages. That diversity, coupled with easy accessibility to the city's business district and sporting and cultural events, is the charm of living here. When families decide to live in Allegheny County, they realize their property taxes will be slightly higher than those in surrounding counties. It's a trade-off many people are willing to make for the conveniences, including a greater selection of school districts, hospitals, churches and synagogues, and social services; access to many colleges and universities; and much more.

Don't let the neighborhood names in the region's outskirts confuse you. If you hear Carolina or Indiana mentioned, don't automatically assume we mean "off in another state," for these are towns in Western Pennsylvania. Little Washington certainly isn't near the Pacific or our nation's capital. It's Washington, Pennsylvania, to the southwest of Pittsburgh. Indeed, Allegheny County is much more populated than Beaver, Butler, Armstrong, Westmoreland, or Washington Counties (those we've defined as our coverage area for this book). As a result, most of the attractions, restaurants, and shopping emanate from this area.

Finally, Pittsburgh gained another distinction in 1999. It was named as one of America's most driveable cities by the Surface Transportation Policy Project. The group studied aggressive driving, and found that Pittsburghers drive at less risk than their counterparts in other metropolitan areas.

COUNTY LINES

Beyond Allegheny, there's Beaver County, just a few miles from Pittsburgh International Airport. Towns such as Ambridge (another old steel town) sit along the Ohio River. You might want to visit Old Economy Village, where the Harmonists, a German sect, built their final homestead (see the Attractions chapter). It is beautifully lit for candlelight tours during the holidays. Beaver is the county seat, and Beaver Falls sits at the northern end.

The Beaver River spills into the Ohio, and marinas abound in Beaver County river communities such as New Brighton and Bridgewater. Parks are prevalent. You can visit Raccoon State Park, and the county parks of Brush Creek, Economy, and Brady's Run.

Butler County offers more history in Harmony, where German immigrants first settled in the early 1800s. The city of Butler is the seat of county government, but areas just north of suburban Pittsburgh such as Cranberry Township have seen tremendous growth in recent years. On a leisurely summer weekend, people often drive north to Lake Arthur and Moraine State Park, the state's fourth largest park. Cultural opportunities include the Butler County Symphony Orchestra, which celebrated its 50th season in 1998. (See the Arts chapter.)

In Armstrong County, the Allegheny River runs southward. Towns here include Apollo, Kittanning, Freeport, and Ford City, where the first successful plate glass manufacturing venture in the United States operated as Pittsburgh Plate Glass Company, now named PPG Industries.

Greensburg is the center of action in Westmoreland County. There, you'll find the Westmoreland County Museum of American Art, the Westmoreland Symphony, and the Laurel Ballet. Fort Ligonier Days are popular for outings, as is the Westmoreland County Air Show and the Arts & Heritage Festival. Children can't wait each year for the opening of Idlewild Park, with its family setting in the wooded Laurel Highlands and the memorable trolley ride through Mister Rogers' Neighborhood of Make-Believe (check out the Attractions and Kidstuff chapters).

In Washington County, just off Interstates 79 and 70, Ladbroke at the Meadows brings out the equestrian enthusiasts who enjoy clubhouse dining and harness horse racing. Burgettstown's *Post-Gazette* Pavillion is the site of many summer concerts, with performers John Tesh, Jimmy

For the best, most current information about attractions and events in the Pittsburgh area, contact the Greater Pittsburgh Convention and Visitors Bureau, (412) 281-0482, www.visit pittsburgh.com. You can also stop by the bureau's Visitor Information Center downtown at 420 Liberty Avenue, across the street from Gateway Center's tall, aluminum buildings.

Buffett, and Alan Jackson appearing in past years.

The Pittsburgh Penguins hockey team, now under the ownership of former player and hero Mario Lemieux, practices at the Iceoplex in Southpointe, Washington County. Also, Meadowcroft Village in Avella is a landmark in itself, a 200-acre facility offering a trip into the history of Native Americans, frontier settlers, farmers, coal miners, and conservationists. The Pennsylvania Trollery Museum offers a chance to climb aboard a streetcar and experience the sights and sounds of an earlier era when these vintage cars were the mainstay of transportation throughout Western Pennsylvania. Don't leave Washington County without photographing a few of the covered bridges you'll find in your travels.

Speaking of travels, some day trips and sights make it worth driving into counties outside our coverage area. A trip to see Frank Lloyd Wright's Fallingwater is one of them. This masterpiece was constructed in Fayette County south of Pittsburgh in the 1930s for the Edgar Kaufmann family. Today it's maintained by the Western Pennsylvania Conservancy, which conducts guided tours of the house on the waterfall.

Shoppers also make several obligatory trips to Lawrence and Mercer Counties (northwest of the city) for the Prime Outlets in Grove City, where more merchants than you can imagine are congregated in

Allegheny County has more than 1,700 bridges, with 720 inside the city limits and 15 major bridges crossing waterways in downtown Pittsburgh alone.

one spot. If your Mercer County day trip becomes a weekend getaway, make Tara, a country inn, your romantic hideaway.

Finally, did you know that Indiana, Pennsylvania, bills itself as the Christmas tree capital of the world? Shipping, sightseeing, rekindling romance, and, yes, even chopping down our own Christmas trees are just a few of the reasons we Pittsburghers venture beyond our own communities. (See both the Day Trips and Weekend Getaways and Shopping chapters for further adventurous ideas.)

PITTSBURGH TODAY

We call the time period from 1980 to the present the Post-Industrial Era—and it's still evolving. Corporations continue the diversification of our economy begun in the late 1970s, furthering an infrastructure of finance, research and scientific concerns, high technology, health-care advances, and educational excellence.

Beyond all the accolades, a city is its people. Pittsburgh will remain prominent because it offers a high quality of life for the people who call it home. It maintains a relatively low crime rate, wonderful recreation, championship sports teams, a thriving cultural community, and tremendous warmth tied to its sense of family, ethnic heritages, and traditions. You'll enjoy it here. We just know it!

GETTING HERE, GETTING AROUND

Pittsburgh has a glorious transportation history, reaching back to its days as the "Gateway to the West" with bustling river and railway traffic. While the riverboats are gone and passenger trains have dwindled to a few, Southwestern Pennsylvania remains a busy inland region, within 500 miles of more than half the U.S. population. Because of its proximity to so many vital destinations, US Airways has designated Pittsburgh a hub, assuring a heavy volume of air traffic.

The region has developed a colorful and diversified transportation system to meet the demand. Pittsburgh International Airport is a sparkling facility with impressive room for expansion. Public transportation can take you just about anywhere you want to go, and the system features a variety of shared-ride services targeted to senior citizens and disabled patrons. As you move out from Pittsburgh and population density thins, public transportation options thin as well.

Highway travel is not always as gratifying, thanks to the double whammy of topography and weather. The region is hilly, the city itself squeezed between three rivers. These factors have contributed to the development of narrow urban streets; if you're looking for a town with broad, sweeping boulevards, you've probably come to the wrong place. Moreover, many of the older highways around town, once high-speed routes to and from the city, have seen neighborhoods and business districts spring up around them. As a result, some are ill-equipped to handle the unanticipated influx of traffic. Transportation planners labor to catch up, making highway development a dynamic, ongoing process here. Nevertheless, if you're from Washington, D.C., or New York, you'll think traffic during our rush hour is just breezing along. However, you will want to take note of two 'Burgh things to avoid a potential pileup: Pittsburghers slow down in tunnels and, at lights, they *often* let the person turning left have the right-of-way. That means some people turning left now *take* the right-of-way, so watch out.

Note also that weather does take its toll; winter's freeze-thaw cycles often lead to an annual spring fling of potholes. The good news about winter weather is that it seldom immobilizes the region.

The review of transportation in Southwestern Pennsylvania has been divided into two major segments—travel to and from Pittsburgh, and travel in Pittsburgh, with particular attention paid to three key areas of travel: Pittsburgh International Airport, public transportation, and parking in Pittsburgh's downtown and Oakland neighborhoods. One way or another, developments here likely will affect you, just about every day.

TRAVEL TO AND FROM PITTSBURGH

Air Travel

Pittsburgh International Airport
(412) 472-3525

Pittsburgh International Airport is a marvel. It spans more than 10,000 acres, making it the fourth largest airport complex in the United States. To give you a better sense of its size, consider that Atlanta's Hartfield-Jackson International Airport and Chicago's O'Hare Airport—together—would fit comfortably within Pittsburgh International's borders. The airport routinely handles

In 2002, Travelocity.com ranked Pittsburgh International Airport as number one for the shortest wait at ticket counter check-in lines and security checkpoints, averaging 15 minutes or less.

nearly 20 million passengers annually and by tapping unutilized acreage, it could accommodate more than twice that many.

One reason for its popularity is the airport's proximity to so many important locales. It's within one hour's flying time of such cities as New York, Detroit, and Washington, D.C., and within 90 minutes' flying time of 20 states and much of Canada. Yet another reason Pittsburgh International ranks so highly with travelers is the scope of its amenities and services. The facility debuted in 1992 following an $800 million construction project; you'd swear that its grand opening was yesterday. That's how new and inviting it looks.

You'll find the Pittsburgh International Airport in Findlay Township, about 16 miles west of downtown Pittsburgh. Let's take a tour through Pittsburgh International Airport. We'll call it PIT, as they do in air traffic controller circles, to get a real feel for the place.

DESIGN

PIT features two main buildings: the Landside Terminal, with 25 commuter gates, and the Airside Terminal, which is shaped like a giant X and features 75 jet gates. When you arrive at the Landside Terminal, you'll be shuttled through a one-half-mile tunnel to the Airside Terminal by PIT's people mover system. The subwaylike people mover can transport up to 13,200 passengers per hour at speeds of up to 32 miles per hour. You can't get from Landside to Airside except via the people mover, but don't worry about lengthy waits. No matter when you arrive, the people mover will be at your service in

less than two minutes. Once you're at the Airside Terminal, you'll be at the center of the giant X, with the four concourses spoking off in each diagonal direction.

Because PIT is so large, it can be quite a hike from the most remote gates to the baggage claim area. PIT helps make it a more comfortable trip by providing moving walkways that will take you part of the way through each concourse. In addition, people with physical challenges who are flying on US Airways have the option of being transported through the airport in a large golf-cart-like conveyance. Wheelchairs are available for public use at the Traveler's Aid booth.

AIRLINES

PIT is a major hub for US Airways, which accounts for much of the airport's vitality, to say nothing of the positive impact on the local economy. Without US Airways' commitment to gate leasing and construction of an automated baggage-handling system, PIT might still be on the drawing boards.

There is, however, another side of the coin. While PIT serves more than 100 locations with nonstop flights, to get to most of those cities, you won't find a choice of carriers. For travel to and from such major cities as Los Angeles, Baltimore, Charlotte, and Miami, you'll find that US Airways provides the only nonstop flights. That's the tradeoff at PIT: an airline vital to the well-being of the region, but one so dominant that potential competitors look elsewhere.

Other airlines that serve PIT are Air Canada, American Airlines, Continental Airlines, Delta Airlines, Laker Airways, northwest Airlines, Pan Am, Skyway Airlines, Trans World Airlines, United Airline, and Vanguard. International travelers can take advantage of US Airways service to Frankfurt, Paris, and London.

BAGGAGE

PIT likes to claim that its $32 million automated baggage handling system is reliable

98.9 percent of the time, and travelers seem to agree. Among airlines that serve PIT, US Airways is the only authorized user of the automated system. That shouldn't hold you up if you're flying with another carrier; once US Airways passenger luggage is out of the equation, other carriers have relatively few bags to move.

You'll find the baggage claim area on the ground floor of the Landside Terminal, a pretty fair piece from some of the more remote jet gates. In many cases, since the automated system sorts 400 bags per minute, once you've walked and people-movered from your gate, you'll find your luggage waiting for you. Overhead neon signs will tell you which carousel has your baggage.

GROUND TRANSPORTATION

You'll find many ways to get from PIT to your ultimate Southwestern Pennsylvania destination. One of the most economical is the Port Authority Transit's express bus service called the Airport Flyer. The Airport Flyer links PIT, downtown Pittsburgh, and the Oakland university-medical complex with buses that run every 20 minutes between 5:30 A.M. and 12:30 A.M. The bus also stops at Robinson Town Center, gateway to a rapidly expanding commercial and residential neighborhood near the airport. Perhaps the most attractive feature of the Airport Flyer is its price: $2.25 one way.

Express Shuttle USA, (800) 991–9890, a privately run service, provides transportation to and from downtown hotels hourly. Rates are $16 one way, $30 for a round-trip. Other options include taxi cabs, which typically charge about $33 for a trip to or from downtown. If your destination is east of downtown, expect to pay more.

Another private service, operated by Checker Cab, is Pittsburgh Air Bus, (412) 381-5600, which provides door-to-door bus service to and from PIT. Fares are based on zones traversed but typically range from $20 to $35. If you're traveling

with a companion, the discount for the second fare can be as much as 75 percent.

Eight car rental agencies operate at PIT—all rental counters are located in the Landside Terminal. See this chapter's gray box for their names and phone numbers.

Be advised that if you're outside the terminal waiting for pick-up, you must be on the correct side of the terminal, since one side is dedicated exclusively to commercial ground transportation. If you look up and don't see a parking garage, we suggest you whistle a happy tune and head back through the terminal to the other side. (Where did we pick up this handy tip? Let's call it experience and leave it at that.)

PARKING

PIT's tagline when promoting its services is "You Can't Park Any Closer." It would be hard to argue with that, as the airport offers a variety of parking options that can accommodate a total of 9,528 vehicles. You'll find an indoor garage for short-term parking at $3.00 per hour to a maximum of $17.00 per day. For long-term parking, PIT maintains an outdoor lot with rates of $1.50 per hour to a $9.50 daily maximum. Both the short-term and long-term facilities provide access to an indoor moving walkway to facilitate your trip to the terminals.

For extended parking, PIT provides a 5,200-space lot, with a rate of $5.75 per day. Because these spaces are more distant from the terminals, PIT offers continuous shuttle service to and from the extended lot. No matter which option you choose, the parking areas are patrolled by Allegheny County Police. You'll enjoy complimentary emergency car-starting service, and you can pay for your parking with a credit card.

Convenient as airport parking may be, there are other options. A number of private carriers offer spacious parking lots and shuttle service to the airport. The shuttle services are easy to contact when you're at PIT—all their phone numbers are

By Phone

When you're traveling to or from the region via Pittsburgh International Airport, here's a directory of key phone numbers that can help things go more quickly.

Airlines
Air Canada, (888) 247-2262
American Airlines, (800) 433-7300
British Airways, (800) 247-9297
Continental Airlines, (800) 523-3273
Delta Airlines, (800) 221-1212
Northwest KLM Airlines, (800) 225-2525
Spirit Airlines, (800) 772-7117
United Airlines, (800) 864-8331
US Airways, (800) 428-4322

Commuter Airlines
Allegheny (US Airways Express),
  (800) 428-4322
American Airlines, (800) 433-7300
Chautauqua (US Airways Express),
  (800) 428-4322
ComAir (Delta Connections),
  (800) 221-1212
Continental Express, (800) 523-3273
Mesa (US Airways Express),
  (800) 428-4322

Mesaba Airlines (Northwest KLM Airlink),
  (800) 225-2525
Piedmont (US Airways Express),
  (800) 428-2322
PSA (US Airways Express),
  (800) 428-2322
Trans States Airlines (TWA Express),
  (800) 221-2000
United Express, (800) 864-8331

Car Rentals
Alamo Rent-A-Car, (412) 472-5060
Avis Rent-A-Car, (412) 472-5200
Budget Rent-A-Car, (412) 472-5471
Dollar Rent-A-Car, (412) 472-5100
Enterprise Rent-A-Car, (412) 472-3490
Hertz Corporation, (412) 472-5955
National Car Rental, (412) 472-5094
Thrifty Rent-A-Car, (412) 472-3333

Other Useful Numbers
Airport Information, (412) 472-3525
Airport Lost and Found, (412) 472-3500
Airport Parking Information,
  (412) 472-5050
Travelers Aid Society, (412) 472-3599
Police–General Information,
  (412) 472-5510

grouped on phones that enable you to access them by pushing a single button.
  Prices for these services tend to be market driven; in considering them, be aware of the potential trade-offs involved. For example, if you're paying more at the airport, is the convenience and security

provided by the patrolling county police worth the extra price to you? Each traveler will answer that question differently. The shuttle services typically offer a number of discount programs, such as reduced prices for AAA West Penn/West Virginia members.

AMENITIES

The AirMall, a shopping mall contained within PIT, is so vast and attractive that if you're shopping there, you may have a hard time remembering to make your flight. It's described more fully in our Shopping chapter. While we're here, however, we should at least mention that all the shops and restaurants at PIT are required to charge the same prices inside the airport that they charge at other locations. You won't be paying $6.00 for a travel-size bottle of aspirin here.

You'll find a food court with emporiums offering everything from pizza to deli fare, from baked goods to frozen yogurt. You also may enjoy several full-service restaurants, and you'll find food purveyors and lounges along the concourses as well as at the food court. You won't lack for nourishment here, but if there is a shortcoming at the food court, it's occasional congestion in the limited seating area.

If you're traveling with young children, you'll love Kidsport, a multifaceted play area for children designed to resemble a miniature amphitheater complete with tiered seating, padded floors, and ramps. When PIT's predecessor facility launched Kidsport in 1983, it was the first of its kind in the nation. It has grown substantially and today features displays from some of the region's cultural leaders, including Carnegie Science Center, the Pittsburgh Zoo, the National Aviary in Pittsburgh, and the Pittsburgh Children's Museum—all rotated every six months.

Kidsport also offers continuously running videos that capture entertaining Western Pennsylvania scenes, a map of the United States designed into the floor, children's books, and a ticket counter designed to stimulate imaginative play. You'll find a baby-changing station and a gallery and seating area for sleeping children or nursing mothers. Kidsport is in Concourse C in the Airside Terminal, allowing convenient access to the food court and AirMall. One note: Kidsport is an unsupervised play area.

Other Airports

Allegheny County Airport
**12 Allegheny County Airport, West Mifflin
(412) 461-4300**
This airport, situated on a 432-acre plateau, once served as the region's chief commercial airport and continues to serve as a vital general aviation airport. Dozens of corporate and private aircraft are based at the facility, which functions as a gateway to the Mon Valley. It features three runways, a 23,500-square-foot terminal building, parking for 500 cars, and a range of aviation services. These include fueling, aircraft sales, rental and maintenance, part sand supplies, storage and tie-down services, and flight and mechanical instruction.

Beaver County Airport
**Piper Street, Beaver Falls
(724) 847-4662**
Since 1950 the Beaver County Airport has functioned as a general aviation facility, used primarily for business, training, and recreational flights. The facility is designated a "reliever" airport for Pittsburgh International Airport to provide additional capacity during times of congestion. Air Heritage of Western Pennsylvania, a working museum that restores aircraft of historical interest, is located on the premises. Beaver County Airport sponsors a popular air show each August.

Butler County Airport
**473 Airport Road, Butler
(724) 586-6665**
Both corporate and private plane owners utilize Butler County Airport, which features an asphalt runway; The Runway restaurant; and a full-service fixed-base

If you're driving, watch the car horizontally across from you at the intersection. When the light turns green, the driver is likely to quickly make a left, rather than yielding. It's a 'Burgh thing!

operator that provides fueling, maintenance, training, and charter service. The facility is a designated "reliever" for Pittsburgh International Airport.

Washington County Airport
205A Airport Road, Washington
(724) 228-5151
This facility offers a 5,000-foot runway used by corporate and private aircraft, as well as a fixed-base, aeronational operator to handle fueling and maintenance needs.

Arnold Palmer Regional Airport
200 Pleasant Unity Road, Latrobe
(724) 539-8100
Ground transportation from Pittsburgh International Airport to parts of Westmoreland County can be an exhausting three-hour journey. Another option is to land at Arnold Palmer Regional Airport, a convenient spot if your destination is Greensburg or points east. US Airways services the airport, as do several full-service car charter firms and car-rental agencies. At the airport, you'll find a gift shop and Jimmy Monzo's Blue Angel, a full-service restaurant. Flight training is also available.

Train Travel

Amtrak
1100 Liberty Avenue
(412) 471-6171, (800) 872-7245
www.amtrak.com
Amtrak's Pittsburgh station is located at the eastern edge of downtown, near the Greyhound bus terminal and Liberty Center. It's also convenient to many Port Authority of Allegheny County bus lines. Amtrak offers an automated reservation system that will provide you with schedules and fare information. You can also get that by visiting Amtrak's Web site, www.amtrak.com.

Destinations for the two, reservations-only trains that service Pittsburgh currently include New York, Philadelphia,

Harrisburg-Altoona, Johnstown-Pittsburgh, and Chicago. If you ride the Pennsylvania or Three Rivers, you'll find sandwiches and snacks in the dinette and a lounge area where smoking is permitted during certain times of day. You also may utilize the Amtrak Express Shipping and Checked Baggage Service aboard the Three Rivers.

The Three Rivers offers connections to the Capitol Limited. No matter which train you ride to New York, you'll find buses to connect you to Kennedy and LaGuardia Airports. Amtrak's Pittsburgh station is fully accessible to wheelchair users.

Bus Travel

Greyhound Bus Lines
11th and Liberty Avenues
(412) 392-6513, (800) 229-9424

Mall Circle Drive, Monroeville
(412) 856-3080
www.greyhound.com
Greyhound offers two area terminals, in downtown Pittsburgh and the eastern suburb of Monroeville. The company travels to 1,400 different destinations; you can reach most of them from Pittsburgh, although some involve bus changeovers. You'll find discount programs for advance bookings and kids, as well as "companion fare" program offering reduced rates. While the company's national fleet numbers about 2,400 buses, not all are wheelchair accessible. To find out if a bus can accommodate your needs, it's best to call in advance.

Car Travel—Interstate Highways

The interstate highway system can make car travel to and from Pittsburgh a pretty easy and comfortable mission, although there is one unusual feature of interstate highway travel here. The Pennsylvania Department of Transportation (PennDOT) reports that, while trucks typically

Help for Travelers

Several organizations in the region are dedicated to helping travelers. If you've ever needed emergency road service on a dark and lonely road, you well know the value of the American Automobile Association. The AAA member service center in Southwestern Pennsylvania is AAA West Penn/West Virginia, (412) 363-5100, located at 5900 Baum Boulevard in Pittsburgh's East Liberty neighborhood. AAA operates 58 branch offices in the tristate area, offering a variety of services that go well beyond emergency help.

Services include worldwide air, cruise, and rail tickets; hotel and rental-car reservations; American Express travelers checks at no fee; credit cards, maps, and individually tailored routings, otherwise known as the much-loved Triptiks. AAA also operates travel and insurance agencies. There is an annual membership fee.

Also available for wayward wayfarers is Travelers Aid Society of Pittsburgh, a nonprofit agency that helps travelers throughout the country. The agency assists people stranded here and without the means of reaching home or another destination. Among the group's beneficiaries are runaway youths, the homeless, and those in need of counseling or referral.

You'll find two Travelers Aid Society locations in southwestern Pennsylvania; Pittsburgh International Airport, (412) 472-3599, and the Greyhound Bus Terminal in downtown Pittsburgh, 11th and Liberty Avenues, (412) 281-5466 or (412) 281-5474.

account for about 10 percent of all traffic on interstate highways, the percentage in our region is about 50 percent higher, or 15 percent of all vehicles on the road. Note the variability in speed limits from 55 to 65 mph throughout the region; if you're not paying attention, you could easily cross into a 55 mph zone while doing 65.

Interstate 76
This is the Pennsylvania Turnpike, which covers 506 miles and crosses the Commonwealth, linking the cities of Pittsburgh, Harrisburg, and Philadelphia and connecting with the Ohio and New Jersey Turnpikes. The turnpike also features a Northeast Extension that will take you to Scranton and other Northeastern Pennsylvania locations. Locally, you'll find access to the turnpike at Monroeville, Harmarville, Warrandale, Butler, and Beaver Valley.

The highway is administered by the Pennsylvania Turnpike Commission, which charges 4.1 cents per mile for passenger cars. You must pay your tolls in cash upon leaving the highway. PennDOT maintains a Welcome Center along the turnpike near Beaver Falls. One caution about turnpike driving: exits can be as far as 30 miles apart, so you don't want to miss yours.

Interstate 376
I-376, known locally as the Parkway East, connects the Pennsylvania Turnpike with downtown Pittsburgh and is the principal link between the city and its eastern suburbs. It's heavily traveled, carrying 93,000 vehicles each weekday, and you can expect routine rush hour delays that can make the road look like a genuine parkway, but pile ups usually don't last long. If you travel I-376, you'll course through the Squirrel Hill tunnels at the

city of Pittsburgh's eastern edge. Watch out for delays here; remember, Pittsburgh drivers slow down as they drive through tunnels. Go figure . . .

Interstate 79

This is a major north-south highway that goes from Erie all the way to southern West Virginia. It also intersects with Interstate 70 in Washington County. PennDOT maintains a Welcome Center along I-79 in Greene County.

Interstate 279

I-279 is a loop off I-79 and serves as a vital connection between the heavily populated North Hills, the city of Pittsburgh, and Pittsburgh International Airport. Local residents call I-279 either the Parkway West or the Parkway North, depending on which section they're talking about. The highway exits downtown Pittsburgh across the Fort Pitt Bridge and through the Fort Pitt Tunnels; here, it becomes the state's most heavily traveled highway, handling 148,000 vehicles per day. Rush hour traffic jams are common.

An important feature of I-279 is the region's only High Occupancy Vehicle (HOV) lane, which during morning and evening rush hour is restricted to vehicles with a minimum of two occupants. At all other times, the HOV lane functions as an express lane and is open to all drivers. You'll find the HOV lane between the North Side of Pittsburgh and the city's northern suburbs.

Interstate 70

I-70 is an important highway in Washington and Westmoreland Counties, taking you through the Mon Valley or west into West Virginia, Ohio, and beyond. Penn-DOT maintains a Welcome Center along I-70 in Washington County.

Interstate 80

It's slightly north of our principal coverage area, but I-80—sometimes called the "Keystone Shortway"—is a road you should know about. It's a good route to central and eastern Pennsylvania points, and it will deposit you directly in New Jersey going east or Ohio going west. To reach I-80, take I-79 north to New Castle in Lawrence County.

TRAVEL IN PITTSBURGH

Because public transportation in Southwestern Pennsylvania tends to be organized and administered by county, we'll begin our look at public transportation in the same way. That doesn't mean you can't get from, say, Westmoreland County to Allegheny County. You can, although the options are limited; county boundaries tend to shape the contours of the region's public transportation. That will be important to keep in mind if you're a public transportation user.

Allegheny County

In Allegheny County, public transportation is the domain of the Port Authority of Allegheny County, or PAT as it's popularly known. It's a massive job, as PAT provides service to 250,000 riders per weekday. It accomplishes this by deploying about 750 buses each day along with several nifty features—inclines and the "T" light-rail and subway system—which is described below.

The bus system also features a number of exclusive bus lanes that serve most of the county and cut much of the time from your trip. These include the South Busway, the Martin Luther King, Jr. East Busway, and a High Occupancy Vehicle (HOV) lane that's part of I-279 in the North Hills. The HOV lane is open to carpoolers as well.

PAT offers a number of programs for riders with special needs, including 228 bus routes that are accessible to wheelchairs each weekday; all PAT routes are wheelchair-accessible on Saturday, Sunday, and holidays. In addition, PAT sponsors and administers ACCESS, a door-to-door, advanced-reservation, shared-ride transportation service targeted primarily to senior citizens and those with disabilities. Many ACCESS riders enjoy discounts of up to 90 percent once eligibility has been established. It's a vital service in the county, providing more than two million passenger trips each year. For information about ACCESS, call PAT at (412) 562-5353.

The fare for a ride on a PAT bus depends on how far you need to go. Fares range from free (within the downtown "Free Zone") to $2.75 for a three-zone trip. If you're a frequent rider, PAT offers a number of discount opportunities, including: books of 10 discounted tickets; weekly, monthly, and annual subscription passes; a Weekend Day Pass; and a Summer Ride Pass.

Disabled patrons may ride for half price during off-peak hours, while senior citizens ride for free during off-peak hours on weekdays and all day on Saturdays, Sundays, and holidays. For certification to either program, call PAT at (412) 255-1356 or stop by the PATransit Downtown Service Center, 534 Smithfield Street. Applications for Senior Citizen Transit Cards also are available at senior centers throughout the county.

PAT modifies its routes and schedules several times per year to respond to changing conditions and customer needs. You can keep up with all routes, schedules, and changes by visiting PAT's Web site, www.ridegold.com, or by calling PAT's Customer Service department, (412) 422-2000. They'll send you "The Ride Guide," which is a complete directory of routes, and other helpful information.

Inclines

Imagine a subway car rolling along a track. Now imagine the car and track tilted at about a 35-degree angle to carry you up a mountainside. You now have a mental picture of an unusual transportation mode known as an incline. In Pittsburgh, you don't have to imagine it, as the

Here's a handy tip that can help you avoid a moment of embarrassment when riding a Port Authority of Allegheny County bus. On buses heading to downtown, you pay your fare when you board. On outbound buses, pay as you exit. You'll need the exact fare, as PAT drivers don't carry any change.

city is served by two inclines that function both as tourist attractions and as important daily conveyances for downtown commuters.

Between 1870 and 1901, transportation pioneers in the city erected and operated 15 "inclined planes," as they were formally known, to carry folks up and down Pittsburgh's steep hills. Although most were passenger conveyances, at least one served as a freight incline to haul horses, buggies, furniture, and coal. As the city's roadway and public transportation systems improved, incline ridership declined. Today, only two inclines survive.

Both the Monongahela Incline and the Duquesne Incline link the Mt. Washington and Duquesne Heights neighborhoods to the South Side, more than 600 feet below. The cars traverse Mt. Washington at 6 miles per hour. They're popular with tourists, as a ride on the incline can be combined with a stop at the observation decks atop Mt. Washington, providing breathtaking views of the city and its three rivers. Mt. Washington and Duquesne Heights residents use them to reach the South Side; from there, a walk across the Smithfield Street Bridge gets them to work. Their total commuting costs: $1.75 each way for the incline ride.

The inclines operate from 5:30 A.M. to 12:45 A.M. Monday through Saturday, with reduced hours on Sundays and holidays. Both inclines run on demand; that means, after waiting only a few minutes, ostensibly, you could have the thing to yourself. For information about the Mon Incline, contact the Port Authority of Allegheny County, (412) 442-2000. The Duquesne

Incline is operated by a nonprofit group called the Society for the Preservation of the Duquesne Heights Incline. You can reach them at (412) 381-1665.

Parking

Downtown Pittsburgh offers approximately 2,000 parking spaces, including metered onstreet parking and downtown fringe lots and garages. That may seem like a pretty generous number, but if you consider that 148,000 vehicles whiz past downtown each day on I-279, it's pretty easy to see the peril there. If downtown is the destination for too many of those drivers, there won't be enough parking to go around.

Of course, it seldom is as bad as that. Many of those drivers aren't coming downtown, and those who do aren't necessarily parking all day, so there is some turnover. If you arrive early enough or late enough in the workday, chances are you'll find the space you desire, or one pretty close to it. You will encounter a crunch virtually every midday, when the all-day parkers have yet to depart and downtown crowds are swollen by noontime shoppers and diners.

Moreover, downtown won't pose the only parking challenges for you in the city. The Oakland neighborhood, with its phalanx of important hospitals and universities, is notoriously crowded when the colleges are in session. In some of Pittsburgh's residential neighborhoods, parking is at such a premium that the city has taken to providing permits to local residents for onstreet parking: no permit, no park.

Public transportation and carpooling may be your most reliable alternatives. If you must drive, however, we'll try to give you a wheel up by profiling the largest parking garages in downtown and Oakland, providing some information about PAT's "Park and Ride" program, and offering some insight into Pittsburgh's homegrown parking solution—a chair strategically placed in "your" parking space.

PARKING—DOWNTOWN

Downtown proper offers about 26,000 parking spaces. With a little ingenuity and luck, you can find one. You may need to walk a little farther than you had planned or grab the "T" to reach your destination, but with persistence, you'll find your space.

For each facility the minimum and maximum hourly rates—in other words, what you'd pay to park from 0 to 30 minutes and the maximum that you'd pay to park all day—are provided. Included within the range is what you'd pay to park on a weekend or weeknight; the cost is often a lower hourly rate or flat fee then. If different pricing applies during special events, it is noted. Phone numbers listed are those of garage operators and may ring at corporate offices rather than on-site. Unless otherwise noted, all garages and lots offer security guards, wheelchair-reserved spaces, and discounted evening rates. Downtown garages also provide escort service upon request. Where valet parking is offered, that usually means a charge and/or a tip over and above the standard hourly rate. The entries below are not comprehensive, as you'll find many other surface lots and indoor garages, but these are the largest parking sites, where open spaces are most likely.

11 Stanwix Street
11 Stanwix Street
(412) 323-4455
When other downtown garages are full, you may find a space here. Perhaps the disappearance of Westinghouse from Pittsburgh's corporate scene has freed space in the lot. Whatever the reason, this garage is always worth a shot. Rates for its 341 spaces range from $5.00 to $16.00. Monthly leases are available for $285.

Gateway Center Garage
126 Sixth Street
(412) 391-3380
You'll find this a convenient garage for events in the Cultural District. Rates for the 920 spaces range from $3.75 to

$10.00, and you'll receive a discount when you patronize certain downtown establishments. Monthly lease rate is $220 by day, $100 by night.

Liberty Center Garage
10th Street and Liberty Avenue
(412) 261-6655

You'll be beneath Liberty Center and the Westin Hotel when you park here. The garage offers 500 spaces; the rate is $17 per day. You also may take advantage of valet parking, at $22 per day.

Liberty Parking
1001 Penn Avenue
(412) 344-6565

Part of the David L. Lawrence Convention Center, this 535-space garage provides the closest possible parking for convention center events. It's also connected by an indoor bridge to Liberty Center and the Westin Convention Center Hotel. Rates range from $3.00 to $10.50. Monthly leases are priced at $175 by day, $85 by night.

The Manor Complex Garage
564 Forbes Avenue
(412) 323-4455

This garage is part of the Manor Building and a quick walk from Grant Street, the hub of the city's legal and political activity. Rates for the 750 spaces range from $5.00 to $11.00 with monthly leases available for $185.00.

Mellon Square Garage
Mellon Square
(412) 255-6138

One of the most popular garages because of its central location, Mellon Square Garage offers 1,100 spaces at rates ranging from $5.00 to $18.00. Monthly lease rate is $275, with a discounted monthly lease night rate available.

Mon Wharf Parking
Mon Wharf
(412) 456-2770

If you plan to park on the Mon Wharf, you will enjoy a favorable rate—$8.00 no matter how long you stay—but you need to be aware of certain things. First, this surface lot is only a few paces from the Monongahela River, meaning you will have a bit of a walk to central downtown locations. Perhaps more important, the lot typically is flooded several times each year when the Mon rises, so you need to be aware of river conditions before you park here. The lot offers 850 spaces and security from 1:00 to 9:00 P.M. but no monthly leases.

Ninth & Penn Garage
136 Ninth Street
(412) 560-7250

When you're planning to enjoy a play or performance in Pittsburgh's Cultural District, you'll find this lot a short walk from your venue. It features 581 spaces and rates ranging from $3.75 to $10.00. Monthly leases are available for $220 and monthly night leases are priced at $100. Your hourly rate will be discounted with a purchase from participating downtown merchants.

One Oxford Centre Garage
Smithfield Street and Third Avenue
(412) 263-2180

If you're planning a shopping expedition at trendy Oxford Centre, you can't beat the convenience of this 850-space garage. Rates range from $5.00 to $15.00 with discounts when you patronize certain shops in Oxford Center. Cost for monthly leases is $310—slightly less for Oxford Centre tenants.

The garage is connected by a series of bridges to both the Forbes Avenue Garage and the Boulevard of the Allies Garage.

PPG Place Garage
Third Avenue and Market Street
(412) 323-4455

As the name suggests, this garage is part of the six-building PPG Place complex, headquarters to many important Pittsburgh companies and adjacent to the popular dining spots of Market Square. Rates for the 673 spaces range from

The Pittsburgh Downtown Partnership, (412) 566-4190, provides a free guide to downtown parking with basic information about parking spaces, garages, and lots as well as a listing of retail establishments that participate in discount parking programs.

$4.00 to $16.00 with monthly leases ranging from $280.53 for open parking to $326.33 for a reserved space.

Sixth & Penn Garage
Sixth Street and Penn Avenue
(412) 323-4455

On many nights, there's a palpable excitement around this garage—it's the closest parking garage to Heinz Hall, home of the Pittsburgh Symphony Orchestra and many touring troupes and plays. The garage offers 500 spaces, with rates ranging from $3.00 to $12.00 and monthly leases for $200.00.

Smithfield Street & Liberty Avenue
629 Smithfield Street
(412) 391-1952

An indoor tunnel connects this 620-space garage to the Duquesne Club, making it a convenient parking site when you're dining at the club. Rates range from $5.00 to $14.00 with monthly leases priced at $275.00. Your fee will be discounted with a purchase at participating downtown establishments.

Third Avenue Garage
Third Avenue at Wood Street
(412) 323-4455

This centrally located garage offers 550 spaces, with rates ranging from $3.75 to $13.00 and monthly leases for $250.00.

USX Tower Garage
600 Grant Street
(412) 263-0440

When you have an appointment at USX Tower, one of the city's most important

headquarters facilities, you can't beat the convenience of this 650-space garage. Rates range from $3.00 to $16.00 with monthly leases available for $275.00 and valet parking offered.

Wood Allies Garage
228 Boulevard of the Allies
(412) 560-2504

This 538-space garage is convenient to PPG Place and Market Square, both of them just a few paces across the Boulevard of the Allies. Rates range from $3.75 to $10.00 with monthly leases priced at $220.00 by day, $100.00 by night. The garage offers discounts with a purchase from participating downtown merchants.

DOWNTOWN FRINGE

Many commuters avoid high downtown parking rates by parking in lots that dot the fringes of downtown. These are among the largest parking sites in the city, offering about 16,000 spaces. From some sites, you'll need to walk a bit to reach your ultimate destination, while others provide complimentary shuttle-bus service. Commuters on a budget put the fringe on top.

Allegheny Center Parking Garage
Allegheny Center
(412) 323-4455

You'll find 2,500 indoor parking spaces at this garage, which is just across the Seventh Street Bridge from downtown. Rates range from $4.00 to $10.00, with monthly leases priced at $115.00. You can enjoy discounts by purchasing the garage's coupons or parking stamps, or through purchases at participating merchants.

Boardwalk Lot
15th and Smallman Streets
(412) 323-4455
www.alcoparking.com

This 1,500-space surface lot is in the Strip District, a short walk from the David L. Lawrence Convention Center and Liberty Center. The lot provides complimentary shuttle service to and from several down-town locations. You'll pay by day-part. For example, you can park from 5:00 A.M. to 4:00 P.M. for $5.00 and 4:00 P.M. to close for $4.00 Monday through Friday. All day Saturday or Sunday is $4.00.

Chatham Center Garage
54 Chatham Center
(412) 261-0809

Located in the uptown section near the Mellon Arena, Chatham Center offers 2,281 indoor spaces. The garage is about a five-minute walk from Grant Street in down-town. Rates range from $2.50 to $10.25, with monthly leases priced at $214.00. You can get a discounted "early bird" monthly lease, good Monday through Fri-day from 5:30 A.M. to 6:30 P.M. for $192.

Mellon Arena Lots
Center Avenue
(412) 642-4284
Washington Place, Bedford Avenue, Lemieux Place, and Crawford Street

You'll find 2,500 spaces to welcome you in the arena area—unless an event at the Mellon Arena causes a jam. The regular daily rates range from $5.75 to $7.75, 6:00 A.M. to 6:30 P.M. Monday through Friday. During Mellon Arena events, which usually take place on the weekends, rates are higher, varying with different events.

Expect to walk no longer than 10 min-utes to reach downtown; the most distant Mellon Arena lot is only 4 blocks from Grant Street. If you work in USX Tower, park in the Mellon Arena lot nearby and sprint to work in five minutes or less; you may even be able to look down on your car from your office window.

Be sure to check out the Melody Tent lot above the Mellon Arena if you're a commuter. You won't find the Civic Light Opera crooning tunes there as you would have in the 1960s, but you might be inter-ested in the shuttle bus that operates on weekdays from 6:00 to 10:00 A.M. and 3:00 to 6:30 P.M. The other four Mellon Arena lots are named after the points on the compass in which you'll find them. Not nearly so groovy as the Melody Tent, but you'll know where you are.

Greyhound Garage
11th and Penn Avenues
(412) 765-1775

Though not among the most spacious garages—it has 190 spaces—this facility is worth noting because it is adjacent to the Greyhound Bus Terminal. Rates range from $4.00 to $13.00, with monthly leases priced $175.00.

Second Avenue Parking Plaza
Second Avenue
(412) 323-4455

This surface lot in the Uptown neighbor-hood offers 800 parking spaces for a daily rate of $5.00, monthly leases for $100.00, and free shuttle service to down-town points.

Station Square Parking
One Station Square
(412) 261-1993

This popular shipping/office complex fea-tures two surface lots and a garage pro-viding a total of 3,500 parking spaces. You will need to walk across the Smithfield Street Bridge to reach town. Indoor rates range from $3.00 to $16.00 with outdoor rates in the East lot ranging from $1.00 to $14.00. You also may park for a $5.00 daily fare in the West lot. During Steelers and Pirates games, expect a rate hike—up to almost twice the price for the day. Monthly lease prices from $115 to $145.

PARKING—OAKLAND

As the hub of the region's higher-education and medical sectors, Oakland frequently has more would-be parkers than it can comfortably accommodate. You'll find plenty of metered on-street parking, but you can't use most of those spaces during morning and evening rush hours. You'll also find plenty of garages, only to be frustrated by the "Permit Parking Only" warnings, indicating that

You'll find America's shortest interstate highway in Pittsburgh. I-579, all 0.5 mile of it, connects the Liberty Bridge and I-376 (via the Boulevard of the Allies) to the Veterans Bridge across the Allegheny River and I-279. This mighty little highway often goes by an alternate name: the Crosstown Expressway.

the garages are reserved—often for University of Pittsburgh personnel. When classes are in session, there's no real remedy for the parking crunch. Here are some garages and lots that can help.

Forbes & Semple Garage
410 Meyran Avenue
(412) 621-5922

This 450-space garage is part of Oakland's commercial district. Rates range from $3.00 to $9.00 with monthly leases priced at $190.00 by day, $100.00 by night. Discounts are offered through participating professional and university offices.

University Parking
3915 O'Hara Street
(412) 624-4034

O'Hara Garage provides a convenient location between the University of Pittsburgh's lower and upper campuses. From here, you're within walking distance of most of Oakland's hospitals and medical offices. Rates for the 455 spaces range from $4.00 to $10.00 with discounts for Pitt personnel and students. Leases are available through the university for its faculty and staff only.

Schenley Plaza
Schenley Plaza
(412) 560-PARK

This is a great location for a surface parking lot. It separates the Carnegie Library of Pittsburgh and the University of Pittsburgh's Hillman Library, and it can be considered part of the campus of both Pitt and Carnegie Mellon University. It features 250 spaces with rates ranging from $3.00

to $12.00. You won't find much turnover at this lot. Once people find spaces here, they tend to milk them for all they're worth. When the universities are in session, people actually line up to get in here.

Webster Hall Garage
101 North Dithridge Street
(412) 621-6751

This garage provides 245 spaces at rates ranging from $5.00 to $17.00, with discount for purchases at participating merchants. It also offers valet parking and monthly leases priced at $120—you also must provide a $50 security deposit for a lease. Webster Hall is a former elegant hotel now serving as an office and apartment building.

PARK AND RIDE LOTS

One way of avoiding downtown parking expenses is to utilize the Port Authority of Allegheny's Park and Ride lots. These 35 lots offer more than 5,000 parking spaces, most free or with a nominal charge. They're all located adjacent to public transportation routes, so you can park cheaply and ride the bus or "T" to town. If you call PAT at (412) 442-2000, they'll send you a free map of Park and Ride lots.

PITTSBURGH NEIGHBORHOODS

As you tool through Pittsburgh's residential and commercial neighborhoods, you'll notice a chair standing unattended before the curb. Then another. Then another. These are not the products of some mass sheriff's evictions. Rather, Pittsburghers use chairs to stake their claims to parking spaces in front of their homes or businesses. They're especially prevalent on snowy days, when residents who have shoveled out their parking spaces feel particularly protective about them. The chairs are a colorful facet of Pittsburgh residential life, but don't take them lightly. Many a neighborhood brawl began when someone shoved aside a chair to trespass on a reserved parking space.

The need for such a homegrown strategy stems from the tightness of parking spaces in some city neighborhoods. Many Pittsburgh streets are narrow and can't accommodate parking on both sides of the street. In addition, neighborhoods with institutions such as hospitals draw many visitors in search of on-street parking to beat the prices of lots, garages, and meters.

The city has implemented a more rational approach to the problem through its Residential Parking Permit Program. Through RPPP, residents of 26 residential areas—including Beechview, Bloomfield, The Bluff, Garfield, Lawrenceville, Lower Hill district, Mt. Washington, North Squirrel Hill, Oakland, and Shadyside—enjoy exclusive on-street parking rights from 8:30 A.M. to 4:00 P.M. each weekday. To acquire a permit that admits you into the program, you'll need to provide proof of residency and car ownership, a driver's license, and an annual fee of $20 per vehicle. You'll also be entitled to one guest car per household for an annual fee of $10. For more information or an application, contact the Pittsburgh Department of City Planning, (412) 255-2200.

If you don't live in an eligible neighborhood, we advise that you pick up a couple of folding chairs.

Subway

Pittsburgh's subway system, known as the "T," is an unusual blend of subterranean and aboveground features. When it courses through the city's South Hills, the "T" is largely an aboveground conveyance that resembles a trolley line, although it's officially called a "light-rail system." When it reaches Downtown, the "T" dives beneath the surface to provide riders with an unobstructed trip below city streets. Actually, three downtown stops—Gateway Center, Wood Street, and Steel Plaza—are underground, while the "T" stops at Penn Park and Station Square are aboveground. By combining these features, the "T" serves as both a convenient means of downtown-

only travel as well as a key component of the region's commuting infrastructure.

For downtown travel, it would be hard to beat the price of the "T"—there's no charge for travel between the three underground stations. When you visit those stations, you'll enjoy the soothing strains of classical music provided by PAT. For longer "T" rides for which there is a charge, PAT encourages riders to purchase tickets and passes by imposing a surcharge, ranging from $1.25 to $1.75, on cash payments. For more information, call (412) 442-2000.

ARMSTRONG COUNTY

In Armstrong County, the Mid-County Transit Authority, (724) 548-8696, provides three bus programs. The first features fixed-route service in the county's central communities—Applewold, Ford Cliff, Ford City, Kittanning, Manorville, and West Kittanning. The buses run about once every hour, Monday through Saturday, at a base fare of 75 cents plus additional charges for zones traversed. All buses are wheelchair accessible. As a bonus, MCTA provides service to hospitals and shipping malls in East Franklin.

The second service, called Armstrong Rural Public Transit, is a shared-ride program available to all Monday through Friday. You must reserve your transportation at least 24 hours in advance, with cost on a zones-traversed basis. The buses are primarily, though not exclusively, wheelchair accessible. While service normally runs from 8:00 A.M. to 5:00 P.M. the program will transport you to doctors' office visits from 6:00 A.M. until 8:00 P.M.

The third MCTA service provides transportation for children in the county's Head Start program.

BEAVER COUNTY

The Beaver County Transit Authority (724-728-8600) manages public bus transportation throughout the county. You'll find routes that operate exclusively within Beaver County as well as express

In 1985 the Port Authority of Allegheny County selected the name "T" for its subway light-rail system through a public contest. The losing submissions included "The Unda Grunda Wonda," "The Gazunder," and "YGDT (Yunz Goin'd Dathn-Tahn?)" Now you know why they chose "T."

and local routes between Beaver County and the city of Pittsburgh. Your fare will depend on the number of zones traversed; a one-way fare from Pittsburgh ranges from $2.25 to $3.00. Exact fare is required, unless you pay by tickets purchased at the BCTA Transportation Center in Rochester. Transfers are free. An important note to remember: BCTA buses do not operate on major holidays.

Senior citizens may ride BCTA's Beaver County routes free of charge during off-peak hours and all day Saturday. To get your senior citizen transit card, call BCTA at (724) 728–8600 or visit the transportation center. For riders who use wheelchairs, most routes are accessible. You may want to check with BCTA to determine which routes might be right for you. The county also provides a shared-ride service called Demand and Response Transit (DART) for people with disabilities. Call DART at (724) 728–4200 for more information or to schedule a ride.

The county maintains several Park 'n Ride lots in close proximity to BCTA stops throughout the county. In addition, you'll find a convenience lot just outside the transportation center where you can park while conducting any short-term activity at the center. Beaver County officials call these lots "Kiss 'n Ride," but these activities are not mandatory when visiting the transportation center . . . at least we don't think they are.

BUTLER COUNTY

Bus service in Butler County is something of a mix-and-match affair. In the city of

Butler and environs, bus service is provided by the Butler Township-City Joint Municipal Transit Authority, (724) 285–4124.

Travel between Butler County communities is handled by the Butler County Commissioners through a demonstration program supported by the Pennsylvania Department of Transportation and the Pennsylvania Livery. This service links the communities of Butler, Connoquenessing, Harmony, Evans City, Zelienople, and Cranberry. The one-way fare is $1.00.

Exact change is required. Senior citizens age 65 and older ride free during off-peak hours once they have acquired appropriate transit cards. Patrons with disabilities and wheelchair users can access the buses in this demo program.

The schedule varies from day to day. On Wednesdays, for example, the city of Butler is not part of the route. Call the county at (724) 283–0445, extension 217, for complete schedule and fare information.

WASHINGTON COUNTY

You'll have several options for bus service in Washington County, depending on your needs. For Pittsburgh or locations in or near the city of Washington, GG&C Bus Lines, (724) 222–2320, provides express service from Washington County to downtown Pittsburgh, connecting with the "T" at South Hills Village Station, as well as local service throughout the city of Washington.

For service in the Mon Valley and along the Route 88 corridor, Mid-Mon Valley Transit Authority, (724) 489–0880, provides local service as well as commuter service to downtown Pittsburgh.

WESTMORELAND COUNTY

Westmoreland County Transit Authority operates a far-reaching, sophisticated bus system that includes 19 routes and features service throughout the county as well as buses to Pittsburgh. For schedules, call WCTA at (724) 834–9282 or (800) 221–9282, or visit them at the Westmoreland Transit Center, 41 Bell Way, Greensburg. Please note that WCTA buses do not operate on major holidays.

As with many municipal transportation systems in the region, fares are based on the number of zones traversed; for travel within Westmoreland County, expect your fare to range from $1.20 to $4.00. Transfers are free when needed to complete one-way travel, but you must use your transfer within one hour from the time it's issued. While exact fare is not required, drivers will change $1.00 bills only. You can avoid the need for cash by purchasing "Ten Trip Tickets" that offer a 10 percent discount off the total ticket price. Drivers carry the ticket books for your convenience.

Senior citizens age 65 and older ride free during off-peak hours on weekdays and on Saturdays and holidays. Patrons with disabilities ride for half fare at all times. Seniors should apply for their eligibility cards at the transit center, while those with disabilities may apply by calling the center at (800) 221-9282. If you're a wheelchair user, WCTA asks that you call them at (800) 221-9282 two days to one week before you need their service.

For disabled persons unable to utilize public transportation, the county operates a paratransit service in association with several local taxi cab companies. The paratransit service operates in the same communities, and during the same hours, as WCTA's bus routes. Fares, however, are twice the amount charged for a similar bus trip. To apply, call WCTA at (800) 221-9282.

Taxi Cabs

The first thing you must appreciate about travel by cab in Southwestern Pennsylvania—if you wave your arm for a cab here, you're likely to get a tired arm. Typically, you won't find cabs cruising city streets. The demand is relatively small for standard cab service, and companies size their fleets to match that demand. In fact, most of the cab companies here also provide

paratransit and shared-ride service to complement their cab fleets.

You will find cabs aplenty at Pittsburgh International Airport and downtown Pittsburgh's major hotels. If you're anywhere near the airport or a hotel, the best way to get a cab is to call and book one. All companies profiled here offer round-the-clock service each day of the year.

Also, a word about jitneys. You'll find these private operators, who transport customers at negotiated fees, in several Pittsburgh neighborhoods. Residents contend that, because licensed cab companies seldom ventured into these neighborhoods in years past, jitneys arose and thrived to meet a pressing need. Jitneys are unlicensed by the state and have no official standing, so you'll have very little recourse should something go awry. Patronize them at your discretion. Frequent jitney users often know their drivers.

Checker Cab
4001 Clariton Road
(412) 664-5600
www.taxicabusa.com/Pittsburgh/checker
_cab_pgh.htm

These distinctive cabs, with their green checkerboard patterns accented by gold striping, operate in downtown Pittsburgh and the city's western suburbs. You'll find a fleet of 25 cabs that await you at major hotels and are authorized to transport you to and from Pittsburgh International Airport. Checker also operates shared-ride service as part of the Port Authority of Allegheny County's ACCESS program.

Peoples Cab Company
1140 Washington Boulevard
(412) 441-5343

To reserve your red and white Peoples Cab, you must call ahead. They can provide you with service to—but not from—Pittsburgh International Airport, where Yellow Cab operates an exclusive contract. Peoples Cab provides vehicles and drivers to serve schools and school districts with established contracts.

City, county, and state government all have responsibility for highway mainte-nance in Southwestern Pennsylvania.

S&S Transit
400 Eden Park Boulevard, McKeesport
(412) 751-6780

You won't see many S&S cabs around. They have a fleet of six green cabs that serves the Monongahela Valley. The company maintains a much larger fleet—70 vehicles—for its shared-ride programs in Allegheny and Westmoreland Counties. Rented vans, complete with drivers, are available for rental on an hourly basis.

Yellow Cab Co.
5931 Ellsworth Avenue
(412) 665-8100

By far the largest provider in the region, Yellow Cab offers a fleet of about 360 vehicles. It serves corporate accounts, stands at major hotels, and deploys about 60 cabs at any given time at Pittsburgh International Airport. As a special service, Yellow Cab offers several regional phone numbers to spare residents of those areas toll calls. If you live in the South Hills, call the company at (412) 344-TAXI. In Monroeville, the number is (412) 374-TAXI.

Local Driving

Driving in and around Pittsburgh can be at once rewarding and frustrating. When you drive here, you'll travel along roads that take you through charming towns with attractive river views. The hills and mountains provide breathtaking vistas that attract international tourists. Those same hills, however, can become treacherous in bad weather. Even more maddening is the way many streets in the region are named.

Take the city of Pittsburgh, for example. In downtown Pittsburgh, you'll find avenues numbered from 1 to 7. At the same time, you'll encounter numbered streets that begin with 6 and go all the way to the 50s in the city's Lawrenceville neighborhood. If that weren't confusing enough, South Side cross streets begin at 1 and go into the 20s. Got it? Now, when someone says to meet him on 6th, what on earth do you do?

You'll get used to it soon enough, and the charm of Pittsburgh's streets will prevail. The following is a look at some of the principal state routes, city streets, and bridges with which you'll become familiar.

STATE ROUTES

The primary state routes in the region are similar in a number of key respects. They pass through residential and commercial districts, offering only the occasional high-speed sections. They're great for local travel, but you'll probably prefer the inter-state network for longer hauls.

Allegheny County also offers a belt-way of five concentric rings—designated blue, green, yellow, orange, and red—with the city of Pittsburgh at the center. These were developed many years ago as alter-natives to driving through the city. They may have been effective at one time, but with the growth of commercial and resi-dential districts along the belts, and the concomitant increase in traffic and traffic signals, you frequently won't make good time if you use the belts. When you get to know them well—if you're one of the few who does—you'll find the belts can help you detour around local traffic snarls.

Route 8
This is an important connector between the city of Pittsburgh and Butler County, passing through the city's northern sub-urbs en route.

Route 19
Route 19 spans both the North Hills and the South Hills of Pittsburgh, reaching all the way to Washington County. The high-way offers separate truck spurs in both the North Hills and South Hills.

Route 22

A major route from Pittsburgh to the east, Route 22 provides access to such communities as Indiana and Johnstown. Many folks traveling to Penn State University travel Route 22 to State College.

Route 28

Route 28 reaches from the city of Pittsburgh north to Kittanning in Armstrong County, pretty much paralleling the Allegheny River, which is intermittently visible along the way. You can follow Route 28 well into Northwestern Pennsylvania, though with the development of I-79, few would do that.

Route 30

This highway takes you east, through Westmoreland County and into the Laurel Highlands region. Route 30 is linked to Route 22 by a 14-mile high-speed highway called the Amos K. Hutchinson Bypass. It's a toll road maintained by the Pennsylvania Turnpike Commission.

Route 51

You can travel Route 51 from Pittsburgh southeast to Uniontown, passing through some of the South Hills and the Mon Valley along the way.

Route 60

Route 60 links most of Beaver County's major towns and extends north all the way to I-80. A 17-mile stretch of the road between Beaver Falls and New Castle is a high-speed toll road, maintained by the Pennsylvania Turnpike Commission, called the Beaver Valley Expressway.

Route 65

Route 65 offers a scenic drive along the Ohio River as it carries you from Pittsburgh west to Beaver County.

Route 422

This Butler County road links Route 28 with I-79. It's an important highway for residents of Armstrong and Butler Counties.

PITTSBURGH STREETS

Two of the city's most important streets are Fifth Avenue and Forbes Avenue, which run roughly parallel from downtown about 6 miles to the city's eastern neighborhoods. Forbes is one-way outbound through Oakland, while Fifth is one-way inbound from Oakland. When you drive these streets, you'll pass by five colleges or universities—Duquesne University, Carlow College, the University of Pittsburgh, Carnegie Mellon University, and Chatham College. You'll find it positively enlightening.

When you're looking to avoid traffic jams on the Parkway East, Second Avenue and the Boulevard of the Allies might help. The Boulevard of the Allies reaches from downtown to the Squirrel Hill neighborhood, providing a pleasant drive through Schenley Park. The Second Avenue trip also is interesting, paralleling the Monongahela River and passing the gleaming Pittsburgh Technology Center as it takes you to Hazelwood.

Penn Avenue and Liberty Avenue also are important routes to and from town, connecting the central business district and eastern neighborhoods. Penn is one-way inbound near downtown. Two steep streets, Perrysville Avenue and Mt. Troy Road, will take you from the Allegheny River to the city's northern neighborhoods.

One of the city's most interesting streets is Carson Street—it's East Carson Street or West Carson Street, depending on which side of the Fort Pitt Bridge you find yourself. The street provides you with views of the city's West End and the town of McKees Rocks, passes through the vital

You can rent a variety of styles of bicycles and even a "bike trailer," to seat two toddlers, from Golden Triangle Bike Rentals, LLC (412) 600-0675. Guided group bike tours of Pittsburgh's riverfront trails and downtown are also available.

Located in Southwestern Pennsylvania, Pittsburgh is about halfway between Chicago and New York City. It's within a two-hour flight or a day's drive of more than 70 percent of the U.S. population and 50 percent of the Canadian population, according to our visitors bureau.

South Side and its brace of trendy restaurants and galleries, and continues through to West Homestead in the Mon Valley, offering glimpses of former industrial sites now being recycled as residential, office, and entertainment complexes. Not a bad tour of the city . . . and you never have to leave Carson Street.

BRIDGES

If you like bridges, you'll love Pittsburgh. In Allegheny, Beaver, and Lawrence Counties alone, you'll find an estimated 167 bridges, many of them beautiful and distinctive, sporting ornate metalwork and a vast variety of architectural approaches. Since you'll be using them every day, you'll probably think of them more as convenience than art, but it's nice to appreciate their design every so often.

You'll become familiar with such Allegheny River bridges as the Fort Duquesne Bridge, Veterans Bridge, the Sixth Street Bridge, the Seventh Street Bridge, the Ninth Street Bridge, the 16th Street Bridge, the 31st Street Bridge, the 40th Street Bridge, the 62nd Street Bridge, the Highland Park Bridge, and the Hulton Bridge, with its lavender superstructure.

Across the Monongahela, you'll find the Fort Pitt Bridge (although it could be argued that this bridge is above the Point and therefore crosses all three rivers), and the Liberty Bridge, a major artery—along with the companion Liberty Tunnels—between Pittsburgh and the South Hills. Other Monongahela River crossings include the 10th Street Bridge (remember what we told you about street numbering here?), the Birmingham Bridge, and the Ranking Bridge.

Near Pittsburgh, you'll cross the Ohio River at the West End Bridge, the McKees Rocks Bridge, and the Sewickley Bridge.

The McKees Rocks Bridge is the longest at better than 1.5 miles, while Veterans Bridge covers the most deck area with its six lanes. Clearly, we've presented only a selection of the region's bridges, those that are most heavily used.

HISTORY 🏛

When the first hardy 18th-century traders gazed upon the land that would come to be known as Pittsburgh, they saw a valley of verdant hillsides cut by a triangle of rivers, with majestic, unspoiled forests rising as sentinels above. The strengths they viewed were formidable. On the one hand, the flatter land between and along the rivers would serve for trading posts, forts, and settlements. On the other hand, the rivers would provide convenient and economical transport routes—both to the settled cities of the East and the unexplored domains of the West—while the virgin woods would offer game as well as timber for building.

It's impossible, of course, to know what really went through the minds of those intrepid early traders as they surveyed for the first time the site of the future Pittsburgh. But it is clear that the assets they saw—and those that they couldn't see, such as abundant coal beneath the soil—would form the foundation of a city that would become the industrial giant of America, as well as a home to generations of immigrants. The story of Pittsburgh is a story of boom, bust, and rebirth, the rise and decline of a great manufacturing center recreated as a thriving, progressive metropolis based on economic and social diversity.

All who observed this land recognized its commercial and strategic importance as the Gateway to the West. Even before 1750, the French had successfully navigated the river network all the way from the Point, where the Allegheny and Monongahela Rivers merge to form the Ohio River, to the Mississippi River. In fact, well before Pittsburgh was officially founded or named, the French and the British, each allied with different Indian nations of the region, extended their European battle for dominance to what was then known as the Ohio Country. The struggle was protracted and bloody, the outcome far from certain.

In 1754, the French held dominion over the Ohio Country from Fort Duquesne, the redoubt constructed at the point. It was in that year that a young major named George Washington led a group of Virginians against the French, only to meet ignominious defeat. A 1755 expedition against the fort, this one led by Gen. Edward Braddock, suffered even worse consequences. Braddock and many of his officers were killed; Washington, miraculously, defied death in the Ohio Country for the second time in two years.

It was only in 1758, as Britain began to gain the upper hand all across the New World, that the French occupation of the Ohio Country ended. On November 24, as the British army prepared for its final assault on the fort, a scouting party delivered the news: the French had abandoned Fort Duquesne. Three days later, Gen. John Forbes, the British commander, solemnly renamed the fort in honor of British prime minister William Pitt.

The prolonged struggle for control of the Ohio Country may have been over, but the growth of the settlement continued at a measured pace. This, after all, was the wilderness. Beautiful as the land was, life remained harsh. Home very often was little more than a hut along the rivers that could be swept away by the fury of a spring flood. In 1760, two years after the final conquest of the French, the settlement that surrounded Fort Pitt numbered 151 people. Even at the close of the Revolutionary War, the population still numbered in the hundreds.

Slow though growth may have been, the late 18th century brought several important developments. The year 1787 marked the founding of the Pittsburgh Academy, forerunner of today's University of Pittsburgh. On April 22, 1794, the city became a borough and staged its first elections.

ℹ️ **Check the Web site www.frenchand indianwar250.org for new events through 2010 honoring the 250th anniversary of the French and Indian War, which started in 1754.**

THE RIVERBOAT ERA

As the century closed, the city began to fulfill its promise as the Gateway to the West. With the young nation expanding, Pittsburgh became an excellent launching point for traffic that could navigate the inland waterways all the way to New Orleans.

From the turn of the 19th century, Pittsburgh served as a significant center for flatboat traffic. The craft not only transported cargo but were also a primary transportation mode for immigrants seeking to settle the West. Since Pittsburgh merchants often loaded flatboats with goods for sale at ports of call along the way, the colorful craft resembled nothing so much as floating department stores. Lacking a way to float the boats upstream, the owners typically disassembled the craft and sold them for their lumber at journey's end.

Upstream traffic required a different kind of vessel—the keelboat, long and narrow, pointed at the ends, propelled by human rowers, or polers. The upstream journey was tedious and arduous for passengers, as the trip from Louisville to Pittsburgh might last a month. More difficult still was the work of the polers, a hard-drinking, hard-living breed.

The riverboat era produced one of the most colorful characters in Pittsburgh history—Mike Fink, self-proclaimed King of the Boatmen, whose brawls and benders took on mythic proportions.

Pittsburgh even became an early hub of shipbuilding, a natural given the volume of its river traffic. With the development of steam-powered vessels, however, shipbuilding died out in Pittsburgh, and the era of flatboats and keelboats lasted no more than a few decades. Mike Fink, frustrated by the advent of steam-powered vessels, took off for the badlands of the Rockies and departed Pittsburgh's history forever.

The city's future would not lie in shipbuilding. But the riverboat era proved conclusively that Pittsburgh and its waterways could serve the nation well as a transport center, a role the city would continue to play throughout the period of America's industrialization.

FROM EUROPE THEY CAME... AND CAME... AND CAME

During the 19th century and the first part of the 20th century, Pittsburgh developed its modern identity as a melting pot for dozens of nationalities and cultures, and as the most important steel manufacturing center in America.

Blessed with the natural elements used for manufacturing, the city needed only the human component to complete the equation. In the 19th century, seemingly endless waves of immigration satisfied that need.

Early in the century, a steady stream of uprooted Europeans settled in Pittsburgh, drawn to the city for a number of reasons. Among that early group were Irish fleeing famine in their homeland and finding work in Pittsburgh's mining industry; Scots-Irish, Scots, Welsh, and Dutch who were among the earliest settlers; and skilled Belgians who answered a call for help from a fledgling Pittsburgh glass manufacturer. Still others came as indentured servants or criminals, working off their contracts or sentences in the New World.

In the 1840s the trickle of immigration grew to a flood, with the influx of new

Pittsburghers primarily from Germany and Ireland. Yet another wave, in the 1890s, brought immigrants from Central and Southeastern Europe.

The contributions of these new resident cannot be overestimated. The immigrants tended to settle with their fellow displaced countrymen in neighborhoods ringing the burgeoning downtown that reflected their distinct cultures and religions. Many Italians, for example, settled in Bloomfield, a few miles east of downtown Pittsburgh. Even today, Italian can be heard spoken on Bloomfield's streets.

The Irish gathered in downtown itself before fanning out to neighborhoods such as Garfield. Many German immigrants found new homes in the hilly area north of downtown that would become known as Troy Hill. European Jews congregated in the Hill District; later, this neighborhood adjacent to downtown would become the city's most important African-American community with the 19th-century wave of migration from the American South. Polish immigrants settled in a number of new neighborhoods, including Lawrenceville along the Allegheny and South Side along the Monongahela.

Even relatively small immigrant groups made an impact. Scandinavians, for example, never settled in Pittsburgh in large numbers. Yet Swedish immigrants who came for work in the steel mills gathered in the working-class suburb of McKeesport, where they erected churches that conducted services in their native tongue well into the 20th century. Finnish immigrants clustered in the Monongahela River towns of Glassport and Monessen, building schools, churches, and fraternal organizations.

These distinctive neighborhoods, insular in their way but steeped in the traditions and culture of the Old World, would provide Pittsburgh with a foundation of ethnicity that, to this day, is a defining characteristic of the city. Pittsburgh became the very embodiment of the "melting pot," and the effects continue to be profound. A mid-20th-century study found that, years after the principal waves of European immigration had ended, 42 percent of the population of Allegheny County (of which Pittsburgh is the seat) were foreign born or children of those born outside America.

THE HEART OF STEEL

With all the components in place, manufacturing in Pittsburgh was set for takeoff. As early as the 1820s, Pittsburgh boasted eight rolling mills driven by steam power. Between that period and the Civil War, several developments facilitated the transformation of the fledgling steel industry to a growing giant.

One such development was the discovery that bituminous coal, so plentiful in the region, could be used to create coke, an abundant and relatively cheap fuel, to power the mills. A second was the almost simultaneous development, by England's Henry Bessemer and Pittsburgh's William Kelly, of air cooling the molten iron to strengthen and purify the product. With these refinements in the production process, and others that would follow, such as the creation of the open-hearth process in the early 20th century, Pittsburgh was poised to become the steelmaking heart of America.

It had the economic muscle, through such financiers as the Mellon family. It had the natural resources necessary for steel production and the river and railroad networks to ship products anywhere. It had a willing and skilled labor force. And it had the entrepreneurial talent.

Many of the giants of industrialism grew in Pittsburgh along with the city's manufacturing base. In 1881 a Scottish immigrant named Andrew Carnegie joined

At the Forks of the Ohio in 1753, George Washington was thrown into the half-frozen Allegheny River from his raft, where he named the site for a fort.

Preserving the History of Big Steel

Rivers of Steel National Heritage Area
(412) 464-4020

Reel Steel. Monday through Saturday
11:00 A.M. to 4:00 P.M.

From 1875 to 1980, southwestern Pennsylvania was the steelmaking capital of the world, producing the steel for some of America's greatest icons, such as the Brooklyn Bridge and the Empire State Building. During World Wars I and II, this region's steel-workers carried a nation's defense on their backs, producing more steel, armor, and armaments in a single year than entire countries. While many of the region's legendary mill sites have been dismantled and it has been decades since the mills belched fire and smoke over Pittsburgh's skyline, the enormity of the region's steel-making contributions and its historical significance to the nation demand its story be told and its sites be preserved.

Created by Congress in 1996, the Rivers of Steel National Heritage Area is committed to preserving, interpreting, and managing the historic, cultural, and natural resources related to Big Steel and its related industries. Encompassing 3,000 square miles in the seven counties of Allegheny, Armstrong, Beaver, Westmoreland, Greene, Fayette, and Washington, Rivers of Steel is building on this area's remarkable transition from heavy industry to high technology and diversified services, as well as bolstering the new regional economy by promoting tourism and economic development based on this region's historic industrial saga.

A multifaceted program, the Rivers of Steel National Heritage Area's mission includes historic preservation, cultural conservation, education, recreation, and resource development. Currently, the Heritage Area has bills in Congress to create the Homestead Works National Park. The proposed park would be located on 38 acres surrounding the Carrie Furnaces, the last of the giant blast furnaces from the Homestead Works, and the Pump House, site of the bloody 1892 Homestead Steel Strike.

—With thanks to Rivers of Steel

with his six brothers in a venture that later would become Carnegie Steel Company, itself a predecessor of the giant U.S. Steel Corp. (today known as USX). In one of those ironies of history, Carnegie located his first major mill, the Edgar Thomson Works, on the site where the ill-fated General Braddock fell to the French.

Other early steel and coal magnates included Henry Phipps, an early Carnegie partner, Henry W. Oliver, and Henry Clay Frick. Nor was entrepreneurship limited to the steel industry. In 1869, George Westinghouse invented the air brake in Pittsburgh, a development that advanced the continuing growth of the railroad industry. A protean figure, Westinghouse helped found or operate an estimated 60 companies, including the business that would become a 20th-century giant—Pittsburgh-based Westinghouse Electric Corp.

These titans of industry left an indelible mark on the region, in a number of ways. Their impact on the area's economy, of course, was profound. But so, too, was their perpetuation—if not downright origination—of the concept of philanthropy. The Carnegie Museums of Pittsburgh, the Carnegie Library (a thriving institution in so many western Pennsylvania towns), the Frick Art & Historical Center, Phipps Conservatory and Botanical Gardens, Mellon Park, Mellon Square—all remain vital features of contemporary Pittsburgh, and all are living testament to the philanthropy of Pittsburgh's leading industrialists.

Aided by such corporate largesse as well as the traditions that the transplanted Europeans brought with them, culture and education in Pittsburgh flourished in this period. These years marked the founding of such foundation arts institutions as the Pittsburgh Symphony in 1895 and the Pittsburgh Opera in 1938.

In education, Carnegie Tech University—later to become Carnegie Mellon University with an infusion of Mellon family money—was founded in 1900, Duquesne University in 1878. The development of the University of Pittsburgh speaks volumes about the community partnership that was at the heart of Pittsburgh's growth.

To finance its landmark 42-story Cathedral of Learning, the University of Pittsburgh asked residents to participate by "buying" bricks for the edifice at a dime apiece. In the 11 years between 1926 and the Cathedral's completion in 1937, the university "sold" bricks to 114,000 people. The Cathedral of Learning still towers over the city as a symbol of Pittsburgh's commitment to education and to the cohesiveness and community spirit of Pittsburghers.

THE RISE OF LABOR

The impact of the leading industrialists of the 20th century was evident in yet another way—the rise of organized labor. As more and more men went to work in the mines and mills, they realized they would need representation to assure them of fair wages and safe working conditions. The nascent labor movement would not be readily accepted by the same men who had dotted the community with the libraries and museums that spoke of their generosity.

In 1858, as recorded by Arthur C. Bining in *Pennsylvania's Iron and Steel Industry,* a group of steelworkers formed a secret organization called the Iron City Forge of the Sons of Vulcan, the first permanent labor association in the iron industry. In 1876 the Sons of Vulcan merged with three other newly formed organizations to create the national Amalgamated Association of Iron and Steel Workers.

Forming a union was one thing; persuading management to recognize it was another. The growth of steel in Pittsburgh was marked by regular confrontations between management and labor, none more infamous or bloody than the Homestead strike of 1892. In a dispute over wages and the right to organize, workers at U.S. Steel's Homestead plant along the city's southeastern border seized the factory and captured 300 Pinkerton detectives sent in to quell the strike. The situation degenerated into a series of pitched battles along the Monongahela River and a failed assassination attempt against U.S. Steel board chairman Henry Clay Frick. By the time the Pennsylvania Militia restored order, 10 were dead.

Far from hastening management-labor accord, the Homestead strike served only to polarize the parties. It was 45 years after the strike that U.S. Steel officially recognized the steelworkers' union, breaking the impasse in the industry. Finally,

Pittsburgh lost the "h" in its spelling in 1891. Twenty years later, bowing to popular pressure, the U.S. Board on Geographic Names approved restoration of the "h."

If you'd like to read an in-depth account of regional history, complete with hundreds of photographs, get a copy of the comprehensive coffee-table book **Pittsburgh: Story of an American City** *by Stefan Lorant, now in its fifth edition.*

with labor and management at relative peace, the boom could roll on.

Pittsburgh's role as the industrial heart of America reached its full flower during World War II, when the Commonwealth of Pennsylvania produced one-sixth of the world's iron and steel.

The city's reputation reached international proportions. On his historic visit to the United States during the height of the cold war, Soviet premier Nikita S. Krushchev included Pittsburgh on his itinerary. While in the city, he was heard to remark that if the Soviets really wanted to cripple America, they would drop a bomb on the Duquesne Club, where Pittsburgh's leading industrialists gathered for lunch and hosted their guests overnight. It was thought to be a joke, but Khrushchev, perhaps mindful of his words, chose to spend the night at the Carlton House.

A RENAISSANCE DRAMA, IN TWO ACTS

The city in the Golden Triangle, as the land near the Point was called, was a stunning success. Yet as America settled into postwar normalcy, Pittsburgh was in danger of choking on that very success. The problems were twofold. First, the same plants that were the city's lifeblood also were spewing smoke into the air, creating deadly dark clouds that, at their worst, literally blocked the rays of the sun and created virtual 24-hour-a-day nights. Ask Pittsburghers of a certain age about that era, and what they remember most is the smoke, the gasping for air, the clothes that would turn pitch-black when hung on the line to dry.

The second problem was the helter-skelter pattern of development that had left the Golden Triangle an unattractive warren of dirty warehouses and untended tracks to nowhere. If Pittsburgh were to continue its growth, both problems would have to be addressed.

Pittsburgh Mayor David L. Lawrence and leading industrialist and financier Richard K. Mellon had, independently, reached that conclusion. Lawrence was more than the city's top official and the future governor of Pennsylvania; he controlled the Democratic party, which in the labor-dominated city was the only party that mattered. Mellon was perhaps the city's' most powerful industrialist, one who could lead others in important new directions. They joined forces in a new entity called the Allegheny Conference on Community Development, an organization that, more than 50 years later, continues to play an important role in Pittsburgh's growth.

Their collaboration was historic, as government to that point had played little role in the city's development. John P. Robin, who worked for the Allegheny Conference and would be a pivotal player in Pittsburgh's growth for five decades, described that historic collaboration in a 1997 oral history.

"It was really a different climate that had existed," Robin said. "There was excitement and willingness. There never was a precise plan for development. The appetite, I usually say, grew with the eating. There was a contagion, a belief that nothing was impossible and we ought to try it."

The result was an unprecedented redevelopment that became known as the Renaissance. The partnership set out to improve their city on both key fronts. On smoke control, the city passed a series of abatement measures that, with the blessing of Mellon and other corporate leaders, industry implemented without complaint.

On the land use front, the partnership in 1947 persuaded the Pennsylvania Legislature to enact a new body, the Urban Redevelopment Authority of Pittsburgh, that would have sweeping powers to acquire and assemble land. With those new powers the city went to work on its Golden Triangle. At the very point where the Allegheny and Monongahela Rivers converge to form the Ohio River, the city and the Commonwealth of Pennsylvania created Point State Park, a 36-acre urban oasis with riverfront benches, a majestic fountain, and the Fort Pitt Blockhouse, the sole surviving section of the old Fort Pitt.

Adjacent to Point State Park, the partnership demolished the rat's nest of tracks and warehouses and created Gateway Center, a six-building office cluster that became a prestigious downtown address. It remains so today, with entities such as the United Steelworkers of America headquartered there.

Uptown from the Golden Triangle, the URA acquired properties and assembled them in a tract that in 1961 became the home of the Mellon Arena (formerly known as the Civic Arena), a pioneering sports and entertainment complex that features a retractable silver dome.

This period of ongoing prosperity also marked the suburbanization of Pittsburgh. Decades of success had provided thousands of Pittsburghers with the wherewithal to seek larger homes in more pastoral settings. Not all abandoned the inner city, of course, as Pittsburgh's distinctive neighborhoods remain a compelling feature of the city. But people relocated in sufficient numbers that a new term—Greater Pittsburgh—entered the local lexicon. In 1960, the Greater Pittsburgh population soared to nearly 2.4 million.

With the city scrubbed clean of deadly smoke and the public-private development partnership both secure and experienced, Pittsburgh entered the second phase of its Renaissance in the 1970s and 1980s.

As visitors drive through the Fort Pitt Tunnel to enter the city for the first time, they typically are stunned by the unexpected beauty of Pittsburgh's skyline, defined by towering skyscrapers so architecturally and functionally diverse

that, in aggregate, they defy quick or easy description. The most common response is a sharp intake of breath and a determination to explore them all.

Even more remarkable is that most of these signature buildings were created during Renaissance II. Their import is so great that they deserve to be mentioned at some length, and an entire chapter of this book (Architecture) is devoted to doing just that.

During Renaissance II, these multiple downtown building projects generated about $2 billion in private and public investment while creating more than $21 million annually in new local tax revenues. While the redevelopment efforts of cities are difficult to quantify, let alone compare, it seems fair to say that few cities have accomplished so much over such a short period. Between the first and last of these developments, only about 15 years elapsed.

Once again the world took notice of Pittsburgh's remarkable achievements. It was during this period that the city reaped a number of prestigious honors. *Places Rated Almanac* judged Pittsburgh "America's Most Livable City" in 1985. *Health* magazine ranked Pittsburgh in its top 10 American cities. *Savvy* called the city the sixth-best in the nation for raising kids. *Fortune* cited Pittsburgh on two fronts: it had the eighth-best business climate and was the third Most-Conducive-To-Marriage City.

The distinctive fountain at Point State Park, at the confluence of the Allegheny, Monongahela, and Ohio Rivers, is fed by a glacial formation and sprays 6,000 gallons per minute.

Several Fortune 500 companies are headquartered in Pittsburgh: Alcoa, Consolidated Natural Gas, Heinz USA, Mellon Bank, PNC Bank, PPG Industries, and USX. Pittsburgh is the sixth-largest software center in the United States, in terms of number of employees.

The two phases of Pittsburgh's Renaissance extended the unbroken record of prosperity in Pittsburgh and promised even more for the future. That promise, however, would not be fulfilled, at least not at once.

DECLINE, THEN DIVERSIFICATION

At first, it was just a few troubling signs. In 1984, Chevron acquired Gulf Oil, a bulwark of Pittsburgh's economy, and relocated its functions and employees to California. By 1986, only seven Gulf staff remained in Pittsburgh. In 1989, Pittsburgh's Rockwell Manufacturing fell victim to a similar fate—acquisition and relocation to California.

A casual observer might have viewed these defections as aberrations, blips on an otherwise prosperous economic map. But such optimism would not survive the collapse of Big Steel.

The decline was precipitous. In the 1980s, Greater Pittsburgh lost an estimated 127,500 jobs in steel and related manufacturing industries. All the support industries that had grown up around steel also felt the blow.

Analysts differ in their assessment of steel's collapse. In his book *And The Wolf Finally Came*, labor writer and historian John Hoerr points to such factors as incursions by foreign manufacturers and "mini-mills," which could produce steel at lower cost. He also fingers the inability of Big Steel to adequately respond due to a cumbersome organizational structure and the age-old credibility gulf between management and labor.

Whatever the reasons, the impact on the region was severe. Without a healthy manufacturing industry to provide jobs for its young, the region—for the first time in its history—experienced significant out-migration. By 1990 the population of the city proper had plunged to just under 370,000, its lowest mark since 1900. The total for Greater Pittsburgh dipped below 2 million. During its economic heyday, Pittsburgh ranked as America's third-largest headquarters city, behind only New York and Chicago. Between 1984 and 1994, nine "Fortune 500" companies left Pittsburgh or vanished from the rankings.

Throughout its history, the hearty folk who had settled Pittsburgh proved themselves a can-do people; now, more than ever, they needed to do it again. With desperate determination, the city, led by the administration of mayor Tom Murphy, in concert with the Commonwealth of Pennsylvania, the private sector, foundations and neighborhood-based development organizations, unveiled a two-pronged approach to revitalization. First, the partnership would reclaim abandoned industrial sites and develop in their wake a more diversified economy. Just as important, the partnership would exploit the city's rivers, just as Pittsburgh's original settlers had, with exciting new developments that would contribute to the region's emerging economic diversity.

In short order, the city and its partners made significant progress on both fronts. Along the Monongahela, the partnership constructed 300 attractive housing units, with as many as 1,000 more homes to follow. Along the Allegheny, the partnership developed 230 luxury apartments at a site adjacent to new headquarters for Alcoa, the giant aluminum company that renewed its commitment to the city.

In building economic diversity, the region had considerable help from its two largest research universities, Pitt and Carnegie Mellon, sources for dozens of technology-based spin-off companies. Today the city ranks sixth in the nation in software sector employment, while the broader technology sector employs more than 100,000.

Encouraged by Pittsburgh's emergence as a fertile bed for the growth of technology-based industries, the National Aeronautics and Space Administration in 1996 committed $50 million to help launch a national robotics consortium, along the banks of the Allegheny, to be operated in conjunction with Carnegie Mellon. That development has pushed Pittsburgh to the forefront of robotics.

So complete was Pittsburgh's transformation that in 1996 manufacturing, mining, and construction accounted for only 17.5 percent of Pittsburgh's jobs.

THE NEW PITTSBURGH

Throughout the city, there are compelling symbols of the region's transformation. Washington's Landing, an Allegheny River island 2 miles north of downtown, had long been used for industrial operations, including the rendering of animal byproducts; when industrial companies abandoned the island, they left a legacy of contaminated soil. In the 1990s, Pittsburgh's public-private development team entombed the tainted soil and readied the land for redevelopment. Today, Washington's Landing is the site for light manufacturing, office buildings, a marina, townhomes, and recreation.

In Hays, in the city's southeast corner, the U.S. Army Ammunition Plant served as an important cog in the nation's military machine but had been vacant since the Vietnam War. The city's Urban Redevelopment Authority acquired the site from the Army for $1.00 and prepared it for new uses. Now, it is the home of GalvTech, a technology-based company that zinc coats steel coils.

Perhaps the most persuasive symbol of the region's rebirth is the Pittsburgh Technology Center, a gleaming complex along the Monongahela near the Oakland cluster of universities and hospitals. The

Pittsburgh's KDKA-AM delivered the nation's first regularly scheduled radio broadcast in 1920, coverage of the Harding-Cox presidential election. Because of their role as radio pioneers, KDKA and Pittsburgh's KQV-AM are among the three radio stations east of the Mississippi River permitted to begin their call letters with "K." (Philadelphia's KYW is the third.)

site just east of downtown was once home to J&L Steel's Hot Strip Mill; it glowed round the clock as one of the brightest lights of steelmaking.

When the site was abandoned in 1983, the city acquired it and began its conversion to a technology center. The complex currently is home to the University of Pittsburgh Center for Biotechnology and Bioengineering, the Carnegie Mellon Research Institute, Union Switch & Signal (a company founded by the ubiquitous Mr. Westinghouse), and a brace of support organizations of technology-based companies.

To stand on the campus of the Pittsburgh Technology Center is to see the city's history encapsulated. Gaze to the west and you see the gleaming skyscrapers that have defined the downtown since Renaissance II. Look toward the east and you notice the hot metal bridge spanning the Monongahela, still connecting the site to the mill's former coking operations across the river. And all of it wrapped by a latticework of highways, as if bound and determined to enclose and preserve the contrast for posterity.

In its roughly 250 years of settlement, Pittsburgh has experienced the booms and busts of an economic roller coaster, rising through most of its years to a position of prominence among the world's manufacturing centers, feeling the sting when that manufacturing declined, and emerging as a region of multiple strengths. Its impressive downtown, inviting suburbs,

 **HISTORY**

Washington's Landing, an Allegheny River island home to manufacturing, office buildings, recreation, and residence life, is so named because George Washington found refuge there during a 1753 storm.

and distinctive, close-knit neighborhoods are appealing for residents and visitors alike. It offers a rich mix of cultural and entertainment amenities, a reflection of the diverse heritage of its residents.

Above all, it retains the two most important characteristics of its spectacular, sometimes surprising development. Pittsburgh remains within 500 miles of more than half of America's population, making it a preferred site for business and residential location. By land, by water, by air, you can get there from Pittsburgh.

And it continues to boast a population imbued by the work ethic brought to America by its forebears, a population that epitomizes the ideals of America's melting pot, a population ready to roll up its sleeves and get the job done together.

MOVING INTO THE 21ST CENTURY

Amid protests and political controversy, several new initiatives and projects will be unveiled in this new century. Among them will be two new stadiums for the Pittsburgh Pirates and Pittsburgh Steelers sports teams. Already, Pitt Stadium has been razed to make room for a convocation and events center at the University of Pittsburgh.

The David L. Lawrence Convention Center will undergo expansion and revitalize the riverfront even further. The O'Reilly Theater attracts more patrons to the city's Cultural District.

A new form of government takes its place in Allegheny County with the newly created position of County Executive to work with the County Council. A champion of county concerns, former commissioner Tom Foerster passed away in January 2000, leaving his mark on the Community College of Allegheny County, the Kane Hospitals, and the Pittsburgh International Airport, which he worked tirelessly to see to completion.

Both major banks—Mellon and PNC—are moving ahead with new operations centers. The toppling of the LTV Steel stacks in Hazelwood makes way for additional riverfront revitalization in that area as well. With the purchase of Westinghouse's nuclear business in Monroeville, new owners are not only keeping the Westinghouse name but growing the business, adding jobs, and maintaining a vital part of that community's commercial base.

In the years ahead, there will be more abandoned rails made into bicycle and walking trials, and more worn-down properties converted to modern shops, restaurants, and entertainment venues. Indeed the pages of Pittsburgh history will move into new chapters in the new millennium.

ACCOMMODATIONS

Looking to overnight in Pittsburgh? Well, options for you abound. You can stay in a large, happening hotel in the heart of the city; repair to the suburbs for the quiet of a country inn; luxuriate in an all-seasons resort; or grab a room near the airport so you'll be sure to catch the early flight. All are attractive options in Pittsburgh and environs.

Accommodations in Pittsburgh are, in a word, accommodating. You'll find a setting, style, and price range to suit you. Note that one popular category of accommodation—the bed-and-breakfast inn—has its own chapter.

With so many options in greater Pittsburgh, you might think that dropping in and finding the room of your choice would be no problem. In most cases, that's true. Keep in mind, though, that the city is a business center and a popular site for conventions. If we're hosting a major convention, or even several medium-sized gatherings, accommodations in the city are snapped up, forcing visitors to more distant sites. Even there, availability during these occasional crunch times is no guarantee.

Therefore, the wise traveler plans ahead when coming to Pittsburgh. Take the time to make a few phone calls and reservations where appropriate. You'll find the effort rewarded with a guaranteed room you're sure to like.

Most of the time, though, there's more than enough capacity, resulting in sometimes keen competition for business. This has brought some important benefits to customers. For example, virtually all places of lodging in Pittsburgh offer both smoking and non- smoking rooms; any exceptions are noted in the individual write-ups below.

Policies on pets have changed as well. It was not too many years ago that, if you wanted to bring Bowser along with you, you needed to hide him in your picnic basket. With the boom in rooms, many hotels are accommodating pets as an added attraction for guests. You'll find pet policies detailed in the individual write-ups.

Accessibility for the disabled is another area of growing concern, for both operators and customers. Rare is the establishment in Pittsburgh that doesn't consider itself wheelchair accessible. As anyone who requires such facilities knows, however, there can be quite a difference between compliance with the letter of the law and convenience and comfort for you. When you're making those phone calls, be sure to ask specific questions about facilities and amenities for disabled guests as well as guests with other special needs.

Most establishments offer discount programs, such as those available through AAA or AARP. Many also maintain frequent traveler programs that help you reduce the cost of your stay. Make sure you inquire about these as well as special packages and offers for which you may be eligible. In Allegheny County, be prepared to pay a 7 percent room tax; elsewhere, the room tax varies from county to county. All establishments described below accept major credit cards.

In many instances the write-ups describe facilities that are part of well-known national chains, of which there are many that have a strong presence in our area. While the chains are so prominent that you know pretty much what to expect when you stay with them, such facilities are included where their locations make them potentially important to you.

For example, most hotels and motels near Pittsburgh International Airport are included for the convenience of those traveling here by air. All hotels and motels in the Oakland neighborhood's university-medical complex, which attracts many visitors in need of convenient lodging, are described. For those occasions when

Need help locating a hotel? Try the Greater Pittsburgh Convention & Visitors Bureau, (412) 281-7711, for information about hotels and other Pittsburgh attractions. The bureau offers two recorded phone messages detailing current activities: Tourism Information Line, (800) 366-0093, and Weekend Package Hot Line, (800) 927-8376.

Downtown's finest are booked, a number of facilities on the perimeter of Downtown that are good sites for overflow traffic are featured.

After the section on Hotels & Motels, look for listings for Extended-stay Accommodations, Resorts, and Hotels. We tried hard to include something for everyone.

Exploring Pittsburgh's lodgings will be a joy for you. Whatever your choice, you'll find your enjoyment enhanced by the legendary hospitality of Pittsburghers. If you don't mind our saying so, we'll make any room you choose seem like your home away from home.

PRICE CODE

The area of rates is not easily summarized. It might not appear so on the surface, but Pittsburgh is a community with peak seasons. The summer season is heaviest, fueled in part by convention business. Traveling in Pittsburgh also spikes around holidays and the skiing season. In light of all this, most operators maintain a range of rates rather than a set charge. Asked about her typical rates, one operator replied, "It depends on the day."

That kind of variability makes reporting on rates difficult. With each description, we've indicated rate categories with

Even children can partake of afternoon tea at The Omni William Penn hotel. Ask for the Mad Hatters Tea, a selection of tasty cookies and confections kids will love!

from one to four dollar signs. The rates are for standard rooms, double occupancy. Here's the key:

$	$30 to $65
$$	$66 to $100
$$$	$101 to $135
$$$$	$136 and over

Remember that when capacity is tight, your rate may be appreciably higher than the standard charge.

HOTELS & MOTELS

Downtown

Duquesne Club   **$$$**
325 Sixth Avenue
(412) 391-1500
The Duquesne Club is one of the city's most prominent and traditional institutions. Since the turn of the 20th century, business and civic leaders have gathered here to relax and forge plans for the city's growth. Less well-known are the 30 overnight rooms that the club offers to visitors (provided they are guests of members). The experience here is Old World, with attentive staff and quiet surroundings. Many who stay here return each time they're in town, enamored of the ambience.

You'll be in the heart of downtown Pittsburgh, within walking distance of virtually every center-city attraction. The club does not permit pets. See the Architecture chapter for a few of the Duquesne Club's aesthetic details.

The Omni William Penn   **$$$**
530 William Penn Place
(412) 281-7100
www.omnihotels.com
Relaxing in the Palm Court lobby of the Omni William Penn is one of the city's most civilized experiences. While you enjoy a beverage and bask beneath the ornate chandeliers, you can laugh with

friends and watch the swells stroll through the lobby. It's such a comfortable experience that you might not want to leave.

Once you manage to get past the lobby, you'll find 603 guest rooms offering mahogany furnishings, plush carpeting, and marble baths. The hotel welcomes your pets. Ask about the special amenities at the select guest level.

In 1998 the hotel finished a three-year, $25 million renovation that gave facelifts to meeting rooms on the conference level, including new names that reflect Pittsburgh's industrial history—names such as Frick, Heinz, Oliver, Phipps, and Vandergrift. Many of the luxury suites have also been updated. Each boasts multiple bedrooms, living and dining rooms, sitting areas, and full kitchens. Electronics throughout the hotel were improved as well, so guests now enjoy two phone lines and voice mail.

The hotel features more than 52,000 square feet of meeting space, capped by the two-story grand Ballroom. For your dining pleasure, you'll choose from several restaurants, including the Terrace room, one of the city's most popular spots for breakfast meetings. The Palm Court lobby is a grand space flanked by seven arches on each side.

The Omni William Penn sits in the center of the city, within walking distance of all the cultural amenities as well as Grant Street political happenings. Turn to the Architecture chapter, where this hotel, commissioned by Henry Clay Frick, appears as part of the walking tour of downtown Pittsburgh. Don't miss afternoon tea in the Palm Court lobby, a simply splendid tradition (albeit borrowed from the British).

Pittsburgh Hilton and Towers $$$$
600 Commonwealth Place
Gateway Center
(412) 391-4600, (800) HILTONS
www.hilton.com
If you arrive at the Hilton and wonder about that attractive greenery across the

The Pittsburgh Hilton and Towers claims the world's largest revolving door.

street, wonder no longer. That's Point State Park, the unusual urban park that's the site for many entertainment and cultural events, including the annual Three Rivers Arts Festival (see the Annual Events chapter). Stay at the Hilton and the park and its attractions will be at your doorstep—literally. And so will the new home of the Pirates, PNC Park.

The hotel is the city's most capacious, offering 713 guest rooms that include a complement of concierge-class rooms. In your room you'll enjoy two phone lines with voice mail, writing desk, in-room movies, a coffeemaker, and an iron set. Each guest room boasts a river or city view.

If business beckons, the Hilton is well equipped to meet your needs. Its Executive Center is sequestered in a quiet corner of the first floor and offers boardrooms, computers, and secretarial service. If it's a meeting that you're planning, consider the Hilton's 18,200-square-foot ballroom, said to be the largest between New York and Chicago.

The health center includes Universal weights, treadmills, Stairmasters, rowing machines, and stationary bicycles. You'll enjoy both casual and more elegant dining in the hotel's two restaurants and two lounges.

The Hilton will allow small pets with management's prior approval.

Pittsburgh Marriott City Center $$$
112 Washington Place
(412) 471-4000, (800) 228-9290
www.marriott.com
While some urban hotels struggle to find space for exercise equipment, Pittsburgh Marriott City Center has no such problem. It offers a 40-foot indoor pool, a health club, and a sauna. Parking, another possible headache for urban hotels, also is hardly a problem here, as hotel guests have access to a 2,100-space indoor garage.

The hotel offers 402 guest rooms as well as 5 parlor suites and the deluxe Presidential Suite, complete with Jacuzzi and wet bar.

When you're ready to eat, you'll find fare that will match your mood. You'll want to try the Steelhead Grill, the on-premises seafood restaurant that has won national awards. In the mood for something lighter? Try Domino's Pizza selections, available through room service for late-night snacks.

While the hotel is only a few blocks from the center of downtown, it offers complimentary shuttle transportation to key downtown points.

Ramada Plaza Suites $$$
One Bigelow Square
(412) 281-5800, (800) 2RAMADA
www.ramada.com

Life is suite at Ramada Plaza. That's because all accommodations here are suites. Your suite features a kitchen or kitchenette, microwave oven, coffeemaker, utensils and dishware, dining and work areas, cable television, and recliners. Street-level retail shops provide a variety of valuable services. You'll find a hair stylist, a florist, a travel agency, and same-day laundry and valet services.

The health club is impressive, featuring 10,000 square feet including an indoor track, a free-weight room, aerobics classes, a pool, a sauna, a steam room, and a tanning bed. The hotel also offers meeting and banquet facilities.

For dining, the Ruddy Duck Restaurant and Lounge is popular with hotel guests and downtown visitors alike. The restaurant and hotel are just a few paces from Grant Street, the hub of Pittsburgh's professional activity.

Renaissance Pittsburgh Hotel $$$$
107 Sixth Street
(412) 562-1200, (800) 468-3571
www.marriott.com

The Renaissance is not only the city's newest hotel, but also the only one located right in the Cultural District downtown. A historic 1906 building that once housed offices and later—in one metamorphosis—became a dance club in the waning disco days, the Renaissance has been restored to its former glory. It's resplendent with a granite, brick, and copper exterior and an interior that showcases a spectacular lobby done in mosaic tile, with a grand marble staircase that winds upward. The building itself is notable for its three-story rotunda and roof of leaded glass and copper. In fact, the three-year renovation of the Renaissance became the largest copper restoration project in the United States since the restoration of the Statue of Liberty.

This luxurious hotel offers 286 guest rooms and 14 luxury suites. There is on-site and valet parking. Amenities include high-speed Internet access, voice mail, Web TV, an exercise room and whirlpool, plus an adjacent fitness center. Off the lobby the fashionable restaurant Opus has garnered rave reviews for its Mediterranean cuisine, as well as its wine bar.

Overlooking the Allegheny River, the Renaissance is within walking distance of theaters, restaurants, nightclubs, and the convention center. It's also less than a 10-minute stroll across the Roberto Clemente Bridge to the Andy Warhol Museum, PNC Park, and Heinz Field.

Sheraton Station Square Hotel $$$
7 Station Square Drive
(412) 261-2000, (800) 325-3535
www.sheraton.com

Station Square is a vibrant urban riverfront shopping center with 60 upscale shops. It's actually situated on the city's South Side, but it's so close to Downtown (right across the Smithfield Street Bridge) we decided to include it here. Stay at the Sheraton Station Square and you'll be only a few excited paces from all that activity.

The hotel offers 396 guest rooms as well as a club level with special amenities. Many rooms provide dramatic views of Pittsburgh's rivers and skyline, while all guest rooms offer cable television, in-room movies, and coffee service. You'll enjoy an indoor pool, whirlpool, sauna, and fitness center, while massage therapists stand at the ready to soothe any aches and pains. Meeting and banquet facilities can accommodate up to 1,500 people.

The atrium lobby is a must-stop, whether you're staying at the hotel or dropping by for refreshments. There, you'll see a waterfall that cascades seven stories into a charming lily pond. The water show makes the Pittsburgh Rare Lounge and Restaurant particularly appealing. Reflections Dining Room serves a popular Sunday brunch.

The Sheraton is just across the Smithfield Street Bridge (see our Architecture chapter for more details and the start of a walking tour). The hotel welcomes pets.

Westin Convention Center Hotel $$$$
1000 Penn Avenue
(412) 281-3700
www.westin.com

This is definitely one of the deluxe hotels in town, and very convenient to the David L. Lawrence Convention Center across the street. With 616 rooms, including 3 luxury suites and 22 junior suites, guests who want a little luxury while on business in the downtown area may opt to stay here. The banquet room seats approximately 960 people, and there are 19 meeting rooms. Guests enjoy two-line dataports with speaker phones and ironing supplies in each room. There are four restaurants, including the Fish Market. Parking is convenient underneath the hotel, but because parking is at a premium in downtown it's $17 a day for guests. Valet parking is available at $22 per day.

North

Clarion Hotel $$
300 Tarentum Bridge Road
New Kensington
(724) 335-9171, (877) 424-6423
www.clarioninn.com

Looking to hold a banquet or meeting in the New Kensington area? This may be your place, with facilities that can accommodate up to 900 and complete audiovisual equipment offered on-site.

Stay in one of the 115 guest rooms and you'll have access to an outdoor pool. If you're willing to sign for responsibility for any cleanup or damages, you're welcome to bring your pets.

Conley Resort Inn $$
740 Pittsburgh Road, Butler
(724) 586-7711, (800) 344-7303
www.conleyresort.com

While the designation "resort" may be a little highfalutin', Conley Resort Inn does offer a number of attractive amenities. It features an 18-hole golf course, a putting green, tennis courts, and an indoor pool. If the kids are along, dare them to try either the 100-foot waterslide or the speed slide. Pets are not permitted.

When you stay in one of the 56 guest rooms, you'll receive complimentary breakfast. Ask about specially priced golf packages. Conley Resort Inn is located along Route 8, a major state highway that connects Pittsburgh and Butler.

Days Inn—Butler/Conference Center $
139 Pittsburgh Road, Butler
(724) 287-6761, (800) 329-7466
www.daysinn.com

As the name suggests, conferences are popular at Days Inn, which offers meeting and banquet space for up to 1,200 people. That's far from the only attraction. The 138 guest rooms feature cable television, and you can also enjoy the pool, Jacuzzi, Brentwood Café, and Frisco's Night Club. Bring your pet, but be prepared to pay a $10 nonrefundable pet fee.

The facility offers specially priced golf packages that allow you to test as many as four Butler-area courses. Days Inn is located along Route 8.

Fairfield Inn Butler $$
200 Fairfield Lane, Butler
(724) 283-0009

Operated by Marriott, Fairfield Inn offers complimentary continental breakfast, in-

The New David L. Lawrence Center

The innovative, new David L. Lawrence Convention Center brings an elegant, functional, and environmentally intelligent facility to Pittsburgh's riverfront. The facility is the first certified "green" convention center in the United States, using features such as natural ventilation, natural daylight, water conservation, and energy efficiency. Stunning, spacious, and unique, the convention center triples Pittsburgh's capacity for meetings, conventions, and exhibitors.

The Sports & Exhibition Authority is responsible for the construction of the new convention center. Rafael Vinoly Architects, P.C. is the architect of record for the project. The convention center contains a main hall; a secondary hall; meeting rooms; two lecture halls; 330,000 square feet of exhibition space; a 33,000-square-foot ballroom; and a 700-space parking garage.

room work areas, an indoor pool, and a whirlpool. Feel free to use the hotel's fax service. Pets are not permitted in the 64 guest rooms.

While Fairfield Inn is about 25 miles from Pittsburgh, it is convenient to the many attractions of Butler, including Butler Memorial Hospital and the fairgrounds, host to the annual Big Butler County Fair in early July (see our Annual Events chapter).

Holiday Inn Allegheny Valley—RIDC Park $$$
180 Gamma Drive, O'Hara
(412) 963-0600
www.holiday-inn.com
If you expect your stay to last longer than a day or two, consider this Holiday Inn's leasing opportunities. The hotel offers 40 apartment-style suites with kitchen facilities and patios. You can take advantage of short- and long-term rates. "RIDC" is short for Regional Industrial Development Corporation, which developed the business park in which the hotel is located. Many who are in town on business in the park take advantage of this Holiday Inn's long-term rates.

Guests can relax in the fitness room, the Cabana Club bar (in the warmer

months), and Accolade's Restaurant and Nitescape Lounge. Meeting space can accommodate up to 600 people. The hotel welcomes your pets.

Holiday Inn Pittsburgh/McKnight $$$
4859 McKnight Road
(412) 366-5200
www.holiday-inn.com
Stay at this Holiday Inn and you'll hear the "Call of the Mall." It's located in the suburban North Hills on McKnight Road, an active strip of malls sure to satisfy your every shopping need.

The hotel offers 146 standard-issue guest rooms with cable television, computer access, voice mail, coffeemakers, and iron sets. Dine at the on-premises restaurant. Holiday Inn welcomes pets.

Holiday Inn Pittsburgh North $$
10 Landings Drive, Harmarville
(412) 828-9300
www.holiday-inn.com
One of the principal attractions of this hotel is a host of unusual entertainment opportunities nearby. Within a few minutes' walk are Blade Runners Ice Complex, featuring two regular ice-skating surfaces, and Ladbrokes, an off-track wagering facil-

ity where you can watch and wager on as many as 25 horse-racing tracks per day.

Located just off exit 5 of the Pennsylvania Turnpike, the hotel offers four suites in addition to its 63 standard rooms, as well as a small indoor pool. Sorry, but this Holiday Inn prefers no pooches.

The Priory—A City Inn $$$
614 Pressley Street
(412) 231-3338
www.thepriory.com

In the late 19th century, Benedictine priests traveling through Pittsburgh would take respite at the Priory. Current owners have restored the facility with

Victorian-style furnishings in its 24 guest rooms. If you need an office-away-from-the-office, this probably isn't the place. If you're looking for an Old-World experience in elegant surroundings, you'll find it at the Priory.

The inn is unobtrusive, located on a North Side residential street, but the appointments are splendid. You'll enjoy complimentary breakfast and evening wine around the fireplace. You can walk in the garden courtyard or to any of the city's nearby attractions, including Three Rivers Stadium and The National Aviary.

If you like, you can use complimentary limousine service for the half-mile trip across the Ninth Street Bridge into downtown Pittsburgh. Or you can sip your wine, gaze across the Allegheny River at the hustle and bustle of downtown, and contemplate how good life can be. Pets are not permitted. Parking is complimentary.

Rodeway Inn $
RD#6, US 422 East, Kittanning
(724) 543-1100

Here's a quaint establishment with only 20 rooms; what it lacks in volume it makes up in dedicated customer service. The hotel keeps records on all its guests. When guests come for return visits, staff have their customers' favorite touches waiting for them. Everyone who stays here will enjoy the free continental breakfast.

Guest rooms feature cable television, computer access, and coffeemakers. Bring your small pets, but you must provide a $25 refundable deposit. This Rodeway Inn is in Armstrong County, about 30 miles north of Pittsburgh.

Sheraton Inn Pittsburgh North $$$
910 Sheraton Drive, Mars
(724) 776-6900
www.sheraton.com

Don't worry about being on Mars. This community is part of Pittsburgh's growing suburban North Hills, which means you'll be close to many attractions.

This Sheraton Inn offers 189 rooms with a number of compelling views. You can request a room with a balcony or one that faces the hotel's atrium. All rooms offer cable television, computer access, coffeemakers, hair dryers, and iron sets. You'll also have access to fax and copier service.

For a workout, try the on-site health club, indoor/outdoor pool, and Jacuzzi. You can slake the thirst you work up at the on-premises lounge, Legends Pub. Sheraton Inn does not permit pets.

East

Al Monzo's Palace Inn $-$$
Routes 22 and 48, Monroeville
(412) 372-5500, (800) 545-6600

This hotel offers the distinctive touch of owner Al Monzo, who stages such unusual and attractive events as boxing cards on-site. Other entertainment options include indoor and outdoor swimming pools, a Jacuzzi, an exercise room, and a tanning salon. The Casa Di Monzo restaurant features weekend entertainment, and you also can sample lighter fare at Daisy's Coffee Shop.

Guest rooms include cable television and in-room movies, and suites are available. Pets are not permitted. Weekdays bring complimentary breakfast. The facility is a popular site for meetings, offering a Grand Ballroom with seating for 2,000.

You can reach Al Monzo's Palace Inn via the Pennsylvania Turnpike or Interstate 376 (the Parkway East).

Antiochian Village $$
P.O. Box 638, Ligonier, PA 15658
(724) 238-3677
www.antiochianvillage.org

Antiochian Village specializes in lodging for groups and conferences; it offers 11 meeting rooms. The experience here is quiet and thought-provoking. There are no televisions or other distractions in any of the 100 guest rooms, but you will find televisions in two common areas.

Antiochian Village provides plenty of amenities for group activities, including a baseball diamond, a football field, and basketball courts. For meals, a full-time chef is waiting to serve you. Antiochian Village does not permit pets.

Best Western University Hotel $
3401 Boulevard of the Allies
(412) 683-6100, (800) 245-4444
www.bestwestern.com

Stay at Best Western University Hotel and you'll be at the doorstep of Magee Woman's Hospital and the other health-care providers that constitute Pittsburgh's most important medical center. The hotel provides free shuttle service throughout the Oakland university-medical complex. Pick up your shuttle schedule at the front desk.

The 117 guest rooms include cable television and private balconies, and you'll have access to fax service, meeting space, and an on-site restaurant. You also can request an executive room and enjoy such amenities as a hair dryer, coffeemaker, and complimentary breakfast.

Comfort Inn of Greensburg $$
1129 East Pittsburgh Street, Greensburg
(724) 832-2600, (800) 228-5150
www.comfortinn.com

This Comfort Inn offers 77 rooms, including 24 whirlpool minisuites and two specialty suites. All rooms include cable television and complimentary continental breakfast, as well as access to fax and copier service. Staying here affords plenty of shopping opportunities, as the Westmoreland Mall is only a mile away, and there are plenty of other stores (Barnes & Noble, Toys R Us) and restaurants in the immediate area. When you're finished shopping, take a dip in the outdoor heated pool (if it's summer that is!). Pets allowed for an additional $10 per night.

Days Inn—New Stanton $
127 West Byers Avenue, New Stanton
(724) 925-3591
www.daysinn.com

If you're traveling the Pennsylvania Turnpike, Days Inn will be a welcome stop—it's close to the New Stanton exit where the turnpike meets Interstate 76. You'll find 135 guest rooms with many attractive features, including cable television, computer access, voice mail, hair dryers and iron sets.

When you're ready to relax, try the outdoor pool, the weight room, the restaurant, and the lounge. Days Inn does not permit pets.

Four Points Hotel by Sheraton $$
Route 30 East 100 Sheraton Drive
Greensburg
(724) 836-6060
www.sheraton.com

Don't be surprised if you hear wedding bells ringing as you near Four Points. Not only does the hotel offer an old-fashioned bridal suite but it also maintains a wedding coordinator to help you with the details of your nuptials.

Even if you're not in the matrimonial mood, you'll find the experience here pleasing. The hotel offers 146 rooms—the Deluxe Rooms and Bridal Suites have Jacuzzis—that feature cable television, in-room movies, and computer access. You'll enjoy the indoor pool, but if you need a more vigorous workout, you can hit the weights at a nearby fitness center for a $10 fee. The hotel's fitness room is less equipped.

Relax at the Prospect Lounge and the Vista Plateau, both on-site. Four Points does permit pets if you're willing to pay the additional $10.

Hampton Inn Greensburg $$
1000 Towne Square Drive, Greensburg
(724) 838-8800, (800) HAMPTON
www.hamptoninn.com
This Hampton Inn is much like any other location, only with a few differences. There's an outdoor pool, exercise facility, and 69 guest rooms at this location. You'll find restaurants within 2 miles, and this hotel is not far from the Westmoreland Mall. No pets allowed here, however. All Hampton Inns feature complimentary continental breakfast and free local telephone calling.

Hampton Inn Monroeville $$
3000 Mosside Boulevard, Monroeville
(412) 380-4000, (800) HAMPTON
www.hamptoninn.com
The Hampton Inn is one of Monroeville's newer hotels, strategically located just off the Pennsylvania Turnpike, the Parkway East, and Route 22. There are 140 guest rooms and two meeting rooms for business or conferences. Enjoy the indoor pool, fitness room, and complimentary continental breakfast. Guests can also enjoy the Outback Steakhouse attached to the Hampton Inn. Situated in Monroeville, you're close to shipping with the Miracle Mile Shopping Center right up the road and Monroeville Mall five minutes away. Just drive down Business Route 22 and you're never at a loss for a gas station or store! Boyce Park is approximately 10 minutes away in nearby Plum Borough. And that's a good thing since pets under 20 pounds are indeed allowed at this Hampton Inn location.

Holiday Inn Parkway East $$$
915 Brinton Road, Wilkinsburg
(412) 247-2700
www.holiday-inn.com
This hotel offers 177 guest rooms, with suites also available. You'll enjoy the indoor pool as well as privileges at a local fitness center that offers tennis and racquetball courts. For on-site dining, try the 915 Cafe. The Alleghany Room can accommodate up to 300 for banquets and meetings. The hotel welcomes small pets.

Holiday Inn Pittsburgh-Monroeville $$$
2750 Mosside Boulevard, Monroeville
(412) 372-1022
www.holiday-inn.com,
www.holiday-inn.com/monroeville
All 188 guest rooms at the hotel offer cable television, designated phone lines for modem connection, hair dryers, iron sets, and coffeemakers. Pets are permitted.

Amenities include an outdoor swimming pool and an on-premises restaurant called Finnegan's, which serves breakfast, lunch, and dinner, plus a Sunday brunch. Meeting and banquet facilities can accommodate up to 300 people.

The hotel is a quarter mile from exit 6 of the Pennsylvania Turnpike.

Pittsburgh's most elegant hotel during the 19th century was the Monongahela House, which stood next to the Monongahela Wharf. Six presidents, including Abraham Lincoln, stayed there during Pittsburgh's heyday as a river port.

Holiday Inn Select $$$
100 Lytton Avenue
(412) 682-6200
www.hiselect.com
When you stay here, you'll be smack-dab in the middle of the University of Pittsburgh campus. The historic Cathedral of Learning is several hundred yards away, and you'll enjoy the compelling sight of students on their way to class. You can reach all of Oakland's hospitals by walking or a short bus ride.

All 251 guest rooms feature cable television, in-room movies, coffeemakers, hair dryers, iron sets, and voice mail. Business travelers might prefer Executive Edition Rooms, with refrigerators and a daily buffet. Small pets are permitted.

Recreational opportunities include an indoor pool, a sauna, and exercise equipment. For dining, try the on-premises Foster's Grill, which features a popular Champagne Jazz Brunch each Sunday.

The hotel offers 7,500 square feet of meeting and banquet space. While you're here, treat yourself to a tour of the Cathedral of Learning's impressive Nationality Rooms. For more on those, see the Attractions chapter.

Mountain View Inn $$
Route 30 East, Greensburg
(724) 834-5300, (800) 537-8709
www.mountainviewinn.com

Built in 1924, Mountain View Inn has remained under continuous ownership of the Booher family since 1940. They have maintained the Early American setting, with guest rooms featuring antique furnishings as well as brass or canopied beds. You can opt for a suite or schedule a meeting for your group in the facility's spacious banquet rooms.

You'll enjoy the outdoor pool and take special pleasure in dining at the Mountain View Inn, acclaimed for its decor and excellent food. If you're looking for understated elegance, you'll find it at Mountain View Inn.

This inn also makes for the perfect romantic getaway with some suites featuring small fireplaces, spacious Jacuzzis, and the lavish touch of fresh floral arrangements.

Radisson Hotel $$
101 Mall Boulevard, Monroeville
(412) 373-7300, (800) 333-3333
www.radisson.com

A compelling attraction of the Radisson is its proximity to Pittsburgh ExpoMart, a popular venue for a wide variety of exhibits and trade shows. If you're participating in or visiting one of those events, you won't beat Radisson's convenience.

You can select from 322 guest rooms and penthouse suites that feature dataports, wet bars, and whirlpools. All guests can swim in the pool, relax in the Jacuzzi, or drink and dine in the Iron City Grille and the Oxford Dining Room. You also will enjoy privileges at the nearby Oxford Athletic Club, a full-service fitness center.

If that doesn't tire you out, the 160-shop Monroeville Mall and Borders Books & Music are a quick walk from the hotel, which is accessible from both the Pennsylvania Turnpike and I-376 (the Parkway East). The hotel does not permit pets.

Ramada Inn & Conference Center $$
699 Rodi Road, Wilkins
(412) 244-1600, (800) 2RAMADA
www.ramada.com

Travel up the long winding road that's the driveway, and you'll reach a scenic view of Pittsburgh's eastern communities. You'll also find such amenities as indoor and outdoor pools, saunas, a whirlpool, and lighted tennis courts. This hotel was newly remodeled in 1999.

In-room telephones are computer adaptable, and you may utilize the hotel's fax services. Showtime is available in all rooms. Pets, however, are not permitted. Indigo Blue Restaurant, located within the hotel, takes pride in its wine list.

This Ramada is accessible from the Pennsylvania Turnpike (by only a few miles) and I-376 (the Parkway East).

Ramada Inn at Historic Ligonier $$
216 West Loyalhanna Street, Ligonier
(724) 238-9545
www.ramada.com

You'll find 66 guest rooms with computer access, as well as deluxe rooms that feature a large work and sitting area. In addition, there are seven suites with Jacuzzis and minikitchens. All rooms have access to fax and copier service, and all guests can enjoy the Bistro, located on-site. In season you can splash in the outdoor pool. The hotel does not permit pets.

At the Ramada, you'll be in the scenic Laurel Highlands recreation area, close to many attractions. Make sure you inquire about special guest packages featuring the Seven Springs Mountain Resort and Idlewild Park, a popular amusement park (see the Kidstuff chapter for details).

South

Days Inn Pittsburgh $
1150 Banksville Road
(412) 531-8900, (800) 325-2525
www.daysinn.com

This is a serviceable hotel with 70 rooms, an outdoor swimming pool, and banquet facilities that can seat up to 150 people. You also can request a room with a Jacuzzi. Fax service is available, and all rooms offer cable television.

The most important feature of this facility, however, is its central location, less than 2 miles from downtown Pittsburgh. When convention or holiday traffic causes congestion at downtown hotels, many travelers look to Days Inn as a convenient alternative. The hotel does not permit pets.

EconoLodge $
1385 West Chestnut Street, Washington
(724) 222-6500

If you're looking for economical, serviceable lodgings in Washington, this might be the place. The 62 rooms offer cable television, and guests enjoy complimentary, continental breakfast. Pets are not permitted. Find this motor inn at exit 4 off I-70.

Holiday Inn Meadowlands $$$
340 Racetrack Road, Meadowlands
(724) 222-6200
www.holiday-inn.com

If horse racing is in your blood, then this Holiday Inn is in your future. It's about a furlong from Ladbroke at the Meadows, a harness-racing facility that features both live and simulcast racing (see the Spectator Sports chapter). The hotel offers several Ladbroke packages that include box seats at the track and race programs.

Stay in one of the 138 guest rooms and you'll enjoy the pool, Jacuzzi, and steam room. A lounge and restaurant are on the premises, and you can repair to your room to watch cable television. You also may take advantage of golf privileges at a nearby club. The hotel welcomes pets.

Because Racetrack Road is an important connector between Interstate 79 and Route 19, the hotel is a popular and convenient site for banquets.

Perhaps you'll get lucky and pay for your stay with your Ladbroke winnings. Should you come up a loser, the hotel probably will expect you to pay your bill anyway.

West

Best Western Parkway Center Inn $$
875 Greentree Road, Green Tree
(412) 922-7070
www.bestwestern.com

Location is an important plus for this hotel. It's 2 miles west of downtown Pittsburgh along the Interstate 279 corridor. That means it's only a 15-minute drive or ride to Pittsburgh International Airport, and you can utilize the hotel's airport shuttle service. The hotel is adjacent to the 85-store Parkway Center Mall, which will provide you with such amenities as shopping, dining, a post office, a travel agency, and automobile rentals.

The hotel offers 138 rooms, a complimentary breakfast buffet, and complimentary cocktails—enjoy them around the indoor pool. You can take advantage of the fitness center. Pets are not permitted.

As you drive along I-79 (the Parkway West), you'll spot the inn by the distinctive "P" on the building. Trouble is, it's a red "P" that looks suspiciously like the Philadelphia Phillies logo. In Pittsburgh? Nah, couldn't be.

Comfort Inn Pittsburgh Airport $$
7011 Old Steubenville Pike, Oakdale
(412) 787-2600
www.comfortinn.com

One of the neatest attractions of this hotel—it's adjacent to the Tonidale Restaurant, well known locally for its extensive menu and homemade fare. In fact, the hotel used to be known as the Tonidale.

It features 47 guest rooms, such business services as a fax and a copier, a fitness center, and courtesy transportation to Pittsburgh International Airport, which is about 7 miles away. You can lodge your pet with you for an additional $7.00 per day, but if you're smart, you won't let Rover anywhere near your Tonidale pie.

Courtyard by Marriott $$$
450 Cherrington Parkway, Coraopolis
(412) 264-5000, (800) 321-2211
www.courtyard.com

At Courtyard by Marriott, you can relax while you work, or work while you relax. Either way, you'll find accommodating facilities here.

The 148 guest rooms offer large working areas as well as two telephones with modems, coffeemakers, and cable television. When you're ready for a break, try the minigym, indoor pool, and whirlpool. Later, you can enjoy the on-site restaurant.

The facility can provide meeting rooms for up to 60 participants as well as fax and copier service. The establishment does not permit pets.

Crowne Plaza Hotel $$
1160 Thorn Run Road, Coraopolis
(412) 262-2400
www.crowneplazacom

The 193 guest rooms at the Crowne Plaza offer in-room work areas and telephones with modem ports. For a special treat, try the Concierge Level, where you'll enjoy complimentary breakfast and cocktails, or swim in the outdoor pool. There is a restaurant and lounge on property.

No matter which room you choose, feel free to bring your pets. The hotel's meeting space can accommodate up to 550 people. You also can access round-the-clock courtesy transportation to and from Pittsburgh International Airport, which is about 6 miles away.

Embassy Suites Hotel $$$$
550 Cherrington Parkway, Coraopolis
(412) 269-9070
www.embassy-suites.com

As the name suggests, you'll find well-appointed suites here, each with a refrigerator, microwave, coffeemaker, voice mail, and computer access. Take advantage of the pullout sofa and meeting area within each suite. You'll enjoy cable television and in-room movie.

The hotel offers a health club and swimming pool as well as the Foggy Bottom Restaurant on-site. You won't go hungry here, as you'll feast on a cooked-to-order breakfast.

No pets are allowed here. Embassy Suites is several miles from Pittsburgh International Airport.

Fort Pitt Motel $
7750 Steubenville Pike, Oakdale
(412) 788-9960

Fort Pitt Motel is an unusual little budget-type establishment with only 19 rooms. The story here is the surprising amenities. Seven rooms offer heart-shaped whirlpools, while a number of rooms feature balconies, patios, and working fireplaces. It's pretty spartan otherwise, but the unusual features and location about 10 miles from Pittsburgh International Airport make this one worth checking out.

Hampton Inn Green Tree $$
555 Trumbull Drive, Green Tree
(412) 922-0100
www.hamptoninn.com

The Hampton Inn is among a cluster of three hotels in the Pittsburgh suburb of Green Tree. All offer great locations, only 3 miles from downtown Pittsburgh and just a 15-minute ride from Pittsburgh International Airport. The hotel offers free airport shuttle service.

Its 132 rooms offer work tables and telecommunication ports. If you're getting in a little work during your visit, feel free to use the copier and fax machine as well as the hotel's meeting rooms. These can accommodate up to 35 people.

If you have a pet under 50 pounds, bring it along. Of course, you must sign a pet policy for any potential damages.

Hampton Inn Pittsburgh Airport $$
8514 University Boulevard, Coraopolis
(412) 264-0020
www.hamptoninn.com

Hampton Inn offers complimentary shuttle service to and from Pittsburgh International Airport, which is a convenient 7 miles away. If you're visiting Robert Morris University, the hotel is only a mile from campus. Bring your pets along for the visit—they're welcome here.

Accommodations include 127 guest rooms featuring cable television and a complimentary breakfast buffet. With Robinson Town Centre and the Pointe at North Fayette about five minutes east (toward the city), you'll have plenty of shopping and restaurants to keep you entertained and fed.

Holiday Inn $$$
401 Holiday Drive, Green Tree
(412) 922-8100
www.holiday-inn.com

The Holiday Inn is part of the Green Tree cluster of hotels, with that great location convenient to both downtown Pittsburgh and Pittsburgh International Airport.

The hotel's 201 rooms offer phone modems, work areas, and balconies, so you can work a little and relax a little. If you're looking for a workout, try the outdoor pool or fitness center. Afterwards, you can repair to the Greenery Restaurant and Lounge, the in-house restaurant that stages a daily lunch buffet that's popular with hotel guests and others in search of a good meal. Bring your pets—they're welcome here.

For banquets, the hotel's Grand Ballroom can seat up to 1,000 guests. You can deploy the dozen breakout rooms as well.

Holiday Inn Beaver Falls $$
7195 Eastwood Road, Beaver Falls
(724) 846-3700
www.holiday-inn.com

The fitness buffs in your party will love the hotel's Holidome, which features a pool, a sauna, a whirlpool, a video arcade, billiards, and a jungle gym. When you're ready to eat and drink after your workout, you'll find a restaurant and a lounge on the premises.

The hotel offers 156 rooms with cable television, computer access, hair dryers, and iron sets, and it welcomes your pets. You can reach Holiday Inn easily—it's just off exit 13 (old exit 2) of the Pennsylvania Turnpike.

Holiday Inn Pittsburgh Airport $$$
8256 University Boulevard, Coraopolis
(412) 262-3600, (800) 333-4835
www.holiday-inn.com

You can almost see Pittsburgh International Airport from the Holiday Inn, and the courtesy transportation the hotel provides will get you to the airport in a few moments. The hotels' 255 rooms include work areas and in-room movies; you also can opt for an executive room with a king-size bed and an over-sized chair with ottoman. Stuck with work on your trip? The hotel's computer ports, fax, copier, and secretarial assistance will help you get it done more quickly.

The highlight of the hotel's recreational facilities is the indoor "aquacade," featuring a pool and whirlpool. You can dine at the on-site Bridges Bar & Grill or choose from the many restaurants along University Boulevard. For meetings and banquets, the hotel offers almost 11,000 square feet of conference space.

Your pets are welcome here.

Holiday Inns in Pittsburgh offer special golf packages, including the opportunity to build your own custom package. Call (800) HOLIDAY or visit www.holiday-inn.com for more information.

While in Pittsburgh with his orchestra in the 1940s, Lawrence Welk "discovered" his trademark bubble machine at the Omni (formerly the Westin) William Penn. The original machine, devised by a staff chef, remains on the premises.

Hyatt Regency Pittsburgh
International Airport $$-$$$
1111 Airport Boulevard
(724) 899-1234, (800) 233-1234
www.pittsburghairport.hyatt.com
After touching down at the Pittsburgh International Airport, what could be easier than *walking* to your accommodations? Directly connected to the enclosed moving walkway, this full-service hotel offers 325 comfortable guest rooms and 11 suites, plus meeting and banquet space in its conference center. Amenities include high-speed Internet access.

Approximately 20 minutes from downtown Pittsburgh, the hotel is a surprisingly tranquil spot in the airport complex amid flight departures and arrivals. And nothing reduces the stress of modern travel like the Hyatt's 1,000-square-foot fitness center, with its whirlpool and 50-foot, heated lap pool.

Its Olive Press restaurant serves Mediterranean cuisine in stylish surroundings, a coffee bar delivers the prerequisite caffeine jolt needed to catch your next flight, and you have direct access to some of the Airmall's shops and less pricey eateries.

La Quinta Inn $$
8507 University Boulevard
Moon Township
(412) 269-0400
www.lq.com
Stay at La Quinta and you'll be treated to complimentary continental breakfast. You'll enjoy in-room movies and complimentary airport transportation.

For business purposes, each of the 128 rooms and three suites features dataport phones and access to voice mail and fax service. The hotel permits small dogs in rooms.

Radisson Hotel $$$
101 Radisson Drive, Green Tree
(412) 922-8400, (800) 333-3333
www.radisson.com
The hotel is conveniently located in the airport Parkway West corridor and only 3 miles from downtown Pittsburgh.

The Radisson offers 465 guest rooms, 5 suites, and 9 parlors (meeting rooms with a Murphy bed). In your room you'll find cable television, in-room movies, a heat lamp, and voice mail. If you're of a mind, check out the enhanced amenities (including free local calls, one free in-room movie, and a full breakfast) on the Concierge Level.

For a workout, try the health club, indoor pool, outdoor pool, sauna, and gym. You can relax in the lounge and two restaurants, all located on-site. One restaurant is full-service, and the other is a small deli. The hotel features 30,000 square feet of meeting and banquet space, highlighted by the grand ballroom.

Bring your pets along—they're welcome here.

Sewickley Country Inn $$
801 Ohio River Boulevard, Sewickley
(412) 741-4300
www.sewickleyinn.com
For an experience that will take you back to a kinder, gentler era, try the Sewickley Country Inn. You'll be situated right along a scenic section of the Ohio River; the view alone will relax you.

The innkeepers have not ignored modern amenities. The 147 guest rooms feature cable television, and you'll have access to an outdoor swimming pool in the summertime as well as a dining room and a lounge on premises. The inn is about equidistant from downtown Pittsburgh and Pittsburgh International Airport, with complimentary airport transportation offered. Meeting space can accommodate up to 250 people.

As you might expect in an establishment of such old-fashioned charm, small pets are welcome for a $10 fee. Sewickley Country Inn does weddings, meetings, showers, and dinners.

Wyndham Pittsburgh Airport $$$
777 Aten Road, Coraopolis
(412) 788-8800
www.wyndham.com

There are quite a few hotels in Pittsburgh International Airport corridor, but the Wyndham Pittsburgh Airport physically stands out, rising like a pastel palace of the Parkway West. Its lobby, grand and inviting, extends the palatial theme.

The hotel offers 314 guest rooms as well as a Concierge Level and 5 minisuites. Your pets are welcome here. On-site recreational opportunities include indoor and outdoor pools, an exercise room, a whirlpool, and a sauna. Try Meritage Grill for dining and drinking pleasure.

The hotel offers 12,000 square feet of meeting space (16 rooms) and free airport transportation.

EXTENDED-STAY AND TEMPORARY ACCOMMODATIONS

One product of Pittsburgh's rich corporate history is a tradition of company teams traveling to headquarters here for extended assignments. While massive corporations no longer are the rule in Pittsburgh, they remain sufficiently numerous to provide a basis for a strong extended-stay and temporary accommodations sector.

Even as many corporations have downsized, the booming film production business has brought many actors, technicians, and executives to town. They, too, require temporary accommodations, enhancing the presence of this hospitality sector.

If you're seeking such accommodations, keep some key questions in mind: do prospective providers offer accommodations in a variety of locations, so you can select one that's convenient for you? Can they provide for your family? Do their

rate schedules dovetail with the projected length of your stay? If you get the right answers, you'll know you've found the right temporary digs.

Rather than list these places geographically, we've included the whole region in one listing and present your options in alphabetical order.

AmeriSuites Pittsburgh/Airport
6011 Campbells Run Road
(412) 494-0202, (888) 774-6467

AmeriSuites Pittsburgh/Cranberry
136 Emeryville Drive, Cranberry
(724) 779-7900
www.amerisuites.com

Billed as America's all-suite hotels, guests enjoy separate living and sleeping areas, a refrigerator, microwave, wet bar, and a coffeemaker with complimentary coffee in every suite. There is also 26-inch cable TV, ironing supplies, voice mail, and data-port telephones in each suite. Do partake of the bountiful breakfast buffet, the indoor heated pool, the fitness center, and the MBE Business Express Center. If you need to do laundry, there are both valet service and laundry facilities available. With a free *USA Today* thrown in, it's just like being at home—well, almost.

Bridgestreet Accommodations
1501 Reedsdale Street
(412) 322-3999
www.bridgestreet.com

You'll find a diverse selection here, as Bridgestreet offers 150 units at 11 locations. By visiting them on the Web, you can take a virtual tour of each location. All units are in Allegheny and lower Butler Counties. You'll enjoy cable television, a complete kitchen, a washer and dryer, and housekeeping services. If you've been forced from your home for any reason, you'll find temporary housing options at Bridgestreet.

Daily rates range from $71 to $106, while the range for monthly rates is $1,980 to $2,550.

Corporate Accommodations
15 Chestnut Street, Carnegie
(412) 429-5165, (800) 899-5456

Corporate Accommodations offers a broad selection of units—175 units in 13 complexes, primarily in Allegheny County, but fast-growing Butler County also is represented. Your apartment will feature cable television, housekeeping and linen service, and a furnished kitchen.

To assure that their rooms meet your needs, customer service personnel inspect the preparations of the housekeeping staff before turning the unit over to you. Corporate Accommodations also provides short-term housing options for those forced from their homes by catastrophes.

Daily rates range from approximately $72 to $98, while the range for monthly rates is $1,920 to $2,700. There are lower rates for longer stays.

Extended StayAmerica
520 North Bell Avenue, Carnegie
(412) 278-4001

3851 Northern Pike, Monroeville
(412) 856-8400
www.exstay.com

Extended StayAmerica offers both daily rates, ranging from $49 to $59, and weekly rates, ranging from $239 to $299. As appropriate for an extended stay, you'll find your room equipped with a refrigerator, stove top, and microwave oven, and you can utilize the on-site laundry.

The Carnegie facility is located in the Pittsburgh International Airport corridor and is convenient to both downtown Pittsburgh and the airport. If you stay here, though, better give your pets a big good-bye hug—they're not permitted.

Studio Plus Pittsburgh Airport at the Pointe is affiliated with this extended-stay hotel group, and the accommodations are very similar but with studio apartments that have a full kitchen. The address is 200 Chauvet Drive (in North Fayette). Call them at (412) 490-0979.

Shadyside Inn
5405 Fifth Avenue
(412) 441-4444, (800) 767-8483

You're more than welcome to stay at Shadyside Inn for one night only, but the facility also can meet your temporary housing needs for weeks or months. All accommodations are suites featuring cable television and a VCR, a telephone-answering machine, and an equipped kitchen. You also may utilize the on-site laundry and a complimentary pass to a local fitness center. For business needs, optional amenities include fax, copier, and secretarial service. There are 100 guest suites here.

Daily rates range from $99 to $160, while the range for weekly rates is $540 to $770. If you prefer the monthly rate, the range there is $1,795 to $2,595.

Once here, you're within walking distance of the popular Shadyside shopping and dining district, and you're a short bus ride from Oakland's university-medical complex, making this an attractive option for those visiting Pittsburgh's colleges or hospitals for an extended period.

Bring your pets if they're under 25 pounds, but expect to pay a one-time fee of $60 for the privilege.

SpringHill Suites by Marriott—Pittsburgh Airport
239 Summit Park Drive
(412) 494-9446
www.springhillsuitespittsburghairport.com

Nestled among many other properties and retail establishments at the Pointe in North Fayette Township, you'll find SpringHill Suites with 102 guest rooms. Guests enjoy the continental breakfast provided. Each suite offers a microwave, refrigerator, in-room coffeemaker, and hair dryer. See the Shopping chapter for more information about all that's offered at the Pointe, for there is much shopping and many restaurants to choose from. This property is also along the airport corridor, so you're not far from catching your flight. There is a whirlpool and an indoor pool.

RESORTS

When you start to discuss resort communities, Pittsburgh may not be the town that springs to your lips. Think about it, though. We have warm, beautiful summers that are just the ticket for golf. We have plenty of inland waterways, the ideal setting for a variety of water sports. We have mountains and snow; last time we checked, those were a couple of the key ingredients in skiing. So who needs a beach and boiling temperatures?

With all these elements, Pittsburgh offers a number of resorts that take full advantage of the four seasons to vary their offerings and assure year-round attractions. While the resorts are a bit outside this guide's five-county geographic coverage area, they're included here rather than in the Day Trips chapter because each is no more than a 90-minute trip from Pittsburgh.

While we've adhered to the rate code for the resorts below, remember that seasonal swings in rates may be severe. Unless otherwise noted, the resorts offer smoking and nonsmoking rooms but do not permit pets.

East

Hidden Valley Resort   **$$$$**
One Craighead Drive, Hidden Valley
(814) 443-8000, (800) 458-0175
www.hiddenvalleyresort.com
Place a gorgeous community in the heart of the Laurel Highlands, sprinkle with beautiful fall foliage, crisp air, and pure snow, and you have the recipe for Hidden Valley Resort. Located about 60 miles east of Pittsburgh in the Laurel Highlands, the resort is primarily a community of homes. You're welcome to stay for a night or weekend, however, as owners often rent out their homes. That means a treat for you.

You'll enjoy a golf course, tennis courts, four swimming pools, and a playground with basketball and volleyball. The resort stocks its freshwater lake seasonally with trout and bass, and you'll also enjoy canoeing, paddleboating, kayaking, and sailboating. The sports club in the conference-center complex features racquetball courts and exercise equipment, as well as a whirlpool, sauna, suntan bed, massage room, hair salon, and video arcade.

Skiing is particularly popular at the resort (see the Recreation and Golf chapters for fuller descriptions of these features), as are hiking and biking. You'll find more than 30 miles of trails, and you'll enjoy complimentary use of the resort's mountain bikes and helmets.

Hidden Valley offers more than a half dozen restaurants and lounges; it's hard to imagine staying hungry very long. With so many attractions, it's no wonder that so many permanent residents became familiar with the resort as weekend guests.

Seven Springs Mountain Resort $$$$
777 Waterwheel Drive, Champion
(814) 352-7777, (800) 452-2223
www.7springs.com
Seven Springs is justifiably known for its excellent skiing—more about that in the Recreation chapter. The resort offers so much more than that it's become one of the region's premier sites for conferences. If you're looking for a romantic getaway, you'll find that here as well.

The resort can accommodate 5,000 overnight guests in its lodges, 10-story high-rise, chalets, condominiums, and cabins. They need every bit of that capacity, as Seven Springs each year hosts more than 700 conferences and meetings that take advantage of exhibit and festival halls and the many indoor and outdoor recreational activities.

If a fresh snowfall calls to you, try the snow tubing park or the alpine slide. Indoors, you'll enjoy a swimming pool, massage, an exercise room with a whirlpool, a universal gym and a sauna, miniature golf, bowling, racquetball, roller skating, and a variety of video games.

Downtown Pittsburgh offers more than 2,300 "committable" hotel rooms. Hoteliers save a few beyond that for emergencies and their own needs.

Outdoor activities include golf, tennis, hiking, horseback riding, and volleyball.

You'll work up an appetite with such active participation; Seven Springs is prepared to satisfy the heartiest of appetites with 10 restaurants and 6 lounges, some of which feature live entertainment. Be sure to check out Helen's, the original home of the resort's founders that now serves as a slopeside restaurant serving intercontinental cuisines.

Seven Springs is about 50 miles east of Pittsburgh, reachable from both exit 9 and exit 10 of the Pennsylvania Turnpike.

South

Linden Hall $$
432 Linden Hall Road, Dawson
(724) 529-7543

This splendid mansion derives its name from the linden trees imported from Berlin by the original owner, Sarah Cochran, widow of coke and coal pioneer Philip Cochran. The estate has been transformed by its current owners, United Steelworkers of America, into a crackerjack resort and conference center with overnight facilities for up to 300 guests, all at working persons' rates.

Recreation is a key theme at Linden Hall. You'll enjoy golf, tennis, biking along the scenic Yough River Trails, and fishing in a 25-acre lake. The picnic pavilion features sand volleyball and boccie courts, softball and soccer fields, and a children's playground.

You can relax in the sports pub and the charming country restaurant. The Great Hall can host your reception, while the outdoor gazebo provides a splendid backdrop for photographs. Make sure you inspect the Great Hall's Aeolian pipe organ, said to be one of only three in the world.

The resort is near Uniontown, 37 miles from Pittsburgh via Route 51 south. Linden Hall is closed from mid-December through mid-March; the golf course remains open year-round, weather permitting.

Nemacolin Woodlands
Resort & Spa $$$$
1001 LaFayette Drive, Farmington
(724) 329-8555, (800) 422-2736
www.nemacolin.com

Nemacolin was named for a Native American chief. His name does not translate even loosely into "lap of luxury." Perhaps it should, because when you arrive at Nemacolin, you'll think you've fallen there. The artwork alone is indicative of the ambience. You'll encounter pieces by Tiffany, Audubon, Calder, and Remington, just to name a few.

Your experience in this 1,000-acre jewel begins with your accommodations, whether in the inn, the condominiums, or the 124-room the LaFayette, modeled after the Ritz in Paris. Rooms and suites are spacious and well lighted, with plush footstools and scenic views of the resort. Enjoy the view in your terrycloth robe—it will be hanging in your room for you.

You'll enjoy golf, skiing, an equestrian center and polo field (there's more about Nemacolin's golf, skiing, and equine activities in the Golf and Recreation chapters), tennis, hiking, biking, and a broad range of water activities including canoeing, and fishing. Looking for less demanding activities? How about croquet and billiards—they're both available as well.

When you're ready to be pampered after your workout, attendants at the three-story spa await your bidding. The spa, of polished marble tiles, may be Nemacolin's pièce de résistance. It offers a fitness center, cardiovascular equipment, an aerobics room, and a lap pool. You can try it all under the watchful eye of your personal trainer. The spa's salon offers more than 60 treatments. When you arrive at the spa, the scent of aromatherapy convinces you to try out additional pampering such as the 16 different types of massages, nine body therapies, seven hydrotherapies, and nine facials. The Woodlands Spa boasts a signature treatment in the Water Path, an adaptation of European thermal therapy that stimulates circulation and improves immune function. The Woodlands Vitamin Facial is also special, for it features vitamin repair and hydroxy exfoliation, improving skin tone and elasticity.

Seasons is the on-site restaurant for the Woodlands Spa, giving guests as healthy a cuisine as the treatment they've just enjoyed. Dining at other restaurants, too, is a rich experience at Nemocolin, especially if done at the Golden Trout. Don't worry about ordering an obscure wine. The wine cellar has a capacity of 10,000 bottles. Lautrec is the French restaurant featuring a Sunday brunch from 10:00 A.M. to 2:00 P.M. Reservations are required. But dining here is a lovely experience any time.

In all, Nemacolin offers six restaurants, each with its own theme, as well as a '50s-style ice-cream parlor. Nemacolin is accessible from the Pennsylvania Turnpike, about 60 miles from Pittsburgh. If you'd really like to make a grand entrance, taxi up the resort's 4,000-foot private air strip. Everything else about Nemacolin says class—why shouldn't your arrival?

**The R&R Station Family
Restaurant and Inn**   **$**
19 West Main Street, Mt. Pleasant
(724) 547-7545
Located in the same large building as the restaurant (featured in our Restaurants chapter), the R&R Station Family Inn offers 17 rooms decorated in railroad themes. You'll find rooms honoring the Baltimore–Ohio (B&O) Railroad, the Union Pacific, and the Santa Fe, as well as the legendary railroad worker Casey Jones. All rooms have private baths and full amenities, including air conditioning, telephones, and cable television. There'll even be a chocolate mint on your pillow when you

Where do celebrities stay when in Pittsburgh? Jodie Foster stopped at the Shadyside Inn, while Gregory Peck opted for the Duquesne Club. Jack Nicholson chose the Vista (predecessor of the Westin Convention Center Hotel, which was formerly the Doubletree Hotel) and had television coverage of his beloved Los Angeles Lakers piped in via special arrangement.

get ready to turn in. The delicious home-cooked food available at the restaurant downstairs will complete that cozy, well-cared-for feeling you'll cultivate here.

The R&R Station Family Restaurant and Inn is nestled in the foothills of the Laurel Highlands, and you'll be only 30 minutes or so from major attractions such as Seven Springs ski resort, Frank Lloyd Wright's Fallingwater, white-water rafting at Ohiopyle, and Fort Necessity in Uniontown. Right in Mt. Pleasant, there's the West Overton Museum, a 19th-century rural industrial village. Children will especially enjoy nearby attractions such as Idlewild and Living Treasures Animal Park. Each September, there's an annual glass festival (this used to be the home of the Lennox factory) and an annual coke and coal festival five minutes away in Scottdale. The R&R Station Family Restaurant and Inn is 30 to 40 minutes southeast of Pittsburgh. You'll find this family-owned gem on the east end of town in Mt. Pleasant, near Cook's Lumber.

West

**Oglebay Resort and
Conference Center**   **$$$$**
Route 88 North, Wheeling, West Virginia
(304) 243-4000, (800) 624-6988
www.oglebay-resort.com
This 1,500-acre resort was once the elegant summer estate of Cleveland industrialist Col. Earl W. Oglebay but now is

A brothel once flourished near the Priory when that city inn was a home for Benedictine monks in the 1880s. When the bishop discovered the house of ill repute, he ordered the front curtains closed and relocated the priests to the back room.

operated by the city of Wheeling, West Virginia. Oglebay is so fun filled that it will take you several days just to sample it all.

It features two golf courses, including the Speidel Championship Golf Course, which has played host to a number of Ladies Professional Golf Association events, as well as a par 3 course. (For more on Oglebay's golf delights, see the Golf chapter.) You'll enjoy miles of jogging trails that crisscross the estate, as well as Bissonnette Gardens, which glows with such seasonal flowers as tulips, daffodils, and mums. Wedding parties travel for

miles to Bissonnette Gardens to stage their nuptial pictures.

The Good Children's Zoo showcases bears, otters, bison, and rare red wolves in natural settings. The Crispin Center offers outdoor swimming and tennis courts, and you'll find a number of venues for shopping.

You'll work up quite an appetite with all that activity, and you'll satisfy it just as surely in the Ihlenfeld Dining Room in Wilson Lodge, the principal guest house. If you'd like to get a little more rustic than the lodge, Oglebay offers a number of cottages where you can snuggle by the fireplace—the resort provides the firewood, you provide the rest. Pets are permitted only in cottages.

The highlight of the year at Oglebay is the Winter Festival of Lights, featuring more than one million lights. Travelers come from miles around to enjoy the 6-mile driving tour. You can reach Oglebay from Pittsburgh by taking I–79 south, then Interstate 70 west.

BED-AND- 🛏️ BREAKFAST INNS

Up until eight or ten years ago, accommodations in Pittsburgh tended toward the traditional. And city ordinances weren't too friendly to the potential bed-and-breakfast industry. Nowadays, while within the city limits Pittsburgh still can offer only about 30 bed-and-breakfast rooms, these accommodations are first-class—some of them downright luxurious. You'll also find about 150 more rooms around the city in the surrounding county areas, some of which are quite convenient to the downtown business district.

In the rural county areas, several farms have jumped on the haywagon of the farm-stay craze, generating extra revenue by converting underutilized space to guest accommodations. A number of these agrarian facilities are set on working farms, with guests invited to pitch in with chores. Your kids will love it!

It is important to remember, however, that as numerous as they are, bed-and-breakfast inns typically offer no more than five or six guest rooms. In addition, as small-business owners, proprietors of bed-and-breakfast inns may take off for vacation or suspend their services for long periods of time for other reasons. Some accommodate guests by reservation only. Under these circumstances, it makes a lot of sense for you to reserve your room, rather than dropping by and hoping for the best.

Planning is also important in the area of amenities; some bed-and-breakfasts do not offer the conveniences we take for granted in hotels and motels, such as in-room baths, telephones, television, air-conditioning, and computer accessibility. Some establishments welcome children, a few permit pets, and only a handful allow indoor smoking. The write-ups will indicate policies on pets and children. Unless otherwise indicated, smoking is permitted only outdoors. If a particular amenity is important to you, check with the proprietors when you call to make your reservation.

In a number of cases where inns prohibit children and pets, owners have indicated that they try to be as accommodating as circumstances allow. If they're fully booked with adult parties, they'll probably enforce their prohibitions. If your party is the only guest, they may be more flexible about children and pets. The bottom line: always ask, and don't be afraid to negotiate.

In summary, it's important that you consider all your needs—even those you customarily take for granted—in selecting a bed-and-breakfast. Pick the right one and you'll have the ideal opportunity for a memorable experience. You might even make a new friend or two.

PRICE CODE

We've included with our listings a rate guide to help you pick the establishment that best fits your budget. With each write-up, you'll see from one to five dollar signs to help you place the inns within these categories.

$	$45 to $70
$$	$71 to $90
$$$	$91 to $135
$$$$	$136 to $210
$$$$$	$211 to $275

Rates represent average charges for double occupancy. Keep in mind that rates will vary with season and availability, and that many establishments maintain discount programs through such organizations as AAA, AARP, or their own frequent guest programs. The room tax in Allegheny County is 7 percent: elsewhere, it varies from county to county. Except as noted, all bed-and-breakfast inns profiled here accept at least one major credit card.

NORTH

An Inn Between $$–$$$
161 Deer Creek Road, Saxonburg
(724) 352-4899
www.innbetween.us

When you arrive at An Inn Between, you'll be treated to homemade pie and ice cream. You'll be staying in your own private, air-conditioned apartment on the 200-acre estate, and you'll enjoy a fireplace, balcony, and your own secluded garden.

You'll be 25 miles from Pittsburgh and only 9 miles from the Pennsylvania Turnpike. You're in golfers' heaven, and you're also near Moraine State Park, the historic town of Saxonburg, a planetary observatory, a chocolate factory, and plethora of antique shops. (See the Golf chapter for information on nearby courses.) You might choose to stay right where you are, however. There's certainly enough to do, what with the walking and biking trails; the opportunities for bird-watching; the tennis court; and the two-acre pond where you can row, fish, and swim. Watch for osprey, egrets, and Canada snow geese seasonally at the pond.

If you're going to be in town on business, note that you can set up your computer and plug in your modem. Don't worry about the phone being busy; it's your own private line. The full-sized apartment, which sleeps four people, is also spacious enough to accommodate small meetings. In addition, you'll have access to the fax machine and the copier in the nearby inn office.

Your children are welcome here. You may smoke on the balcony or outside the barn.

Note: Discounts are available for staying here three or more nights, making this splendid accommodation in the same price range as nearby, moderately priced motels.

Armstrong Farms
Bed and Breakfast $$–$$$
1020 Ekastown Road, Saxonburg
(724) 352-2858
www.armstrongfarms.com

Armstrong Farms Bed and Breakfast is a 200-year-old farm/inn, still operating a large, purebred cattle herd on 1,000 unspoiled acres of Pennsylvania farmland. Located only 45 minutes from Pittsburgh in southeast Butler County, Armstrong is only minutes away from the National Historic District of downtown Saxonburg, where guests can enjoy fine dining, antique and gift shopping, and walking tours of the town. Guests can stay in Drake's Guest House, the Love Cottage at Westminster Preserve, and the Bonnie House, for a total of 13 rooms, some with working fireplaces. Television and telephone can be enjoyed in a common room. A hearty, country breakfast is served in the private dining room at the main farmhouse, which was built in 1816. Miles of farmland offer safe, gorgeous terrain for outdoor activities such as hiking, horseback riding (stalls available), biking, cross-country skiing, snowshoeing, fishing, bird-watching, wildflower conservation, and still-life painting.

This bed-and-breakfast has received numerous awards, including *Arrington's Bed & Breakfast Journal*'s Best horse Lovers Inn in 2001 and the National Cattlemen's Beef Association 2002 Environmental Stewardship Award. It has also been featured in *Range Country* magazine. Special packages are available for several holidays; for parties, such as weddings; and for small, corporate retreats. From June 1 to November, "chuckwagon" retreats are offered, with a unique emphasis on farm life. Children are welcome at Armstrong, and so is one housebroken pet per party, with the innkeeper's pre-approval.

Ber-Nita Acres Bed & Breakfast $
RD 2, 151 Bennett Drive, Ellwood City
(724) 752-1455, (888) 297-5396
www.pafarmstay.com/bernita
Ber-Nita Acres, a 92-acre working farm, offers three guest rooms in the owners' large home. Private baths are accessible to, but not adjoining, all of the rooms. A phone is available in the large living room, where there's also a television, VCR, and an abundance of family-oriented movies on videotape. You'll be treated to a full country breakfast in the morning.

Your children are welcome to help feed the sheep, cows, and ostriches! From March to September, they'll also be able to watch baby ostriches hatch from eggs in the incubator. For adults and children alike, there are two fishing lakes and a paddleboat, and you won't have to worry about bringing along your fishing poles or lifejackets—it'll all be there waiting for you, just like at grandma's house.

After a long day of play, sink into the Jacuzzi on the covered deck; it's open all year. Smoke under the stars, but not in the house or in any of the outbuildings, and please leave the pets at home.

Heather Hill Bed & Breakfast $$–$$$
268 Rader School Road, Renfrew
(724) 789-7911
bedandb.isrv.com/
Heather Hill offers seven air-conditioned guest rooms—five with private baths, three with wood-burning stoves. The bed-and-breakfast sits on a secluded 180-acre farm about 30 miles from Pittsburgh in Butler County. You can enjoy hiking trails, swimming, paddleboats, a soak in the hot tub after a round of boccie, and interaction with the farm animals that share the space. There's also a game room with a pool table and other recreational delights, such as air hockey.

If you plan to bring children or pets, you'll need to review that with management. You'll also want to remember there's a large hall here, convenient for

receptions, business meetings, and retreats.

Credit cards are not accepted.

The Inn on Grandview $$–$$$$
310 East Grandview Avenue, Zelienople
(724) 452-0469
www.fyi.net/~grandinn
Originally known as the Zimmerman Hotel, the facility has been completely restored and now features four guest rooms furnished with antiques. All offer private baths, air-conditioning, televisions, and telephones. Two rooms also offer working fireplaces, and one offers a whirlpool. Well-behaved children are welcome, but pets are not.

The Inn on Grandview is just a few miles from both the Pennsylvania Turnpike and Interstate 79. That places it in the heart of some splendid outdoor recreation country. Opportunities for golf, tennis, boating, and antiquing will beckon when you stay here. Enjoy a full breakfast at the inn before setting out to enjoy your activities.

The Inn on the Mexican
War Streets $$$–$$$$
604 West North Avenue
(412) 231-6544
http://members.aol.com/_ht_a/innwarst
/collect/
Locals in the know are still surprised that more out-of-towners than actual Pittsburghers know—and enthusiastically praise—this gem on the North Side. A registered historical building more than a century old, the Russell H. Boggs mansion was renovated several years ago to become the Inn on the Mexican War Streets, which offers eight attractively furnished suites with private baths and TV/VCR combinations, with two of the suites including kitchens and offices.

With exterior walls of quarry-faced stone and an arched Romanesque front porch, the inn is impressive. Innkeepers Jeff and Karl have recently converted the stone carriage stable behind the mansion into two additional dining rooms on the second floor to seat 50 people and a

All members of the Western Pennsylvania Bed and Breakfast Association subscribe to the organization's code of ethics.

forthcoming country-style French restaurant on the main level.

In a city neighborhood in transition, the Inn on the Mexican War Streets is ideally located across from a public park and within walking distance of many major attractions on the North Side—the Andy Warhol Museum, the Mattress Factory, Heinz Field, and PNC Park—and a leisurely stroll across the Allegheny River to the Cultural District downtown.

The Inn on Vine $$-$$$
241 Vine Street, Kittanning
(724) 545-7744, (888) VINE INN
www.innonvine.com

This restored Georgian colonial home features two guest rooms and one suite, all furnished with Victorian antiques.

In the heart of downtown Kittanning in Armstrong County, the inn is only 1 block away from the Allegheny River, and there's a $4 million amphitheater carved into the riverbank, where the Pittsburgh Symphony and other groups perform from time to time. In the summer the *Gateway Clipper* docks along the river, and boat and Jet Ski rentals are available a short distance down the street from the Inn on Vine. The inn is also just around the corner from a genealogy library and 2 blocks from the "Rails to Trails" bike and walking trail. Children ages 16 and older are welcome, but pets are not permitted.

Maggie West Bed & Breakfast $
605 Pittsburgh Street, Springdale
(724) 274-8906

This 1860s mansion, only a few blocks away from the Allegheny River, is within walking distance of small, local shops and restaurants in the heart of Springdale. Of the 20 rooms in the house, four are rented to guests. All rooms, decorated in Victorian style appropriate to the house, feature access to a parlor and tearoom, while one offers a private bath.

If you need to make a call, use the inn's portable phone. There are televisions in all the rooms. Children are welcome, but pets are not. Maggie West Bed & Breakfast is about 20 minutes from Pittsburgh when the traffic along Route 28 is light.

Credit cards are not accepted.

The Main Stay B&B of Saxonburg $$-$$$
214 Main Street, Box 547
Saxonburg, PA 16056
(724) 352-9363
www.mainstaybnb.com

The Main Stay is a beautifully restored 150-year-old home in the heart of Saxonburg, about 25 miles north of Pittsburgh. Accommodations include two guest rooms; one suite; and one apartment with a kitchen, living room, and telephone. All accommodations offer air-conditioning, private baths, and cable television. If you stay in the rooms or the suite at the Main Stay, you'll share a common phone.

The Main Stay is renowned for its peaceful surroundings and attention to detail, as well as its "earth-friendliness." It's decorated in English country style, with hardwood floors, lace curtains, teapots, soft floral fabrics, and a lovely antique quilt collection. Linens are soft, green cotton. Guests are greeted with cookies and fresh flowers and are served a full breakfast each morning. Many of the ingredients are organic, and dietary restrictions can be accommodated. Afterwards, you might want to go outside and relax in the Peace Garden, intended as a sacred space in which to contemplate personal peace as well as the possibility of peace in the world.

You also can utilize the inn's parlor and library for visiting with old pals or the new friends you'll meet during your stay. The Main Stay is a nonsmoking facility. Children are welcome, but no pets, please. Senior citizens and those staying two or more nights enjoy discounted room rates. Credit cards are not accepted. The Main Stay also provides space for small parties, showers, receptions, and business meetings.

The Outside Inn $$
980 Route 228, Mars
(724) 776-0626, (800) 947-2783
www.outsideinnpa.com

The Outside Inn's four rooms, each decorated differently, offer something for everyone, much like the area where the inn is located. Nestled on 50-plus acres of secluded land, the inn, surprisingly, is just 1 mile from a local fitness center, where you'll enjoy complimentary membership during your stay. You'll be near the Cranberry business district and only 3 miles from the Pennsylvania Turnpike and I-79.

Your room will have a private bath and a television with satellite programming. If you're planning to bring a small child, you might want to ask for the room with the nursery adjacent to it. Please leave your pets at home.

Computer and modem hookups and phones are located in each of three sitting rooms, where you're free to host a business meeting, if you like. You'll also have access to a fax machine in the office. When you've had enough work, venture on down to the working wine cellar, sniff the bouquet, and taste a few. You might take the path back through the woods and visit the hidden garden, where there are ponds, a waterfall, and a gazebo among the trees. You could also just sit on one of the decks and enjoy the view, or soak in the sumptuous outdoor hot tub. You'll enjoy a full, gourmet breakfast in the morning.

Step Back in Time $-$$
224 North Washington Street, Butler
(724) 283-7509

This charming colonial-style home offers three guest rooms furnished with Victorian period antiques. All of the rooms have private baths, telephones, and televisions, so even as you soak in the claw-foot tub and dream of yesteryear you'll

rest assured knowing that all the modern amenities are at your fingertips. Step Back in Time is conveniently located in the heart of downtown Butler, within easy walking distance of offices, shops, restaurants, and area churches.

The facility is an hour from Pittsburgh, 30 minutes from I-79, and quite near Moraine State Park. Just imagine waking up the morning, taking a hike through the park, then feasting on scones, clotted cream, raspberry jam, and warm hospitality—that's what you'll find at Step Back in Time.

Your children are welcome here. Smoking, pets, and alcohol are not allowed.

Sun and Cricket Bed
and Breakfast $$$
1 Tara Lane, Gibsonia
(724) 444-6300
www.sunandcricket.com

You'll be struck by the appealing blend of old and modern on this 35-acre country estate about 15 miles north of Pittsburgh. Of the two spacious guest cottages, one is a log cabin adjoining the main house, the other a carriage house about 500 feet from the main house. Each is enhanced by antique furnishings and handmade quilts. On the modern side, you'll enjoy private baths, color television, a VCR and stereo, a refrigerator, and air-conditioning. The cozy log cabin offers a telephone and accommodations for children that offer their parents some privacy. Each cottage has a separate entrance and porch, so you can relax alone while you enjoy the view of the woods surrounding you. (You won't even be able to see the road from where you're sitting!) You'll enjoy a full, gourmet breakfast served in your own, private sitting area.

The owner notes that at least 12 golf courses are within a 5-mile radius from here, including the acclaimed Deer Run. (See the Golf chapter for more information.) While other pets are not permitted, Sun and Cricket will board your horse in a pasture you can view from your window.

EAST

**The Inn at Oakmont
Bed and Breakfast** $$$-$$$$
300 Route 909, Verona
(412) 828-0410
www.pittsburghbnb.com

The emphasis at this newer, federal-style inn is on charming surroundings and gracious service. The facility features eight rooms with private baths; two of the rooms also offer a fireplace and whirlpool bath. All of them are furnished with antiques. A special feature in each room is a sleep machine that lulls you off to dreamland with the sounds of tropical rain or the Hawaiian surf.

You'll have a phone in your room and use of the house fax machine, as well as access to an in-house fitness center and massage services. Children age 6 and older are permitted, but leave the pets at home. Inquire about discounts for extended stays.

One of the chief attractions of the inn is its accessibility to the city. It's a short hop from the Pennsylvania Turnpike and about 20 minutes from downtown Pittsburgh along Route 28.

When you stay here, enjoy this picturesque town with its quaint, notable shops, such as the Mystery Lovers Bookstore. You'll also find a public golf course right across the street from the inn.

For the enjoyment of their guests, a number of Pittsburgh bed-and-breakfast inns collaborate on Murder Mystery Weekends.

The Inns on Negley $$$$-$$$$$
703 and 714 Negley Avenue
(412) 661-0631
www.theinnsonnegley.com

Still under the same ownership and still beautifully appointed, the popular Appletree Bed & Breakfast in the heart of Shadyside now has a sister inn just down the street and just as lovely. Looking at the intricately designed decorative ceilings and exquisite fireplaces, you'll think you stepped back into the 1800s. Yet there are some reminders of the amenities of modern life in the newly renovated rooms. All of the rooms in both inns feature Egyptian cotton sheets, imported down comforters, and a high-speed Internet access port. Some of them also feature a Jacuzzi.

The inns are especially popular with corporate travelers, because the homes are only five minutes from downtown and are in many cases a better value and much more comfortable than many hotels. They're even closer to the medical-university complex in Oakland, the neighborhood on Shadyside's border.

Ask about the special facilities and discounts available for corporate meetings and events. The inns are also luxurious spots for weddings, receptions, and other types of celebrations.

The Inns are just one block from Walnut Street and Ellsworth Avenue, which offer some of the finest shopping, dining, and entertainment experiences in Pittsburgh.

SOUTH

**Campbell House
Bed & Breakfast** $$-$$$$
305 East Main Street, Ligonier
(724) 238-9812

Amenities abound at Campbell House, where the three guest rooms and two suites are what owner Patti Campbell describes as "eclectic" in decor. Whichever room you choose, you'll find a private bath, air-conditioning, cable television, a VCR and complimentary snacks and beverages. You also can utilize the common phone and fax machine and receive e-mail messages. Pets and children are not permitted.

Campbell is the owner of a large collection of Campbell's Soup artifacts—her license plate reads "Soup Kid." At breakfast, make sure you sample one of her

"Campbell's Babies," large pancakes with fruit, powdered sugar, and optional chocolate. With her "babies" she also passes out "cigars"—sausage links, of course. Mmmmm, mmmmm good.

**Champion Lakes
Bed & Breakfast** $$-$$$
**Route 771 North
P.O. Box 724, Ligonier, PA 15658
(724) 238-5440
www.pagolf.com**
This facility is located on the grounds of Champion Lakes Golf Course, right next to Champion Lakes Restaurant. (See the Golf chapter for more information about the course.) Owned by two retired Pittsburgh Pirates, Dick Groat and Jerry Lynch, the bed-and-breakfast has nine rooms. (Get it? Like nine innings?) Each room has a private bath, phone, television with HBO, and heating and air-conditioning system with its own controls.

All of the rooms are named after baseball players, and each room has its namesake's autographed uniform and picture on the wall. You'll choose your breakfast, which is included in the price of your room, from the menu at the restaurant next door.

Ask about special golf getaway packages when you call for reservations. Your children are welcome, however, your pets are not.

Foggy Mountain Lodge $$-$$$
**190 Old Distillery Road, Stahlstown
(724) 593-1000
www.foggymt.com**
Foggy Mountain Lodge is unusually large by local standards. Not only does it offer 12 rooms, but it's also set on 120 lush acres dotted with wooded trails, fields, and a lake. The air-conditioned rooms offer private baths, televisions, and phones, and you'll enjoy the game room, which features a pool table and darts. When you're ready to relax, try the outdoor hot tub and Bootlegger's Bar & Grill. Proprietors Rena and Jeff Stumpf think of Foggy Mountain primarily as a couples retreat, but if you want

to bring your children and discuss it with them, they'll probably approve it. Pets are not permitted. Note: The rooms are spread over two buildings, a lodge, and a guesthouse, and the nightly rate is higher for the lodge. Foggy Mountain Lodge is near Ligonier in Westmoreland County, 1.3 miles from Route 711.

**The Inne at
Watson's Choice** $$$-$$$$$
**234 Balsinger Road, Balsinger
(724) 437-4999, (888) 820-5380
www.watsonschoice.com**
Serenity and relaxation is a significant draw at this early-19th-century brick farmhouse in the Laurel Highlands, 60 miles from Pittsburgh. Situated on a land-grant farm from the 1820s, the Inne at Watson's Choice surveys a 42-acre working farm with cattle. Before you go inside, sit on the wraparound porch and gaze at the picturesque hay fields and wooded hills.

While the charm is 19th century, the amenities are 21st. Innkeepers Bill and Nancy Ross have decorated the seven guest rooms individually according to themes, such as bluebirds or a particular flower, with distinct colors and matching fabrics—in fact, when guests make reservations they've already made their selection from the Web site. Each room has queen- and king-size beds; a modern private bath, some with a whirlpool; a private phone; and computer access. All rooms are air-conditioned.

In a rustic dining room, Nancy serves a country breakfast, such as fresh fruit, Amish sausage and bacon, and Belgian waffles with strawberries, and vegetarians are always given appropriate choices.

The red oak floors and all doors are original. The great room is impressive, with its huge, working fireplace and exposed wooden beams from a local barn. The recently added Harvest House, which was authentically reproduced, has a gathering room, four guest rooms, and one suite. Children are welcome, but pets are not permitted. The inn is a smokefree facility.

You may be tempted not to stray from the Inne at Watson's Choice, but a short drive away you can visit Frank Lloyd Wright's Fallingwater and Kentuck Knob; George Washington's first battleground, Fort Necessity; antiques shops; and Touchstone Center for the Arts. More demanding activities include white-water rafting on Youghiogheny River, biking, horseback riding, golf, hunting, fishing, and cross-country and downhill skiing.

The John Butler House $-$$
800 Rock Run Road, Elizabeth
(412) 751-6670
www.butlersgolf.com
About 40 minutes from downtown Pitts-burgh, this facility is located by both the Monongahela and Youghiogheny Rivers on the grounds of Butler's Golf Course. (See the Golf chapter for more informa-tion on the course.) A deck on the house overlooks the course, and you'll be only a mile from the Youghiogheny Trail.

Two of the four guest rooms offer pri-vate baths, while a television and phone are available in the common living room and kitchen, respectively. You'll be served a full breakfast at the adjacent restaurant, the Rock Run Inn. You'll also enjoy games in the sunroom . . . and the opportunity to learn the correct spelling of Monongahela and Youghiogheny once and for all.

Children are permitted; pets are not. If you have a large party, you may rent all four guest rooms. Check with manage-ment for the appropriate fee.

Lady of the Lake Bed & Breakfast $$$
157 U.S. Route 30 East, Ligonier
(724) 238-6955
www.ladyofthelakebandb.com
There is indeed a lake at Lady of the Lake, a 25-acre lake, to be specific. It's a sea-sonal home for swans and Canada geese, and it's a picturesque element at this lovely Westmoreland County inn. It offers four rooms in the main house, one cot-tage, and the opportunity to spend the night on the 60-acre grounds in a tent (you can bring your own or they'll rent

you one). The rates for these lodging modes vary quite a bit. The listing of $$$ applies to the main house while a night under the stars would be $ or less. The rooms offer private baths and television—you're welcome to use the office phone. Lady of the Lake is available for company picnics, and it offers a tennis court, in-ground pool, and rowboats and canoes for use at the lake. Lady of the Lake wel-comes children—a useful feature, since the inn is adjacent to Idlewild Park and Story-book Forest, both popular attractions for kids. You'll find more about them in the Kidstuff chapter. Lady of the Lake wel-comes small pets only.

Lesley's Mountain View Country Inn $$$$
10 Mountain View Road, Donegal
(724) 593-6349, (800) 392-7773
www.shol.com/mtviewbb
Mountain View offers spectacular views of the surrounding Laurel Highlands from each of its six rooms. These are furnished with period American furniture, including tall-poster beds, and feature televisions, phones, and private baths. The inn permits children but does not allow pets. In-room smoking is not permitted, but you can light up at the bar of Lesley's, the restau-rant within the inn that also is operated by inn owners Lesley and Gerard O'Leary. For more on Lesley's, see the Restaurants chapter.

The inn is about 1 mile east of the Donegal exit of the Pennsylvania Turnpike. By the way, don't confuse this inn with Mountain View Inn in Greensburg, a sepa-rate Westmoreland County establishment. You can read about Mountain View Inn in the Accommodations and Restaurants chapters.

Ligonier Country Inn $$-$$$
US 30, Laughlintown
(724) 238-3651
www.ligoniercountryinn.com
This inn may be the region's most capa-cious and diverse—it offers 26 rooms and 2 cottages. Each room is furnished differ-

Finding a Bed-and-Breakfast

Bed-and-breakfast inns tend to limit their advertising, so it can be tough to find out where they are and what they offer. In Pittsburgh you can get current information from a trade group, the Western Pennsylvania Bed and Breakfast Association. You can reach them at (888) 400–6380. Their Web site is www.western pabandb.com.

You can obtain information specific to Pittsburgh and the surrounding six counties on the Web site for the Pittsburgh Bed & Breakfast Association, www.pittsburghbnb.com.

---

ently; here you'll find a brass bed, there a four-poster. All rooms feature private baths, air-conditioning, televisions, and telephones with computer ports. The cottages also are different from each other. One is family-oriented and sleeps up to seven people. The other, which offers a working fireplace, is known informally as the "romance cottage." Both cottages sport porches that overlook Mill Creek.

Wherever you stay here, you're invited to enjoy the outdoor pool and the adjacent restaurant, also known as Ligonier Country Inn. For more on that, see the Restaurants chapter. You're welcome to use the office fax and copying services, and the good proprietors even will provide massage services for you. Smoking and nonsmoking accommodations are available. Discounts are available for stays of at least two nights. Children are welcome in certain rooms only. If you're staying in the cottages, you may bring your dog but no cats, please. Ligonier Country Inn is located about 3 miles from Ligonier in eastern Westmoreland County.

Morning Glory Inn $$$$
2119 Sarah Street
(412) 431–1707
www.morningglorybedandbreakfast.com
Morning Glory Inn is a restored 1862 brick, Italianate Victorian home on Pittsburgh's South Side. Not only will you enjoy gracious appointments, but you'll be in the perfect position to experience one of Pittsburgh's most captivating and "hot" neighborhoods. South Side is an unusual blend of professional offices; trendy restaurants and clubs; art galleries; and unusual shops, such as the Bead Mine, where you can string your own necklaces from gem or glass beads. From the Morning Glory, you'll also be able to stroll through the friendly streets to the City Theatre, which offers innovative, New York–quality performances.

The five guest rooms at the Morning Glory Inn offer private baths, televisions, wireless Internet connections, and speaker phones with digital answering machines, as well as Swedish pressure-relieving mattresses for extra comfort. The rooms are all well-appointed. For instance, the Margaret Jackson suite offers a queen-size canopy bed, a desk and several chairs, and a sitting-room bathroom complete with chaise lounge. You'll enjoy a walk in the Victorian garden after relaxing on the Spanish porch or in the guest parlors, one of which features a restored 1890 grand piano.

Smoking areas are available on the porch or in the garden. A corporate discount is offered, and you may make use of the office fax machine and copier. You can also hold your business meeting or special event at the Morning Glory Inn. For children's and pet's accommodations, discuss your circumstances with Nancy, the innkeeper. She pledges to be as flexible as she can.

Oak Noggin $$$
209 Waterman Road, Jefferson Hills
(412) 714-3571
www.oaknoggin.com

Oak Noggin is the only bed-and-breakfast in the South Hills area of Pittsburgh, and a fine one it is. Stay here in a separate, log-hewn guesthouse that is an accurate representation of an early America home—except for the modern amenities, of course. The oak logs used to build the home are from two small 18th-century settler's cabins, the earliest recorded houses built in the Jefferson Hills area, which is approximately 45 minutes from downtown Pittsburgh.

Oak Noggin boasts two working fireplaces, including one especially large in the "keeping room," or living area, that would have been used for cooking during settlers' times. Don't worry if you're not familiar with frontier culinary artistry, however: You'll enjoy your own modern kitchen, and a full breakfast will be delivered to your door. There's one bedroom and a bath in the guesthouse, and the large bed has a twin trundle that slides out from underneath, ideal for accommodating children. A crib can also be provided. No pets, please!

Quiet House Bed
& Breakfast $$$-$$$$
667 Elliotsville Road, Farmington
(724) 329-4606, (800) 784-8187
www.quiethousebnb.com

You probably won't find a more romantic stay than at Quiet House, which offers a champagne dinner at an award-winning French country inn followed by the "pure seclusion" that a guesthouse on 234 acres of woodland provides. It's one of the many package deals Quiet House arranges throughout the year. In fact, owners Marty and Judy Anker will help you create your own special package from a surprisingly large number of options, such as massages, bouquets of roses, and wine tasting at a local winery.

Open year-round, Quiet House is a pre–Civil War Georgian farmhouse with seven guest rooms with private baths. For even more solitude, Quiet House offers the Carriage House Loft or Spring House, Cozy Cottage, or John's Cottage, some of which have wraparound decks. All units are air-conditioned. A full gourmet breakfast is delivered to your cottage, and as one satisfied customer from Wales noted, "It was worth crossing the Atlantic just for Grandma Judy's breakfast."

There is a stocked trout lake on the property and even a small chapel, since Marty is a minister who performs wedding ceremonies. An easy walk uphill awards you with a panoramic view of the entire valley.

Only 60 miles from Pittsburgh, your stay in the Laurel Highlands is a short drive to Frank Lloyd Wright's Fallingwater and Kentuck Knob, Ohiopyle State Park, Laurel Caverns, and Nemacolin Woodlands.

Children ages 14 and older are welcome, but your pets will have to find other accommodations. Smoking is not permitted.

Sunnyledge
Boutique Hotel $$$$-$$$$$
5124 Fifth Avenue
(412) 683-5014

With eight rooms, intimate enough to be a bed-and-breakfast, Sunnyledge is Pittsburgh's only boutique hotel—and a sumptuous one it is. All suites have Jacuzzis, and they all boast marble baths, wet bars and minibars, fluffy bathrobes, king-size beds made up with Egyptian cotton linens, two-line speakerphones with modem hookups, and cable television. The decor is contemporary with eclectic touches, similar to what you might find in a Ritz Carlton or Four Seasons.

You'll find a restaurant and full bar and room service in this restored mansion; note that, as Sunnyledge is not a true bed-and-breakfast (it's included here because of its size), breakfast is not included in the price of the room. In the meantime, we'll tell you that the hotel offers a delicious Sunday brunch with such tempting entrees as lobster club sandwiches, spinach and feta streudel, and banana rum French toast. Sunnyledge is within walking distance of Shadyside, Carnegie Mellon University, and the Oakland medical complex; it's a 10-minute car or bus ride from downtown.

**Weatherbury Farm
Bed and Breakfast** $$$–$$$$
**1061 Sugar Run Road, Avella
(724) 587-3763
www.weatherburyfarm.com**
If a vision of more than 100 acres of rolling meadows, gardens, fields, and valleys appeals to you, then you're the ideal guest for Weatherbury Farm. Your kids will like it too—they're welcome here. Pets are not permitted. This is a working farm with cows, sheep, ducks, and geese, and you can expect a hearty and filling breakfast—bountiful, they call it here. In fact you are cordially invited to help with the farm's chores after you eat in the morning.

The three guest rooms feature private baths but no phone or television, in keeping with the agrarian theme. Three suites are also available. Feel free to enjoy the outdoor swimming pool while the kids cavort on the playground.

Woolley Fox Bed and Breakfast $$$
**132 Woolley Fox Lane, Ligonier
(724) 238-3004**
The two guesthouses at Woolley Fox impart distinctly different personalities, but both luxurious houses offer separate bedroom and kitchen areas, private baths, air-conditioning, and working fireplaces. One of the guesthouses features a balcony overlooking a pond and waterfall, while the second boasts a cathedral ceiling and an awning-covered back deck. Both are furnished with antiques and original hooked rugs. The rooms have no telephones, but you can use the phone in the common area. The inn, surrounded by stone walls, is perched on a secluded woodland hillside in Westmoreland County, remote enough to promote privacy and romance yet not far from the attractions of downtown Ligonier. Woolley Fox does not permit children or pets.

WEST

Country Road Bed & Breakfast $$$
**199 Moody Road, Clinton
(724) 899-2528
www.pittsburghbnb.com**
This country estate near Pittsburgh International Airport offers you an appealing 200-year-old log cabin with a fireplace. It is equipped with a small kitchen, private bath, television, and VCR. Children are permitted, but management needs to review your plans for pets.

You'll enjoy a fully stocked fishing pond and an outdoor pool, and you can take advantage of complimentary airport transportation.

Credit cards are not accepted.

**The Inn on College Hill
Bed & Breakfast** $
**3233 Sixth Avenue, Beaver Falls
(724) 843-6048**
The mission oak–style inn draws its name from its location near Geneva College, about 3 miles south of the Pennsylvania Turnpike. Often, guest lecturers and performers at Geneva College stay here, and you'll love conversing with them.

The facility offers four air-conditioned guest rooms furnished mostly with antiques; two have private baths. A telephone and television are available in a common area. Review your plans for bringing children age 12 and older with the management. Neither pets nor smoking are allowed.

When you wake up well rested, you'll be ready to feast on the country continental breakfast. If you tuck one of the fresh muffins or biscuits into your overalls as a tasty reminder of the inn, chances are no one will mind. Note that you'll need to make a reservation to stay here, as the inn can't accommodate drop-ins.

Credit cards are not accepted.

McKinley Place
Bed & Breakfast $$-$$$
132 McKinley Road, Beaver Falls
(724) 891-0300, (866) 891-7502
www.mckinleyplace.com

McKinley Place offers four rooms with televisions, VCRs, phones, computer/modem ports, and private baths. Rooms are decorated in English country style, with Laura Ashley prints and wicker and antique furniture in each room.

While the address for McKinley Place is Beaver Falls, the 60-plus-year-old colonial house is actually a mile from the town of Chippewa, near chain stores, a large antiques mall, and all of the good restaurants. You'll still have that secluded feeling, though, because the bed-and-breakfast is on 3½ wooded acres.

You and other guests will have a private entrance. Breakfast time is the social time at McKinley Place, and you'll enjoy a full, gourmet breakfast that takes into account your special dietary needs.

The Pittsburgh International Airport is only 20 to 25 minutes away. Your children are welcome, and your pets may stay at the nearby kennel. (Check with the proprietors for kennel reservation information.)

The Whistlestop Bed and Breakfast $
195 Broad Street, Leetsdale
(724) 251-0852
www.pittsburghbnb.com

This 1888 brick Victorian about 12 miles west of Pittsburgh was constructed by the Harmonists, an order that founded several western Pennsylvania towns. It features two guest suites with private baths, and two rooms that share a bath, phones, air-conditioning, and cable television. Two of the suites have kitchens. The Whistlestop is only 2 miles from Sewickley, a charming Ohio River town with many galleries and antiques shops for you to explore. It's also very near the popular historic site Old Economy Village, where the Harmonists once lived. Children are welcome, pets are not.

RESTAURANTS

If you thumb through this chapter, you'll notice that it's a very large one. Pittsburgh and the surrounding areas boast everything from the traditional meat-and-potatoes, old-style restaurants you'd expect to Cambodian, Indian, and Middle Eastern restaurants. On Pittsburgh's trendy South Side, there's even an all vegetarian/vegan restaurant, art gallery, and antiques store combination, Zenith Tearoom.

As in most places, the diversity of Pittsburgh's ethnic restaurants is largely dependent on the diversity of its immigrant population. One of the largest populations of immigrants, historically, is Italian. Thus, you might expect that one of the largest categories of ethnic restaurants is Italian. Another factor in Pittsburgh's restaurant scene is the large college crowd. Some students seek out traditional America youth fare, hot dogs and fries, likely to be found at the Original Hot Dog Shop, or "The O," as it's known by insiders. Other, more health-conscious types seek organic or vegetarian fare, easily found at the Co-op Café at East-End Food Co-op, at Zenith, or at most ethnic restaurants.

As you travel outside the city of Pittsburgh into the six-county surrounding areas, you'll find less ethnic diversity and more good home-cooking, as in Butler, where Morgan's Diner has been a local fixture for decades. Don't even say "soup starter kit" while you're at Morgan's; it would be like hitting a wrong note with a master pianist in the audience.

In short, if you're in our area, you're likely to have access to almost any kind of food you've got a craving for. Now, what we can't promise is that it will be right next door, unless you're inside the city proper. Suppose you just want to wander around an area and choose a restaurant with the shortest wait list or the most delicious-sounding specials posted on the menu outside its door. Then we suggest you head for Downtown, Shadyside, or Atwood or Craig Street in Oakland.

To find the area where you'd like to dine, take note of where it is in relation to Downtown: north, south, east, or west of it. To check out the restaurants serving the type of food you're looking for, see the descriptive headings in each of those sections. For instance, if you want to eat Chinese or Japanese in Shadyside, find the East section, then the respective headings within it.

Now get out there and go to dinner, or lunch, or breakfast, or tea . . . and don't be afraid to venture into a place we just didn't have room to include. If it looks good to you, it probably is. We hope you'll enjoy dining in the Pittsburgh area—we sure do.

PRICE CODE

In addition to aiming to include representative, good restaurants of every flavor, we've also aimed to include places for every pocketbook and occasion. You'll find economical lunch spots as well as places where you'd want to propose or close that most important business deal. Here's how we've indicated the price range at each establishment.

$	$1 to $16
$$	$17 to $28
$$$	$29 to $62
$$$$	$63 to $100

In this town of business travelers and independent-minded individuals, we're not assuming you'll be dining with anyone else, so each price range is based upon the range of entree costs, from lowest to highest for one person. For instance, when we checked, at the Red Bull Inn in Robinson, the lowest price for an entree was $9.00 and the highest, $20.00; thus, we've characterized the price range of entrees there as $–$$. Get it?

DOWNTOWN

American

Boulevard Deli $
322 Boulevard of the Allies
(412) 281-4300
Boulevard Deli is a popular spot for take-out lunches, and it also offers a seating area for 26 patrons. Sandwiches here all bear the names of Pittsburgh neighborhoods and features, such as "The Mt. Washington," mountainous roast beef piled high over cheddar cheese and snow-capped with coleslaw; and "The Mon," tuna salad on a bagel with rivers of melted cheddar. You also can order salads and soups, and you can select from a small number of continental breakfast items. Boulevard Deli offers extensive catering services as well. It does not accept reservations or credit cards, and it does not serve alcohol. Smoking is not permitted. Boulevard Deli is open for breakfast and lunch Monday through Friday.

The Carlton $$-$$$
500 Grant Street
(412) 391-4099
www.thecarltonrestaurant.com
You're in for an elegant dining experience at The Carlton, which is located in One Mellon Bank Center. It would be hard to cite the restaurant's specialties, because the menu changes each day to keep the dining experience fresh. You can always count on veal and fresh seafood. Lunch and dinner specials might include seafood Wellington, veal portabella, sesame-seared mahimahi, or crab potato cake with citrus ponzu and wasabi aioli.

The wine list is extraordinary. It covers 43 pages and 500 selections, with each selection priced just $10 above cost, per the philosophy of proprietor Kevin Joyce, named Pittsburgh Restauranteur of the Year four years in a row. The wine list also won the city's *Wine Spectator* award six years straight. Reservations are recommended, and the Carlton accepts major

credit cards. While the restaurant does not offer banquet facilities as such, it can accommodate private parties of up to 150 people. The Carlton is open Monday through Saturday but does not serve lunch on Saturday.

The Common Plea $$$$
310 Ross Street
(412) 281-5140
www.commonplea-restaurant.com
You are summoned to an important duty at the Common Plea, to wit: "The Bearer is summoned to savor a selection from the following menu and to adjudicate the value thereof." That's what the menu, in the form of a legal summons, advises patrons. As you can see, the restaurant gets plenty of mileage from its location in the city's legal and political district. As for its food, service, and atmosphere, the verdict is in, and it's thumbs up.

The Common Plea serves its food in a seemingly endless succession of courses, so bring a hearty appetite. Entrees include pasta, seafood, veal, beef, and lamb selections, many of them priced daily with the market. The lounge provides an intriguing selection of single-malt Scotch whiskeys as well as such specialty cocktails as Chocolata, a martini concocted with vodka and white crème de cacao. The wine list is extensive. If you're of a mind, you can pamper yourself with a five-liter bottle of 1993 Robert Mondavi "reserve" Pinot Noir—for $600.

The restaurant offers banquet facilities for up to 70 people. It serves dinner Monday through Saturday, lunch Monday through Friday. The Common Plea closes from 2:30 to 5:00 P.M. though the lounge remains open during those hours. Smoking and nonsmoking sections are available during lunch and dinner.

Eadies Kitchen $
One Mellon Bank Center
(412) 391-3993
This restaurant in One Mellon Bank Center specializes in lighter fare for breakfast and

lunch, and is a popular spot among Grant Street workers for a quick and affordable meal. The menu, chalked on a blackboard above the ordering counter, features soups, pastas, burgers, hoagies, and salads, as well as four or five hot entree specials. Eadies also provides catering services for downtown offices, including cakes prepared by the pastry chef at the Carlton. The restaurant is open Monday through Friday for breakfast and lunch.

Eadies operates a companion restaurant at the same address called Eadie's Market, which specializes in take-out lunches Monday through Friday. Actually, you'll have to take your Eadie's Market lunch out, as there's no seating. Neither restaurant serves alcohol, and neither accepts reservations or credit cards.

Frenchy's Restaurant & Cocktail Lounge $$$
136 Sixth Street
(412) 261–6476

You will find French-inspired entrees at Frenchy's, but they're a small part of a diverse menu that also includes seafood, beef, chicken, pasta, and veal selections. Frenchy's offers lunch and dinner specials, which might include twin filet mignons with seasoned mushrooms or boneless chicken pepperoni with red sauce and cheese. The restaurant offers a full-service bar and a wine list, and it accepts reservations.

A fixture in downtown's theater district for more than three decades, Frenchy's offers lunch and dinner Monday through Saturday. It's usually closed on Sunday but opens on show nights. When you call for the Sunday schedule, you also can ask about the restaurant's catering services and its banquet facilities, which can accommodate up to 50 people.

Froggy's $-$$
100 Market Street
(412) 471–3764

Owner Steve "Froggy" Morris is one of the region's most colorful restaurateurs, a devotee of sports who once hosted a local sports radio show. The decor reflects Froggy's interests, with sports memorabilia covering nearly every inch of wall space without any apparent organizing principle. In one section, for example, you'll find pictures of Don Shula and Joe Louis above a four-shot sequence of Ben Hogan and his golf swing . . . all of it framing a photo of Froggy himself in harness-racing regalia. Dominating this tableau are 15 LeRoy Neiman prints and an elk head hung over the bar, with sports caps adorning the antlers.

The decor sets the mood for the fun experience here, which includes large portions and strong cocktails. Froggy's specializes in steaks and ribs, but you'll also find such lunch and dinner specials as seafood Devonshire and mussels Parmesan, and many seafood, dinner salad, and sandwich selections. You can enjoy outdoor dining on the third-floor deck in season—a rock band performs there Friday evenings. On Wednesday Froggy's also features live piano entertainment. Reservations are suggested on weekends. Froggy's accepts major credit cards. It's generally closed on Sunday but is open then when the Steelers play at home.

The Garden Cafe $$
Penn Avenue and Sixth Street
(412) 392–4879

You'll enjoy this outdoor cafe at Heinz Hall, the glittering performing-arts hall. The cafe is set in the courtyard and features a fountain and a waterfall, creating an inviting, relaxing atmosphere. The Fluted Mushroom, a prominent Pittsburgh caterer and Heinz Hall's concessionaire, provides sandwiches and salads, and the cafe can accommodate up to 250 for outdoor events. The cafe serves alcohol, although it does not offer a bar or wine list. It accepts reservations for parties of six or more. As the dining area is outdoors, smoking is permitted anywhere. The Garden Cafe serves lunch Monday through Friday from May through September—weather permitting, of course.

Jimmy's Post Tavern　　　　　$
110 Smithfield Street
(412) 562-0238

Owner Jimmy Costanzo says this about his operating philosophy: "We've been in business 20 years, and we're still dedicated to the working man. We have no frills, no specials, just good quality food and large portions." Whether you enjoy lunch or early dinner here, you'll find a menu that's true to Jimmy Costanzo's philosophy. The restaurant is open Monday through Friday and closes at midnight.

"Jimmy's Famous Fish" is the signature sandwich, and you'll find many other sandwich and burger selections as well as soups, salads, and a few vegetarian options. Jimmy's offers a full bar as well as catering services through a separate company called Jimmy's Corporate Catering.

Jimmy Costanzo operates two other restaurants downtown, including Up Over Jimmy's, which as you might guess, is upstairs from Jimmy's Post Tavern, and Jimmy's Downtown Pizza & Lounge, which is just across the street from the tavern.

Mahoney's Restaurant　　　　$$
949 Liberty Avenue
(412) 471-4243

Mahoney's is a quick walk from the David L. Lawrence Convention Center, thus a popular spot for conventioneers. It serves lunch and dinner Monday through Friday, closing on Saturday and Sunday. While the menu is diverse, the most popular items are dinner salads, such as the steak salad and the grilled chicken salad. Mahoney's offers daily specials for each meal. You'll find an upstairs billiards room as well as a full-service bar with daily happy-hour specials and a complimentary buffet on Friday evening. Reservations are accepted. Mahoney's offers banquet facilities for up to 60 people.

Michael's　　　　　　　　$
400 Fifth Avenue
(412) 232-2887

Michael's is part of the 11th-floor dining complex of Kaufmanns department store.

Michael's serves lunch Monday through Saturday, focusing on lighter fare and quick service as a courtesy for busy Downtown shoppers and workers. You'll enjoy the salad buffet as well as Michael's Marketplace Salad, cashew chicken salad served with a frozen fruit mold and homemade nut bread. Michael's offers a lounge and banquet facilities for up to 40 people. Reservations are accepted. Michael's is closed on Sunday.

Mitchell's Restaurant,
Bar & Banquet Center　　　$
304 Ross Street
(412) 471-3663

Since 1903 the Mitchell family has operated restaurants in Pittsburgh, first in East Liberty, now in Downtown in the heart of the city's legal and political center. Many city and Allegheny County employees dine here; if you want the latest political buzz, you'll likely hear it at Mitchell's. The restaurant specializes in inexpensive, home-cooked meals. The menu features seafood and poultry items, dinner salads, and sandwiches. Mitchell's offers a full-service bar and capacious banquet facilities, which have hosted 400 people.

Mitchell's accepts major credit cards but not reservations. It serves lunch and dinner Monday through Friday. On Saturday, only the bar is open. While the restaurant is formally closed on Sunday, it will host banquets on those days.

Morton's of Chicago　　$$$-$$$$
625 Liberty Avenue
(412) 261-7141

You'll know pretty early in your experience at Morton's that you're in a classy restaurant. As you enter, you'll spy the private liquor lockers where such celebs as Mario Lemieux keep their supplies for entertaining guests. Even if you don't achieve that status, you'll enjoy the attentions of a staff that won *Pittsburgh Magazine*'s 1997 award for excellence in service, and also in 2001. That award also cited Morton's steaks, for which the restaurant is known. The menu also offers such entrees as Sicilian veal chops, domestic rib lamb chops, and seafood selections that include shrimp Alexander and broiled Brock Island swordfish steak. When you're ready for libations, Morton's offers a full-service bar and wine list that won mention in 2001 *Wine Spectator* magazine. You can smoke in a small section of the dining room and in the bar, and also buy your cigars here. Morton's serves dinner daily, and it can accommodate banquets of up to 80 people—it also entertains private parties for lunch. Reservations are recommended. You'll find Morton's on the ground level of CNG Tower.

The Mozart Room $$$
Penn Avenue and Sixth Street
(412) 392-4879

Here's a find known primarily to Insiders—a group that now includes you. The Mozart Room is a dining room within Heinz Hall, one of the region's principal halls of the performing arts. The Mozart Room offers pre-performance or pre-concert dinners prior to events in Pittsburgh's Cultural District; your ticket to that evening's event gains you admission to the Mozart Room (you still have to pay for the food). Contemporary American meals are prepared and served by Truffles and Flourishes, a prominent Pittsburgh caterer and Heinz Hall's concessionaire, and are drawn from a seasonal menu that features such entrees as pan-roasted loin of veal.

One of the most appealing aspects of the experience here is the decor, notably the crystal chandeliers and Corinthian columns found throughout Heinz Hall. The Mozart Room, which is entirely nonsmoking, offers a wine list. Reservations are required, and you must wear what management calls proper attire. Banquet facilities can accommodate up to 80 people. The Mozart Room offers occasional Sunday brunches, and it sometimes opens before events staged at venues other than Heinz Hall. Call for details about brunches and those special dinner performances.

Opus, the Renaissance Hotel $$
107 Sixth Street
(412) 992-2005

The last time I was at Opus, the party at the table next to me was toasting Pittsburgh. I'll drink to that—and to the restaurant itself, I might add. The food, the wine list, the atmosphere, and the service are all lovely here, as befits the hotel. Opus isn't just another hotel restaurant; it's a place to add to your favorites list.

Some representative entrees include grilled Alaskan halibut, served with black rice and fruit chutney; seared ahi tuna, with mashed potatoes and pickled ginger relish; and New York strip steak, with sautéed leeks and onions and béarnaise butter. Two particularly wonderful appetizers are fried calamari with saffron aioli (perfectly done and the portion was enormous) and field greens served with buffalo mozzarella, beefsteak tomatoes, red onions, and red wine vinaigrette. By the way, the quality of the seafood here is great and the presentation beautiful, so enjoy.

The wine list is truly extensive, with more than 60—in a range of varieties and moderate prices. By the bottle and glass, there are wines, for example, from vineyards in France, Italy, Spain, the United States, Chile, New Zealand, Australia, and the Russian River Valley. There's also a small, good selection of champagne, sparkling wines, and dessert wines and ports, too. In fact, Opus was recently granted an Award of Excellence by *Wine Spectator*.

In addition to the regular menu, you'll find the restaurant offering two specials

---

The Strip District, just east of Downtown Pittsburgh, is the city's most vital food marketplace, offering fresh produce, meat, and seafood brought in daily. Many of the region's restaurateurs shop there every day. You'll find it a lively, exciting venue for your own fresh food shopping.

---

each evening during the week and more on the weekends. The only thing less than pleasing was the one so-so vegetarian entree. Opus is open for lunch and dinner daily, and there's also a Sunday brunch—particularly bountiful on Steelers Sundays.

Original Fish Market $$$
1001 Liberty Avenue
(412) 227-3657

Seafood is the principal theme here, with a seemingly endless variety of tasty variations. Watch for items such as Chilean sea bass, Florida black grouper, Maine wolffish, and Alaskan halibut under "Today's Catch." The extensive wine list offers a taste guide to help you distinguish those that are dry, for example, from those that are sweet. You also can select from 17 varieties of bottled beer, 11 types of beer on tap, and 4 varieties of sparkling water. Original Fish Market is located adjacent to the Westin Convention Center Hotel. Open daily. All major credit cards accepted.

The Original Oyster House $
20 Market Square
(412) 566-7925

Since 1870, the Original Oyster House has been delighting downtown patrons with its variety of seafood—crab cakes, fish sandwiches, clams, shrimp, and, of course, its signature oysters. This is a lively, informal spot, with many patrons preferring to sit or stand at the bar/counter while they eat. Booths are available, and around them you'll see one of the oddest collections of photographs you're ever likely to find in a restaurant. Staring at you, with toothy smiles each, will be Miss America contestants in group photos representing many years of the pageant. These have been preserved from the collection of the restaurant's original owner, a Miss America buff. Each time he attended the pageant, he returned with a group photo. The Original Oyster House is open from 9:00 A.M. to 11:00 P.M. Monday through Saturday. It's closed on Sunday. Credit cards and reservations are not accepted.

The Promenade Cafe $$-$$$
600 Commonwealth Street
(412) 391-4600, ext. 5304

Part of the Hilton hotel, the Promenade Cafe is open daily for breakfast, lunch, and dinner, and it also serves brunch each Sunday. The dinner menu offers extensive selections of dinner salads and sandwiches, and a more limited selection of entrees. Breakfast and lunch are fun here. The breakfast menu runs to three pages. For lunch, try the Chinese buffet each Monday, featuring a "Wok It to Me" stir-fry station, or the Wednesday buffet that highlights foods of a different nationality each week.

Reservations are accepted, and the cafe offers a wine list and banquet facilities (through the hotel). For cocktails, you can repair to the adjacent Scenes lounge, which features jazz on Friday and Saturday evenings. For more on that, bop over to the Nightlife chapter.

The Ruddy Duck $-$$
1 Bigelow Square
(412) 281-3825

Finding a place to dine on a major holiday sometimes can be a problem. That problem is solved by the Ruddy Duck, which serves breakfast, lunch, and dinner 365 days a year. It's part of the Ramada hotel, so you'll find banquet facilities that can accommodate up to 1,000 people. The menu features veal, pasta divalo, and a stuffed Parmesan chicken dish as highlights. In season, you're welcome to dine on the patio, though there's no view to speak of.

The Ruddy Duck offers a full-service bar and a wine list. During happy hour, from 5:00 to 7:00 P.M. Monday through Friday, you'll enjoy half-off appetizers and drink specials. The restaurant accepts major credit cards, and you can reserve a table at all times except those nights when the nearby Mellon Arena is hosting an event. The Ruddy Duck offers a schedule of ethnic food festivals as well as specially priced cocktails; to keep up with these, ask for a monthly schedule. By the way, if you forget the phone number, it spells 281–DUCK.

Ruth's Chris Steak House $$$
6 PPG Place
(412) 391–4800

If you've visited a Ruth's Chris Steak House in other cities, you'll be familiar with the menu and high quality of service at this restaurant. Steaks, of course, are the specialty, but the restaurant also offers an appealing selection of fresh fish that varies daily with the catch. You usually can find fresh lobster and grilled salmon on the menu, as well as coconut shrimp with a honey mustard sauce that makes an unusual appetizer.

The restaurant offers a full-service bar and a 14-page wine list, with prices up to $500 a bottle. Reservations are suggested for both lunch and dinner. While the restaurant is open seven days a week, lunch is served Monday through Friday only. The dinner menu is available all day.

Seventh Street Grille $$$
130 Seventh Street
(412) 338–0303

Set in the heart of the theater district, Seventh Street Grille is a popular spot before and after shows and concerts. It serves lunch and dinner daily, which is somewhat unusual, as many theater-district restaurants close on Sundays. Mesquite-grilled items are among the specialties here, as you'll enjoy such items as tuna nicoise, salmon fillet, lite chicken, and boneless breast of duck from the grill. Quesadillas, with your choice of six fillings, also are popular. The restaurant offers a bar and a wine list as well as a selection of 77 bottled and 13 draft beers. Reservations are accepted. Seventh Street Grille offers banquet facilities for up to 70 people.

The Smithfield Cafe $-$$
639 Smithfield Street
(412) 281–5452

The Petrolias family has operated the Smithfield Cafe at the same location since 1933. If that's not a record, it's still a heck-

uva lot better than average. The restaurant serves breakfast, lunch, and dinner Monday through Friday, breakfast and lunch only on Saturday; it accepts reservations for lunch and dinner. It opens on Sundays only to accommodate large conventions in downtown. Breakfasts are quite popular here. Breakfast specials are economically priced, and waffles are a regular feature of the menu.

"The Famous Smithfield Devonshire" is a favorite of lunch patrons, while the diverse dinner menu offers beef, chicken, and seafood selections as well as salads and "mix & match" pasta—you select the pasta and match it with your choice of sauces. The cafe offers a full-service bar and banquet facilities for up to 150 people On Friday evenings, the Smithfield Cafe hosts karaoke.

Souper Bowl Restaurant & Lounge $
910 Fifth Avenue
(412) 471–0416

Here's an unpretentious spot in the Uptown neighborhood, a few blocks from both Downtown and the Mellon Arena. You'll find a variety of soups and sandwiches, several specials each day, and a taco salad special each Wednesday. During happy hour, from 4:00 to 6:00 P.M., you'll enjoy special prices on cocktails and the extensive selection of beers. Souper Bowl is open Monday through Friday. It accepts major credit cards and offers banquet facilities for up to 100 people. Reservations are not accepted.

Southwest Bistro $-$$
129 Sixth Street
(412) 261–8866

Run by native Texan Michael Crawford and his wife Cheryl Lowitzer, Southwest Bistro features menu selections unlike any others we know of in Pittsburgh. While the number of entrees is around only 10, you're certain to find plenty of taste packed in each. The bistro's specialty is smoked duck with ancho-chile demi-glacé and shiitake mushrooms. Another dinner entree often ordered is grilled center-cut pork

Pittsburghers, per capita, are said to drink more coffee than people in any other city on this continent.

loin topped with roasted red pepper jelly and a pineapple-jicama salsa. On the vegetarian side, you'll find saffron rice topped with black beans, with a medley of side dishes surrounding it: ginger carrot puree; braised red cabbage; brandied portobella mushrooms; green chile grits; grilled garlic tomatoes; and a poblano, leek, and red pepper side dish. Michael orders all the wines himself from special, smaller vineyards (we give them a thumbs-up), and you'll get a great price on a bottle—$10 above cost. To complement your Southwest experience, beer and margaritas are also available. Something else to look forward to at the bistro is the desserts; two of our favorites are the Belgian chocolate mousse and the caramel flan.

Southwest Bistro is open for lunch during the week from 11:00 A.M. to 2:00 P.M. and for dinner Tuesday through Thursday 5:00 to 9:00 P.M. and Friday and Saturday from 5:00 to 10:30 P.M. Formal banquet facilities are not available, as this really is a bistro; however, you may be able to book the entire restaurant for your party of up to 55 people. With occasional exceptions during odd hours, Southwest Bistro is a nonsmoking zone.

The Terrace $$-$$$
530 William Penn Place
(412) 553-5235

Sitting in the lobby of the Omni William Penn Hotel is one of our town's most enjoyable experiences, when you dine at the hotel's restaurant, known as the Terrace, you'll enhance that experience. The Terrace offers breakfast, lunch, and dinner Monday through Saturday, brunch only on Sunday. Each meal has a distinct personality, and power breakfasts are popular here.

Dinner is a more leisurely affair. Wheeling and dealing gives way to lingering dinners over such entrees as seared duck breast, roast lamb rack, curry roasted cod, and bronze-skin salmon. On Tuesday and Friday evenings, you'll enjoy a special package that includes hors d'oeuvres, a cigar (Sinatra label), cognac or Scotch whiskey, and a local Jazz entertainer every Friday night. The Terrace offers two full-service bars, a wine list, and banquet facilities for up to 150 people.

The Tic Toc Restaurant $
400 Fifth Avenue
(412) 232-2307

The ornate clock outside Kaufmanns department store is one of the city's most recognizable landmarks. As far back as the 1930s, Kaufmanns appreciated the importance of this landmark, and so it named its first-floor restaurant to reflect the clock's popularity. Today, it's still convenient to look up and catch the time while dashing about downtown.

While the Tic Toc Restaurant has the look and feel of a coffee shop, it goes beyond that to offer such breakfasts as homemade waffles and a dessert menu that's about 15 items strong. It's open from 10:00 A.M. to 8:00 P.M. Monday through Saturday, closing at 6:00 P.M. on Wednesday and all day Sunday. The Tic Toc restaurant serves beer and wine. It does not accept reservations.

Up Over Jimmy's $
110 Smithfield Street
(412) 562-0239

Located upstairs from Jimmy's Post Tavern, this restaurant—which serves lunch only—is true to owner Jimmy Costanzo's philosophy of serving working people on a budget. You'll find reasonably priced entrees such as Maryland crab cakes and broiled swordfish, as well as a diverse selection of sandwiches and several specialty salads. And of course, "Jimmy's Famous Fish Sandwich" is always available. Up Over Jimmy's is a popular spot for banquets and meetings, often hosting political functions. Up Over Jimmy's is open Monday through Friday.

Cambodian

The Lemon Grass Cafe $$-$$$
124 Sixth Street
(412) 765-2222

Restaurateurs are a colorful breed with engaging tales to tell. Spend some time, however, with the Lemon Grass Cafe owners Kim Hong and her son, Bophanara "Bo" Meng, and if the mood is just right, you'll hear stories shocking in their cruelty and nearly incredible with their examples of commonplace heroism. It's the story of native Cambodians Kim and Bo, of course, who in 1979 escaped Khmer Rouge "killing fields" and re-education camps that claimed the lives of 21 members of their immediate family. After enduring four years of re-education, they escaped to Thailand as the first part of their journey to Pittsburgh.

Now, they operate both the Lemon Grass Cafe and a sister Downtown restaurant called Phnom Penh (see write-up below). The menu at the cafe offers a variety of Cambodian dishes, including red and green curry; spicy mussels; and fried rice with sausage, eggs, carrots, peas, and scallions. For many of the entrees, you have the option of chicken, beef, or shrimp as the base. You'll also enjoy the green papaya salad; the signature lemon grass soup; and the shark fin soup, which includes crabmeat, roast pork, egg, shredded ginger root, bamboo shoots, black mushrooms, and scallions. The cafe does not use butter or cheese in any of its dishes.

The cafe serves lunch and dinner Monday through Saturday, dinner only on Sunday. It does not serve alcohol. Reservations are accepted. The cafe does not designate smoking or nonsmoking sections. It can accommodate banquets of up to 80 people.

When you're here, take a minute to shake hands with Kim and Bo. If the mood is just right, they might have some tales to tell you.

Phnom Penh $-$$
410 First Avenue
(412) 261-4166

The second of the downtown restaurants operated by Kim Hong and Bo Meng, Phnom Penh offers a menu similar to that of its sister restaurant, the Lemon Grass Cafe. Phnom Penh, however, supplements its Cambodian cuisine with a generous selection of Chinese entrees such as General Tso's Chicken and cashew chicken or shrimp. You also can enjoy lemon grass soup here. Phnom Penh serves lunch and dinner Monday through Friday, dinner only on Saturday. It's closed on Sunday. Reservations are accepted. Phnom Penh does not serve alcohol—you're invited to bring your own—and it does not designate smoking and nonsmoking sections. It provides banquet facilities for up to 55 people.

Caribbean

Kaya $$$
2000 Smallman Street
(412) 261-6565

The Caribbean food and decor in this casual Strip District restaurant attracts a noisy, younger crowd. Great hot and cold tropas (like Spanish tapas) and vegetarian selections complement a collection of microbrews. In summer sit outside and watch the nightclubbers pass by. Open daily for lunch and dinner. Bar hours differ, often extending until 1:00 A.M. Most major credit cards are accepted.

Chinese

Chinatown Inn $$
520 Third Avenue
(412) 261-1292

The Yee family has operated Chinatown Inn for three generations, serving Cantonese, Szechuan, and Hunan selections.

It's located near Grant Street, the center of city and Allegheny County political and legal activity, so you'll be rubbing shoulders with politicos when you dine here. The lunch and dinner menus include beef, seafood, and poultry entrees as well as limited vegetarian menu. Chinatown Inn offers a full-service bar and a wine list, as well as banquet facilities for up to 100 people. Lunch and dinner reservations are accepted, as are major credit cards.

Mandarin Gourmet   **$–$$**
305 Wood Street
(412) 261-6151
Mandarin Gourmet serves lunch and dinner Monday through Saturday. You'll find a broad selection of pork, beef, poultry, seafood, and pasta items as well as vegetarian selections. Check out the "Chef's Suggestions" section for a number of interesting combinations, like sizzling two delicacies, featuring beef and scallops, and dragon and phoenix, with lobster and General Tso's chicken. Hot and spicy items are marked with a red star. Mandarin Gourmet offers a full-service bar, and it accepts reservations. It offers banquet facilities for up to 300 people. You'll find a sister Mandarin Gourmet in the North Hills, which offers a buffet as well as a full menu.

Greek

Christos Mediterranean Grill   **$–$$**
130 Sixth Street
(412) 261-6442
For three years, Christos Malacrinos served as a chef for Jackie Onassis aboard the yacht *Christina*. Now, he's bringing the benefits of that experience to Downtown Pittsburgh diners. Christos serves lunch and dinner daily, offering such entrees as spanakopita, lamb kabob, chicken kabob oreganato, and moussaka—you can complement them all with Greek Easter bread. But the real star of the menu is a dessert called ekmek, which Malacrinos says he

developed and prepared especially for Onassis. It's a white cake topped with honey syrup, custard, cinnamon, and whipped cream, and you can order a version with a chocolate cake base as well.

Christos offers an outdoor dining area and banquet facilities for up to 55 people. It does not serve alcohol—you're invited to bring your own—and it does not designate smoking and nonsmoking sections. Christos normally does not accept reservations, but it will take lunch reservations for parties of six or more on days when the nearby theaters are staging performances. Open 11:00 A.M. to 9:00 P.M. Sunday through Thursday and 11:00 A.M. to midnight Friday and Saturday. Credit cards are not accepted.

Italian

Asiago   **$$–$$$**
One Oxford Centre
(412) 392-0225
This elegant restaurant in One Oxford Centre on Grant Street features European cuisine of French and Italian influence. The selections include pasta, beef, veal, poultry, and fresh seafood. Among its most popular items are crabcake Valencia with a scarlet orange beurre blanc and veal siago, which is topped with roasted peppers, Asiago cheese, and pesto, and laced with chianti bordelaise sauce. You'll find a full bar and an outstanding wine list, as well as banquet facilities for up to 70 people. Reservations are suggested for dinner and accepted for lunch parties of five or more. Parking is complimentary with dinner reservations. The restaurant, which accepts all major credit cards, is closed on Sunday.

Bravo Franco Ristorante   **$$$**
613 Penn Avenue
(412) 642-6677
Located in the heart of the Cultural District, Bravo Franco offers both indoor dining in an intimate room and dining al fresco on its sidewalk patio. The menu fea-

tures chicken, seafood, pasta, and beef selections, with the steaks cut thick. A popular selection is the bowtie and salmon pasta, served with a light tomato cream sauce. Bravo Franco offers a full-service bar, and extensive wine list and banquet facilities for up to 100 people. Reservations are requested. Bravo Franco does not designate smoking and nonsmoking sections, but it tries to accommodate patrons of each persuasion. The restaurant offers lunch and dinner Monday through Saturday. It's open on Sunday only when the nearby theaters are staging performances. Call ahead to check the Sunday schedule.

Caffé Amante $$
120 Fifth Avenue
(412) 391-1226

Caffé Amante is the principal restaurant in Fifth Avenue Place, the retail and office complex that features distinctive needle-type ornamenting. Caffé Amante specializes in continental and Northern Italian fare, with seafood, veal, chicken, and pasta entrees. The restaurant offers a full-service bar and an extensive wine list, and it can accommodate banquets. Reservations are suggested. Caffé Amante serves lunch and dinner Monday through Saturday. It's closed on Sunday.

Carmassi's Tuscany Grill $$$
711 Penn Avenue
(412) 281-6644

Carmassi's specializes in Northern Italian fare. You'll enjoy such entrees as chicken and shrimp saute; penne arrabiatta, which consists of grilled lobster and shrimp with red onions in a spicy tomato sauce over a penne bed; and veal San Remo, which features veal medallions sautéed with artichoke hearts, roasted peppers, and a marsala demi-glacé. Carmassi's also serves a pretheater "Prix Fixe"—a fixed-price feature with a different entree each day. Carmassi's offers a full-service bar, an extensive wine list, and banquet facilities for up to 80 people. Reservations are accepted. Carmassi's serves dinner Monday through Saturday, lunch Monday

through Friday. It opens on Sunday only on performance days at the nearby theaters. If you're thinking about Sunday dinner here, it's best to call ahead.

Costanzo's Italian Bar and Grill $-$$
240 Fourth Avenue
(412) 232-0706

Costanzo's offers two separate personalities, both of them appealing. By day, it's a popular spot for lunches. By night, it swings, offering DJs or bands Friday and Saturday nights. The menu features steak, veal, chicken, seafood, and pasta selections. Banquets are an important service of Costanzo's, as it can accommodate up to 200 people. It offers a full-service bar. Reservations are recommended for lunch; not usually needed for dinner. Costanzo's is open every day except Sunday.

F. Tambellini Seventh Street $-$$
139 Seventh Street
(412) 391-1091

F. Tambellini offers a wide variety of lunch and dinner selections, including beef, veal (including ossu bucco, or veal shank), seafood, and pasta selections. The common denominator among longtime patrons, however, is considerable affection for the restaurant's fried zucchini—a must when you dine here. The restaurant offers a full-service bar and an extensive wine list, and it accepts reservations for parties of eight or more. The Puccini room hosts banquets for up to 100 people. F. Tambellini is open Monday through Saturday; with its location in downtown's theater district, it also opens on Sunday show nights. It's best to call to determine F. Tambellini's status on any Sunday.

Jamie's On The Square $$-$$$
435 Market Street
(412) 471-1722

Jamie's offers a diverse menu that includes beef, seafood, veal, chicken, and pasta selections. Popular entrees include crab cakes, which are deep fried with jumbo lump crabmeat and served with Dijon mustard sauce, and Jamie's Surf and Turf,

If you're having one of those days when you just don't feel like leaving the house to eat, order your meal from Wheel Deliver. The service will deliver your order from any of more than 30 restaurants, primarily but not exclusively in the city's eastern neighborhoods. You'll pay restaurant prices plus a 15 percent delivery charge, with minimum and maximum orders and delivery charges applied. Wheel Deliver accepts credit cards, cash, and checks. It's available for dinners daily, for lunches Monday through Friday. The delivery territory is limited.

featuring charbroiled beef tenderloins and skewered shrimp and scallops, served with a tomato caper sauce. Jamie's offers a full-service bar and a wine list. It serves lunch and dinner Monday through Saturday, closing on Sundays. Reservations are recommended for dinner, but not accepted for lunch. You'll find Jamie's in the busy Market Square section of Downtown.

La Scala Ristorante $$-$$$
144 Sixth Street
(412) 434-6244

This classy restaurant in the heart of the theater district features primarily Northern Italian selections, including seafood, veal, beef, chicken, and pasta entrees. If you're in the mood for light dining after the theater, you'll enjoy La Scala's homemade desserts. The restaurant offers a bar and a wine list, as well as banquet facilities for up to 80 people. The dining room normally is nonsmoking, but La Scala will waive that rule if the restaurant isn't too full. Reservations are recommended. La Scala offers lunch and dinner Monday through Friday, and only dinner on Saturday. It's usually closed on Sunday but opens on show nights. Call to confirm La Scala's status on any Sunday.

Lidia's $$$
1400 Smallman and 15th Streets
(412) 522-0150

Still relatively new to the Strip, Lidia's serves Northern Italian cuisine in a grand setting. For a set price you can sample from three pastas of the day, such as homemade ravioli with thyme butter or fettuccine with beef, and it's all-you-can-eat. The price also includes a Caesar salad and tiramisu. The quail with cherry-balsamic sauce melts in your mouth. An extensive all-Italian wine list with almost half the bottles around $20 helped earn Lidia's the *Wine Spectator*'s Award of Excellence.

Named after Lidia Bastianich, the TV cooking personality and cookbook author, the restaurant opened with a built-in fan base. Balcony seating increased the capacity for this always busy restaurant, and there's often a bargain selection of wines by the glass and appetizers during happy hour at the long bar facing the kitchen. Open daily for lunch and dinner, Lidia's offers brunch on Sunday. Reservations are suggested for larger groups, and all major credit cards are accepted.

Piccolo Piccolo Ristorante $$$
1 Wood Street
(412) 261-7234

Piccolo Piccolo is one of the restaurants people often name when asked about the finest in town. The restaurant specializes in Roman-style food. Among its most popular selections is the antipasto buffet, which comes with your entree or serves as a meal in itself. You'll find veal, chicken, seafood, and pasta selections, as well as steaks and chops. When you're really hungry, try the delizia del mare, a mixture of lobster, crab claws, shrimp, and other shellfish simmered in garlic and white wine and served on a bed of angel-hair pasta.

Piccolo Piccolo offers a full-service bar and a 12-page wine list, as well as banquet facilities for up to 65 people. It accepts major credit cards and recommends reservations for lunch and dinner. The restaurant is open on weekends from 4:00 to 10:00 P.M. General manager Frank Sacco is the second generation of his family to participate in Piccolo Piccolo's ownership. Shuttle service is available to and from hotels and major events in the area.

Pizza

Jimmy's Downtown Pizza & Lounge $
107 Smithfield Street
(412) 394-9600

The ubiquitous and hard-working Jimmy Costanzo operates this restaurant, along with two others just across Smithfield Street. One of the strongest attractions here is that you can place your orders for pizza, hoagies and submarines, and soups and salads as late as 1:30 A.M. making it one of the latest-closing restaurants in all of Downtown. The menu also includes several pasta entrees and of course, "Jimmy's Famous Fish Sandwich."

Monte Cello's Italian Restaurant & Pizzeria $
Seventh and Liberty Avenues
(412) 261-2080

When you have time for a quick lunch only but still want to get away from the office, hurry on down to Monte Cello's. You can avoid the lines at the counter by helping yourself to pizza by the slice and sandwiches at the express lunch buffet—and enjoy your meal in the dining area. Monte Cello's offers such unusual pizza toppings as steak and onions, and chicken and broccoli. You also can choose from a limited number of entrees, soups, and salads. Monte Cello's does not serve alcohol. It accepts reservations for parties of 10 or more, and it offers catering and delivery services. Monte Cello's serves lunch and dinner Monday through Sunday.

Villa Reale $
628 Smithfield Street
(412) 391-3963

Villa Reale calls its pizza "perfect." That may be an exaggeration, but only a slight one, as downtown shoppers and workers have been enjoying the restaurant's pizza since 1976. You can order yours with such unusual toppings as roasted red peppers or pineapple. Villa Reale also features a limited selection of entrees—pasta with broccoli and pasta with ricotta cheese are among patrons' favorites—and plenty of sandwiches and salads. The restaurant offers a lounge and a limited wine list, as well as banquet facilities for up to 50 people. It serves lunch and dinner Monday through Sunday.

Seafood

The Steelhead Grill $$$
112 Washington Place
(412) 394-3474

When the Steelhead Grill opened in 1997, it was named by *Esquire* magazine as one of America's top 10 new restaurants. It's operated by Myriad Restaurant Group, the force behind such restaurants as Montrachet, TriBeCa Grill, Layla, and Nobu in New York, and Rubicon in San Francisco. As you would expect, Steelhead boasts all the features—excellent food, classy environment, attentive service—that you would expect in a restaurant that attracts national attention. Specialties include grilled steelhead salmon and tuna seared rare with soba noodles and a mushroom broth. You'll also find beef, chicken, and pasta entres, as well as a vegetarian "plate of the day."

Steelhead offers a lounge, an extensive wine list, and banquet facilities for up to 50 people. It serves breakfast, lunch, and dinner Monday through Friday and a breakfast buffet on Saturday and Sunday. While Steelhead closes each Monday through Friday from 2:00 to 5:00 P.M., the lounge remains open for eating and drinking during those hours. Reservations are recommended for dinner and lunch. When you call for reservations, remember that the phone number above spells FYI–FISH. The principal dining area is nonsmoking, but smoking is permitted in the lounge.

The Steelhead Grill is located in the Pittsburgh Marriott City Center near the Mellon Arena. For more on the hotel and its banquet facilities, see the Accommodations chapter.

NORTH

American

Bonello's Family Restaurant $–$$
353 Butler Road, Kittanning
(724) 545-2601
For buffet buffs, Bonello's is boffo. On Wednesday and Thursday, you can sample the chef's buffet, a dinner spread that features such entrees as lasagna, cabbage rolls, and chicken. Friday brings the super seafood buffet, while the highlight of Saturday and Sunday is the American buffet, offering ribs and roast beef. Did we mention the breakfast buffet each Saturday and Sunday? The salad bar at Bonello's seems like a buffet itself, offering about 50 items. Banquet facilities for up to 100 people are available. This Armstrong County restaurant accepts reservations. Bonello's is open daily for breakfast, lunch, and dinner. And don't worry about getting lost trying to find this old-time gem; there's a giant plastic cow out in front of the restaurant.

The Clark Bar & Grill $–$$
503 Martindale Street
(412) 231-5720
Although this building housed the original Clark Bar production facility, you won't find any of those chocolate bars here, as the candy company now is based in Pittsburgh's northern suburbs. You will find a restaurant that serves lunch and dinner Monday through Saturday, and each Sunday that brings an event to Three Rivers Stadium. The menu is limited but trendy, offering ribs, steak, grilled crab cakes, sandwiches, and dinner salads. The wine list is limited, but the bar is exceptionally well stocked, offering 12 brands of vodka

and 10 types of single-malt Scotch whiskey, among other delights. The restaurant accepts reservations. The restaurant designates smoking and nonsmoking sections. It's a long field goal from the stadium on the city's' North Side.

Crow's Nest $$
19th Street and River Road, Sharpsburg
(412) 782-3701
When you dine at Crow's Nest, the Allegheny River will be your cheerful companion. The restaurant takes full advantage of its riverfront location by offering a nautical decor, outdoor dining with a view of the river and the dam at Highland Park, and bands performing on a barge in the river each weekend throughout the warm weather months. (Sorry, there's no food available on the barge.)

The lunch and dinner menus offer primarily lighter fare as well as daily specials. But you will find such dinner entrees as shrimp scampi, filet mignon, and pan-fried Maryland crab cakes. You'll enjoy a full-service bar with a broad selection of beers as well as a limited wine list. The restaurant offers banquet facilities for up to 150 people. It accepts reservations for parties of six or more.

Crow's Nest is a few miles north of Downtown. It's open Tuesday through Friday in the summer, Tuesday through Saturday at other times.

Damon's $$$
855 Freeport Road, Fox Chapel
(412) 782-3750

7221 McKnight Road, North Hills
(412) 367-7427

Miracle Mile Shopping Center
Monroeville
(412) 858-7427

511 Clairton Boulevard, Clairton
(412) 653-7427
You'll find four Damon's restaurants in the area—two in the North Hills, one in Monroeville in the eastern suburbs, and one in the South Hills. Each offers the same com-

bination of fun food, around-the-wall TVs, and unusual games. The Fox Chapel restaurant, set in Waterworks Mall, is the original Damon's in this region, so we'll tip our cap to them and profile that Damon's in this section.

The restaurant may be best known for its prime rib and ribs; prime rib is available after 4:00 P.M. Monday through Saturday, but the St. Louis–style ribs are available for lunch and dinner. In fact, the lunch and dinner menus are identical, with the exception of the prime rib noted above. You'll also find chicken, pasta, seafood, and sandwich selections, as well as a special menu for kids younger than age 10. For an unusual appetizer, try the onion loaf—if you're really in a daring mood, go for the "Mother Loaf." Adults will enjoy a full-service bar, a wide selection of beers, and a more limited wine list, plus happy hours that run from 5:00 to 7:00 P.M. Monday through Friday and 9:00 P.M. to closing Monday through Thursday. Enjoy half-price appetizers during these extended get-happy times.

If you'd like some upbeat entertainment with your meal, try the Damon's clubhouse, which features computer keyboards that offer trivia games viewed on wide-screen TVs; kids enjoy their own cartoon time, 5:00 to 7:00 P.M. each Wednesday. Damon's accepts major credit cards as well as reservations every day. You may also call ahead for priority seating when you're en route. Damon's offers banquet facilities.

Ford City Steak & Seafood Company $
418 Third Avenue, Ford City
(724) 763-2901
The Ford City Steak & Seafood Company serves dinner only from Tuesday through Sunday. The menu offers diverse American fare, with beef, poultry, and veal selections as well as sandwiches and daily pasta and seafood specials. It offers a full-service bar and a wine list, and it can accommodate up to 120 people for banquets.

Hardwood Cafe $
646 Pittsburgh Road, Butler
(724) 586-5353
On those cold Southwestern Pennsylvania nights, you'll enjoy dining by the fire at Hardwood Cafe, which features a two-story fireplace. You'll also enjoy a diverse menu that offers pasta and chicken dishes as well as pizza and burgers. You can opt for lunch and dinner specials each day except Sunday, when you'll still be able to choose from the wide variety of selections on Hardwood's menu. Reservations are needed on weekends and accepted on weekdays. The Hardwood Cafe offers banquet facilities for up to 50 people. The restaurant is conveniently located on Route 8. Like the entrees available, prices at the cafe encompass a broad range.

J-Barn Country Inn $-$$
495 Monroe Road, Sarver
(724) 353-3300
This Butler County restaurant is a pleasant country inn that offers such appealing country-style fare as ribs, ham, seafood, steak marinated on the premises, marshmallow fruit salad, fried mushrooms, and homemade banana bread and apple butter. Outdoor grilling is one of their specialties. If you like what you're eating, you can stop at the inn's country store and pick up J-Barn baked goods and other branded foods. The store also features crafts fashioned by local artisans. J-Barn is open Wednesday through Sunday for dinner, with lunch served on Sunday only. Reservations are recommended for Saturday, accepted at other times.

James Street Restaurant $$-$$$
422 Foreland Street
(412) 323-2222
For good food and good jazz, try James Street Restaurant on Pittsburgh's North Side. The restaurant features a number of Cajun- and Creole-style dishes, including chicken and shrimp jambalaya and andouille gumbo, and sautéed chicken in a

stew of onions and peppers over rice. You'll find lunch and dinner specials, a full-service bar, and a wine list.

James Street also is one of the city's most popular havens for jazz. On Tuesday, Thursday, Friday, and Saturday evenings, the stage typically is turned over to such top local performers as drummer Roger Humphries and saxophonist Kenny Blake. Wednesday brings a double treat. First, the Pittsburgh Banjo Club holds an open practice session at the restaurant. Then Five Guys Named Moe treat patrons to a show featuring jazz from the '40s and '50s. There's a cover charge only for the occasional national act.

Reservations are recommended. James Street offers banquet facilities for up to 150 people. It's open for lunch and dinner Tuesday through Saturday, and you can enjoy Sunday brunch here when the Steelers play at home. If you're wondering about the name, you do turn on James Street to get there.

Kaufman House $
105 South Main Street, Zelienople
(724) 452-8900

You can have a memorable dining experience here, as each month brings wild-game specials that include such dishes as elk, ostrich, and wild-boar sausage. The less adventuresome will enjoy the prime rib and fried chicken selections from the regular menu.

The restaurant offers a bar, a wine list, and banquet facilities for up to 50 people. You'll need reservations on Friday, Saturday, and Sunday. Kaufman House serves breakfast, lunch, and dinner daily.

Luma $$
8 Brilliant Avenue
(412) 781-0355

This popular neighborhood restaurant on a quiet tree-lined street in Asinwall made a welcome replacement for the dark burger joint previously located there. Now a light airy bistro offering American cuisine with an emphasis on fresh seafood,

poultry, and beef, Luma does not stint when it comes to large entrees and accompanying side dishes. Their wine list offers sufficient selections with a 20-for-20 section of reasonably priced wines at $20 a bottle. Save room for dessert, like warm chocolate mousse cake by Tallulah's Catering. Dining inside can be noisy; out on the patio it's delightful, with evenings extended through the fall by tall outdoor heaters. All major credit cards are accepted. Making reservations on weekends is a wise decision. Open daily.

Morgan's Diner $$
127 Oneida Valley Road, Butler
(724) 282-2800

Here's a pleasant throwback—a diner that serves breakfast all day and hearty American fare for lunch and dinner. Beyond the signature steakburgers, Morgan's offers daily specials that include creamed chicken and biscuits, sirloin tips and noodles, and scalloped potatoes and ham. Morgan's accepts no reservations.

You'll find real home-cooked food at Morgan's; even the pastries are made from scratch. The diner is especially famous for its fried chicken, homemade soups, the shakes made from real ice cream and milk, and its apple dumplings. There's an extensive menu, and you'll feel like you're at Grandma's house when you see the five kinds of potato dishes available. That reminds us, if you're a vegetarian, you're not likely to find a conventional entree, but you can load up on veggie side dishes and maybe one of those yummy shakes. It's worth it. If you're in Butler, don't miss this tasty landmark.

The 1901 Tavern & Grill $$$
143 North Main Street, Butler
(724) 283-6061

Owners Greg and Laura Walter traveled throughout the world when Greg served in the Air Force, sampling exotic fare. They've brought a touch of that exotic flavor to The 1901 in downtown Butler. In addition to the standard steak, seafood, pasta, and chicken dishes served for lunch and dinner, you can sample such unusual dishes as elk, caribou, black bear, rattlesnake, and wild boar—or whatever else chef Don Potter has bagged that day. Alligator is a staple of the appetizer menu, and you'll enjoy the raw bar each Friday.

The 1901 offers more than 100 micro-brews and 17 varieties of beer on tap. If you want to enjoy a post-alligator cigar, you'll find a humidor on the premises. Reservations are accepted for lunch and dinner.

Shamrock Inn $
917 Western Avenue
(412) 231-2468
Shamrock Inn is an unpretentious restaurant on the North Side. You'll find a solid selection of sandwiches, as well as entrees and a few dinner salads. The salad bar is a particularly popular feature. You can enjoy the lounge and choose from a limited wine list. Reservations are accepted; you might want to consider them, as Shamrock Inn typically draws large crowds. The restaurant offers banquet facilities for up to 200. Shamrock Inn serves breakfast, lunch, and dinner Monday through Friday. Only the lounge is open on weekends.

Tata's Family Restaurant $$
5 Lyn-Mar Plaza, Lyndora
(724) 287-7359
Since 1971, the Milasincic family has operated Tata's—you pronounce it TUH Tuh's, by the way—and it has the feel of an old-time family restaurant. Located just outside the city of Butler, Tata's offers daily lunch and dinner specials; all entrees include visits to the food bar, a buffet of salads and hot foods. You'll also find specially priced seniors' and children's menus. Reservations aren't required, but Tata's will accept them for larger parties. The restaurant offers banquet facilities for up to 110 people. Entrees are priced at the lower end of $$. Smoking is not permitted in the restaurant.

W. Ricks Taproom & Grill $-$$
269 Meridian Road, Meridian
(724) 482-2970
Located just outside the city of Butler, W. Ricks offers a diverse menu that includes steak, seafood, and lamb selections regularly; prime rib is available after 4:00 P.M. on Wednesday, Friday, and Saturday. You'll find daily lunch and dinner specials and a children's menu. W. Ricks offers a full-service bar and a wine list. Reservations are accepted but not required.

Asian

Mandarin Gourmet $$$
4812 McKnight Road, North Hills
(412) 261-6151
Mandarin Gourmet serves lunch and dinner daily, including a buffet for each. You'll find a broad selection of pork, beef, poultry, seafood, and pasta items as well as vegetarian selections. Check out the "Chef's Suggestions" section for a number of interesting combinations, such as sizzling two delicacies, featuring beef and scallops, and dragon and phoenix, with lobster and General Tso's chicken. Hot and spicy items are marked with a red star. Mandarin Gourmet offers a full-service bar, and it accepts reservations. If you're Downtown, try Mandarin Gourmet's sister restaurant on Wood Street.

Tai Pei Chinese Restaurant $-$$
1124 Freeport Road, Fox Chapel
(412) 781-4131
When you choose Tai Pei for lunch or dinner, you can select from a limited wine list or enjoy the full-service bar. The extensive menu offers plenty of beef, lamb, chicken, pork, and seafood selections, ranging from such traditional favorites as General Tso's chicken (the General's shrimp is available as well) and Peking duck to more daring entrees, such as crispy prawn, Szechuan style. You'll know if you're ordering a "hot and spicy" selection—these are highlighted in red on the menu.

Tai Pei offers a limited selection of "Dieter Gourmet" entrees as well as specially priced family dinners; entree selection for family dinners is limited. The restaurant accepts major credit cards and reservations for lunch and dinner, and provides free lunch delivery for take-out orders. The Fox Chapel location is about 10 miles north of Pittsburgh and only 1 mile south of Sichuan House, while you'll find its sister restaurant in Pittsburgh's Shadyside neighborhood.

German

Max's Allegheny Tavern   **$–$$**
537 Suismon Street
(412) 231-1899
If it's sausages, schnitzel, and other German delights you hunger for, you'll find them at Max's Allegheny Tavern on the city's North Side. The restaurant offers daily lunch and dinner specials. If you can't settle on just one German entree, try Max's Sampler Platter—you'll get three entrees with your platter. The restaurant also offers beef and seafood selections prepared with a German touch. You'll find a full-service bar and a wine list, as well as banquet facilities for up to 80 people. Max's accepts reservations for parties of five or more. It's open daily for lunch and dinner and features brunch each Sunday.

Penn Brewery Restaurant   **$$**
Troy Hill Road and Vinial Street
(412) 237-9402
www.pennbrew.com
Gemutlich! That's how you'll describe Penn Brewery after you visit this bright, informal restaurant on Pittsburgh's North Side. Tom and Mary Beth Pastorius operate both the restaurant and the adjoining microbrewery, which produces Penn Pilsner and a variety of other beers. There's more than a touch of authenticity here, as Tom Pastorius traces his lineage to Franz Daniel Pastorius, who is credited with

establishing the first German settlement in America in 1683.

The menu features such German fare as schnitzel, sauerbraten, schweinbraten, and potato pancakes, as well as dinner salads and beef, chicken, and seafood entrees. You'll find lunch and dinner specials, a full bar, a limited wine list, and banquet facilities for up to 200 on Sunday, up to 100 on other days. If you're planning to hold a birthday party here, you can bring in your own cake, but be sure to ask about the restaurant's "cutting fee," which applies even if the staff doesn't actually cut the cake; this cost can be on the prohibitive side.

You'll be entertained on Wednesday evenings by a strolling accordion player, on Friday and Saturday evenings by a live band. Special events also are fun here. These range from Oktoberfest and Caribbean Night to the annual Pennsylvania Microbrewery Fest, when patrons can sample the wares of more than 30 brewers. But for Oktoberfest, these events are irregularly scheduled, so it's best to call for details about these special events.

The restaurant accepts reservations for parties of eight or more. Penn Brewery serves lunch and dinner Monday through Saturday.

Indian

Taj Mahal   **$$**
7795 McKnight Road
(412) 364-1760
Taj Mahal serves Mughlai, North Indian, South Indian, and authentic regional Indian cuisine. In 2003, it was awarded *Pittsburgh Magazine*'s Gold Medal award for "Excellence in Serving Indian Food," as well as the magazine's Gold Medal award for "Best Overall Sunday Brunch." The restaurant also offers full-service catering.

Some of my favorite items from the daily, plentiful lunch buffet are the delicious vegetable *pakora* (vegetable fritters), *tikki* (small potato pancakes), special lemon rice, vegetable korma, *palak paneer,* and the creamy mango dessert. One of the nice things about the buffet is that, often, many unusual items are also offered.

Taj Mahal's full menu is one of the most extensive of any Indian restaurant in the area. The restaurant is particularly well-known for the fresh naans, kebabs, and *dosas* prepared there. Overall, in fact, dining at Taj Mahal retains a quality of true "home-cooked" Indian food, and the environment is gracious.

Irish

**Blarney Stone Restaurant
and Catering Service $$$
30 Grant Avenue, Etna
(412) 781-1666**
When proprietor Tom O'Donoghue came to Pittsburgh from County Kerry in 1974, he brought a piece of the "oulde sod" with him. It's preserved in a glass-topped square on Blarney Stone's ceramic floor. When you enter Blarney Stone, you have the opportunity to set foot on Irish soil.

Be that as it may, the good folks at Blarney Stone asked us to advise you that they serve American as well as Irish dishes. Consider yourself advised. You'll find such Ireland-inspired selections as County Cork Salad, Channon Chef Salad, and Irish smoked salmon, as well as American entrees that include Maryland crab cakes, prime rib, duck breast, and lamb chops. The restaurant serves dinner Tuesday through Sunday, lunch Tuesday through Friday, and a Sunday brunch. It's closed on Mondays. Blarney Stone offers a full-service bar, a wine list, and banquet facilities for up to 700 people—it's a popular spot for corporate functions. Reservations are accepted. Smoking and nonsmoking sections are designated for lunch, but the dining room is nonsmoking for dinner.

It's in the area of entertainment that Blarney Stone shows its Irish. It celebrates St. Patrick's Day with a week of lunch and dinner shows as well as an Irish buffet. During November, it hosts Irish singing groups. And there's swing dancing on Friday.

Italian

**Bravo! Italian Kitchen $$
4976 McKnight Road, Ross
(412) 366-3556**
This is a family restaurant that understands families, passing out crayons, coloring books, and pizza dough to each youngster who visits. While your kids are occupied with those pursuits, you get a chance to enjoy the signature Pasta Bravo, rigatoni with wood-grilled chicken and button mushrooms in a roasted red pepper sauce. Chicken scaloppini romano also is popular here. Located in the North Hills, Bravo! serves lunch and dinner daily. It offers a full-service bar and a wine list. Reservations are not accepted, but you may call ahead for priority seating.

**Falsetti's Villa $$
Route 128, North Buffalo
(724) 763-2266**
This Armstrong County restaurant specializes in Italian food and seafood selections. Among the most popular items are the Italian platter, which includes spaghetti, lasagna, rigatoni, ravioli and a meatball, and scrod Villa. The restaurant offers a full-service bar and a wine list. Reservations are accepted Sunday through Thursday. Located near the county seat of Kittanning, Falsetti's Villa serves lunch and dinner daily. Credit cards are not accepted.

**Mama Rosa's Restaurant
& Lounge $-$$
263 Old Plank Road, Butler
(724) 287-7315**
Yes, Virginia, there is a Mama Rosa—Mama Rosa Fusca, who founded this restaurant with her family. Mama Rosa no longer is active in the business, but she still drops

in to watch as the staff prepares the handmade pasta that is the restaurant's signature. In addition to pasta, you can select from steak, seafood, chicken, and veal dishes. The restaurant offers daily lunch and dinner specials as well as a wine list. Mama Rosa's offers catering services as well banquet facilities for up to 50 people.

Michael's Lake Arthur Restaurant & Motel $-$$
970 New Castle Road, Butler
(724) 865-9838

Michael's sits on U.S. Route 422, about 7 miles from Moraine State Park. If you've enjoyed an active day at Moraine, you'll also enjoy repairing to Michael's to sample the rock shrimp linguini, chicken parmigiana, and barbecued ribs. Michael's serves lunch and dinner, offers a full-service bar and wine list, and can accommodate up to 65 people in its banquet facilities. Reservations are available. The number of rooms at the motel is limited.

Natili Restaurant & Lounge $$
104 West Wayne Street, Butler
(724) 287-5033

Natili Restaurant & Lounge is a familiar sight at the corner of Wayne and Main in downtown Butler; it's been operated continuously by the same family since 1939. It features what owner Vince Tavolario describes as traditional dishes from the Abuzzi region of Italy, including many selections based on Natili's homemade pasta. The restaurant, which is closed on Sunday, offers lunch and dinner specials as well as a full-service bar and wine list. Reservations are accepted. The restaurant's banquet facilities can accommodate up to 75 people.

Live bands, fronted by such noted Pittsburgh performers as trombonist Harold Betters, are featured each Friday and Saturday evening. Twice each month, a guest pianist sits in. It's none other than Vince Tavolario, who dazzles his dinner guests with an eclectic repertoire that fea-

tures jazz, rock, and standards. Tavolario and his family also operate the nearby Natili-North Restaurant & Carry Out.

Serventi's $-$$
438 South Chestnut Street, Butler
(724) 287-4474

Serventi's is an institution in downtown Butler—it's been serving its popular Italian-American fare there since 1973. You'll find a broad selection of steak, seafood, chicken, and veal dishes, as well as daily lunch and dinner specials. Serventi's offers a full-service bar, a wine list, and banquet facilities for up to 30 people. Reservations are accepted but not required.

Mexican

Mad Mex $-$$
7905 McKnight Road, Ross
(412) 366-5656

370 Atwood Street
(412) 681-5656

You'll find Mad Mex in both the North Hills and near the University of Pittsburgh campus in Oakland. We're not sure what Mex is mad about—it's certainly not the menu, which is varied and entertaining. You'll find a broad selection of dishes that the restaurants consider "California-Mexican." These include such interesting variations as Heavy Duty Judy's Curry Chicken Burrito, with marinated chicken, white rice, pineapple, and raisins topped with a curry sauce, and grilled chicken chick pea chili burrito, packing a lot of tastes into one burrito. The restaurants offer a generous selection of microbrews as well as "Big Ass Margaritas," which probably don't require further explanation, and happy-hour specials. Each location serves lunch and dinner daily, and the Atwood Street restaurant is open until 2:00 A.M. each day. Reservations are not accepted.

This is a fun place with good food, but take it from an Insider—don't expect a quiet rendezvous here. Mad Mex is for an evening when you feel like good background music and loud conversation.

EAST

American

Baldonieri's Mill Creek Restaurant $$
Springer Road, Ligonier
(724) 238-3636
You'll dine in style here in a restored 18th-century barn furnished in wormy chestnut and boasting a working fireplace and a 2½-story cathedral ceiling. The diverse menu is particularly strong on seafood selections, such as lobster ravioli and Po River catfish. Choucroute, a traditional Alsacian dish featuring braised pork loin, sausage, and sauerkraut, also is popular. Reservations are accepted. Baldonieri's offers a full-service bar, a wine list, and banquet facilities for up to 350 in the barn's loft. That's also the scene of entertainment—acoustic guitarists on Saturday nights. Baldonieri's serves dinner only Wednesday through Sunday. It's closed on Monday and Tuesday.

Baum Vivant $$$
5102 Baum Boulevard
(412) 682-2620
At this unobtrusive Shadyside restaurant, owners Toni and Beck Pais have created an unusual and compelling menu that blends elements of French, Northern Italian, and Portuguese cuisine—often in the same entrees. That approach is so innovative that Baum Vivant captured *Pittsburgh Magazine*'s Blue Ribbon Award as Pittsburgh's best restaurant for six consecutive years. Don't miss this place if you're making a tour of Pittsburgh's finest dining spots.

The menu changes up to eight times each year, but entrees typically include such items as tiger shrimp Mediterranean; wild boar medallions with braised white cabbage in a Riesling sauce; a medley of shrimp, lobster, scallops, clams, and mussels with Israeli couscous; and caribou

tenderloin with figs in a port wine sauce. Appetizers include ostrich as well as tenderloin of kangaroo with kiwi sauce, and you can choose from four types of caviar. Baum Vivant offers a full-service bar and a wine list with roughly 150 selections. Smoking is permitted at the bar only. The restaurant can accommodate banquets for up to 20 people. It serves dinner only Monday through Saturday, and is closed on Sunday. Reservations are highly suggested.

The Bistro $$$
216 West Loyalhanna Street, Ligonier
(724) 238-9545
You'll find the Bistro at the Ramada Inn Historic Ligonier. Specialties include crab cakes, pasta dishes, grilled steak, salads, and sandwiches. You also can dine more informally at Cappy's Deli, which features the same wine list and much of the same menu as the Bistro.

The Bistro serves breakfast, lunch, and dinner—including a buffet—each day but Sunday and Monday. There is no breakfast on Monday and brunch is offered on Sunday. The Bistro does not designate smoking or nonsmoking sections. The hotel offers banquet facilities for up to 80 people. The restaurant offers occasional special events, such as theater nights; these are irregularly scheduled, so you'll need to call for details. The Bistro is closed from 1:30 to 4:30 P.M. daily.

Buffalo Blues $-$$
216 South Highland Avenue
(412) 362-5837
This Shadyside restaurant specializes in wings, barbecued foods, and blues. The wings come topped with your choice of 12 different sauces, ranging from "Who Do Voodoo" to "Hotter 'an Hell." The barbecue menu includes ribs, chicken, and seafood, and you can pick from three different sauces. Fresh fish, jambalaya, and fajitas round out the menu. Buffalo Blues offers a full-service bar and a limited wine list. It offers both catering services and banquet facilities for up to 50 people.

Only restaurants with Sunday licenses can serve liquor on Sunday and on election day when the polls are open. If you're not sure if your favorite restaurant has this license, don't hesitate to ask.

On Friday and Saturday evenings, you'll enjoy the restaurant's signature live blues performances. There's often a cover charge for national acts but none for local groups. By the way, the restaurant's phone number is easy to remember—36 BLUES. The most expensive entrees are priced at the lower end of $$.

Cappy's $
5431 Walnut Street
(412) 621-1188
If you're trying to keep your diet free of fried foods but still love to eat out, try this Shadyside restaurant. Cappy's does not fry any of its foods, preparing them instead on the grill or in a high-heat convection oven. The restaurant offers a diverse selection of burgers, sandwiches, and salads. Cappy's features a full-service bar but does not designate smoking and nonsmoking sections. Reservations are not accepted. Cappy's serves lunch and dinner daily, breakfast on Saturday and Sunday. Late breakfasts are available on weekdays.

The Carnegie Cafe $
4400 Forbes Avenue
(412) 622-3225
For one of the most engaging and civilized dining experiences in town, try the Carnegie Cafe, a feature of The Carnegie in Oakland. The cafe serves lunch only, and you don't have to pay admission to the museum to dine here. The cafe specializes in sandwiches and salads, including roasted vegetable Napoleon salad and portabella mushroom panini. You'll find a bar as well as wine and beer lists. You'll enjoy the view of the museum's fountains, a series of geyser-like water jets. In fair weather, you can dine al fresco in the Fountain Court. (Be warned that the view

outclasses the food; however, dining here is still worth doing.)

When the Carnegie Theater is staging performances, the cafe often hosts themed dinners for theater patrons. It can entertain up to 160 patrons at those dinners, and it's also available for wine-tasting parties and sponsored or corporate conferences. Lunch reservations are recommended. The entire cafe, including the Fountain Court, is non-smoking. The Carnegie Cafe serves lunch Tuesday through Saturday, but it does open on Mondays when the museum is open. It's best to call to determine the Monday schedule.

Carson St. Deli $
17th and East Carson Streets
(412) 381-5335
This is a popular South Side spot for après performance eats. Not only does the deli offer a broad selection of sandwiches (including vegetarian selections), soups, salads, and desserts, but it also stays open until 2:00 A.M. on summer Fridays and Saturdays. Many musicians repair here after their South Side gigs—you can compare notes with them as you enjoy the sidewalk cafe tables. On occasion, the musicians perform impromptu concerts here, but you never can be sure when that might happen. It's all part of the ambience that helped Carson St. win the Best Deli in Pittsburgh award from *In Pittsburgh* from 1996 to 2002.

The deli does not designate smoking and nonsmoking sections, and it does not serve alcohol. Credit cards and reservations aren't accepted. Carson St. provides catering and delivery services. It's open daily but closes at 6:00 P.M. on Sunday.

Chelsea Grille $-$$
515–519 Allegheny Avenue, Oakmont
(412) 828-0570
Chelsea Grille is part of Oakmont's one-two culinary punch operated by brothers Danny and Tommy Monaco. It serves dinner daily, lunch Monday through Saturday. The menu covers a lot of ground, offering beef, seafood, and chicken entrees, fajitas,

barbecued ribs, pasta and Italian selections, and dinner salads. Chelsea Grille offers a full-service bar, a wine list, and facilities that accommodate up to 60 people for banquets. Reservations are accepted.

Dunning's Grill $
1100 South Braddock Avenue, Swissvale
(412) 243-3900

Here's a pleasant neighborhood restaurant that's popular with those who live and work in Pittsburgh's eastern suburbs. Burgers, pasta, and grilled chicken salad are among the hottest sellers. Don't let the salads fool you. They're served over a bed of mixed greens and with French fries; you'll want to bring a hearty appetite when you order one. Dunning's offers a full-service bar and banquet facilities, available only on Sundays, for up to 55 people. The restaurant does not accept reservations. Dunning's serves lunch and dinner Monday through Saturday; it's closed on Sunday except for private parties.

The Elbow Room $-$$
5744½ Ellsworth Avenue
(412) 441-5222

The Elbow Room has been a fixture in the city's Shadyside neighborhood for more than 40 years, offering a diverse lunch and dinner menu that's particularly strong on salads. Steak salads may be the most popular selections, but you'll also find portabella, grilled eggplant, grilled chicken, spinach, and many other dinner salads. You also may choose from an extensive sandwich selection and a more limited entree list.

The restaurant offers a Sunday brunch, a full-service bar, and a limited wine list. It accepts reservations and provide banquet facilities of up to 100 people. In fair weather, you'll enjoy dining on the patio, which is especially nice as it boasts a large tree in the center and is surrounded by vine covered garden walls. The Elbow Room is next door to Club Havana, which features Latin dance classes and other evening entertainment, so you can make a night of it at these side-by-side establishments. For more on Club Havana, see the Nightlife chapter.

Gullifty's $
1922 Murray Avenue
(412) 521-8222

Gullifty's won *Pittsburgh Magazine*'s award for the best desserts in town for 17 years in a row! It was back on top in 2002 after being ousted in 2001. When you're ready to indulge your sweet tooth, you can sample the restaurant's peanut butter truffle pie, its macadamia truffel torte, or its chocolate intemperance. The pièce de résistance is the "Killer Cookie," featuring a chocolate chip and walnut cookie topped with vanilla ice cream, bananas, chocolate syrup, and whipped cream. It's so loaded with taste that Gullifty's requires 15 minutes to prepare it.

The restaurant's menu features soups, dinner salads, sandwiches, burgers, Mexican fare, pasta, and a limited entree list. Gullifty's offers a significant number of meatless dishes; these are so noted on the menu. Among the most popular sandwiches is Gullifty's Meshugna, grilled corned beef served open-face with cole slaw and Russian dressing on two potato pancakes. Gullifty's offers a full-service bar, a limited wine and beer list, and banquet facilities for up to 40 people. It does not accept reservations. It serves lunch and dinner daily as well as Saturday and Sunday brunches. You'll find Gullifty's in the center of the Squirrel Hill business district.

Hemingway's Cafe $
3911 Forbes Avenue
(412) 621-4100

The spirit of Papa Hemingway comes alive each Tuesday evening when this restaurant on the University of Pittsburgh campus hosts poetry readings. Some readers are scheduled, while other Tuesdays feature open sessions. If the hunger for literature makes you literally hungry, you can select from a varied menu including sandwiches; salads; pasta dishes; and some poultry, seafood, and beef dishes. Hemingway's offers a full-service bar, wine and beer lists, and banquet facilities for up to 60 people. The cafe serves lunch and dinner daily, and it accepts reservations.

Hoffstot's Cafe Monaco Restaurant & Lounge $$$
533 Allegheny Avenue, Oakmont
(412) 828-8555

Hoffstot's is a pleasant restaurant near the Allegheny River and the Hulton Bridge. Along with the neighboring Chelsea Grille—the restaurants are operated by brothers Danny and Tom Monaco—it gives Oakmont an attractive dining tandem. Hoffstot's offers a diverse menu with beef, seafood, veal, an Italian selections, as well as dinner salads. Steaks are popular, as is the shrimp Monaco—shrimp and jumbo lump crabmeat baked in butter, garlic, lemon, white wine, and oregano—and sea scallops Palermo. You'll find a lounge and a wine list that includes 11 "reserve" or premier wines. Hoffstot's offers weekday banquet facilities for up to 50 people. It serves lunch and dinner daily; make it a late lunch on Sundays, when the restaurant opens at 1:00 P.M. reservations are accepted.

Jaden's $
4727 William Penn Highway, Monroeville
(412) 373-8575

Jaden's is a family restaurant that's open daily for breakfast, lunch, and dinner, with daily specials offered for each meal. If you're hankering for a hearty breakfast, try Jaden's Ultimate, featuring two hot cakes topped with your choice of strawberries, blueberries, or cherries; two eggs; potatoes; and a side of bacon, sausage, or ham. Dinner entrees include beef, chicken, pastas and seafood selections. Save room of a slice of homemade pie or the waffle sundae. As a family restaurant, Jaden's doesn't serve alcohol.

John Harvard's Brew House $-$$
3466 William Penn Highway, Wilkins
(412) 824-9440

John Harvard's serves lunch and dinner daily. Among the most popular entrees are chicken pot pie, meatloaf, and fish and chips, and you'll also find beef, seafood, and pasta entrees as well as daily specials. You'll find a full-service bar and a wine list; as befitting a brew house, John Harvard's also offers an extensive selection of ales and lagers. Other features include a humidor and cigar list and a retail area for merchandise imprinted with John Harvard's logo. The restaurant offers banquet facilities for up to 35 people. Reservations are recommended for weekends for eight people or more, accepted at all times. John Harvard's is located on U.S. Business Route 22.

Kazansky's Restaurant and Delicatessen $
2201 Murray Avenue
(412) 521-4555

Kazansky's has been pleasing Squirrel Hill patrons for decades. It features Jewish-style specialties, including homemade soups, dinner salads, a limited entree list, and a broad selection of sandwiches. These include the Yoy (prounoced oi-ee), the Double Yoy, and the Triple Yoy, all built around corned beef and based on a characteristic exclamation of Pittsburgh Steelers commentator Myron Cope, as in "Another penalty? Yoy." You'll also find the Marv Albert, comprised of beef tongue and Swiss cheese on pumpernickel. "Sink your teeth into this one," the menu advises. Hey, we don't endorse 'em, we just report 'em.

Kazansky's offers a retail section and a take-out counter, which is one of the region's busiest places on Christmas Eve, when patrons line up to purchase meat and dairy trays for their guests. Kazansky's serves beer but no other alcohol, and it does not accept reservations. You won't find designated smoking and non-smoking sections. Kazansky's serves breakfast, lunch, and dinner daily.

The Lamplighter Café $$
330 U.S. Route 22, Delmont
(724) 468-4545

For more than 40 years, the Lamplighter has been a hub for dining and entertainment in Westmoreland County. In fact, the restaurant offers so many activities and specials—such as a daily early bird menu, a full-course weekly special, and dance bands each weekend—that you're advised to pick up your monthly activities calendar in the lobby. Prime rib and fresh seafood are the menu headliners, and you'll also enjoy the Monday-to-Friday lunch buffet and the Sunday breakfast and dinner buffets. The Lamplighter offers a lounge, a wine list, and banquet facilities for up to 400 people. Reservations are suggested. The Lamplighter serves breakfast, lunch, and dinner daily.

Lesley's Tea Room $$$
10 Mountain View Road, Donegal
(724) 593-6349, (800) 392-7773
www.shol.com/mtviewbb

Lesley's offers intimate dining in a restored chestnut barn nestled in the foothills of the Laurel Highlands at Mountain View Country Inn. Dining is leisurely and memorable here, as you'll enjoy such entrees as scallop pasta with roasted peppers and Beef Wellington. The menu changes weekly, but you can get a preview—as well as some of Lesley's most popular recipes and wine list—by visiting the restaurant's Web site. The site also will introduce you to the companion Lesley's Mountain View Country Inn. For more on that, see the Bed-and-Breakfast Inns chapter.

Lesley's offers a full-service bar and an extensive wine list. Smoking is permitted at the bar only. The restaurant serves dinner Monday, Tuesday, and Thursday through Saturday, and reservations are suggested. You'll find the restaurant about 1 mile east of the Donegal exit of the Pennsylvania Turnpike.

Ligonier Country Inn $-$$
U.S. Route 30 East, Laughlintown
(724) 238-3651

Located in eastern Westmoreland County, Ligonier Country Inn serves dinner Thursday through Sunday, as well as a Sunday breakfast and a Sunday brunch buffet. It's closed Monday through Wednesday. The menu features beef, chicken, pasta, and seafood selections, as well as specials and a vegetarian feature of the day. You'll find a full-service bar, a wine list, and banquet facilities for up to 300 people. Reservations are recommended.

You can transform your trip here into a relaxing vacation by staying at the adjacent bed-and-breakfast inn, which shares the name Ligonier Country Inn. For more on that, see the Bed-and-Breakfast Inns chapter. Both the restaurant and the bed-and-breakfast are owned and operated by P.J. and Maggie Nied, so you can be assured of uniform service whether you're lodging or dining. There's an outdoor pool here, and the Nieds plan a busy summer schedule of pool parties featuring live music. Call them for details.

Ligonier Tavern $-$$
137 West Main Street, Ligonier
(724) 238-4831

This is a fun spot, where everyone seems to have a good time, whether they're dining indoors or alfresco on the front porch or balcony. Your enjoyment will increase when you discover that the tavern makes all its sauces and desserts from scratch. Popular menu items are the crab cakes and fresh mozzarella and tomato chicken. Make sure you save room for the signature Loyalhanna cheesecake—two layers of New York and chocolate cheesecake over an Oreo cookie crust and topped by fudge icing. Try it and you'll know why everybody's smiling.

The tavern offers a full-service bar and a wine list, as well as catering services and banquet facilities for up to 275 people. It recommends reservations on Friday, Saturday, and Sunday. Ligonier Tavern is open daily for lunch and dinner.

New York New York $-$$
5801 Ellsworth Avenue
(412) 661-5600

New York New York is not especially near Pittsburgh's Cultural District, but the Broadway theater posters on the walls of this Shadyside restaurant will make you feel as if you're treading the boards. The menu is eclectic, featuring beef, pork, chicken, seafood, and pasta entrees. The restaurant offers a full-service bar, a wine list, and live piano entertainment Wednesday through Saturday evenings. Reservations are accepted, recommended for parties of eight or more. One of the most memorable features of New York New York is its upstairs patio, a colorful enclosed porch decked with flowers. The patio seats 100 diners. Ask for it when the weather is right. New York New York is open daily for dinner only, and it also features Sunday brunch.

Through its "Dining With Heart" program, University of Pittsburgh Medical Center designates selections at local restaurants that meet program standards in cholesterol, fat, and sodium content. Participating restaurants usually mark those entrees with a small red heart. You can get your free list of participating restaurants from UPMC at (412) 647-UPMC or (800) 533-UPMC.

Original Hot Dog Shops $
3901 Forbes Avenue
(412) 621-7388

When you consider the University of Pittsburgh, you may think of such wonders as the towering Cathedral of Learning or the Nationality Classrooms that celebrate the region's ethnic heritage. Ask alumni what they recall about their undergraduate days, however, and the landmark they're most likely to name is the "O," the affectionate nickletter for Original Hot Dog Shop. Since 1960, the O has been serving up hot dogs, burgers, wings, subs, and pizza. French fries are particularly popular here—the O goes through 40,000 pounds of them every 10 days. (*Note:* A small order of fries could fill a dinner plate, so don't dare order two unless you're dining with four or five people! Also note that

you won't be eating heart healthy here.) You'll find a full-service bar and a broad selection of beers. The O serves lunch and dinner daily, staying open until 3:30 A.M. during the week and 5:00 A.M. on weekends. It does not accept credit cards or reservations, of course. If you're looking for a leisurely candlelight repast with muted string music in the background, this is not the place for you. But if you want to experience the sights and cacophony of an urban college hangout in motion, the O is a go.

Pamela's $
5527 Walnut Street
(412) 683-1003

3703 Forbes Avenue
(412) 683-4066

5813 Forbes Avenue
(412) 422-9457

If you like your hotcakes stacked high and stuffed full, Pamela's is the place for you. Each of Pamela's three locations—Shadyside, Oakland, Squirrel Hill—specializes in breakfasts that are available in the afternoon as well. Pamela's offers banana walnut, strawberry, chocolate chip and apple walnut hotcakes, a variety so tasty and appealing that Pamela's has won the silver medal for Best Breakfast in *Pittsburgh Magazine* Reader's Choice Awards for the last nine years running. Breakfast fare also includes waffles, omelets, and French toast. For lunch, Pamela's offers sandwiches and salads. Pamela's does not serve alcohol and does not accept reservations or credit cards. The restaurants are open daily for breakfast and lunch.

Peppermill Inn $$$
4733 William Penn Highway, Monroeville
(412) 372-9878

You won't find many restaurants with a separate lobster menu, but that's an attraction of Peppermill Inn. You can enjoy lobster tails, lobster Newberg, or lobster in a surf and turf combination. The eclectic menu also offers homemade pasta selections as well as beef, veal, chicken, and additional seafood entrees. It would be hard not to find something you like at the Peppermill. The restaurant offers a full-service bar, a wine list, catering services, and banquet facilities for up to 70 people. Reservations are recommended for weekends and accepted at all times. Peppermill Inn does not designate smoking and non-smoking sections. It serves lunch and dinner daily.

Pittsburgh Deli Co. $
728 Copeland Street
(412) 682-DELI
www.pghdeli.com

This bright, airy Shadyside deli serves lunch and dinner daily; you also can enjoy a late-night bite, as the deli is open until 2:00 A.M. daily. You'll find gourmet sandwiches, Jewish-style foods, and homemade baked goods, and you can enjoy it all in the downstairs dining area or the bar area upstairs. Speaking of the bar, Pittsburgh Deli Co. offers a full array of drinks and roughly 100 varieties of beer. It provides catering services and can accommodate banquets of up to 100 people on-site. Smoking is permitted in the second-floor bar area only. The deli features live jazz, rock, and acoustical bands on some Friday evenings. The entertainment schedule is irregular, so it's best to call for details.

The R&R Station Family
Restaurant and Inn $
19 West Main Street, Mt. Pleasant
(724) 547-7545

While the Pennsylvania Railroad that once served the Mt. Pleasant railroad station is gone, the still-active Highlander steam train shuttles past on its way to Scottdale. All that railroad history is the inspiration for the R&R Station Family Restaurant and Inn, which includes both a restaurant and a 17-room hotel. For more about the hotel, see the Accommodations chapter.

The restaurant, furnished with rails, flashing lights, and other railway memorabilia, serves breakfast, lunch, and dinner daily; it's open 7:00 A.M. to 9:00 P.M. Sunday through Thursday and 7:00 A.M. to

midnight on Friday and Saturday. You'll find daily specials for each meal and over 100 items on the regular menu including plenty of homemade favorites like meatloaf and spaghetti. Particularly popular are such homemade desserts as Death By Chocolate—chocolate cake topped by chocolate ice cream, chocolate syrup, hot fudge, and chocolate whipped cream. That can put a little kaboom in your caboose. Speaking of which, libations are served in the Caboose Lounge. R&R Station offers banquet facilities for up to 50 people. Note that it is located on the east end of town, near Cook's Lumber.

Ritter's Diner $
5221 Baum Boulevard
(412) 682-4852

Most of the region's night owls know Ritter's—not only has it been a fixture since 1951, but it's also one of the few round-the-clock restaurants in the area, closing only on major holidays. The menu is diverse, offering entrees, salads, sandwiches, and daily lunch and dinner specials. Make sure you save room for the rice pudding, a specialty of the house. Ritter's does not serve liquor or accept reservations. Credit cards are not accepted either. It offers banquet facilities for up to 75 people. Don't expect to eat heart healthy here; just enjoy yourself at this quintessential diner.

The Road Toad $-$$
US 30 East, Ligonier
(724) 539-7623

The Road Toad is one of those places that fairly hops with energy—diners indoors, diners outdoors, the Loyalhanna Creek rushing by just below the restaurant. The menu features beef, chicken, seafood, and pasta selections as well as a lengthy list of sandwiches and pitas. Outdoors at the Back Bay Grill, they'll grill just about anything you order. The Road Toad offers a full-service bar and accepts reservations for parties of eight or more. It can accommodate 50 people for indoor banquets, 150 for outdoor affairs. The restaurant offers occasional live music; it's best to call for details. The Road Toad offers lunch and dinner Tuesday through Sunday.

Ruthie's Diner $
US 30 East, Ligonier
(724) 238-9930

If you're a diner fan, make sure you drop by Ruthie's for the homemade soups, pies, and apple dumplings. The fare is filling and economically priced. Ruthie's serves breakfast, lunch, and dinner daily, and it's open until midnight on Friday and Saturday. Ruthie's does not serve alcohol, and it does not accept credit cards. It accepts reservations Monday through Friday only.

Tessaro's $$
4601 Liberty Avenue
(412) 682-6809

Hardwood-grilled steaks, the best hamburgers in town, and fish top the menu at this bustling spot in the Bloomfield neighborhood. The atmosphere is casual, but don't be surprised if you wait a long time for a table and then get seated near a local celebrity—everyone goes to Tessaro's, unless they're vegetarian, that is. Open Monday through Saturday for lunch and dinner until late. Most major credit cards are accepted.

Union Grill $-$$$
413 South Craig Street
(412) 681-8620

South Craig Street is a happening venue in Oakland, situated between the campuses of the University of Pittsburgh and Carnegie Mellon University and drawing considerable traffic from each. Union Grill is one of the chief contributors to the bustle of activity, offering indoor and outdoor dining and a menu that's sure to please almost everyone. It offers such specialties as Bourbon Street Pasta, fresh vegetables and fettuccine tossed in a spicy Cajun sauce and flavored with a shot of Jim Beam bourbon, and calypso chicken, a chicken breast rubbed with Calypso spices and topped with peppers, mushrooms, onions, tomatoes, and mangoes.

The selections don't stop there. Union Grill offers seafood and salsa specials each evening, a "Build a Burger" feature, dinner salads, sandwiches, and vegetarian selections. For libations, you'll find a full-service bar and a wine list offering what the house calls "rock bottom prices." Union Grill serves lunch and dinner daily, and it also offers a late night menu each day. Reservations are accepted for parties of seven or more.

Caribbean

Donsvilles' Jamaica, Jamaica $
6008 Broad Street
(412) 361-1631

Donsvilles' specializes in such Jamaican dishes as curry shrimp; curry goat; jerk chicken; and escovitch, a red- or yellow-tailed snapper fried and sautéed with spicy peppers, vinegar, tomatoes, and onions. The menu is rich in Jamaican foods—make sure that's what you want, since you won't find any alternative selections. Donsvilles' accepts reservations. It does not serve alcohol or designate smoking and nonsmoking sections. The restaurant serves lunch and dinner daily. You'll find Donsvilles' in Pittsburgh's East Liberty neighborhood near North Highland Avenue, one of the neighborhood's principal thoroughfares.

Chinese

China Palace $$
5440 Walnut Street
(412) 687-7423

4059 William Penn Highway, Monroeville
(412) 373-7423

409 Broad Street, Sewickley
(412) 749-7423

China Palace offers some of the best Chinese food in the area, with the nicest ambience. China Palace offers a compelling variety of entrees, including salmon sizzler; orange-flavored beef; and Three's Company, which combines lemon chicken, General Tso's chicken, and chicken with vegetables. You'll find a broad variety of seafood, beef, chicken, and pork selections, with hot and spicy items noted on the menu. China Palace offers a bar and a wine list, but it does not accept reservations. It serves dinner daily, lunch Monday through Saturday. Note that the phone number of each restaurant sports the same last four digits, which spell the word RICE.

Chopsticks $$
2018 Murray Avenue
(412) 421-1920

Since 1960, Chopsticks has been pleasing Squirrel Hill diners with its broad menu representative of all Chinese regions. You'll find such entrees as Szechuan spicy eggplant; ginger chicken with spicy sauce; and happy family, a medley of shrimp, beef, chicken, and roast pork with Chinese vegetables and topped by a brown sauce. Hot and spicy items are so noted on the menu. Chopsticks serves lunch and dinner daily and offers a limited wine list. It accepts reservations, but it does not permit smoking.

Evergreen Chinese Restaurant $
3500 William Penn Highway, Wilkins
(412) 825-8088

Evergreen offers a varied menu that features beef, chicken, pork, and seafood selections, but the most popular item here is the daily lunch and dinner buffet. The buffet features nearly 40 items, including about one dozen entrees. Evergreen offers a special buffet price for children, and senior citizens receive a discount on any order. The restaurant accepts reservations, and it offers banquet facilities for up to 70 people. It does not serve alcohol. Evergreen is located about 2 miles from exit 6 of the Pennsylvania Turnpike on U.S. Business Route 22, a commercial corridor that spans Wilkins Township and Monroeville.

The House of Chiang $-$$
120 McKee Place
(412) 681-5169

The House of Chiang, located near the western edge of the University of Pittsburgh campus, serves lunch and dinner daily. It specializes in Cantonese and Szechuan fare, including such favorites as moo goo gai pan over rice and cashew chicken. The diverse menu offers an uncommon number of lunch specials, highlighted by 20 combination plates. Although you won't find a bar here, the waitstaff will serve alcohol you've brought yourself. Reservations are not accepted.

Jade Garden $-$$
4450 William Penn Highway, Murrysville
(724) 733-2281

If you like to share plates with your dining companions, try Jade Garden's "Happy Family Dinners." They're specially priced, and you can select from 13 entrees. The menu also offers beef, lamb, pork, chicken, vegetarian, and seafood selections. General Tso's chicken is a popular pick, as is seafood in bird's nest, which features sautéed shrimp, scallops, and lobster with Chinese vegetables over a crispy base. The restaurant offers a full-service bar and a wine list, and it can accommodate banquets of up to 40 people. Reservations for parties of five or more are accepted. You'll find Jade Garden on US 22 in Westmoreland County, just east of the Allegheny County line.

Jimmy Tsang's Chinese Restaurant and Korean Grill $$-$$$
5700 Centre Avenue
(412) 661-4226

Jimmy Tsang's offers selections representing the four major Chinese styles—Mandarin, Hunan and Szechuan, Shanghai, and Cantonese. Popular features of the lunch and dinner menu include shrimp with lobster sauce; Manchurian noodles; and a whole fish, which might be red snapper or sea bass. If you order that whole fish, the folks in the kitchen will need about 40

If you spot unsanitary conditions at an Allegheny County restaurant, call the county health department, (412) 687–ACHD. They pledge to investigate.

---

minutes to prepare it. The restaurant in Pittsburgh's Shadyside neighborhood also offers an extensive roster of vegetarian entrees, combination dinners for up to six people, daily lunch specials, and a limited early bird menu with specially priced entrees.

Jimmy Tsang's features a full-service bar and an extensive wine list, as well as banquet facilities for up to 300 people. Reservations are accepted for parties of four or more. Jimmy Tsang's is open daily but serves only dinner on Sunday. Prices for the most expensive entrees are at the lower end of $$$.

P. F. Chang's China Bistro $$
148 West Bridge Street, Waterfront
(412) 464–0640

Once impossible to get into without a long wait, Chang's is no longer the new kid at the waterfront. Yet depending on when the last movie ended at nearby Lowe's Cineplex, there can still be a line; whiling away the time at the small bar is a pleasant enough pastime. The atmosphere is geared toward adults with mood lighting and upbeat background music. The cuisine is from Canton, Shanghai, Hunan, and Mongolia, and there's wine by the glass, as well as a decent by-the-bottle list. Start with Chang's spicy chicken or vegetarian wraps, where you'll scoop ground chicken or wok-seared tofu into lettuce leaves that you fold and then drizzle with a selection of sauces—a tasty appetizer. Even the wonton soup tastes fresh and different here. Mild to spicy entrees—typical Chinese fare but again with a flair—are served with steamed rice. The prices are reasonable, and all major credit cards are accepted. Chang's is open every day, 11:00 A.M. to 10:30 P.M., later on

weekends, and reservations are not accepted.

Sichuan House $$
1900 Murray Avenue
(412) 422–2700

1717 Cochran Road, Mt. Lebanon
(412) 563–5252

If you like broad menu variety, you'll love Sichuan House, which features 175 distinct entrees at both of its locations—in the city's Squirrel Hill neighborhood, in the South Hills, only a few miles from Downtown. Beef, seafood, chicken, pork—all are well represented at Sichuan House, which serves both lunch and dinner. Among diners' favorites here are shrimp with snow peas; stuffed bean curd; pan-fried Cantonese noodles with seafood; and leeks with smoked ham, Taiwanese style.

The menu clearly highlights "hot and spicy" items in red, so you'll always know what's in store for you. Sichuan House offers a small selection of "lean" entrees and free delivery, within a limited service area for take-out selections. The restaurants accept reservations for parties of five or more.

When you want to enjoy the food at Sichuan House at a slightly reduced rate, try their "family dinner." It features a flat rate for each member of your party, no matter what entree each selects. It's a great way to work your way through that menu.

Soba Lounge $$$
5847 Ellsworth Avenue
(412) 362–5656

Rising like a phoenix from the ashes of an electrical fire that closed the building for more than a year, Soba has been reborn with revamped, award-winning Pan-Asian cuisine and a cozier ambience, complete with two-story waterfall and wood-burning fireplaces. Try the seared rare tuna with Korean barbecue sauce or one of the many vegetarian dishes. The wine list is now more extensive. Reservations are suggested on weekends.

The new rooftop patio offers a breeze in summer and a warm meeting spot when the heaters are on. The side bar downstairs with banquet seating makes a much-needed addition to this very hip restaurant.

Continental

Café Zhino $$-$$$
238 Spahr Street
(412) 363-1500

This garage-turned-bistro features tasty nouveau continental cuisine—French, American, and Portugese influenced—that changes seasonally. Just off Ellsworth Avenue, this sister restaurant to Baum Vivant (sharing the same owners) has its own young, top-gun chefs turning out terrific food at a surprisingly reasonable price. Many appetizers prove meals in themselves. Daily specials are definitely special.

The funky decor plus outdoor dining when weather permits made this an instant hit with fashionable East-Enders as soon as it opened. Disappointingly, on the other hand, there's little for vegetarians here. Open Tuesday through Saturday for lunch and dinner. Cash only. You're welcome to bring your own wine.

Casbah $$$
229 South Highland Avenue
(412) 661-5656

Feast on French, Italian, and Spanish offerings with influences from the Middle East and North Africa. Dine downstairs in a more formal setting, upstairs in the noisy bar and adjacent area packed with Gen Xers, or relax outside on the front patio. Dress ranges from casual to dressy.

The award-winning food is a main draw, and as a wine bar, Casbah has no equal. Several cheese plates make a good accompaniment to the two-ounce selections in the wine flights—more than 40 wines by the glass or the large selection of wines by the bottle and half bottle. Check for new wine listings on the blackboards behind the bar.

Open every day for lunch and dinner, Casbah serves a popular brunch on Sunday. It accepts reservations.

Lucca $$-$$$
317 South Craig Street
(412) 682-3310

Lucca styles its food as European, inspired by Italian flair. Read the menu and you'll get an idea of the international flavor. You'll find Crisfield County crab cakes, calamari gaetta, lump crabmeat spring roll, and shrimp taquito. The menu changes daily for lunch and dinner and offers seasonal complements; for instance, it features lamb in the spring, pasta in the summer. Staples of the menu are the mixed grille, which combines samplings of filet mignon, lamp chop, leg of duck, and Italian sausage, and the seafood mixed grille.

You'll find a full-service bar, and a sommelier will guide you through the ample wine list. Reservations are recommended. Lucca offers banquet facilities for up to 30 people. The restaurant serves lunch and dinner Monday through Saturday. Eat out on the patio when the weather is nice—if you can grab a table.

Filipino

La Filipiana Teody's Restaurant $-$$
5321 Butler Street
(412) 781-8724

This restaurant is located in the city's Lawrenceville neighborhood along the Allegheny River, not known for restaurants, but inside you'll find the only Filipino restaurant in the region. A feature on the menu is the Taste of La Filipiana, a seven-course dinner for two that features entrees representing three geographic regions of the Philippines. Groups of 10 or more can make arrangements to dine any day of the week. The restaurant is open all week from 5:00 to 10:00 P.M. for dinner, and 11:30 A.M. to 2:30 P.M. for lunch. Bring your own wine or beer, but La Filipiana bans liquor.

Greek

The Harris Grill Cafe $-$$
5747 Ellsworth Avenue
(412) 363-0833

Delightful front and back patios with tables sheltered by umbrellas are the signature of this Shadyside restaurant. You'll enjoy such Greek entrees as chicken or lamb souvlaki and such Greek appetizers as spanakopita and grape leaves. The menu also offers a limited number of beef, chicken, and seafood entrees, as well as sandwiches, salads, and pizza. The cafe serves lunch and dinner daily, and it offers a full-service bar and a wine list. It does not accept reservations in the summer, when the patios are in particular demand, but you can reserve tables in the other seasons. The cafe does not designate smoking and nonsmoking sections.

Indian

India Garden $-$$
328 Atwood Street
(412) 682-3000

3815 William Penn Highway, Monroeville
(412) 372-0400
www.indiagarden.net

India Garden's dining room is large and inviting, and the daily lunch buffet features more than 25 items. India Garden prepares its food in a clay oven, giving it a distinctive taste. The extensive menu offers popular tandoori entrees as well as a generous selection of vegetarian entrees.

India Garden does not serve alcohol, but patrons may bring their own. Reservations are required. The restaurants, which serve lunch and dinner daily, offer banquet facilities for up to 230 people. You'll find the Pittsburgh restaurant on the University of Pittsburgh's Oakland campus, the Monroeville location on U.S. Business Route 22 near the Pennsylvania Turnpike.

Prince of India Restaurant
and Tavern $-$$
3614 Fifth Avenue
(412) 687-0888

Located near the University of Pittsburgh campus and the Oakland medical complex, Prince of India serves lunch and dinner daily. Its daily lunch buffet is popular, as is its mix grill tandoori, a medley of seekh kabob, boti kabob, chicken tikka, and tandoori chicken and shrimp, served with chutney. The menu includes beef, lamb, seafood, vegetarian, and biryani entrees, and you'll enjoy the selection of 10 breads baked in Prince of India's clay oven. The restaurant offers a bar and a wine list. Smoking is permitted at the bar only. Prince of India does not accept reservations.

Sree's Foods $
2107 Murray Avenue
(412) 422-0663

606 Main Street, Sharpsburg
(412) 781-4765

Where else but Sree's can you find an entire Indian meal to go for under $5.00? Mr. and Mrs. Sree started their business with a take-out cart at Carnegie Mellon. Now, they offer takeout from more prestigious digs as well—restaurants in Squirrel Hill and Sharpsburg. Prices are a couple of dollars higher at the restaurant in Sharpsburg, but you can eat in there on Friday and Saturday evenings when the restaurant is open for dinner. You can't eat in at the Squirrel Hill location, but when you get home you'll enjoy this delicious, medium to very spicy food. Vegetarian entrees are always offered.

Star of India $-$$
412 South Craig Street
(412) 681-5700

Dinner fare includes a variety of chicken, lamb, beef, and shrimp selections as well as biryani, a rice and raisin base topped by shrimp, chicken, lamb, or beef. You'll find a number of vegetarian entrees, and the Monday-through-Thursday lunch buffet includes vegetarian choices. Star of India does not serve alcohol, but you can bring in your own. It accepts reservations. The restaurant does not offer designated smoking or nonsmoking sections. If you become a regular patron here, the personable Star of India waiters will greet you as a friend.

International

Road to Karakesh $$
320 Atwood Street
(412) 687-0533

We really didn't anticipate an "International" category; technically, there is no international cuisine. But how else do you categorize Road to Karakesh, an under-appreciated jewel of a restaurant that features foods from a wide variety of Asian and African nations and regions? You'll find such unusual entrees as doro wat, Ethiopian chicken curry in spiced herb butter; Moroccan beef tagine, beef stew with onion, mushrooms, tomato, and cauliflower; Parsi shrimp curry; and Malaysian devil's pork curry. Other selections include Yemeni lentil stew, and aush, an Afghani noodle soup served with split peas, kidney beans, and a spiced mint yogurt cream, all topped with lamb and tomato sauce.

Located near the University of Pittsburgh's Oakland campus, Road to Karakesh serves lunch and dinner Monday through Saturday, closing on Sunday. It does not serve liquor or accept reservations. The dining room is nonsmoking. Road to Karakesh likes to call itself "a spice odyssey." It's a trip you'll want to take.

Italian

Carbone's $-$$
U.S. Route 119, Crabtree
(724) 834-3430

Carbone's accepts reservations for parties of six or more, but you probably don't

have to worry about getting seated here. With a seating capacity of 650, Carbone's can pretty much guarantee a table whenever you arrive. It's operated by Natale "Buzzy" Carbone and his sister Natalie Carbone—Carbone's has been in their family since its opening in 1938. An interesting bit of family lore: Natale and Natalie were named to honor their grandfather, who was born on Christmas—"Natal" in Italian.

It will seem like Natal when you dine here. A house specialty is braciole, steak stuffed and rolled in tomato sauce. Save room for Carbone's homemade desserts such as angel pie, made with strawberries, coconut, and whipped cream cavorting on a vanilla wafer crust. Carbone's offers a bar, a wine list, and banquet facilities for up to 300 people. It serves dinner only Monday through Saturday, closing on Sunday. Carbone's is about 6 miles north of Greensburg in Westmoreland County on US 119.

Del's Bar & Ristorante DelPizzo $-$$
4428 Liberty Avenue
(412) 683-1448

Del's, as this establishment is popularly known, has been a Bloomfield fixture since the DelPizzo family opened it in 1949. It offers lunch and dinner daily, providing a broad selection of steaks and chops, pasta, chicken, veal, and seafood dishes. You can easily make a meal of Del's Gourmet pizza. The restaurant offers daily luncheon specials, with specially priced drinks if you eat at the bar. On Wednesday, there is a lunch buffet. Del's offers irregularly scheduled entertainment in the form of karaoke—it's best to call for details. The restaurant offers a wine list, and it accepts reservations. Banquet facilities for up to 100 people are available.

DeNunzio's Italian Restaurant $$
700 Lowry Avenue, Jeannette
(724) 527-5552

You'll enjoy the creative menu at DeNunzio's. It features veal, chicken, beef, and seafood entries, as well as two pages of pasta entrees. But the show stoppers may be the tenderloins of beef garnished with shrimp and prepared in a Cajun style, and the veal Florentine, which is layered with shrimp and lump crabmeat and prepared in a white wine sauce. DeNunzio's offers a bar, an extensive wine list, and banquet facilities for up to 100 people. The restaurant can accommodate two banquets simultaneously. Reservations are recommended. DeNunzio's serves lunch and dinner daily. You'll find it in Westmoreland County about 1 mile north of US 30.

DeNunzio's Italian Restaurant $$–$$$
2644 Mosside Boulevard, Monroeville
(412) 374-7120
This is a sister restaurant of the Jeannette DeNunzio's but offers a somewhat less extensive menu. It also aims more for families, offering more booths than its Jeannette counterpart and covering the tables with paper on which kids are invited to color. In fact, the restaurant holds occasional coloring contests for its young patrons. Another difference: the Monroeville restaurant cooks in a wood-fired oven, providing a distinctive taste for its food. The restaurant offers a full-service bar and an extensive wine list. It serves lunch and dinner daily. Reservations are accepted for parties of four or more; others may call ahead for priority seating. The Monroeville DeNunzio's is about 1 mile west of the Pennsylvania Turnpike.

D'Imperio's Restaurant $$–$$$
3412 William Penn Highway, Wilkins
(412) 823-4800
D'Imperio's is a classy restaurant with an appetite for fun as well. Shrimp Sorrento, enhanced with a taste of lemon and vodka, is a popular selection, and you'll find a wide variety of veal, lamb, chicken, seafood, and pasta entrees. Executive chef Joseph Schilling offers at least three soups—including his signature seafood bisque—for every meal, and he also offers what D'Imperio's calls its "Culinary Geek" showcase of daily entree specials. The restaurant accepts reservations, and it offers a full-service bar and banquet facilities for up to 250 people. It serves dinner

Monday through Saturday, lunch Tuesday through Friday. D'Imperio's is closed on Sunday.

A restaurant that calls its specials a "Culinary Geek" showcase clearly knows how to entertain, and you'll find a number of entertaining touches here. As you walk in, you'll enjoy viewing the ample wine collection in cabinets decorating the lobby areas. You can participate in the restaurant's wine-tasting events, held on most Friday evenings, and you can trip the light fantastic at a summer series of "Al Fresco Friday Feasts," which feature dinner and drinks as well as dancing. Al and the geeks move indoors if it rains on their feast. Call D'Imperio's for a schedule of special events.

DiSalvo's Station Restaurant and Banquet Facilities $$–$$$
325 McKinley Avenue, Latrobe
(724) 539-0500
Some enterprising entrepreneurs locate their businesses in renovated train stations. The DiSalvo family has gone them one better, creating a dining complex in an active train station. You'll find this Westmoreland County restaurant, as well as a sister restaurant called Prima Classe, in the Latrobe Train Station, where two Amtrak trains stop daily. In addition to deploying a railway motif in their decor, the DiSalvos have created a special Steelers training-camp package built around Amtrak's service. The package, offered only when the Steelers are training at nearby St. Vincent College in July and August, includes round-trip train fare from Pittsburgh, lunch at DiSalvo's, and an afternoon at training camp.

The menu offers beef, chicken, seafood, and pasta selections. Favorites include Filet DiSalvo, filet mignon stuffed with prosciutti ham and provolone cheese and laced with bordelaise sauce and mushrooms; and DiSalvo's Station Seafood Platter, a medley of lobster, clams, shrimp, scallops, deviled crab, oysters, and sole. You'll also enjoy the early bird menu featuring a limited selection of specially priced dinner entrees from Tuesday through Sunday. Reservations are suggested for all meals. DiSalvo's offers an extensive wine list and can accommodate up to 350 people for banquets. The restaurant is nonsmoking, but if you want to light up, you can repair to the adjoining Joey D's Sala Da Fumo, a cigar smokers' lair that's part of the complex.

DiSalvo's serves dinner Tuesday through Sunday, lunch Tuesday through Friday, and lunch on Sunday. It's closed on Monday. The most expensive entrees are priced at the lower end of $$$. For more on Prima Classe, see below.

Girasole $$
733 Copeland Street
(412) 682-2130

This basement restaurant with tables lining the walls may be tiny but its portions are large, and as soon as Girasole opened, it became a popular (nonsmoking) addition to the Shadyside scene. Start with bruschetta or an antipasto platter, then a fresh house salad with olives, garbanzo beans, and Gorgonzola, and pick a fresh selection of the season. Most of the yummy desserts are made in-house. There is some seating on the patio, and it too is close together—you'll get to know your neighbors. Closed Monday. No reservations.

Lombardozzi Restaurant
& Lounge $-$$
4786 Liberty Avenue
(412) 682-5785

Lombardozzi is one of a number of fine Italian restaurants in Pittsburgh's Bloomfield neighborhood, where you can still hear Italian spoken all along Liberty Avenue. The restaurant features pasta, seafood, veal, chicken, and beef entrees. It's particularly proud of its fettucine Lombardozzi, which includes lump crabmeat, shrimp, scallops, and clams in a red or white sauce, and its veal Lombardozzi, which is crowned with lump crabmeat and shrimp. Lombardozzi offers a popular lunch buffet—the lineup changes daily—as well as a full-service bar and an extensive

wine list. It accepts major credit cards and reservations for lunch and dinner. The restaurant provides banquet facilities, with a special menu for up to 150 people. Several entrees are priced slightly higher than $$.

Mariani's at the Pleasure Bar $-$$
4729 Liberty Avenue
(412) 682-9603

Mariani's at the Pleasure Bar has been a fixture in Bloomfield since the 1940s; the Mariana family has operated it since 1963. The atmosphere is cozy here, the menu strong on pasta dishes. The Pleasure Bar, as it's popularly known, also offers beef, chicken, veal, and seafood selections, as well as a children's menu. Patrons are especially fond of the Italian tripe, served with mushrooms and sweet or hot peppers in tomato sauce, as well as the eggplant parmigiana and the homemade manicotti. The list of daily specials is extensive. The Pleasure Bar offers a full-service bar, a limited wine list, and banquet facilities for up to 50 people. It accepts reservations for parties of four or more on weekends, for parties of any number at other times. It's open daily Monday through Thursday until 10:30 P.M., Friday and Saturday until 11:30 P.M., and on Sunday from 4:00 to 9:00 P.M.

Minutello's Restaurant & Lounge $-$$
226 Shady Avenue
(412) 361-9311

The Minutello family has operated this East Liberty restaurant for more than 40 years, attracting a loyal clientele. The restaurant features a diverse menu, with veal, beef, chicken, seafood, and pasta entrees. You'll also find specialty pizzas and salad and sandwich selections. Minutello's offers a full-service bar, a wine list, and an extensive selection of domestic and imported beers and microbrews. Reservations are accepted. The restaurant is open daily for dinner and serves lunch Monday through Friday; it's open from 1:00 to 9:00 P.M. on Sunday. Takeout, catering, and delivery are available.

Moré Restaurant $$-$$$
214 North Craig Street
(412) 621-2700

Since 1971 this Oakland restaurant has been pleasing its patrons with a varied lunch and dinner menu that includes beef, seafood, chicken, veal, and pasta entrees; Virginia spots and shrimp scampi are among the most popular selections. Nor does the variety stop there, as more lists 16 appetizers and 10 desserts, ensuring that your dining experience here can be complete. The restaurant offers a full-service bar, an extensive wine list, and banquet facilities for up to 80 people. It serves lunch and dinner daily. Reservations are recommended. On Wednesday through Saturday evenings, feel free to sing along at the piano bar.

Persichetti's $-$$
Third and Magee Streets, Jeannette
(724) 527-5553

This Westmoreland County restaurant offers a diverse menu that's especially strong on seafood, with such selections as Persichetti's Lobster Crock and the land and sea trio, a medley of chicken breast, jumbo gulf shrimp, and sea scallops. You'll also find beef, veal, chicken, and pasta selections as well as dinner salads, sandwiches, and pizza. Persichetti's offers daily specials; on Wednesdays, the special is barbecued ribs. The restaurant offers a lounge, a wine list, and banquet facilities for up to 30 people. It serves lunch and dinner Tuesday through Sunday, closing on Monday. Reservations are accepted on weekends for parties of five or more, on weekdays for parties of any size.

Prima Classe $$$$
325 McKinley Avenue, Latrobe
(724) 539-0500

This small, elegant restaurant is set in a turn-of-the-20th-century railway dining car. That's fitting, since it's located at the still-active Latrobe Train Station, where Joseph DiSalvo and his father Gaetano have created a dining complex. The DiSalvos will make your dining experience here memorable. Joe himself will wait on you, while Gaetano—the executive chef for the complex—will prepare your food. The menu is aural, so you won't need your glasses here. It features such gourmet Italian entrees as veal stuffed with proscuitto and provolone and sautéed in a wine and mushroom sauce, and shellfish in a red bouillabaisse.

Prima Classe offers an extensive wine list. Reservations and proper attire are required. The restaurant is nonsmoking, but you can puff to your heart's content at the adjoining Joey D's Sala Da Fumo, a cigar salon that hosts several cigar-based special events each year and offers private lockers for members. Prima Classe serves only dinner, and only on Friday and Saturday evenings. For a visit to its sister restaurant, DiSalvo's Station Restaurant and Banquet Facilities, see above.

The Tarentum Station Restaurant $$-$$$
101 Station Drive, Tarentum
(724) 226-3301

The Tarentum Station was constructed in 1892 as a stop for the Pennsylvania Railroad. Such notables as William Howard Taft, William Jennings Bryan, Kit Carson, Carrie Nation, and Chief Ironstone rode the Pennsylvania to Tarentum, an Allegheny River town. When train traffic declined, the station was converted to a restaurant in 1983. When you dine here, you'll get a little flavor of the train station—and a lot of flavor in your meal.

The menu features beef, seafood, veal, chicken, and pasta selections, as well as dinner salads, such as an enticing grilled eggplant salad. Among the most popular selections is the Pittsburgh steak, a New York strip steak marinated in seasoned butter, then placed in a white-hot cast-iron skillet, resulting in a charred exterior and a rare interior. You'll find a bar and a wine list that includes domestic, Italian, and Australian selections but eschews French brands. Tarentum Station offers banquet facilities for up to 40 people. It serves dinner daily, lunch Monday through

Friday. Reservations are recommended. You can get here by taking the Tarentum exit off Route 28.

Tivoli Restaurant $$-$$$
419 Rodi Road, Penn Hills
(412) 243-9630

Rodi Road is a busy commercial thoroughfare that doesn't look like it could easily accommodate fine dining. That's just what you'll find, though, at Tivoli, which features a menu rich in seafood, veal, and homemade pasta selections. Veal roaise, prepared with artichokes, mushrooms, provolone, prosciutto, and sherry, is a popular entree, and you can order it in a combination with scrod. Sole belle meunierie also rates highly with Tivoli patrons. You can select from nine types of pasta—including whole-wheat linguini—and top your pasta with your choice of 17 sauces. Tivoli offers a full-service bar and an extensive wine list as well as banquet facilities for up to 225 people. Reservations are suggested.

Tivoli serves dinner Tuesday through Sunday, lunch Tuesday through Friday. It's closed on Monday. You can reach Rodi Road, in the eastern suburb of Penn Hills, from U.S. Business Route 22.

Vallozzi's $-$$
US 30 East, Greensburg
(724) 836-7663

Vallozzi's is a veritable oasis amid the arid shopping malls and heavy traffic that mark this section of US 30. It's a warm and inviting restaurant—an Italian villa, the proprietors call it—that's been honored by Distinguished Restaurants of North America, The National Restaurant Association, and *Wine Spectator*. The menu has a distinct Italian flavor, with such entrees as cappelletti lobster, with spinach and portobella mushrooms in a buttery tomato sauce, and Salmon Vallozzi, grilled salmon with artichokes, tomatoes, scallions, and portobella mushrooms, served in an Asiago cream sauce over angel-hair pasta.

The wine list offers 325 different selections, and you'll also find a lounge. Parties up to 16 people will enjoy seating in the secluded Wine Cellar or the semiprivate Arbor Room. Reservations are recommended. Vallozzi's serves lunch and dinner Monday through Friday, dinner only on Saturday. It's closed on Sunday.

Japanese

Sushi Too $-$$
5432 Walnut Street
(412) 687-8744

As its sister restaurant on the South Side, this Shadyside establishment features sushi—its phone number spells out 68-SUSHI—and such other Japanese fare as tempura and teriyaki. You'll find an attractive list of chef's specials, including garlic shrimp and lemon chicken. You'll enjoy a visual treat if you order the beef or seafood shabu shabu; both of these meals for two are prepared at your table. Sushi Too offers a bar, a wine list, and a Tatami Room that can accommodate banquets of up to 30 people. Reservations are accepted for parties of six or more. When you enter Sushi Too, take a minute to admire the replica Japanese garden in the lobby; it will help set an appropriate mood for your meal. (By the way, no smart comments about the editors. The Shadyside restaurant is Sushi Too; the South Side restaurant is Sushi Two.)

Korean

Young Bin Kwan $-$$
4305 Main Street
(412) 687-2222

In ancient times, Young Bin Kwan was the name of a house in Korea that hosted the Chinese ambassador and his retinue on official visits. That blending of cultures is the defining feature of this Bloomfield restaurant, which features Korean, Chinese, and Japanese fare—and a separate chef for the dishes of each nationality. Be advised that because the menu is so eclectic, prices vary widely. Young Bin Kwan serves lunch and dinner. It offers a full-service bar, a limited wine list, and banquet facilities for up to 100 guests. Reservations are accepted.

Kosher

Yacov's Restaurant $
2109 Murray Avenue
(412) 421-7208

Yacov's selections all are meatless, which makes the diversity of the menu that much more interesting. You'll find Israeli and Italian entrees, as well as soups and vegetarian chopped liver. When you eat at this restaurant in the heart of Squirrel Hill, you'll be intrigued by the art on Yacov's walls, including a series of primitive-style paintings that depict biblical scenes—Moses receiving the commandments, the Tower of Babel, David about to slay Goliath.

The dining room is nonsmoking. Yacov's does not serve alcohol, and it does not accept reservations or credit cards. It offers catering services. The restaurant serves lunch and dinner Sunday through Thursday, lunch only on Friday until 2:00 P.M. as it closes for the Jewish Sabbath.

Mexican

Casa Chapala $-$$
122 North Market Street, Ligonier
(724) 238-7399

This is a bright, airy restaurant in downtown Ligonier that features foods primarily from the Mexican interior. Among diners' favorites are chile Colorado, chicken en mole—chicken in a salsa of tomato and spice, served with rice and beans—and mole ranchero, an especially hot and spicy blend with chunks of pork and cactus. The restaurant offers a full-service bar and banquet facilities for up to 120 people. It accepts reservations. Casa

Chapala is open for lunch and dinner Tuesday through Sunday. It occasionally offers such entertainment as a guitarist—you'll need to call for coming attractions.

Cozumel $-$$
5507 Walnut Street
(412) 621-5100

US 30 East, Greensburg
(724) 836-2653

Cozumel offers a diverse menu at both its Shadyside and Greensburg locations, but you're most likely to remember the ostrich fajitas and taco salad. The restaurant features a number of tempting combination platters as well as limited children's and vegetarian menus. Cozumel offers a full-service bar, a wine list, and a broad selection of Mexican beers. It features live music each Saturday night—there is a cover charge even if you're dining there. Cozumel serves lunch and dinner daily.

The Fajita Grill $$
5865 Ellsworth Avenue
(412) 362-3030

This Shadyside restaurant offers dishes from four Mexican regions—Central, Puebla, Gulf Coast, and Caribbean. In addition to a broad selection of fajitas, you'll find such intriguing entrees as marinated jumbo shrimp in chipotle sauce and chicken in a pumpkin seed sauce. The restaurant does accept reservations and does not serve alcohol—you're invited to bring your own. There's no smoking here, even if you're dining on the patio. The Fajita Grill serves lunch and dinner daily.

Middle Eastern

Ali Baba $-$$
404 South Craig Street
(412) 682-2829

Ali Baba has been pleasing Oakland patrons since 1972. Particularly popular are its shish kebab and its hummus, which are part of a broad selection of entrees and a la carte items. The restaurant serves beer but no other alcohol, and it accepts reservations for parties of five or more. It provides take-out service. Ali Baba serves dinner daily, lunch Monday through Friday. It's located between the campuses of the University of Pittsburgh and Carnegie Mellon University and easily accessible from each. Don't miss it.

Khalil's II $-$$
4757 Baum Boulevard
(412) 683-4757

Before he opened Khalil's II, Mikhail Khalil worked for years as the chef at a predecessor restaurant at the same Shadyside site, so you know this restaurant is a labor of love. Shish kebab is a popular entree, as is samket el pasha, catch of the day baked in lemon and garlic and topped with pine nuts and sesame sauce. You won't find much in the way of fried foods here, as Khalil grills, broils, or oven-bakes most of the fare. The restaurant features a full-service bar, a wine list, and banquet facilities for up to 130 people. It's open for dinner only from Tuesday through Sunday, and it's closed on Mondays. If you're wondering about the name, Khalil also operated Khalil's I and Khalil's III some years ago, but these no longer are extant.

Open Flame $
2103 Murray Avenue
(412) 422-8170

Until another Insider told us about the homemade Middle Eastern food here, we just walked right by this unassuming, small restaurant. That was years ago; we've enjoyed many tasty bites since then. Open Flame is known mostly for its takeout and delivery; it's a favorite of Carnegie Mellon students too hard at work to leave their dorm rooms, even for a trip to nearby Squirrel Hill. However, there are six tables and a small counter inside the restaurant, and it's a fine place to dine very informally and fairly quickly. It sure beats fast food! Enjoy the variety here; even vegetarians will find plenty to choose from. We especially like the falafel sandwiches, the spinach pies, and the baklava.

Pan Asian

The Spice Island Tea House $
253 Atwood Street
(412) 687-8821

When you visit Spice Island, you'll be embarking on a culinary journey of Southeast Asia. The restaurant features the cuisine of Burma, Indonesia, Malaysia, Singapore, Thailand, and lesser-known regions of Southeast Asia. Among the intriguing selections are five-spiced chicken of Malaysia; Burmese barbecued chicken; pad Thai; Singapore rice noodle; Java fried rice; Sumatran corn and shrimp fritters; and gado gado, an Indonesian salad. There are plenty of vegetarian choices. Dining here is a fulfilling—and filling—journey; it's a trip you'll want to take. The restaurant is near the University of Pittsburgh campus in Oakland, and is owned by a Carnegie Mellon graduate. It serves lunch and dinner Monday through Saturday, closing on Sunday. It does not serve alcohol, and it does not accept reservations. The Spice Island dining room is nonsmoking.

Peruvian

La Feria $
5527 Walnut Street
(412) 682-4501

Unique is an overused word, but we're pretty sure La Feria is unique in this regard: you won't find another combination Peruvian restaurant and imported crafts store in Southwestern Pennsylvania. Owners Luisa Porras and Pamela Cohen founded this Shadyside complex in 1992, not really sure how the market would respond. They needn't have worried. Residents and visitors alike have been charmed by the products of Peruvian artisans as well as the Peruvian cuisine.

The restaurant features rotating specials—there's always a vegetarian dish—that include such entrees as locro de zapallo, a pumpkin and potato stew; tacu

tacu, a black bean and rice casserole baked with hot peppers and served with fried bananas and sweet potato chips; and ajide gallina, shredded chicken cooked in a creamy sauce with crushed peanuts, aji peppers, garlic, and onions. La Feria serves lunch and dinner Monday through Saturday, closing on Sunday. It does not serve alcohol but invites patrons to bring their own. The restaurant seats only 36 people, so the smoking section is rather small. Reservations are accepted for parties of six or more.

Pizza

Mineo's Pizza House $
2128 Murray Avenue
(412) 521-9864

713A Washington Road, Mt. Lebanon
(412) 344-9467

Most pizza lovers have their favorites; for many Pittsburgh residents, their favorite pizza comes from Mineo's. In fact, Mineo's was named the town's best pizzeria for six years in a row by *City Paper*. The restaurant offers outlets in Pittsburgh's Squirrel Hill neighborhood and in Mt. Lebanon in the South Hills. In addition to its standard pizza, Mineo's offers Sicilian and white varieties as well as options for thick crust and extra sauce. The menu also features subs, calzones, and largely pasta-based entrees. You can order pasta party trays as well. Mineo's does not serve alcohol, and it doesn't accept reservations or credit cards. It does not designate smoking and non smoking sections, as most orders here are for takeout rather than to be enjoyed in the small dining area. It's open daily for lunch and dinner.

Vento's Pizza & Dairy $
420 North Highland Avenue
(412) 361-9197

How important is this 50-plus-year-old establishment to its East Liberty neighborhood? In 1998 when the city moved to acquire the buildings in this block to make way for an important new Home Depot store, it worked with Al Vento to find a convenient new location for his restaurant. The result: Vento's and Home Depot are neighbors.

In addition to its signature pizza, Vento's offers such lunch and dinner specials as pepper steak, fish, and chicken parmesan, as well as a variety of hoagies and other sandwiches. Vento's does not serve liquor, and it does not accept reservations or credit cards. The seating area is small, so there are no smoking and non-smoking sections. Vento's is closed on Sunday.

Seafood

The Nest $$$
407 Clay Avenue, Jeannette
(724) 527-9880

Lobster and shrimp dominate the interesting menu at this Westmoreland County restaurant. No fewer than 11 entrees feature lobster or shrimp, and the lobster and shrimp scampi includes both. The headliner of the lobster group is the 22-ounce lobster tail; this must have been one of those tails that wagged the lobster. You'll also find crab cakes, orange roughy, and scallops on the menu as well as a few beef, veal, and lamb selections. The Nest offers a full-service bar, a wine list, and banquet facilities for up to 150 people. Reservations are suggested for weekends and accepted at all times. The Nest serves dinner only from Tuesday through Saturday, closing on Sunday and Monday.

Simmie's Restaurant and Lounge $-$$
8500 Frankstown Road, Penn Hills
(412) 731-4689

Located just over the city line in Penn Hills, Simmie's offers such seafood dishes as Caribbean shrimp scampi and twin Maine lobster tails and a variety of fresh fish specials that change with the catch. Barbecued ribs also are popular here. If you'd like to enjoy both seafood and beef, try the surf and turf combination. Happy hour each Monday through Friday from 5:00 to 7:00 P.M. brings specially priced cocktails and hors d'oeuvres, and senior citizens enjoy a discount on their meals each Wednesday.

Simmie's serves lunch and dinner Monday through Saturday, opening at 1:00 P.M. on Saturday. It opens on Sunday only for some holidays. It offers a full-service bar and a wine list, and it accepts reservations for parties of seven or more. If you leave Simmie's with an enduring taste for fresh fish to take home, you can satisfy your urge at the adjacent Frankstown Fish Company.

Thai

My Thai $
5401 Walnut Street, Third Floor
(412) 688-0729
The first time we went to beautifully and simply decorated My Thai, three waitresses were seated around a table carefully stripping the leaves from a mountain of fresh herbs. We knew we were going to enjoy our food! The freshness of the ingredients is evident in all the tasty dishes we have had here, and there are many items to choose from—an extensive menu at dinner and a shorter, but still plentiful lunch menu.

Some favorites include the *pla-goong,* a salad of grilled jumbo shrimp, marinated in chiles, lime juice, and lemongrass, served with fresh grapefruit on a bed of greens; the green curry tofu; and the eggplant delight, stir-fried with fresh basil leaves in bean paste sauce. There's a nice dessert menu, with traditional items such as fresh mango with sticky rice. I especially recommend the coconut ice cream, served with pieces of young coconut and mango over warm sticky rice. The portion is quite large—nice to share—and can be ordered with or without peanuts. If you're lucky, you'll enjoy yours at one of the tables over by the windows, where you'll have a view of the trees along Aiken Avenue and a few of the shops, too.

Thai Place $$-$$$
5528 Walnut Street
(412) 687-8586
When you're in Pittsburgh's Shadyside neighborhood and ready for a taste of pad Thai, that signature Thai dish that here is prepared with shrimp and ground peanuts in a flavorful sauce, Thai Place is the place to go. The diverse menu also includes such favorites as tiger prawns, which are spiced with red curry sauce and coconut milk and served with mixed vegetables, as well as a broad selection of beef, chicken, pork, seafood, curry, vegetarian entrees. Thai Place offers a wine list and a retail section, where you can purchase crafts, silk products, and neckties— all fashioned in Thailand. The restaurant offers a wine list, and it recommends reservations. Thai Place serves lunch and dinner daily.

Vegetarian

East End Food Co-op Cafe $
7516 Meade Street
(412) 242-7726
Many Pittsburgh shoppers appreciate the East End Food Co-op as a great source of organic and natural foods. In the rear of the co-op is a nice find for vegetarians and vegans, and anyone else wishing to have a healthy, tasty meal—the Co-op Cafe. The cafe offers seating for about 20 people, and foods are served cafeteria-style from a hot bar and a salad bar. The cafe features breakfast, lunch, and dinner daily from 9:00 A.M. to 9:00 P.M. The breakfast menu includes hotcakes, omelets, and a variety of tofu dishes. The lunch and dinner menu offers a limited number of soups, salads, and entrees that change daily, including linguine primavera and spinach quesadilla. The cafe's soups are vegan, and other vegan options are available. Smoothies and fresh juices are also

served, and you may want to pick up one of the cafe's cookies made without white flour and sugar, if you've got a sweet tooth. They're really satisfying.

The Co-op Cafe does not serve alcohol, and it does not accept reservations or permit smoking. The cafe can be a little noisy, what with shoppers checking out the adjacent deli case and the kids that are a constant feature of this environment, so don't plan that crucial business lunch or romantic rendezvous here. Come here if you want to meet other like-minded souls or enjoy a quick bite, though—and pick up your groceries at the same time. If you're interested in joining the Food Co-op, management would be happy to explore that with you. The Co-op Cafe is in the North Point Breeze neighborhood, about 2 miles from the Edgewood-Swissvale exit of Interstate 376 (the Parkway East).

SOUTH

American

Armstrong's Restaurant $
Baptist and Grove Roads
Castle Village Shopping Center
Whitehall, Castle Shannon
(412) 885-1033

When you're out shopping at Castle Village Shopping Center, you'll enjoy a respite at Armstrong's which is located in the mall. You'll find the same menu for lunch and dinner here, an Italian-accented menu with selections such as pasta and manicotti. Daily specials include such items as stuffed chicken breast, beer-battered fish with macaroni and cheese, and meat loaf. It's hearty fare. In fact, Armstrong's has received a "Best Buy for the Buck" award from *Pittsburgh Magazine*. The restaurant features a full-service bar. It offers catering services, and its entire menu is available for takeout. Armstrong's doesn't take reservations.

The Back Porch $$
114 Speers Street, Belle Vernon
(724) 483-4500

The Back Porch is set in a restored, antique-packed 1806 home along the Monongahela River in Washington County. You'll enjoy dining on the veranda or on the sunporch and choosing from a diverse menu. Appealing selections include charcoal-broiled ribs marinated in brown sugar and soy sauce, tuna topped with feta cheese and a lemon herb vinaigrette, and a mixed grill that highlights three different items each day. The Back Porch offers a full-service bar, an extensive wine list, and banquet facilities for up to 50 people. (The banquet space is not available on Saturday.) Smoking is permitted only in the Side Door, a casual dining room located downstairs. The Back Porch serves dinner Tuesday through Sunday, lunch Tuesday through Saturday, and reservations are recommended for all meals. It's closed on Monday.

Barry's on the Avenue $$
939 Jefferson Avenue, Washington
(724) 222-6688

In Washington Country, Barry's is a popular spot for seafood and steaks. Seafood selections include blackened tuna, swordfish, and salmon, while if you're hungry for beef, it would be hard to look past Barry's 40-ounce porterhouse steak. Barry's offers a lounge that's cigar friendly as well as an extensive list of California wines. Reservations are accepted. The restaurant hosts banquets—primarily on weekdays—for up to 40 people. Barry's on the Avenue serves lunch and dinner daily. You'll find it just off exit 6 of Interstate 70.

Blue Lou's Bar & Grill/
Mario's South Side Saloon $-$$
1514 East Carson Street
(412) 381-5610

Blue Lou's and Mario's once were distinct, although commonly owned, establishments that stood side by side on East

Carson Street. In recent years, however, the owner has knocked out the interior dividing walls, so they function as a single entity with a common menu and amenities. It's a lively, vital place with a pool table and a fun menu headlined by "Blue Lou's Famous BBQ Ribs," which are roasted for eight hours before they hit the grill. You'll also find seafood, chicken, and pasta selections, as well as dinner salads and an extensive sandwich menu. The creative dessert menu features chocolate chip baked potato and chocolate razz-a-matazz pie, cheesecake swirled with fudge and topped with a layer of raspberry and white chocolate.

The restaurant offers a broad selection of specialty coffees and cocktails; order one of the cocktails and you can keep the imprinted glass as a souvenir. (Note: The cocktails carry sexually explicit names that probably aren't appropriate for children.) As another tip of the cap to regular patrons, those who drink 10 yards of beer—not necessarily at the same sitting—have their achievement commemorated on a small plaque that will hang in the restaurant. Drink prices are reduced during happy hours, and ladies enjoy specially priced drinks and free wings each Wednesday evening.

The restaurant accepts reservations and offers banquet facilities for up to 80 people. While the restaurant accommodates nonsmokers, management advises that smoke from the bars tends to affect all dining areas.

Bobby Rubino's Place for Ribs $$–$$$
4 Station Square
(412) 642-7427
Like the man says, this Station Square restaurant is a place for ribs, for both lunch and dinner. Other barbecued selections include chicken and ribs, and you can order prime rib after 4:00 P.M. daily. Other entrees include rainbow trout, served for lunch and dinner, and lunch specials like roasted turkey platter and a jumbo chicken sandwich.

Bobby Rubino's offers an appealing variety of specialty cocktails, such as "TopNotch Butterscotch" with butterscotch schnapps, and "Buoys 'n Berry," concocted with tropical schnapps and raspberries. The wine list is more limited. You can reserve a table Monday through Thursday. Bobby Rubino's offers banquet facilities for up to 150 people.

Cafe Allegro $$–$$$
51 South 12th Street
(412) 481-7788
The Pittsburgh Steelers may have won four Super Bowls, but Cafe Allegro has an even more impressive championship record. For six consecutive years, 1993 through 1999, *Pittsburgh Magazine* and its readers named Cafe Allegro Pittsburgh's "Best Overall Restaurant." Considering that the region sports about 7,200 restaurants and taverns, that's a remarkable distinction, indeed. When you visit Cafe Allegro, you'll see the blue quartz trophy emblematic of the title.

Chef Nolan changes the menu with the seasons. Depending on the season, you may find such entrees as horseradish-crusted red snapper with garden salsa; veal saltimbocca; or Chef Nolan's bouillabaisse, prepared with market-selection seafood. One specialty impervious to seasonal changes is the grilled calamari—it's enjoyed a run on the menu year after year. Cafe Allegro offers a full-service bar and an extensive wine list, as well as banquet facilities for up to 40 people. It's open daily for dinner only.

Cafe du Jour $$
1107 East Carson Street
(412) 488-9695
Discovered and rediscovered several times over the years by food critics, this little restaurant on the less rowdy end of Carson Street hasn't yet built the following it deserves; still, that means seating is never a problem, either inside the narrow cafe or out back in the charming, brick-wall-enclosed patio. The atmosphere is casual,

with the two owner/chefs and usually one waitperson chatting with diners before or after the dinner. A large fresh salad divides into two satisfying starters with crunchy nuts, greens, and homemade dressings. The portions of comfort food are large, satisfying, and reasonably priced. For example, we found the roasted chicken accompanied by a heaping portion of garlic mashed potatoes quite filling. Bring your own bottle of wine. Cash only. Closed Sunday.

Callahan's Sports Grill $
Great Southern Shopping Center
Bridgeville
(412) 221-2235
Callahan's is a popular spot for kids' parties—and adult bashes for that matter—and you'll know why as soon as you step inside and get the full impact of the 32 televisions that surround you. Partygoers will enjoy the pool table, electronic darts game, and video/pinball arcade where kids can win prizes for their performance. You'll also enjoy the lunch and dinner menus, which feature primarily lighter fare such as sandwiches and wings. Callahan's offers a full-service bar. The restaurant accepts reservations for parties of eight or more. The grill opens at 4:00 P.M. during the week and at noon on weekends.

Cheese Cellar Café $$
25 Station Square
(412) 471-3355
While the menu is diverse, many diners choose Cheese Cellar to enjoy its specialty fondues. In fact, you can "fondue" your way through each course of lunch or dinner, starting with the Sam Adams cheddar and beer fondue for your appetizer and topping off your meal with chocolate fondue, which is flavored with orange liqueur and served with fresh fruit, pound cake, and marshmallows.

Another attraction of Cheese Cellar is its outdoor seating. The restaurant offers an extensive list of specialty coffees and cocktails, as well as a more limited wine list. Cheese Cellar accepts reservations Sunday through Thursday. It offers banquet facilities for up to 60 people.

Cheese Cellar offers several discount programs. Through one, you'll get your discount card punched each time you dine at Cheese Cellar, with a free lunch when your ticket is completely punched. The other discount program is for birthday celebrants. If you dine at Cheese Cellar on your birthday, you'll enjoy a discount that's equal in percentage to your birthday. If you eat here when you turn the big Four-Oh, for example, your discount is 40 percent. And they throw in a free chocolate mousse besides.

City Grill $-$$
2019 East Carson Street
(412) 481-6868
When you're cruising the South Side and get that hankering for something from the grill, try City Grill. Burgers are the most popular items here, but City Grill also grills steaks, shrimp, and a variety of appetizers. Salads and a delicious grilled chicken sandwich are also available. The desserts are popular here, too. City Grill offers a full-service bar and a wine list, but it does not accept reservations or designate smoking and nonsmoking sections.

Fat Head's South Shore Saloon $
1805 East Carson Street
(412) 431-7433
When you have an appetite that won't quit, bring it to Fat Head's for one of their oversized sandwiches called "Headwiches." They headline a menu that includes primarily informal selections—burgers, subs, wings, salads, and munchies—as well as a limited selection of full entrees. Fat Head's offers a full-service bar that draws heavy evening crowds. It does not accept reservations, and it does not designate smoking and nonsmoking sections. Fat Head's serves lunch and dinner daily. *Note:* Be aware there is a mural depicting near-naked women.

Grandview Saloon $$
1212 Grandview Avenue
(412) 431-1400

Grandview Saloon combines a great view of the city from the top of Mt. Washington with hearty, informal dining. If you're really into the view, try the saloon's outdoor deck, which will put you right out on the mountain. Reservations aren't accepted for the deck, but you can reserve a table indoors for both lunch and dinner.

Portions are large here, but perhaps none larger than the one-pound fish sandwich, one of the saloon's most popular items. You'll find a broad selection of burgers, salads, and pasta, and you can kick things off with such unusual appetizers as Greek spinach pie and pepperoni roll. Grandview Saloon offers a limited wine list and a full-service bar, which celebrates a daily happy hour from 6:00 to 8:00 P.M. with discounted drinks and hors d'oeuvres. The saloon accepts major credit cards, and its banquet facilities can accommodate up to 30 people.

Houlihan's $-$$
15 Freight House Shops, Station Square
(412) 232-0302

You'll usually find something inviting happening at Houlihan's. The Station Square restaurant serves lunch and dinner daily, and it also offers a late-night menu, serving until 12:30 A.M. For dinner, you'll find beef selections that are prepared on a wood-fired grill, as well as chicken and fajita entrees and salads and sandwiches. A specialty of the house is an appetizer called 'Shrooms—jumbo mushroom caps filled with herbs and garlic cheese, then lightly battered and fried and served with a horseradish and Dijon sauce. The restaurant offers a lounge, a wine list, and banquet facilities for up to 75 people. For entertainment, Houlihan's provides either a DJ or a band—sometimes both—each evening as well as nightly happy hours with complimentary hors d'oeuvres and specially priced drinks. The restaurant accepts reservations Sunday through Thursday but not on Friday and Saturday.

The dining room offers a section for smokers after 5:00 P.M.; before then, you can smoke in the lounge.

LeMont Restaurant $$-$$$
1114 Grandview Avenue
(412) 431-3100

LeMont has been an important Pittsburgh institution since 1960, offering both a splendid Mt. Washington view of Pittsburgh from 20-foot windows and an elegant dining experience. LeMont has been honored by the Distinguished Restaurants of North America and *Wine Spectator*, and it earned *Holiday Magazine*'s award for dining excellence for 37 consecutive years. That recognition suggests the comprehensive excellence you'll enjoy here. Popular entrees include roasted raspberry duck and steak Diane, which is prepared tableside, as well as such game specials as antelope and zebra. Vegetarians will enjoy the vegetable strudel, an herb-laced medley of garden vegetables and rice nestled in streudel dough.

The wine list is extensive, as is the selection of coffees and the array of desserts. Crepes Suzette and strawberries and bananas flambe are two of the more tantalizing desserts. Banquets are an important component of LeMont's services, so important that they've captured their banquet menus in a helpful four-color pamphlet that you can request. The restaurant can accommodate up to 250 people for a special event. LeMont serves dinner daily, and reservations are suggested.

Louis Tambellini Restaurant $$
860 Saw Mill Run Boulevard
(412) 481-1118

Just for the heck of it, we counted the entrees Louis Tambellini restaurant was offering on the night we visited. When we reached 44 regular entrees and 19 dinner specials, we were too hungry to bother with the salads and sandwiches, though those are plentiful as well. We were more than ready to eat. The extensive menu here will tempt you, and the restaurant will satisfy your temptation. You'll find beef, veal, seafood, and pasta selections. Specials include such entrees as filet of Norwegian salmon, filet of Florida grouper, and steak filet with sweetbreads and bacon strips. The restaurant offers a full-service bar, a wine list, and banquet facilities for up to 120 people. Banquets are not booked for Saturday night. Louis Tambellini Restaurant serves lunch and dinner Monday through Saturday, closing on Sunday. Reservations for parties of eight or more are accepted. You'll find the restaurant just south of the Liberty Tunnels on Route 51.

Maxwell's $-$$
340 Race Track Road, Washington
(724) 222-6200

Located in the Meadow Lands Holiday Inn, Maxwell's offers a varied selection of food and entertainment. Its menu features such unusual specialties as shrimp Jessica, shrimp stuffed with provolone cheese, wrapped in bacon and broiled; and pecan-crusted walleye, which is served with an herb sauce. Maxwell's also offers beef, chicken, veal, and pasta selections, and it features prime rib on Friday and Saturday. It offers a lounge, a wine list, and banquet facilities (through the hotel) for up to 550 people.

For entertainment, Maxwell's provides a jazz band on Friday evening from 9:30 P.M. to 1:30 A.M. In addition the adjoining Nitelite nightclub features live music and dancing Thursday through Saturday evenings. Maxwell's serves breakfast, lunch, and dinner daily as well as a Sunday brunch. The dining room closes from 2:00 to 5:00 P.M. daily. But you're welcome to eat in the lounge during those hours. Reservations are accepted; they're recommended for Sunday brunch and for weekend evenings.

Peppercorns $-$$
3821 Willow Avenue, Castle Shannon
(412) 344-7856

Peppercorns is an intimate South Hills restaurant that lavishes considerable care in the selection and preparation of its food. They prepare their own ravioli, which is featured in such dishes as lobster ravioli and salmon ravioli. You'll also enjoy the roasted sesame salmon, served with spicy peanut noodles. The menu offers beef, veal, chicken, and seafood selections. Peppercorns does not serve alcohol, but you're invited to bring your own for a nominal service fee. The restaurant offers banquet facilities for up to 50 people. It serves dinner Monday through Saturday, closing on Sunday. Reservations are recommended. The dining area is nonsmoking.

Pittsburgh Steak Company $$
1924 East Carson Street
(412) 381-5505

This South Side steak restaurant is more than just a steak restaurant. To be sure, you'll find a broad selection of steaks, but you also can choose from seafood, chicken, and pasta entrees as well as salads and sandwiches. Fried zucchini is a popular appetizer here. Pittsburgh Steak Company offers a full-service bar and a wine list, and it accepts reservations for parties of eight or more. It provides banquet facilities for up to 96 people. The restaurant serves dinner daily, with lunch offered Monday through Saturday.

Shootz Cafe & Billiards $
2305 East Carson Street
(412) 488-3820

Shootz describes itself as "an upscale cafe and billiards club," rather an unusual combination for these parts, where billiards clubs don't necessarily cater to the upscale. Shootz combines dining, drinking, and billiards so well that *City Paper* named this South Side establishment the region's best bar for billiards for five consecutive years. The menu features primarily lighter fare, including sandwiches, salads, and pizza, as well as a limited list of full entrees. You won't go thirsty here, as Shootz offers a number of drink promotions, including nightly beer specials and a highlighted "Brewery of the Month."

When you're ready to take cue in hand, 18 billiards tables await you. Shootz hosts regular leagues and tournaments, but players of any skill level are welcome. In fact, many corporations host staff parties at Shootz, which can accommodate up to 500 people for such events. You'll also find a small retail area, where you can pick up a Shootz golf shirt and other logo-emblazoned material. Shootz serves lunch and dinner Monday through Sunday and remains open until 2:00 A.M. on Friday and Saturday. Reservations are required for parties of eight or more. Shootz does not designate smoking and nonsmoking sections.

The Tin Angel $$$$
1200 Grandview Avenue
(412) 381-1919

When you dine at the Tin Angel, you'll enjoy that splendid Mt. Washington view of the city below, as well as the delights of an innovative menu. You'll get that sense of creativity right away, with the restaurant's signature fresh vegetable boat and homemade clam dip. The boat brings such unusual starters as stuffed grape leaves and baby pickled eggplant. When you're ready for your entree, try the Black Forest Filet, charbroiled filet mignon stuffed with pitted black cherries and topped with a bernaise sauce. You'll also find other beef, chicken, veal, and seafood selections. The Tin Angel offers a full-service bar, a wine list, and banquet facilities for up to 50 people on weeknights, up to 30 people on Saturday nights. The restaurant serves dinner Monday through Saturday, closing on Sunday. Reservations are suggested.

Chinese

Golden Palace $
206 Shiloh Street
(412) 481-8500

Golden Palace can't boast of the spectacular city view that other Mt. Washington restaurants offer, but it does provide a diverse menu and tasty food. If offers entrees representing all regions of China. Among the more interesting selections are Golden Palace Seafood Combination—shrimp, scallops, lobster, and crabmeat with black mushrooms, broccoli, baby corn, and snow peas—and The Four Happiness, chicken, shrimp, beef, and roast pork sautéed with vegetables in a brown sauce. Golden Palace serves lunch and dinner daily. It offers a full-service bar, a wine list, and banquet facilities for up to 75 people. Reservations are accepted for parties of 10 or more.

Sesame Inn $
Station Square
(412) 281-8282

715 Washington Road, Mt. Lebanon
(412) 341-2555

2975 Washington Road, Canonsburg
(724) 942-2888

711 Browns Lane, Ross
(412) 366-1838

Sesame Inn operates four restaurants in our primary service area—one at Station Square, two in the South Hills, the fourth in the North Hills. The menu is the same at each, so no matter which one you choose, you can be sure of the quality that persuaded both the *Pittsburgh Post-Gazette* and the *Tribune-Review* to name Sesame Inn the region's Best Chinese Restaurant.

The lunch and dinner menus are quite extensive, featuring poultry, beef, lamb, pork, seafood, and vegetarian selections. Among the most popular dinner choice are General Tso's chicken, salmon with black bean sauce, and the four duck entrees on the menu. Hot and spicy dishes are marked with a star, so you shouldn't be taken by surprise. Sesame Inn offers a full-service bar and a wine list, and it accepts reservations and major credit cards. Each restaurant offers banquet facilities for up to 60 people.

Continental

Cliffside Restaurant $$$
1208 Grandview Avenue
(412) 431-6996

Through its large picture windows, Cliffside offers one of Mt. Washington's best views of the city and three rivers below. A piano player performs on Friday and Saturday evenings to enhance the atmosphere. The menu is attractive as well, drawing from a variety of sources and traditions. Cliffside's most popular entree is Veal LaFayette, veal medallions sautéed with artichoke hearts, Butler County mushrooms, black olives, and Marsala wine and laced with scallions. You'll also enjoy the chicken dragina, chicken breast stuffed with cheddar cheese and apple and glazed with a sauce of raisins and honey, and the pepper steak, a New York strip steak lightly marinated and topped with whole green peppercorns, heavy cream, and brandy. Cliffside serves only dinner daily. It offers a full-service bar, an ample wine list, and banquet facilities for up to 60 people. Reservations are recommended. While Cliffside does not designate smoking and nonsmoking sections, it will try to accommodate those who prefer nonsmoking areas.

English

London Grille and Pub $$
1500 Washington Road, Mt. Lebanon
(412) 563-3400

Located in the Galleria Mall in the South Hills, London Grille and Pub offers formal and informal English-accented dining. In the dining room, you'll enjoy such traditional English dishes as fish and chips; shepherd's pie, a lamb-based dish with onions and potatoes; and steak and Guiness pie, beef tips braised with Guinness Ale, beef gravy, onions, carrots, and potatoes. If you're in a particularly British mood, try the bangers, grilled British sausage served with English mustard and mashed potatoes. The pub offers lighter fare and features the same menu for lunch and dinner.

In addition to a full-service bar and a wine list, London Grille offers a broad selection of bottled beers and English ales. Reservations for the dining room are recommended on weekends. London Grille offers banquet facilities for up to 40 people in its glass-covered atrium. The dining room and pub are open daily for lunch and dinner, and the restaurant offers a Sunday brunch.

French

Le Pommier $$$
2104 East Carson Street
(412) 431-1901

The number of French restaurants in the region is seriously limited; once you've dined here, you'll likely agree that one is more than enough when it's as satisfying as Le Pommier. Among the specialties are Muscovy duck, served on currant red wine sauce, and Elysian Fields farm lamb, served with spicy brown mustard sauce. Also featured are a nightly seafood selection and chef's specials, which include such unusual fare as Thai-style curried seasonal vegetables. French wines dominate the extensive wine list, but you'll also find American wines. Le Pommier offers a full-service bar and banquet facilities for up to 90 people. It serves dinner only Monday through Saturday, closing on Sunday. Reservations are accepted.

Italian

Angelo's Restaurant $-$$
955 West Chestnut Street, Washington
(724) 222-7120

You won't have to worry about the track record here. The Passalacqua family has operated Angelo's at the same location for more than 60 years, a tribute to the quality of the food and service. It's fitting that one of the signature entrees bears the family name. It's called Pasta Lacqua, and it features sautéed green beans tossed with a light tomato sauce and served with fettuccini and Romano cheese. You'll find a full-service bar and an extensive wine and liquor list. Angelo's is a nonsmoking restaurant. Reservations are preferred at Angelo's, which is located in downtown Washington.

Bruschetta's $$-$$$
19th and East Carson Streets
(412) 431-3535

Bruschetta's is a cozy South Side spot that features both indoor and outdoor dining. The menu offers beef, chicken, seafood, and pasta entrees as well as such interesting veal selections as veal Zurich, which is sautéed with fried onions and Swiss cheese in a marsala wine sauce. If you're in the mood for pasta, try the rotolo, pasta rolled with sausage, mushrooms, and onions and topped with marinara and fontinella cheese. Bruschetta's serves lunch and dinner Monday through Saturday, closing on Sunday. The restaurant offers a full-service bar, and it accepts reservations for parties of six or more. It does not designate smoking and nonsmoking sections.

Calabria's $-$$
3107 Library Road, Castle Shannon
(412) 885-1030

Hearty portions are the theme at this South Hills restaurant. Each dinner entree comes with two side dishes, a popular feature with patrons. The diverse menu includes pastas and seafood selections as well as such specials as meat loaf and stuffed chicken breast. Each Monday, Calabria's offers a lunch buffet—it's never the same as it was the previous Monday. The restaurant offers a wine list, a limited-service bar, and banquet facilities for up to 65 people. Calabria's accepts reservations for parties of six or more.

Paparazzi Ristorante $$-$$$
2100 East Carson Street
(412) 488-0800

Paparazzi specializes in Northern Italian fare . . . and a whole lot more. Regulars at this South Side restaurant particularly enjoy the veal and shrimp cangelosi, which is sautéed with artichokes, mushrooms, and red roasted peppers and served in a wine, lemon, and butter sauce. You'll find other veal and seafood entrees, as well as pasta and chicken selections and an appealing variety of freshly baked breads. The entertainment doesn't end with the food, however, as Paparazzi feature live blues and jazz bands Wednesday through Sunday evening, and you can enjoy both your meal and the sounds in an outdoor seating area. Paparazzi offers a full-service bar, a wine list, and banquet facilities for up to 100 people. Paparazzi serves dinner daily, lunch Monday through Saturday. Reservations are accepted Friday and Saturday only.

Pasquarelli's Restaurant $$
1204 Grandview Avenue
(412) 431-1660

631 Painters Run Road, Upper St. Clair
(412) 221-0350

The Pasquarelli brothers—Gino, Joseph, · and Mario—emigrated from Italy in 1970 and founded these restaurants only 10 years later. They brought rich Northern Italian flavors and tastes with them, as represented by a variety of veal dishes including ossu buco alla Melanese and Veal Chop Alla Pasquarelli, veal stuffed with prunes and broiled in the brothers' special sauce. You'll also find beef, chicken, seafood, and pasta entrees. The restaurants offer full-service bars; if you ask to see the wine list, they'll bring you a volume so thick and authoritative that it's called "The Bible." The Grandview Avenue restaurant, which offers a great Mt. Washington view of the city, serves dinner each day and accepts reservations for parties of any number. The Upper St. Clair restaurant serves dinner Tuesday through Sunday, and it accepts reservations for parties of five or more. Each restaurant offers banquet facilities for up to 90 people.

Union Grill $$
13½ East Wheeling Street, Washington
(724) 222-2860

The diverse menu at Union Grill is likely to satisfy most tastes. Italian selections include an appealing assortment of pastas and specialty pizzas as well as fried zucchini. If you're in the mood for American fare, try the popular Rueben sandwich. Union Grill—not to be confused with a different but similarly-named restaurant in Pittsburgh's Oakland neighborhood—offers a full-service bar, a wine list, and banquet facilities for up to 40 people. Reservations are suggested for weekends and accepted at all times. Union Grill serves lunch and dinner Monday through Saturday, closing on Sundays.

Japanese

Kiku Japanese Restaurant $-$$$
6 and 7 Commerce Court, Station Square
(412) 765-3200

Sushi and tempura for lunch and dinner are Kiku's specialties and its most popular menu items. You'll find plenty of other entrees at this Station Square restaurant, however, including chicken and swordfish teriyaki and shabu shabu, featuring thinly sliced beef and fresh vegetables. You dip the ingredients into a boiling broth, cook them to your liking, and enhance to taste with ponzu and sesame sauce.

Kiku offers an interesting selection of specialty cocktails and Japanese wines and beers, as well as a list of domestic and European wines. Reservations are suggested for dinner. Kiku accepts major credit cards and can accommodate up to 30 people for banquets.

Sushi Two $-$$
2122 East Carson Street
(412) 431-7874

As the name implies, sushi is the star at this South Side restaurant, but you'll find many other options such as tempura, teriyaki, and such "Chef's specials" as chicken cheese roll; eggplant and string beans; and fantasy shrimp, which is sautéed with asparagus in a creamy sauce. Sushi Two offers a full-service bar and can accommodate banquets of up to 30 people in its Japanese Tatami Room. The restaurant offers lunch and dinner daily, although you'd better make it a late lunch on Sunday, as opening time is 1:00 P.M. Also note that the restaurant closes from 3:00 to 5:00 P.M. Monday through Friday. Its sister restaurant, Sushi Too, is located in Pittsburgh's Shadyside neighborhood.

Mexican

Hungry Jose's $
227 South Main Street, Washington
(724) 228-1311

If business takes you to Washington, take your dining business to Hungry Jose's—it's only 2 blocks from the county courthouse. In addition to a wide variety of Mexican fare, Hungry Jose's also offers Italian and American entrees. The restaurant's the Cantina bar offers a number of specialty margaritas as well as a generous selection of beers on tap. Hungry Jose's offers banquet facilities for up to 50 people. It does not designate smoking and nonsmoking sections. The restaurant serves dinner each day and lunch each day but Sunday.

Jose and Tony's Mexican Restaurant $
1573 McFarland Road, Mt. Lebanon
(412) 561-2025

Here's an unpretentious restaurant in the South Hills. You'll order at the counter and transport your food to your table without the intervention of waitstaff, but you'll be pleased with the broad selection of tacos, burritos, tostadas, and other Mexican treats. The restaurant offers combination entrees, Mexican-style pizzas, and a limited children's menu. From Monday through Thursday, you'll enjoy "Taco Hour" from 5:00 to 7:00 P.M. when tacos and pitchers of beer and soda pop are half price. Jose and Tony's offers a full bar—with specially priced margaritas each Monday—and a limited wine list.

Margaritaville $
2200 East Carson Street
(412) 431-2200

Margaritaville specializes in varieties of margaritas, of course. The menu offers both Mexican and American fare, including some hearty Mexican combination platters that will test your appetite. You'll find a bar and a beer list, and you can enjoy your meal or drink in an outdoor seating section. Margaritaville does not designate smoking and nonsmoking sections. It serves dinner daily and lunch during the week. Reservations are accepted on weekends only.

Middle Eastern/ Mediterranean

Amel's $
435 McNeilly Road, Baldwin Township
(412) 563-3466

Amel's is an institution—it's been serving customers in the South Hills since 1952 and has been operated continuously by the Reiland family since 1968. You'll appreciate that experience and commitment when you dine on fresh seafood on a bed of homemade pasta, or the lamb kabobs that may be the most popular menu item. Amel's offers daily lunch and dinner specials as well as a full-service bar. It accepts reservations, and provides banquet facilities for up to 30 people.

Seafood

Grand Concourse $$-$$$
1 Station Square
(412) 261-1717

The former P&LE Railroad Station is now a national historic landmark and restaurant, where you can dine surrounded by near regal architecture. The restaurant concentrates on seafood and has an all-you-can-eat Sunday brunch that won acclaim in *Pittsburgh Magazine*'s readers' poll. The River Room's view of the city on the water is worth the wait. Open daily for lunch and dinner, the concourse is a popular tourist attraction, so reservations are suggested, but they're not accepted for Sunday brunch.

Monterey Bay Fish Grotto $$
1411 Grandview Avenue
(412) 481-4414

If you have any doubts that this is a bright, classy Mt. Washington establishment, take a close look at the waiters. They're all sporting bright aqua vests with schools of fish cavorting across them. The menu and its rich selection of seafood will provide another clue. Among the favorite entrees here are Maryland crab cakes, ahi tuna—served sesame style with a lemon butter soy sauce—and an Atlantic salmon dish called Rido Grille House, salmon marinated in a house teriyaki sauce, chargrilled and topped with a honey lime glaze. The restaurant also offers beef, chicken, and pasta selections.

You'll find a bar and an extensive wine list; Monterey Bay pledges to sell its wines at only $10 more than cost. It also offers banquet facilities for 50 to 90 people. It serves dinner daily, lunch Monday through Friday. Reservations are recommended. We probably don't have to remind you, but don't forget to admire the particularly fine view of the city, enhanced by Monterey Bay's 10th-story location and its glass elevator.

Solomon Seafood $$
222 Hall Avenue, Washington
(724) 222-0898

Solomon is a popular Washington County spot for salmon, orange roughy, and tuna, and it supplements its seafood offerings with steak and pasta entrees. It's located near I-70 and a few minutes from the campus of Washington and Jefferson College. The Solomon waitstaff will serve your liquor orders. The restaurant serves lunch and dinner Monday through Thursday from 11:00 A.M. to 9:00 P.M. and Friday and Saturday from 11:00 A.M. to 10:00 P.M. and is closed on Sunday. You can't reserve tables on Friday and Saturday, but your reservations will be accepted at other times.

Spanish

Mallorca $$
2228 East Carson Street
(412) 488–1818

As the sun streams through the skylight, accenting the colors in the hanging plants, and the tuxedoed waitstaff attends your every need, you'd swear you were actually in Spain, enjoying the creative recipes of proprietor Antonio Pereira. It's a touch of Spain on the South Side. Mallorca offers a full-service bar, a robust wine list more than 200 brands deep, and outdoor garden seating seasonally. It accepts weekday reservations for parties of any number and weekend reservations for parties of five or more. Mallorca serves lunch and dinner daily. In fact, it closes only one day—Christmas Eve. "My staff cooks for me 364 days a year," Periera says. "On Christmas Eve, I cook for them."

Vegetarian

Zenith Tea Room $
26th and Sarah Streets
(412) 481–4833

Zenith Tea Room offers soups, salads, sandwiches, and daily specials for lunch and dinner. Representative specials include linguini with onions, walnuts, and Gorgonzola, and wild rice pilaf with celery, onions, cashews, and mushrooms. The menu changes weekly. If you leave your e-mail address with owners Mary Kay Morrow and David Goldstein, they'll send out weekly updates. Also, if you follow

the stricter vegan diet, Zenith Tea Room can accommodate your needs with various menu items as well on request, in some cases.

Zenith does not serve alcohol, but you're invited to bring your own. It does not accept reservations or allow smoking. The tearoom can accommodate up to 40 people for banquets. It's located in the same South Side building as the delightful and quirky Zenith Gallery and antiques shop—in fact, you'll be seated among antiques and art in the dining area.

The tearoom serves lunch and dinner Tuesday through Saturday, brunch only on Sunday. Zenith is closed on Monday. It's located in a residential area and is not particularly well marked. You'll find it just by following the numbered streets. Don't give up; this is one of our favorite restaurants. Vegetarian is gourmet here, and the portions are large, too.

WEST
American

Alexion's Bar & Grill $
141 Hawthorne Avenue, Green Tree
(412) 276–2018

Here's a nice neighborhood restaurant where you can enjoy lighter fare and sports—both spectator and participant. For your culinary enjoyment, Alexion's offers a large sandwich menu as well as salads, pizza, and wings. You'll enjoy lunch and dinner specials as well as discounted drinks during happy hour each Monday through Friday. If you're a sports buff, you'll enjoy the restaurant's seven televisions and its darts and other games as well as the sports posters that grace the walls. Alexion's offers a full-service bar. It does not accept reservations, and it does not designate smoking and nonsmoking sections for dinner. For lunch, nonsmokers are invited to eat in the upstairs dining room away from the bar. Alexion's is near the Crafton-Green Tree exit of Interstate 279 (the Parkway West), a few miles from Downtown. It serves lunch and dinner Monday through Saturday and offers special entertainment on Christmas, Halloween, and St. Patrick's Day. Call for details.

Casey's Grill $-$$
7195 Eastwood Road, Beaver Falls
(724) 846-3700

You'll enjoy breakfast, lunch, and dinner at Casey's Grill, which is located in the Holiday Inn on Route 18. (For more on this Holiday Inn, see the Accommodations chapter.) The dinner menu includes steak and seafood selections as well as such specialty salads as tuna almond salad, steak salad, and Cajun chicken salad. Each Saturday night there's a surf and turf buffet and a champagne brunch each Sunday.

Casey's Grill provides entertainment—either a disc jockey or a band—on Friday and Saturday night. The restaurant offers a full-service bar and a wine list. Reservations are suggested for Friday and Saturday and holidays. Casey's is open daily but closes from 2:00 to 4:30 P.M. each day. It's located just off exit 2 of the Pennsylvania Turnpike.

Clark's Restaurant $$
333 Rouser Road, Coraopolis
(412) 269-9100

Airport Office Park, with its impersonal buildings, is an unlikely setting for a top restaurant. Don't be fooled by Clark's location in the park, for you'll find a restaurant that's warm and classy. The flower-bedecked dining room is an oasis in the desert of gray concrete, getting you in the right mood for the menu, which features beef, seafood, and pasta selections, as well as sandwiches, burgers, and dinner salads. Clark's offers a full-service bar and an extensive wine list. If you're in the mood for a $225 bottle of Chateau Lafite de Rothschild, you'll find it here. Reservations are recommended. Clark's offers banquet facilities for up to 100 people. It serves dinner Monday through Saturday, lunch Monday through Friday. Clark's is closed on Sundays.

Dockers Restaurant and Tavern $-$$
500 Market Street, Bridgewater
(724) 774-7071

Dockers is a delightful spot along the Beaver River, near exit 13A of Route 60. In season, you can dine outdoors on a deck that overlooks the Beaver, and you can feed the ducks—Dockers will provide the bread—that call the river home. If watching those ducks dine sparks your appetite, repair to the restaurant to select from a diverse menu that includes prime rib, burgers, seafood and dinner salads. Dockers offers a full-service bar, and it provides banquet facilities for up to 110 people. It accepts reservations but for Friday and Saturday after 6:00 P.M.

Grand Valley Inn $$$
452 Constitution Boulevard, Fallston
(724) 843-9000

This Beaver County restaurant offers a menu that's interesting and diverse. Entrees range from crab cakes to a filet mignon dinner for two, to dinner salads, including a popular pork loin salad. You'll also find chicken and pasta selections as well as lunch and dinner specials. Grand Valley offers a full-service bar, a wine list, and banquet facilities for up to 100 people. It accepts reservations. Grand Valley is open Tuesday through Sunday. If you enjoy the restaurant's player piano music, you might seek out Grand Valley co-owner Scott Watson and tip your cap. He created the instrument from an unused piano he had around the house.

Idlewood Inn $
2749 Noblestown Road, Green Tree
(412) 922-9560

There's never an idle moment at the Idlewood Inn. On Thursday, Friday, and Saturday evenings, you'll enjoy live entertainment, ranging from bands to DJs. Thursday is karaoke night. On Sunday, large crowds gather to watch NASCAR races and Steelers games and to enjoy the accompanying free buffet, live guitar entertainment, and specially priced beer. Did we mention the free happy-hour buffet

Monday through Friday from 5:00 to 7:00 P.M.? The scene is so lively that Idlewood captures it all in a monthly schedule that you can pick up when you're here.

The food is primarily lighter fare, including burgers, wings, and salads. Each Tuesday through Thursday evening, wings—in 10 different flavors—are priced at 15 cents each. Idlewood offers a full-service bar. It does not accept reservations, and it does not designate smoking and nonsmoking sections. It offers banquet facilities for up to 150 people, and it serves lunch and dinner daily. You can reach it off the Green Tree-Crafton exit of I-279 (the Parkway West).

J. W. Hall's Steak and
Seafood Inn　　　　　　　$-$$
2284 Brodhead Road, Hopewell
Shopping Center, Aliquippa
(724) 375-6860

As the name suggests, J. W. Hall specializes in steak and seafood for both lunch and dinner. It also features such homemade desserts as Dutch apple pie; peanut butter fudge pie; and turtle cheesecake, which is covered with caramel, hot fudge, and pecans. Maybe they need to add desserts to their name. The restaurant offers a full-service bar and a wine list, as well as banquet facilities for up to 40 people. It does not accept reservations.

Kathy's Country Kitchen　　$
3403 Old Darlington Road, Darlington
(724) 827-2558

Kathy's is one of those old-fashioned restaurants that offers solid American food at reasonable prices. Breakfast, lunch, dinner—you can get them all here seven days a week, and Kathy's stays open round the clock on Friday and Saturday. Staples of the menu include sausage over homemade biscuits, breaded vegetables and zucchini, and Kathy's Large Steak and Cheese Sandwich. For dessert, try the bread pudding or rice pudding. Kathy's does not accept reservations or credit cards, and it does not serve

alcohol. Kathy's will close off part of the dining room to accommodate banquets.

Manny's Rook Station Cafe　　$
201 Hawthorne Street, Green Tree
(412) 429-9353

Manny's is a neighborhood restaurant, set near an abandoned railroad station, and it offers primarily informal fare. Wings, sandwiches, turkey burgers, and Maryland crab cake sandwiches are popular selections. Manny's offers lunch and dinner specials as well as a full-service bar, where you'll enjoy happy hour discounted beers. Reservations are not accepted. Manny's serves lunch and dinner every day.

Red Bull Inn　　　　　　　$-$$
5205 Campbells Run Road, Robinson
(412) 787-2855

Located just off the Parkway West about 6 miles from Pittsburgh International Airport, Red Bull Inn serves dinner daily, lunch Monday through Friday. Specialties include an extensive salad bar, prime rib, and the restaurant's trademarked Lobster Pot. You'll enjoy live piano entertainment in the two-story lounge each Wednesday, Friday, and Saturday. The lounge is large enough that if you sing off key, no one will be sure the offender is you. Red Bull Inn offers a full-service bar, a wine list, and banquet facilities for up to 80 people. It accepts reservations for parties of six or more.

Red Hots Cafe　　　　　　$-$$
11 West Mall Plaza, Carnegie
(412) 276-2853

Ribs and wings are the hot items at Red Hots Cafe, which also offers Cajun-style dishes and such unusual selections as buffalo burgers and special salads. The restaurant offers a full-service bar and a limited wine list. For entertainment, try the pool room and the live bands and DJs on Friday nights. Red Hots Cafe can accommodate up to 50 people for banquets. It accepts reservations for parties of six or more. The restaurant serves dinner Monday through Sunday (except from May through

August, when it's closed on Sunday), and it's open for lunch Monday through Friday.

Tramp's Grill & Bar $
412 Greentree Road
(412) 921-7194

The owners of this West End establishment operated a downtown restaurant for years but found they preferred a neighborhood atmosphere. You'll like it, too. Tramp's offers lunch and dinner specials, a lot of sandwiches, and a limited dinner entree list. Its "jumbo cut" wings are a popular selection. You'll find a full-service bar and draft beer specials each Monday and Thursday. Tramp's offers banquet facilities for up to 50 people. Reservations are not accepted, and there is no designated smoking section. It's open Monday through Saturday and on Sunday when the Steelers play at home.

Willows Inn Family Smorgasbord $
1830 Midland Beaver Road, Industry
(724) 643-4500

No need to describe the menu here—there isn't any. This newly remodeled Beaver County restaurant offers exclusively buffet dining, serving dinner Tuesday through Sunday, lunch Tuesday through Saturday, and brunch Sunday. That's not to say that the fare is the same every day. The DiMaggio family, which owns both the restaurant and the adjoining Willows Inn hotel, vary the buffet lineup to provide some fun. Wednesday is Italian Night, while the Friday buffets feature seafood. On Thursday and Saturday, barbecued pork ribs are the featured item. Willows Inn offers a lounge and banquet facilities for up to 215. Reservations are recommended for parties of eight or more. Willows Inn is near Beaver, the county seat of Beaver County. Note that seniors get a discount on the cost of the buffet.

Wooden Angel Restaurant $$-$$$
308 Leopard Lane, Beaver
(724) 774-7880

For more than 30 years, Alex Sebastian has operated this Beaver County restaurant on his personal philosophy of customer satisfaction. For example, Wooden Angel offers an extensive wine list that feature only American brands, which Sebastian believes should be promoted. It's a personal vision to be sure, but Wooden Angel executes it so well that many regard it as one of the region's finest restaurants.

The menu is attractive and diverse. Featuring such entrees as rack of lamp; lobster cannelloni; Tuscany sautéed chicken; and angel hair Cantonese, with gulf shrimp and sea scallops atop the pasta bed. Wooden Angel offers a full-service bar. It can accommodate up to 100 for banquets. Reservations are recommended. If you want to smoke, you can sit in the more informal Casual Cafe, a bistro located within Wooden Angel, which shares the same service and menu as the larger dining room. The Wooden Angel and the cafe are closed Sunday and Monday.

Greek

Evergreen Family Restaurant $
816 Ohio River Boulevard, Rochester
(724) 775-8885

One of the attractions of this Beaver County restaurant is its availability. It's open seven days a week for breakfast, lunch, and dinner. You'll find steak and seafood selections and many homemade entrees and deserts. Evergreen Family Restaurant does not serve alcohol, and it does not accept reservations.

Italian

Aracri Greentree Inn $
1006 Greentree Road, Green Tree
(412) 921-4601

Aracri serves lunch and dinner Monday through Saturday, offering a healthy selection of special entrees that changes regularly. You'll find seafood, pasta, beef, chicken, and veal selections, including such entrees as Norwegian salmon prepared "lightly Cajun" with linguini and red calm sauce, and linguini al Scoglio, a linguini base topped with clams, shrimp, scallops, and lump crabmeat in a white or a red sauce. Aracri offers a full-service bar and a limited wine list as well as banquet facilities for up to 75 people. It accepts reservations.

Giuseppe's Italian Restaurant $–$$
Route 18, Beaver Falls
(724) 843-5656

In addition to its broad selection of Italian food for lunch and dinner, Giuseppe's offers dining themes Thursday through Sunday evenings. Thursday's specialty is prime rib. Fresh seafood is featured on Friday, while family style dining is Sunday's concept. The restaurant offers a full-service bar and a wine list, and it offers banquet facilities for up to 20 people in one room and 30 in another.

Mario's Family Italian Restaurant $
926 Brodhead Road, Moon
(412) 262-3020

The breadth of its menu and wine list is a strong appeal of Mario's, which is located near Pittsburgh International Airport. The menu offers beef, veal, seafood, and pasta selections, as well as homemade soups. A favorite of diners is Mario's own Hot Sausage Casserole, featuring ziti and hot Italian sausage baked with provolone cheese and a plum tomato sauce. The wine list runs to 190 selections, and you can enjoy the full-service bar as well.

Mario's can accommodate banquets of up to 20 people. It offers dinner only Monday through Saturday. Reservations are accepted Monday through Saturday. The restaurant is closed on Sunday.

The Primadonna Restaurant $–$$
801 Broadway Avenue, McKees Rocks
(412) 331-1001

Primadonna has won a clutch of awards for its food and service. The *Post Gazette*, *Pittsburgh Magazine*, and *City Paper* have all called it the Best Local Italian Restaurant. But the most important tribute to Proprietor Joseph Costanzo Jr., that hangs on a Primadonna wall is from one Tommy Lasorda, Los Angeles Dodger executive and sometime gourmand, when he's not hawking weight control products. "You, the Dodgers, and the Italians are all great," Lasorda wrote. We agree with all that, except maybe the part about the Dodgers. You will find great things on the menu here, highlighted by 33 different made-to-order pastas. Seafood, beef, chicken, and veal entrees complement the pasta selections. Popular selections include portafoglio-delizia—a pocket of veal filled with ham, cheese, artichokes, and mushrooms and simmered in sauce—and chicken zummo, chicken breast filled with a hot stuffed pepper, pepperoni, melted provolone cheese, and prosciutto ham, all breaded, baked, and topped with a tangy tomato sauce.

Primadonna serves dinner from Monday through Saturday. Reservations are accepted for parties of six or more. It offers a full-service bar and a wine list. You'll find it in the western suburb of McKees Rocks, about 5 miles from downtown Pittsburgh.

Mexican

Chi Chi's Restaurante $
600 Beaver Valley Mall, Monaca
(724) 774-9206

This chain restaurant is located in Beaver Valley and offers lunch and dinner daily. Among its most popular menu items are fajitas and fried ice cream. Chi Chi's offers a full-service bar, and it accepts reservations for parties of six or more. Each Monday through Thursday, you can take advantage of specially priced mixed drinks. While Chi Chi's does not feature banquet rooms, it sometimes can provide its dining room to host events for up to 50 participants.

Seafood

Wright's Seafood Inn $$–$$$
1837 Washington Street, Heidelberg
(412) 279–7900

Wright's Seafood Inn has been a tradition with local seafood lovers since 1898 when it was opened by the Wright family. It's still operated by their descendants, who have added a few touches here and there, such as outdoor dining in the summer months.

While the menu offers token beef entrees, tasty seafood is the name of the game here. You'll find shrimp, crab, and lobster selections flow in fresh seasonally as well as seafood pasta and some tempting combination platters. Particularly appealing is Bedford broil, a medley of Boston scrod, Atlantic Salmon, Maine lobster, swordfish, and sole broiled with lemon dill or teriyaki. For dessert, you'll enjoy the confections from Wright's made-from-scratch bakery. Wright's offers a lounge, an ample wine list, and banquet facilities for up to 120 people. Reservations are accepted. You'll find Wright's just off Route 50, less than 10 miles from downtown Pittsburgh.

MULTIPLE-LOCATION RESTAURANTS

Our region boasts a number of locally owned restaurant chains. Each offers family dining, and each is quite popular. Rather than numb you with lengthy lists of addresses and phone numbers, the food and experiences that pretty much apply to all restaurants in the chain are described. The phone number and address listed are those of corporate headquarters; they'll be happy to help you locate a specific restaurant within the chain.

Eat 'n Park $
100 Park Manor Drive
Robinson Township
(412) 788–1600

It was in 1949 that Eat 'n Park rolled out its first restaurant, a 13-seater in the South Hills section that featured a revolutionary concept: patrons, attended by carhops, could eat in their automobiles. The concept was wildly popular, so popular that Eat 'n Park had to close early on opening day due to the crush of curious patrons. Carhop service has vanished along with the Ramblers, Packards, and Studebakers that queued up that first day, but Eat 'n Park's popularity remains. It's the region's largest restaurant chain, boasting more than 70 locations in Pennsylvania, Ohio, and West Virginia. With more than 7,000 employees and annual sales exceeding $150 million, Eat 'n Park is a major corporate player in the region . . . and a responsible one. It donates at least 5 percent of its annual pretax profits to community initiatives.

The restaurants are family-oriented, featuring menus with more than 150 choices. Most offer such features as a breakfast buffet; a soup and salad bar; a Sunday brunch; and a bakery, where you can order homemade pies for takeout and pick up some of Eat 'n Park's signature Smiley cookies. Many of the restaurants are open 'round the clock and offer a midnight buffet. If you contact Eat 'n Park, they'll send you a directory of their restaurants, complete with maps and a checklist of features. The restaurants don't serve liquor, and they don't accept reservations. They serve breakfast, lunch, and dinner daily.

Kings Family Restaurants $
1180 Long Run Road, McKeesport
(412) 751–0700

Hartley C. King opened his first restaurant in the eastern community of North Versailles in 1967. His concept of economical family restaurants with signature desserts grew so popular so quickly that today, Kings Family Restaurants includes 36 locations in Allegheny, Butler, Westmoreland, Crawford, Mercer, Vanango, Blair, and Lawrence Counties. All Kings restaurants serve breakfast, lunch, and dinner daily, and all offer 20 daily dinner specials priced under $5.00.

When you're ready for dessert, you'll enjoy Hartley's Choice ice cream, which also is available for takeout. The Hartley's Choice private label also features tea and coffee selections. Kings does not serve alcohol. Some, but not all, restaurants offer banquet facilities.

Primanti Bros. $
3191 Industrial Boulevard, Bethel
(412) 854-2700

In the 1930s when Pittsburgh was primarily a factory town, Primanti Bros. had a brainstorm: why not pile everything—meats and side dishes—on a sandwich and create a meal that could be eaten during a rushed lunch hour? Some 70 years later, that idea is still popular, even though the region no longer depends as heavily on manufacturing. Sandwiches here begin with thick slices of Italian bread; wedged between them are your choice of meats as well as any coleslaw or French fries you order. The result; just about the most robust sandwich you'll find anywhere, imitated by many but equaled by few. If you must break down and cut your sandwich with a knife and fork, it's okay—you won't be the first.

Primanti Bros. offers restaurants in Downtown, Oakland, South Side, the Strip District, Robinson, and Three Rivers Stadium. They serve lunch and dinner—hours at the Three Rivers location depend on the day's activities at the stadium—and the Strip District restaurant is open 'round the clock. Most serve alcohol, but none designates smoking and nonsmoking sections. Reservations and credit cards are not accepted.

Valley Dairy $
1562 Mission Road, Latrobe
(724) 537-7111

Valley Dairy offers old-fashioned, unpretentious dining where meals are filling and economical. It serves breakfast, lunch, and dinner daily and is especially popular for its breakfasts. If you serve two eggs, hash browns or home fries, and toast for $2.09, chances are you will be pretty popular, too. Valley Dairy, which has been in business for more than 60 years, boasts award-winning ice creams and desserts. And the desserts are plentiful here; you have more than 20 to choose from, including such traditional favorites as All American Banana Split and rainbow parfait. Valley Dairy does not accept reservations, and it does not serve alcohol. In our six-county service area, you'll find Valley Dairy restaurants in Kittanning, Richland, Butler, Greensburg, Latrobe, and Washington. Other Valley Dairy locations are in Fayette, Indiana, and Cambria Counties.

NIGHTLIFE 🍸

In this chapter, a sampling of entertainment possibilities throughout the coverage area is given. Admittedly, some Allegheny County neighborhoods, like the Strip District and Station Square, really party the night away in sharp contrast to the more sedate evenings in rural counties. Yet you'll probably find something appealing from the list of jazz clubs, bars and brewpubs, coffeehouses, lounges and nightclubs, sports bars and movie theaters. Each of these categories has been segmented by the traditional geographic breakdown used throughout this guide.

Rest assured, Pittsburgh nightlife isn't always synonymous with roaring crowds and pulsating music. You'll find those elements, for sure. But you'll also discover neighborhood cafes where patrons play board games, sip cappuccino, and make their own entertainment through lively conversation. If artistic venues of the performing arts appeal to you, turn to the Arts chapter for myriad ideas.

For those who do enjoy a spirited evening in the literal sense, let's discuss a few caveats. First, the drinking age in Pennsylvania is 21. Restaurants with a liquor license are permitted to serve alcohol until 2:00 A.M. Sunday sales are based on a formula involving the establishment's ratio of food to alcohol sales. You won't find sales in the state liquor stores (except at a few sites where Sunday sales are being tested) or at beer distributors on Sundays, however.

Second, you may be asked for identification, so be prepared if you have that youthful look about you. Also, be ready to pay a cover charge at some clubs. The amounts vary even from night to night at the same club or nightspot, depending upon that night's entertainment.

Third, always designate a driver who won't partake of alcoholic beverages. Be sure to consult this chapter's taxi listing to arrange cab transportation, for your own safety and everyone else's. Unlike some cities, you usually must call for a cab in Pittsburgh unless you're at the airport or a major hotel—you won't necessarily find the cabbies cruising the streets for fares.

Fourth, dress appropriately, or call the phone numbers provided if you're unsure of the dress code. Remember, as a former industrial town, Pittsburgh is a bit more conservative than New York, Los Angeles, or cities in Florida (like Key West, for example).

Finally, there are two factions that deserve mention, and I didn't want you to think I'm excluding them. One is the teen scene, and the other is gay nightlife. In our region, neither has a wealth of clubs devoted to them, although they're out there if you look. When clubs, concert venues, or other entertainment may be of particular interest to these crowds, it's noted in the text in order to give you some guidance.

Above all, enjoy your night out on our town. Pittsburgh might lag behind a few other major metropolitan areas, but sure enough, it's a happening kind of place!

ALL JAZZED UP

Downtown/Uptown

Crawford Grill
2141 Wylie Avenue
(412) 471-1565

Though the days of the legendary jazz greats in the 1930s and '40s and '50s are long gone, the enthusiasm for the music hasn't waned. You'll sway at this club while enjoying soul food and drinks every Friday and Saturday night. The Crawford Grill is in the heart of Pittsburgh's African-American community, close to Downtown.

> *Check out live theater productions by consulting the Arts chapter.*

Hill House
1835 Centre Avenue
(412) 392-4400
Mellow out every Sunday evening at the Hill House in Pittsburgh's Hill District in this uptown area that's the center of the African-American community. Local and visiting jazz artists take the stage. There's free parking at Hill House or in lots nearby.

Scenes Outdoor Café
Pittsburgh Hilton and Towers
600 Commonwealth Place
(412) 391-4600
Don't miss the nightly jazz bands, martinis, and cigar bar here at the Pittsburgh Hilton and Towers outdoor cafe. Of course, this nightspot is open only in the warmer weather months, so call ahead if you're unsure. The summer menu specializes in grilled salads, burgers, turkey wraps, and portobello sandwiches. It's open daily until 9:00 P.M.

Tequila Willies
1501 Smallman Street
(412) 281-3680
Tequila Willies, on the shores of the Allegheny River in what's known as the Strip District, attracts boaters who dock and climb aboard these floating barges anchored to the shore. Other music is featured on other nights, including disco, oldies, and steel band rhythms.

North

James Street Tavern
422 Foreland Street at James Street
(412) 323-2222
Jazz bands, quartets, and trios perform here on the North Side many nights each week. Dinner, snacks, drinks, and a fun atmosphere are the highlights beyond the cool tunes you'll hear. Menu specialties from New Orleans like jamabalaya are particular hits. Reservations are suggested for this nightspot with two floors of fun and entertainment.

East

Foster's Bar & Grill
100 Lytton Avenue
(412) 682-6200
Set in the Holiday Inn in Oakland, this local night spot features live jazz each Sunday evening from 7:00 until 11:00 P.M. Pittsburgh Jazz Society bands perform, and anyone joining the society at the door receives a discount off drinks and food. Sunday brunch includes a jazz performance as well, as do Friday and Saturday evenings.

South

Paparazzi
21st and Carson Streets
(412) 488-0800
Various local artists perform in this South Side establishment. The upstairs dining room serves Italian cuisine for those who want a little dinner before listening to jazz and blues tunes. Tuesday is Euro-Club night with a disc jockey, and ladies receive half off drink prices. No entertainment is typically planned for Monday.

West

Temperanceville Tavern
424 South Main Street
(412) 920-1300
If you want jazz and blues on the west side of the rivers, come to the Temperanceville Tavern Wednesday through Saturday. Located in the West End community, this nightspot attracts a happy-hour crowd that comes out to hear local bands perform.

BARS AND BREWPUBS

Downtown

Real Luck Cafe
1519 Penn Avenue
(412) 566-8988

This bar on the edge of the Strip District is a comfortable place where gay men and lesbians socialize. The young crowd relaxes downstairs around a large bar. Upstairs most patrons are older. At the dance bar on the upper floor, disco still plays, and there's a side room for not-so-serious pool players.

Ruddy Duck
Ramada, One Bigelow Square
(412) 281-3825

Cheese and fruit plus hot items are on the hors d'oeuvres menu for the professionals needing to unwind following their Downtown workdays. Check out events on the Ruddie Buddie Calendar, published each month. In fact, if you visit this local lunch and evening spot, be sure to ask them to add your name and address to the mailing list. It's free. Different nights feature microbrew samples, snack attacks, and special promotions for sporting events.

North

Blarney Stone
30 Grant Avenue, Etna
(412) 781-1666

You won't want to miss this hot spot, especially around St. Patrick's Day when Irish musicians and dancers put on an extra entertaining performance. Various performers come here, and reservations are suggested for dinner theater packages. For one fixed price, usually on weekends, you get your meal and entertainment. This ranges from approximately $15 to $20 per person. On nights when individuals perform, expect to pay a slight cover charge.

Moondogs
378 Freeport Road, Blawnox
(412) 828-2040

Just 2 miles north of the Highland Park Bridge, Moondogs features some of Pittsburgh's finest local rock 'n' roll talent. On different nights you'll hear from local musicians including native rocker Norm Nardini. Most bands and comedy acts are booked in advance and advertised in the alternative weekly papers (see the Media chapter). Past events have included Pajama Party night, open stage comedy, and contests to win a $1,000 guitar. The tunes range from country and rock to reggae and blues. Moondogs' menu is limited to pizzas, tacos, nachos, and a variety of other light snacks.

Penn Brewery
Troy Hill Road and Vinial Street
(412) 237-9402

Enjoy the ambience of restored 19th-century brewing buildings as you sample at least a dozen varieties of German beers brewed on the premises. This North Side hangout offers an award-winning selection of microbrews, plus its own famous Penn Pilsner beer. There is live entertainment each Saturday. On the last Thursday of every month, enjoy the sounds of live swing and jazz. German and American cuisine is served in the dining hall with traditional family-style tables (see the Restaurants chapter). The outdoor biergarten is fun in warm weather. Plus, there's free parking in the covered lot next door.

East

Baggy Knee Cafe
9 East Pittsburgh Street, Greensburg
(724) 832-5733

This upscale bar attracts what locals call the courthouse crowd comprised of after-hours professionals. Occasionally a live band will perform, but this is a rarity. It's mostly an eatery for dine-in or take-out

If you're a recovering alcoholic, head to Club Alternative at 615 McClure Street in Homestead. There's a big dance floor, a house disc jockey, and a snack bar. Call (412) 462-5777.

service as well as a place to imbibe favorite beers or mixed drinks. It is reported that Harrison Ford enjoyed himself here while in town to make movies.

Bloomfield Bridge Tavern
4412 Liberty Avenue
(412) 682-8611

Local bands, including alternative rock, rhythm and blues, and new wave artists, perform here in Bloomfield, where ethnic food such as pierogies (a Polish specialty) always hits the spot as a late night treat. And be sure to wash them down with imported beers.

Church Brew Works
3525 Liberty Avenue
(412) 688-8200
www.churchbrew.com

Does the name intrigue you? We admit, it might seem strange, but in Lawrenceville you'll find handcrafted ales and lagers served in a turn-of-the-20th-century Catholic church-turned-pub. In fact, you'll find a gleaming steel and copper kettle sitting behind glass on the famous altar. Strange, we know, but it's true.

Brews featured include Pipe Organ Ale, Bell Tower Brown Ale, and Pious Monk Dunkel. You won't go hungry either, with wood-fired pizzas, buffalo strip steak, and other American cuisine. The outdoor Hop Garden is open every day. If you come because you're curious, you won't be the only ones. The Food Network visited Church Brew Works and Primanti Brothers (see the write-up in the chapter's Coffeehouses section) for separate shows.

Holiday Bar
4620 Forbes Avenue
(412) 682-8598

Some things never change, like this 40-year-old neighborhood gay bar situated between two universities. This dark, friendly spot attracts men of a certain age, probably because there's no dancing here, although it can get noisy as conversation vies with the loud music and ubiquitous go-go dancers. A more quiet room in back has a pool table and another bar. Supposedly Andy Warhol was a regular.

John Harvard's Brew House
3466 William Penn Highway
(412) 824-9440

Nestled into the Shoppes at Penn Center in Wilkins Township, John Harvard's is certainly a restaurant with wonderful appetizers, entrees, and desserts to go with any beverage. There are those, however, who only go for the microbrews and the ambience of looking in at the stainless-steel tanks. Each month, John Harvard's hosts a brewery dinner with samples of their brews, with complementary food dishes at one all-inclusive price (see the Restaurants chapter for details). If you sit in the bar area, you can watch sporting events or whatever else happens to be on the television as entertainment.

Mullaney's Harp and Fiddle Pub
24th Street at Penn Avenue
(412) 642-6622

Not just on St. Patrick's Day, but every day it's Irish Old World atmosphere here in the Strip District. Enjoy at least 10 different draft beers, grilled specialties, outdoor seating, and traditional live music. Tuesdays feature Celtic dancing. Be prepared to pay a $5.00 cover charge after 8:30 P.M. on weekends, when you'll find Irish bands playing.

Yuppies
241 East Main Street, Mt. Pleasant
(724) 547-0430

Run by the owners of the Casa Nova Lounge in Somerset County, this bar is frequented by gay clientele. It has been in business for 10 years and has become a popular watering hole.

South

Excuses Bar & Grill
2526 East Carson Street
(412) 431-4090
If the music menu of live blues, R&B, plus rock 'n' roll doesn't tempt you, then the 24 imported beers surely will. Feast on wings and munchie delights. Thursday night enjoy a jam session. Depending upon the entertainment on Saturdays, there may be a cover charge of $2.00 or $3.00.

Gandy Dancer Saloon
Landmarks Building, One Station Square
(412) 261-1717
In what was once the main passenger waiting area of the Pittsburgh & Lake Erie Railroad, the Gandy Dancer makes natives and those from out of town feel right at home. Crowds come here for the cozy feel this bar affords, complete with music from the baby grand piano. Listen to every tune imaginable, from Gershwin to ragtime and even the Pittsburgh Steeler fight song. Enjoy free hors d'oeuvres Monday through Friday.

Margaritaville
2200 East Carson Street
(412) 431-2200
You won't go hungry here with a plentiful Mexican and Tex-Mex menu. Reservations are suggested if you have a large group coming here. Of course, as the name implies, this spot is famous for its substantial margaritas. Band entertainment is limited to Friday evening, as most other nights it's too crowded.

Nick's Fat City
1601-1605 East Carson Street
(412) 481-6880
www.nicksfatcity.com
Enjoy live music almost nightly. Don't miss seeing the Hall of Stars, or stars of local entertainment, that is. Doors open at 8:00 P.M. in this art-deco club reminiscent of the 1930s nightclubs. There's no cover charge Tuesday through Thursday. Beer specials are offered from 8:00 P.M. to midnight

daily, and happy-hour drinks come at $1.00 per drink from 10:00 to midnight.

Rock-a-Bye Café
4962 Library Road, Bethel Park
(412) 835-9915
Here at Rock-a-Bye Café, enjoy music (including country western) with a disc jockey, bands, and karaoke too. If the variety of sounds doesn't get you on the dance floor, entertainment like the dartboard will ensure a fun time.

The Sandbar
Sandcastle Park
(412) 462-6666
If you didn't spot a glimpse of the Gateway Clipper Fleet, you'd think you were on Venice Beach. So says their ad for this beach bar along the banks of the Monongahela River. Having experienced Sandcastle's family fun during the day (see the Kidstuff chapter), adults claim this spot at night to enjoy a little alcoholic refreshment.

West

Kelly's Down By The Riverside Saloon
1458 Riverside Drive, Bridgewater
(724) 728-0222
Kelly's is one of a kind in this Beaver County community. Set on the banks of the Beaver River, you'll enjoy the tropical island they've set up outdoors with palm trees, equatorial plants, and lots of sand. Inside, there's also action at the bar. Tuesdays are devoted to different Irish balladeers. During the summer months there is live music. During the winter, it's usually blues bands for your listening pleasure. A bar menu features sandwiches and burgers.

Quaker Steak & Lube
The Pointe, 110 Andrew Drive
(412) 494-3344
Now fans of Quaker Steak & Lube's famous chicken wings don't have to travel all the way to Sharon in Mercer County. The eatery's newest location is off the Parkway West at the Pointe. Don't miss

the many flavors of wings, but do watch out for the atomic ones. They're potent, and if you want them, you'll have to sign a release form. Of course, there are burgers, steaks, and other fare on the menu. The ambience isn't quite what made the Sharon store a favorite, but the car motif is still prevalent. At the bar, you can even purchase beer to go.

COFFEEHOUSES

Downtown

Barnes & Noble
339 Sixth Avenue
(412) 642-4324
www.barnesandnoble.com
This chain of bookstores is famous for its Starbucks coffee bars. Consult the newsletter in the store nearest you to see when poetry readings might occur. Barnes & Noble is also located on Murray Avenue in Squirrel Hill, at the Pointe in North Fayette Township, in Cranberry Township, at the Waterworks Mall, and in Greensburg near Westmoreland Mall (see the Shopping chapter).

   Of course, if you're savoring Starbucks coffee, know the choices include cafe au lait (a French staple of espresso served piping hot and mixed with steamed cream), caffe latte (a large espresso served with a double shot of steamed milk), cappuccino (espresso coffee served steaming hot, topped with frothed milk), and regular espresso (finely ground dark coffee).

North

Borders Books & Music
1170 Northway Mall
(412) 635-7661
www.borders.com
The Borders chain of book and music stores has three locations in Pittsburgh.

Each provides a monthly newsletter with its literary as well as music offerings. If you're looking for a more sedate evening sipping a cappuccino and listening to the sounds of jazz, guitar, acoustic music, and many other varieties, then hang out here. Other locations include Monroeville Mall Boulevard in the east suburbs and at Norwin Center in the South Hills (see the Shopping chapter).

East

Dick's Diner
Route 22, Murrysville
(724) 327-4566
Open every day, Dick's Diner isn't opulent, but that doesn't matter to its followers. This late-night coffee shop and restaurant is known by east suburbanites for its great prices, tasty food, homemade desserts, and casual atmosphere.

Enrico's Tazza D'oro
Café & Espresso Bar
North Highland Avenue
(412) 362-3676
Owner Amy Enrico grew up in an Italian family and created this cafe with European flair. She searched the entire country for a coffee broker and now conducts "cupping" sessions some evenings, where coffee drinkers learn to appreciate the qualities and characteristics of particular types of coffee. Entertainment occurs Friday evenings, with brunch on Sundays. Dine on the great sandwiches made on the European panini grill.

Hemingway's Cafe
3911 Forbes Avenue
(412) 621-4100
Enjoy poetry readings every Tuesday at 8:30 P.M. While there's no live musical entertainment here, you can savor the delicious menu items including appetizers, wings, seafood dishes, and a full range of pastas in addition to the full bar.

Primanti's
46 18th Street
(412) 263-2142
If you took a poll of Pittsburghers' favorites for late-night bites to eat and early morning cups of coffee, we bet Primanti's (pronounced Pra-MAN-tees) in Pittsburgh's Strip District would rank at the top. We know of no place else where you'll find the fries and slaw inside (yes, inside!) the sandwich.

Primanti's is open 24 hours. Besides the very reasonable prices, people come here for the camaraderie and the reputation. You've just got to say you've been to Primanti's! And while other Primanti locations have popped up on the Pittsburgh landscape (East Carson Street on the South Side, Forbes Avenue in Oakland, Market Square and Cherry Way, Downtown, and in Robinson Township), this is the flagship location—the one and only that counts, according to some!

South

Beehive Coffee Shop
1327 East Carson Street
(412) 488-4483
There is no planned entertainment here at this South Side coffee shop. Feel free, however, to simply hang out with friends and create your own form of recreation. Board games and chess sets are available to use if you want to join in with this hip, laid-back crowd.

Cafe Au Lait
1224 East Carson Street
(412) 431-5910
With coffees like "Funky Monkey" and "Milky Way Cappuccino," you can tell there's some true brew and specialty teas served here on the South Side. The menu is a bit more extensive, though, with cakes, pastries, bagels, sandwiches, and soups. This nightspot stays open until midnight Sunday through Wednesday (they stay open until 1:00 A.M. on Thursday). On Fri-

day and Saturday, the doors don't close until 2:00 A.M. Until then, enjoy live entertainment, the Internet, computer and board games, as well as library selections.

If you're single, check out Sophisticated Singles dances every Friday at 8:30 P.M. at the Holiday Inn Green Tree in Pittsburgh. Call (412) 572-5259.

Cafe Bean
31 East Wheeling Street, Washington
(724) 228-1799
Close to Washington & Jefferson College, this spot attracts an eclectic crowd. Occasionally, there is music provided by the local radio station, but the ambience here is created more by the conversation and diversity among the patrons. Some of those customers comment that this place is a throwback to the '60s with its rhythmic sounds as background music.

West

Cappuccino City And Gourmet Coffee
441 Beaver Street, Sewickley
(412) 749-0766
If you're in the mood for excellent pastries, gourmet coffees, and herbal teas, stop in. There's no regular entertainment, but look for signs posted in the window (or call to inquire) because the owner books occasional music events. The atmosphere here is a little more casual than in some of the neighboring cafes (like Starbucks).

Common Grounds
234 Bridge Street, Beaver
(724) 728-5282
Special coffees, cappuccino, and lattes make this a literal perk-up spot. But if the beverages don't do it, the acoustic music will. Occasionally, you'll find Mario singing Frank Sinatra and Tony Bennett tunes on selected Saturdays. For serious tea

drinkers, the fancy tearoom can be reserved for parties of 2 through 20 people. Dress in this room is more formal than in the rest of the cafe.

Starbucks Coffee
425 Beaver Street, Sewickley
(412) 741-9184

415 Seventh Avenue
(412) 471-3422

210 Sixth Avenue
(412) 642-9066

1719 Penn Avenue
(412) 281-4898

1717 Cochran Road
(412) 563-7813

6304 Forbes Avenue
(412) 421-6244

3460 William Penn Highway
(412) 823-5328

Brewing is their business. In recent years, Pittsburgh has seen an increase in stand-alone Starbucks coffee shops beyond those in the Barnes & Noble bookstores (which are mentioned above). So stop by not only in the morning, but also well into the evening. Downtown locations include Chamber of Commerce Building and at One Olive Plaza. Also, enjoy the Strip District shop, the Mt. Lebanon location, the Squirrel Hill's Starbucks, and the Wilkins Township store. Some Starbucks offer periodic entertainment such as acoustic guitar or folk music, usually on weekends.

Tuscany Cafe
1501 East Carson Street
(412) 488-4475
www.tuscanysouthside.com

Tuscany Cafe is the real deal and not part of a chain, a coffeehouse with a unique personality all its own that's close to restaurants and the City Theatre. During the day it's a hip, friendly coffeehouse serving espresso or cappuccino with a muffin or sandwich. In the evening it's a comfortable "alternative" full-service bar in back where the younger crowd watches episodes of *Will and Grace* or *Queer as*

Folk. If you aren't won over by the wide assortment of coffees and desserts, happy-hour specials or Sunday brunches, sip your coffee at one of the tables in the front window above the rest of the cafe. You'll catch the rest of the South Side going by and feel as if you're starring in your own independent film.

LOUNGES, DANCING, MUSIC & MORE

Downtown

Pegasus
818 Liberty Avenue
(412) 281-2131

It's got a glittery look and a techno sound for dancing. Watch for drink specials as well. This is perhaps Pittsburgh's most visible gay bar.

North

Ghost Riders
1805 North Main Street, Butler
(724) 283-4401

Even though it plays primarily country music, Ghost Rider draws a diverse crowd. There's no liquor license here, so it's bring your own bottle.

Jetz
2801 Freeport Road, Harmarville
(412) 828-9500

Jetz attracts the younger, under-21 crowd, on Friday, Saturday, and Sunday. Since there aren't that many clubs for this age group, you can see it's a popular place on weekends.

Pittsburgh Eagle
1740 Eckert Street
(412) 766-7222
www.pitteagle.com

This is *the* club for gay men; nothing in Pittsburgh touches it. But first you need wheels, then you gotta find it. Take Chateau Street on the North Side and head toward the penitentiary, several miles from Downtown. At night the building is most impressive: four brick stories stretch toward a bridge high above. Inside is even better; a pressed-tin ceiling, 14-feet high, covers a spacious bar where a diverse gay crowd, some women and all ages, mingles. The pace picks up on the second floor, where the beat and the heat hit you immediately. Unwind in the third-floor lounge where couches surround a huge TV showing dance videos. On weekends the dance floor is packed to the beat of Hi-NRG music from years past. Expect a weekend cover, typically $3.00 to $5.00 depending on the theme or entertainer.

3 B's Lounge
309 South Main Street, Zelienople
(724) 452-9959

There's a lot to entertain you here in Butler County. Thursday, play pool here. A disc jockey is on hand Friday, and a different band performs every Saturday night. Roughly once a month (usually on Wednesday or Thursday) it's open stage. If you feel like playing the hockey game, or joining in at the pool tables, you're in luck. Dartboards and pinball machines are popular fun here also.

3 B's features a full menu with everything from salads to prime rib.

East

Club Havana
5744 Ellsworth Avenue
(412) 661-2025

Martinis, cigars, and Latin sounds are all here at Club Havana. In the warm weather months, the patio is open. Salsa and merengue dance lessons are offered many evenings between 8:00 and 10:00 P.M.

Four Points Hotel—Prospect Lounge
Route 30, 100 Sheraton Drive
Greensburg
(724) 836-6060

Tuesday through Sunday you'll find various bands performing top-40 dance

Board the Gateway Clipper Fleet for occasional rhythm and blues cruises. Call (412) 355-7980 or turn to the Attractions chapter for more information regarding the fleet.

music. A different band rotates on the schedule each week. The dress code here is rather casual.

Metropol
1600 Smallman Street
(412) 261-2232

There's a semiprivate club upstairs, with a multilevel (and large) dance floor downstairs. If you like to dance, you can surely work up a sweat here with the variety of sounds ranging from new wave and modern hits to electronica. There are plenty of disc jockeys to keep the music hot.

Sanctuary Club
1620 Penn Avenue
(412) 263-2877
www.sanctuarypittsburgh.com

Convert a 19th-century Slovak Catholic church into a nightclub and what do you get? The hottest new dance club in the Strip for slightly older, better-dressed sophisticates. Walk past the crowd dancing through fog and strobe lights to a techno beat and order a drink at the 60-foot fiberglass bar, which stretches along one side of the room. Ascend the striking steel-and-fiberglass staircase to a mezzanine with a smaller bar, comfy seating, and a view of the dancers below. Expect to pay a cover.

South

Blues Cafe
1832 East Carson Street
(412) 431-7080

Stop in for a Monday-night jam session here on the South Side. Various artists are featured most weekends with different blues bands all the time. The Blues Cafe now serves Primanti sandwiches (read more about Primanti's above under Coffeehouses). Typical cover charge is $2.00.

CJ Deighan's
2506 West Liberty Avenue
(412) 561-4044
While the clientele at many of the other alternative bars and nightclubs in Pittsburgh is mostly men, CJ Deighan's is a happening place for women, with the majority of patrons being of that gender. During winter months, the nightclub's busiest season, Friday and Saturday nights boast DJs, and there are often bands or other live entertainment scheduled. In the summer, there's a DJ on Saturday night only. If dancing isn't really your thing, belly up to one of the two bars or shoot some pool. Call CJ Deighan's to check the live entertainment schedule year-round. And get yourself over there; it's a nice place.

Funny Bone
Station Square
(412) 281-3130
www.funybonepgh.com
If you couldn't guess from the name, this club will keep you laughing with its evenings of comedy, music, and magic. Showtime is 7:30 P.M. most nights. Tuesday features karaoke and open mike. Friday and Saturday be prepared for shows at 8:00 and 10:15 P.M. Reservations are recommended.

Lava Lounge
2204 East Carson Street
(412) 431-5282
Most every night disc jockeys keep the pace hopping at the Lava Lounge. On Monday, there is a variety show. The mood here is set by the different decor—the feeling of a subterranean organic environment with a deep-cushioned pit booth. Wednesday and Thursday give you the chance to visit with no cover charge, but expect to pay $2.00 to $4.00 on other evenings.

Nitelite
Holiday Inn Meadowlands
340 Racetrack Road, Washington
(724) 222-6200
Join the upscale crowd assembled here for dancing, drinks, and wonderful evening entertainment. Nitelite isn't far from the race track, so once your wagering is finished for the evening, head on over.

Pepsi-Cola Roadhouse
Route 18, Burgettsown
(724) 947-1900
www.pepsiroadhouse.com
Pepsi-Cola Roadhouse is a unique dining and entertainment experience, with a seating capacity in excess of 800. With tables of four, every seat yields an up close and personal view of the performers, who range from country and western entertainers to pro boxing and night-at-the-races events. Take Route 22 west (off the Parkway West) and continue until you reach the Burgettstown-Florence exit.

Quail Hill
Route 19 South, Washington
(724) 745-0333
One mile north of Racetrack Road, you'll find Quail Hill, a restaurant lounge with light fare, cocktails, and live music. Performers vary, but previous groups and individual artists have included jazz, blues, rock, and country music.

West

Boots Texas Roadhouse
1420 Riverside Drive, Beaver
(724) 728-8002
If you're into country and western music come to Boots, where beers are served from plastic boot glasses (that double as take-home souvenirs).

But that's not the only thing that makes this quite a different hangout. The menu (try the ribs) is presented as a newspaper. Peanut shells get thrown on the floor. If you time your visit right, you'll get to witness one of the many line dances the waitstaff occasionally performs. However, that's not all they're known for. Servers here at Boots also write the daily specials on each table cloth—upside down!

SPORTS BARS

North

Clark Bar & Grill
503 Martindale Street
(412) 231-5720
Housed in the old Clark Candy Building on the North Side, there's a definite sports atmosphere to this popular hangout across from Gate B at Three Rivers Stadium. Come in for the great grilled entrees, delicious salads, and sandwiches, and supreme pastas. Drinks are moderately priced. Even better than the food and libation, however, is the art deco atmosphere, including autographed jerseys, baseballs, hockey sticks, and much more celebrating Pittsburgh sports.

East

Champs
5832 Forward Avenue
(412) 422-6414
This Squirrel Hill haunt is a favorite for Steeler games and other local sports. It's open every day from midafternoon until 2:00 A.M. However, for Steelers' Sundays, come on in at noon to start the fun.

Damon's
Miracle Mile Shopping Center
Monroeville
(412) 858-7427

7221 McKnight Road
(412) 367-7427

511 Clairton Boulevard
(412) 653-7427

855 Freeport Road
(412) 782-3750
This is certainly the place for barbecued ribs, but you'll also find sports fans congregating here. Other house specialties include reasonably priced sandwiches, salads, and entrees for the whole family. In the Pittsburgh area, visit other Damon's locations in the North Hills, South Hills, and at the Waterworks Mall.

Dino's Sports Lounge
Route 30, Latrobe
(724) 539-2566
Dino's is a popular spot for sports fans. If you don't want to watch the 10-foot big-screen television, park yourself near one of the 16 to 18 smaller sets. In addition to the great sandwiches and wings for which the lounge is known, there are also two Indy race-car simulators, pinball and golf machines, and a dartboard.

Oakmont Tavern
814 Allegheny River Boulevard, Oakmont
(412) 828-4155
With five televisions that let you see your favorite sports action, we'll term this a sports bar, even though you can have lunch or dinner also. After all, the walls are adorned with old photos of Forbes Field, Pirates baseball, and more. The menu features sandwiches, hoagies, and appetizers. Mexican dishes are apparently the hit of the house.

South

Forbes Field Tavern
2901 Sarah Street
(412) 431-9500
Forbes Field, for those with a primitive Pirates baseball background, was the predecessor of Three Rivers Stadium.

Centered in Oakland, the baseball park was demolished to make room for expansion at the University of Pittsburgh. Today, this tavern bears its name with old memorabilia adorning the walls, including scorecards and plenty of photographs.

West

Butya's Tavern
5576 Steubenville Pike, Route 60
(412) 787-1919
The autographed memorabilia hanging on the walls gives just the right team spirit to watch popular games on television while enjoying good food and drink. Recently completed for the summer season is a sand volleyball court with an adjacent pavilion for outdoor serving. Based in Robinson Township, Butya's is known for its tasty fish sandwiches.

Zooky's Sports Tavern
Route 51, Fallston
(724) 843-9464
Between Beaver and Chippewa, Zooky's offers more than just great wings and beer. There's the trivia game patrons play on television, competing against participants in other bars around the country. Of course, that's when fans aren't watching a major sporting event. So whether it's food, beverages, or just plain fun, Zooky's has all three.

MOVIE THEATERS

This obviously is not a comprehensive list, but here we've given the largest and the most popular theaters and spots for movie lovers.

Andy Warhol Museum
117 Sandusky Street
(412) 237-8300
www.warhol.org
While the art comprises most of the attraction here, there is a theater that screens Andy Warhol films. It's on the first

floor of the museum, and sometimes easily missed by those who only browse the exhibits or eat in the cafe. The Warhol is open Tuesday, Wednesday, Thursday, Saturday, and Sunday from 10:00 A.M. to 5:00 P.M. and Friday from 10:00 A.M. to 10:00 P.M. It's closed Monday. Admission to the theater is included in the cost of a museum ticket. Adults will pay $10.00, seniors $7.00, and students and children $6.00 for admission. Carnegie members pay nothing to enter.

Carmike Cinemas—Cranberry
Route 19 North, Cranberry
(724) 772-3180
www.carmike.com
Carmike Cinemas is a chain with several suburban locations throughout the Pittsburgh region. This cinema in Cranberry has eight screens showing popular first-run movies. Try the others closer to you at South Hills Village, (412) 835-7700; the Galleria in Mt. Lebanon, (412) 531-5720; Pleasant Hills, (412) 655-0511; Century Square Plaza, (412) 655-8123; and Delmont, (724) 468-3555.

Carnegie Science Center Omnimax
One Allegheny Avenue
(412) 237-3400
www.carnegiesciencecenter.org
Read more about this attraction in both the Attractions and Kidstuff chapters. However, here we wanted to highlight the Rangos Omnimax Theater, which shows one or two different films on any given day. Double-feature presentations are the norm on weekends. Expect to pay approximately $6.00 to $8.00 for tickets, unless you attend a double feature. Members are admitted at lesser charges.

Dependable Drive-In
Moon Clinton Road, Coraopolis
(412) 264-7011
Drive-in theaters are so rare, we've chosen to list this one. Why not enjoy a throwback to the 1950s and take the family out to this theater? Enjoy the per car admission as opposed to per person charges too!

Destinta Theatres
Route 30 and Route 48, North Versailles
(412) 824-9200
www.destinta.com
Opened in June 1999, this 20-screen complex bills itself as "luxury for less" because it boasts VIP luxury boxes, highback recliner seats, large party rooms, a video arcade, a full concession stand, and a gourmet coffee bar. Visit another location in the west suburbs at Route 50 West in Ridgeville, (412) 914-0999.

Harris Theater
809 Liberty Avenue
(412) 471-9700
The Harris Theater is often the site of films for Pittsburgh Filmmakers. You can read more about both the theater and the organization in the Arts chapter.

Loews Cineplex
Route 30 to Warren Drive
North Versailles
(412) 823-3992
There's a tough competition in this area of North Versailles, with Loews Cineplex opening less than six months after Destinta Theatres. Built on the site of the former Greater Pittsburgh Drive-In, Loews offers 22 screens showing recent Hollywood releases.

Loews Waterfront Theatre
300 West Waterfront Drive, Homestead
(412) 462-6923
www.loewscineplex.com
If bigger is better, the newest 22-screen Loews Theatre, at the Waterfront entertainment/shopping complex in Homestead, wins as "best." Outside, giant pillars and oversize architectural features resemble movie palaces of old. Inside, "big" also applies: from its vast lobby with a high ceiling, a huge concession stand, and a cafe for a leisurely coffee to a full service restaurant and bar upstairs. The screens and sound are big, too. Some of the theaters offer VIP areas with the opportunity to purchase tickets in advance.

Check the weekend entertainment sections in your local newspapers for listings of movies currently playing and a whole host of other nightlife possibilities. Most of these sections appear on Friday, although some may be published on Thursday.

Regent Square Theater
1035 South Braddock Avenue
(412) 241-2332
Like the Harris Theater, this facility hosts the Pittsburgh Filmmakers. Find out about the showings by calling the phone number, checking the Web at pghfilmmakers.org, or reviewing the listings in the alternative weekly papers.

Showcase Cinemas
McKnight Road
(412) 931-1870
www.showcasecinemas.com
Built in the 1970s, many of these cinemas have been added on to. The North Hills location on McKnight Road boasts 12 screens. There's Showcase Cinemas West in Robinson Township, (412) 787-5788, with 15 screens, and Showcase East in Wilkins Township, with 12 screens.

Getting A Cab

Remember: You can't hail a cab in Pittsburgh. It's just one of those things.
And be sure to call one if you're unable to drive home safely.

Yellow Cab Company of Pittsburgh
(412) 665-8100

Peoples Cab Company
(412) 681-3131

A Limousine Service
(412) 782-5466

SHOPPING ⊛

If you've read other chapters so far, you probably know that Pittsburghers are proud of our sports teams. But there's one sport we love that you won't read about in that chapter: shopping.

Indeed, browsing for bargains, finding fresh produce, or uncovering valuable antiques is a true treasure hunt in these parts. Then, there's gearing up for your garden, outfitting the kids, or finding a fun flea market. If all these venues don't complete your search, your local mall surely will. Throughout the region, major malls and strip plazas dot the landscape.

However, there has been controversy surrounding shopping as well, most notably concerning the proposed Market Place at Fifth and Forbes Avenues. This issue has been in the news so much that headline writers merely write "Fifth/Forbes" and everyone knows what it means.

Essentially, Mayor Tom Murphy has pushed for development of a historic but slightly run-down retail corridor in downtown Pittsburgh. Chicago-based Urban Retail Properties planned to transform this space into an 18-hour mecca of upscale shops, restaurants, and movie theaters. The plan collapsed in 2000 under pressure from preservationist groups and local residents and retailers, who feared that the project would destroy the charm and character of Downtown. A new Philadelphia-based consulting firm, Kravco, presented the mayor's office with its three-phase development plan in July of 2003. Kravco plans to take an approach that is more respectful of existing buildings and their tenants. Well, we can't solve the ongoing debate here, but architecture aficionados can turn to the Architecture chapter to learn about preservation groups, and die-hard shoppers can merely dream that someday we may have an FAO Schwartz, Tiffany's, or Nordstrom to call our own.

For the moment, shoppers will not go through withdrawal or have to do without. Whether it's window-shopping or stockpiling for the next snowstorm, you're set. Peruse the following list, which we hope will help you on your way. Using this guide's normal geographic breakdown for the most part, this chapter is also broken into other sections, beginning with places where you can boost the Downtown economy, then focusing on shopping within the city limits before heading out to the suburbs. In addition, particular types of stores were felt to deserve their own sections within this chapter, so look for added focus on books and music, specialty merchants, consignment shops, antiques dealers and flea markets, and farmers' markets as well. Hardly comprehensive, we've tried to include the highlights such as major malls and outlets, while also steering you toward out-of-the-way shops and independent merchants you won't want to miss. Several of these entrepreneurs have stellar reputations in the region for providing only the finest.

DOWNTOWN SHOPPING

Pittsburgh is fortunate to have a rather compact central business district, defined by the banks of its rivers on each side. From Point State Park to the Mellon Arena, we call this area the Golden Triangle. Within the Triangle, there are three major department stores Pittsburghers rely upon for their shopping needs.

Kaufmann's
400 Fifth Avenue and Smithfield Street
(412) 232-2000
This is the home of the famous Kaufmann's clock, which hangs outside the store. If anyone tells you to meet them

under this famous landmark, now you'll know exactly what they mean. Inside, you'll find plenty of merchandise as it is Pittsburgh's oldest department store (in the Architecture chapter you'll read about the Kaufmann family and their legendary summer retreat). This is the original Kaufmann's, and the oldest name in Pittsburgh retailing. The store carries moderately priced to expensive merchandise including jewelry and cosmetics, men's, women's, and children's fashions, home furnishings, and housewares. You'll also find that in the downtown store, space is rented out to private vendors selling everything from a quick bite to eat to gourmet chocolate or books.

This downtown flagship store offers a parking garage across the street with a convenient skyway. Watch out for the Day & Night sales, which bring patrons mostly to the suburban locations including Beaver Valley, Ross Park, Monroeville, and Westmoreland Malls, Robinson Town Centre, Century III Mall, South Hills Village, and Shenango Valley Mall in Mercer County.

Lord & Taylor
514 Smithfield Street
(412) 261-3000
When Lord & Taylor opened here in fall 2000, it became another anchor in an upscale shopping quadrangle within the Golden Triangle, the 10-block district at the heart of downtown Pittsburgh. Controversial for remodeling a historic landmark, a classical-styled bank from the 1920s, Lord & Taylor maintained the building's facade but reconfigured the marble interior to create a 135,000-square-foot store that offers fashionable, high-end clothing and gifts. While some criticized the renovation, others praised Lord & Taylor for attempting to revitalize the downtown shopping area.

You'll find menswear on the lower level, with a separate entrance for speedy shopping; cosmetics, accessories, and shoes for women on the main floor; dresses and petite sportswear on the second floor; women's career and sportswear

on the third floor; and intimate apparel and the children's department on the fourth floor. While Lord & Taylor offers an elegant atmosphere and merchandise comparable to that at Saks, as Insiders, we're here to tell you that sales at L&T can offer merchandise at prices that beat Kaufmann's. In case you want to compare prices for yourself, it's an easy walk to the other major department stores.

Saks Fifth Avenue
513 Smithfield Street
(412) 263-4800
While much smaller than the world-famous Saks Fifth Avenue in Manhattan, this location lends a certain appeal to certain upscale clientele. It's got all the same top names in fashion and fragrance as its New York counterpart. It's within easy walking distance of the other major department stores and rounds out Pittsburgh's list of major downtown retailers. For the moment, that is.

Other Downtown Stores

Respected names in fine clothing—Brooks Brothers (600 Smithfield) and Larrimor's (Grant Street & Fifth Avenue)—have stand-alone stores Downtown.

During the city's second Renaissance, new downtown office towers and retail centers sprouted. The Shops of One Oxford Centre along Grant Street and Fourth Avenue nest inside a five-level atrium and showcase such fine fashion labels as Armani and Ralph Lauren. Hardy & Hayes, with its selection of Tiffany and Baccarat merchandise, is another anchor tenant in Oxford Centre. The White House is a store with one dominant color in clothing! Shoppers wishing to boost their economy don't even need to venture outdoors for there is a skywalk that connects Oxford Centre to covered parking and Kaufmann's.

Closer to Gateway Center at Third and Stanwix sits PPG Place, an architectural jewel that includes specialty shops, mostly

It's a taxing subject, but you will want to know that in Pennsylvania, most clothing is not subject to the state's 6 percent sales tax. Within Allegheny County, the sales tax levied is 7 percent.

with interesting cards and gifts. Just blocks away, Fifth Avenue Place Arcade Shops (at Fifth & Liberty Avenues) features two floors of boutiques, fashionable shops, and gift merchants.

Other finds within the Golden Triangle include Warner Centre, a retail arcade fashioned out of a former movie palace along Fifth Avenue; Burlington Coat Factory, at Sixth and Smithfield; and several jewelry stores making up what is known as the diamond district right around the Clark Building along Liberty Avenue.

SHOPPING DISTRICTS ON THE OUTSKIRTS

While not within the Golden Triangle, many other areas boast wonderful shopping. Several are within city limits.

East

South Craig Street Shopping
Oakland section of Pittsburgh
In the heart of Pittsburgh's education and health-care community, you'll find one-of-a-kind gifts and other worldly surprises. Among the local merchants are Caliban Book Shop, (412) 681-9111, for books of the scholarly variety; the Irish Design Center (412) 682-6125, filled with such Irish imports as sweaters, fashionable woolens, and decorative household items.

Shadyside Shopping
Along Walnut Street and Aiken Street as well as Ellsworth Avenue
Not far off Fifth Avenue, heading east is the fashionable Walnut Street of Shadyside. This community is known for cafes,

restaurants, retail chain stores, and local specialty shops and galleries. The best finds may be at the independent establishments such as Clay Place, (412) 682-3737, with sculptures and ceramics; Glassworks, (412) 682-5443, boasting names such as Baccarat, Lalique, and Swarovski; and Feathers, (412) 621-4700, which as the name implies is filled (literally!) with comforters, quilts, and pillows. You can read about S.W. Randall Toyes & Giftes in the Kidstuff chapter and review the Specialty Shops section below for Journeys of Life information.

Squirrel Hill Shopping District
Forbes and Murray Avenues
Searching for perhaps the best homemade bagels in Pittsburgh? In the heart of Pittsburgh's Jewish community, you won't want to miss Bageland, (412) 521-1067. Other favorites include Linton's, (412) 421-9700, for women's designer clothing and bridal selections and Little's Shoe Store, (412) 421-3530, which is actually big! That's right, no matter whose feet you intend to fit into the shoes, you should be able to find a pair here. And after a day of heavy duty shopping, why not walk to Barnes & Noble (see Books & Music below) for some coffee in the cafe and a relaxing book.

Strip District
Several blocks from Downtown at 11th Street to 33rd Street
Named for the strip of flat land that runs from the edge of downtown to the beginning of Lawrenceville, one thing is for sure: People come to the Strip for the hectic atmosphere, novel merchandise, and above all else, great food! As stated in other chapters, the Strip is very decent!

Gourmet delights abound, with everything from authentic Mexican ingredients at Reyna Foods, (412) 261-2606, to the wonderful seafood selection at Robert Wholey & Co. (412) 261-3693, and Benkovitz Seafoods, (412) 263-3016.

Looking for Italian bread, buckets of fresh olives, imported cheeses, and a variety of pastas? Head to the Pennsylvania Macaroni Co., (412) 471–8330, Jimmy & Nino Sunseri Co., (412) 255–1100, or Stamoolis Brothers, (412) 471–7676.

While it's true that you'll breathe in a new aroma on virtually every corner of the Strip, there are a few other nonedible finds in this trendy shopping district. Known for its noise-activated toys and wacky gadgets, the Mike Feinberg Co., (412) 471–2922, supplies everything from partyware and gifts to Pittsburgh sports team merchandise. Come Halloween, look your spookiest with the help of Costume World, (412) 281–3277.

Sidewalk vendors in the Strip peddle everything from T-shirts to compact discs and cassette tapes. And you will not go hungry while you shop. Sidewalk grills offer barbeque ribs, chicken, and pork, Chinese specialties, as well as hot dogs and hamburgers. Stop in at a coffee shop or bakery for a cup of fresh brew, and a freshly baked pastry or biscotti. It's all here—dozens of stores to tempt your palate and pocketbook—in Pittsburgh's Strip District.

South

The Shops at Station Square
Across the Smithfield Street Bridge
at Carson Street
(412) 261–9911
www.stationsquare.com

Imagine an old railroad station with its freight house and passenger operations. That hurried exchange of merchandise between boxcars and wagons is somewhat replicated today as savvy shoppers dart in and out of the chic stores comprising the Shops at Station Square.

Since the 1970s when the Pittsburgh History & Landmarks Foundation launched a site study and plan for a retail complex, the Shops at Station Square have brought distinction to this section of the South Side.

Today this indoor mall boasts restaurants and maybe one or two chain retailers, but mostly purely Pittsburgh establishments. S.W. Randall Toyes & Giftes carries the obvious. St. Brendan's Crossing features Celtic charm with fisherman's knit sweaters, woolens, and wraps. And the Landmarks Store is the place to go for books about Pittsburgh as well as a few unique souvenir items.

Shoppers who want charming boutiques and off-the-beaten-path stores that focus on Pittsburgh's diverse ethnic heritage come to Station Square. Parking and restaurants are nearby, as is the Monongahela Incline, taking visitors or commuters to the heights of Mt. Washington. The "T" light-rail station is also a permanent fixture. Indeed, many downtown shoppers park at Station Square and ride the "T" across the river.

The Waterfront
300 Waterfront Drive, West Homestead
(800) 366–0093

The Waterfront is Pittsburgh's newest shopping and entertainment development—and also its biggest, occupying more than 260 acres. It's been attracting crowds since it opened. On the site of the former Homestead steel mills, this complex features a mix of stores, from Filene's Basement to Barnes & Nobles to Abercrombie and Fitch, a Loew's Cineplex, and restaurants in every price range. There's even a village square surrounded by upscale shops. Take the Homestead Hi-Level Bridge over the Monongahela River. The huge brick chimneys to the right mark the spot, and there's plenty of free parking.

SUBURBAN MALLS

East

Westmoreland Mall
Route 30 East, Greensburg
(724) 836–5025

Anchor tenants here include Kaufmann's, JC Penney, Sears, and the Bon-Ton. In terms of size, Westmoreland ranks second

in the region. You'll find the usual stores here, and a few unique ones, including the Disney Store, Victoria's Secret, Limited and Limited II, Champs, and Old Navy. The Waldenbooks is a large-format store. Gloria Jean's coffee stand is a fixture in the food court. Built in the late '70s, Westmoreland Mall was refurbished in the mid-'90s, taking on a thoroughly modern look.

Monroeville Mall
Monroeville Mall Boulevard
off Route 22, Monroeville
(412) 243-8511

Built in 1969, this was one of the region's first major malls. In addition to large department stores such as Kaufmann's, Lazarus, and JC Penney, Monroeville Mall boasts the usual regimen of franchises and national chains, including Victoria's Secret, the Disney Store, Payless Shoes, Lechter's, Lerners New York, Warner Brothers Studio Store, Kay's Jewelers, and more. Behind the mall itself sits the Monroeville Mall Annex with Burlington Coat Factory, Office Max, Dick's Sporting Goods, and other merchants. The food court and full-service restaurants keep you well fed. There's the Playground Day Care Center for the kids, valet parking, and stroller rentals available.

South

Century III Mall
Route 51, Clairton Road, West Mifflin
(412) 653-1220

The largest mall in the region (in terms of square footage), Century III boasts anchor department stores Kaufmann's, JC Penney, and Sears, in addition to specialty retailers Old Navy and Wickes Furniture as well as nearly 200 other stores and services. National chains such as American Eagle Outfitters, Gap and Gap Kids, Lerners New York, and Motherhood Maternity, Parade of Shoes, and Fredericks of Hollywood are offered here. In past years, shoppers have been rewarded with the

Mallperks program as they earn points toward huge discounts on travel, entertainment, and merchandise. A food court and full-service restaurants are available.

Washington Crown Center
(formerly the Franklin Mall)
1500 West Chestnut Street, Washington
(724) 228-4270

Anchor tenants at this Washington County mall include Kaufmann's, Sears, and the Bon-Ton (a smaller regional department store). Banks, jewelers, and shoe stores are found here in addition to names you'll recognize such as the Gap, Old Navy, American Eagle, Victoria's Secret, and Bath & Bodyworks. There is a small food court on the premises. Customer services include stroller rental and wheelchair loans, shopping bags, and senior citizen discount cards.

The Galleria
1500 Washington Road, Mt. Lebanon
(412) 561-4000

Opened in 1989, this upscale mall property boasts some national chains and other retailers that operate solely at this location in Pittsburgh. Enclosed parking for inclement weather is one perk at the Galleria. Shops include Godiva Chocolatier, Sox Appeal, Restoration Hardware, Williams-Sonoma, Talbots, and Ann Taylor. The London Grille is one of the restaurants within the complex.

South Hills Village
Route 19 and Fort Couch Road
Bethel Park
(412) 831-2900

Built in 1965, and revamped in 1993, South Hills Village is a fixture in the South Hills communities of Bethel Park, Mt. Lebanon, and Upper St. Clair. Kaufmann's, Lazarus, and Sears department stores anchor this mall, with the usual national chains and franchises such as Banana Republic, Brookstone, Elizabeth, Eddie Bauer, Discovery Channel Store, Museum Company Store, Natural Wonders, and the Disney

Store. In recent years, strip malls and other merchants have taken up camp nearby.

Washington Mall
301 Oak Spring Road, Washington
(724) 222-7390

Outside of JC Penney, there are no major department stores here. However, the mall has a Toys R Us and Home Depot outside the main building as well as several banks, barbers and hair salons, a general store, and local Victorian gift boutique and ladies apparel store called Lang's.

West

Airmall
Pittsburgh International Airport
(800) ITS-FAIR
www.airmall.com

If you arrive at the airport early for your flight, you might want to consider carrying more than your suitcase on your next trip. Try a shopping agenda and credit cards! That's right, the Airmall makes it possible to shop for much more than last-minute souvenirs. In fact, Pittsburgh International consistently scores as one of the nation's leading airports based upon the stellar shopping alone.

BAA Pittsburgh oversees the airport shopping mall, and one rule for retailers here is that prices are guaranteed to be the same as they are at local malls. And while you will find some familiar names here (Eckerd Drugs, the Body Shop, and Victoria's Secret), you'll also find such niche stores as Waterstone's Booksellers, the Discovery Channel Store, Perfumania, Tie Rack, and the PGA Tour Shop. Most shops require going through security checks to the airside building, although a handful of merchants are located landside. Food court vendors as well as sit-down restaurants are available, and there is Kidsport if the youngsters need to play a spell. (See the Getting Here, Getting Around chapter for more details on the airport.)

General Nutrition Center (GNC), located in many malls throughout the country, was founded in Pittsburgh in 1935 as a health-food store. Back then, the main product was yogurt. Today, GNC stocks a variety of vitamins, health foods, and natural products.

The Mall at Robinson
100 Robinson Centre Drive
Robinson Township
(412) 788-0816
www.shoprobinsonmall.com

Located off Parkway West between the airport and downtown Pittsburgh, opposite the Pointe at North Fayette and behind Robinson Town Centre, The Mall at Robinson is the most recent addition to this rapidly growing shopping district. The two-story enclosed mall is anchored by Kaufmann's, Sears, JC Penney, and Dick's Sporting Goods and contains more than 100 shops and a food court with large TV screens that just can't be ignored.

Robinson Town Centre
Park Manor Boulevard
Robinson Township
(412) 391-7887

An outdoor strip mall with some free-standing stores and buildings, this complex just keeps on growing. Kaufmann's Department Store is the most significant recent addition. Ikea (see Specialty Stores in this chapter) is an anchor retailer along with Dick's, Marshalls, and T.J. Maxx. Family Bookstores have a location here, along with Pier 1 Imports and many other chains.

The Pointe at North Fayette
Summit Park Drive at Quinn Drive
North Fayette Township
(412) 394-4355

Directly across from Robinson Town Centre on the other side of the Parkway West sits the Pointe, which looks a little like a strip mall but is almost more of a shopping district because its buildings are not connected in many locations. Don't miss

Barnes & Noble, Home Place, Sam's Club, Wal-Mart, Home Depot, Half-Price Books, Petsmart, and many other major retailers. You won't go hungry either. Turn to the Restaurants chapter for more detail on dining options here. To get to the Pointe, take the bridge from Robinson Town Centre, or if you're coming from the airport on Interstate 279, exit at Montour Run. You'll find Summit Park Drive about a half-mile up the road on your left.

Parkway Center Mall
Parkway Center Mall Drive, Green Tree
(412) 922-1741
Just off the Parkway West and having its own exit, Parkway Center Mall offers shopping to local residents. Don't expect to find major department stores. There's merely a Kmart, Syms, Phar-Mor, Comp USA, and Giant Eagle. But there are also a few smaller chains.

Beaver Valley Mall
380 Beaver Valley Mall, Monaca
(724) 774-5573
Beaver County's major shopping locale, this mall has all the major department stores in the region—Lazarus, Kaufmann's, Sears, and JC Penney. In addition, you'll find the typical mall stores such as Lerners New York, Victoria's Secret, the Disney Store, and Waldenbooks, a convenient food court, and two sit-down restaurants—Chi Chi's and Humphrey's.

North

Ross Park Mall
1000 Ross Park Mall Drive
Ross Township
(412) 369-4400
Nestled in the North Hills, Ross Park Mall includes a collection of major department stores such as Kaufmann's, Lazarus, JC Penney, and Sears. Here you'll find all the other stores you've grown accustomed to in mall locations such as Ann Taylor, Casual Corner, Baby Gap and Gap Kids,

Lane Bryant, Talbot Kids, Victoria's Secret, and the Disney Store. Ross Park Mall was built in 1986.

The Waterworks Mall
Freeport Road, O'Hara Township
(412) 784-1537
This outdoor strip mall is located in the Fox Chapel Area with the usual merchants you would find at most indoor locations such as Lechter's, Dress Barn, Toy Kingdom, Old Navy, and Famous Footwear. No major department stores have branches here except for discounters Marshall's, T.J. Maxx, and Dunham Sports. However, you will find gourmet groceries within the Giant Eagle supermarket, as well as musical selections in the Barnes & Noble.

Clearview Mall
101 Clearview Circle, Butler
(724) 285-5722
Anchor tenants include JC Penney, Sears, the Bon-Ton, and Boscov's. Typical mall outlets and chain stores such as Zale's and King's jewelry stores, Casual Corner, Bath & Bodyworks, American Eagle, and Lerner New York also make their home in the Clearview Mall. There is a food court, as well as plenty of restaurants and eateries within the complex and along the mall periphery.

BOOKS & MUSIC

Downtown

Barnes & Noble Booksellers
339 Sixth Avenue
(412) 642-4324
A frequent lunchtime hangout for the working crowd, this Barnes & Noble location also offers a handy selection of computer software. As with all Barnes & Noble stores in the area, there is a Starbucks coffee bar serving up cappuccinos, fancy desserts, and other goodies. Author events and children's story times are held regularly. Check the in-store bulletins for

dates and times. There are several Barnes & Nobles in Greater Pittsburgh. Additional locations are on Murray Avenue (Squirrel Hill), the Pointe (North Fayette, across from Robinson Town Centre), Cranberry Township, and at the Waterworks and Westmoreland (along Route 30 East). Both the Waterworks and Westmoreland locations offer music departments in addition to cafes.

Bradley's Book Attic
400 Fifth Avenue
(412) 232-9506

Browse for books here on the ninth floor of Kaufmann's Department Store. Bradley's carries a full selection of fiction, nonfiction, and children's books. The store stocks remainders and some new releases.

Eide's Entertainment
1121 Penn Avenue
(412) 261-0900

Billing itself as "the only store that matters," Eide's—to some—isn't exaggerating. Founded in 1972, Eide's quickly became Pittsburgh's first and foremost comic shop, winning *City Paper's* award for best comic-book store nine years in a row. Eide's also began hawking videos, magazines, and music, winning awards as "best record store" and "best place to buy used CDs" as well. Today this "entertainment superstore" offers alternative press and cutting-edge books and magazines.

Kirner's Catholic Bookstore
219 Fourth Avenue
(412) 261-2326

Since Kirner's carries much more than books within this family-run store, we classify this as more of a gift shop. It's been in business for more than 115 years. Merchandise includes a most extensive selection of Catholic Bibles, books, clerical apparel, first communion merchandise, and gifts for all occasions, including Christmas, Easter, weddings, baby congratulations, and confirmation.

East

Basilica Gift Shop
St. Vincent College, Latrobe
(724) 532-5060

Gifts for the soul abound here. This shop is a project of the St. Vincent Archabbey, whose 190 Benedictine monks, many of whom teach at the college, operate priories worldwide. The spiritual stock includes religious medals, prayer books and Bibles, small statuary, and artwork, as well as cookbooks and gift items.

Borders Books & Music
200 Mall Boulevard, Monroeville
(412) 374-9772

The most recent location in the Borders chain to open in Pittsburgh, the Monroeville store offers book lovers and music fans a "wall-less" concept in shopping. Unique spaces are designed for the children's area and the cafe, which includes coffee, soft drinks, pastries, salads, and desserts. The store's music department sits at the center behind the information desk. Author signings and discussions are regularly held, along with a full array of children's story times and events, as well as live entertainment in the cafe on weekends. Check the current newsletter for details. Additional Borders locations in the area are at Route 19's Norman Center (South Hills) and along McKnight Road, Ross Township (North Hills).

Caliban Books
410 South Craig Street
(412) 681-9111

A great little store with a surprisingly large number of books on hand, Caliban is one of the few local bookstores still offering used and rare first editions. In addition to poetry, fine arts, and travel, Caliban also stocks contemporary fiction. The bookstore is well situated in a lovely little shopping area near the Carnegie Museums, where you'll also find some excellent restaurants, such as Ali Baba, serving Middle Eastern fare, and Star of India.

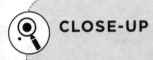

Farmers' Markets

Most communities offer farmers' markets beginning in May or June and running through the fall harvest season. Check with your municipality or borough for more details, but here's a list of a few more popular farmers' markets.

Downtown
City-County Building Farmers' Market
400 Grant Street
Friday from 10:00 A.M. to 2:00 P.M.

East
East Liberty Farmers' Cooperative Market
344 North Sheridan Avenue, Pittsburgh
Saturday from 5:00 A.M. to noon, open year-round

Greensburg Market
West Second Street, Greensburg
Thursday from 4:00 to 6:00 P.M.

Highland Park Farmers' Market
Pittsburgh Zoo parking lot
Thursday from 3:30 to 7:30 P.M.

Ligonier Country Market
Baldonieri's Mill Creek Restaurant parking lot
Saturday from 7:00 A.M. to noon

Monroeville Lions Club Farmers' Market
Gateway Campus Drive, Monroeville
Saturday from 9:00 A.M. to 12:30 P.M.

Verona Borough Farmers' Market
736 East Railroad Avenue, Verona
Thursday from 4:00 to 8:00 P.M.

South
Mt. Lebanon Farmers' Market
Washington Road and Shady Drive East
Wednesday from 4:00 P.M. until dusk

South Side Farmers' Market
South 18th Street and Carson Street
Tuesday from 3:30 to 7:30 P.M.

Washington Farmers' Market
Washington
Monday, Wednesday, Friday from 5:30 P.M. to dusk

West
Ambridge Farmers' Market
Park Road and Route 65
Thursday from 4:00 to 7:00 P.M.

Beaver Farmers' Market
Beaver County Courthouse parking lot
Saturday from 10:00 A.M. to 1:00 P.M.

North
Farmers' Market
Chestnut Street and West Diamond Street, Butler
Mondays and Wednesdays from 3:00 to 6:00 P.M.
Saturday from 7:00 A.M. to noon

North Side Farmers' Market
East Park (across from main entrance to Allegheny General Hospital at Cedar Avenue)
Friday from 3:30 to 7:30 P.M.

Chapters
195 Hillcrest Shopping Center
Lower Burrell
(724) 337-7303

Nestled in a suburban shopping center, you'll find friendly staff who help shoppers find books they love—usually a hallmark of this kind of independent bookseller. Chapters offers gift certificates and special orders for hard-to-find titles. Check to see when there might be story times for children. This store used to be a Little Professor Book Center until early in 2000.

Jay's Book Stall
3604 Fifth Avenue, Oakland
(412) 683-2644

It was at this popular independent bookstore that novelist Michael Chabon once worked part-time while he was a student at the University of Pittsburgh. Jay's offers a general selection of fiction and nonfiction, children's literature, and more.

Media Play
4100 William Penn Highway, Monroeville
(412) 374-1266

The media superstore, as it calls itself, offers 60,000 CDs and 20,000 video titles in addition to thousands of children's and adult books, toys, and interactives. In essence, Media Play is comprised of four smaller stores in one—music, video, books, and computer software/video games. Other locations within Greater Pittsburgh include Ross Park Mall and Robinson Towne Centre.

Mystery Lovers Bookshop
514 Allegheny River Boulevard
Oakmont
(412) 828-4877

The only bookstore in Pittsburgh devoted exclusively to the passion of mystery novels, Mystery Lovers Bookshop offers a warm atmosphere, knowledgeable staff, author signings, writers' group meetings, children's events, and an in-store coffee bar. Orders by phone can be placed using their toll-free number, (888) 800-6078.

The Book Center
University of Pittsburgh
(412) 648-1455

The main supplier of textbooks to University students, this store (colloquially called the Pitt Book Store) also offers a full range of consumer and trade books as well as periodicals and children's books. Merchandise such as Pitt sweatshirts, T-shirts, mugs, and other mementos are also available.

North

Cokesbury Books & Church Supplies
19015 Perry Highway, Mars
(724) 776-6150

Stocking church supplies and curriculum materials, this store also carries books and gift items merchandised to the general public. Compact discs, cassettes, videos, pictures, and greeting cards are also available.

Family Christian Stores
Morning Star Bible Bookstore
10517 Perry Highway, Wexford
(724) 935-9460

Carrying a full range of Christian Bibles, storybooks, music, gifts, and church supplies, this chain used to be known as Family Bookstores. You'll find additional locations at Robinson Town Centre, Bridgeville, West Mifflin, Monroeville, and Natrona Heights.

Record Rama Sound Archives
1130 Perry Highway
(412) 367-7330

Boasting more than three million sound recordings in stock, this is the place to browse for a day's (or several) worth of music. Compact discs, CD singles, cassettes, and more are carried here. There's a large selection of used CDs, cleaning and storage products, reference material, and phonograph needles for those of you who still spin vinyl. This store is so busy, the ad states that they do not answer the telephone on Saturdays!

Waldenbooks
Highland Mall, Natrona Heights
(724) 224-5444

There are many Waldenbooks locations throughout Western Pennsylvania. Some are larger than others. At Westmoreland Mall, for instance, there is a large-format store with a more extensive children's book and product selection. Each store offers author signings throughout the year. Additional locations at Century III Mall and South Hills Village (South Hills), Ross Park Mall (North Hills), Monroeville Mall, Waterworks Mall, Clearview and Butler Malls (Butler County), and at the Beaver Valley Mall (Beaver County).

South

FYE
477 South Hills Village, Bethel Park
(412) 835-6930

This chain of music stores can be found all around Pittsburgh with locations at Ross Park Mall, Beaver Valley Mall, and Century III Mall as well.

Sam Goody
South Hills Village, Bethel Park
(412) 831-9557

Another chain establishment for music lovers, you'll also find two stores downtown (at Warner Centre and Fifth Avenue Place). Additional locations are at Forbes Avenue, Oakland, Beaver Valley Mall, and Westmoreland Mall.

West

Coconuts Music
1990 Park Manor Drive
(412) 788-0223

Located at Robinson Town Centre, this is the only Coconuts store locally, and perhaps one of the largest music stores around. Coconuts carries the latest in compact discs, cassettes, and music accessories as well as videos and DVDs.

National Record Mart
Various Locations
(800) 860-8863

Known as National Record Mart or NRM Music, this chain has more than two dozen stores throughout Western Pennsylvania. By calling the toll-free number, you're sure to find a location near you carrying compact discs, cassettes, videos, and more. Other stores within the NRM chain include Oasis, Music X, Vibes, and Waves.

Penguin Book Shop
420 Beaver Street, Sewickley
(412) 741-3838

Here's another independent bookstore of general nature. Kids can browse upstairs while adults look over the selection of fiction, nonfiction, current best sellers, and greeting cards.

SPECIALTY SHOPS

Downtown

Candy-Rama
212 Fifth Avenue
(412) 281-7350

Generations of Pittsburgh kids (and grown children!) have enjoyed discovering the plentiful selection of candy at this downtown store. Indeed, it's a favorite stop during the lunch hour or on virtually any shopping trip to the city. Candy-Rama has an additional location at 264 Fifth Avenue, and you can stop by its warehouse at 3340 Smallman Street in the Strip District.

Curtain Call
Penn Avenue and Sixth Street
(412) 392-3313

Stop by this coffee bar and retail store run by the Pittsburgh Symphony—a perfect complement to the Cultural District according to many arts patrons. In this 2,100-square-foot space, you'll find CDs, books, jewelry, and symphony-related merchandise. Demonstrations and lectures are offered occasionally so call for more information.

Bailey Banks & Biddle Jewelers
One Mellon Bank Center
(412) 391-4440

You'll find this store in the lower lobby of One Mellon Bank Center along Grant Street, Downtown. This leading jeweler offers the finest in jewelry, better watches, corporate gifts, and giftware, including crystal and porcelain pieces. Clients come here for custom design work and repairs. With 29 windows, it's a great place to window-shop as well! Look for additional locations at South Hills Village and Ross Park Mall.

Honus Wagner Co.
320 Forbes Avenue
(412) 471-3045

Sports fanatics will flock to this store named for one of the greatest Pirate players ever, since many sporting goods and apparel items are stocked here. This includes athletic shoes, team merchandise, brand-name athletic workout suits, coats, shorts and shirts, footballs, baseballs and gloves, tennis, racquetball and squash racquets, and golf accessories. Really, anything that's sports-related and small is available here. Because of its downtown location, Honus Wagner Co. doesn't stock golf clubs and other large items. But with almost 75 years in business, it's a store to check out.

J.R. Weldin Co.
413 Wood Street
(412) 281-0123

A favorite stationer and travel supply store, you'll find the usual office supplies that most businesses and professionals need. But here, you'll also discover wonderful gifts for the career-minded, including fine pens, stationery, desk accessories, and much more. There's a bountiful selection of greeting cards and unusual gifts that you typically don't find elsewhere.

Mon Aimee Chocolate
2101 Penn Avenue
(412) 395-0022

A chocoholic's fantasy, this boutique store in the Strip specializes in candies from

Drive toward New Wilmington from the Prime Outlets (along Route 208) and you can't miss the Volant Mill, a major tourist stop and shop! Built in 1812, it operated as a grist mill and flour mill until 1963. Today it sits across the street from the minimall of refurbished train shops.

more than 20 countries. Sample treats from the nostalgia section and, of course, try their chocolates from around the world—mmmm!

Pennsylvania Culinary Institute
717 Liberty Avenue
(412) 566-2433

Gourmet cooks head for the retail store at Pennsylvania Culinary School in the Clark Building, Downtown. You'll find cookbooks (why of course!), textbooks, small wares, cutlery, chef wear, and other culinary products. And if they don't have what you want in stock, they'll be happy to locate it for you.

East

A Pleasant Present
2301 Murray Avenue
(412) 421-7104
www.apleasantpresent.com

A Pleasant Present is a card and gift store with, as its tag line asserts, something "for every taste, every budget, and for everyone." With that, the store appeals to both a general market and a niche gay and lesbian one, carrying specialty items that rarely can be found elsewhere in Pittsburgh. A Pleasant Present also carries tickets to local events, so it's a good place to find out what's going on in Pittsburgh and get involved.

Plus, you'll simply have a good time looking around here, starting even before you step inside—soap "champagne" bubbles drift from the store's entrance down

the street. They still make me smile every time I drive or stop by.

In addition the store has quite a good reputation for its specialty gift baskets, serving many corporate clients. And the friendly owner, who designs most of them, also works with a party planner to create gift bags for out-of-town guests, as well as balloon greetings.

Basket Styles
901 Elizabeth Street, Churchhill
(412) 351-2742

No request is too big or small for a custom-made gift basket for personal celebrations or corporate gift giving. Baskets created for the usual occasions of holidays, new babies, weddings, birthdays, and Valentine's Day. Nontraditional baskets include new promotion, comfort, and the ever-popular Pittsburgh baskets. Owner Pamela Price will arrange personal delivery to area hospitals or ship worldwide. Corporate accounts can be established, and credit-card orders are also accepted by phone.

Delallo Italian Market Place
Route 30, Jeannette
(724) 523-5000

Since 1950 this family name has supplied its own brand of pastas, peppers, tomato sauce, oils, and vinegar to Pittsburgh-area supermarkets. In Jeannette, you can visit the large Italian market where the complete selection of Delallo products is stocked on the shelves. In addition, you'll find an extensive counter of ready-made foods (both hot and cold entrees and salads), fresh breads, candies, and Italian supplies.

Journeys of Life
810 Bellefonte Street, Shadyside
(412) 681-8755

You'll find New Age gifts that are hard to come by—things such as feng shui cures, handcrafted meditation fountains, candles, and aromatherapy products—on the store's first floor. Upstairs, discover a selection of wonderful books for kids and adults, many with creative and alternative spiritual themes. Lots of 12-step recovery books and materials are found here as well.

Phantom of the Attic
3766 William Penn Highway
Route 22, Monroeville
(412) 856-4403

There aren't many stores specializing in comic books, magic cards, and collectible cards. But you'll find those items here.

Pittsburgh Center for the Arts Shops
6300 Fifth Avenue
(412) 361-0873

The Pittsburgh Center for the Arts Shops feature original and handcrafted jewelry, ceramics, paintings, prints, glassware, and more. You'll find this location at Fifth & Shady Avenues in Shadyside. Galleries and shops are open Monday through Saturday, from 10:00 A.M. to 5:30 P.M. and on Sunday from noon to 5:00 P.M. The store is accessible for those with physical challenges. In prior years there were other suburban locations, but all operations and sales have been consolidated into this location.

Rolling Rock Gift Shop & Visitor's Center
Behind the brewery on Ligonier Street
Latrobe
(724) 539-3394

Operated by the Latrobe Brewing Company, this gift shop offers sweatshirts with different logos as well as glassware, gift items, baseball caps, can coolers, jackets, and golf shirts. No beer is for sale here because of the state liquor laws, but there is a beer distributor about 2 blocks up the road. It's open Monday through Friday from 9:00 A.M. until 5:00 P.M., and on Saturday it closes at 3:00 P.M.

The Toy Box
108 South Market Street, Ligonier
(724) 238-6233

Quality toys, games, and puzzles for children of all ages are found here. Phone orders are welcome as well. Popular brand names include Avanti, Brio, Bburago, Erector, Folkmanis, Playmobile, Steiff, and Tucker Jones.

Willi's Ski Shop
3838 William Penn Highway
Route 22, Monroeville
(412) 856-1230
www.skiandboard.net
Complete ski furnishings including clothing and equipment in addition to snowboarding and tennis accessories. Additional locations are at Seven Springs Ski Resort, in the North Hills and South Hills.

West

The Country Mercantile
220 Route 30, Imperial
(412) 695-7251
Country crafts fill the shelves of this quaint little store in rural Imperial, not far from Pittsburgh International Airport and just minutes from Robinson Town Centre. Fresh ground coffees, unique teas, candles, crafts, bears, baby items, and other gift suggestions stock the store. Visitors who sign the guest register are invited to special open houses held throughout the year for refreshments and an advance peek at new holiday-themed merchandise.

Ikea
2001 Park Manor Boulevard
Robinson Town Centre
(412) 747-0747
The only store of its kind in the Pittsburgh region, this Swedish furniture and home furnishings retailer offers a thoroughly modern and well-stocked showroom, cafeteria-style restaurant and cafe areas, and a supervised ballroom for young children, as well as convenient self-service and efficient checkout. Known for its inventiveness and thriftiness, the Ikea concept will be kind on your budget. Most components are easy to assemble, but it's best to take your measurements carefully before coming to the store. Design specialists are on hand to assist you. Ikea is open every day except Thanksgiving, Christmas, and Easter Sunday.

The Open Mind
439 Beaver Street, Sewickley
(412) 741-1888
New Age, spirituality, self-help, and recovery books stock the shelves along with a limited children's selection. Gift items include jewelry, incense, candles, bath salts, greeting cards, music, and video. Call to find out when you might catch appearances by a massage therapist, palm reader, or psychic.

Volkwein's Music
138 Industry Drive, RIDC Park West
(412) 788-5900
www.volkweins.com
Anyone who is serious about music in Pittsburgh knows Volkwein's for its fine reputation selling musical instruments, band and orchestra accessories, and sheet music. Private instruction, voice lessons, and instrument rentals are also available. Phone orders are welcome.

North

Carlisle's
409 East Ohio Street
(412) 321-2421
www.bridalwear.com
Carlisle's is truly a Pittsburgh wedding tradition, offering only the finest in bridal gowns and fashions for bridesmaids and mothers. You'll find names such as Vera Wang and Janell Berté on the racks. Carlisle's has been serving Pittsburgh since 1888. Carlisle's is conveniently located on the North Side, just off I-279 North. Many shop here for formal wear for other occasions as there is also an adjacent tuxedo shop.

Duncan Comic Books and Accessories
1047 Perry Highway
(412) 635-0886
Find more than just comic books here, for there are toys, gifts, and cards to choose form as well as a large selection of action

CLOSE-UP

Pittsburgh Products

Pittsburgh Pride extends to gift giving. No matter if you're a sports fan, beer connoisseur, Christmas collector, or card player, there's a Pittsburgh product for you or your loved one. Here's a sampling of some of the most popular and useful items we've found:

- Couch potatoes will want to curl up with nearly 20 different videos produced by WQED/Pittsburgh. From Frank Lloyd Wright's *House on the Waterfall* or *Kennywood Memories* to *The Strip Show* or *Pittsburgh's Greatest Sport Heroes,* each video costs $19.95 plus tax. These are available at WQED Store of Knowledge locations or by calling (800) 274-1307 or (412) 622-1307.

- Hometown Treasures reproduces local landmarks such as the Allegheny County Courthouse in ceramic. Perfect for your Christmas train displays, these reproductions are available at The Landmarks Store in Station Square or can be ordered by phone at (412) 765-1042.

- A made-to-order basket from The Brewery Store pretty much proves that Iron City Beer is indeed "a 'Burgh thing." Place a gift basket order by calling (412) 692-1114.

- Pittsburgh playing cards and Pittsburghese mugs from ABEL Express will give your next bridge or card club gathering something to talk about. Showroom visits are by appointment only, but you can order by phone at (412) 279-0672.

- Afraid of getting lost? *Finding Yourself in Pittsburgh* ($5.95) is a colorful

figures. You'll also find a plentiful array of used books to browse through.

New Dimension Comics
20550 Route 19, Mars
(724) 776-0433
Located in Cranberry Township, New Dimension stocks more than 60,000 back issues of comic books, and a 40-foot wall of new releases. This is the place to browse for collectible card games, too. Your children will also delight in the action figures.

Wendell August Gift Shoppe & Forge
620 Madison Avenue, Grove City
(724) 458-8360
Allow some time for a tour of the Wendell August Forge in Mercer County, established in 1923 in Brockway and moved to Grove City in 1932. Signs are well-placed along major routes into town. It's one of the few remaining forges in the country that continue to produce forged aluminum, pewter, bronze, sterling, and silver articles entirely by hand, using no production machinery.

The showroom houses a historical collection of artifacts and a complete line of giftware that has been commissioned by corporate executives, leading companies, and even the U.S. Congress. Visitors witness the artisans hammering and chiseling artforms as part of the free, self-guided tours available Monday through Saturday.

series of maps to help you navigate across Pittsburgh's bridges and boulevards. Published by Informing Design, this map is carried in many local bookstores.

- And while you're buying books, don't forget to read *Mario Lemieux: Final Period* (Triumph Books), the inspirational story told mostly through pictures of how this shy Canadian teenager overcame battles on and off the ice to become one of hockey's all-time greats.

- Job seekers will appreciate the professional contacts found in *The Pittsburgh Job Source,* a book published by Benjamin Scott Publishing. This resource retails at $16.95 and is in most major bookstores. Adams Media publishes the *Pittsburgh Job Bank 2000,* which retails for $16.95.

- Learn all about Pittsburgh's history by reading *Pittsburgh: Story of an American City* by Stefan Lorant. It sells for $39.95 at area bookstores.

- Sacred Heart Elementary School has published a cookbook from historic Pittsburgh. It's called *The Heart of Pittsburgh* ($17.95). Call (412) 441-1582.

- *Pittsburgh For Kids: A Guidebook and Directory for Grown-ups and Kids* is published by the McEwan School. Copies are sold in local bookstores as well as through mail order. Call (412) 361-7559.

- Kids and their grownups will enjoy buying up prime real estate such as Station Square, The Benedum, or Isaly's as they play the "Pittsburgh In A Box" board game ($24.95), produced by Late for the Sky Production Company. Find it in specialty gift shops or Kaufmann's, especially around the holidays.

Do call before making the trip to make sure that the forge and/or showroom is open, since it's a bit of a drive from some communities in our coverage area.

South

Gram & Gramps
1720 Washington Road, Bethel Park
(412) 831-4726
Not only will you find a great selection of top-quality toys (including Brio, Thomas, and Playmobile), but you'll also be able to outfit the kids in this all-in-one store. Named for doting grandparents, it's probably appropriate. While prices on the toy merchandise are competitive, the clothing lines are a little upscale. But then, grandparents want only the best!

McGinnis Sisters Specialty Foods
3825 Saw Mill Run Boulevard
Route 51, Brentwood
(412) 882-6400
If you're in the market for supreme cuts of meat, plentiful produce, fresh fish, gourmet cheeses, and ready-made pasta salads, McGinnis Sisters is the place to go. With one other location at 4311 Northern Pike, Monroeville, the McGinnis Sisters stores host occasional Saturday events with samples of seasonal items. Special orders are accepted. Why not join in a

cooking class also? Find out more by calling the store near you.

Send Me No Flowers
606 Weyman Road, Whitehall
(412) 885-4888
Gift baskets that express what flowers cannot are the idea here. Choose from many selections including baskets to pamper, celebrate special occasions, comfort with chocolate or coffee, or welcome home a new baby. You can place your orders toll-free at (800) 680-3277.

The Riverside Shoppes
127 Speers Street, Lower Speers
(724) 483-2290
Situated midway between Washington and New Stanton and just two minutes off Route 70, this complex sits along a wooden walkway and cozy courtyard. In this colonial setting, you'll find 16 shops awaiting you with everything for the home, for the luxurious bathroom, for a gourmet kitchen, and much more.

CONSIGNMENT STORES

East

Music Go Round
Holiday Center, Route 22, Monroeville
(412) 856-8742
If you need musical instruments that don't cost bundles, then head here. This store is great for the parents of aspiring musicians just taking up an instrument in school. You'll find guitars, drums, clarinets, flutes, and all the other popular instruments as well as speakers, amplifiers, and accessories.

Play It Again Sports
Holiday Center, Route 22, Monroeville
(412) 372-3380
You'll find all types of used sports equipment here—everything but hunting, fishing, and archery equipment. Weights, benches, and accessories; in-line skates; hockey,

baseball, golf, tennis, exercise, croquet, volleyball, skiing, snowboarding, and lacrosse equipment fill the store. Other locations within the region are found at Edgewood Town Center, Pleasant Hills, North Hills, Cranberry (Butler County), Bridgeville, and McMurray (Washington County).

Repeats
5871 Forbes Avenue, Squirrel Hill
(412) 422-3340
This clothing shop for women carries better sportswear, formal wear, suits and dresses, and accessories such as shoes, purses, some jewelry, and hats. Name brands such as Armani and Liz Claiborne are common. You'll find extended Thursday hours but the store is closed Sunday.

Second Chance Resale Shop
500 Garden City Drive, Monroeville
(412) 372-4308
Established in 1985, this shop offers only the finest in family clothing in all sizes as well as select, small household items. Designer labels in women's fashions are sought after and displayed the most.

South

Yesterday's Best
141 Main Street, New Eagle
(724) 258-8112
Here in Washington County, this old house is full of everything on consignment that's related to the home. Dishes, pots and pans, linens, furniture, and antiques are here, but no clothing.

West

Second Hand Rose
411 Walnut Street, Sewickley
(412) 741-5909
Men's, women's, and children's gently worn apparel is found here, along with accessories, ties, shoes, and hats. Some

designer labels are available, as well as selected formal wear, suits, and dresses.

North

Kids' Consignment III
3463 Babcock Boulevard
(412) 364-7282
This store carries gently used children's items including baby through childhood clothing, cribs and furniture, sports equipment, toys, accessories, and books.

Once Upon A Child
10648 Perry Highway, Wexford
(412) 933-1660

3747 William Penn Highway, Monroeville
(412) 374-9932
www.ouac.com
Outfit the kids for less here at Once Upon A Child. Not only will you find play and dressy clothing for the kids, but a selection of quality used toys and children's furnishings. Strollers, portable cribs, and potties prevail too. The Monroeville location is in Holiday Center Shopping Plaza (near Phar-Mor).

OUTLET SHOPPING

North

Prime Outlets at Grove City
Interstate 79 at the Grove City/
New Wilmington exit
(888) 545-7221
In 1994, the Grove City Factory Shops, smack between the towns of New Wilmington and Grove City, put this region in the news as savvy shoppers combed racks and roamed aisles of outlets in search of the ultimate bargain. Now the complex is called the Prime Outlets. With the fourth phase completed, the shops now include 533,000 square feet—a virtual shopper's mecca. The more than 130 stores here include Ann Taylor, Liz Clai-

Thrift stores such as Goodwill, Salvation Army, and St. Vincent De Paul stores are plentiful throughout the region. Turn to your Yellow Pages directory for a complete listing, for there are dozens to choose from.

borne, Calvin Klein, Eddie Bauer, London Fog, and many other popular retailers.

From downtown Pittsburgh, count on at least an hour's drive (perhaps less from northern suburbs). Shuttle buses run daily to take shoppers around the outlets—it's *that* big. Customer services (located in the food court) include gift certificates, stroller rentals, wheelchair loans, area tourist information, coupon books, and lost and found services.

East

Horizon Outlet Center
Route 601 North, Somerset
(814) 443-3818
Just off the Pennsylvania Turnpike at Somerset lies another outlet complex that has been serving up finds for outlet shoppers for many years. Opened in April 1990, the Horizon Outlet Center is approximately one hour from Pittsburgh (less perhaps from the eastern suburbs). Retailers here include Bass Shoes, Levi's, and Van Heusen.

During the winter months these outlets may close a little early (say 6:00 P.M.) whereas they are open into the evening in the summer and busy holiday months. You'll find abbreviated hours on some holidays as well.

Lenox Factory Outlet
Route 31 East, Mt. Pleasant
(724) 547-9555
Located in Mt. Pleasant, the Lenox Factory Outlet saves you 15 to 20 percent off suggested retail prices on quality china and crystal gifts, dinnerware, stemware,

and barware. At the Lenox Factory Clearance Center, save up to 60 percent off suggested retail prices of seconds, overstocks, and discontinued and special products. The outlet is open from 10:00 A.M. to 5:00 P.M. Monday through Saturday and 12:00 to 5:00 P.M. on Sunday.

L.E. Smith Glass Company
1900 Liberty Street, Mt. Pleasant
(724) 547-3544

At L.E. Smith Glass Company, they've been crafting handmade glass for nearly a century. Using many techniques of original artisans, today's craftsmen mold, shape, heat, and cool beautiful glassware. Factory tours are available Monday through Friday from 9:00 A.M. to 2:00 P.M. The Factory Outlet & Giftware Store is open daily until 5:00 P.M. but it's closed on weekends from January through March, and on all national holidays. Don't miss the annual "Christmas in July" sale held during the first two weeks of the month.

ANTIQUES & FLEA MARKETS

East

Ages Ago Antiques
722 Allegheny River Boulevard, Verona
(412) 828-9800

Moderately priced antiques here include furniture, lamps, lace, glassware, pottery, rugs, collectibles, toys, and paintings. The

For antiquing, try the main drag in the little town of Blawnox, past Fox Chapel on Route 28 North or the "16:62 Design Zone" along Butler Street, between the 16th Street Bridge in the Strip and the 62nd Street Bridge in Lawrenceville. You'll also find numerous other sorts of shops—about 70 in the Design Zone, most of them arts-related in some way.

store is open Monday through Saturday from 10:00 A.M. to 4:30 P.M. but it's closed Sunday. In the evenings, the hours are by appointment only.

East End Galleries
600 Clyde Street
(412) 682-6331

Popular with Pittsburgh antiques lovers, East End Galleries displays paintings, objéts d'art, and furniture—genuine antiques only, not reproductions.

Hanna's Town Antiques & Collectibles Show
Between Routes 119 and 819 in Historic Hanna's Town
(724) 836-1800

Three miles north of Greensburg, in a large open field, you'll find this show and sale held several times each year. This one-day market ends up being more like a two-day event, according to those who frequent it. Technically held on Sunday, some bargains can be found throughout Saturday. Antiques and collectibles are offered as well as some yard-sale-type articles.

Mullin House Antiques
16 Mullin Avenue, Mt. Pleasant
(724) 547-4690

Specializing in antique furniture, Mullin House also offers lamps, clocks, decorative items for the home, old music boxes and musical instruments, glassware, prints, pictures, and lots more. Browse through the six rooms filled with furniture and accessories, each according to a theme.

South

Antiques Downtown
88 South Main Street, Washington
(724) 222-6800

This store carries a general line of antiques, including Duncan & Miller and other American handmade glass. They specialize in glass and china. Bring your Civil War (or any war) collector here because the shop offers swords, badges, pins, books, and other military memorabilia.

The Antiques Fair at the Meadows
Race Track Road
North Strabane Township
(724) 228-3045

Voted the best flea market by *Pittsburgh Magazine* readers, this Washington County flea market offers some 600 different dealers who put out their wares the last Sunday of each month from February through November. Better quality antiques and collectibles are featured. There are indoor as well as outdoor dealers from 8:00 A.M. to 3:00 P.M.

Trader Jacks
99 Steen Road, Kirwan Heights
(412) 257-8980

This year-round indoor and outdoor flea market usually offers lower end merchandise for true bargain hunters. The feel here is definitely more like a yard sale, but you may find some antiques and collectibles among the merchandise. Come on the weekend and holiday Mondays from 7:00 A.M. until 3:00 P.M.

Where The Toys Are
45 West Pike Street, Canonsburg
(724) 745-4599

Indeed an antiques store, this place specializes in turn-of-the-20th-century through baby-boomer–era toys, old Barbies and other dolls, trains, vehicles, action figures, TV-show and movie tie-in toys, comic characters, GI Joe and Star Wars figures, and memorabilia. This unusual store is open from 10:30 A.M. until 5:00 P.M. Thursday through Monday. Where The Toys Are is closed on Tuesday and Wednesday.

Whiskey Run Antiques Southpointe
Route 19 South, Canonsburg
(724) 745-5808

Named because of its location in the 1794 Whiskey Rebellion area, this shop sits between Pittsburgh and Washington off Interstate 79. More than 40 professional dealers offer upscale antiques, including 18th- and 19th-century country and formal furniture along with appropriate accessories such as glassware, pottery, and silver. Appraisals, clock repairs, and lamp repairs are offered as well. It's open daily from 10:00 A.M. to 5:00 P.M.

West

Leonard's Antiques & Uniques MegaMall
2586 Constitution Boulevard, Route 51
Chippewa
(724) 847-2304

More than 300 dealers in this former Kmart building offer antiques, some collectibles (though no fad merchandise such as Beanie Babies), and other higher-end items. The rule is "if you can find it selling in typical stores, you won't find it here." You'll find more attractive booths here. It's open daily from 9:00 A.M. to 8:00 P.M. except for Sunday, when it closes at 6:00 P.M. Leonard's is closed also on Christmas, Easter, and Thanksgiving.

Linder's
701 Yunker Street, McKees Rocks
(412) 771-6566

Linder's features fine art and antiques from England, Ireland, Europe, and the United States and also carries new and traditional furniture, oriental carpets, and more. If you're in the mood for upscale merchandise, come here Monday through Friday from 10:00 A.M. until 5:00 P.M. Evening hours are by appointment only. Saturday, you can shop from 10:00 A.M. to 4:00 P.M. and on Sunday browse from noon to 4:00 P.M.

The Antique Emporium
818 Seventh Avenue, Beaver Falls
(724) 847-1919

Here you'll find three floors devoted to antiques and collectibles from more than 75 quality antiques dealers. There are no

crafts and only a few reproductions. But you'll find the usual array of furniture, military wares, glass, and collectibles. Most days the store is open from 10:00 A.M. until 5:00 P.M. but there are extended Friday hours until 8:00 P.M. On Sunday, the hours run from noon to 5:00 P.M.

North

Wildwood Peddlers Fair
2330 Wildwood Road
Hampton Township
(412) 487-2200
This indoor and outdoor flea market is held weekly, featuring an eclectic mixture of brand-new items, coins, collectibles and antiques to typical yard-sale quality merchandise. It's open on Sunday from 6:00 A.M. until 4:00 P.M.

ATTRACTIONS

Sightseeing around this diverse city is more than an afternoon's entertainment or a day away from it all. Pittsburgh is particularly rich with memories of eras past, parks as pleasurable as you'll find, and culture that flourishes here.

Whether you choose to spend your leisure time learning, poking through Pittsburgh's past, exploring nature, or simply seeing the sights, opportunities abound for you throughout the entire region.

Note that the usual geographic headers are being deviated from in this chapter—most of these attractions are worth driving to, even if they're not in your immediate area. You can look forward to learning about educational venues, touring famous homes, venturing out to parks and other fun places, and browsing through some of our notable museums.

While many of the most popular attractions are situated in or near the city of Pittsburgh, and within Allegheny County, a fair number await your discovery in surrounding counties. So enjoy the listing presented here. Your fun-filled opportunities will soon transform into fond memories. And you'll keep coming back for more!

EDUCATIONAL ATTRACTIONS

The Carnegie
4400 Forbes Avenue
(412) 622-3131
www.cmoa.org
www.carnegiemuseums.org
www.clpgh.org
Culture, history, and art appreciation abound in our area because of renowned turn-of-the-20th-century Pittsburgher Andrew Carnegie, who resolved at an early age to use his phenomenal wealth for benevolent purposes. This led to the creation of Carnegie Institute, Carnegie Library, as well as the Carnegie Music Hall and Lecture Hall, the Museum of Art, and the Museum of Natural History. Today, these entities all fall under the organizational banner of the Carnegie.

Since Mr. Carnegie, who rose from working-class ranks, was committed to creating resources he could have used in his formative years, he was deeply concerned about details of architecture in the buildings that are now landmarks in the Oakland neighborhood.

Inside, pick up a visitor orientation map of the Museums of Art and Natural History. This will guide you through three floors of exhibits including the famed Dinosaur Hall (see Kidstuff), the natural history gallery, the Benedum Hall of Geology, Hillman Hall of Minerals & Gems, Walton Hall of Ancient Egypt, and the Heinz Architectural Center (see Architecture). Additional displays feature African and North American wildlife, botany, fossils, insects, amphibians, and reptiles, as well as the Wyckoff Hall of Arctic Life.

Upstairs is the permanent collection of the Scaife Galleries as well as exhibitions of limited runs. Concerts are held in the Music Hall. (See the Arts chapter.)

Before leaving the Carnegie, walk through the Hall of Sculpture, made famous as a backdrop in the movie *Flashdance*. Each holiday season, the Hall of Architecture hosts a display of beautifully decorated Christmas trees (see Festivals and Annual Events).

A coffee cart is available inside the complex, and the Museum Cafe serves meals during certain hours (see Restaurants). A brown bag lunch area is located in the basement with vending machines for sandwiches, snacks, and beverages.

Finally, Andrew Carnegie's legacy is predominantly felt through his contribution to literacy with the entire system of Carnegie Libraries, with branches through-

CLOSE-UP

Sandra Budd, Exhibit Designer

Sandra Budd is the lead exhibit designer at the Carnegie Museum of Natural History. Her challenge is to take the dense, often-groundbreaking scientific research curators provide her with and find ways to present it to the public that are as exciting as the discoveries themselves. She explains, "That's where artistic ability and creativity come into play."

Sandra holds a Masters of Fine Arts from Carnegie Mellon University (CMU) and a Bachelor of Fine Arts from the Center for Creative Studies in Detroit. Sandra's work as an artist began with painting and evolved when she was at CMU, influenced by trends in conceptual art, to a form she calls, "interactive installations." Installation art invites viewers to be participants, to climb inside, to make choices, to somehow "interact" with the work beyond the scope of standing and seeing. Ecology and habitat have long been subjects Sandra's work deals with, and so it seems a natural segue that she

is now designing exhibits at the Carnegie, where all these concerns are at the forefront. Sandra notes that the Carnegie Science Center, in the 1980s, was one of the first institutions to develop exhibits with an "interactive edge" and that now top museums are doing "a lot of computer interactive work."

Sandra's artwork is quite layered, employing found earth and consumer artifacts, as well as the juxtaposition of text and image. This, too, positions her especially well to design exhibits at the Carnegie, which as one of the most prominent and advanced museums in natural history, is on the cutting edge in terms of exhibit design, producing displays that are interdisciplinary and "layered" so that museumgoers "from five to sixty-five" can enjoy them.

Sandra's role as lead designer, she explains, is to develop the "basic concept and look of a piece." She's particularly excited about the Lewis and Clark exhibit

out the city. The main library is part of the Oakland complex, next to the Music Hall and post office. Highlights here include the Pennsylvania Room, the Foundation Center, and the Ready Reference telephone unit, as well as the general holdings of the book, video, and periodical collections.

Hours at the museum are Monday through Saturday from 10:00 A.M. to 5:00 P.M. and Sunday from noon to 5:00 P.M.

Carnegie Library is open Monday through Thursday from 10:00 A.M. to 8:00 P.M., Friday and Saturday from 10:00 A.M.

to 5:30 P.M., and Sunday from 1:00 to 5:00 P.M. Admission to the library is free of charge. Admission to the Carnegie Museum of Natural History and Museum of Art is $10.00 for adults, $7.00 for senior citizens, and $6.00 for children (ages 3 to 18). Children younger than age three and members are admitted free of charge.

Carnegie Science Center
One Allegheny Avenue
(412) 237-3400
www.carnegiesciencecenter.org

she designed. She constructed a "dramatic entrance" for the exhibit, and she carefully "pulled stuff from as many different departments as possible" to inform the exhibit. For example, along with examples of specimens Lewis and Clark collected on their journey, she used all-original illustrations from the early to mid-1800s, rather than photography. She also focused on finding "touchable" artifacts that will allow museumgoers to explore the natural world Lewis and Clark catalogued for President Jefferson. Without giving away the whole story museumgoers will find when they visit, she promises that the exhibit "pushes the envelope" of previous interdisciplinary models.

Sandra is most excited, however, about a long-lasting change the museum is making—its $15 million expansion of Dinosaur Hall by 25,000 square feet. Over a period of two to three years, the museum will be remounting and repositioning its collection, arguably one of the finest in the world, so that the dinosaurs are in poses that reflect the types of activity scientists recently have found they engaged in. For example, while once it was presumed that the large dinosaurs, such as T-Rex, dragged their tails on the ground, it seems these were actually very active appendages! On an even larger scale, the museum will be redesigning the hall to reflect the dinosaurs' "whole world." Sandra explains this is in keeping with a larger trend in scientific research now focusing around biodiversity, in which whole environments and the interdependency of the species within them are studied.

Finally, Sandra reminds visitors that they may also encounter some dinosaurs around town in Pittsburgh. Sandra spearheaded the "Dinomite Days" fund-raiser for the new hall, which augmented money from the Commonwealth of Pennsylvania, calling on artists to design sculptures of dinosaurs that would be placed locally, then auctioned off.

Along the north shore of the Ohio River is the Carnegie Science Center, recognizable because the USS *Requin* submarine moors along the banks of the river. This facility grew out of the older institution known as Buhl Planetarium. Now, it boasts not only a new planetarium and observatory, but indoor displays of science, technology, and health care as well as the miniature railroad display that's open almost year-round (see Annual Events).

Rangos Omnimax Theater film presentations, hands-on learning, and a guided tour of the submarine, commissioned during World War II, are available (see Kidstuff). The center extends its hours in the summer at times. Regular hours, Sunday through Friday 10:00 A.M. until 5:00 P.M. and Saturday 10:00 A.M. to 7:00 P.M. An Explorer Pass for adults costs $14, $10 for children.

Tickets are also sold separately for Omnimax, submarine and laser shows, and exhibits, if you prefer to see only one part of the center. For instance, to see the exhibits only, admission costs $14 for

> **i** *A total of 218 covered bridges remain standing throughout Pennsylvania. The common nickname for many of these structures was "the kissin' bridges." Well, you can probably figure out why!*

adults, and $10 for seniors (ages 65 and above) and children (ages 3 through 18). For the Omnimax theater alone, expect to pay $8.00 or $6.00. Combination ticket packages are available and prices are listed at the desk and given by telephone on the automated information line (call number given above). Senior discounts are extended on Tuesday. Purchasing a membership to the science center allows complimentary admission. Parking is free.

Nationality Rooms
157 Cathedral of Learning
University of Pittsburgh
(412) 624-6000
www.pih.edu/~natrooms
Twenty-six classrooms (and the number continues to grow) in this towering cathedral depict the city's diverse ethnic heritage through their individual architecture and decor. In the 1920s, over a quarter of Pittsburgh's population had been born abroad, and another fifth were the offspring of foreign-born parents. At Pitt, one of every three students was foreign-born or the child of immigrants.

Thus, chancellor John Baggert Bowman and others conceived of these special rooms so as not to disappoint visitors who saw the impressive structure outside. Each was funded by ethnic committees, designed by native architects, and built with materials from the countries they represent. Access to the classrooms is by tour only. Recorded tours are offered if you like. Tours are also available between 11:00 A.M. and 2:30 P.M. on most days. The Nationality Rooms are open Monday through Friday, 9:00 A.M. to 2:30 P.M., Saturday 9:30 A.M. to 2:30 P.M., and Sunday, 11:00 A.M. to 2:30 P.M. Admission rates are $3.00 for adults, $2.00 for seniors (ages

60 and older), and 50 cents for children (ages 8 to 18). Children age 7 and younger are free.

UPMC SportsWorks at Carnegie Science Center
333 Allegheny Avenue
(412) 237-3400
Fly an F-18, drive a bobsled, play ball, and do a lot more in a giant playroom that covers all the bases and lives up to its billing as the "world's largest science and sport exhibition." There are more than 40 displays and 60-plus interactive adventures in one 36,000-square-foot arena to entertain and challenge even the most timid sports fan.

SportsWorks combines the allure and mystery of virtual-reality experiences with athletic tests of physical ability—run a track race against Olympian Jackie Joyner-Kersee; tee off and test your golf power swing; design a perfect roller coaster, then take your ride; climb a 25-feet-high rock wall; ride a unicycle 15 feet off the ground; shoot basketballs in vision-distorting goggles that will challenge you with angle anxiety. Little stars, ages three to seven, can enjoy SportsWorks Jr., with its obstacle course, pitching cage, and other sized-right attractions.

Open Monday through Friday and Sunday 10:00 A.M. to 5:00 P.M.; Saturday 10:00 A.M. to 7:00 P.M. Adult tickets $14, children (ages 3 to 18) and seniors (ages 62+) $10. Free with Carnegie museum membership. Reserve overnight and birthday party events, too. Tickets subject to availability.

HISTORICAL ATTRACTIONS

Air Heritage Museum
Beaver County Airport, 15 Piper Street
Beaver Falls
(724) 843-2820
www.airheritage.org
This museum boasts a rich heritage of aviation with vintage aircraft, war planes, and aeronautical artifacts. Volunteers at this

museum work hard to make some of these old "war birds" or aircraft fly again. Some of the aircraft date from the 1920s. Visitors can shop for flying paraphernalia in the gift shop. Proceeds from the planes' appearances in air shows, movies, and commercials help to support the restoration process, as do donations from the public and gift shop sales. Here, you'll find that behind every plane is, of course, a war story to go along with it! The Air Heritage Museum is open to the public from 10:00 A.M. to 5:00 P.M. Monday through Saturday, 11:00 A.M. to 6:00 P.M. Sunday. A small donation per person is requested.

Senator John Heinz Pittsburgh Regional History Center
1212 Smallman Street
(412) 454-6000
www.pghhistory.org
Named in memory of the late U.S. Senator John Heinz, this center in the Strip District is home to the Historical Society of Western Pennsylvania and serves as a museum and depository of regional history. Four floors of exhibits tell of building a life in Western Pennsylvania from 1750 to the present. Many of the displays are interactive, informative and entertaining. A library and archives are housed on the sixth floor.

The center's first floor offers a video inside an actual trolley car, reminiscent of Pittsburgh's past. There are also famous neon signs depicting well-known merchants and companies through the years. Large staircases and elevators take you to the exhibit areas, starting with the second floor and its dramatic contrast of Pittsburgh in the pioneer days with its status today (as seen through a large screen image). A 10-minute orientation video introduces the exhibits you'll see on this floor of the permanent collection.

On the museum's third floor, children enjoy the Discovery Place (see Kidstuff). Changing exhibit galleries grace the fourth floor where past displays have included Toy Bop, Glass: Shattering Notions, and

the History of Heinz 57 (a history of the Heinz Company).

The Heinz History Center is open daily from 10:00 A.M. to 5:00 P.M. The library is open Thursday through Saturday, 10:00 A.M. until 5:00 P.M. The Center is closed Easter, Thanksgiving, Christmas, and New Year's Day. Cost for adults is $6.00, $4.50 for seniors (65 and above) and students (with ID), and $3.00 for children (ages 6 to 18). Children younger than age six are admitted at no cost.

Beaver Area Historical Museum
East End Avenue, Beaver
(724) 775-7174
www.bchistory.org/beavercounty/Beaver
CountyCommunities/Beaverfolder/
HistoryMuseum/HistoryMuseum.html
Housed in the renovated Pittsburgh and Lake Erie Railroad freight station, this museum tells the story of Beaver County. Residents and visitors alike will enjoy the collection of artifacts and information about life in years past. Some of the exhibits include a Revolutionary War uniform and equipment, Civil War weaponry, archaeological specimens from area digs, and examples of local pottery. Publications and gifts are features in the museum shop. The historical attraction is open on Wednesday and Saturday from 10:00 A.M. until 4:00 P.M. and on Sunday from 1:00 to 4:00 P.M. Admission is free of charge. Donations are welcome.

Butler County Heritage Center
119 West New Castle Street, Butler
(724) 283-8116
www.butlercountyhistoricalsociety-pa
.org/heritagecenter.html
After searching for more than 20 years for a place to archive its artifacts and memorabilia, residents of Butler County found just such a site. In 1994, the Butler County Heritage Society purchased a three-story building that opened the following year, with a 4,500-square-foot exhibit entitled "Made in Butler County," which includes an original Bantam jeep, the Bantam

Hollywood prototype convertible sports car, and displays representative of Butler industries both past and present. Metered on-street parking is available. The Heritage Center is open weekends May through October.

Pennsylvania Trolley Museum
Off Race Track Road, Washington
(724) 228-9256
(877) PA-TROLLEY
www.pa-trolley.org
South of Pittsburgh in Washington County, vintage streetcars depict transportation from another era. Home of "A Streetcar Named Desire," this museum rebuilds and restores these relics for your enjoyment. Kids especially enjoy the special events such as Santa's visit each year (see our Kidstuff and Annual Events chapters).

Allow at least two hours to completely experience the museum. Please note the museum is closed during the months of January, February, and March, but reopens on weekends in early April through December 31 from 11:00 A.M. to 5:00 P.M. It's open weekdays also, Memorial Day through Labor Day, from 10:00 A.M. to 4:00 P.M. Admission costs $6.00 for adults, $5.00 for seniors (ages 65 and older), and $3.50 for children (ages 2 to 15). Children younger than age 2 receive free admission.

Meadowcroft Museum of Rural Life
401 Meadowcroft Road, Avella
(724) 587-3412
www.meadowcroftmuseum.org
Experience life in the 19th century, as it was in Western Pennsylvania. This 200-acre living-history museum in Washington County offers lessons on rural life for the entire family (see Kidstuff). Meadowcroft introduces you to the Native Americans, frontier settlers, farmers, lumbermen, coal miners, and conservationists who have shaped rural Western Pennsylvania. You'll get to try your hands at spinning wool or attend a class in a one-room school. Included on the grounds are wooden paths, gardens, a picnic area, a gift shop, a cafe, and a modern visitor center. Meadowcroft is open Memorial Day through Labor Day Wednesday through Saturday from noon to 5:00 P.M. and on Sunday from 1:00 to 5:00 P.M. Groups of 20 or more can call for appointments. To enter, adults pay $6.50; children (ages 6 through 16), $3.50; and children younger than age 6 are admitted free of charge.

Harmony Museum
218 Mercer Street, Harmony
(724) 452-7341, (888) 821-4822
www.harmonymuseum.org
Surrounding the diamond in the village of Harmony are many of the original buildings erected by the Harmonists, immigrant German separatists in the early 1800s. Johann George Rapp was a German vinetender-turned-prophet. Several of his followers traveled with him to the New World, fleeing religious persecution and finding the freedom they could not have in their European homeland. Rapp purchased acreage in Western Pennsylvania. Their religious fervor prospered, until in 1807, they adopted celibacy, a step toward the ultimate extinction of the group. Subsequently, the Mennonites settled here from 1815 through much of the 19th century.

The Harmony Museum, including the Wagner House and Ziegler log house, as well as the Harmonist cemetery, Father Rapp's hillside seat, and the Mennonite meetinghouse and cemetery, are under the direction of Historic Harmony. Appointments are recommended for the weekends. Tours are given Tuesday through Sunday, 1:00 to 4:00 P.M. year-round. General admission is $3.50; seniors (ages 60 and older) pay $3.00; children (ages 6 through 12) get in for $1.50; children age 6 and younger, free of charge.

Old Economy Village
270 Sixteenth Street, Ambridge
(724) 266-4500, (724) 266-1803
www.oldeconomyvillage.org
Visit the third and final home of the Harmony Society here at Old Economy Village

in Beaver County. This National Historic Landmark is administered by the Pennsylvania Historical and Museum Commission. The Harmonists were one of America's most successful Christian communal groups. Wearing Harmonist dress, interpreters take you through the museum building, cabinet shop, community kitchen, baker house, wine cellar, store, and George and Frederick Rapp Houses, all of which were built between 1825 and 1830. Browse through four buildings and the gardens independently. Original objects owned by the Harmonists are displayed. Tours are conducted Tuesday through Saturday, 9:00 A.M. to 5:00 P.M. and Sunday noon to 5:00 P.M. If you're visiting in the fall or winter, the tours end at 2:30 P.M. Old Economy Village is closed Mondays and winter holidays and during January and February. Special holiday decorations and activities are seen at particular times throughout the year (see Annual Events). Admission costs $7.00 for adults (18 years and older), $6.00 for seniors (60 years and older), $5.00 for youths (6 years to 17 years), and no charge for those younger than 6 years old.

**Fort Necessity National Battlefield
and Braddock's Grave
One Washington Parkway, Farmington
(724) 329-5512
www.nps.gov/fone/home.htm**
Along what's called the National Road (otherwise known as Route 40), there's a little bit of history from the French & Indian War. Here, on July 3, 1754, a French and Indian force surrounded George Washington's "fort of necessity" and forced his only military surrender. Fort Necessity park grounds and visitor center are run by the National Park Service and open to the public, daily from 9:00 A.M. to 5:00 P.M. throughout the year (except for November 11, Thanksgiving, Christmas Day, January 1, Martin Luther King, Jr.'s birthday, and Washington's birthday). Besides the battlefield, don't miss other related sites, including the grave of British general Edward Braddock, a commanding officer who was mortally wounded in the war

and buried just up the road. Jumonville Glen was the site of Washington's first skirmish with the French. And the park also operates the Mount Washington Tavern, built in 1828 to serve travelers along the National Road.

Picnic facilities are available during summer months. Start at the visitor center with the audiovisual program and exhibits before moving through the grounds, where on a warm day you'll see Indians demonstrating crafts and telling the story of survival at Fort Necessity.

**Fort Ligonier
Routes 30 and 711, Ligonier
(724) 238-9701
www.fortligonier.org**
Another battle site of the French & Indian War, Fort Ligonier is located on U.S. Route 30 and Route 711 in Westmoreland County. On October 12, 1758, the British overcame a few French and only a few hundred Indian forces. The fort is open daily May 1 through October 31 from 10:00 A.M. to 4:30 P.M., Monday through Saturday and noon to 4:30 P.M. Sunday. Fort Ligonier Days occur each October (see the Annual Events chapter). Admission fees are $6.75 for adults, $3.75 for children ages 6 to 14, and $5.50 for seniors. Children younger than age 6 are admitted free of charge.

HERALDED HOMES

**Armstrong County Historical Museum
300 North McKean Street and Vine
Street, Kittanning
(724) 548-5707**
This Federal-style house was built in 1842 and added on to with a spacious wing in 1990. It was known as the McCain House before the change to its present name. Today, it's a museum offering the public seasonal exhibits, a historical and genealogical library, and an educational classroom center. It's open Wednesday noon to 4:00 P.M. During the winter months, this attraction is closed. Special tours can be arranged by appointment.

Clayton
Penn Avenue and Homewood Avenue
(412) 371-0600
www.frickart.org/home

Henry Clay Frick and his wife Adelaide purchased this as their home in Pointe Breeze in 1882. Clayton, as the house was called, was an example of the Italianate homes built following the Civil War. But the Fricks, wanting a new look, had the house remodeled, giving it steep roofs and gables. (See the Architecture chapter.)

The Fricks' daughter Helen Clay Frick inherited the home, and after she died in 1984, it was willed to the family's foundation. In 1990, Clayton opened to the public and is now part of the Frick Art & Historical Center (see the Arts chapter). There is free parking. The center is open Tuesday through Saturday, from 10:00 A.M. until 5:00 P.M. and on Sunday from noon until 6:00 P.M. Clayton is closed on Monday. Tours of Clayton cost $10.00 for adults, and $8.00 for seniors and students. Members are admitted free of charge.

Hartwood
200 Hartwood Acres
(412) 767-9200

In the northeastern suburbs of Pittsburgh lies the Hartwood estate, 629 equestrian acres with stables, gardens, and summer music and theater performances. The Tudor mansion is fully furnished with English and American antiques, and there is a gate lodge designed by Alfred Hopkins. This is the site of the special holiday lights tour (see Annual Events). Mansion tours are conducted by reservation only. Hartwood is closed January through March and major holidays, but is open April 1 through December 31. Hartwood opens its doors Wednesday through Saturday, 10:00 A.M. to 3:00 P.M. and Sunday, noon to 4:00 P.M. It's closed Monday and Tuesday. Admission costs $5.00 per adult, $3.00 for seniors (age 60 and older), $3.00 for children ages 13 to 17, $2.00 for children ages 6 to 12, and $1.00 for children age 5 and younger.

Passavant House & Buhl House
243 South Main Street and 221 South Main Street, Zelienople
(724) 452-9457
boro.zelienople.pa.us/historical_society.htm

Local history abounds in this Butler County community where these two homes have been converted to museums. Baron Dettmar Freiderich Basse, an aristocrat, invited daughter Zelie and her husband Philipp Louis Passavant to join him at the land he'd purchased in the early 1800s. The couple's five children were born in Passavant House, which dates from 1808. Their progeny continued their hardworking tradition, establishing churches, hospitals, orphanages, and schools in the area.

Son Charles married the granddaughter of Christian and Fredericka Buhl, another famous name to Western Pennsylvania, associated with the Buhl Planetarium and the former Boggs and Buhl Department Store on the city's North Side. Buhl House, built in 1805, houses a museum of the Buhl family in its 10 rooms. Contact the Zelienople Historical Society (telephone listed above) for tours. Admission includes a guided tour of both homes, with the general admission price set at $3.50 per person. Children (younger than age 18) and students cost $2.50. Children (younger than age 6) are admitted free of charge.

Rachel Carson Homestead
613 Marion Avenue, Springdale
(724) 274-5459
www.rachelcarsonhomestead.org

At the birthplace and childhood home of ecologist Rachel Carson (1907–1964), there are guided tours available to homestead visitors. Carson's 1962 best seller *Silent Spring* helped launch the environmental movement. This legendary home has seasonal hours. You'll want to call before heading there. Admission costs $4.00 for adults, $3.00 for seniors, and $2.50 for kids ages 5 to 12.

Fallingwater
Mill Run (off Route 40), Fayette County
(724) 329-8501
www.wpconline.org/fallingwaterhome.htm
Frank Lloyd Wright's spectacular house set atop a waterfall is an architectural masterpiece of the 20th century. Back in the 1930s, Pittsburgh department store owner Edgar J. Kaufmann and his wife, Liliane, commissioned Wright to design their weekend retreat at Bear Run, 90 minutes south of Pittsburgh. Tucked among the rhododendrons, the house uses cantilevers, enabling the terraces of the living and bedroom levels to extend over the rushing falls without visible support.

Now under the care of the Western Pennsylvania Conservancy, the house can be toured by visitors, but reservations are suggested. Children younger than age 6 are not permitted, but there is group baby-sitting at $2.00 per hour per child at the Visitors Pavilion. With the many stairs, considerable walking is required, so make arrangements for special assistance in advance if you feel you'll need it.

Fallingwater is closed January through February. Admission for the regular tour is $12.00 for adults, $8.00 for youth (ages 6 to 18) on weekdays, and $15.00 for adults, $10.00 for youth on weekends. In-depth tours are available at 8:30 A.M. for $40 (weekdays) or $50 (weekends). Children under the age of 9 are not allowed on in-depth tours. This famous architectural masterpiece is open March through December, Tuesday through Sunday from 10:00 A.M. to 4:00 P.M.

Kentuck Knob
Chalk Hill, Ohiopyle
(724) 329-1901
www.kentuckknob.com
High above a mountain overlooking the Youghiogheny River Gorge near Fallingwater is another of Frank Lloyd Wright's creations. Built of native stone and tidewater cypress, this house was commissioned by the I. N. Hagan family of Uniontown. Contemporary sculpture and historic artifacts enhance the secluded setting. Children younger than age 9 are not permitted (no child care provided). Though not as renowned as Fallingwater, Kentuck Knob is available for touring. Kentuck Knob is open daily, 9:00 A.M. to 4:00 P.M. In-depth tours are available at 8:30 A.M. for $50. Or take a regular tour, available on weekdays during the summer at $12 per person and $15 per person on weekends.

LeMoyne House
49 East Maiden Street, Washington
(724) 225-6740
www.wchspa.org/html/house.htm
Discover why LeMoyne House is a trail to the Civil War. This historic 1812 structure once was an abolitionist home and shelter to escaping slaves. The house is named for Dr. Francis Julius LeMoyne, who converted words into action, at great personal risk, as he sheltered escaping slaves on the Underground Railroad, established a college for African Americans, and rescued Washington College from bankruptcy. LeMoyne House is administered by the Washington County Historical Society, which makes tours available. The property is open from February through mid-December, Tuesday through Friday, 11:00 A.M. to 4:00 P.M. and Saturday by appointment. Admission is $4.00 for adults and $2.00 for students.

Linden Hall
RD 1, Dawson
(724) 529-7543, (800) 944-3238
www.lindenhallpa.com
Listed on the National Register of Historical Sites, Linden Hall Mansion and Recreation Center was built in Fayette County in 1913, with its grand view of the Laurel Highlands. Enjoy 35 rooms of the exquisite English Tudor mansion featuring signed Tiffany windows, an Aeolian pipe organ, wonderfully restored Victorian furnishings, and original paintings. In addition, there are gardens and trails for warm-weather walks. The estate offers lodging, dining, and recreation. Tours are conducted daily April through October, 11:00 A.M. to 3:00

P.M. (weekends, by reservation). Tours are available only for groups of 25 or more. If you want to visit in November and December, you may, but by appointment only. To enter, each person can expect to pay $7.00.

ON THE WILD SIDE

Idlewild Park
Route 30, Ligonier
(724) 238-3666
www.idlewild.com
Set in the Laurel Highlands of Westmoreland County, Idlewild is an amusement park where you'll want to pack for a picnic. Theme areas include Story Book Forest, Mister Rogers' Neighborhood of Make-Believe, Soak Zone, Jumpin' Jungle, Hootin' Holler, and Raccoon Lagoon. Enjoy major amusement rides in the Olde Idlewild area, and live entertainment occurring on stage. (See the Kidstuff chapter for more.) This family fun land is open from May 26 to Labor Day, but is closed every Monday in June. Adults and children pay $20.95 every day, and seniors (age 55 and older) are charged $14.50. Children age two and younger are admitted free of charge. For those who discover there is simply too much fun to explore in one day, ask about the "Next Day Pass" at guest services. There's no cost to park at Idlewild.

Kennywood Park
4800 Kennywood Boulevard
West Mifflin
(412) 461-0500
www.kennywood.com
A historic park and roller-coaster capital, Kennywood has long had a commitment to upgrading its rides and keeping its Allegheny County grounds family-friendly. (See the Kidstuff chapter.) Kennywood has brought generations of Pittsburghers lots of thrills and old-fashioned fun. Enjoy live performances, community and school picnics, ethnic pride days, and fall fantasy parades. Ride-all-day passes cost $28.95.

General admission tickets (rides not included) are available to adults for $8.00 and to seniors (ages 65 and older) for $7.00. During the last week of August, there is a Fun Finale each evening. A ride-all-evening pass costs $13.95.

Sandcastle
1000 Sandcastle Drive, West Homestead
(412) 462-6666
www.sandcastlewaterpark.com
Set along the Monongahela riverbanks in Allegheny County, this is where Pittsburgh beats the heat during the summer. That's because there are 15 twisting and turning waterslides, a gentle Lazy River to float down, several pools, and the self-proclaimed World's Largest Hot Tub for adults. The park has undergone renovations that added the 20,000-square-foot Mon-Tsunami wave pool.

Landlubbers play volleyball, snack on food, or visit the gift shops along the old-fashioned boardwalk. Oasis Miniature Golf and the exciting Formula 1 Speedway give your trip to Sandcastle added activities. The adjacent Riverplex entertainment complex boasts an amphitheater, big-top circus tent, grassy areas, and tree-lined walkways.

Sandcastle is open daily from early June through early September. Hours are 11:00 A.M. to 6:00 P.M. in June and September and 11:00 A.M. to 7:00 P.M. in July and August. A Whitewater Pass entitles you to all water attractions and costs $21.95 for adults and $16.95 for seniors. The Season Pass costs $39.95. To ride the Formula 1 Speedway, you must be at least 58 inches tall and pay $5.00. Children age 2 and younger are admitted free of charge; parking is $5.00 and boat docking is free of charge.

Whitewater Rafting
Ohiopyle
(800) 272-4141
Ohiopyle Falls in Fayette County had its name derived from the native words "Ohio pehelle" which means white frothy water.

Indeed, thousands enjoy white-water rafting in this most famous site in the Appalachians. Ohiopyle State Park has hiking and bicycle trails, picnic areas, camping, as well as cold- and warm-water fishing. During the winter months, many enjoy sledding, cross-country skiing, and snowmobile trails. White-water rafting trips are available through Wilderness Voyageurs (telephone listed above), April 1 through November 1. The reservation office is open year-round. Anyone can use the bike trail, free of charge, but it's best to call when reserving pavilions or organizing a rafting trip.

NATURE'S BEST

Pittsburgh Zoo & Aquarium
One Wild Place
(412) 665-3640, (800) 474-4966

If you feel like monkeying around, head to Highland Park, where the primates show off just for you. The elephants, zebras, and giraffes roam the African Savanna, and the Siberian tigers and snow leopards explore the Asian forest. Youngsters can enjoy Kids Kingdom (see Kidstuff) and the young elephant, born in 1999. (If you're counting on seeing the baby elephant, call ahead for the exact times.) In addition, a recent capital campaign allowed for a renovated aquarium, making the Pittsburgh Zoo one of only six zoos in the country with a major aquarium.

Did you know that the zoo is open year-round? Well, it is, and it closes only on Thanksgiving, Christmas Day, and New Year's Day. Don't miss the special evening hours during the holiday season (see the Annual Events chapter). At all other times, the zoo is open Memorial Day through Labor Day from 10:00 A.M. to 6:00 P.M. Labor Day through Memorial Day, the zoo opens at 9:00 A.M. until 5:00 P.M. Entrance gates close an hour before the park closes. Admission is as follows; Adults, $8.00; seniors, $7.00; and children (ages 2 to 13) $6.00, April through Novem-

Powdermill Nature Reserve, in the Laurel Highlands, offers woodlands, streams, fields, and ponds for its educational programs run through The Carnegie Museum of Natural History. It's open during the warm-weather months.

ber; adults, $6.00; and seniors and children, $5.00, December through March. Children younger than age 2 are admitted free. Members of the zoo are also admitted free of charge. Strollers are available for rent at a nominal charge.

National Aviary
Allegheny Commons West
(412) 323-7235
www.aviary.org

This bird zoo is indeed called the National Aviary. Though it receives no federal funding, Congress granted the North Side aviary the national designation in 1993. More than 600 of the world's most colorful and exotic birds live here in this, the nation's largest indoor bird display, independent of a larger zoo. The aviary is open daily, except Christmas Day, 9:00 A.M. to 5:00 P.M. Adults will pay $6.00 and seniors (age 60 and older) $5.00. Admission for children (ages 2 to 12) costs $4.50 and those younger than age 2 are admitted free of charge.

Phipps Conservatory and
Botanical Gardens
Schenley Park
(412) 622-6914
www.phipps.conservatory.org

Donated by Henry Phipps, one of the city's turn-of-the-20th-century millionaire industrialists and philanthropists, this conservatory is a 13-room Victorian glasshouse full of beautiful gardens. Visit one of the country's finest bonsai collections or take the kids to the Discovery Garden (see Kidstuff). You don't need to fly to Arizona to view desert plants, or head to the Caribbean to see tropical palms, ferns, and other flora that are right here for you to enjoy. A $30 million expansion project that will quadruple the size of this facility broke ground in mid-2003.

Phipps is open Tuesday through Sunday, 9:00 A.M. to 5:00 P.M. On Friday, it is open until 9:00 P.M. Phipps admission is $6.00 for adults, $5.00 for seniors ages 60 and older, $4.00 for students with ID, and $3.00 for children (ages 2 through 12). Children younger than age 2 and Phipps members enter without charge. Metered parking is right in front of the conservatory.

PIVOTAL POINTS OF INTEREST

Andy Warhol Museum
117 Sandusky Street
(412) 237-8300
www.warhol.org

Pop artist Andy Warhol, born into a Pittsburgh family that emigrated from Eastern Europe, began his career right in this city. After attending Saturday art classes and college at Carnegie Institute and what now is Carnegie Mellon University, Warhol moved to New York, working as a commercial artist and becoming famous for his experimentation with silk-screens (from which he made photographically derived paintings). Upon his sudden death in 1987, The Andy Warhol Museum was constructed on the city's North Side. Seven floors house celebrity portraits, pop paintings (including Heinz Boxes, Marilyns, and Campbell's soup cans), Warhol's sketchbooks, and a film gallery. The Warhol is open Tuesday, Wednesday, Thursday, Saturday, and Sunday, 10:00 A.M. to 5:00 P.M. It's closed Monday, open Friday from 10:00 A.M. to 10:00 P.M. Adults will pay $10.00, seniors are charged $7.00, and students and children older than age 3 pay $6.00 for admission Carnegie members pay nothing to enter.

Jimmy Stewart Museum
845 Philadelphia Street
Third Floor, Indiana
(800) 83-JIMMY
www.jimmy.org

Though an attraction of Indiana County, this museum is a definite Western Pennsylvania highlight for those who follow Hollywood and its legends. Located in Jimmy's hometown of Indiana, where his father once owned a hardware store, the museum gives you a chance to see many of Stewart's accomplishments in film, radio, and television. Tributes to Jimmy Stewart's military service, family life, and public service are also housed here. The museum is closed Christmas Eve and Day, New Year's Eve and Day, Good Friday, Easter Sunday, and Thanksgiving. However, it's open 10:00 A.M. to 5:00 P.M. six days a week, and on Sunday noon to 5:00 P.M. Adults pay $5.00; seniors (ages 60 and older), students, and military, $4.00; and children (ages 7 to 17), $3.00. Children younger than 7 get in for free.

Pittsburgh's Inclines
Carson Street
(412) 442-2000 (Monongahela Incline)
(412) 381-1665 (Duquesne Incline)
members.tripod.com/~riid/inclines.html

Pittsburgh had over a dozen working inclines at the turn of the 20th century. Now, only the Monongahela and Duquesne Inclines remain, transporting commuters and tourists to and from Grandview Avenue atop Mt. Washington to the city of Pittsburgh below. The Monongahela Incline was the city's first in 1870. Declared a historic structure by the Pittsburgh History and Landmarks Foundation, it's been registered a National Historic Landmark as well. Today, it's operated by the Port Authority Transit (PAT). For a panoramic view, a ride on one of these is a must, night or day. (See the Getting Here, Getting Around chapter.) The inclines operate daily starting at

5:30 A.M. until 12:45 A.M. On Sunday, service begins at 8:45 A.M.

Washington County Covered Bridges
**Various Locations, Washington County
(800) 531-4114**
Travel back in time to some century-old covered bridges (of which there are 25 in this county alone). All are listed on the National Register of Historic Places. Romantics call these "kissing bridges" for their seclusion, and animal lovers herald their barnlike appearance for helping the animals cross streams. A helpful map is offered through the Washington County Tourism office (telephone number listed above). A covered bridge festival is held each fall (see Annual Events).

KIDSTUFF

To see the world through a child's eyes lends a new perspective, particularly on Pittsburgh. Kids, this chapter is for you mostly, but also for Mom and Dad, family and friends, and anyone else who simply wants to have fun.

Since play is the child's work, it's impossible to list every spot across so many counties where kids can enjoy themselves as they learn and grow. In these pages, you'll find the highlights and the things you most definitely won't want to miss.

Savvy parents might also peruse the Attractions and even the Arts chapters, particularly for older children or those who have interests in more sophisticated subjects such as history, art appreciation, and landmarks. As another entire chapter, Recreation offers a range of equally fun activities that can burn off some of that boundless energy.

Separate chapters cover Shopping and Restaurants as well, so if you're looking for family-friendly places to eat or shops in which to outfit the kids, or if you need to stock your home with a few new toys, it's best to turn to these listings. However, you'll find that most of the museums and attractions listed in these pages do offer gift shops with appropriate memorabilia and merchandise. That may come as a double-edged sword, bringing on the chorus of "Mom, can I have that?" but these stores are often very educational in nature.

Because children teach us to throw structure to the wind sometimes, the usual geographic breakdown has been abandoned for this chapter. Instead, get ready to stretch your mind, discover and explore, go a little crazy in between, and savor the delights of Pittsburgh's seasons.

We've tried to present current prices, but there are instances where class or exhibit fees do fluctuate. Thus, it's best to call before heading out (and perhaps disappointing a child).

So lace up your sneakers and get ready to enjoy a day (or several) of being inquisitive, overjoyed, and yes, probably tired at the end of it all. Oh, but the fun you'll have!

STRETCHING THE MIND

Kids' Classes
Community College of Allegheny
County Main Campus
800 Allegheny Avenue
(412) 237-3100

Think of this as kids' college of sorts, as youngsters attend a variety of classes at one of the community college campuses near you. There are offerings at the Boyce, North, South, and Allegheny campuses. Most sessions meet on Saturdays, with some classes held on particular evenings. Kids can acquire new skills or sharpen existing ones as they take art, acting, basketball, babysitting, cheerleading, dance, computer, language, writing, fencing, swimming, or other classes. Sessions are also offered for SAT preparation and verbal self-defense, just to name a few of the courses available for your child's educational advancement.

In outlying counties, many community colleges offer similar fare for the younger set. It's best to contact the schools in your area for their continuing-education brochures. Use these numbers to help you:

Butler County Community College (724) 287-8711

Contact the Special Kids Network at (800) 986-4550 for information on services for children with special health needs. Directories of summer day camps, residential camps, and leisure and recreational activities are available.

Community College of Beaver County (724) 775-8561

Westmoreland County Community College (724) 925-4000

Classes at The Carnegie
4400 Forbes Avenue
(412) 622-3288
Culture, history, and art appreciation abound here at the home of the Carnegie Museum of Natural History and the Carnegie Museum of Art. The schedule changes each semester, so it's best to call for a catalog, or perhaps pick one up at your local library. Previous offerings have included painting, puppet-making, sculpting, and architectural classes on the art side. Explore everything from bugs and bears to dinosaurs, Disney animals, reptiles, and archeological findings. Also, there are classes specifically designed for home-schoolers. The prices for these always fluctuate, so it's best to call for further details.

Dinosaur Hall
Carnegie Museum of Natural History
4400 Forbes Avenue
(412) 622-3131
This world-famous collection of dinosaur bones and fossils is perhaps the most popular attraction at the museum with children of all ages. Eleven different species are on display in addition to the other fossils of animals that lived around the same Mesozoic Era. For children, these non-threatening monsters are simply amazing, especially in size. The Tyrannosaurus rex stands 20 feet tall here, and dominates the far end of Dinosaur Hall. While at the Museum of Natural History, don't miss Bonehunters Quarry, an interactive exhibit that re-creates an area of Dinosaur National Monument in Colorado and Utah.

Hours at the Carnegie museums are Tuesday through Saturday, 10:00 A.M. to 5:00 P.M. and Sunday noon to 5:00 P.M. The museums stay open until 9:00 P.M. on Friday from June through August and is open on Monday in July and August from 10:00 A.M. to 5:00 P.M. Admission to The Carnegie Museum of Natural History and Museum of

Art is $10.00 for adults, $2.00 for senior citizens and $6.00 for children (ages 3 to 18). Children younger than age 3 and members are admitted free of charge.

Children's Discovery Room
Carnegie Museum of Natural History
440 Forbes Avenue
(412) 622-3131
Tucked away downstairs in this museum is a room where kids can touch, explore, ask questions, and find answers to many intriguing facts. Individual boxes of artifacts can be checked out to explore while in the room (grown-up supervision with these sets is requested). The room's handful of aquariums contain fish, hermit crabs, and turtles.

Kids can sniff spices and learn where they come from, and in general, explore to their heart's (and hands'!) content. All children younger than age 12 must be accompanied by an adult.

Discovery Room hours are Tuesday through Friday 1:00 to 3:00 P.M., Saturday 10:00 A.M. to 4:00 P.M., and Sunday 1:00 to 4:00 P.M. during the school year. In the summer the room is open weekdays and Saturdays 10:00 A.M. to 4:00 P.M. as well as on Sunday from 1:00 to 4:00 P.M. Admission to The Carnegie Museum of Natural History and Museum of Art is $10.00 for adults, $4.00 for senior citizens and $6.00 for children (ages 3 to 18). Children younger than age 3 and members are admitted free of charge.

Pittsburgh Children's Museum
10 Children's Way
(412) 322-5058
www.pittsburghkids.org
In the historic landmark Old Post Office Building on the city's North Side, this museum offers outstanding exhibits throughout its three floors. Luckey's Climber is an amazing two-story indoor jungle gym. Riverscape re-creates Pittsburgh in the 1920s where children can roleplay, while the Studio is a section where kids create their own silkscreens. The little ones won't want to miss the

puppet exhibit featuring some of Fred Rogers' famous puppets as well as some Jim Henson (of Muppets fame) creations. Stuffee, the museum's health-teaching exhibit, doesn't mind at all if he's poked and prodded.

Previous exhibits have included the Welcome to Mister Rogers' Neighborhood exhibit, made possible by the Grable Foundation. In honor of Mister Rogers' 30th anniversary on public television, this exhibit will travel to other children's museums but come back for a permanent stay in Pittsburgh.

The Children's Museum is closed on major holidays, but open Monday through Saturday from 10:00 A.M. to 5:00 P.M., and on Sunday, the museum opens from noon to 5:00 P.M. Adults pay $5.00 per person for admission, with $4.50 charged for seniors and children (ages 2 to 18). Children younger than age 2 are admitted free of charge, and museum members receive complimentary admission as well. Each Thursday, everyone's admission is discounted to $3.50.

Carnegie Science Center
One Allegheny Avenue
(412) 237-3400
www.carnegiesciencecenter.org

With its focus on science and technology, it's no wonder the Carnegie Science Center on the North Side makes kids feel like inventors, young astronauts, and even magicians. The center isn't limited to children's activities, but certainly kids can learn so much from the interactive exhibits and Omnimax large-format films. They can momentarily pretend they are meteorologists on the evening news, and they can watch a demonstration of science in the kitchen.

Ports of Discovery is a three-part water-related area featuring a living Pacific coral reef aquarium. Kids can explore the planets and stars at the Henry Buhn, Jr. Planetarium & Observatory. Young history buffs shouldn't miss a tour of the USS *Requin,* a World War II diesel-electric submarine moored on the banks

of the river (this one's not recommended for very young children). And do note that the miniature train display, while closed each February for refurbishing, is open most other months of the year. You'll avoid the crowds if you time your visit outside the holiday season (see the Annual Events chapter).

The center features an educational division with programs for school groups, students, families and educators. Scouts can earn badges at the science center's scout workshops. Using NASA resources, there's even a young astronauts program exploring space travel. Periodically, school students compete in science fairs, and the Carnegie Science Academy for teens fosters a fun, interactive environment for students in grades 9 through 12 with a love of science and exploration.

The center extends its hours in the summer at times. Regular hours are Sunday through Friday 10:00 A.M. to 5:00 P.M., and Saturday 10:00 A.M. to 7:00 P.M. An Explorer Pass costs $14 for adults, $10 for children.

General admission tickets include entry to the exhibits, UPMC SportsWorks, Buhl Planetarium, and the submarine. For the Omnimax theater alone, expect to pay $6.00 to $10.00. Combination ticket packages are available and prices are listed at the desk and given by telephone on the automated information line (call the number given above). Senior discounts are extended on Tuesday. Purchasing a membership to the science center allows complimentary admission. Parking is free.

Kindermusik
Various locations
(800) 628-5687

This flexible curriculum that brings out the magic in music appeals to children between the ages of 18 months and 5 years. The goal isn't necessarily to make a musician out of your child, but to make your little one eager to learn and more alive through musical activities. These include 30-minute classes of singing, moving, listening, and playing simple instruments for those younger than 3, and 45-minute classes for kids ages 3 to 5. Those who enroll can take advantage of the parent orientation, family newsletters, and bring-a-friend days. Early registrants receive a 10 percent discount. The eastern suburbs location at Beulah Church may provide information for this site. Contact them at (412) 798-SONG. To find a Kindermusik location closer to you, try the toll-free number above or do a class locator search on the kindermusik.com Web site.

DISCOVERING HISTORY

Senator John Heinz Pittsburgh Regional History Center
1212 Smallman Street
(412) 454-6000
www.pghhistory.org
Home of the Historical Society of Western Pennsylvania, this museum and depository of regional history isn't limited to children alone (see the Attractions chapter). However, there are several displays and features that will interest your youngsters. Start on the first floor of the Strip District museum, where kids can board an old streetcar, the way it used to be in Pittsburgh before the days of light-rail transit and PAT buses. Kids will also delight at the robots giving them directions.

Children are certainly welcome to browse the exhibits throughout the building, but they will especially enjoy the Discovery Place (no relation to the Discovery room mentioned above) on the third floor, which is just for them. This room offers hands-on exploration with interactive exhibits and games. Kids can interview an object, travel through time, interview a shoe, and climb in a steel mill. Past exhibits at the History Center have included Top Bop, a collection of the best toys ever created.

The Heinz History Center is open from 10:00 A.M. to 5:00 P.M. The library is open Thursday through Saturday, 10:00 A.M. until 5:00 P.M. The Center is closed Easter, Thanksgiving, Christmas, and New Year's

Bookstores throughout the region often feature story times, Saturday craft and story sessions, and other events for children during the school breaks and throughout the summer months. Check with your local bookseller, particularly the large superstores, for their individual offerings.

Day. Cost for adults is $6.00, $4.50 for seniors (age 65 and older) and students (with ID), and $3.00 for children (ages 6 to 18). Children younger than age 6 are admitted at no cost.

Pennsylvania Trolley Museum
Off Race Track Road, Washington
(724) 228-9256, (877) PA-TROLLEY
www.pa-trolley.org
Just 30 minutes south of Pittsburgh, kids can climb aboard a streetcar, hear the clang of the bell, and feel the powerful electric motors and the heavy clatter of steel wheels over the rails. These vintage streetcars are fun to ride and learn about. Volunteer craftsmen rebuild and restore these relics. Allow at least two hours to completely experience the museum. Please note the museum is closed during the months of January, February, and March, but reopens on weekends in early April through December 31 from 11:00 A.M. to 5:00 P.M. It's open weekdays also, Memorial Day through Labor Day from 10:00 A.M. to 4:00 P.M. Admission costs $6.00 for adults, $5.00 for seniors (age 65 and older), and $3.50 for children (ages 2 to 15). Those children younger than age 2 receive free admission.

Meadowcroft Museum of Rural Life
401 Meadowcroft Road, Avella
(724) 587-3412
This 200-acre living-history museum in Washington County offers lessons on rural life for the youngsters as well. Each summer, there's a hands-on history day camp where children experience life in 19th-century Western Pennsylvania. Kids

CLOSE-UP

Everyone's Favorite Neighbor

Fred Rogers' life was honored formally in a public memorial service at Heinz Hall in Pittsburgh on May 3, 2003; it was attended by more than 3,000 people. Fred's life was also honored informally in myriad ways, at a special gathering at Carnegie Mellon University for students, for example.

Fortunately, for Mister Rogers' "television neighbors," the series continues to be broadcast on public television stations across the country. Fred Rogers' intention over the years was to produce the Neighborhood series as a "video library" of programs that could be available to children in future years. Thus, for children, the relationship with their "television neighbor" didn't change with his death. As one child said, "But I can still see him on TV, can't I?" Through these "television visits," Mister Rogers can still help children feel good about who they are and appreciate others and the world around them.

Fred McFeely Rogers (1928–2003) was born in Latrobe, Westmoreland County. After graduating from Rollins College, Fred surprised everyone with his decision to work in television. He rejected the pies-in-the-face humor aimed at young audiences in the 1950s and was determined to find a better approach to this powerful medium.

In New York he worked briefly as an NBC floor manager, but later, he wanted to return to Pittsburgh and a start-up station, the first community-supported public television station in the country. "My friends thought I was crazy. I was in line to be a network director," he told us in a 2000 interview. And though it took eight years to complete additional studies at Pittsburgh Theological Seminary, Rogers was ordained with the special mission of working through the media.

While gaining that seminary degree, Rogers was influenced by what he calls the "giants" in the field of child development—people like the late Margaret McFarland, Benjamin Spock, and Eric Erikson. Much of the *Mister Rogers'*

---

shop at the general store, visit the blacksmith, and join Ma in preparing a meal on a woodstove. Then, after lunch, there's class in a one-room school, learning a craft skill, and playing historical games. This five-day camp is for ages 8 through 13, and runs from 10:00 A.M. to 3:00 P.M. Registration costs $160 per child. (See the Attractions chapter for more information on Meadowcroft.)

Fort Necessity National Battlefield & Braddock's Grave
One Washington Parkway, Farmington
(724) 329-5512
www.nps.gov/fone/home.htm
Most kids have had to study about the French & Indian War in school, so why not show them a little history to supplement the studies! Right off Route 40 in Fayette County, or what is commonly called the

Neighborhood material, all written by Fred himself, emerged from the insights he gained from his mentors.

Family Communications, Inc. (www.misterrogers.org), the nonprofit company that Fred Rogers founded in 1971, carries on his legacy. Building on its beginnings in broadcast television production, Family Communications has expanded into a wide range of media—books for children and adults, audio and video tapes, training workshops, the Internet, DVD, a planetarium show, and traveling exhibits. The company's ongoing work continues to be guided by Fred Rogers' mission of communicating in open, honest, and nurturing ways—ways that support the relationships between children and their families as well as those with the professionals who often care for them.

While, over the years, some parents have poked fun at Mister Rogers and his slow, quiet approach, most have grown to admire the way he reaches out to their youngsters, becoming an important teacher in their lives, even now, as his broadcasts continue. "Any adult who is honest with children and cares to spend time with them and cares to appreciate them can make a difference," he asserted. "Parents need to know how important they are in the life of their children. They really are their pre-school child's world. They are their axis."

The world showed its thanks with numerous awards and recognition. During the course of his lifetime, Fred Rogers received two Peabody Awards; four Emmys; a "Lifetime Achievement" award from the National Academy of Television Arts and Sciences; and the nation's highest civilian honor, the Presidential Medal of Freedom.

A favorite quote that guided Fred Rogers perhaps gives us the most personal insight into this man. Translated from Saint-Exupery's *The Little Prince:* "What is essential is invisible to the eye." Indeed, this great television neighbor appreciated every day, every person, "just the way they are." We Pittsburghers cherished him—and still cherish the legacy his television program and the staff at Family Communications continue to provide.

National Road, visit George Washington's "fort of necessity," so named because a large force of French and Indians attacked Washington's army of 400 here. While this battle wasn't a success for Washington, the war's outcome had great impact on global affairs. The French lost much influence in North America, while the English colonies began to pay taxes levied upon them to help pay for this expensive war.

Independence became a dream of some settlers.

Quietly up the road from Fort Necessity, a single marker memorializes the final resting place of British Major General Edward Braddock. Braddock was the leader of an ill-fated expedition along the Ohio River trying to capture the French-held Fort Duquesne. Don't drive too fast along this road, for you just might miss it.

Fort Necessity park grounds and visitor center open daily from 9:00 A.M. to 5:00 P.M. Picnic facilities are available during summer months. It's best to start your visit at the visitor center with its audio-visual program and exhibits before moving through the grounds. On a warm day, you'll find costumed Indians demonstrating crafts and telling the survival story at the fort.

In addition to the battlefield and the aforementioned grave of General Braddock, Fort Necessity features other historical sites of interest to kids. Jumonville Glen was the site of Washington's first skirmish with the French. And the park also operated the Mount Washington Tavern, built in 1828 to serve travelers along the National Road. Admission to Fort Necessity, which includes the fort, the museum exhibits, and the Mount Washington Tavern, costs $3.00 per person. Children age 16 and younger are admitted free of charge.

Fort Ligonier
Routes 30 and 711, Ligonier
(724) 238-9701
www.fortligonier.org
If your children studied the French and Indian War, visit Fort Ligonier in Westmoreland County, which served as a staging area for the 1758 Forbes campaign that resulted in the capture of Fort Duquesne (Pittsburgh). The enemy arrived here October 12, 1758, with about 1,200 French and only a few hundred Indians, who were retreating to begin preparations for the long winter ahead. With their strength in numbers and mortar fire, the British were victorious. The new battery, constructed in a $2.3 million restoration project, is built on the site of the original defense fortification of 1758. This historic site is open daily, May 1 through October 31. Fort Ligonier Days occur each October (see the Annual Events chapter). It's open from 10:00 A.M. to 4:30 P.M. Monday through Saturday and noon to 4:30 P.M. on

Sundays. Admission rates are $6.75 for adults, $3.75 for children ages 6 to 14, and $5.50 for seniors. Children younger than age 5 are admitted free of charge.

GOING CRAZY

Idlewild Park
Route 30, Ligonier
(724) 238-3666
www.idlewild.com
This family theme park in Westmoreland County includes Storybook Forest, Mister Rogers' Neighborhood of Make-Believe (the only one in the country), Soak Zone (water slides and pool), Jumpin' Jungle, Hootin' Holler, and Raccoon Lagoon (kiddie rides). Kids will enjoy such major amusement rides as a Ferris wheel and other traditional amusement park attractions in the Olde Idlewild area, and live entertainment on stage. Idlewild offers shaded picnic tables and grills, so be sure to pack a basket in this beautiful area of the Laurel Highlands. Pavilions can be reserved for large groups. Refreshment stands are numerous, and there's a large restaurant.

Previous highlights at Idlewild have included the Royal Hanneford Circus, and annual appearances of everyone's favorite characters from *Mister Rogers' Neighborhood*. Height requirements apply on the park's faster rides. There are changing facilities for the water attractions, and lockers for rent to store your belongings. But they aren't large, so pack light.

This family fun land is open from May 26 to Labor Day, but is closed on Mondays in June. Adults and children pay $20.95 everyday and seniors (age 55 and older) are charged $14.50. Children age 2 and younger get in free. For those who discover there is simply too much fun to explore in one day, ask about the "Next Day Pass" at guest services, which gives you a discount on your second day's visit. There's no cost to park at Idlewild.

Kennywood Park
4800 Kennywood Boulevard
West Mifflin
(412) 461-0500
www.kennywood.com
Named as a Pennsylvania Historic Landmark and having celebrated its 100th year
anniversary in 1998, Kennywood in
Allegheny County is a roller-coaster capital. The park has been named the favorite
traditional amusement park of the
National Amusement Park Historical Association for more than a decade running.

One of the most popular rides is the
Pitt Fall, which hoists riders to the top of a
black and gold tower, then plummets
them at a free fall of nearly 65 miles per
hour. Technology and innovation have set
Kennywood apart for years. Noah's Ark, a
walk-through "haunted" ark built in the
1930s, was totally refurbished in 1996-1997
so that it might sail into the 21st century.
Guests are now thrilled by high-tech
scenes such as the Elevator of Doom,
which provides the illusion that you're in a
falling, crumbling elevator.

Coasters at Kennywood are the main
attraction. Don't miss the Thunderbolt and
the Jack Rabbit roller coasters, if your children are old enough (and brave enough!).
There's also the Racer and the Extermina-
tor to thrill you. Be prepared to get
drenched on the Log Jammer flume ride.
And, here at Kennywood, you don't need a
learner's permit to drive the Turnpike.

Throughout the year, but especially
in the summer, Kennywood features live
performances, community and school picnics, ethnic pride days, and fall fantasy
parades. A cafeteria-style restaurant is
available as well as numerous refreshment
stands. Height requirements do apply on
some rides.

Ride-all-day passes cost $28.95. Gen-
eral admission tickets (rides not included)
are available to adults for $8.00 and to
seniors (age 65 and older) for $7.00. Dur-
ing the last week of August, there's a Fun
Finale each night. Ride-all-evening passes
cost $13.95 per person.

In 2002, the trade magazine Amusement Today *voted Kennywood the
fourth-best amusement park in the
nation.*

Sandcastle
1000 Sandcastle Drive, West Homestead
(412) 462-6666
www.sandcastlewaterpark.com
This is Pittsburgh's wettest playground,
just minutes outside the Golden Triangle
along the Monongahela River in Allegheny
County. With 15 twisting and turning waterslides, a gentle Lazy River to float down,
several pools, and the self-proclaimed
World's Largest Hot Tub (for adults), you
understand why people flock to Sandcastle
when the mercury soars. Little tykes love
Wet Willie's Waterworks.

There's plenty of fun on land as well,
with volleyball, food and gift shops, and
an arcade on the old-fashioned boardwalk. Oasis Miniature Golf and the exciting
Formula 1 Speedway add landlubber fun
to your trip to Sandcastle.

Sandcastle is open daily from early
June through early September. Hours of
operation are 11:00 A.M. to 6:00 P.M. June
and September, and 11:00 A.M. to 7:00 P.M.
in July and August. A Whitewater Pass
entitles you to all water attractions and
costs $21.95 for kids and adults and $16.95
for seniors. The Season Pass costs $44.95.
To ride the Formula 1 Speedway, you must
be at least 58 inches tall and pay an additional $4.00. Children age three and
younger are admitted free of charge, and
parking is $5.00. Boat docking, if you get
here via the river, is free.

Just Ducky Tours
Station Square
(412) 402-DUCK
www.justduckytours.com
It's a boat, it's a truck . . . no, it's a duck!
That's right, Just Ducky tours offers an
amphibious tour vehicle to shuttle passengers throughout the city as they learn a

little about Pittsburgh and its waterways. This fully narrated tour begins at Station Square, a building formerly housing the Pennsylvania and Lake Erie Railroad and now a shopping/restaurant mecca on the city's South Side. Quacking your way along, you'll see Pittsburgh's past and present along Grant Street and the historic Penn Station before moving into the Strip District (yes, it's G-rated—the Strip is the infamous produce/food shopping area) and then the Cultural District.

Kids squeal with delight at the tour's highlight, when the Duck boat makes its way effortlessly off the dry land, splashing down into the Allegheny River to continue the tour! Adults ride for $16.00, with students (with ID) and seniors costing $15.00, and children ages 3 to 12 $12.00, and children age 2 and under $2.00. The duck tour is wheelchair accessible, and the boats are equipped with heat and canopies for inclement weather. Tours operate from April through November at various times throughout the day beginning at 10:30 A.M. and ending at 6:00 P.M. (except October and November, when it gets dark earlier). Call to book your reservation and get ready to quack away!

Chuck E. Cheese
1025 Washington Pike, Bridgeville
(412) 257-2570

3800 William Penn Highway, Monroeville
(412) 856-5044

Chuck E. Cheese and his band are on stage for you in the Chartiers Valley Shopping Center, and in Monroeville. So take the kids to this popular restaurant for pizza, music, and lots of fast-paced, indoor fun. Watch them climb their way to the skycrawls or shimmy down a slide. Older kids and tiny tots are bound for the ball pit, and there are plenty of arcade games for your preteens too.

Chuck E. Cheese has a hand-check, child-identification system to keep children from leaving without their parents. Party packages available, but do make weekend party reservations at least one month in advance. Enjoy the nonstop fun (and noise!) Sunday through Thursday from 9:00 A.M. to 10:00 P.M. On Friday and Saturday, hours are 9:00 A.M. to 11:00 P.M. Prices vary on the menu, so call if you're curious.

Wildwood Highlands
2330 Wildwood Road
(412) 487-5517

Wildwood Highlands is North Park's family fun center, with miniature golf, go-karts, bumper boats, a driving range, an arcade, and a complete menu for meals and snacks. Woody's Den is an area of the park especially suited for kids age 10 and younger. This site can accommodate small groups of children as well as large corporate gatherings. Teen parties are also available. Wildwood Peddlers Flea Market is adjacent to this family fun center (see the Shopping chapter).

The center sells tickets for go-karts, bumper boats, and Woody's Den. Tokens are required for the driving range, miniature golf, and game room. Call the automated information line (number above) for complete price information. However, miniature golf costs $5.25 for adults and $3.75 for children ages 4 to 10, and it's free for kids age 3 and younger with a paying customer. Indoor play costs $4.00 for children age 4 and older, $3.00 for two- and three-year-olds, and it's free for babies age one and younger. Tickets are available in different price amounts, but for $20 you can receive 25 tickets.

Wildwood Highlands is open year-round, but the hours vary seasonally. Generally, it's open Sunday through Thursday from 11:00 A.M. to 10:00 P.M. and on Friday and Saturday from 11:00 A.M. to 11:00 P.M.

Caddie Shak
Route 31 East, Donegal
(724) 593-7400

From sports to animals—there's something sure to please young and older kids alike. Try the challenge of two miniature golf courses, bumper boats with water cannons, three go-kart tracks, batting cages, an arcade, driving range, beach volleyball, a kiddie area, horseback riding, paintball, and a picnic grove that's perfect for birthday parties. Height requirements apply on all tracks and bumper boats.

Caddie Shak, in Westmoreland County, is open Memorial Day through Labor Day, Monday through Thursday, 10:00 A.M. to 10:00 P.M. and Friday through Sunday 10:00 A.M. to 11:00 P.M. Spring and fall hours are more limited, generally from 4:00 to 8:00 P.M. on weekdays and 10:00 A.M. to 10:00 P.M. on weekends. Admission is free, but each activity costs a certain number of tickets. Tickets cost $1.00 apiece, but you can purchase 25 tickets for $20.00, 65 tickets for $50.00, and 140 tickets for $100.00. Paintball costs $21 and more.

Fun Fest Entertainment Center
2525 Freeport Road, Hamarville
(412) 828-1100
Kids will enjoy the range of activities at this indoor entertainment complex. Pick from cosmic bowling with laser lights and fog rising above the lanes, laser-tag games with computerized scorekeeping and much more. Fun Fest is open from 9:00 A.M. until midnight Sunday through Thursday. On Friday and Saturday, the center stays open until 3:30 A.M.

Bowling costs $4.00 per game Monday through Thursday. On weekends, it costs a little more at $4.50 per game, per person. Laser Storm costs $5.00 per game per person during the week, but after 6:00 P.M. and on weekends, the price goes up to $5.25. Reservations are strongly suggested.

Safari Sam's
8001 Rowan Road, Cranberry Township
(724) 779-1991
For a ball-jumping, tunnel-crawling, game-playing good time, head to Safari Sam's in Cranberry in Butler County. This is an indoor playground like others designed for

Pittsburgh For Kids *is a guidebook published by the McEwan School that's quite resourceful for children and their grown-ups. Purchase a copy for $14.95 by calling (412) 361-7559 or get one at your local bookstore.*

kids age two to early teens where tokens operate the interactive games. A full-service restaurant menu features pastas, salads, sandwiches, and pizza. Birthday party packages are available.

Safari Sam's is open Sunday through Thursday 10:00 A.M. to 9:00 P.M. and Friday and Saturday 10:00 A.M. to 10:00 P.M. Adults are admitted free (with children); but older children (age 5 and older) cost $5.99; children ages 2 to 4 get in for $4.99; and children younger than age 2 are admitted free.

Gymboree Play Programs
1500 Washington Road #120
Galleria Mall
(724) 933-0033

Fox Chapel, Boyd Community Center
1220 Powers Run Road
(724) 681-1183

Monroeville Music Center
4280 Northern Pike, Monroeville
(412) 856-8771

Wexford Plaza
10628 Perry Highway, Wexford
(724) 933-0033
Gymboree specializes in developmental play programs for newborns through five-year-olds, with more than 40 pieces of colorful play equipment, upbeat music, movement, creative games, and activities to improve self-esteem. It's a great opportunity for youngsters to socialize with children their own age. To enroll a child, the fee is generally $168 for a period of 14 weeks. There is also a first-time enrollment fee of $25. Additional siblings can attend at a slightly lesser rate, so ask at the location near you.

TALKIN' TOYS

The Center for Creative Play
1400 South Braddock Avenue
(412) 371-1668
www.center4creativeplay.org
Your children can play with more than 1,000 toys and computer programs, climb the three-story playhouse, create their own puppet shows, experience the sensory room with its unusual lighting and relaxation (designed for special-needs children but enjoyed by all), and romp in the ball pit.

Family membership entitles you to borrow any of the toys or software for an entire month. The center's lab has software for both PCs and Macs, with packages for all ages, plus access to the World Wide Web for parents. Developmentally appropriate toys are plentiful for all ages. Perhaps the most appealing part of this center is that you can bring the whole family. Young children and their teen siblings will not be bored.

Fully accessible for children with disabilities and special needs, this fun zone is right across from the subway stop at Station Square. Party packages are available in a special, brand-new room. Adults are $2.50 and all children enter for $5.00 apiece. Babies less than a year old pay nothing. Family memberships begin at $100 per year and entitle you to unlimited visits for your immediate family and the ability to borrow three toys at a time for one month. Higher membership levels, including some that include grandparents, are available with additional benefits and discounts.

September through May, the center is open Monday, Wednesday, Friday, and Saturday from 10:00 A.M. to 5:00 P.M.; Tuesday and Thursday until 7:00 P.M.; and Sunday 1:00 to 5:00 P.M. During the summer it is open Monday through Saturday 10:00 A.M. to 5:00 P.M. and Sunday 1:00 to 5:00 P.M.

Pittsburgh Toy Lending Library
5401 Centre Avenue
(412) 682-4430
trfn.clpgh.org/toylibrary/
Created as a safe, clean, inexpensive place for children, parents, and caregivers, the Toy Lending Library operates from the First United Methodist Church at the corner of South Aiken Avenue and Baum Boulevard. Children from birth through kindergarten are welcome to come and explore or attend free classes. Developmentally appropriate toys enhance motor, social, sensory, cognitive, imaginative, and language skills.

A resource reference library helps parents and caregivers, and informal meetings provide friendly information exchange of such topics as nursing and potty training to selecting a school. The Parent Enrichment Program features speakers from Children's Hospital leading various sessions. Family memberships cost $30 per year for those who can volunteer to help. For nonvolunteers, it's $60 annually. Visitors are also welcome to stop by on a pay-per-visit basis. Cost is $4.00 per child older than one year of age. Members enjoy toy borrowing and party privileges as well as newsletter subscription. This toy library is open Monday through Saturday, generally 9:30 A.M. until 2:00 or 2:30 P.M. but it varies depending upon the day. Please call before heading out with your little ones!

Disney Store
South Hills Village, Bethel Park
(412) 831-5010
Save the trip to Orlando by coming to one of six Disney Stores in the Pittsburgh area. Cast members will assist you in finding Disney collectibles, clothing, toys, videos, and stuffed animals. And if you think the

Giant Eagle supermarkets make shopping just a bit easier with the Eagle's Nest play center in many of the larger stores. It's free for children ages three to nine. Check with your store for requirements.

Disney Store is strictly for children, you'd be mistaken. There are plenty of adult items, such as desk accessories, books, and apparel, including ties for men and sleepwear for all ages. Don't miss the sale rack, and enjoy Disney's trademark customer service. In fact, if you purchase an item at one of the Disney theme parks and need to return it, the cast members at the Disney Stores can often assist you. In addition to this South Hills Village location, you'll find the Disney Store at Monroeville Mall, Ross Park Mall, Century III Mall, Beaver Valley Mall, and Westmoreland Mall.

Gram & Gramps
1720 Washington Road
(412) 831-4726

Not only will you find a great selection of top-quality toys (including Brio, Thomas, and Playmobile) but you'll also be able to outfit the kids in this all-in-one store in the South Hills. Named for doting grandparents, it's probably an appropriate moniker. While prices on the toy merchandise are competitive, the clothing lines are a little upscale. But then, grandparents want only the best!

Once Upon A Child
10648 Perry Highway, Wexford
(724) 933-1660

Holiday Center, Route 22, Monroeville
(412) 374-9932
www.tradeyanow.com

Outfit the kids for less here at Once Upon A Child, featuring gently used merchandise. Not only will you find play and dressy clothing for the kids, but also a selection of quality used toys and children's furnishings. Strollers, portable cribs, and potties prevail too. If you'd like to sell children's items you no longer need, please note that the stores accept only top-quality merchandise, which clerks check for missing pieces and stains. Appointments aren't necessary, but you can arrive with your sale items from 10:00 A.M. until 6:00 P.M. Monday through Saturday. You should plan to return that same day to collect what they will not buy from you, and, of course, receive payment.

S.W. Randall Toyes and Giftes
806 Ivy Street
(412) 687-2666

630 Smithfield Street
(412) 562-9252

5856 Forbes Avenue
(412) 422-7009

Station Square
(412) 471-8800

Generations of Pittsburgh families have shopped at S.W. Randall for classic toys such as Brio and Lego sets, quality stuffed animals, dolls, board games, and other children's favorites.

The Toy Box
108 South Market Street, Ligonier
(724) 238-6233

Quality toys, games, and puzzles for children of all ages are found here. Phone orders are welcome as well. Brand names include Avanti, Brio, Erector, Folkmanis, Playmobile, Steiff, and Tucker Jones. The Toy Box is open Monday through Saturday, 10:00 A.M. to 5:00 P.M.; and Sunday, from noon to 5:00 P.M.

Toys R Us
Route 18 and Valley View Drive, Monaca
(724) 728-0525

4000 Oxford Drive, Bethel Park
(412) 831-3410

2003 Cheryl Drive
(412) 364-4062

275 Clairton Boulevard, West Mifflin
(412) 655-0677

2001 Park Manor Boulevard
(412) 787-1770

Donahue Road, Greensburg
(724) 836-8813

The Pittsburgh region is well covered when it comes to popular toy stores. Toys R Us is the national chain of toy superstores featuring everything from infant clothing, cribs, layettes, and diapers to children's toys, bicycles, outdoor play equipment, electronic games, even Halloween costumes. There are extended hours during the months preceding the holidays so do call prior to heading out. Most of these stores are found near our major suburban shopping malls.

EXPLORING NATURE

Round Hill Farm
651 Round Hill Road, Elizabeth
(412) 384-8555

Take the kids to see a real working farm, while there's one still left! Open year-round with tours conducted from April through November, Round Hill in southern Allegheny County has picnic areas in the summer, so be sure to pack a lunch. Kids will enjoy the self-guided tour, especially if there's a cow that needs some milking. Though retired, the county police department's riding horses remain on the farm along with their friends, the sheep and chickens. In fact, exotic chickens that they are, some even lay beautifully colored eggs. Ask about the "Day on the Farm" program for fifth and sixth graders whereby the students go on hayrides, have snacks, and fix their own lunches on the farm. Normal hours are from 9:00 A.M. to 2:30 P.M.

Pittsburgh Zoo & Aquarium
One Wild Place
(412) 665-3640, (800) 474-4966
www.zoo.pgh.pa.us

If your idea of fun is seeing others act out, head to the Pittsburgh Zoo. At this 77-acre natural habitat facility, primates show off their antics in the fog-shrouded indoor rain forest; elephants, zebras, and giraffes roam the African Savanna; and Siberian tigers and snow leopards explore the Asian forest. Your own children can act as animalistic as they like (under your supervision, of course!) at Kids Kingdom, where they'll have a roaring good time on play equipment that replicates animal motions

and behaviors. They'll pass through a petting area to touch a friendly goat or see the Australian grey kangaroos up close.

In 1994, the zoo became a nonprofit organization owned and operated by the Zoological Society of Pittsburgh. Privatization has been a tremendous success with zoo attendance soaring. In 1998 the zoo celebrated its 100th birthday, amidst celebrations including national broadcasts on *Good Morning America*. The centennial year's work included a few surprises, among them an exotic dragon and a pair of koalas.

The Pittsburgh Zoo is open year-round. Special evening hours are held during the holiday season (see Annual Events). Otherwise, the zoo is open from Memorial Day through Labor Day 10:00 A.M. to 6:00 P.M. Labor Day through Memorial Day the zoo opens from 9:00 A.M. until 5:00 P.M. Entrance gates close an hour before the park closes. Admission is $8.00 for adults, $7.00 for seniors, $6.00 for children ages 2 to 13, and children younger than age 2 pay nothing. Members of the zoo are also admitted free of charge. Strollers are also available for rent at a nominal charge.

National Aviary
Allegheny Commons West, Ridge Avenue
(412) 323-7235
www.aviary.org

While it receives no federal funding, the National Aviary on Pittsburgh's North Side was granted the national designation by Congress in 1993. This sanctuary proves that the Pittsburgh Penguins hockey players aren't the only birds in town! More than 600 of the world's most colorful and exotic birds live here in this, the nation's largest indoor bird display, independent of a larger zoo. Kids will love the cacophony and the mysterious-looking birds flying overhead. The Aviary is open daily, except Christmas Day, 9:00 A.M. to 5:00 P.M. Adults will pay $6.00 and seniors (age 60 and older) $5.00. Admission for children (ages 2 to 12) costs $4.50, and those younger than age 2 are admitted free of charge.

SAVORING THE SEASONS

Discovery Garden
Phipps Conservatory and Botanical
Gardens, Schenley Park
(412) 622-6914

Located in Schenley Park in Pittsburgh's Oakland section, among the blossoms and bonsai, the indoor and outdoor Discovery Garden is designed especially for children. Kids can pot their own plants, learn about botany with the garden ambassadors, and partake of other special activities. Phipp's Discovery Garden is open May 2 through October 31, and the hours vary depending upon the weather. A $30 million expansion project that will quadruple the size of this entire facility began construction in mid-2003.

Phipps is open Tuesday through Sunday, 9:00 A.M. to 5:00 P.M. weather permitting. Admission is $6.00 for adults, $5.00 for seniors age 60 and older, $4.00 for students with ID, and $3.00 for children (ages 2 to 12). Children younger than age 2 and Phipps members enter without charge. Metered parking is in front of the conservatory.

Pumpkin farms
Various locations

Picking your way through a pumpkin patch each October is a fun way for the kids to enjoy autumn's colorful changes. The only thing more exciting than picking your own great pumpkin is carving it once you get it home.

Many pumpkin farms exist in the Greater Pittsburgh area, offering selections as tiny as two pounds to giant-sized ones needing a small truck to haul it home. Besides picking a pumpkin, however, children can often find their way through cornstalk mazes, take a hayride, play on outdoor equipment, enjoy a petting zoo, have a pony ride, and help the family shop for other produce, including fall specialties and baked goods. Here are a few of the better-known pumpkin patches around Pittsburgh:

Janoski's Farm, Route 30, Clinton (3 miles from the airport), (724) 899-3438

Kaelin Farm Market, 2547 Brandt School Road, Franklin Park, (724) 935-6780

Reilly's Summer Seat Farm, Ohio Township, (412) 364-8662

Schramm's Farm Market & Greenhouse, 291 Criswell Road, Butler, (724) 282-3714

Schramm's Farms & Orchard, Harrison City Road, Westmoreland County, (724) 744-7320

Soergel's Farm, Brandt School Road, Wexford, (724) 935-1743

Trax Farms, Route 88, Finleyville, (412) 835-3246

Simmons Farms, 170 Simmons Road, McMurray, (724) 941-1490

Bridgewater Pumpkinfest
Bridge Street, Bridgewater
(724) 774-7615

Held the second weekend in October, this giant pumpkin contest and Little Miss Pumpkinfest contest are things the kids will love. Children will enjoy the games, food, crafters, and a fireworks display. (See the Annual Events chapter.) Visit the Pumpkinfest in Beaver County on Saturday from 10:00 A.M. to 8:00 P.M. and on Sunday from noon to 6:00 P.M.

Houston Pumpkin Festival
American Legion Picnic Grounds
Houston
(800) 531-4114

Sponsored by the Houston Volunteer Fire Department, there's more pumpkin fun at this Washington County fall festival. Kids will enjoy the petting zoo, pony rides,

Even Mister Rogers came to meet the baby elephant at the Pittsburgh Zoo & Aquarium. His production crew taped an episode of Mister Rogers' Neighborhood *featuring the African elephant calf and her family herd.*

pumpkin decorating, and an orange pumpkin bouncer. (See the Annual Events chapter for more.) This festival takes place on October Saturdays from 10:00 A.M. to 7:00 P.M. as well as Sundays from 10:00 A.M. to 6:00 P.M.

Great Miniature Railroad & Village
Carnegie Science Center
One Allegheny Avenue
(412) 237-3400

A true Pittsburgh holiday tradition, this display is a great way for families to teach children what the region looked like decades ago. Strollers are welcome. (See the Annual Events chapter for additional information.) Closed for a week in June and again from September 27 through mid-November, regular hours are Sunday through Friday 10:00 A.M. to 5:00 P.M. and Saturday 10:00 A.M. to 7:00 P.M. To see the exhibits only (including the railroad), admission costs $14 for adults, and $10 for seniors (age 65 and older) and children (ages 3 to 18). Combination ticket packages are available and prices are listed at the desk and given by telephone at the number listed above. Senior discounts are extended on Tuesday. Purchasing a membership to the science center allows complimentary admission. Parking is free.

Penn Hills Train Display
Penn Hills Municipal Building
12245 Frankstown Road, Penn Hills
(412) 798-2147

During December, this monthlong train display is brought to the community by the Penn Hills Police Department, which converts its shooting range into a holiday exhibition each year. Kids will enjoy unusual scenes such as the Batcave and the military airport. Browse the display on weekdays from 5:00 to 9:00 P.M. and weekends from 1:00 to 9:00 P.M. A $1.00 per person donation toward local charities is asked at the door.

Santa's Trolley
Pennsylvania Trolley Museum,
Off Race Track Road, Washington
(724) 228-9256
www.pa-trolley.org/eventscd.htm

Kids can make special crafts at the trolley museum and ride with Santa aboard one of the vintage trolley cars this museum is known for. A Lionel train display is also a part of the holiday season. Visitors can even operate the Lionel trains on the museum's large "you run it" display. (See the Annual Events and Attractions chapters.) Hop aboard the trolley from 11:00 A.M. to 5:00 P.M. Admission rates are $6.00 for adults, $5.00 for seniors (age 65 and older), and $4.00 for children (age 2 to 15). Those younger than 2 are admitted for free.

FESTIVALS AND ANNUAL EVENTS

No matter what your favorite interest, hobby, sport, or recreation, chances are good you'll find events throughout the Greater Pittsburgh area that will make you smile, and keep you plenty busy. Perusing this list will give you an overall picture of the broad range of activities and events our area has to offer at special times of the year—everything from county fairs and farm shows, marathons and parades, to ethnic celebrations and holiday festivities.

Unless indicated otherwise, events can be enjoyed free of charge, though specific portions of a festival or event—like food or a special performance—might require some cash outlay. For those festivals or special events that require an admission or entry fee the most current price level is given, but please know these are subject to change each year so it's best to check before heading out.

Also given are approximate dates and times for anything particularly special occurring within the activities and celebrations listed, but again, it's always best to call the sponsoring organization or group before making plans to attend. Where expositions are listed spanning many days, even entire weekends, the times are left out because they vary. Again, call in advance. Many of the shows at the David L. Lawrence Convention Center run well into the evenings. And of course, bring along enough money to any festival to cover the food, beverages, and crafts you might want to purchase. This is often the case even if there is no formal admission charged.

Rather than format this chapter geographically, I've followed the calendar, starting in January and ending up at the holidays. So grab your camera, put on your walking shoes, and get ready to have some fun.

JANUARY

Beaver County Annual Snow Shovel Contest
Economy Park, Legionville Hollow Road, Ambridge
(724) 846-5600
Contestants in this event ride on their favorite snow shovels, trying for the fastest time, as they slide down a 160-foot hill. You must be at least five years old to participate. Four different divisions are offered—for boys age 13 and younger, girls age 13 and younger, and adults, with a modified race for all ages. This modified class simply means those with "improved shovels." Registration starts at 11:00 A.M. and the contest begins at 1:00 P.M. The winner is the person with the fastest time to the bottom, where a trophy awaits. There is no charge to participate so bundle up, grab your shovel, and enjoy!

Recreational Vehicle Show
David L. Lawrence Convention Center
1001 Penn Avenue
(412) 565-6000
www.pghrvshow.com
The latest in recreational vehicles, including travel trailers, motor homes, fifth wheels, custom and conversion vans, campers, park models, pop-up camping trailers, truck caps, and utility trailers are on display on the convention center floor. Representatives are handy to answer questions you might have or help put you behind the wheel of your own Winnebago. If nothing else, just seeing the limitless camping possibilities primes you for sum-

mer and all its allure in the months ahead. Admission costs $7.00 for adults, $6.00 for seniors, and $5.00 for children (ages 6 to 16). Those younger than age 6 are admitted free of charge.

Pittsburgh Boat Show
David L. Lawrence Convention Center
1001 Penn Avenue
(412) 798-8858
www.pittsburghboatshow.net
This annual display of boats, big and small, along with the latest in other assorted watercraft, makes people in this boat-crazy region pray for an early spring on the three rivers. Included on the show-room floor are personal watercraft (such as Jet Skis), fishing boats, ski boats, plus house boats. You can even take boating exams and classes for various safety certi-fications, though advance registration may be necessary. Beginning January 2000, anyone operating a personal watercraft in Pennsylvania must possess a valid boating-safety certificate. Be sure to enter the contests (sometimes there's a cash give-away contest) and peruse the accompa-nying flea market to find a bargain treasure to add to your watercraft. Admis-sion costs $8.00 with children age 12 and younger admitted free of charge if accom-panied by an adult. Each person who completes a boating-safety class for certi-fication receives free admission to the Boat Show as well.

FEBRUARY

Winterlude Festival
Various locations throughout
Greensburg
(724) 838-4362
This monthlong major arts extravaganza celebrates the performing and visual arts all across Westmoreland County. The Grand Finale will conclude the event at the restored Palace Theatre, Greensburg. Hours do vary, with locations throughout the county. As the event is diverse with many different activities, please check

your local paper for particular listings and the prices charged at any particular show, display, concert, or screening.

CARQUEST World of Wheels
David L. Lawrence Convention Center
1000 Fort Duquesne Boulevard
(412) 565-6000
This unusual show features automobiles, hot rods, motorcycles, and monster trucks for the car fanatics, or simply the mildly curious. If you've ever fathomed sitting on a Harley, imagining the wind flowing through your hair, this is the place to come live out that fantasy! Celebrity appearances are also a part of the week-end. Adults can expect to pay $12.00, children (ages 6 to 12) $4.00, and those 5 and under are admitted free.

Pittsburgh Automobile Show
David L. Lawrence Convention Center
1001 Penn Avenue
(412) 565-6000
A Pittsburgh tradition, this show brings out the best in local automobile dealer-ships. Local dealers' newest models, plus manufacturers' prototypes of cars of the future, are on display. So picture yourself driving the car of your dreams. Here, you can hop right in behind the wheel (at least for a brief moment of glory!). The admis-sion charge for adults is $8.00, with chil-dren (ages 6 to 16) paying $6.00, and those younger than age 6 admitted free of charge.

MARCH

Charter Day
Old Economy Village
14th and Church Streets, Ambridge
(724) 266-4500
This free one-day event at Old Economy Village features exhibits of many old hand-crafts, including spinning and black-smithing, with the intent to introduce you to how the Harmonists lived (see the Attractions chapter for details about the Harmonists). There are crafts available for

purchase and musical entertainment every year. You'll feel you're stepping back in time with craft demonstrators dressed in clothing of centuries past. Plus, German food is typically on each year's menu. Do note that the hearty meals are served inside, which might be a welcome reprieve from the still-chilly temperatures. Though depending upon what the winter has allowed, you might see an early preview of the flowering spring bulbs and perennial herbs sprouting. Tours of Old Economy Village are conducted Tuesday through Saturday, 9:00 A.M. to 5:00 P.M. and Sunday noon to 5:00 P.M. Old Economy Village is closed Monday and winter holidays.

Pittsburgh Home & Garden Show
David L. Lawrence Convention Center
1001 Penn Avenue
(412) 565-6000
www.pghhome.com

A very large and popular event among Pittsburghers, the Home & Garden Show usually features more than 1,400 exhibits highlighting the latest in products for your house, yard, and garden. Information on interior design, landscaping, lawn care, furnishings, cooking, and other related topics is plentiful, and of course, you won't want to miss your chance at winning any number of prizes in various contests and giveaways. Adult admission costs $9.00, and children (ages 6 to 12) pay $4.00. Those younger than age 6 are free of charge.

St. Patrick's Day Parade
Downtown
(412) 621-0600
www.pittsburghirish.org/parade

Usually held the Saturday morning before St. Patrick's Day, this annual parade brings out the best Irish eyes in the city. The parade runs from Mellon Arena down Grant Street to the Boulevard of Allies, and there's a reviewing stand at Stanwix Street. Sponsored by the Irish Society for Education and Charities, the parade includes everything you'd expect on St.

Patty's Day: floats, celebrities, and lots of green on display. Usually you can count on seeing approximately 200 different parade entries, and it seems to be a tradition to watch the parade from parking garages (for a better view, and to stay dry in the unpredictable March weather). Of course, there's no charge to view the parade, so come out, wear your green shirts and hats, and be a little Irish for the day! Plenty of parties follow throughout the day in the Downtown area.

Spring Flower Show
Phipps Conservatory and Botanical
Gardens, Schenley Park
(412) 622-6914

The arrival of spring brings new blossoms and a bouquet of color at this Schenley Park conservatory in the Oakland neighborhood. Call for notice of special activities, including the annual Mother's Day Flower Sale, held each spring. The Flower Show lasts for about a month, while the Mother's Day sale runs the weekend of that special holiday. Phipps is open Tuesday through Sunday, 9:00 A.M. to 5:00 P.M. Phipps admission is $6.00 for adults, $5.00 for seniors age 60 and older, $4.00 for students with ID, and $3.00 for children (ages 2 to 12). Children younger than 2 years old and Phipps members enter without charge. Metered parking is right in front of the conservatory.

APRIL

Shrine Circus
Mellon Arena, 66 Mario Lemieux Place
(412) 642-1800

The Shriners have all that it takes for a festive circus adventure, with traditional clowns, wild animals and their trainers, magic tricks, illusions, and other zany surprises. Kids' eyes may light up at the fire rings lit for animals to jump through in the darkened arena. Ticket prices average approximately $10. There are usually eight shows (including three on Saturday) over the course of a long weekend.

Easter Egg Hunts
Trax Farms, 528 Trax Road, Finleyville
(412) 835-3246
www.traxfarms.com/events.htm
Held on numerous weekends leading up to Easter in this South Hills town, kids hunt for Easter eggs, enjoy pony rides, learn button making, have their faces painted, and walk away with a bag of goodies, treats, and other surprises. Of course, no egg hunt would be complete without a visit from the celebrated rabbit himself—the Easter Bunny. There's no admission charge for kids to hunt, though some of the other activities require money.

Antiques Show at the Carnegie
The Carnegie, 4400 Forbes Avenue
Oakland
(412) 622-3131
This show runs concurrently with other regular museum attractions and exhibits and features fine quality glass, furniture, jewelry, porcelain, silver, and various other works of art. The antiques are brought in and displayed by more than 50 different dealers, representing many states across the country. This isn't garage-sale stuff—they can be quite pricey, but certainly worth the look and price of the extra charge. Tickets for the Antiques Show cost $10.00 for members of the Carnegie and $15.00 for nonmembers. To browse the exhibits and/or make a purchase, you'll spend your time in the Music Hall Foyer and Hall of Architecture for the most part, which are consumed by this annual show.

Maple Syrup Festival
Brady's Run Park, off Route 51
Beaver County
(724) 774-7090
Held at the Brady's Run Park Lodge, this festival celebrates the annual spring bounty of the area's millions of maple trees. Come for the all-you-can-eat pancake breakfast and stay for demonstrations and old-time crafts, including lace making. The lines for breakfast can be long, but the wait is worth it, locals report. The concept is to tap the trees and explain the boiling-down process through which maple syrup is made. Admission rates (including breakfast) are $4.00 for adults. Children age 10 and younger are admitted free of charge. The event runs from 8:00 A.M. until 4:30 P.M.

Spring Festival
Trax Farms, 528 Trax Road, Finleyville
(412) 835-3246
www.traxfarms.com/events.htm
Step into spring with three days of celebrating flowers and sunshine and getting back into the fresh air at this South Hills farm. Garden lectures, display gardens, kids' activities, farm animals, demonstrations, giveaways, and other prizes are all part of this long weekend of celebrating the outdoors. There's no admission charge for the spring festival, so come, learn, and just have fun.

MAY

Cinco De Mayo
Station Square, Smithfield and
Carson Streets
(412) 562-9900
This Mexican festival marks the anniversary of the day the Mexicans defeated the French at the Battle of Puebla in 1862 (Cinco de Mayo means May 5th). Music, drinks, and food all have a Mexican flair here. There is no cover charge to attend, but individual vendors may charge for food and beverages.

Fort Pitt Museum Colonial Fair
Point State Park
(412) 281-9285
www.fortpittmuseum.com
The Fort Pitt Colonial Fair weekend is usually held one or two weekends before Memorial Day at the Fort Pitt Museum downtown in Point State Park. The museum itself is located in part of a re-created 18th-century British fort at the

confluence of the mighty Allegheny and Monongahela Rivers, which converge to form the Ohio River at this location. Military reenactments and performances are the attraction.

Greek Food Festival
419 South Dithridge Street
(412) 682-3866

In years past, more than 20,000 people have stopped in for an appetizing dose of Greek food and culture at this weeklong festival in the Oakland neighborhood. Greek lunches and dinners, plus dancing and live entertainment each evening are found at St. Nicholas Greek Orthodox Cathedral's community center. Imagine smelling the aroma of dishes you typically do not cook at home such as moussaka, pastita, and baklava. Normal hours run Sunday noon to 8:00 P.M., Monday through Friday 10:00 A.M. until 2:00 P.M. (lunch), and Monday through Thursday 5:00 to 9:00 P.M. (dinner). On Friday, dinner is served from 4:00 until 10:00 P.M. Prices for various parts of the festival vary each year so do call closer to the actual event.

Ambridge Nationality Days
Merchants Street from Fourth to
Eighth Streets, Ambridge
(412) 266-3040
www.nationalitydays.org

Held as an open-air street fair, this is a three- or four-day celebration of ethnic pride that offers tasty foods from all over the world along with live entertainment, crafts, and special children's activities and attractions. Traditional dancing has always been a part of the event, and you can count on 3 blocks of fabulous food stands with the aromas of Greek, American, Italian, and other cuisines wafting through the air. Italian, German, Croatian, Greek, Russian, Vietnamese, Scottish, Caribbean, Argentinean, Peruvian, Polish, Bosnian, and African-American dishes are represented. The festival begins at 10:00 A.M. and lasts until 9:30 P.M. As this is a street fair, there is no admission charge, just the cost of your food and beverages purchased.

National Pike Festival
Route 40, Washington, Fayette, and
Somerset Counties
(724) 437-9877, (800) 840-0274

Numerous towns in several counties participate in this festival along the historic National Pike, which we know today as Route 40. Washington (Washington County) and Uniontown (Fayette County) are two of the larger cities the road passes through as it cuts diagonally across the southwest corner of the state. Arts and crafts, antique cars, displays, food, and entertainment are all a part of the event. In years past, two wagon trains started at opposite ends of the route, traveling along and making encampments along the way. The best advice we can give you is to check the local newspapers closer to the actual festival (or call the number above) for particular offerings you're interested in, as this event covers three large counties. So get ready for a full range of fun, traveling back in history.

Many boroughs or municipalities host community days over the summer. Keep tabs with the local newspapers for dates and times.

Pittsburgh Children's Festival
134 Allegheny Center
(412) 321-5520

Youngsters will enjoy all the festivities, many of which are educational, at this North Side festival for the performing arts. Past performers have come from as far as South America, Europe, Asia, Australia, and certainly from other North American cities to perform. The event typically spans five days filled with puppetry, acrobatics, storytelling, participatory art projects, face painting, and sometimes paddle-boat rides. Look forward to the parade that's been a part of previous children's festivals. Local schools may even have booths of their own with children's activities. There is a $3.00 per person admission charge, but do know that shows are additional.

Pittsburgh Folk Festival
David L. Lawrence Convention Center
1001 Penn Avenue
(412) 565-6000

Usually held around Memorial Day weekend, this is a festive three-day ethnic event. More than 20 nationalities prevalent in the Pittsburgh area celebrate their heritages with colorful costumes, authentic folk dancing, native dishes, delicious desserts, and an international marketplace. In years past, tickets cost $5.00. Children age 12 and younger enjoy free admission.

JUNE

Three Rivers Arts Festival
Gateway Plaza and Point State Park
(412) 281-8723
www.artsfestival.net

A Downtown tradition for decades, new exhibitions and performers are introduced daily as a part of this 17-day festival. All types of art, crafts, dance, music, and food make this a memorable start to anyone's summer. Lunchtime for downtown office workers will never be the same after meandering the line of food booths at the entrance of Point State Park.

Just imagine the aroma of sizzling steak sandwiches and fried vegetables, let alone hot sausage, Chinese foods, and dozens of other tasty treats.

Most artists offer their work for sale, including handcrafted jewelry, pottery, photography, paintings, fiber art, and finished calligraphy. As years go by, the expanse of the arts festival has covered more of the downtown urban setting including the Art Institute of Pittsburgh and Wood Street Gallery (on the second floor of the Wood Street T station at Liberty Avenue).

The Three Rivers Arts Festival runs from the beginning of June through mid-month, and is free to the public. See the Getting Around chapter for tips on parking downtown or taking public transportation.

Historic Harmony House Tour
Harmony Museum, 218 Mercer Street
Harmony, Butler County
(724) 452-7341

Normally held the first Saturday in June, this event gives visitors the chance to tour the historically and architecturally significant Harmony House that lies in the historic district (exit 27 off Interstate 79, east of Zelienople). The site actually consists of five houses in addition to the museum buildings. Since the tour is self-guided, you can use the map to go at your own pace, and it costs $20 per person. Tours are given Tuesday through Sunday, 1:00 to 4:00 P.M., year-round. General admission is $3.50 for adults, $3.00 for seniors (age 60 and older), and $1.50 for children ages 6 through 12. Children younger than 6 years of age are admitted free of charge.

Mountain Top Bluegrass and Craft Festival
Mountain Top Park, Tarentum
Armstrong County
(724) 224-1511

Some of the top national bluegrass pickers and strummers come to Pittsburgh for the region's premier bluegrass festival. It brings a touch of Appalachia to Pittsburgh no doubt! This event, typically the first weekend in June, features the family fun of live music, crafts, workshops, horsedrawn wagon rides, camping, a petting zoo, and much more. There's also been a pig roast in previous years. A day pass costs $25 per person Thursday and Friday and $30 per person on Saturday. Children ages 10 to 16 get in for half price, and children younger than 10 years old are admitted free.

JULY

Big Butler Fair
Butler Fairgrounds, Route 422, Prospect
(724) 865-2400

Usually run from the end of June through July 4, this event takes place along Route 422, 6½ miles east of I-79. Livestock, horse and farm product demonstrations, exhibitions, and rides are all a part of this traditional county fair. In addition, browse the food stands, and enjoy country entertainment, harness racing, and other grandstand events. In years past, there's been a petting zoo and a Confederate railroad, too. Gates open at 9:00 A.M. and the carnival begins at 1:00 P.M. Cost is $8.00 per person, but if you come before 4:00 P.M. pay only $6.00 per person. Children younger than 2 years old are admitted free of charge, and parking comes at no cost as well.

Ellwood City Arts, Crafts & Food Festival
Ewing Park, Ellwood City
(724) 758-5630
www.ellwood-city-festival.net
More than 200 craft booths, art shows, entertainers, and food booths are offered at this annual Beaver County event held in Ewing Park, Ellwood City. The fun begins at 11:00 A.M. and keeps going strong until 10:00 P.M. Enjoy the free admission. On-site parking is available for $3.00 though you might park at no charge in outlying areas if you're willing to walk a few blocks.

Fourth of July Fireworks at the Point
Point State Park
(412) 471-0235
Fireworks displays are ignited in numerous Western Pennsylvania communities, but this one is perhaps the most spectacular. The Pittsburgh Symphony Orchestra performs a rousing patriotic concert under the stars and fireworks at the Point. Fireworks are courtesy of Zambelli International of New Castle, Lawrence County (also known as the fireworks capital of the world). The music and fireworks extravaganza comes at no cost, but do bring a blanket to spread out in Point State Park, and be prepared for the massive crowds and traffic jam exiting the city. The festivities get under way at dusk.

Greenberg's Train & Dollhouse Show
ExpoMart, 105 Mall Boulevard
Monroeville
(412) 856-8100
This is America's premier toy train and

At the 16th-century Renaissance Festival in Westmoreland County, early reservations for tickets usually means a slight reduction on price. So plan to order your tickets before June 10.

miniature railroad event, complete with a dramatic train layout, displays, and a huge dollhouse marketplace. In addition, there are ongoing how-to clinics, door prizes, and the latest in hobby books. This show will definitely give you plenty of project ideas to fill the remaining winter days! Adults will pay approximately $7.00 and children younger than 11 are free. The show also comes to ExpoMart in November.

Pittsburgh Vintage Grand Prix
Schenley Park
(412) 471-7847
Since 1983 the Pittsburgh Vintage Grand Prix has grown from a one-day vintage car race to a full week of activities. In addition to a rally at Point State Park and the main attraction, the race itself, which weaves along twisty turns in a gem of a city park, you can watch drivers compete in qualifying races, check out several classic car shows, buy automotive memorabilia, and perhaps participate in a mystery run as well.

Three Rivers Regatta
Point State Park
(412) 875-4841
www.pghregatta.com
This free, family-oriented weekend is full of thrilling air shows, on-land events, Formula 1 powerboat races, hot-air balloon races, fireworks, and waterskiing demonstrations. In prior years, the live music made coming out to the Regatta special even if you never saw the water attractions. Local musician Donnie Iris has performed as well as the group Blood, Sweat and Tears. The "Anything That Floats Race" has also been a regular event, with teams creating some type of seaworthy (in theory, anyway) transportation out of

materials not usually used for boatmaking. And one year, beer lovers not only sipped their favorite brew but also learned how it was made in a trailer-classroom created for the event.

Westmoreland Arts & Heritage Festival
Twin Lakes Park, off Route 30
Westmoreland County
(724) 834-7474
www.artsandheritage.com

Art comes alive at the kaleidoscope of creative expression usually held around the July 4th holiday in Unity Township. What makes the booths appealing are their juxtaposition around the lake. Get ready for arts, crafts, and music—everything from woodworking, painting and photography. Past festivalgoers have enjoyed poetry readings and performances by the Westmoreland Symphony, polka bands, fiddlers, and oldies music, country, and rock 'n' roll groups. International food booths offer a culinary complement as well. This festival begins at 11:00 A.M. and runs until 8:00 P.M. Shuttles and wheelchair-accessible vans run from the University of Pittsburgh at Greensburg. Round-trip shuttle tickets cost $2.00 per person.

South Side Summer Street Spectacular
East Carson Street
(412) 481-0651

A carnival-like atmosphere with a parade, fireworks, riverfront races, and live entertainment makes this Pittsburgh's largest neighborhood festival, held amid the South Side's coffee shops and novelty stores. As the event is an open-air celebration of fun and food, there is no admission charge, but be prepared to pay for food and drinks.

AUGUST

Beaver County Riverfest
Ohio River at Riverfront Park, Rochester
(724) 775-1200

This celebration of the region's rivers brings out residents of Beaver County for outdoor activities, fireworks, food, and great music. Bands typically perform on a stage constructed on the riverfront, and boaters enter a contest to determine the best decorated among them. Look up and you'll see skydivers, too. As this is open air, there's no admission charge, but you'll pay for food and other purchases.

Two Shadyside Arts Festivals
Walnut Street and Ellsworth Avenue
(412) 621-8481

Note there is a little rivalry of sorts between these two Shadyside festivals, but we couldn't alert you to one without the other. One festival encompasses the area between Walnut Street from South Negley to South Aiken Avenues. The Ellsworth Avenue celebration takes place between Maryland Avenue to Spahr Street.

Nightly outdoor jazz performances, workshops, and more than 200 designers of American collectibles exhibiting their wares are a part of these large community events. Recycled art and neon art plus multidimensional pieces have been on display for serious art aficionados in years past. Both festivals showcase local talent, and there is running shuttle service from various points in Shadyside to avoid any parking nightmares. A few of these shuttle points include Shadyside Hospital, the Pittsburgh Center for the Arts, and Sacred Heart Academy.

Washington County Agricultural Fair
Washington Fairgrounds, 2151 North
Main Street, Washington
(724) 225-7718

Agricultural and commercial exhibits, rides, games, entertainment, tractors, animals, the 4-H and FFA exhibits, a market livestock sale and refreshments are all a part of this weeklong county-wide fair, now more than 200 years old. Trolley service to fairgrounds is provided by the Pennsylvania Trolley Museum. Admission costs $6.00 for the event that runs from 8:00 A.M. until 11:00 P.M.

Hookstown Fair
**One mile from Route 168 and
Route 30, Hookstown, Beaver County
(724) 573-4512
www.hookstownfair.com**
This weeklong fair, more than 50 years
old, has entertainment, tractor pulls, rides,
a demolition derby, fireworks, food, and
plenty of other fun, including live country
music. There is no official Beaver County
fair, but this one takes on that type of
ambience. Admission costs $7.00 for
adults and children. However, seniors can
enter free before 5:00 P.M. (rides not
included). Parking is plentiful in this open
area that resembles a big old farm.

Westmoreland County Fair
**Westmoreland Fairgrounds, R.D. 2
Greensburg
(724) 423-5005**
Generally held during a week in the middle of August, this county fair has the
usual rundown of rides, entertainment,
food, and fun that residents look forward
to each summer. Look to the local papers
or call the number listed above for the
current admission charges and any special
attractions taking place.

Greater Pittsburgh Renaissance Festival
**Route 31E, west of New Stanton
(724) 872-1670
www.pgh-renfest.com**
From August 14 through September 19,
this re-creation of a 16th-century village
brings together crafters, acting troupes,
combat jousting, musicians, and food purveyors in a village setting to celebrate the
arrival of the king and queen. The Westmoreland County festival is an appealing
history experience for all ages. Children
will particularly enjoy the Children's Dell
and petting zoo. Held over five weekends,
the event was moved to a new site in
recent years on Route 31 East, 7 miles
west of New Stanton in Southwestern
Westmoreland County. Take exit 51A on
Interstate 70 (for those of you traveling
that route). Admission is $11.95 in advance
or $13.95 at the gate for adults, and chil-

dren (ages 5 to 12) pay $3.95 in advance
or $5.95 at the gate.

SEPTEMBER

Ligonier Highland Games
**Idlewild Park, Route 30, Ligonier
(724) 851-9900**
The first weekend after Labor Day brings
a Scottish fair to Ligonier, featuring bagpipe bands, highland dancing, Scottish
fiddling, children's games, exhibits, and
more. Friday and Saturday evening activities include dinner and entertainment at
Mountain View Inn, by reservation only.
Event hours for Saturday and Sunday are
9:00 A.M. until 6:00 P.M. Admission charges
are $15.00 for adults and $5.00 for children ages 6 to 12. Those younger than age
6 enter at no cost. Parking is free as well.
Group discounts are available.

Annual Pennsylvania Arts & Crafts Colonial Festival
**Westmoreland Fairgrounds, R.D. 2
Greensburg
(724) 863-4577**
Experience the pride and skill of colonial
men and women in more than 170 booths
as they create hand-thrown pottery, handcrafted furniture, dried floral arrangement,
stained glass, tole and decorative painting,
and much more. In years past there have
been military encampments, a fife and
drum group, a Civil War string band, carriage rides, children's activities, and
refreshments at this multiday event. Rates
for adults are $5.00, $4.50 for seniors,
and $1.00 for children ages 6 to 12. There
are indoor as well as outdoor exhibits, so
come rain or shine!

Pittsburgh Irish Festival
**Chevrolet Amphitheatre, Station Square
(412) 422-1113**
Irish and Celtic folk music is the focus
of this festival, usually held around the
second weekend in September, running
from Friday night through most of Sunday. Get ready for a long list of perform-

ers and bands. Previous years the talent
has included the Great Big Sea band,
Tommy Makem and the Makem Brothers,
David Kincaid, and Mike Gallagher. There's
plenty of traditional Irish dancing too.
Admission in past years has been $9.00
for adults, $3.00 for children (ages 3 to
12), and complimentary tickets for children
age 2 and younger. A three-day pass
costs around $16.

Penn's Colony Festival
Allison Park, Allegheny County
(724) 352-9922

This is the closest thing you'll find to
Colonial Williamsburg, and we've got it
here in Western Pennsylvania! This is an
18th-century colonial marketplace featuring 230 American folk artists and cottage
craftsmen with authentic entertainment
and food. Demonstrations here have
included sheep clipping and wool preparation, soapmaking as done in colonial
times, and hand stenciling for the kids.
Come Friday from 1:00 to 5:00 P.M., Saturday from 10:00 A.M. until 6:00 P.M., and
Sunday 10:00 A.M. until 5:00 P.M. Admission in prior years has been $6.50 for
adults, $4.50 for seniors (ages 65 and
older), and $3.50 for children (ages 8 to
15). Children age 7 and younger receive
complimentary admission. Parking is free
of charge.

Covered Bridge Festival
Various locations throughout
Washington County
(724) 228-5520

Traditionally held the third weekend in
September, there's old-fashioned hospitality in store at this festival among the
rolling hills of southwestern Pennsylvania. Old-time fiddlers perform in addition
to the arts and crafts, antique cars and
engines, guns, and other artifacts that
are displayed. Country-style food is also
available at different covered bridges
throughout Washington County. In prior
years just under a dozen of the covered
bridges in the county were featured, and

each one has its own natural flavor.
There are approximately 218 covered
bridges that remain standing in the
Commonwealth of Pennsylvania. The
exploring begins at 10:00 A.M. and continues until 5:00 P.M. Admission and
parking for this covered bridge festival
are free of charge.

Richard S. Caliguiri/City of Pittsburgh
Great Race & Walk
Frick Park to Point State Park
(412) 255-2493

This race is always held the last Sunday
in September. Nearly 11,000 runners from
around the world, many donning hilari-
ous costumes, compete in this annual
10K great race, 5K run, and 5K walk, held
in honor of the late Richard S. Caliguiri,
former mayor of Pittsburgh. Caliguiri
died in 1988 after a lingering illness in the
prime of his political career. The race
begins at Frick Park and moves to Point
State Park downtown, where it con-
cludes. Early bird registrations save you
money. If you submit them before July
16, the fee is $16.00. Then, those register-
ing before September 3, pay $18.95.
Thereafter, it costs $25 to register.

Oktoberfest
Penn Brewery, Troy Hill Road
and Vinial Street
(412) 237-9402

This traditional event is held on the last
two weekends in September to coincide
with the actual Oktoberfest in Germany.
The North Side's German heritage is in
full swing as the Pennsylvania Brewing
Company marks this event. Dine in the
brewery restaurant on such traditional
German fare as schnitzel, sauerbraten,
and potato pancakes. In the outdoor tent,
there's often grilled wurst and chicken,
pork, and strudel. Ongoing entertainment
provided by German bands and a
strolling accordionist complete the ambience. And of course, there are plenty of
beers to sample. Celebrate your German
heritage (or pretend to!) on Friday and

Saturday from 5:00 P.M. to midnight, or on Sunday from 4:00 to 10:00 P.M. The hearty aromas will tempt you, so bring along money for your food and beverage purchases.

OCTOBER

Bridgewater Pumpkinfest
214 Bridge Street, Bridgewater
(724) 774-7615
The second weekend in October, the Beaver County community of Bridgewater blocks off several streets to celebrate autumn in this charming area filled with antiques and specialty stores. Previous favorites of this festival include the pumpkin pie bake-off, the giant pumpkin weigh-off, and Little Miss Pumpkinfest. There have also been adult and children's games, food vendors, crafters, and a spectacular fireworks display. Of course, the prime attraction is the weigh-off, which often requires flatbed trucks and farm equipment just to maneuver the pumpkins, some of which weigh hundreds of pounds. If nothing more, bring the kids out to watch! This pumpkinfest is held Saturday, 10:00 A.M. until 8:00 P.M., and on Sunday from noon until 6:00 P.M. As it's open air in nature, there is no admission charge except for your purchases.

Meadowcroft Maize Days
Meadowcroft Museum, 401 Meadowcroft Road, Avella
(724) 587-3412
This festival is usually around the third weekend in October. Experience autumn in its glory with this celebration of corn and Western Pennsylvania's farming heritage, featuring corn shelling and grinding, cornhusk doll making, blacksmithing, flax scotching, children's games, and old-time music. Learn to make apple butter and enjoy horse-drawn wagon rides too. Meadowcroft is only open on Saturday and Sunday this time of year. To enter, adults pay $6.50 and children pay $3.50.

Houston Pumpkin Festival
American Legion Picnic Grounds
Houston
(800) 531-4114
Sponsored by the Houston Volunteer Fire Department in Washington County, this fall festival features baked goods, crafts, entertainment, a children's petting zoo, pony rides, pumpkin decorating, and an orange pumpkin bouncer. Bring the kids on Saturday from 10:00 A.M. until 7:00 P.M. or on Sunday from 10:00 A.M. until 6:00 P.M.

During the month of December, many churches offer dramatic presentations of the journey to Bethlehem, free of charge, as a gift to their communities. Keep an eye out for mentions of these in community newspapers, church bulletins, and through word of mouth.

American Indian Gathering
Community College of Beaver County
One Campus Drive, Monaca
(724) 775-8561
Usually held around the second weekend in October, this weekendlong event is held at the college's Golden Dome. There's Native American dancing, crafts on display and for purchase, food, as well as seminars about American Indians. In past years the organizers charged $2.00 for admission for adults, seniors, and older children. Those ages 5 to 12 enter at $1.00 and children younger than age 5 are admitted free of charge.

Fort Ligonier Days
Route 30 and Route 711, Ligonier
(724) 238-9701
This three-day Westmoreland County festival commemorates the battle at Fort Ligonier in 1758 during the French and Indian War. It's the largest celebration in town with 150 juried craftspeople, merchant sidewalk sales, entertainment, antique window displays, and a huge

parade on Saturday at 11:00 A.M. There are more than 30 food booths around the diamond, or bandstand area. Look for an official program to guide you through the festival. It's a supplement to the *Ligonier Echo* newspaper. Admission rates are $6.75 for adults and $3.75 for children (ages 6 to 14). Children younger than age 6 are admitted free of charge.

Fall Foliage Cruises
Along the Allegheny River
Armstrong County
(724) 548-3226

All month long, you're invited to board boats of the Gateway Clipper Fleet to experience the beautiful autumn foliage along the Allegheny River in Armstrong County northeast of Pittsburgh. The atmosphere is relaxing as you see the region from a totally different (waterfront) perspective. Cruises, which have in the past cost around $20 per person, are offered throughout the month of October and sail from 1:30 until 4:30 P.M.

Fall Flower Show
Phipps Conservatory and Botanical
Gardens, Schenley Park
(412) 622-6914

Fall foliage is on display indoors with the splendor of autumn accented in the various rooms of the Schenley Park conservatory in Oakland.

Phipps is open Tuesday through Sunday, 9:00 A.M. to 5:00 P.M. Phipps admission is $6.00 for adults, $5.00 for seniors age 60 and older, $4.00 for students with ID, and $3.00 for children (ages 2 to 12). Children younger than 2 years old and Phipps members enter without charge. Metered parking is right in front of the conservatory.

The Pennsylvania Arts & Crafts
Christmas Festival
Washington Fairgrounds
2151 North Main Street, Washington
(724) 863-4577

This festival, held in late October and early November, boasts more than 165 exhibit booths with artists and craftspeople displaying hand-thrown pottery, handcrafted furniture, dried floral arrangements, stained glass, clothing, quilts, children's toys, wrought iron, and lots more. Santa Claus and Emmett the Elf are here for children. Trolley rides are also available. Exhibits are displayed in five heated buildings, Friday, Saturday and Sunday 10:00 A.M. until 6:00 P.M. Admission is $5.00 for adults $4.50 for seniors (ages 65 and older), $1.00 for kids (ages 6 to 12), and complimentary for children younger than age 6.

NOVEMBER
AND DECEMBER

Sparkle Season & Light Up Night
Various locations throughout Downtown
(412) 566-4190

Light Up Night traditionally kicks off the holiday shopping season within the Golden Triangle, known as Sparkle Season. Light Up Night begins at 5:00 P.M. on a Friday evening and lasts until midnight. Downtown office buildings remain lit, and retailers have their holiday displays illuminated.

PPG Place is aglow in luminaria and its own towering tree. Several trees, including the Unity Tree (formerly the Joseph Horne Co. tree) at Penn Avenue Place, are unveiled, and there is the creche at the USX Plaza. (Read more about it in the Worship chapter.)

Looking down at the city from Mt. Washington is a great vantage point, especially for the fireworks.

Throughout the rest of Sparkle Season, activities, events, and displays appear throughout the city to celebrate Christmas, Chanukah, Kwanzaa, and New Year's. One such display is the Santa Exhibit at the PPG Wintergarden. The "Celebrate the Season" parade is the Saturday after Thanksgiving. And if you feel worn out, take the Holly Trolley shuttling downtown shoppers throughout the Golden Triangle. It's free of charge, and stops at the major plazas, department stores, in the Cultural

District, and at the Heinz History Center in the Strip District.

Sparkle Season brochures are available at the major Downtown buildings with a complete list of events and special shopping hours during the holiday season.

Beaver County Festival of Trees
Brady's Run Park, off of Route 51
Beaver County
(724) 846–2411
www.beavercountyfestivaloftrees.org
This winter wonderland—indoors, mind you—lasts a long weekend and has approximately 58 decorated trees, continuous entertainment, a Santa snack bar, visits by Santa, and a talking Frosty the Snowman. Community groups and businesses decorate these trees, which are sold at the end of the festival. There's a Santa's gift shop and a model railroad on display in the park's large recreation center. Thursday hours are from 5:00 to 9:00 P.M. All other days, come around noon and stay until 9:00 P.M. Admission costs $3.00 for everyone ages 13 to 60, $2.00 for seniors, 50 cents for children ages 6 to 12, and free for those age 5 and under.

Overly's Country Christmas
Westmoreland Fairgrounds, R.D. 2
Greensburg
(800) 9OVERLY
One of America's largest light displays (according to *Good Housekeeping* magazine), this extravaganza began at the home of the late Harry E. Overly years ago. But it grew too massive and was moved to the fairgrounds.

Another drive-through event, Overly's Country Christmas boasts animated displays, more than 800,000 lights, a gift shop, outdoor barbecue, cookie barn, bonfires, and a manger scene with live animals. Rides on a horse-drawn sleigh or wagon are also part of the fun. Overly's Country Christmas is open daily for a couple of weeks before Christmas, usually from 5:30 to 10:00 P.M. Cost is $8.00 per car.

Don't miss the display of life-size Santas from around the world at the PPG Place Wintergarden in downtown Pittsburgh each holiday season.

Clayton Holiday Tours
The Frick Art & Historical Center
7227 Reynolds Street
(412) 371–0600
www.frickart.org
From mid-November through the New Year's holiday, visitors to the Frick Art & Historical Center can enjoy extended hours and special holiday tours of Henry Clay Frick's Clayton. This 23-room, turn-of-the-20th-century residence is the only surviving estate in Pittsburgh's East End (Pointe Breeze), the once-fabled millionaires' row. Watchful holiday guests at Clayton might even catch a glimpse of Father Christmas, dressed in Victorian costume. They certainly gather a sense of the closeness associated with Frick holidays at Clayton. Of course, the mansion is decorated with pine, poinsettias, and other winter blooms, and the scent of evergreens prevails. For families with children ages 6 to 12, the Frick presents Family Holidays at Clayton, special tours for kids, on several Saturdays in December from 9:30 until 11:30 A.M. Cost is $10.00 for one adult/one child for nonmembers, and $7.00 for members. Additional children cost $5.00 ($3.00 for members).

Hours during the holiday season are Tuesday through Saturday from 10:00 A.M. until 5:00 P.M. and Sunday from noon until 6:00 P.M. Evening tours (which run until 8:00 P.M.) are offered on selected days so it's best to call for the exact dates each year. Tours of Clayton cost $10.00 for adults, $8.00 for seniors, and $6.00 for students. Members are admitted free of charge.

For more information about Clayton and the Frick museums, turn to the Architecture and Arts chapters.

ZooLights
Pittsburgh Zoo & Aquarium
One Hill Road
(412) 665-3640
Brought to the zoo by AT&T, ZooLights transforms the zoo into a display of more than 500,000 lights from 5:30 until 8:30 P.M. closing time each night for approximately six weeks. Visitors can stop at various indoor locations for hot cocoa, to see the indoor zoo exhibits, or merely to warm up from the brisk night air. The Pittsburgh Zoo is closed on Christmas Eve and Christmas Day. Admission to ZooLights costs approximately $4.00 for nonmembers and $3.00 for zoo members. Parking for Zoo-Lights is free.

Santa's Trolley
Pennsylvania Trolley Museum, off Race
Track Road, Washington County
(724) 228-9256
www.pa-trolley.org
The trolley begins operation the day after Thanksgiving and runs for three weekends. All aboard the Santa Express! Kris Kringle arrives in true trolley fashion to kick off the holiday season's popular Santa's Trolley. Children and their families can ride with Santa aboard one of the vintage trolleys while listening to the sounds of Christmas carols. Kids can make special crafts, and visitors can operate the Lionel trains on the museum's large "you run it" display. Santa's Trolley pulls out regularly from 11:00 A.M. until 5:00 P.M. Admission rates are $6.00 for adults, $5.00 for seniors (age 65 and older), and $4.00 for

children (age 2 to 15). Those younger than age two are admitted free.

Great Miniature Railroad & Village
Carnegie Science Center, next to Three
Rivers Stadium, One Allegheny Avenue
(412) 237-3400
Whereas many other train displays close up shop after the holiday season, this North Side one stays open Thanksgiving through the end of January, and throughout many months of the year.

This is a true Pittsburgh tradition. The railroad display began in the 1950s, but because of the limited space, had to be dismantled each spring. Now, the 2,300-square-foot exhibit, featuring new models each year, is left in place, closed only periodically for refurbishment (for a week in June and again from September 27 through mid-November). The miles of train display feature an O-gauge railroad and beautiful animated scenery showing the region's history.

Regular hours run Sunday through Friday from 10:00 A.M. until 5:00 P.M. and on Saturday from 10:00 A.M. to 9:00 P.M.

Admission costs vary. Adults can see the exhibits for $14, children (ages 3 to 18) and seniors (age 65 and older) pay $10, and science center members are free. For more detailed prices for the rest of the science center facility and attractions, turn to the Attractions chapter.

LeMoyne House Candlelight Tours
East Maiden Street, Washington
(724) 225-6740
Typically this event is held the first weekend in December. Sponsored by the Washington County Historical Society, these evening candlelight tours show the LeMoyne House decorated for Christmas with costumed actors portraying members of the LeMoyne family. Admission rates are $5.00 for adults and $3.00 for students. Candlelight hours run from 5:00 to 9:00 P.M. on Saturday and 2:00 to 6:00 P.M. on Sunday.

If you plan to attend the Great Miniature Railroad Village at the Carnegie Science Center, know in advance that holidays are the peak period. More than 6,000 visitors each day pass through in the week between Christmas and New Year's. So plan to stand in line.

Candlelight Christmas at Old Economy Village
Old Economy Village, 14th and Church Streets, Ambridge
(724) 266-1803, (724) 266-4500

Traditional German Christmas decorations and legends are displayed in the historic village of the 19th-century Harmony Society, here in Beaver County. Food, crafts, and entertainment are always a part of the annual festivities. More than 25 rooms are decorated for the season, nightly from 5:00 until 9:00 P.M. Please know that this event is held for only two days, usually at the start of December, so do call in advance or you might miss out. The village, lit only by the glow of candlelight and with the scent of pine prevailing, is sure to put you in the holiday spirit! The tour takes you out of the hustle and bustle of the season, allowing you to focus on simplicity. Cost is $6.00 per person. For those interested in the special Christmas Dinner Tour, cost is $45 per person, and reservations are necessary. The dinner typically takes place after the two-day tours, but again, call for the exact day and times.

Holidays at The Carnegie
The Carnegie, 4400 Forbes Avenue
(412) 622-3131

Stop in to see this annual Christmas tree exhibit that illuminates the Hall of Architecture. Each year, there's a different theme. Past trees have celebrated the Russian czars, French impressionists, and Victorian England. Traditional carols echo throughout the great halls of the museum and art galleries. Previous exhibits have included rare nativity scenes and spiritual paintings. Concerts are performed most days.

Admission to the Carnegie Museum of Natural History and Museum of Art is $10.00 for adults, $7.00 for senior citizens, and $6.00 children (ages 3 to 18). Children younger than age 3 and members are admitted free of charge. Call for the Carnegie's Holiday Program Guide.

Many small train displays are presented locally each December, such as the one the Penn Hills Police display at their municipal building. Call your own borough or municipality for local exhibits.

Festival of Lights
Ligonier Valley Library, West Main Street, Ligonier
(724) 238-6818

This is a monthlong display of decorated trees and wreaths designed by local families within Westmoreland County along with those contributed by area businesses and the Ligonier Valley Historical Society. There's also a holiday boutique with handcrafted items. Cost for adults is $2.00. Children are admitted for 50 cents.

Holiday Open House at the Nationality Rooms
Cathedral of Learning, Fifth Avenue and Bigelow Boulevard, University of Pittsburgh
(412) 624-6000

For the month, 24 nationality rooms representing European, Middle Eastern, Asian, and African cultures are on display with holiday decorations representing their individual traditions and heritages. Guides appear in national dress, and there are continuous performances, and sometimes also delicious ethnic foods. Rooms are open from noon until 4:00 P.M. daily.

Candlelight Evenings at Phipps Conservatory and Botanical Gardens
Phipps Conservatory and Botanical Gardens, Schenley Park
(412) 622-6914
www.phipps.conservatory.org

Throughout December the conservatory remains open later than usual during the holiday season each year. The rooms are dressed for the holidays with lights and festive decorations. Special tours can be arranged.

Phipps admission is $6.00 for adults, $5.00 for seniors age 60 and older, $4.00 for students with ID, and $3.00 for children (ages 2 to 12). Children younger than age 2 and Phipps members enter without charge. Metered parking is right in front of the conservatory.

First Night
Various locations throughout Downtown
(888) PGH–FEST
www.firstnightpgh.com
Go out with a big bang, as the expression says! Pittsburgh's First Night Celebration occurs each year for families. It's the city's way of planning a safe alternative for New Year's Eve. Events and locations vary, but package deals are available so that families can book a room at a downtown hotel.

Public transportation into the downtown area is also offered. Performances in years past have included Joe Negri from *Mister Rogers' Neighborhood* and Margo Loveland puppets, among others. Fireworks are courtesy of Zambelli International of New Castle, Lawrence County (also known as the fireworks capital of the world).

In past years, those who wanted to attend all events had to purchase a First Night button costing $15.00 for adults and $5.00 for children (ages 6 to 12). Children younger than 6 did not have to pay. But if you just want to see what's happening in the open-air spaces, there is no cost for First Night. Check the daily newspaper for particulars each year, including special parking and public transportation hours.

ARCHITECTURE

As the sun sets on Pittsburgh's Golden Triangle, it lights the pinnacles of PPG Place and reflects off several other shimmering skyscrapers that are the city's architectural gems. These dominant corporate headquarters, including the mighty USX Tower, add aesthetically as well as economically to the city. Often the modern buildings reflect the transitions our companies have undergone—companies such as PPG industries (Pittsburgh Plate Glass decades ago) and USX Corporation (formerly United States Steel).

Today, nothing is half-veiled in smoke the way many buildings erected in 19th-century Pittsburgh were back when heavy industry polluted the skies. And plenty of these structures merit close attention, especially for aficionados of great architecture. In this chapter, discover the highlights, including the works of famous architects and a brief tour of architectural masterpieces you won't want to miss.

Of course, with any remarkable achievement and improvement comes controversy, and Pittsburgh has had its share. For instance, downtown Pittsburgh was a picture of urban vitality back in the late 1940s. Well before shopping malls, many downtown merchants thrived in Italianate, Victorian Gothic, or art deco buildings.

In an effort to restore such commercial vitality to the downtown area, Mayor Tom Murphy and the city's Urban Redevelopment Authority have struggled with a plan that will forge ahead into the future while saving at least some semblance of the past. As you might guess, it's hard to merge the wishes of the preservationists with the needs of modern merchants. At this writing, it's hoped that many important architectural facades can be maintained while making way for new construction of shopping and entertainment complexes.

You will notice in this chapter that we depart from the geographic breakdown used in other chapters throughout this book. Instead, we start with information on history and preservation efforts and close the chapter with a short list of important buildings and bridges, some of which are broken down by region. The highlight of the chapter is our downtown walking tour, which features many of Pittsburgh's most important buildings. If you've never taken a walking tour, now's your chance.

In keeping with the architectural theme, this chapter focuses more on the structural aspects of design than the historical appeal. So you won't find descriptions of buildings simply because they are old. Of course, architecture and history overlap, and where appropriate, you might want to refer to the History chapter.

Now, get ready to read about the fascinating creations and works of building art brought about by names such as Hornbostel, Janssen, Klauder, Osterling, Richardson, and Wright. Their contributions quite literally made our city what it is today.

ARCHITECTURAL PERIODS

From the formation of Fort Pitt after the British took hold of the Pittsburgh Point in 1758, this city has enjoyed a rich discussion of its structural heritage. This settlement phase was followed by the Georgian simplicity of 1785 to 1830. The latter-day form of Georgian style is what we now call the Federal style.

The Greek Revival period came next, followed by the mid-Victorian era. The Manchester and Mexican War Streets neighborhoods on the city's North Side remain primarily Victorian examples of architecture. Unfortunately, this mid-Victorian style was thought by some to have a harsh appearance.

New ideas characterized the years following the Civil War. Helping to propel these insights was the American Institute of Architects, which became a national organization in 1857. Architectural schools, exhibitions, and journals became recognized forces. All of this focus culminated in a time of experimentation, most notably in East Coast cities such as Boston and Philadelphia. Henry Hobson Richardson was one of these experimental architects.

Richardson, his firm based in Brookline, Massachusetts, submitted his plans to rebuild the Allegheny County Courthouse and Jail in 1883. (In May 1882, fire had gutted the rotunda of the second county courthouse, reducing the building to a sandstone shell.) The first and original jail structure had been built in the Downtown Market Square area (known as the Diamond in years prior).

The simplicity of Richardson's Romanesque design was alluring with its rounded arches, rugged stone walls, and Byzantine leaf carving. He was formally chosen for the job from among competitors in 1884.

Of course, the original jail and courthouse site was 10 feet higher due to a hump, commonly referred to as Grant's Hill, that was eventually lowered in 1912. Subsequent widening of Grant Street required that the entrances be lengthened in the 1920s. But to look upon the finished structure is to see the beauty of the intricate carvings, the rise of the tower, the way in which the sun grazes the exterior stone, and most certainly the handsome grand staircase Richardson created.

The Allegheny County Courthouse and jail are regarded as the finest works of architecture in the city. Richardson is quoted as saying, "If they honor me for the pygmy things I have already done, what will they say when they see Pittsburgh finished?" Sadly, the architect passed away before his vision was realized. Work did not conclude on these structures until 1888, two years after he died. (See walking tour below.)

ADDITIONAL ARCHITECTURAL STRIDES

As the application of architecture became more professional around the country, Pittsburgh felt the effects as well. The Carnegie Technical Schools, founded in 1900 and the predecessor of today's Carnegie Mellon University, incorporated architecture into its curriculum in 1905. Architects sought more modern ways of designing. American architects practicing their trade between 1890 and 1930 are loosely categorized as Eclectics.

Henry Hornbostel, a partner in the New York firm of Palmer & Hornbostel, won the 1904 competition for the master plan of the Carnegie Technical Schools. During the next two decades, Hornbostel carved out his architectural domain, quite literally, in the Oakland-Shadyside area. Among the buildings he designed were the Rodef Shalom Temple, Soldiers' and Sailors' Memorial, the U.S. Bureau of Mines building (now a part of CMU), the Schenley Apartments, and the University Club in Oakland. Two downtown buildings, the City-County Building and the Grant Building, are also among Hornbostel's creations.

Major Eclectic buildings erected during the Great Depression include the Gulf Building and Mellon Institute (both Downtown), East Liberty Presbyterian Church (in East Liberty), Buhl Planetarium (on the North Side), and the Cathedral of Learning and Heinz Chapel (both in Oakland at the University of Pittsburgh). Engineers, contractors, and suppliers were accustomed to the whims, even fantasies, of architects during this time. However, as material became more expensive and money in short supply during the war years, Eclecticism steadily declined. (Read more detail of these noteworthy buildings later in this chapter.)

PITTSBURGH'S RENAISSANCE

It wasn't until the 1950s that the architectural effects of Pittsburgh's first Renaissance could actually be seen, although plans for revitalization had begun years before. Soon after World War II ended, smoke abatement became one of the city's priorities. Business and government leaders—Republican Richard King Mellon and Democrat David L. Lawrence, chief among them—joined forces for the future. Mellon and Lawrence were indeed a powerful pair, convincing the city's populace to listen to their ideas for Pittsburgh's Renaissance.

The Fort Pitt Blockhouse was saved, but freight terminals at what is now Point State Park gave way to create the Gateway Center office complex. It's interesting to note that many ideas had surfaced to create the Point as we know it today. Among the visions tabled were those Edgar J. Kaufmann, the department store owner, commissioned from his own architect, Frank Lloyd Wright. Grandiose schemes were quietly put aside for they lacked any concern over cost and were considered to be extravagant for the times.

The building boom continued all over the region. In the 1950s the lower Hill District was cleared to make room for the Civic Arena, now known as the Mellon Arena. Structures on the North Side in the former city of Allegheny made way for Allegheny Center. Other buildings, particularly those of historical significance, were saved in part by the Pittsburgh History & Landmarks Foundation, founded in 1964.

Also during this time, buildings began to display their corporate products. The firm of Harrison & Abramovitz showed off the functional and decorative uses of aluminum in the Alcoa Building, erected in the early 1950s. The firm did the same years later in 1970, designing the U.S. Steel Building (now the USX Tower).

In the mid-1970s, Landmarks turned its attention to another large-scale property, the Pittsburgh & Lake Erie Railroad complex. With an eye toward commercial revitalization, Landmarks saw potential in this site along the south shore of the Monongahela River. Why not try the notion of historic preservation coupled with urban development? The result is what we know today as Station Square on the South Side. Five historic railroad buildings were saved and adapted beside several new buildings.

Renaissance II

Pittsburgh's second Renaissance altered the skyline yet again. Although the 680-foot main tower of PPG Place still doesn't match the height of the USX Tower (at 841 feet), the complex architecturally changed the city forever. Perhaps no other structure since Klauder's Cathedral of Learning or Richardson's County Courthouse has had the impact of PPG Place.

Here we see Gothic translated into plate glass by architect John Burgee with Philip Johnson. The six buildings that comprise PPG Place were completed in 1984 and are leased to various retailers and businesses.

Also in the 1980s, the old Jenkins Arcade was razed to make way for Fifth Avenue Place. This and the CNG Tower are smaller, yet substantial additions to the city as well, since the former houses an upscale shopping complex (see the Shopping chapter) and the latter the corporate headquarters of Consolidated Natural Gas.

Since the city is home to two internationally known programs in architectural education, at Carnegie Mellon University and the University of Pittsburgh, this region will surely see more forward movement in the architectural scheme of things. Whether it's a new engineering marvel spanning one of Pittsburgh's famous rivers, or a new skyscraper designed for aesthetic as well as economic purposes, rest assured the future of Pittsburgh will be beautiful to behold.

Thinking Green

Pittsburgh boasts more green buildings—including the new David L. Lawrence Convention Center—than any other city in the nation. FYI, according to the Green Building Alliance, green buildings incorporate design and construction practices that reduce or eliminate the negative impact of buildings on the environment and occupants in five broad areas: sustainable site planning, safeguarding water and water efficiency, energy efficiency and renewable energy, conservation of materials and resources, and indoor environmental quality. Energy savings of between 25 and 50 percent are common for green buildings, and a few cases have documented 90 percent savings!

ARCHITECTURAL EXHIBITS

Hall of Architecture
The Carnegie, 4400 Forbes Avenue
(412) 622-5550
www.cmoa.org/html/hilites/framearc.htm
In this grand space, architecture has been an important part of the Carnegie since it opened in 1895. Carnegie Institute, designed by Longfellow, Alden & Harlow, was an outstanding example of academic Classicism. The Hall of Architecture, which opened in 1907, became a major feature of The Carnegie, with 144 full-scale plaster casts of building fragments—pulpits, columns, portals, and pediments, even an entire facade capturing the history of Western architecture.

Here you can see the east and west fronts of the Parthenon as well as a portal of the north transept of the Cathedral of Sainte-Andre at Bordeaux. Browsing through this skylit space, designed especially for the display of these casts, you will see samples of columns, pillars, and doorways from Romanesque, Italian Byzantine, French Gothic, and many other periods of historic architecture.

The Hall of Architecture is one of three surviving cast courts today, and it is the only one in North America. It's not uncommon to see groups of students gathered within the room studying the displays. Indeed, the purpose of the hall's creation was so that everyone, not just those who could afford to travel abroad, could study the form and detail of architecture in full scale.

The Hall of Architecture is open during regular museum hours, Monday through Saturday 10:00 A.M. to 5:00 P.M. and Sunday, noon to 5:00 P.M. Admission is $10.00 for adults, $7.00 for senior citizens, and $6.00 for children (ages 3 to 18). Children younger than age 3 and members are admitted free of charge.

The Heinz Architectural Center
Carnegie Museum of Art
4400 Forbes Avenue
(412) 622-5550
www.cmoa.org/html/hilites/heinz.htm
Founded in 1990, the Heinz Architectural Center honors the memory of Henry J. Heinz II, who during his lifetime combined a deep interest in architecture with a commitment to Pittsburgh. Here you'll find architectural drawings, photographs, models, artifacts, and related items. While the center's scope is international, it still places significance on the architecture of Western Pennsylvania.

Cicognani Kalla Architects designed the Heinz Architectural Center with galleries specifically suited for the exhibition of drawings, a study room, and support spaces. Every few months these exhibits change.

On permanent display, however, is the office designed and used by esteemed architect Frank Lloyd Wright in San Francisco from 1951 until his death in 1959. In this unique space, Wright divided a nondescript 20 x 40-foot room into three interlocking spaces—a reception area, drafting room, and a personal office. Wright's fondness for Asian art is very much apparent. Those interested in further details can tour this office the first Saturday of every month from 1:00 to 3:00 P.M. Meet at the Museum of Art Store. Although reservations aren't necessary, space is limited.

Throughout the rest of the center, much of the collection of drawings, models, prints, and photographs represents the 19th and 20th centuries. Designs for residential, institutional, commercial, and industrial buildings as well as examples of engineering, landscape, furniture, and interior design are included.

A special affiliation between the Heinz Architectural Center at the Carnegie Museum of Art and the Royal Academy of Arts in London allows these two institutions to collaborate on exhibitions, publications, and programs of mutual interest.

The Architectural Center is open during regular museum hours: Tuesday through Saturday, 10:00 A.M. to 5:00 P.M. and Sunday, noon to 5:00 P.M. Admission is $10.00 for adults, $7.00 for senior citizens and $6.00 for children (ages 3 to 18). Children younger than age 3 and members are admitted free of charge.

ARCHITECTURAL PRESERVATION

**Pittsburgh History & Landmarks Foundation
One Station Square, Suite 450
(412) 471-5808
www.phlf.org**
This nonprofit historic preservation organization was founded in 1964 to explore

and assess regional architecture and preserve Pittsburgh's history.

Landmarks, as the foundation is known, compiled the first countywide architectural site survey in the nation and has published many studies of regional architects, buildings, and landscape design, including the hefty book *Pittsburgh's Landmark Architecture*, written by Walter C. Kidney and published in 1997. Many books and publications produced by Landmarks can be found at the Carnegie Library or in local bookstores.

Since 1965 the Pittsburgh History & Landmarks Foundation has offered a variety of walking tours throughout the Golden Triangle where visitors and even lifetime Pittsburghers can learn from trained docents. These range from one-hour walking tours of the downtown area to customized, in-depth excursions filling one or two days. Walking tour field trips for school groups can also be arranged. Hours are Monday through Friday, 9:00 A.M. to 5:00 P.M. excluding holidays.

By becoming a member of the Pittsburgh History & Landmarks Foundation, you'll save on tours, publications, and educational programs, get special invitations and a newsletter, and have access to the foundation's James D. Van Trump Library of architecture and historical materials.

DOWNTOWN WALKING TOUR

Though there are guided tours available, there's nothing to keep you from discovering Pittsburgh's streets, structural facades, and architectural highlights on your own. Lace up your comfortable walking shoes, and come along on our own Insiders' tour of Downtown. The tour will be as brief or as long as you prefer. There may be some buildings you'll want to browse for a while, and other facades you may want to skip. The choice is yours. But if you took a few minutes to stop, read, and look at each mention, we're guessing you'll complete the tour in about two hours. As we said, it all depends upon your gait and your curiosity.

Our starting point will be Station Square, where you can easily park your car in the parking garage or outdoor lot. Our best advice is to bring along this book, and plan your walking adventure in good weather. That way, you can stop along the sidewalk, follow the directions of where to turn next, and read about the structure you're passing.

Station Square
South Side
On a 40-acre site on the south bank of the Monongahela River that was once the center of a bustling railroad and a complex of operational buildings sits a major tourist attraction, office complex, and shopping mall called Station Square.

In the late 1870s, the Pittsburgh & Lake Erie Railroad consisted of coal freight, boxcar leasing, and passenger service at the northwest corner of Carson and Smithfield Streets.

Architect William George Burns was chosen to create a new train station, which was extolled in an 1896 issue of *The American Architect*. Building began in 1899. Upon completion, the structure and its interior were extensively praised. The Chicago firm of Crossman and Sturdy was responsible for the interior, and the watercolor for the waiting room was written about in the *Pittsburgh Architectural Club Exhibition Catalog of 1900*.

The vestibule and waiting room were filled with decorative details—marble, mosaic, and stained-glass elements. Pittsburgh historian James Van Trump called it "the finest Edwardian interior in the city," second only to the Carnegie Music Hall foyer.

By 1970, when other forms of transportation had made the railroad somewhat obsolete, the ornate spaces were empty, and the terminal complex, with a great barrel-vaulted ceiling in the waiting room, was a prime focus of restoration. The Allegheny Foundation, a Scaife family trust, provided the necessary funding to the Pittsburgh History & Landmarks Foundation to sponsor this restored site, which would be dubbed Station Square.

Today, the old waiting room is now the Grand Concourse restaurant (see the Restaurant chapter), and natural light shines through the clean stained glass. The Gandy Dancer Bar was fashioned out of part of the former baggage area.

The dingy, tarnished, and faded facades have been polished in other buildings as well. The former shovel warehouse was transformed into an office complex. The freight house underwent a metamorphosis into a modern-day arcade of shops, restaurants, and entertainment possibilities. Smaller structures such as the gatehouse and express house were also remodeled.

Plenty of commuters find the parking at Station Square convenient for workdays or stadium games as they board the Gateway Clipper Fleet of sightseeing and dinner cruise vessels. Special events are sometimes held on the grounds as well (see Annual Events).

Standing just outside the Landmarks Building at Station Square, we'll step on to the bridge deck to continue our tour. One of the oldest and most remarkable bridges in Allegheny County, the Smithfield Street Bridge used to be called the Monongahela Bridge.

Smithfield Street Bridge
Downtown and South Side
Visitors to Station Square can't miss this bridge spanning the Monongahela River, for it's one of Pittsburgh's oldest and most remarkable. When engineer Gustav Lindenthal designed it in 1981–1983 (with Stanley L. Roush, the architect for the bridge's portals), it replaced the Monongahela Bridge, a covered wood truss. The forces of the two 360-foot main lenticular-truss type spans seem to cancel each other out. An arch thrusts outward on the upper cord. The lower cord pulls inward. Several restorations have taken place since the original design. In 1995, the Roush portals and main spans were

repainted in their original colors—deep blue for the trusses, brown for the flooring, and a creamy yellow for the portals. Designated a national historic civil engineering landmark, notice as you walk across the bridge that the upper cord visually cancels out the lower cord.

Victorian Fronts
Various locations along Fort Pitt Boulevard

Standing at the traffic light across the bridge, you'll see to your left the Victorian fronts of the buildings along the 200 block of Fort Pitt Boulevard that comprise a commercial row of dwellings.

Cross Fort Pitt Boulevard at the light and walk 1 block north on Smithfield Street to First Avenue.

Keep walking 3 more blocks, crossing the Boulevard of the Allies and Third Avenue and stopping at Fourth Avenue. Here at the corner of Smithfield Street and Fourth Avenue, you could take a rest if you like on one of the outdoor benches right outside Dollar Savings Bank.

Dollar Savings Bank
348 Fourth Avenue
(412) 261-7538

Philadelphia architects Isaac Hobbs & Sons created this bank in a era when the word Victorian was usually the equivalent of "monstrosity." This structure was begun in 1868 and completed in 1871. The strong columns at the Fourth Avenue entrance suggest solidity. The lions on each side are masculine in detail. Fourth Avenue used to be the investment district, and many buildings here have a rather masculine look to them.

When you get up from your brief bench reprieve, turn left down Fourth Avenue, quickly passing the Times Building (336 Fourth Avenue). This is one of architect Frederick J. Osterling's most successful designs, in Richardson Romanesque fashion, with its rounded arches.

Shortly across the street you'll see the awnings and brass sign that designate the Bank Tower (307 Fourth Avenue), built in the 1890s. Architects Alden and Harlow are responsible for the semicircular, grand staircase. Cross the street and stroll into the Bank Tower's lobby (if the building is open). Glancing up the stairwell, you'll see the marble intarsia of the balustrade.

Once you're finished admiring the building, exit on Fourth Avenue and turn right, continuing toward the shimmering glass tower we know as PPG Place. You'll cross Wood Street, passing both the Investment Building (239 Fourth Avenue) and the Benedum-Trees Building (221, 223, 225 Fourth Avenue) on your right.

Burke's Building
209 Fourth Avenue
www.city.pittsburgh.pa.us/wt/html/burke_s_building.html

Immediately before PPG Place on the right is a tiny building of great architectural significance. This is the Burke's Building, Pittsburgh's oldest commercial structure.

As the oldest commercial building in the Golden Triangle, the Burke's Building is what remains of the Greek Revival period. When the great Downtown Fire of 1845 destroyed many buildings, this one was fortunately spared. This small building was designed by architect John Chislett in 1836, and is now the home of the Western Pennsylvania Conservancy. It's small, but with the plaque outside, you shouldn't have any trouble finding it. It's literally right next door to PPG Place.

PPG Place
One PPG Place

Witness the spectacle of PPG Place, the shimmering tower we've been saying you'd find. You can't miss this plate-glass complex with the tower rising 680 feet into the downtown sky. In fact, young movie fans affectionately refer to the structure as "the Inspector Gadget building," since that Disney film used Pittsburgh and PPG Place as its backdrops. But this is only its more recent claim to fame.

In 1979, PPG Industries, wanting to make a one-time gift of significant proportions to the city, commissioned architects to show off the company's product of plate glass. The site chosen was a stretch of land from the Boulevard of the Allies, through Third and Fourth Avenues to Market Square. But you don't just decide to construct a towering complex without much scrutiny.

PPG heard the many fears that their design might block the midday light and forever harm the appeal of nearby Market Square. The company involved city planners in selecting architects Philip Johnson and John Burgee. While the original intent might have been to build a single tower, the final plan included six buildings, with the tower (One PPG Place) serving as corporate headquarters for PPG Industries. The complex was completed in 1984.

To meet the city's 20 percent open space requirement, the architects and planners created a formal plaza on the east side of the tower between Third Avenue and Fourth Avenue. This area not only allows the sun to shine down upon the concrete, but also provides the lunchtime crowds a pleasant site for brown bagging it. Festivals sometimes use the space for outdoor events, and the plaza has also been the venue for special receptions. During December, you can't miss the brightly decorated Christmas tree—the focal point of the plaza.

Philip Johnson saw Pittsburgh as Gothic. The tower, with its silver-gray glass that you can't see through, has eight wonderful pinnacles reaching up to the sky. In fact, the building is glazed with nearly 20,000 pieces of reflective glass—the company's flagship product—that catch the sunset over the Point nightly. Inside the lobby of this headquarters building sits the PPG Wintergarden, where the annual Christmas Santa display is a popular attraction (see the Annual Events chapter).

From the Burke's Building, keep walking along Fourth Avenue, literally a few steps, and open the glass doors to Two PPG Place, one of the complex's six buildings, on your right. Go through the second set of doors entering the retail arcade (the food-court escalators greet you, should you need a beverage by now). Out the glass doors directly ahead of you is Market Square, once known as the Diamond. From the mid-1790s until 1852, it accommodated not only market stalls but also the First Allegheny County Courthouse.

Market Square is currently used as a small, open-air space for rallies, political announcements, and even concerts in warm weather. Workers often eat lunch on the benches, appreciating the ambience and sunshine. But now, Market Square has the added distinction of controversy. Mayor Tom Murphy is proposing a retail development plan that, if approved, would mean the razing of several buildings of historical or architectural significance. Preservation groups have their own propositions for saving the buildings, and it seems every day the newspaper includes a new development in this back-and-forth saga.

Continue straight from your glass door departure point with one warning. Duck the pigeons! They do flock in Market Square, much to the chagrin of most every resident and visitor. As you walk, you will pass several small shops, and the 1902 Landmark Tavern. This building, along with the Oyster House restaurant, are Market Square's oldest structures.

The street you are walking on is not marked with a street sign. When you get to the intersection at Fifth Avenue, however, you will find an inscription on the curb stating this is Graeme Street.

From Fifth Avenue On

Turn right onto Fifth Avenue and begin walking east toward Kaufmann's Department Store. A 2-block walk will put you at the intersection of Fifth Avenue and Smithfield Street, with Kaufmann's on the far right corner. Notice the popular Kaufmann's Clock, under which many a rendezvous for Pittsburghers have taken place. But wait! Don't cross the street (unless you're meeting someone, of course).

We want you to turn left at this juncture, crossing Fifth Avenue as you proceed north on Smithfield Street. Walk 2 blocks (passing Saks Fifth Avenue on your left) until you come to Sixth Avenue, where you will take another left to explore two of Pittsburgh's architecturally significant churches, and a club for the powers that be.

Trinity Cathedral
328 Sixth Avenue
(412) 232-6404
www.trinitycathedralpgh.org

You'll know you're in the right place when you see Trinity Cathedral. Detroit architect Gordon Lloyd designed this house of worship in 1871, using the decorated Gothic of early 14th-century England as his style for this Episcopal cathedral. While a fire in 1969 damaged portions of the structure, the interior still reflects its original mid-Victorian appeal. Outside, there's a historic courtyard, and some of Pittsburgh's oldest graves inhabit the cemetery.

First Presbyterian Church
320 Sixth Avenue
(412) 471-3436
www.fpcp.org

First Presbyterian Church is next door to Trinity, just a step away. On property donated by the Penn family (William Penn was the founder of Pennsylvania), Philadelphia architect Theophilus Parsons Chandler began constructing the church in 1903, completing it two years later. The cathedral-like front is reminiscent of 13th- and 14th-century English Gothic. Inside, the nave windows (all but one) are by the Tiffany Studios, and the sanctuary itself boasts rectangular preaching space. Notice also the raised side galleries.

Duquesne Club
325 Sixth Avenue
(412) 391-1500
www.city.pittsburgh.pa.us/wt/html/
duquesne_club.html

Directly across the street from First Presbyterian on Sixth Avenue, sits the bastion of what some would say was the "old boy network" in Pittsburgh. At the Duquesne Club, women were once excluded as leading industrialists conducted countless business transactions. The architectural firm of Longfellow, Alden & Harlow designed the club between 1887 and 1889. Alden & Harlow added to the main front in 1902, and further remodeling was completed by Janssen & Cocken, as they added a tower in 1930 to 1931.

Return up Sixth Avenue to Smithfield Street and proceed past Mellon Square on your right, an outdoor park atop an underground parking garage. This puts you at a street called William Penn Place (the same street is named Cherry Way a few blocks south of here). Walk 1 more block to Grant Street, and cross it. You can't miss the skyscrapers such as the USX Tower, the tallest building in downtown Pittsburgh.

Turn left and walk past the USX Tower, which we'll describe in detail soon. En route, notice how Grant Street offers a handsome view of old architecture juxtaposed next to modern-day skyscrapers.

There's the First English Evangelical Lutheran Church (615 Grant Street), the Gulf Tower, and the Koppers Building (both at Seventh Avenue and Grant Street). Continue your walk to the end of Grant Street.

At the traffic light, you will see where Port Authority buses turn onto the East Busway. Cross this stretch of pavement at the light to the Pennsylvanian.

The Pennsylvanian
Grant Street and Liberty Avenue

You'll know you are in the right place as you peer up at the former train station's beaux-arts rotunda—a 1900 architectural student's dream, and the first sight rail passengers used to see of the city upon arrival.

Inside the rotunda, on pendentives beneath the skylit dome, four women's heads once smiled down upon tablets naming four destinations of the Pennsylvania Railroad. Passenger service diminished in the 1940s, and soon buses used the rotunda, so large was its scale. Eventually the bus traffic ceased as well. In 1988, a restored Union Station became the Pennsylvanian apartment complex. Many of the architectural highlights from the heyday of the trains remain in place today.

We'll soon end the walking tour, taking you past the gem of Pittsburgh architecture—Richardson's Allegheny County Courthouse. But there a few more substantial structures for you to recognize. For instance, there's the USX Tower as you make your way south back along Grant Street (in the opposite direction you came from).

USX Tower
600 Grant Street

At 841 feet high, the USX Tower is the tallest building in downtown Pittsburgh, and one of the tallest buildings between New York City and Chicago. Once known as the U.S. Steel Building (before the company merged with Marathon Oil), it towers 64 stories into the sky. Harrison & Abramovitz started construction in 1968 and completed the project in 1971. The skyscraper is made of an exposed frame of Cor-Ten weathering steel, a rust-resistant steel originally developed for the insides of grain hopper railcars that could not be painted. However, the Cor-Ten finish did need to be painted, as the rust that formed washed off onto other nearby buildings. Interestingly, the columns and girders are filled with water to resist fire (and antifreeze to prevent the expansion of frozen water).

If you keep walking on the left sidewalk next to the USX Tower, you will pass One Mellon Bank Center, corporate headquarters of Mellon Bank. If you're on the other side of Grant Street (across the street from the USX Tower), you'll pass both the Omni William Penn Hotel and Two Mellon Bank Center on your right.

Omni William Penn Hotel
530 William Penn Place
(412) 281-7100
www.omnihotels.com

The Omni William Penn Hotel is an American Renaissance masterpiece erected by industrialist Henry Clay Frick between 1914 and 1916. Designed by Janssen & Abbott, the hotel was enlarged in the late '20s by their successor firm, Janssen & Cocken.

Inside, the Palm Court Lobby has been restored to its original splendor. This is where guests today enjoy afternoon tea and piano music. For a lovely dining experience, the setting is the Terrace Room, framed in carved walnut with original rococo detailing and murals depicting Fort Duquesne during the Revolutionary War.

The centerpiece of this hotel, however, is the art deco classic of black marble and Carrara glass, gold detailing, and exotic murals in the Urban Room, named for designer Joseph Urban. This famed room resides on the 17th floor. For years, this hotel was known simply as the William Penn Hotel—named after Pennsylvania's founder—until its purchase by the Westin hotel chain in 1984, and its more recent change from Westin to Omni.

Two Mellon Center/Union Arcade
501 Grant Street

First called the Union Arcade, this was one of Henry Clay Frick's buildings all in a row. He chose architect Frederick J. Osterling to build the Union Arcade, with its prominent rotunda roof. The project was begun in 1915 and finished two years later. Osterling designed this 237-foot Gothic building using carved gray sandstone, terra-cotta, and green granite exterior trim, and plenty of bronze, marble, and terra-cotta inside. You'll also notice the specially designed light fixtures and leaded glass.

In 1922 the Union Trust Company purchased the building from the Frick estate and quickly remodeled the building the next year, naming it the Union Trust Building. The main vault held more than a billion dollars in silver, cash, and securities. The most significant architectural change was Grecian, but it blended well with the original Gothic design.

As then Mellon National Bank merged with the Union Trust Company in 1946, the character of the building changed a bit as the new owner allowed closing in and flooring over the excess corridor space from the second through fourth floors. When Mellon completed its new corporate headquarters in the 1980s, this site later became Two Mellon Bank Center. Though offices occupy the upper floors, the first floor still has several shops. If nothing more, cut through the building on a rainy day to escape the elements and admire the rotunda.

From where you stand on either side of the street, you can't miss the beautiful detailing of Richardson's Romanesque design in the Allegheny County Courthouse and Jail.

Allegheny Courthouse and Jail
Between Grant Street and Ross Street
(412) 350–5300 (for courthouse tours)

New technical approaches to design may have originated elsewhere, but they soon found their way into downtown Pittsburgh. When Henry Hobson Richardson's Romanesque design was selected, its simplicity was the alluring element, with its rounded arches, rugged stone walls, and Byzantine leaf carving. Richardson was formally chosen from competitors in 1883 to move ahead with this project to replace the second County Courthouse, which had been gutted by fire.

Since Richardson hailed from Boston (where his famous Trinity Church stands), the stone brought in for the courthouse was quarried in Massachusetts, and many Boston stone carvers and contractors came to Pittsburgh to work for the architect.

Richardson designed each court facility to be self-contained and lighted both from the courtyard and the street. Judges'

chambers, jury, and consultation rooms were planned for the building's turrets. The tower, at 325 feet high, dominated the skyline until the Frick Building forever altered the view in 1901.

One courtroom—Judge Raymond Novak's courtroom—has been restored to its original splendor. The lighting and paint were replicated, and a beam in Richardson's work exposed (rather than have drop or artificial ceilings). Much of the furniture used in the restored courtroom today is vintage. Shepley, Rutan & Coolidge, an architectural firm led by Richardson's son-in-law, George Shepley, designed and purchased much of the courthouse furniture.

County offices frequented by the public were situated below the courtrooms. Prisoners were transported securely across a built-in bridge, known as the "bridge of sighs" over Ross Street. One theory regarding this peculiar name was that prisoners walking the raised bridge would sigh upon finishing their route to the courthouse. Others say the name comes from the 16th-century bridge between the Doge's palace and the city prison in Venice, Italy.

A plaque affixed to the courthouse details what used to be called Grant's Hill. This section of street you are standing on used to be significantly higher, so much so that the original entrance was on what's now the second floor. In 1912, the hump was leveled to ease traffic.

The Allegheny County Courthouse and Jail are regarded as the finest works of architecture in the city. Because Richardson passed away in 1886, the buildings were completed after his death. The inscription near the grand staircase at the entrance of the old law library reads "In memory of Henry Hobson Richardson, architect (1838–1886). Genius and training made him master in his profession. Although he died in the prime of life, he left to his country many monuments of art, foremost among them this temple of justice."

Classical and Gothic architecture were used when Richardson employed the rounded arch, his best-known element adapted from Romanesque architecture of the early-11th century. Indeed, his style has been called Richardson Romanesque, and this particular distinction means that the architect built the structure. A building said to be Richardsonian Romanesque was inspired by the famous architect but not built by Richardson himself. Two Rs, one written backwards and sharing the straight line with the next R, is the signature logo carved into one of the architect's great works.

Richardson used granite in such a way that the stone carver's skill revealed rather than concealed the natural stone. Frank Ellis Alden, a senior member of Richardson's design staff, supervised the construction of both the courthouse and jail. Eight months after the jail's completion in June 1886, and by now after his boss's passing, Alden formed his own architectural firm in Pittsburgh—Longfellow, Alden & Harlow, later Alden & Harlow. The courthouse was completed in April 1888 by Shepley, Rutan & Coolidge, a firm that completed several Richardson designs and went on to construct others in the Pittsburgh area.

In 1904 Frederick J. Osterling was commissioned to expand the county jail. A new round tower at Fifth Avenue and Ross Street was added in keeping with Richardson's original ideas. In 1976 trees and shrubbery were planted and benches added, making the courthouse courtyard into a public park that's now a popular summer lunchtime spot for downtown workers.

Having outgrown the space, the jail was vacated in 1995, and prisoners are now housed in a new facility along Second Avenue, with its exceptional view of the river. Thus, the accommodations have been jokingly dubbed "the Hilton on the Mon." The old jail that Richardson built is being renovated for additional courtroom space.

You can tour the Allegheny County Courthouse, and you have many options, including an organized tour sponsored by the Pittsburgh History & Landmarks Foundation. If you want to do a self-guided tour, obtain the booklet "H.H. Richardson's Allegheny County Courthouse and Jail." One caveat of guiding yourself through this masterpiece—stop to admire the design of the three-story staircase, made of Indiana limestone with original lighting fixtures. It's a celebration of the Richardson Romanesque arch—the new architectural style this famous architect created with his artistry and talent!

City-County Building
414 Grant Street

Next door to the courthouse, the City-County Building, along Grant Street between Forbes and Fourth Avenues, is one of Henry Hornbostel's contributions to the skyline. Civil proceedings within Allegheny County take place here. It represents work toward the end of this architect's career in the art deco mode.

Beginning his work in 1915, and finishing two years later, the architect had one distinct advantage in that by the time he began working, the hump on Grant Street had been lowered. The open corridor inside the structure allows light to shine through. At the bottom of the outside steps, a statue of Pittsburgh's beloved mayor, the late Richard S. Caliguiri, stands as a tribute to his legacy.

This ends the walking tour of downtown Pittsburgh. From reading other entries in this chapter, there might be additional buildings or bridges you'd like to explore. However, this tour has given you the highlights (and a little healthy exercise!).

From the City-County Building, return to your origins at Station Square by following Fourth Avenue 1 block west to

Special Distinctions

As you tour the region, take special note of buildings bearing the National Historic Landmark designation, which acknowledges the highest possible recognition conferred upon a building or site by the Secretary of the United States Department of the Interior.

Additionally, the National Register of Historic Places is the official listing of the country's historic sites worthy of preservation. Here, the Pittsburgh History &

Landmarks Foundation awards the Historic Landmark plaque to architecturally significant buildings in Allegheny County. Though such a plaque identifies the property for its heritage, it does not guarantee protection. In Pittsburgh, however, there are City Historic Districts and City Historic Structures, and these cannot be legally altered or demolished without approval of a review commission.

Smithfield Street, turn left, and walk back to the Smithfield Street Bridge, crossing it to Station Square. Or, if you're tired out, take the "T" (light-rail transit) from Gateway Center, Wood Street, or Steel Plaza Stations, and get off at Station Square. The fare is minimal.

OTHER ARCHITECTURE IN DETAIL

Downtown

Frick Building
437 Grant Street
(412) 281-1260

Directly across the street from the courthouse, Henry Clay Frick made a number of real-estate investments in a closely aligned group of buildings. His Frick Building robbed the county buildings of their dominance. Finished in 1902, the building included the new and unusual for that time, things such as hydraulic elevator machinery, a basement generating plant, and washrooms for the whole building (on the tenth floor). Bronze telephone booths remain in the lobby. D.H. Burnbaum & Co. were the Chicago architects that created this building between 1901 and 1902.

Heinz Hall
Sixth Street and Penn Avenue
(412) 392-4900

In the late 1960s, the Heinz endowment bought the old Penn Theatre, one of many silent-movie theaters that also had a stage. Originally built between 1925 and 1926 by the Chicago firm of Rapp & Rapp, Heinz Hall was remodeled in the early 1970s by the local firm of Stotz, Hess, MacLachlan & Fosner. The firm turned the old entrance into a large foyer window, and it used the architectural terra-cotta to match the off-white exterior. Viennese baroque is the style for this center of performing arts that is home to the Pittsburgh Symphony (see the Arts chapter).

Bouquet's Redoubt
Point State Park

This 1764 structure is better known as the Fort Pitt Blockhouse. Of the original Fort Pitt, only one structure remains, known as Bouquet's Redoubt (better known as the blockhouse). Built too late to see any action in the French and Indian War, it has suffered its drama during peacetime through floods and a variety of uses. In 1894 the wealthy Mary Croghan Schenley gave the blockhouse to the Daughters of the American Revolution. The Fort Pitt

Society restored the structure and maintained it as a museum that is open to the public, to this day.

Koppers Building
436 Seventh Avenue
(412) 227-2001
www.aviewoncities.com/building/koppersbuilding.htm
The Koppers building, completed in 1929, was the headquarters of Heinrich Koppers' company. Koppers was the 1908 inventor of a byproduct coke oven, one that captured wastes, recycling and utilizing a product that would have otherwise been dispersed into the air and rendered useless. He had moved his business to Pittsburgh in 1915. This building's chateau roof was made of copper, of course, and the lobby spaces are among the best art deco works in the city.

Gulf Building
707 Grant Street
(412) 263-6000
In the 1920s, Grant Street was extended northward. More real estate became available in the city. Directly opposite the new Koppers Building, the Gulf Oil Company built a 44-story, 582-foot tower that would be the city's tallest building until the USX Tower was constructed in 1970. Trowbridge & Livingston, an architectural firm from New York, were commissioned. E.P. Mellon served as an associate architect for the project. At the top of the building, neon tubes forecasted the weather. When Gulf and Chevron merged in 1984, New York developers acquired the property, and today it has become office space rented out to companies.

Regional Enterprise Tower
Sixth Avenue and William Penn Way
www.spcregion.org/about_ret.shtml
Built by Alcoa in 1953, this building served as the company's headquarters until 1999, when everyone moved to a new facility on Pittsburgh's North Side. The firm of Harrison & Abramovitz designed the building

that sits between Smithfield and Grant Streets, and of course, the idea was to showcase aluminum in every possible way—from the electrical work to cladding. It's a wonder of industrial design, with a system in place that allows all windows to be washed from the inside. In fact, the windows swing completely around, and are sealed with inflatable gaskets that have rounded corners. And the rounded corners, necessitated by the window-cleaning system, change this structure's entire appeal. When completed, the building was hailed as a daring experiment in modern office buildings. Today, the 30-story Regional Enterprise Tower has become a regional resource center, housing economic development groups, among others.

North

Allegheny Post Office (now the Pittsburgh Children's Museum)
10 Children's Way
(412) 322-5058
www.pittsburghkids.org
Though now converted into a museum for children (see our Kidstuff chapter), the former Allegheny Post Office on the North Side is architecturally significant for its Early Italian Renaissance style. The central domed space inside is tall and much like a mosque. In a sense, Pittsburghers get to see more of the building as a children's museum, since they were restricted to the counter and outer corridors when it was a post office.

Armstrong County Courthouse
Market Street and Jefferson Street
Kittanning
(724) 548-3226
This courthouse is a late Greek Revival structure that boasts a Corinthian porticoed central pavilion. It was erected in 1858, and a left wing was added in 1871. While the courthouse was constructed first, the jail was built in 1873. Clarion County sandstone was used in each.

Butler County Courthouse
Main Street, Butler
(724) 285-4731
Built in 1886, the Butler County Courthouse is Richardsonian in its style, of mixed Gothic and French architecture. James P. Bailey of Pittsburgh was its architect. Later enlarged and modernized between 1907 and 1908, this building contains a clock at least 100 years old, which dutifully ran without motorized assistance until 1940.

Carnegie Library of Pittsburgh
(Allegheny Regional Branch)
Allegheny Square
(412) 237-1890
www.carnegielibrary.org/locations/ allegheny/
Completed in 1890, this was the first Carnegie Library commissioned. Designed by architects Smithmeyer & Pelz of Washington, D.C., the library interior has been updated over the years. The adjacent Carnegie Hall is now a theater rather than an auditorium where such speakers as evangelist Kathryn Khulman held services. Still, there are some excellent finials to look at as well as the urn on the Library tower, and a lyre on the Carnegie Hall gable.

Hartwood Acres
215 Saxonburg Boulevard
(412) 767-9200, (412) 767-4738
New York architect Alfred W. Hopkins constructed this large country estate in 1929 in Indiana Township. It was the property of Mary Flinn Lawrence, daughter of the well-known contractor William Flinn. Its main house, which can be toured by the public, is typical of 1920s rural Tudor styling. Allegheny County maintains the property today for recreational and cultural use. (See the Attractions chapter.)

Mother House of the Sisters of Divine Providence
La Roche College
9000 Babcock Boulevard
(412) 367-9300
Religious and academic buildings are clustered around the towering Mother House with its chapel, here on the North Hills campus of La Roche College. John E. Kauzor was its architect in 1927. While many of the other buildings are nondescript, the Mother House maintains a North Italian Romanesque style that's splendid.

East

Allegheny Cemetery
(Butler Street Entrance)
4734 Butler Street
www.alleghenycemetery.com
John Chislett was the architect for this gateway to the Allegheny Cemetery in 1847. You can see his work on the Butler Street entrance. It's a Tudor Gothic gateway in warm gray sandstone. The cemetery was enlarged 20 years later with a chapel and office. In addition, the Penn Avenue gates were added in 1887.

Board of Education Building
341 South Bellefield Avenue
(412) 622-3500
Built between 1926 and 1927, this structure resembles an Italian Renaissance town palace with a few Baroque touches. Architects Ingham and Boyd deserve the honors. Inside, you'll find a landscaped courtyard.

The Carnegie
4400 Forbes Avenue
(412) 622-3131
www.clpgh.org
On land donated by Mary Croghan Schenley, another renowned philanthropist, Andrew Carnegie, offered Pittsburgh a cultural entity that reigns today. Architects Longfellow, Alden & Harlow created Carnegie Institute and the Carnegie Library of Pittsburgh in 1892.

The Italian Renaissance library building was first on the scene, followed by the Music Hall and museums. Outside the institute, you can't miss the four statues—Gallileo, Michelangelo, Bach, and Shakespeare, representing the four branches of science, art, music, and literature.

Learn more about Armstrong County architecture by taking a walking tour where you can walk past private properties and see inside some public ones. To obtain a brochure guide on Apollo, Dayton, Ford City, Freeport, Kittanning, Leechburg, or Parker City, call (724) 548-3226.

The wealthy Sarah Mellon Scaife donated a massive collection of art. To house it, Edward Larabee Barnes built the Scaife Gallery at the Carnegie Museum of Art in 1974 (see the Arts chapter).

Year-round hours at the museums are Monday through Saturday 10:00 A.M. to 5:00 P.M. and Sunday noon to 5:00 P.M. The library is open year-round Monday through Thursday 10:00 A.M. to 8:00 P.M., Friday and Saturday from 10:00 A.M. to 5:30 P.M., and Sunday 1:00 to 5:00 P.M. Admission to the library is free. Admission to the Carnegie Museum of Natural History and Museum of Art is $10.00 for adults, $7.00 for senior citizens, and $6.00 for children (ages 3 to 18). Children younger than 3 and members are admitted free of charge.

Cathedral of Learning
At the University of Pittsburgh
Bigelow Boulevard and Fifth Avenue
(412) 624-4141
www.discover.pitt.edu/tour/tour-080
.html

John Gabbert Bowman, who was named chancellor of the University of Pittsburgh in 1921, inherited a less than spectacular campus. Although a university skyscraper was virtually unheard of, Bowman had a vision for one here, and he hired Charles Zeller Klauder to ignite and carry it through.

Klauder, an eclectic architect from Philadelphia and a specialist in college design, tried to create the perfect plan. Bowman insisted that the building must inspire his students. The chancellor's concept was best articulated when, upon hearing the Magic Fire Music from *Die Walkure*, Bowman suggested that he wanted a climax building, towering higher and higher.

Indeed, Bowman had quite a selling job on his hands. However, with the help of benevolent donors, ordinary laborers, and even young children who took up collections to create the cathedral, the campaign was successful.

Most considered the results beautiful, though some thought it absurd. It's said that Frank Lloyd Wright called the creation "the world's largest keep-off-the-grass sign." Today the Gothic Cathedral of Learning, at 535 feet with 42 stories, towers over much more modest Oakland rooftops.

The Commons Room inside is cavernous and inspiring. On any given day, you'll find students at quiet study or occasionally at a special event like Oktoberfest, with the wafting aroma of ethnic foods, only without the beer.

Chancellor Bowman wanted to use the Cathedral of Learning to showcase world cultures. Thus, dozens of classrooms within the cathedral depict the city's ethnic diversity through their individual architecture. Since so many immigrants settled here in the 1920s, these Nationality Rooms seemed a fitting tribute to that heritage (see the Attractions chapter).

But an important caveat in creating these nationality displays was that each room had to be used as a classroom. In addition, no person who was alive could be portrayed in the room. Each is different. The English is patterned after the House of Commons in 16th-century Tudor. The Yugoslav room features pocketknife wood carvings. And the French were the only group that selected the room's location, in this case to be closer to Heinz Chapel. Each room was funded by ethnic committees, designed by native architects, and built with materials from the countries they represent.

Taped recorded tours are offered if you like. Tours are also available between 11:00 A.M. and 2:30 P.M. on most days. The Nationality Rooms are open Monday through Friday 9:00 A.M. to 2:30 P.M., Saturday 9:30 A.M. to 2:30 P.M., and Sunday 11:00 A.M. to 2:30 P.M. Admission rates are $3.00 for adults, $2.00 for seniors (ages 60 and older), and 50 cents for children ages 8 to 18. Children age 7 and younger are free.

Clayton
Penn Avenue and Homewood Avenue
(412) 371-0606
frickart.org/features/clayton/
In 1882, Henry Clay Frick and his wife, the former Adelaide Howard Childs, purchased this modest example of an Italianate house built after the Civil War in Pittsburgh's Point Breeze neighborhood. Several years later, in 1890, the Fricks decided to expand and remodel the home, hiring Pittsburgh architect Frederick J. Osterling to carry out the task. Although Osterling proposed a much more elaborate vision than what he finally built, today's Clayton boasts a chateauesque appearance, with steep roofs and gables that bespeak Osterling's style. This architect patterned his remodeling efforts after houses in France's Loire River Valley.

Other buildings, including the conservatory, sprouted up along the property. Upon Mr. Frick's death in 1919, his daughter Helen Clay Frick inherited the property. It's reported she was very fond of the home. Though she lived in New York, she visited often and maintained the property. Helen Clay Frick died in 1984, willing the home to the family's foundation. Following her wishes, Clayton was opened as a museum in 1990.

Today, Clayton is part of the Frick Art & Historical Center (see the Arts chapter). You can reserve a spot for a tour of Clayton, where you'll notice the renowned art collection the Fricks amassed during their many trips abroad. The stained-glass window illuminating the main stairs is by Cottier and Company in New York, and depicts heroines from literature. Many of Mr. Frick's acquisitions remain as they were in the oak-paneled sitting room. The family used to gather for meals in the formal dining room, where they received

Theodore Roosevelt in 1902 as the U.S. Marine Corps Band entertained luncheon guests with marches from the lawn.

When you visit Clayton, free parking is available, and there is access for visitors with disabilities. The center is open Tuesday through Saturday from 10:00 A.M. to 5:00 P.M. and on Sunday from noon until 6:00 P.M. Clayton is closed on Monday. Tours of Clayton cost $10.00 for adults, $8.00 for seniors and students. Members are admitted free of charge.

Pittsburgh Athletic Association
4215 Fifth Avenue
(412) 621-2400
Architect Benno Janssen was responsible for the Pittsburgh Athletic Association, a clubhouse in the manner of a Venetian renaissance palace. It was constructed between 1909 and 1911 of limestone and matching terra-cotta. Don't miss the carved ceilings and murals inside.

Soldiers' and Sailors' Memorial
4141 Fifth Avenue
(412) 621-4253
www.soldiersandsailorshall.org
Built between 1907 and 1911 as a memorial to Civil War veterans, this building was also designed to add to Oakland's cultural scene. Architect Henry Hornbostel modeled the memorial after the Mausoleum at Helicarnassus, one of the seven wonders of the ancient world. Today, it contains a museum remembering all American wars, as well as a dining room and large public auditorium.

Stephen Foster Memorial
At the University of Pittsburgh
Forbes Avenue
(412) 624-4141
Built tight against the Cathedral in 1937 is the Stephen Foster Memorial, a museum to the Pittsburgh composer. It's a combination theater, research library, social center, and shrine to honor another of the city's native sons. The auditorium seats nearly 700. The west wing houses the Foster Hall collection of more than 20,000

Altering Your Home?

If you are a resident of the city of Pittsburgh, you will need permission to make any exterior changes to the front of your home. The Historic Review Commission must review and approve all visible exterior alterations, including demolition, new construction, and additions. For more information, call (412) 255-2243.

items pertaining to the late musician. Regular hours for the Stephen Foster Memorial are Monday through Friday from 9:00 A.M. until 4:00 P.M. (except during University holidays). Weekend and library hours are made by appointment only. Guided tours cost $1.50 for adults and $1.00 for seniors and school children.

Westmoreland County Courthouse
North Main Street, Greensburg
(724) 830-3000
Built between 1906 and 1908, this public building's style is French renaissance. The bell from a 1798 brick courthouse has been placed in the old jail tower and preserved by the county's historical society.

South

LeMoyne House
49 East Maiden Street, Washington
(724) 225-6740
www.wchspa.org
LeMoyne House is a fine example of early Greek Revival architecture built in 1812 by a French family that had come to America during the French Revolution. The home was passed down through the generations. Today, tours are available (see the Attractions chapter).

Thomas Jefferson Garden Mausoleum
Jefferson Memorial Cemetery
401 Curry Hollow Road
(412) 655-4500
At this South Hills cemetery, you'll find portions of the former Bank of Pittsburgh

building, which came down in 1944. An admirer of this building asked the property's owner to save the temple front. Thus, its permanent home is this memorial park, which is the final resting place for many generations of Pittsburghers.

Washington County Courthouse
South Main Street and West Beau
Street, Washington
(724) 228-6775
www.courthousecentennial.org
This is the county's fourth courthouse erected between 1898 and the fall of 1900. It's modeled in the beaux-arts classical style from the Italian Renaissance. Rising 25 feet above the courthouse roof are four highly ornamental cupolas whose terra-cotta domes rest on sandstone ionic columns.

Within these cupolas rises a large dome. From this summit rises a cupola on top of which rests an 18-foot bronze statue of George Washington. An original statue of Washington stood atop the building from 1900 until 1917, when lightning strikes damaged it beyond repair. The present-day statue was erected in 1927, and is protected by lightning rods.

West

Beaver County Courthouse
810 Third Street, Beaver
(724) 728-5700
Built between 1876 and 1877, the Beaver County Courthouse is made of stone.

Additions to the building were completed in 1907, remodeling took place in 1933 following a fire the year before, and another later addition was added between 1973 and 1974. Philadelphia architect David S. Geredel was responsible for the present courthouse.

BEST OF THE BRIDGES

When you learn about Pittsburgh's path to progress, you learn of some struggle to bring about improvements. Well, for those who thought Plan B—the plan by which voters registered their thoughts on new stadium construction—was controversial, you should have been around for the debate about bridges back in the 1920s.

In 1924, the county's Ultimate Highway System was designed to carry the road system into the 21st century. New boulevards and radial roads connected the city to outlying areas. But what would span the deep ravines, so prevalent in this region?

The Ultimate Highway System was never quite completed, though portions of the plan were built as late as the 1950s. But the plan's legacy is left behind in the form of magnificent bridges—at Sixth, Seventh, and Ninth Streets, plus the West End and McKees Rocks Bridges, the Liberty, South 10th Street, and Westinghouse Memorial Bridges—all erected between 1924 and 1940. This achievement cemented Pittsburgh's reputation as the "City of Bridges." Here's a peek at the best of these engineering marvels.

Sixth, Seventh, and Ninth Street Bridges
Allegheny River
Affectionately called the "Three Sisters," these three suspension bridges span the Allegheny River between Downtown and the North Side. Their lyrical design was created in the 1920s as they replaced three adjoining Victorian bridges considered to be too ugly for the times. In 1928 the American Institute of Steel Construction bestowed an award on the Sixth Street Bridge. While several engineers

from the Allegheny County Department of Public Works participated in the construction of these impressive spans, Stanley L. Roush served as the architect. In particular, at the site of the Sixth Street Bridge, engineer and designer John Roebling built one of his earlier structures. Roebling, who would go on to construct the Brooklyn Bridge, came from Germany to Pittsburgh in 1832, for he thought Pittsburgh would become the world's industrial center. Roebling invented wire rope and used that technology to build a number of Pittsburgh's early suspension bridges.

16th Street Bridge
Allegheny River
www.pghbridges.com
Spanning the water between 16th Street in the Strip District and Chestnut Street on the North Side, the 16th Street Bridge was designed in 1923 by Warren and Wetmore, the same architects responsible for New York's Grand Central Station. Three truss-arch spans and four masonry piers highlight this bridge. New York's Leo Lentelli created the sea horses that make crossing this bridge even more appealing.

10th Street Bridge
Monongahela River
www.pghbridges.com
This bridge runs between South 10th Street on the South Side and the Armstrong Tunnel on the Bluff (near Duquesne University). Sydney A. Shubin was the engineer in 1931 for this modernistic bridge. Apart from the "Three Sisters" (see description for Sixth Street Bridge), this is Pittsburgh's only extant suspension bridge.

George Westinghouse Memorial Bridge
Route 30
www.pghbridges.com
Connecting East Pittsburgh and North Versailles Township, the George Westinghouse Memorial Bridge served as an entrance for railroad passengers for more than 50 years. Built in 1930, it's got five concrete arches and a total length of 1,596 feet. Each side's entrance has tall concrete

pylons honoring George Westinghouse's development of the Turtle Creek Valley below. The George Westinghouse Memorial Bridge was once compared with other engineering marvels of its era, including the Hoover Dam, the George Washington Bridge, and the Holland Tunnel.

HOUSES OF WORSHIP

Downtown

First English Evangelical Lutheran Church
615 Grant Street
(412) 471-8125
Steep-roofed with a 170-foot spired tower and Gothic elements, this church was built by Andrew Peebles in 1887 and 1888. Inside, worshippers enjoy the Tiffany glass window of the Good Shepherd in the church's sanctuary. Established in 1938, this congregation was the first English-speaking Lutheran congregation west of the Allegheny Mountains.

First Presbyterian Church
320 Sixth Avenue
(412) 471-3436
This Downtown church, with its 13th- and 14th-century English Gothic cathedral front, was covered in the downtown walking tour. Turn to that listing for more detail.

Trinity Cathedral
328 Sixth Avenue
(412) 232-6404
www.trinitycathedralpgh.org
Trinity is right next door to First Presbyterian Church, and this too was covered extensively in the Downtown walking tour, described above.

If you're a high school senior interested in Pittsburgh's history or architecture, apply for the scholarship awarded by the Pittsburgh History & Landmarks Foundation. Call (412) 471-5808.

St. Mary of Mercy Roman Catholic Church
202 Stanwix Street
(412) 261-0110
Somewhat dwarfed by towering PPG Place, this church holds its own simplicity and strength. Built in 1936 by architect William P. Hutchins, there are two redbrick walls gracing the sidewalks on the church's Stanwix Street and Third Avenue sides.

East

East Liberty Presbyterian Church
116 South Highland Avenue
(412) 441-3800
East Liberty Presbyterian Church in its namesake neighborhood of East Liberty was built according to cathedral dimensions, as a gift from Richard Beatty and Jennie King Mellon. Boston architects Cram and Ferguson created this Gothic house of worship that consumes an entire city block.

Heinz Memorial Chapel
East Lawn of the Cathedral of Learning at the University of Pittsburgh
(412) 624-4157
www.discover.pitt.edu/chapel
Next door to the Cathedral of Learning at the University of Pittsburgh is an interdenominational chapel. Chancellor Bowman had insisted upon such a chapel to inspire his students. Thus, in 1938, Charles Zeller Klauder created the 15th-century French, flamboyant Heinz Chapel, with donations from Henry John Heinz and his children. Klauder used several models as inspiration, including Mont-St.Michel, King Louis IV's Sainte-Chapelle, and St.-Maclou at Rouen.

Charles J. Connick, a noted glassmaker from Boston, had responsibility for the spectacular stained-glass windows in this structure that is set off by its tall spire atop the center. Four transept windows represent courage, tolerance, temperance, and truth, and each is 73 feet high.

The present pipe organ in the chapel was made possible through a generous gift of the Howard Heinz Endowment. The third organ to serve this chapel, it has 4,272 pipes (73 ranks) and three electronic pedal stops. The organ, re-created in 1994–1995, represents a trend in American organ building to re-use existing materials in an environmentally friendly and musically sound manner. When you hear the organ in this setting, you can literally feel the vibrations around you.

Heinz Chapel is the site of approximately 1,500 events each year, including lectures, memorial services, weddings, and guided tours. The first funeral to be held in this chapel was that of the late Senator H. J. (John) Heinz III, who died tragically in an airplane accident in April 1991.

Rodef Shalom
4905 Fifth Avenue
(412) 621–6566
One of the two synagogues designed by Henry Hornbostel is Rodef Shalom Congregation in Shadyside. Here, the architect used his favorite materials, cream-colored brick and terra-cotta. Inside, Hornbostel made use of the light from the skylight, which beams down upon his rich mahogany and gilt interior. The temple also contains stained-glass windows and beautiful blue and gold chandeliers.

Sri Venkateswara Temple
1230 South McCully Drive
(412) 373–3380
www.svtemple.org
This Penn Hills temple was the second Hindu temple to be built in the United States and was constructed in 1979. The Indian scientific and professional community contributed greatly to its establishment.

The Tirupathi Shrine from seventh-century southern India served as the model here. Two temple domes are constructed of inch-thick stucco over brick and concrete. The sikhara (spire towers) are similarly made.

Ask for the brochure on Heinz Memorial Chapel weddings if you're thinking of getting married at this historic landmark.

St. Paul's Cathedral
Fifth Avenue and Craig Street
(412) 621–4951
www.catholic-church.org/st.paul cathedralpgh/
Chicago architects Egan & Prindeville designed the twin spires at St. Paul's Cathedral, prominent on the Oakland skyline in this Victorian design. The main structure was built between 1903 and 1906. Two Roman Catholic cathedrals had been downtown on the site of the Union Arcade (see listing for Two Mellon Center), but Mr. Frick's desire to construct the arcade prompted the cathedral's move to Oakland.

This new cathedral turned away from Victorian colors, yet the actual design was reminiscent of Victorian style. There are no flying buttresses as many large cathedrals might have. Two prominent Catholic architects from our city contributed to the entire complex. Edward J. Weber created the Synod Hall and Chancery of 1914, with its 15th-century English look. Carlton Strong built the Rectory in 1926 in a Tudor style.

West

St. Nicholas Chapel
5400 Tuscarawas Road, Beaver
(724) 495–3400
www.gcuusa.com/snc.htm
Constructed in 1992 by architect Tom Terpack, St. Nicholas Chapel, with its three onion domes, is quite a sight in suburban Beaver County. Because it is crafted of cedar logs and shingles, it resembles traditional chapels in eastern Slovakia and western Ukraine. Windows are located in the upper areas of the church so as not to

weaken the main log structure. The wooden entrance doors are carved and framed with logs.

THE WRIGHT STUFF

Since Western Pennsylvania is so fortunate to have two great works of the legendary architect Frank Lloyd Wright, we've chosen to give you the highlights in their own special category. Please note that both of these homes you'll read about are outside the coverage area, but because they're significant in the architectural scheme of things, they're included nonetheless. Turn to the Day Trips chapter for more on these architectural gems.

Fallingwater
Mill Run (off Route 40), Fayette County
(724) 329–8501
www.wpconline.org/fallingwaterhome.htm
Back in the 1930s, Pittsburgh department store owner Edgar J. Kaufmann and his wife, Liliane, commissioned architect Frank Lloyd Wright to design their weekend retreat at Bear Run in the Laurel Highlands, 90 minutes south of Pittsburgh. Tucked among the rhododendrons and sitting atop a waterfall, this masterpiece is more reminiscent of the 1960s than the Great Depression.

A devotee of organic architecture, Wright decided to locate the house on top of the waterfall rather than to the side. Who would have thought? But in the

To learn more about Frank Lloyd Wright's Western Pennsylvania masterpiece called Fallingwater, watch the video House On The Waterfall, produced by WQED-TV. Clayton is featured on the tape Houses Around Here. Videos are available to borrow at many libraries and may also be purchased by calling (412) 622-1307. Prices vary according to place of purchase, but most videos cost $19.95 plus tax.

spring of 1936, construction began with local contractors quickly trained to implement Wright's techniques.

Built of sandstone quarried on the property, Wright used natural stone to reinforce the concrete and create the image of land meeting nature and vice versa. The elements cause the eye to focus outside. Glass and steel were among the other materials used in this massive project, which back in the 1930s cost approximately $155,000 to construct— modest by today's standards, but consider the times.

The architect believed the Kaufmann family should live with the water, not merely look upon it. Cantilevers enable the terraces of the living and bedroom levels to extend over the rushing falls without visible support. A guest and service wing was added in 1939, and Albert Einstein was among the celebrated guests reported to have stayed with the Kaufmanns.

Inside the house, Wright designed the furniture to echo his themes. Southwestern colors were used throughout the property. While touring the home, you'll notice the stairway opens to the sound of the rushing falls. Nature indeed takes over when the windows on the cantilevers are opened, for there is no physical window structure as we normally experience.

When Edgar Kaufmann Jr., the son, turned the home over to the Western Pennsylvania Conservancy in 1963, the family requested that the home remain as original as possible. Thus, you'll also see Tiffany lamps, Japanese prints, and artwork along with Wright's furniture. Much detail was put into the home—from the novel way the windows open to caning in the closet shelves allowing air to flow in such a damp climate. Even ship-quality wood was used to prevent warping. In 1976, the National Park Service bestowed the National Historic Landmark designation to the property.

Ironically, when Edgar Kaufmann had Wright build this home, he was concerned about structural soundness of his project. Thus, he sought the reassurance of a Pittsburgh firm of registered engineers and steel suppliers for concrete. They had advised that Kaufmann use twice the amount of steel his architect had recommended. Kaufmann took the firm's advice, and reportedly, it infuriated Mr. Wright to the point of a near break in the two men's working relationship. Wright felt the steel would weigh too much, causing the terrace to deflect more than it would naturally.

This disagreement was prescient, for in 1997, temporary shoring was installed under the main floor cantilever because of the gradual but continuing deflection of the first and second levels. In fact, at this writing if you stand at just the right part of the surrounding woods, you can see the famous home's slope whereby the master terrace is 7 inches lower than the living room. Computerized analysis along with historical research revealed that the main house had not stopped deflecting since its construction in 1936–1938. This was due to the inadequate steel reinforcement in the concrete beams of the first and second levels. Robert Silman Associates, a structural engineering firm in New York, designed the final repair plan. Strengthening the main floor concrete beams will eliminate the need for further vertical support from beneath. At that juncture, the temporary shoring will be removed. To fund this massive restoration, the Western Pennsylvania Conservancy has conducted a fund-raising campaign.

Despite the restoration, in-depth tours are available at 8:30 A.M. for $40 (weekdays) or $50 (weekends). This famous 20th-century architectural masterpiece remains open through December, Tuesday through Sunday from 10:00 A.M. to 4:00 P.M. Reservations are suggested for the hourlong tour. Children younger than age nine are not permitted, but group babysitting at $2.00 per hour per child is available at the visitor pavilion. For a schedule, call (724) 329–8501. With many stairs, considerable walking is required so call ahead to make arrangements if you need special assistance (see also the Attractions and Day Trips chapters). Note that

staircases are narrow, and the stone can be a bit slippery if you aren't agile. No photos or large bags are allowed.

The best route to Fallingwater is to take the Pennsylvania Turnpike to exit 9 (Donegal). Turn left onto Route 31 East, travel 2 miles, and turn right onto Route 381 South for approximately 19 miles to Fallingwater.

Kentuck Knob
Chalk Hill, Ohiopyle
(724) 329–1901
www.kentuckknob.com

Not far from Fallingwater is another of Frank Lloyd Wright's famous homes, Kentuck Knob, overlooking the Youghiogheny River Gorge. Kentuck (yes, without the "y") Knob was commissioned by the I. N. Hagan family of Uniontown, a family that owned the Hagan Ice Cream Company. They had come to know the Kaufmanns and fell in love with the idea of a Wright creation of their own (only of a little more modest dimension).

This lesser-known Wright home was built of fieldstone boulders found on the site and tidewater red cypress from South Carolina. Wright based the design on a hexagonal modular grid on one main level because it allows for openness. That hexagonal motif is repeated inside and out, even allowing light to shine through in that geometric pattern. It reflects Usonion design, a precursor to the ranch home that most could afford.

Famous for incorporating nature into each site, Wright made sure light permeated in every room at Kentuck Knob. The outdoors is always present, from the morning sun until dusk. A steep, narrow causeway winds its way up from the road and opens to a gravel courtyard, as you ride in the small tour van leading you to the home site. The double glass entry doors welcome guests just as the copper roof offers shelter to curious tourists. The architect also designed the house's furniture, much of which is built-in such as the cypress table that conforms to the angles of the dining room. Today, however,

Wright's furniture sits beside some contemporary pieces reflecting the tastes of its current owners.

The home is now the property of Great Britain's Lord and Lady Palumbo, dedicated patrons of the arts both in the United States and across the Atlantic. Contemporary sculpture and historic artifacts also enhance the secluded setting. In fact, the Palumbo family's photographs give the house a warm, lived-in feel. Do notice the rather striking and now-famous photo of the late Princess Diana, shaking hands in her chic black dress. And do enjoy the many outdoor sculptures that the Palumbos have added throughout the 79-acre property.

But don't expect to meet the owners on your tour. While the Palumbos occasionally entertain in the house when visiting the United States, they live in the nearby valley.

Children younger than nine are not permitted, and no organized child care is provided for touring parents. Though not as renowned as Fallingwater, tours are available. Kentuck Knob is open daily, 9:00 A.M. to 4:00 P.M. In-depth tours are available at 8:30 A.M. and 4:15 P.M. for $50 per person. Or take a regular tour available on weekdays during the summer at $12 per person, $15 per person on weekends.

ARCHITECTURAL TOURISM

It used to be that misbehavior unintentionally rewarded you with a tourist's treat. Yes, career criminals were given a sneak peek at one of the greatest works of 19th-century architecture—the Allegheny County Courthouse and Jail.

Well, now you don't have to misbehave at all to see the same site. "Living Architecture . . . Alive in Pittsburgh" debuted in 1998 to highlight the region's architectural charm. Aficionados of design, engineering, and architecture can book a package tour, and then partake of the work of two of America's most revered architects—H. H. Richardson and Frank Lloyd Wright.

The Greater Pittsburgh Convention & Visitors Bureau (C&VB) gauged the interest in architectural tourism, found it was there, and has marketed a packaged tour ever since. Pittsburgh History & Landmarks Foundation created pamphlets for tours of the courthouse, and cassette tapes also help visitors take self-guided tours of the North Side and Downtown.

If you'd like more information, contact the C&VB at (800) 359-0758, or visit their Web site at www.pittsburgh-cvb.org.

Another tourism option called the "Wright" Touch Getaway package is marketed by the Laurel Highlands Visitors Bureau. It focuses on Frank Lloyd Wrights' Fallingwater and Kentuck Knob exclusively, and is available from July 15 through November. Prices vary considerably depending upon where you choose to stay in the Laurel Highlands. Generally they average around $80 to almost $200 for a two-day, one-night package. If you're interested, contact the visitor bureau at (800) 333-5661 or visit its Web site at www.laurelhighlands.org.

For residents or those nearby who don't require accommodations but do wish to obtain the cassette tape tours, call Pittsburgh History & Landmarks Foundation at (412) 471-5808. The tapes cost $18 plus postage.

THE ARTS

You don't have to be a connoisseur of fine art or a season subscriber to the symphony to appreciate cultural life in Western Pennsylvania. For sure, there are dozens of opportunities for aficionados of all forms of the arts. In fact, it surprises some visitors and newcomers to learn that Pittsburghers are followers of the opera, in addition to being fans of their football team. But such is the scene here.

For a city its size, Pittsburgh has hidden wealth in its passion for excellent performances, dramatic theater, roving exhibitions, unique films, and the latest in literature and poetry. Combine that passion with plenty of raw talent, and the dedication of organizations that support artistic growth, and you have that rare combination that any arts lover needs to feel challenged, yet overwhelmingly satisfied with the offerings.

In this chapter, the usual geographic breakdown is abandoned, as the cultural opportunities available here cross regional boundaries. We'll first explore some of the key places where Pittsburgh takes to the stage, for theater, dance, and film. There's a rundown on local galleries and museums, and a listing of outlets for you creative types, including writers, actors, and musicians. We've also noted some of the area's best artistic support groups.

The Pittsburgh Cultural Trust oversees the development and operation of three of these major theaters—the Benedum Center for the Performing Arts, the Byham Theater, and the Harris Theatre—all located in the 14-block downtown area known as the Cultural District.

The Pittsburgh Cultural Trust was formed in 1984 as the result of the effort of Henry John "Jack" Heinz II. His vision for a downtown cultural district was turned into reality with strikingly restored building facades, murals, and other public art. Handsome brick sidewalks and granite curbs line the district. There's new energy brought about by the economic revitalization of business and the arts community. In December 1999, the O'Reilly Theater opened for public theater patrons to enjoy. Again, Pittsburgh's Cultural Trust was instrumental in this achievement.

Don't forget, I'll close the chapter with a few of the organizations you might turn to for enhancement of your own artistic flair. One thing is certain. In Pittsburgh, you will be pleased with the sounds of symphonies and orchestras, with the sights at major galleries, and with the appeal of theater companies performing a range of works, from Broadway musicals and opera to comedies and dramatic plays.

IN THE LIMELIGHT

Benedum Center for the Performing Arts
719 Liberty Avenue
(412) 456-6666 (tickets and information)
Formerly the Stanley Theater, this building is the cornerstone of Pittsburgh's Cultural District. Reopened in 1987 after a $42 million renovation, the Benedum seats 2,800 and is home to the Civic Light Opera, Pittsburgh Ballet Theater, Pittsburgh Dance Council, and the Pittsburgh Opera. The Benedum Center also hosts first-run Broadway touring productions. Approximately every five years Andrew Lloyd Webber's *The Phantom of the Opera* visits and performs here. Registered with the National Trust for Historic Places, the Benedum (as it's known for short) is one of the few theaters in the country large enough to stage full-cast, first-run Broadway shows.

You'd never guess from the outside the ornate details and ambience you'll find within. Feast your eyes on the sweeping staircases, then let your eyes travel up to the domed ceiling, where the crystal chandelier glitters. This center for the per-

forming arts used to be known as the Stanley Theater, a movie palace dating from 1927.

Byham Theater
101 Sixth Street
(412) 456-1350
Opened in 1903 as a vaudeville house, and later serving as a 1930s talking motion picture house, the Byham today is Pittsburgh's oldest performing-arts facility. With 1,342 seats, the Byham functions as stage for small to mid-size performing arts productions as well as touring companies in music, dance, and the performing arts for children.

Harris Theater
809 Liberty Avenue
(412) 471-9700
The Harris Theater is one of Pittsburgh's newest performing spaces within the Cultural District. Home to the Pittsburgh Filmmakers' presentations of independent and foreign films, the Harris Theater also has smaller, live performances, lecture series, recitals, and experimental theater.

Heinz Hall for the Performing Arts
600 Penn Avenue
(412) 392-4900
No other landmark in this city enjoys the cultural reputation of Heinz Hall, for this great concert hall boasts an international reputation. Back in the 1920s it was called the Penn Theater. But the Howard Heinz Endowment saved this theater, with its Breche opal and Lavanto marble interior, from the wrecking ball after it closed in 1968. Reopened in 1970 after a 16-month, $11 million renovation, it's now known as Heinz Hall. With 2,847 seats, it's home to the Pittsburgh Symphony Orchestra, the Pittsburgh Pops, and the Pittsburgh Youth Symphony Orchestra.

O'Reilly Theater
621 Penn Avenue
(412) 316-8200
The most recent addition to Pittsburgh's Cultural District is the O'Reilly Theater, formerly known as the Pittsburgh Public Theater. Designed by architect Michael Graves and opened in 1999, the theater's balcony overlooks the lobby's floor laid with a checkerboard of green and black slate. This theater replaced the former Hazlet Theater of Pittsburgh's North Side. With only 650 seats, even if you are in the seat farthest from the stage, you're still not more than 18 rows from the actors. There are many elegant elements to Graves' design, including the two-story, semicircular wall of seven windows facing the street entrance. Looking at the theater as you enter, you can't miss the grand overhanging effect created by the windows and the copper-covered roof above you. In honor of his leadership of the H. J. Heinz Co. and undisclosed contributions toward the theater's construction, the building is named for former chairman Anthony J. F. O'Reilly.

Greensburg Garden and Civic Center and the Palace Theatre
951 Old Salem Road, Greensburg
(724) 836-PLAY
This nonprofit organization owns two facilities—the Center and the Palace Theatre. Each promotes cultural, educational, and civic activities benefiting the residents of Westmoreland County. The Garden & Civic Center is located on Old Salem Road off Route 66, north of Greensburg. The Palace Theatre, home to the Westmoreland Symphony Orchestra, sits in downtown Greensburg at 21 West Otterman Street. Occasionally, the River City Brass Band performs at the Palace Theatre as well.

Post-Gazette Pavillion
Route 18 at Route 22, Burgettstown
(724) 947-7400
www.post-gazettepavillion.com
Located in the sprawling countryside of Southwestern Pennsylvania, this amphitheatre attracts approximately 500,000 concertgoers each year, mostly in the warm summer months. Live entertainment, from classical composers to the latest in pop-rock music, plus a variety of festivals occur here. The amphitheatre

holds 23,000 people (7,200 seated within the open-air pavilion). The spacious hillside allows for 15,800 guests who can watch the large video monitors for close-up views of the stage.

DANCE

Pittsburgh Ballet Theatre
2900 Liberty Avenue
(412) 281-0360
www.pbt.org
The Pittsburgh Ballet Theatre celebrated its 30th anniversary in 1999 with Terrence S. Orr as its artistic director. Past performances have included *Dracula, American Salute, The Nutcracker, Coppella, The World Tour, Don Quixote,* and *The Sleeping Beauty*. This dance company takes the stage at the prestigious Benedum Center (see write-up above) for its season each October through May. Tickets range from approximately $16 to $389, depending upon seating in the various tiers and subscriptions. If you become a subscriber, you'll receive the "Spotlight" newsletter, pre-performance lectures, and a liberal ticket exchange policy. To purchase ballet tickets, call the Benedum Box Office at (412) 456-6666.

In addition to fostering its own program, the ballet offers more than 12 levels of dance instruction, with graduates performing with the Pittsburgh Ballet or other national ballet companies. To contact the Pittsburgh Ballet Theatre School, call (412) 281-6727. Classes are offered for children age 4 and older.

Dance Alloy
5530 Penn Avenue
(412) 363-4321
www.dancealloy.org
Committed to exploring dance as a creative performance medium as well as an educational process, this company exhibits a diverse and dynamic art form. Recent seasons have seen the Dance Alloy embark on a series of cross-cultural collaborations, including work with a

Both the Pittsburgh Post-Gazette *and the* Tribune-Review *newspapers have sections devoted to the arts and entertainment before each weekend. Check out "Weekend Mag" in the Friday* Post-Gazette *and "The Ticket" in Friday's* Tribune-Review.

Hawaiian hula company. In 1998 the group joined with the Reichhold Center for the Arts on St. Thomas, U.S. Virgin Islands, and a recognized Calypso artist from Trinidad to produce a new dance. The Dance Alloy School of the Carnegie schedules regular workshops throughout the year, consistent with the group's educational mission and its stature as the region's sole professional contemporary dance school. Tickets for a single performance range from $10 to around $24.

Pittsburgh Dance Council
Benedum Center, 719 Liberty Avenue
(412) 355-0330
The Pittsburgh Dance Council is a hub site of the National Dance Project, a designated consortia of a dozen producers and presenters, each committed to the development of new American work.

Performances are held at the Benedum Center for the Performing Arts, the Byham Theatre, and sometimes the Eddy Theatre at Chatham College. Previous shows have included *The Harlem Nutcracker, American Indian Dance Theater,* and *Choreographers' Continuum*. Each performance is priced differently, but tickets range from $18 to $55.

Laurel Ballet
300 Hamilton Avenue, Greensburg
(724) 837-7230, (724) 832-7391
Founded in the mid-'80s by artistic director Eleanor Tornblom, the Laurel Youth Ballet is a semiprofessional performing company in Westmoreland County introducing hundreds to the world of dance. Former students have gone on to perform with larger companies including the Pitts-

burgh Ballet Theatre and the Pennsylvania Ballet. Each year's schedule includes *The Nutcracker*.

FILM

Academy Travel Adventure Films
Soldiers and Sailors Memorial Hall
(412) 321-7668
www.travelfilms.org
Celebrating well over 100 seasons, this film series has taken locals to such geographic spots as Mexico, Burma and Vietnam, the Santa Fe Trail, Switzerland, France, Peru, Portugal, Australia, and the Great Lakes. Tickets cost $5.00 and one child gets in free with each adult ticket. Single memberships will run $26 for a season and double memberships $46. If you're really a fan, you can purchase a lifetime membership for two for $300. Call for information on upcoming film series with dates and times.

GALLERIES & MUSEUMS

Carnegie Museum of Art
4400 Forbes Avenue
(412) 622-3131
www.cmoa.org
One of Andrew Carnegie's benevolent gifts to this city was the Museum of Art, which is operated under the umbrella of the Carnegie. The Carnegie Institute's original Renaissance-style building was designed by the firm of Longfellow, Alden & Harlow, between 1891 and 1895. Alden & Harlow completed new galleries in 1907. And in 1974, the Sarah Scaife Gallery, designed by Edward Larrabee Barnes, tripled the exhibition space in the Museum of Art.

While many turn-of-the-20th-century art museums focused on amassing work of old masters, Mr. Carnegie envisioned a museum collection consisting of "the old masters of tomorrow." Thus, in 1896, he initiated a series of exhibitions of contemporary art, proposing that the museum's

collection be formed through purchases from this series.

Early acquisitions included work by Winslow Homer, James Abbott, McNeill Whistler, and Camille Pissarro. Today's collection includes a continuum of strength in American art from the late-19th century to the present, along with French impressionists, post-impressionist paintings, and other highly significant works of the 20th century.

The permanent collection is housed in the Scaife Galleries, and special exhibitions are reserved for the Heinz Galleries (or the Alisa Mellon Bruce Galleries for decorative arts). Previous special exhibitions have included *Made in America: The Centuries of American Art* (1996) and *Pittsburgh Revealed* (1997). Current exhibits include *Transmodernity: Contemporary Austrian Architects*. Art classes are available for adults and children (see the Kidstuff chapter). Lunch and Learn programs allow you to learn about the collections with a buffet lunch in the Museum Cafe.

Hours at the museums are 10:00 A.M. to 5:00 P.M. Monday through Saturday, and noon to 5:00 P.M. on Sunday. Admission to the Carnegie Museum of Natural History and Museum of Art is $10.00 for adults, $7.00 for senior citizens, and $6.00 for children (ages 3 to 18). Children younger than age 3 and members are admitted free of charge.

Andy Warhol Museum
117 Sandusky Street
(412) 237-8300
www.warhol.org
Andy Warhola was the son of Eastern European immigrants (he would shorten his name later in life). Beginning in the fourth grade, Warhol attended free Saturday art classes and later graduated from Carnegie Tech's College of Fine Arts.

Warhol moved to New York, working as a commercial artist, taking with him from Pittsburgh an appreciation of working-class life. Thus, he created art that played on everyone's fantasies of inaccessible glamour and celebrity, embodied in his famous works of Marilyn Monroe, Elvis, Jackie Onassis, and Mick Jagger.

Regardless of whether he was correct that everyone would have 15 minutes of fame, Warhol has received that many times over. Who else could create art out of a soup can or ketchup box? Today the Warhol Museum is one of the Carnegie Museums of Pittsburgh and is a collaborative project of the Carnegie Institute, the Dia Center for the Arts, and the Andy Warhol Foundation for the Visual Arts.

The collection includes approximately 900 paintings, 77 sculptures and collaborative works, 1,500 drawings, more than 500 published and unique prints, and more than 400 black-and-white photographs. Also included are wallpaper and books by Warhol, as well as films and videos. Various traveling exhibits come to the museum, including a showing of Disney theme park drawings and artwork.

The Warhol is open Tuesday, Wednesday, Thursday, Saturday, and Sunday from 10:00 A.M. to 5:00 P.M. and Friday from 10:00 A.M. to 10:00 P.M. It's closed Monday. Adults pay $10.00, seniors are charged $7.00, and students and children pay $6.00 for admission. Carnegie members pay nothing to enter.

Concept Art Gallery
1031 South Braddock Avenue
(412) 242-9200
www.conceptgallery.com

One of the oldest galleries in Pittsburgh, the Concept represents established and emerging local and national artists. Gallery hours are Tuesday through Saturday from 10:00 A.M. to 5:30 P.M. and Thursday from 10:00 A.M. to 8:00 P.M. The gallery is closed on Sunday June 6 through September 5.

The Frick Art & Historical Center
7227 Reynolds Street
(412) 371-0600
www.frickart.og

This six-acre complex in Point Breeze is elegantly landscaped with museums and turn-of-the-20th-century buildings, the legacy left by Helen Clay Frick to the people of Western Pennsylvania. Step into the Victorian past to appreciate the architecture and artifacts, in addition to the collection of pre-20th-century European art. Helen, the daughter of industrialist Henry Clay Frick and his wife, the former Adelaide Childs, grew up on the estate in Pittsburgh's fashionable East End. After her parents took to New York, Miss Frick maintained her heartfelt feelings toward the home and property.

Today the Frick Art & Historical Center comprises the Frick Art Museum, Clayton (the restored home of Henry Clay Frick), the Carriage Museum, the Greenhouse, the Museum Shop, the Playhouse, and six acres of sprawling lawns and gardens. Free parking is available in the museum lot. The center is open Tuesday through Saturday from 10:00 A.M. until 5:00 P.M., and on Sunday from noon until 6:00 P.M. Clayton is closed on Monday. Tours of Clayton cost $10.00 for adults and $8.00 for seniors and students. Members are admitted free of charge. Architecture aficionados can turn to that chapter for more information about touring Clayton.

Merrick Free Art Gallery
11th Street and Fifth Avenue
(724) 846-1130

Edward Dempster Merrick wanted to be an artist when he was coming of age in New Brighton, Beaver County, back in the mid-1860s. But like others with similar goals, he was told to find a real job rather than live the life of a starving artist. So he did that, working as a telegraph operator, a soldier, and a cowboy before retiring at age 53 to pursue collecting things, including artwork. Merrick's international travels and studies abroad helped him garner more than 200 19th-century European and American paintings in addition to zoological, entomological, and geological collections.

Perhaps not as wealthy as Frick and Carnegie, who also donated their names and money to museums, Merrick's gallery nonetheless brings art appreciation to the area, and hosts special events such as the Victorian Christmas Toy Show. Ask about Saturday art classes and summer art camp for kids. Gallery hours vary depending upon the season (Labor Day through Memorial Day and the summer months), so do call ahead. Admission is free and group tours can be arranged.

Silver Eye Center for Photography
1015 East Carson Street
(412) 431-1810
www.silvereye.org

This nonprofit organization premieres contemporary photography exhibits in the main front galleries and rotates members' work monthly in the back. Silver Eye offers educational programming, book discussion groups, and workshops. The center's hours are Wednesday through Saturday from noon to 5:00 P.M. and Thursday from noon to 9:00 P.M.

Wood Street Galleries
601 Wood Street
(412) 471-5605

The Wood Street Galleries showcase various artists' work with different exhibitions, sponsored by businesses and local foundations. Illustrations, paintings, and other forms of art are presented. Gallery hours are Tuesday and Wednesday 11:00 A.M. to 6:00 P.M., Thursday, Friday, and Saturday 11:00 A.M. to 7:00 P.M. The Gallery is closed Sunday, Monday, and holidays.

The Mattress Factory
500 Sampsonia Way
(412) 231-3169

No, it's not a place to outfit your boudoir! Rather, we're talking about a former mattress factory warehouse turned art gallery.

This collection of contemporary art is located in the historic Mexican War Streets of Pittsburgh's North Side. Since 1977, the Mattress Factory has had both permanent and temporary collections of site specific installations. More than 100 artists from around the world have been hosted here.

Manchester Craftsmen's Guild
1815 Metropolitan Street
(412) 322-0800
www.manchesterguild.org

Located in an inner-city neighborhood, this minority-directed arts education and presenting organization features both art and jazz musicians. Bill Strickland founded the Manchester Craftsmen's Guild more than 30 years ago to help inner-city youths. Indeed, the guild's profile has risen since then. When the *CBS Evening News* broadcast from Pittsburgh in 1999, the program aired a feature about Strickland and the Guild. Chick Corea, Maynard Ferguson, and many other jazz greats have performed here. Tickets typically cost anywhere from $22 to $30, and children age 18 and younger are admitted for $10 on Thursday evenings. There are discounts for subscribers and Jazz Society members.

Westmoreland Museum of American Art
221 North Main Street, Greensburg
(724) 837-1500
www.wmuseumaa.org

Built at the crest of a hill in downtown Greensburg, the Westmoreland Museum of American Art was established in 1949 with the support of the Woods, Marchand foundation. Ten years later, the museum opened to the public with its mission of acquiring and exhibiting American art. Back in the 1950s, American art was affordable, yet not very prestigious. That's changed today, as exhibitions dedicated to Winslow Homer, Robert Henri, Georgia O'Keeffe, and other great American artists have strong supporters.

Here, contemporary artists counterbalance the more historical nature of some collections, and keep the past and present inextricably woven together for all to appreciate. Educational programs offered include art classes, school outreach, docent-guided tours, lectures, demonstrations, and other special events.

One holiday tradition that families look forward to is the Holiday Toy and Train Exhibition. First begun out of whimsy, it's become a serious collection within the museum. Museum hours are Wednesday to Sunday 11:00 A.M. to 5:00 P.M. and Thursday from 11:00 A.M. to 9:00 P.M. It's closed Monday and Tuesday, as well as most holidays. Admission is free of charge, but there is a $3.00 suggested donation box.

Hoyt Institute of Fine Arts
124 East Leasure Avenue, New Castle
(724) 652-2882
Tucked away from the commercial district of New Castle (Lawrence County) sits the former home of Miss May Emma Hoyt. Today, the mansion is part of Hoyt Institute of Fine Arts, which serves as a local art gallery offering monthly exhibitions upstairs and downstairs. Classes range from watercolors, stained glass, and ceramics to photography, dance, and even writing. The institute is open Wednesday, Friday, and Saturday 10:00 A.M. to 5:00 P.M., Tuesday and Thursday until 8:00 P.M., but it's closed Sunday and Monday. You'll find free admission, but a self-guided tour of the West Gallery costs $3.00 per person.

LITERARY ARTS

Pittsburgh Arts and Lectures
Carnegie Music Hall, 4400 Forbes Avenue
(412) 622-8866
This lecture series is a nonprofit project of Pittsburgh Arts and Lectures. Each year, approximately 12 provocative, entertaining, and informative guests speak in Pittsburgh on a variety of topics. Lectures are normally held at Carnegie Music Hall. Names like Senator John Kerry; authors Tom Wolfe, Andrew Tobias, and Jamaica Kincaid; and humorist Garrison Keillor have presented as part of the series. Indi-

vidual lectures cost at least $18, with partial series or complete series prices available. Admission for the entire series of speakers for fall and spring costs approximately $162.

International Poetry Forum
3333 Fifth Avenue, Webster Hall
(412) 621-9893
www.thepoetryforum.org
Founded in 1966 by Samuel Hazo, Pennsylvania's Poet Laureate, this poetry forum continues as a cultural outreach in Pittsburgh and proves that there is a resurgence of poetry here and around the nation. Poets and performers have included Nobel Prize awardees and many Pulitzer Prize winners. Poets-in-Public is a series at the core of the forum's mission. Poets-at-High Noon presents free poetry events for the public. And Poets-in-Person offers educational outreach and poetry workshops as Pennsylvania poets visit juniors and seniors in high schools. Single ticket prices for readings at the Forum are $15.00 general admission and $8.00 for students and seniors. Subscription and group rates are also available.

MUSIC

Pittsburgh Symphony Orchestra
Heinz Hall, 600 Penn Avenue
(412) 392-4900
www.pittsburghsymphony.com
Under the leadership of Music Director Mariss Jansons, the Pittsburgh Symphony Orchestra continues its heritage of presenting the most talented conductors and musicians. The symphony has completed more than 20 international tours, making the PSO truly a world-class orchestra. Previous conductors have included Maestro Lorin Maazel and André Previn. At home, the orchestra offers 24 weeks of subscription concerts annually between September and May, and a year-round Pops series under the direction of Marvin Hamlisch. Concerts are staged in the elegant Heinz Hall for the Performing Arts. Free summer

concerts are also offered at various parks. Fiddlesticks, the tuxedoed mascot, teaches children lessons in classical music at selected performances (see the Kidstuff chapter for details).

Pittsburgh Opera
801 Penn Avenue
(412) 281-0912
www.pghopera.org

Under the direction of Tito Capobianco, the Pittsburgh Opera is world renowned. One of the first to offer English transla- tions, it breathes new life into the classics, and takes to the stage at the beautiful Benedeum Center in the heart of Pitts- burgh's Cultural District. Past perform- ances have included *Tosca, La Traviata*, and *When A Man Loves A Woman*. Tickets range in price from around $18 to $120. Subscribers get a free opera highlights recording, a subscription to Renaissance magazine, ticket insurance, and easy exchange privileges.

Civic Light Opera
Benedum Center, 719 Liberty Avenue
(412) 281-2822
www.pittsburghCLO.org

Subscribers to the Light Opera enjoy a delightful series of summer Broadway musicals each year performed in the Benedum Center. Past summer series have included Barry Manilow's *Copacabana, Evita, The Pajama Game, Buddy, Anything Goes, Parade, Peter Pan, Joseph and the Amazing Technicolor Dreamcoat, GiGi,* and *Camelot.* Many outreach and education programs are available, including the Academy of Musical Theater. Here, stu- dents from 5 through 85 can attend evening or Saturday classes with the finest training in dance, music, and drama.

Three-show package prices range from $33 to $108 and a six-show package costs between $66 and $216. Thursday matinees are available, and subscribers can secure guaranteed seats, a newsletter, free exchange privileges, and discounts to selected restaurants.

River City Brass Band
Various locations
(412) 322-7222, (800) 292-7222

While the word "band" conjures up images of John Philip Sousa marches, this one is very different. The River City Brass Band is one of just two professional brass bands in the country and by far the most active. Season subscribers enjoy concerts at various locations throughout Allegheny County and in Greensburg, Westmoreland County. Concerts are held at the Carnegie Music Hall in the Oakland neighborhood of Pittsburgh at high schools in the South Hills, North Hills, and Monroeville, and at the Palace Theatre in Greensburg. Take 5 flex plans and single concert ticket sales are available. Senior citizens, students, and groups of 10 or more receive discounted rates. Depending upon the location of the concert, tickets cost between $10 and $31.

Butler County Symphony Orchestra
259 South Main Street, Cutler
(724) 283-1402

Having celebrated its 50th season, the Butler County Symphony Orchestra is a regional treasure. Under the tutelage of Elizabeth "Betsy" Heath Charles, musical director and conductor, the symphony features talented musicians and invited guests. Concerts take place at the Butler Intermediate High School. Single season tickets cost approximately $60 for adults and $30 for students. Other pricing plans are available for contributors.

Westmoreland Symphony Orchestra
Palace Theatre, Greensburg
(724) 837-1850
www.westmorelandsymphony.org

Performing in the beautiful Palace Theatre in Greensburg, the Westmoreland Sym- phony Orchestra has provided a musical experience for decades. The orchestra is under the direction of Kypros Markou. Choose from an eight-week Saturday night series, five classical Saturday night con- certs, four Sunday afternoons, or three pops concerts. Chamber concerts and holiday programs are also presented. Two Young People's Concerts are held during the school day to introduce youth to classical music. The Orchestra also sponsors a 55-member youth symphony. Single tickets range from approximately $10 to $25. Subscription prices vary according to seating.

Calliope House
279 Fisk Street
(412) 687-8800
Founded in 1976, Calliope is a nonprofit educational and presenting organization that promotes traditional and contemporary folk music and its allied arts. All Calliope programs are unique to Western Pennsylvania. The Folk Masters Concert Hall Series, featuring the legends of folk music, holds monthly concerts in the acoustically acclaimed Carnegie Lecture Hall in the city's Oakland area. Classes taught at the Calliope Folk Music School include guitar, banjo, fiddle, harmonic, bagpipe, songwriting, country line dancing, square dancing, and even belly dancing!

Pittsburgh Chamber Music Society
315 South Bellefield Avenue
(412) 624-4129
This society brings various chamber music groups to Pittsburgh. Performances are held each season in Carnegie Music Hall, with most Monday concerts commencing at 8:00 P.M. One previous season included the Juilliard String Quartet, St. Luke's Chamber Ensemble, Beaux Arts Trio, and several more string quartets. The season runs from late October through late April. Ticket prices vary.

Pittsburgh Youth Symphony Orchestra
Heinz Hall, 600 Penn Avenue
www.pittsburghyouthsymphony.org
Comprised of 90 young musicians, ages 11 to 22, the Pittsburgh Youth Symphony Orchestra was selected as one of five youth orchestras to participate in the National Youth Orchestra Festival. The musicians take direction from Daniel Meyer, resident conductor. Since 1962, the youth symphony has enjoyed affiliation

with the Pittsburgh Symphony Orchestra. Free concerts are available in the fall and in the spring. Tickets, however, are required for admission.

THEATER

Pittsburgh Public Theater
O'Reilly Theater, 621 Penn Avenue
(412) 316-1600
www.ppt.org
When this theater burst onto the Pittsburgh scene in September 1975, theater had nearly vanished, except for community and college theater companies. But patrons of the arts and benefactors from many Pittsburgh foundations helped to found the public theater in the early 1970s. Formerly housed on the city's North Side in a building more than 100 years old (the original Carnegie Music Hall, in fact), the theater moved into the state-of-the-art O'Reilly Theater in 1999. Recent productions have included Pirates of Penzance and The Cherry Orchard. In the past, August Wilson and Shakespearean plays have been performed.

More than 100,000 theatergoers attend presentations at the Public every year, and many more are served through educational outreach programs, including student matinees, post-performance discussions, internships, and classes.

Subscriptions range from approximately $114 to $255, with single performance tickets ranging from $29 to $46. Subscribers receive guaranteed and discounted parking, and discounts at selected restaurants.

City Theater
1300 Bingham Street
(412) 431-CITY
www.citytheatercompany.com
On the city's South Side, the City Theater makes its home in the restored building that was once the Bingham Street United Methodist Church. This is contemporary theater at its best, staging a vast array of productions, from satire to rhythm and

The Heinz Chapel Choir presents several concerts during the holiday season. If you miss it, recordings are available from The Book Center at (412) 648-1451.

blues musicals, even romantic comedies. Call for information about workshops and special events, including a workshop series for seniors featuring improvisational theater performed by other seniors.

The Playhouse of Point Park College
222 Craft Avenue
(412) 621-4445

Formerly known as the Pittsburgh Playhouse, this stage is home to the Point Park College Theatre Company, Playhouse Theatre Company, Playhouse Dance Theatre, and Playhouse Jr. The four companies feature students from the Department of Fine, Applied, and Performing Arts at Point Park College. The curtain goes up at the Main Stage of Rockwell & Hamlet Street Theatres, and at the Downstairs Theatre. Cost is approximately $40 for a five-show season. Other package prices are also available.

Theater Factory
Third and Cavitt Avenues, Trafford
(412) 374-9200

This small theater company delights audiences with a variety of performances for adults and families. Previous series have included the comedy *Greater Tuna*. Dinner theater is available for all performances. Kidsworks performances are aimed at younger theatergoers.

Writers requiring library assistance and research by phone can use two regional services. Carnegie Library has a Ready Reference Department at (412) 622-3114, and a similar service is also offered by the Greensburg/Hempfield Area Library at (724) 837-8441.

ARTISTIC & LITERARY SUPPORT GROUPS

Society for Contemporary Craft
2100 Smallman Street
(412) 261-7003
www.contemporarycraft.org

Founded by Betty Raphael in 1971 as The Store for Arts and Crafts and People-Made Things, this organization—now called the Society for Contemporary Craft—is a nationally recognized non-profit contemporary arts organization. Exhibits, family workshops, and a children's studio are open for hands-on activities during all public hours. Previous workshops have included puppet making, creating jewelry from beads, and glass studio tours. Exhibitions are held throughout the city, including at the Carnegie. About 30,000 people annually visit Contemporary Craft (its shortened name). Purchases from the Store benefit the society as well as the individual artist. Guided tours and activities are available for schools. The society is open Tuesday through Saturday, 9:00 A.M. to 5:00 P.M. Closed Sunday and Monday.

Pittsburgh Center for the Arts School
6300 Fifth Avenue
(412) 361-0873

With classes in everything from ceramics, drawing, and music, to yoga stretch and meditation, the Pittsburgh Center for the Arts offers instruction in two locations—Shadyside and in the South Hills. Annually, there are 600 different classes, workshops, and camps provided for adults and children in 20 artistic disciplines. Some say this is the largest community-based art school in the country.

The Center for the Arts Galleries showcase exhibitions of emerging and recognized artists. And the Center for the Arts Shops feature original and handcrafted jewelry, ceramics, functional and decorative works, paintings, prints, glassware, and more. Galleries and shops are open Tuesday through Saturday, 10:00 A.M. to 5:30 P.M. and Sunday, noon to 5:00 P.M. For gallery and shop information, call (412) 361-0873. (See the Shopping chapter.)

Sweetwater Center for the Arts
200 Broad Street, Sewickley
(412) 741-4405

Founded in 1975, this regional center seeks to stimulate broad-based interest in the arts. Artist-instructors have outstanding qualifications for lectures and demonstrations as well as classes for beginners and experienced artists. The center is wheelchair accessible. The schedule of classes and workshops includes ceramics and sculpture, cuisine, drawing, house and home, mind and body, painting, photo and filmmaking, and traditional crafts.

Associated Artists of Butler County
The Art Center, South Main Street
Butler
(724) 283-6922

Dedicated to promoting the arts, this group encourages participation in the creative process and assists the community in finding ways to incorporate the arts into daily life. As the oldest cultural organization in Butler County, the AABC relies upon volunteers and now resides in its own facility on South Main Street. The more than 350 members host exhibits throughout the year and offer classes, each lasting approximately eight weeks. Lectures, poetry readings, musical performances, and children's art classes are also a part of this group's mission.

Pennwriters
Statewide gatherings at
various locations
www.pennwriters.org

Pennwriters is a rapidly growing, independent network of writers covering many genres. Established in 1988, the group includes members from all over the Commonwealth who share their knowledge and support fellow writers penning mystery, science fiction, fantasy, romance, women's fiction, children's books, poetry, nonfiction books

and articles, greeting cards, and other work. The group now boasts more than 400 members.

Held in either Pittsburgh or in the Harrisburg area, a major writer's conference draws attention (and new members) each May. Throughout the year, area groups meet to learn from guest speakers or fellow members, or simply to network over lunch. Pittsburgh is considered to be in Area 3 of the group's six areas. Officers are elected by members. Author advocacy and other services, including a subscription to The Penn Writer newsletter, are the perks of becoming a Pennwriter. Dues cost approximately $35 upon renewal and $45 for first-time members.

Ligonier Valley Writers
Ligonier, Westmoreland County

A nonprofit organization dedicated to encouraging and promoting the craft and business of writing, this group meets informally six times a year to hear from speakers and instructors. Topics tackled by the writers group include travel writing, horror fiction, food criticism, plot development, and the complexities of the publishing industry. An annual conference is held midway through each summer featuring outstanding faculty members.

The Loyalhanna Review provides talented writers with an outlet for their work. Social events, library resource materials, periodic newsletters, and other seminars are the perks of membership. Annual dues

Various literary prizes are offered to area writers. One of these, the Drue Heinz Literature Prize, is administered by the University of Pittsburgh Press and carries a $15,000 cash award and promise to publish. Manuscripts are accepted in May and June for short stories or novellas. For a copy of the rules, write to the University of Pittsburgh Press, 3400 Forbes Avenue, PA 15260.

are approximately $30 for members ($45 for two members at the same address). For information, write in care of Box B, Ligonier, PA 15658.

Pittsburgh Filmmakers
477 Melwood Avenue
(412) 681-5449
www.pghfilmmakers.org

Pittsburgh Filmmakers is a media-arts center devoted to artistic expression through film, video, and photography. It has provided artists with access to necessary equipment since 1971. The organization provides exhibitions of alternative work ranging from off-beat foreign films to radical showings. Classes are available for credit or noncredit learning.

PARKS 🌳

The hills, mountains, streams, and woodlands of Western Pennsylvania provide spacious and splendid settings for parks. In the region, you'll find a happy balance between development and greenways. To its credit, local government has long recognized the value of parks for its citizens. In an era when both the public and private sectors actively seek new revenue sources from growth, they've tended to view the region's parklands as natural resources already producing riches aplenty.

Many of the region's parks were founded through private sector and government cooperation. If you trace the history of parks development here, you'll find that quite a few sit on land once privately owned, then bequeathed to the public by industrialists and philanthropists. Knowing the gems that they inherited, governments tended to buy up adjacent tracts to expand their new parks.

The result is a rich variety of parks ranging from the playground apparatus and tennis courts on the corner to the sweep and majesty of the Allegheny National Forest, Western Pennsylvania's largest scenic and recreation area.

In our descriptions, we've sketched the attractions of 24 municipal parks, 16 state parks, and 6 federal recreation areas. You'll find many more municipal parks that you'll want to get to know. We've tried to capture both the most popular and heavily used parks as well as those with particularly compelling features. For more information on activities offered in the parks, see the Recreation chapter, where you'll find descriptions and opportunities for many sports and activities.

MUNICIPAL PARKS

Municipalities in Western Pennsylvania know the value of parks. Virtually every municipality in the region maintains green areas for the relaxation and enjoyment of its citizens. The city of Pittsburgh, for example, operates 29 parks offering picnic shelters, to say nothing of smaller parks and parklets. Included descriptions are only the "crown jewels" of the Pittsburgh parks system—Frick, Highland, Riverview, and Schenley. Clearly, you'll find a great deal more to explore than we could capture here. An excellent place to begin exploring, on a rainy, early spring day perhaps, is the county parks' Web site, www.county.allegheny.pa.us/parks.

If you want to reserve a shelter or ballfield in the city of Pittsburgh or Allegheny County, you'll need to be familiar with the permitting process in each case. For shelters, the city of Pittsburgh launches its permitting period with a "Shelter Day," held each spring in the lobby of the City-County Building. That opening day is reserved for city of Pittsburgh residents, who participate in a lottery for permits. Thereafter, you can reserve your shelter by calling (412) 255–2370. Fees, which include a mandatory alcohol permit, range from $42 to $262. The city will hold your reservation for seven days, and your payment must be by money order or business check only.

For city of Pittsburgh ballfields, organizations currently using fields are entitled to automatic renewals. For the fields that remain, the city permits time slots of 1 hour and 45 minutes. Fees range from $150 to $300 for the spring season. Call (412) 255–2370 for your ballfield permits.

For the scoop on state parks, forests, rail trails, and other opportunities for outdoor adventure, check out the Department of Conservation and Natural Resource's Web site: www.dcnr.state .pa.us.

Allegheny County's procedures are significantly different from the city of Pittsburgh's. You can reserve shelters, groves, and buildings up to one year in advance—a good idea if you're eyeing one of the large facilities at North Park or South Park. You can make your reservations at the parks (except for Hartwood Acres) or by calling the county at (412) 350-2474. Fees range from $20 to $275. Checks, cash, and money orders are accepted at all the parks, while North and South Parks accept credit cards. For ballfields at North Park, South Park, and Boyce Park, again, call the county at (412) 350-2474; you can reserve fields at other parks at the parks themselves. You must pay your fee in person—$30 for a three-hour slot—within 48 hours.

North

Belmont Complex
415 Butler Road, Kittanning
(724) 548-1067
It would be hard to find a municipal park that offers more comprehensive ice-skating facilities than you'll find at Belmont Complex. Operated by the Armstrong County Recreation Authority, the complex features ice skating and hockey programs August through April. The budding hockey stars in your family will enjoy skating instruction and youth leagues, while adult teams can compete in the league operated by the complex. If you don't belong to a league, complex officials will find one for you.

The complex also hosts skating shows and high-school hockey matches. Perhaps best of all, you can rent the ice complex for your personal or group use. With ice time as precious as it is in the region, that's a rare attraction, indeed.

Skating and hockey are far from the only activities at Belmont Complex. The swimming pool is available on a daily admission basis and to members who pay an annual fee; members are welcome to host their guests. You'll also enjoy various special events. This is a fun place.

Deer Lakes Park
1090 Bailies Run Road, Tarentum
(724) 265-3520
Fishing is the primary theme at Deer Lakes Park, a facility administered by Allegheny County. Over the years, the county augmented the park's existing lake with two additional lakes; all are interconnected and use the same watershed. The state stocks the lake with bluegill, crappie, perch, sunfish, and trout, and bass and catfish also bite. The park's picnic areas all bear the names of fish. Nine picnic shelters and nine groves may be reserved through Allegheny County.

Harrison Hills Park
5200 Freeport Road, Natrona Heights
(724) 295-3570
This 500-acre park in the extreme northeastern corner of Allegheny County offers some of the most enticing vistas of any municipal park in the region. From the Watts Memorial Overlook, you'll view a vast expanse of the Allegheny River, and your view will take in parts of three neighboring counties—Armstrong, Butler, and Westmoreland. You'll find groves and shelters for relaxation as you enjoy the view, and walking trails and soccer fields if you're in the mood for something less sedentary.

Hartwood Acres
200 Hartwood Acres
(412) 767-9200
The centerpieces of Hartwood Acres are the mansion and riding stables that once were the property of the estate's former owner, Mary Flinn Lawrence, who sold the estate to Allegheny County in 1969. The

county has maintained the stables and riding trails and offers tours of the mansion.

Among municipal parks in the region, Hartwood Acres may be unequaled for its beauty, whether lush and green in the summer or a snow-covered picture postcard in the winter. For all that, the principal current attractions are cultural, as Hartwood Acres hosts theater, dance, symphony, and other musical programs in warm weather months. Local restaurants sometimes provide box dinners to patrons of Hartwood performances. Dinner on the lush lawn followed by an evening of theater in the park: Now that's entertainment!

North Park
Pearce Mill Road, Allison Park
(724) 935-1971

North Park and South Park are the reigning monarchs of the Allegheny County park system. Visit this sprawling 3,010-acre park and you'll agree that it deserves its crown. Its 75-acre lake is considered the largest man-made body of water in the county; it's bordered by 4½ miles of natural woodlands. If you're a jogger, you won't earn your spurs until you jog around the lake, a popular pastime for many. Anglers utilize the well-stocked lake; even if you don't fish, you can enjoy the lake by renting a boat from the park's concessionaire.

Bicyclists also circumnavigate the lake—the park provides bicycles for rent. The swimming pool may be the largest you'll ever see. Don't count on lap swimming here, though. There are too many swimmers enjoying the pool to allow for that. North Park's 18-hole golf course is exceptionally popular—you'll find a more detailed description in the Golf chapter.

Other amenities include tennis courts, ballfields, a skating rink, and numerous groves and shelters of varying sizes and amenities. The ballfields and groves attract heavy use. If you're planning an outing, it's mandatory that you reserve your grove or picnic area, and we suggest that you do so well in advance. You can

expect to pay anywhere from $25 to $65 to reserve the space.

Riverview Park
Riverview Avenue
(412) 323-7209

When the North Side of Pittsburgh was a separate municipality known as Allegheny, local residents raised money to purchase land for a park, which they donated to the community. That land became Riverview Park, a 251-acre facility now operated by the city of Pittsburgh. The park offers many attractive features, including 12 hiking trails that will carry you so deeply into thick woods that you'll swear you've left the city for virgin forest.

You'll enjoy bridle trails—rare enough within the city—as well as a swimming pool, three tennis courts, horseshoe pits, a ballfield, and five playgrounds. Picnickers can utilize six shelters—you'll need permits and reservations for three of those.

The Allegheny Observatory stands near the park's main entrance. Used primarily as a research facility by the University of Pittsburgh, the observatory also hosts credit and informal courses and meetings of the region's amateur astronomers.

East

Boyce Park
675 Frankstown Road, Plum
(724) 327-0338

If you're looking for downhill skiing in Allegheny County, Boyce Park is the place. In fact it's the only place. This park at the extreme eastern edge of Allegheny County offers both lifts and a large ski lodge called Four Seasons. For more on Boyce Park's skiing, see the Recreation chapter.

Skiing is one of many attractions here, as the county-run park also features a popular wave pool and a large recreational complex. The 1,096-acre park offers tennis courts and picnic groves and shelters all named with a Boy Scouts motif. That's to honor William D. Boyce, the founder of the Boy Scouts, who was born nearby.

If you visit a federal recreation area, you'll become familiar with Freddie Fish, the mascot of the U.S. Army Corps of Engineers Pittsburgh District.

Cedar Creek Park
RD#4, Belle Vernon
(724) 929-4352
The scenic Youghiogheny River provides the northern border for Cedar Creek . . . as well as a host of recreational activities. The Yough offers fishing and canoeing, with river access through a boat launch. You'll also enjoy hiking and bicycling along the Yough River Trail, a work in progress that features about 20 completed miles. The 10-foot-wide trail is finished with crushed limestone, making it wheelchair accessible.

The park also features 19 pavilions available for rental, bicycle and cross-country ski rentals, ballfields, basketball and volleyball courts, horseshoe pits, and sledding and tobogganing areas. You may hunt in certain areas of the park.

You'll take particular pleasure in several special features of the park. Cedar Creek has cut a deep gorge in the northern section of the park—water cascades down the shale steps amid steep forested slopes. The park's amphitheater accommodates up to 2,500 visitors for its free summer concert series. Finally, the Mon-Yough Model Airplane Club operates from Cedar Creek Park, so you can expect to see some low-flying craft.

Frick Park
2005 Beechwood Boulevard
(412) 422-6538
If there were no Frick Park, someone would want to invent one. Operated by the city of Pittsburgh, this huge urban park

touches five city neighborhoods—Squirrel Hill, Point Breeze, Park Place, Regent Square, and Swisshelm Park—and reaches into the adjacent municipality of Swissvale. At 476 acres, it's large enough to host many simultaneous activities without seeming overly crowded, even when dog lovers and their pooches congregate each weekend morning for socializing and play. Frick's walking and jogging trails wind along the park's hills, giving you a workout that few other municipal parks can.

For recreation, Frick Park offers six clay tennis courts, a basketball court, two playgrounds, three ballfields, and a lawn bowling green. For more on lawn bowling in Frick Park, see the Recreation chapter.

The park was bequeathed to the city by industrialist and philanthropist Henry Clay Frick. In accordance with the bequest, 150 acres of the park have been designated Frick Woods Nature Reserve. The Frick Environmental Center manages the reserve and houses Citipark's Environmental Education program.

Within the reserve, you'll find a meadow, woodlands, and gardens that host a treasure trove of native plant life and are one of the region's most popular birding areas, as home and migratory "stop-over" to more than 150 different species.

Highland Park
Highland Avenue and Bunkerhill Street
(412) 665-3632
For a true Pittsburgh scene, drop by the reservoir at Highland Park any morning at dawn or shortly thereafter. You'll see a parade of walkers and joggers getting in their laps around the reservoir, part of the daily regime for many residents of Pittsburgh's East End. Don't be surprised if you're inspired to join them. Operated by the city of Pittsburgh, the 403-acre park offers eight shelters—all of which you must get a permit to use—woodland trails, a large swimming pool, and a companion wading pool. You'll find 9 tennis courts, a softball field, and 10 areas with play apparatus. Lake Carnegie is popular with

anglers; it's a good place for an afternoon of laid-back fishing, but don't expect to walk away with that trout you've been wanting to mount on your wall. The reservoir notwithstanding, the most popular attraction of the park is the Pittsburgh Zoo & Aquarium, which is detailed for you in the Kidstuff chapter.

Mammoth Park
RD#1, Mt. Pleasant
(724) 830-3950

As you drive through eastern Westmoreland County, you'll come across a lake that's mammoth, ergo the name, Mammoth Park. Mammoth Lake spans 27 acres, and it's stocked with trout by the Pennsylvania Fish Commission. When frozen, the lake provides both ice fishing and ice skating. The park offers wheelchair-accessible fishing decks.

Another popular water-based activity is the giant waterslide, which descends 96 feet from a hillside into the lake. Sounds like a "must-do" for the kids.

When you're dried off and ready for landbased activities, you'll find numerous pavilions available for rental as well as ballfields, play apparatus, sledding and tobogganing areas, and courts for volleyball, boccie ball, shuffleboard, basketball, street hockey, and tennis. You can take it all in from the Mammoth Park observation deck, which provides a panoramic view ranging for almost 10 miles.

Both the Laurel Highlands Radio-Controlled Airplane Club and a BMX club base their operations at the park.

Mt. Odin Park
Tollgate Hill Road, Greensburg
(724) 834-2640

Operated by the city of Greensburg, Mt. Odin Park features several picnic pavilions, tennis courts, and a golf course—for more about that amenity, see the Golf chapter. The most compelling attraction of the park, however, is its play area, where you'll find replicas of downtown Greensburg buildings, including city hall, the Westmoreland County Courthouse, and West-

moreland Hospital. The replicas have an open design, so kids can walk through and play inside them. Sounds like an intriguing way to familiarize your youngsters with life in the city.

Northmoreland Park
Route 356, Allegheny Township
(724) 727-7616

Once you get used to the idea of traveling east to Northmoreland in Westmoreland County (we're dizzy just writing it), you'll find a lovely facility developed around the 17-acre Northmoreland Lake. The lake features a winter and spring trout fishery, as well as quality bass and pan fishing. Since the lake is designated a conservation lake, special Fish Commission rules apply. Northmoreland provides a wheelchair-accessible fishing deck.

The Boathouse Building offers boat rental and picnic facilities. You'll find 11 pavilions available for rental, as well as ballfields, play apparatus, cross-country ski trails, and courts for boccie ball and volleyball. Also available for rental is the Activities Building, which features a small kitchen and an air-conditioned reception/meeting room. You may hunt in some areas of the park. The park sports a model radio-controlled airfield and a BMX track, as well as opportunities for horseback riding and equestrian lessons, using either your own horse or one of the park's.

Renziehausen Park
Eden Park Boulevard, McKeesport
(412) 675-5068

This urban park operated by the city of McKeesport offers both recreational and cultural delights. For recreation you can enjoy the park's ballfield, splash pool for kids, seven shelters and a pavilion available for rental, and fishing in Lake Emily, which hosts an annual fishing derby.

For culture and entertainment, visit the International Village, which since 1960 has been hosting a three-day celebration of the region's ethnic heritage, complete with music, dancing, and food. You'll also enjoy The Little Red Schoolhouse, a replication of the city's first schoolhouse, erected in 1832, and entertainment at the park's band shell. Make sure you save time to tour the Rose Garden maintained by the Garden Club of McKeesport. It features 1,500 rose bushes as well as perennials and beds of grasses and herbs. In addition, the club uses the garden as a test bed to introduce new roses to the region. You'll find it difficult to tear yourself away from this beautiful spot.

Schenley Park
Schenley Drive
(412) 622-6904

Schenley Park, in the Oakland neighborhood bordering the campuses of both the University of Pittsburgh and Carnegie Mellon University, is one of the crown jewels of the city of Pittsburgh park system. You'll enjoy activities that are marvelously diverse. You'll find a swimming pool, 6 playground areas, walking and jogging trails, 13 tennis courts, and 3 ballfields. With permits and reservations, picnickers can utilize all five shelters—and you can rent the park's meeting room, a popular site for receptions.

The park's ice rink is one of the region's most popular venues for ice skating—for more information on this activity, see the Recreation chapter. Schenley hosts a number of popular annual events, including the Vintage Grand Prix, the Smoky City Folk Festival, and the Great Ride bicycle race. For more on the Great Ride, see the Recreation chapter. You can lounge on the lawn at Flagstaff Hill—a popular pastime of CMU students—where the city stages its Cinema in the Parks program each summer, or take in the flower shows at Phipps Conservatory and Botanical Gardens.

Schenley Park is rich in history as well as amenities. Much of the park was donated by philanthropist Mary Schenley, and the park's "Oval" for decades was home to harness racing and horse stables. A horrific fire in the early 1970s destroyed the stables and ended the park's equine involvement.

The park also offers a popular 9-hole golf course—the only golf course within city of Pittsburgh limits—and a flying disc golf course that hosts organized competition. For more on these activities, see the Golf and Recreation chapters.

Twin Lakes Park
Twin Lakes Road, Luxor
(724) 837-8611

The park takes its name from its twin lakes that provide boating, fishing, ice fishing, and ice-skating opportunities. At the Lower Lake's Boating & Concession building, you can load up on fishing and picnic supplies and rent pedal boats, rowboats, and canoes. The park features three wheelchair-accessible fishing decks.

A broad network of recreational trails is a major attraction at this Westmoreland County-operated facility. You'll find trails for walking, cross-country skiing, and jogging—joggers also can test the exercise stations staged along the trails. If you enjoy the Wilderness Trail, you'll also enjoy the park's environmental and nature center, which provides interpretive programs for school, groups, and any interested visitors.

For outings, you can rent any of the seven pavilions or the Activities Building, which features a kitchen and a reception hall/meeting room. Twin Lakes also offers play apparatus as well as hunting in designated areas.

South

Cross Creek Park
Route 50, Rea
(724) 228-6867

Operated by Washington County, Cross Creek Park offers hunting and fishing and boating on the 260-acre lake. Bring your own boat and boating permit. (Annual permits are available from the county.) Picnic sites are available free of charge, but shelters must be rented. All shelters feature grills and electrical outlets. You'll enjoy the park's hiking trails.

Mingo Creek Park
Route 136, Nottingham
(724) 228-6867

Mingo Creek Park features a number of activities with an equine theme. You'll find bridle trails for horseback riding—you're responsible for bringing the horse and purchasing an annual permit—and hourly hayrides from 10:00 A.M. through 2:00 P.M. on weekdays and on weekends in October. Cost for a hayride is $50 per hour for a maximum of 25 people.

The park offers 10 shelters of varying sizes, which must be reserved in season, as well as picnic sites available free of charge. Organized groups may camp in the park, and nature walks are available for all. Mingo Creek Park is operated by Washington County.

Round Hill Park and Farm
651 Round Hill Road, Elizabeth
(412) 384-4701

This is a park with an agrarian theme. In fact, the 1,101-acre park is built around a modern working farm that's a popular destination for student groups. The park offers interpretive sessions to thousands of students and other visitors each year. Other attractions of Round Hill, which is located in the southeastern corner of Allegheny County and administered by the county, include a soccer field and picnic groves and shelters.

South Park
Buffalo Drive, South Park
(412) 835-5710

At about 2,000 acres, South Park is one of the most capacious and diverse of the region's municipal parks, and it offers just about every recreational activity you would hope to find in a municipal facility. Its wave pool attracts about 100,000 people per season, and its two golf courses totaling 27 holes are exceptionally popular. For more on golf at South Park, see the Golf chapter.

You'll find picnic tables and shelters as well as walking, jogging, and hiking trails.

The trails wind through areas that feature both woodlands and open glades. For all that, many joggers eschew the trails for a run along Corrigan Drive, the park's main thoroughfare that was named after the famous "Wrong Way Corrigan." Other amenities include tennis courts, ballfields, horseshoe pits, a deck hockey facility, and a skating rink.

You'll get an eyeful of history at the park as well. Allegheny County, which operates the park, has preserved the homestead of Oliver Miller; it was near that estate that the first shots of the 1794 Whiskey Rebellion were fired. The bathhouse near the wave pool was patterned after the Miller house. You'll also find on Corrigan Drive a memorial to poet Joyce Kilmer, who penned the famous poem "Trees" . . . an appropriate tribute to this lush park.

Ten Mile Creek County Park
Clarksville Road, Fredericktown
(724) 228-6867

As you might guess, the main attraction in 25-acre Ten Mile Creek County Park is the creek, where boating is a popular activity. Bring your own boat and annual permit issued by Washington County, which operates this park. You may also fish from the shore of the creek. Shelters with grills and electrical outlets are available for rental. Picnic sites are offered on a first-come, first-served basis.

White Oak Park
3 Muse Lane, McKeesport
(412) 678-3774

Operated by Allegheny County, White Oak Park is a botanist's delight, featuring a broad variety of plants and trees, some of them found nowhere else in Pennsylvania. You'll get plenty of exercise if you explore the fauna, as some of White Oak's terrain is quite steep. You can unwind in the park's rental picnic groves and shelters when you've finished exploring the 810 acres. Park opens daily from 8:00 A.M. to sunset.

West

Brady's Run Park
526 Brady's Run Road, Beaver Falls
(724) 846-5600
Brady's Run Park is named for Captain Samuel Brady, an early pioneer and merciless killer of Native Americans, whose ferocity was fueled by the death of his father and brother in the Indian wars of the 1770s. In one of the most interesting examples of early American jurisprudence, Brady was charged with killing Native Americans—and acquitted largely on the strength of testimony of Chief Guyasuta, whose tribe had been relentlessly hunted by Brady.

While the park pays homage to Brady, it is a gentle and peaceful facility operated by Beaver County. It features the Beaver County Ice Arena and the Calland Arboretum, a natural area with walking trails. You'll also enjoy Brady's Run Lodge, a popular site for weddings and other special events; an indoor facility for tennis and walking, with an observation deck; an arena for horse shows; and horseshoe courts that have hosted state championship events.

Settler's Cabin Park
1225 Green Road, Oakdale
(412) 787-2750
Settler's Cabin spans 1,589 acres, unusually large for a municipal park, and it has more of a rugged feel than most municipal parks. Named for an 18th-century log cabin that was found on the site, the park's attractive meadows in many cases have been left largely untouched. Allegheny County, which operates the park, has preserved the log cabin for visitors. If you're looking for a getaway only a few minutes from downtown Pittsburgh and Pittsburgh International Airport, you can feel like a settler at Settler's Cabin. It will be easy to feel as if you're exploring a brave new frontier: The park extends to Collier and Robinson Townships, and even into northern Fayette County.

You'll find plenty of amenities, including reasonably priced rental shelters and groves named for Native American tribes. The wave pool and diving platform are extremely popular, as are the park's tennis courts.

STATE PARKS

When the Commonwealth of Pennsylvania established its Department of Environmental Resources in 1971 under Secretary Maurice K. Goddard, it was with the avowed purpose of situating at least one public park within a 25-mile drive of each resident of the state. It might take a surveyor to determine if the state achieved exactly the goal, but one thing the Commonwealth did accomplish was development of a public park system rich in recreational opportunities and environmental wonders.

The state operates 116 parks with a varied and compelling recreational menu. At most, natural or man-made waterways offer fishing, boating, and swimming. Hunting is permitted in most areas of the parks, and you'll find miles of scenic hiking trails, campsites, and picnic areas. Winter brings ice skating, ice fishing, ice boating, sled riding, cross-country skiing, and snowmobiling. Not all activities are offered everywhere, but most parks are diverse enough to satisfy your outdoor needs.

State parks are open year-round, typically from 8:00 A.M. until sunset, although some activities are seasonal. Some activities require fees, reservations, or rentals. You may bring your pets to day-use areas, provided you keep them on leashes. The state imposes a number of restrictions on certain activities and uses, including limitation on the horsepower of motorized boats and the length of your stay at certain cabins and campsites. For instance, to boat, in most cases, you'll also need at least one of the following: 1) a State Park launching permit, available at most State Park offices; 2) a State Park mooring permit; 3) a current certificate and number of watercraft registration; 4) current registration for your motorized (electric) boats; or, for your boat registered in another state, 5) a Pennsylvania State Park launch permit and the boat's current registration.

If you call the Bureau of State Parks at (888) PA–PARKS, they'll be happy to provide you with a useful brochure and map of all 116 parks, indicating the activities that each park offers as well as introducing you to park rules and regulations. They'll also send you more detailed brochures on individual parks—they will charge a nominal fee if you ask for more than a few brochures.

We've profiled 16 state parks. To do so, we've had to step out of the six-county coverage area on occasion. We think you'll find the trip worth taking.

Point State Park
101 Commonwealth Place
(412) 471-0235
www.dcnr.state.pa.us/stateparks/parks/point.aspx

A state park in downtown Pittsburgh? It's not a misprint, as the Commonwealth maintains this 36-acre downtown oasis right at the Point, where the Allegheny and Monongahela Rivers meet to form the Ohio River. The park is steeped in historical significance. It was the site of the original Fort Pitt, where the British routed the French and founded the city. You can see a portion of the old fort at the park's Fort Pitt Blockhouse museum. The park was created just after World War II as part of the city's Renaissance, yet another historical note.

The park hosts the Three Rivers Arts Festival and a variety of concerts and serves as the finishing point for the Pittsburgh Marathon. The emphasis here, however, is not on doing but on relaxing and, dare we say it, contemplating. With benches that provide views of river traffic and the giant fountain, you can slip away from the day's challenges for a few moments of peace and quiet. This is a rare and welcome city amenity.

North

Clear Creek State Park
RR 1, Box 82, Sigel 15860-9502
(814) 752-2368
www.dcnr.state.pa.us/stateparks/parks/clearcreek.aspx

Set in Jefferson County just north of the six-county coverage area, 1,676-acre Clear Creek State Park is popular for its own attractions as well as its proximity to Clear Creek State Forest, Cook Forest State Park, and the Allegheny National Forest. If you want to stay long enough to hit all those highlights, you can use this park's family campground, with 53 tent and trailer sites, or opt for cozier accommodations in one of the park's 2 yurts or 22 rustic family cabins.

Anglers will find stocked and native brook trout in Clear Creek, and northern pike, smallmouth bass, walleye, trout, and panfish in the nearby Clarion River. Hunters can stalk whitetail deer, bear, squirrel, and wild turkey on 677 acres. The park offers 15 miles of hiking trails, a 390-foot guarded swimming beach, more than 300 picnic tables, and 5 pavilions available for rental.

For a special treat while you're here, try canoeing on the Clarion River, one of the region's most scenic and pristine waterways. Canoe rental is available from private concessionaires just outside the park.

Cook Forest State Park
P.O. Box 120, Cooksburg 16217
(814) 744-8407
www.dcnr.state.pa.us/stateparks/parks/cookforest.aspx

Cook Forest State Park spans 6,668 acres in three counties—Clarion, Forest, and Jefferson. It's north of the coverage area but such a recreational and historical gem that you'll want to visit this park. It's named for John Cook, an early settler whose descendants are buried in a private cemetery adjoining the park. In the 1930s, the park was the site of a Civilian Conservation Corps (CCC) camp; CCC workers

Urban, Suburban, and Wilderness Trails

Frick Park Trail System
(412) 422-6538

This is an extensive woodland trail network, including designated areas where dogs may run off-leash. Like the park, it runs from Point Breeze into Squirrel Hill, borders Edgewood, and dips under the Parkway East. A highlight is the Frick Environmental Center, near the Beechwood Avenue entrance in Squirrel Hill, which provides information about the park's history, habitat, and ecology.

Three Rivers Heritage Trail System
(412) 488-0212
www.friendsoftheriverfront.org

This system connects the heart of downtown Pittsburgh with surrounding neighborhoods, including Oakland, the North Shore, South Side, and the Strip District. Built by the city of Pittsburgh in partnership with Friends of the Riverfront, these trails are suitable for walking, running, and biking.

Hartwood Acres Trail System
(412) 767-9200
www.county.allegheny.pa.us/parks/story/hartwood.asp

Trails are set within the "crown jewel" of Allegheny County's parks system in the North Hills. Highlights of a visit to Hartwood Acres include outdoor sculpture placed throughout the park, guided tours of Hartwood Manor, and arts programming at the amphitheater.

Montour Trail
(412) 831-2030
www.montourtrail.org

The Montour Trail stretches for 42 miles between Coraopolis and Clairton and is expanding each year. Suitable for hiking, biking, cross-country skiing, and horseback riding in some areas.

Steel Valley Trail
www.steelvalleytrail.org

When completed, this 19-mile urban trail will connect with the Three Rivers Her-

helped construct the park's cabins, roads, and trails.

The trails remain an attraction. These include 27 miles of hiking trails, featuring a portion of the 140-mile Baker Trail, which stretches from Freeport in Armstrong County to the Allegheny National Forest. The trails wind through magnificent stands of virgin white pine and hemlock timber stands, which have earned the park the nickname "the Black Forest of Pennsylvania." The trail network includes 4.5 miles of bridle trails and 20 miles of snowmobile trails.

Anglers enjoy the scenic Clarion River, which flows along the park's border and itage Trail System and the Montour, Nine Mile Run, and Youghiogheny Trails, as well as numerous historic Pittsburgh areas. It's a highlight of the Rivers of Steel National Heritage Area.

Youghiogheny River Trail
(724) 872-5586
www.youghrivertrail.com
Including 71 miles of limestone-surfaced trail and accessible to individuals of all ages and physical abilities, this trail winds through Allegheny, Westmoreland, and Fayette Counties. Called "one of the world's best walks" by *Travel and Leisure* magazine, the trail draws more than 200,000 visitors each year. Suitable for walking, running, biking, and studying nature.

Laurel Highlands Hiking Trail
(724) 455-3744
This 70-mile path follows the Laurel Ridge from the Youghiogheny River at Ohiopyle to the Conemaugh Gorge near Johnstown. Known among hikers and backpackers, the trail features eight overnight shelter areas, located every 8 to 10 miles along the trail. Overnight

reservations are mandatory; call the number above.

Ohiopyle State Park Trails
(724) 329-8591
www.dcnr.state.pa.us/stateparks/parks/ohiopyle.aspx
This system features more than 41 miles of day hiking trails and is also the terminus of the 70-mile Laurel Highlands Hiking Trail. Each of the trails here offers panoramic views, cascading streams, and a diverse sampling of plants and animals native to the area. Ohiopyle is near many other popular attractions, such as Fallingwater, Kentuck Knob, Fort Necessity Battlefield, and Bear Run Nature Reserve.

Laurel Caverns
(800) 515-4150
www.laurelcaverns.com
Hike inside Pennsylvania's largest cave. Tours for individuals, families, and groups, as well as a more advanced caving excursion or rappelling seminar. Open daily from May to October and on the weekends in March, April, and November.

—With thanks to the Greater Pittsburgh Convention and Visitors Bureau

yields trout, warm-water game fish, and panfish, while hunters utilize more than 4,000 acres in search of deer, squirrel, and turkey. You're welcome to canoe on the Clarion, but you'll have to go outside the park for canoe rentals. Cook Forest offers a swimming pool and such winter activities as ice skating, sledding, and cross-country skiing, with ski rentals available.

Picnickers will find tables and two pavilions available for rental. The park offers 2 organized group tenting areas as well as 24 rustic cabins for rental. Don't miss the Sawmill Craft Center and Theater for plays, musical performances, and displays of crafts by local artisans.

Not all municipalities print and distribute brochures about their parks. For the most useful printed information, try: Westmoreland County Bureau of Parks and Recreation, (724) 830-3950 or (724) 830-3951; Washington County Department of Parks and Recreation, (724) 228-6867; and Armstrong County Recreation Authority, (724) 548-1067.

Jennings Environmental Education Center
2951 Prospect Road, Slippery Rock
(724) 794-6011
www.dcnr.state.pa.us/stateparks/parks/jennings.aspx

You can't swim, snowmobile, hunt, or fish here, as Jennings isn't that kind of park. You can, however, learn about ecological and environmental issues . . . then traverse the 300-acre facility and get a hands-on feel for those issues. Jennings just happens to encompass one of the only prairies left in the Pennsylvania area.

The center strives to protect natural ecosystems and provide public education in ecological responsibility. It does so through displays, exhibits, and the natural wonders of the park. These include the blazing star, a prairie plant that sports a cluster of rose-purple flowers at their most colorful in August, and 220 acres of woodland trails that display nearly 400 species of plants and 134 species of birds. Stay on those trails, please, or you may encounter the massasauga rattlesnake. This guy is endangered and not keen on being disturbed.

Kids, this is one place you'll want to take your parents.

Maurice K. Goddard State Park
684 Lake Wilhelm Road, Sandy Lake
(724) 253-4833
www.dcnr.state.pa.us/stateparks/parks/mauricekgoddard.aspx

The park is named for Dr. Maurice K. Goddard, father of Pennsylvania's environmental movement, who served as the founding secretary of the state's Department of Environmental Resources in 1971. Lake Wilhelm dominates the park, spanning more than 60 percent of the facility's 2,856 acres. As you might expect, water-based activities are popular here.

The park features a 200-slip marina and a 48-space dry land seasonal mooring area; the marina provides parking space for 371 cars and trailers. Other amenities include boat rentals and seven launching areas. Nonpowered boats and those up to 10 horsepower are permitted. Anglers enjoy the lake as well, pursuing largemouth and smallmouth bass, walleyes, northern pike, muskellunge, bluegill, crappie, catfish, perch, and sunfish.

More than 1,155 acres are available for hunting—deer and waterfowl are abundant. You'll find 14 miles of hiking trails, 6 miles of mountain bike trails, and 150 picnic tables in the park. Winter activities include ice skating, ice fishing, ice boating, cross-country skiing, and snowmobiling. The park is just north of the principal coverage area.

McConnell's Mill State Park
RR2, Portersville
(724) 368-8091
www.dcnr.state.pa.us/stateparks/parks/mcconnellsmill.aspx

The centerpieces of McConnell's Mill are the deep gorges of Slippery Rock Creek formed by glacial activity more than 100,000 years ago and a man-made attraction, the restored rolling gristmill from which the park derives its name. The gorge creates some of the region's best—and most challenging—opportunities for modern-day hikers, climbers, and white-water boaters.

Hikers will enjoy 11 miles of rugged trails that provide unparalleled views of the creek. White-water boaters can take to the creek in rubber rafts, white-water canoes, and kayaks, none of which can be rented at the park. Climbing and rappelling are available at the Rim Road Climbing Area and Breakneck Bridge. *Warning:* They don't call it Breakneck for nothing. You may hunt in designated areas—you'll likely encounter grouse, deer, turkey, rabbit, and squirrel.

Anglers will find trout and bass in the creek as well as a "Delayed Harvest—Fly Fishing Only" area. You won't have camping or swimming opportunities at McConnell's Mill, but you can enjoy more than 150 picnic tables and a ballfield.

Moraine State Park
225 Pleasant Valley Road, Portersville
(724) 368-8811
www.dcnr.state.pa.us/stateparks/parks/moraine.aspx

When you take in the majesty of Moraine, you may not believe that this treasured public resource was pocked by the scars of coal mining and oil-well drilling as late as the 1950s. The Commonwealth of Pennsylvania undertook the reclamation of strip-mined land, plugged 422 gas and oil wells, and created the 3,225-acre Lake Arthur, a restoration of the glacial lake that covered most of Northwestern Pennsylvania more than 10,000 years ago. The result: one of the state's most beautiful and useful parks.

Much of the activity at Moraine centers on Lake Arthur. The lake features 10 boat launching areas—motorized boats up to 10 horsepower are permitted—and you can rent canoes, rowboats, paddleboats, motorized fishing boats, and pontoon boats. Sailing is especially popular on the lake, with sailboats available for rental. The colorful sails form an appealing vista that you can view from picnic areas high above the lake. The Barber Point area of the lake is even suitable for wind surfing. Anglers pursue muskellunge, northern pike, tiger muskellunge, striper, largemouth bass, walleyes, channel catfish, black crappie, and bluegill. For swimmers, the park offers two, large guarded beaches.

You'll find plenty to do away from the lake. A 14-mile portion of the North Country National Scenic Trail courses through the park. A 7-mile paved bicycle trail parallels the north shore of the lake, and you'll also find a 6-mile mountain bike trail

that is targeted to experienced off-road bikers. Numerous other trails also offer opportunities for adventure. Approximately 13,600 of Moraine's acres are open seasonally for hunters. Picnickers will discover more than 1,200 picnic tables as well as seven pavilions available for rental.

In the winter, Lake Arthur offers ice skating, ice boating, and ice fishing, and you also may enjoy sledding, tobogganing, cross-country skiing, and snowmobiling. For overnight stays, the park provides 11 modern cabins and 2 organized youth group camping areas. You won't find family campsites, but the area surrounding the park offers plenty of privately operated campsites.

Oh, and just in case you're wondering, "moraine" refers to the soil, rocks, and debris that accumulate at the edges of and underneath a glacier. Now aren't you glad half of Pennsylvania was once covered in ice?

Oil Creek State Park
305 State Park Road, Oil City
(814) 676-5915
www.dcnr.state.pa.us/stateparks/parks/oilcreek.aspx

It was along Oil Creek that Col. Edwin Drake struck oil in 1859, helping to launch the petroleum industry. Part of the mission of Oil Creek State Park is to preserve and perpetuate the heritage of the oil boomtowns that grew up around Drake Well. The park features displays and historical programs at the Petroleum Centre, once a focal point of the petroleum boom and now the park's visitor center.

Hiking is an important activity in the 7,075-acre park. It provides more than 52 miles of hiking trails that double as biking and cross-country ski trails, and there's also one trail exclusively for bikes—and the occasional park maintenance vehicle. You can rent bikes at the Petroleum Centre. One of the neatest aspects of the park's trail system is its two overnight hike-in shelter areas. Each area offers six Adirondack-type shelters with fireplaces, restrooms, and water. You must reserve these shelters

More on Outdoor Activities

Through the guiding principles of aware-ness and training, the Western Pennsyl-vania Field Institute, (412) 255-0564 (www.wpfi.org), strives to promote out-door activities in the Pittsburgh area, as well as serve as a clearinghouse for all other adventure organizations' activities. Those interested in exploring the outdoors can enjoy afternoon, evening, day-long, and weekend excur-sions organized by the institute, as well as informative workshops and training courses in topics such as wilderness first aid, wilderness survival, and wildlife tracking.

—With thanks to the Greater Pittsburgh Convention and Visitors Bureau

in advance. Warning: If you're along the trails and see railroad tracks, stay off the tracks. The railroad is active.

Anglers flock to Oil Creek, which is known for its bass and trout. If you prefer to be on the water, bring your canoe. Oil Creek is classified as a beginner's stream. You'll find a paved portage path around the creek's ice-control dam. Approxi-mately 6,250 acres of the park are open to hunting, with rabbit, deer, squirrel, turkey, and ruffed grouse the most com-mon prey. You'll find picnic areas and shel-ters, although not nearly as many as other state parks offer. Oil Creek State Park is north of our six-county coverage area.

Pymatuning State Park
2660 Williamsfield Road, Jamestown
(724) 932-3141
www.dcnr.state.pa.us/stateparks/parks/
pymatuning.aspx
Pymatuning is somewhat north of the principal coverage area, but if you're an outdoors type, you won't mind the extra drive. An act of the Pennsylvania Legisla-ture decrees that the principal purposes of Pymatuning Lake and dam are for con-trolling floods and the flow of water in the Beaver and Shenango Rivers. The recre-ational opportunities that follow in the wake of those objectives are awesome.

The lake, spanning Pennsylvania and Ohio, is one of the region's most produc-tive for anglers, yielding walleye, muskel-lunge, carp, crappie, and largemouth and smallmouth bass, among many species. In one of those jurisdictional quirks that will drive you crazy, if you're a licensed angler in Pennsylvania, you can't fish from the Ohio shore. Similarly, Pennsylvania bans Ohio licensees on its side of the water. On the water itself, however, licensees from both states are welcome. The lake is a popular site for ice fishing in the winter.

Hunting is available in much of the park, including a Goose Management Area where controlled shooting is permitted during the annual waterfowl season. The park features a large protected area for migratory waterfowl. Swimmers will find four guarded beaches. Nonpowered boats and those up to 10 horsepower are per-mitted on the lake, and you can rent float-boats, rowboats, canoes, and motors, or try ice boating in the winter.

Pymatuning offers a variety of overnight facilities, including 657 family camping sites; an organized group camp-ing area that can accommodate up to 400 people; 194 modern tent and trailer campsites; and modern family cabins. You'll enjoy many picnic tables and 11 pavilions available for rental. Make sure you check out the Linesville spillway, where you may feed the fish and ducks.

Unofficially, this park boasts the most mispronounced name in the region. Try it this way: pie-muh-TOO-ning.

East

Keystone State Park
1150 Keystone Park Road, Derry
(724) 668-2939
www.dcnr.state.pa.us/stateparks/parks/keystone.aspx
If your family has a diversity of outdoor interests, you'll find that Keystone State Park has facilities to match those interests, all within easy driving distance of Pittsburgh. The recreational theme of this 1,182-acre park is variety. Keystone Lake offers up trout and a variety of other fish for anglers and a venue for nonpowered and electric-powered boats. You can rent rowboats, sailboats, and canoes. In winter the lake provides ice fishing and ice skating, while you can sled and snowmobile elsewhere in the park. Swimmers will enjoy a 1,000-foot turf and sand beach.

Hunters can pursue whitetail deer, pheasant, and grouse. Campers will find 100 tent and trailer sites for family camping as well as 11 modern cabins available for rental. Keystone State Park offers 443 picnic tables, several shelters, a ballfield, and hiking and biking trails.

Laurel Hill State Park
1454 Laurel Hill Park Road, Somerset
(814) 445-7725
www.dcnr.state.pa.us/stateparks/parks/laurelhill.aspx
In 1794 during the Whiskey Rebellion, George Washington's troops camped on the site of what is now Laurel Hill State Park. You won't feel the need to rebel here, except perhaps against drudgery. There is much to do and enjoy at Laurel Hill.

The 3,935-acre park offers 12 splendid miles for hiking, including the Hemlock Trail, which features a stand of virgin timber. You'll find four picnic areas with a total of 564 tables, playground equipment, and horseshoe pits. Hunting is permitted in 2,100 acres, and you'll enjoy 70 miles of snowmobile trails in Laurel Hill and the adjacent Forbes State Forest.

Laurel Hill Lake provides many water-based activities, including swimming along a 1,200-foot sandy beach and renting paddleboats, canoes, and rowboats. Both nonpowered boats and electric-powered boats are permitted on the lake. Anglers can test the lake 24 hours a day for bass, trout, catfish, suckers, bluegill, perch, crappie, and sunfish. You'll enjoy ice fishing and ice boating when the lake is frozen. If you want to spend some time to enjoy all the amenities, try the family camping areas. Organized groups may camp in tents or in large cabins.

Though technically a bit outside the six-county coverage area, Laurel Hill is part of a trio of adjacent state facilities—along with Linn Run State Park and Forbes State Forest—well worthy of coverage.

Linn Run State Park
P.O. Box 50, Rector, PA 15677-0030
(724) 238-6623
www.dcnr.state.pa.us/stateparks/parks/linnrun.aspx
Set on 571 acres within the Forbes State Forest, in the heart of the Laurel Mountains, Linn Run is a scenic park used primarily for picnicking, hiking, hunting, and fishing, although it offers other opportunities as well. The Adams Falls and Grove Run areas provide a total of 137 picnic tables; Adams Falls also offers a pavilion and play apparatus. If you find you really

---

Each May, the city of Pittsburgh Department of Parks (Citiparks) publishes a "summer magazine," a comprehensive guide to its recreational facilities, including 31 outdoor pools, 29 picnic shelters, 25 recreation centers, and a variety of special programs. To get your free copy, contact Citiparks at (412) 255-2539.

PARKS

like the place, you can rent one of the park's 10 rustic cabins for up to a week in season—slightly longer out of season.

More than 400 acres are open for hunting, typically providing squirrel, turkey, deer, and black bear. Anglers will like the availability of trout in Linn Run Stream, while hikers will enjoy a variety of delights. The park itself offers 5 miles of trails, and it's near three other trails in Forbes State Forest as well as the Laurel Highlands Hiking Trail, which spans 70 miles from Ohiopyle to the Conemaugh River.

Linn Run offers limited horseback riding and snowmobiling, and it is near such other outdoor attractions as Laurel Mountain Ski Area.

Ohiopyle State Park
P.O. Box 105, Ohiopyle, PA 15470-0105
(724) 329-8591
www.dcnr.sate.pa.us/stateparks/parks/ohiopyle.aspx

Ohiopyle State Park is primarily in Fayette County, just outside our coverage area, but its more than 19,000 acres are so spectacular and rich with recreational opportunities that it would be a significant omission.

The focal point of the park is the more than 14 miles of the Youghiogheny River Gorge that passes through the heart of the park, providing some of the best white-water boating in the mid-Atlantic region. Just watching the churning water is excitement enough for some; if you're in that category, you'll enjoy a number of scenic overlooks.

Bicycling, too, is a popular Ohiopyle activity, as the park features a 28-mile bik-

ing trail, converted from abandoned railroad rights-of-way, that parallels the Yough; bikers will share 9.4 miles of the trail with equestrians. The trail also is suitable for hiking, jogging, and cross-country skiing. Both the Yough and the tamer Meadow Run offer trout to anglers; a wheelchair-access area is available. Nearly the entire park is open for hunting and trapping, with typical quarry including deer, turkey, grouse, rabbit, and squirrel. Winter activities include sledding, tobogganing, and snowmobiling, with numerous snowmobiling trails carved from Sugarloaf Knob at an elevation of 2,640 feet.

Picnic areas feature play apparatus, a pavilion available for rental, a softball field, and a volleyball court. If it's all too much to enjoy in one day, extend your stay by reserving a campsite. Ohiopyle offers 237 campsites that you can reserve from April through December. In addition, you can stay at a nearby Hosteling International facility, (724) 329-4476.

Yellow Creek State Park
170 Route 259 Highway, Penn Run
(724) 357-7913
www.dcnr.state.pa.us/stateparks/parks/yellowcreek.aspx

When winter brings a thick snow cover, Yellow Creek is a wonderland of outdoor activities. These begin with ice skating, ice fishing, and ice boating on Yellow Creek Lake—which comprises about one-quarter of the park's 2,981 acres—and include cross-country skiing, snowshoeing, sledding, tobogganing, and snowmobiling in 350 designated acres.

When the weather warms, you can enjoy your nonpowered boats and boats up to 10 horsepower, swim along an 800-foot guarded beach, and cast your fishing lines for smallmouth and largemouth bass, walleye, muskellunge, tiger muskellunge, northern pike, yellow perch, bluegill, and catfish. The park's picnic and parking areas can accommodate more than 4,000 people.

Most areas of the park are open for hunting. While the facility is not known for hiking, you will find a number of pleasant, short trails, one of which is dotted with wildflowers in season. Yellow Creek is in Indiana County, just outside our six-county coverage area. State parks are so popular, however, that we want to detail all those within a comfortable drive of Pittsburgh.

West

Raccoon Creek State Park
3000 Route 18, Hookstown
(724) 899-2200
www.dcnr.state.pa.us/stateparks/parks/raccooncreek.aspx

Raccoon Creek is one of the larger state parks, spanning 7,323 acres, including the beautiful Raccoon Creek Lake. Camping is a particularly popular attraction here. The park offers 172 tent and trailer sites for family camping from mid-April through mid-December, as well as group camp-sites; group tent camping; and 10 modern family cabins with a furnished living area, kitchen space, and two or three bed-rooms. For a special treat, try Lakeside Lodge, a three-bedroom cottage that sleeps nine and is open all year.

The lake yields a wide variety of fish: bluegill, sunfish, bullhead, catfish, yellow perch, walleye, muskellunge, crappie, sauger, largemouth and smallmouth bass, and brook and rainbow trout. You'll find a turf beach for swimming, a boat launch area, and 42 mooring spaces. Nonpow-ered boats and electric-powered boats are permitted, and you can rent several types of nonpowered boats at the park. You can also ice fish and ice skate on the lake in season and enjoy sledding, snow-mobiling, and cross-country skiing in other areas of the park.

More than 5,000 acres are available for hunting the park's deer, wild turkey, grouse, squirrel, and rabbit. Raccoon Creek offers 16 miles of bridle trails and 5 miles of hiking trails, along which you'll find some of the most singular stands of native wildflowers in the Western Pennsylvania

region. You may want to call the Wild-flower Reserve and Interpretive Center before you head out to check when your favorite flowers will be in bloom; the num-ber is (724) 899-3611. You'll also find 600 picnic tables in the park—some shelters must be reserved. For a historical touch to your outing, visit King's Creek Cemetery on the park's western boundary, where many of the area's pioneers are buried.

Ryerson Station State Park
361 Bristoria Road, Wind Ridge
(724) 428-4254
www.dcnr.state.pa.us/stateparks/parks/ryersonstation.aspx

Technically outside the six-county coverage area, Ryerson Station deserves mention as one of the finest facilities in sparsely populated Green County. Named for the 18th-century Fort Ryerson, which stood nearby, the 1,164-acre park features a varient of winter sports, including ice skating, ice fishing, snowmobiling on 6 miles of trails, and cross-country skiing. You'll find a guarded swimming pool, 10 miles of hiking trails, more than 300 picnic tables, and 5 pavilions—3 of the pavilions are available by reservation only.

Anglers will find trout, warm-water game fish, and panfish in Duke Lake. You can use nonpowered boats and electric-powered boats on the lake. The park pro-vides a launching ramp and a limited number of mooring spaces. For camping, you'll find a 50-site family campground for tents or trailers, as well as organized group tenting areas. Hunting, trapping, and dog training are allowed from the beginning of the fall archery deer season to March 13 of the following year.

FEDERAL RECREATION AREAS

The U.S. Army Corps of Engineers oper-ates 16 flood control projects in the tris-tate area. The principal purpose, of course, is to prevent, or reduce, the damage from flooding. Because the dams hold a pool of water that forms a lake, they also serve a variety of recreational purposes. So popular are these areas that they draw more than 15 million visitors annually.

Generally, you'll find fishing, boating, camping, picnicking, hunting, and cross-country skiing opportunities, as well as hiking, snowmobile, and interpretive trails, although the lineup varies from dam to dam. You may bring your pets to all federal recreation areas. Five of these outdoor playgrounds fall within the six-county coverage area, or close enough to it to merit description below. For unusually well-written and easy-to-follow brochures about all 16 areas, contact the Corps at (412) 395-7152.

Along with descriptions of these recreation areas, we've included information about the Allegheny National Forest. Pennsylvania's only national forest is outside the principal coverage area, but it's such an unusually rich resource that it attracts many visitors from Southwestern Pennsylvania.

North

Allegheny National Forest
222 Liberty Street, Warren
(814) 723-5150
www.fs.fed.us/r9/allegheny/
For outdoor enthusiasts, the Allegheny National Forest is as much paradise as it is park. It spans 513,000 acres in Elk, McKean, Forest, and Warren Counties, about a three-hour drive from Pittsburgh. The only national forest in the state, Allegheny National Forest sits in the rugged plateau country of Northwestern Pennsylvania, with elevation ranging from 1,046 feet to 2,263 feet above sea level. Many creeks and streams cut deeply into the plateau, creating some of the most majestic vistas in the region.

The 12,000-acre Allegheny Reservoir, created by the impoundment of the Kinzua (KIN zoo) Dam, provides a diversity of water-based activities. The reservoir is the centerpiece of 700 miles of waterways

that offer anglers muskellunge, smallmouth bass, walleye, northern perch, channel catfish, and some types of trout. To give you an idea of the scale of fish available, the park is annually the site for Cabela's North American Walleye Anglers Team Event. You can boat in the Allegheny and Tionesta Reservoirs—many launching areas are available—or try canoeing on such venues as the scenic Clarion and Allegheny Rivers or the Brokenstraw and Tionesta Creeks. If swimming or waterskiing is your thing, you'll find the Allegheny Reservoir most accommodating.

Hunters can stalk white-tailed deer, black bear, and wild turkey, while campers will find 16 campgrounds including primitive camping areas that you can reach only by boat or hiking trail. Speaking of hiking, you'll find plenty of opportunities here, as 96.6 miles of the North Country National Scenic Trail traverse the forest. Cross-country skiers, snowmobilers, and dirt bikers will enjoy the loop trails that wind through the hills, while bikers will discover several special treats: both the Iowa to Maine trail and a cross-Pennsylvania bike route pass through the forest.

Many Western Pennsylvanians plan fall foliage excursions to the forest. If you go, check out the Tionesta Scenic Area, part of a 4,000-acre tract of old growth that features venerable beech, hemlock, and sugar maples trees—some of them up to 400 years old. Fall's colors will blaze brightly for you in the Allegheny National Forest. If you're looking for a pretty drive, try the 29-mile Longhouse National Scenic Byway.

You're welcome to bring your pets to the forest, provided you keep them leashed. Saddle and pack animals are permitted in all areas, except on the forest's hiking and cross-country ski trails.

Crooked Creek Lake
RD#3, Ford City
(724) 763-2764
www.lrp.usace.army.mil/rec/lakes/
crookedc.htm
Crooked Creek is a delight for water enthusiasts, no matter the season. In warm

weather, swimmers and sunbathers utilize the sandy peninsula beach, water skiers dot the lake, while anglers reel in bass and sunfish. In cold weather, the park offers two ice-skating ponds, a sled-riding area, and cross-country skiing. You'll also find a boat-launching ramp and no horsepower limit.

Crooked Creek offers hunting; hiking and horse trails; and tent, trailer, and group camping. A special feature is the Environmental Learning Center, an interpretive center for groups. Crooked Creek Horse Park, detailed in the Recreation chapter, adjoins the recreation area.

Mahoning Creek Lake
RD#1, New Bethlehem
(814) 257-8017
www.lrp.usace.army.mil/rec/lakes/
mahoning.htm

Anglers especially will enjoy Mahoning Creek Lake—its waters yield northern pike, walleye, muskie, and bass. (The lake is stocked by the Pennsylvania Fish and Boat Commission.) You can score when you hunt here as well, as the Pennsylvania Game Commission leases nearly 1,300 acres for wildlife management and public hunting.

The lake features two boat launching ramps, with boats up to 10 horsepower permitted. Swimming is not permitted but you will enjoy 28 acres of campgrounds, with all sites featuring restrooms, showers, and electricity.

East

Conemaugh River Lake
RD#1, Saltsburg
(724) 639-3785
www.lrp.usace.army.mil/rec/lakes/
conemaug,htm

The Pennsylvania Game Commission leases 7,000 acres around the lake for public hunting and wildlife management. The park provides a canoe launch but no other public boating due to limited accessibility to the lake. You'll enjoy a picnic area with two pavilions, play apparatus, and nature and hiking trails.

You'll enjoy several sites of historical interest, including traces of the Pennsylvania Mainland Canal and sections of early Pennsylvania railroads.

Loyalhanna Lake
RD#2, Saltsburg
(724) 639-3785
www.lrp.usace.army.mil/rec/lakes/
loyalhan.htm

The Loyalhanna Watershed is one of the most scenic areas in Western Pennsylvania, and Loyalhanna Lake captures that majesty. One of the most popular activities here is picnicking at the Damsite Picnic Area—the view of the dam and surrounding woodlands will soothe your jangled nerves.

If you're looking for more active entertainment, try the Black Willow Water Trail, the lake's self-guided boating trail with stations marking natural and man-made features. Anglers will find inlets and coves that yield bass, walleye, crappie, bullheads, and bluegills. The lake offers two boat launching areas and no horsepower limit. You can camp and hunt at Loyalhanna; the Pennsylvania Game Commission leases 2,115 acres for hunting and wildlife management.

South

Youghiogheny River Lake
RD#1, Confluence
(814) 395-3166
www.lrp.usace.army.mil/rec/lakes/
youghiog.htm

Principal activities at Youghiogheny are boating, waterskiing, and fishing. Just below the dam, the Youghiogheny River offers some of the most popular rafting and canoeing waters in the Mid-Atlantic region. One boulder-strewn stretch is so popular and challenging it frequently hosts national kayak championships. The lake features five boat-launching ramps.

Anglers find the backwaters and coves rich with walleye and smallmouth bass. You can choose from three campgrounds with facilities ranging from primitive to modern.

RECREATION

The recreation scene in Western Pennsylvania is diverse, creative, and inviting. You'll find an arena and an association for just about every sport and activity that might interest you. If you're not sure just what interests you, don't be afraid to jump feet first into something new. Most of the groups profiled below welcome newcomers and offer an instructional component.

Several factors have contributed to the breadth of recreational opportunities. One is the success of the city's professional teams. As the Steelers, Pirates, and Penguins have captured championships that brought them increasing support and media exposure, thousands have been inspired to take to the fields, courts, and rinks to achieve their own levels of athletic enjoyment and rewards. The region's college campuses have played a key role in the growth of certain sports such as rugby; former college players, lacking vehicles to extend their playing days, founded clubs of their own.

Natural geographic resources contribute to the popularity of outdoor activities. The region is blessed with an excellent inland waterway system that provides varied opportunities for fishing, boating, and swimming. The woods of Western Pennsylvania are a hunter's delight, while the region's slopes provide a natural—sometimes stunning—setting for hiking, climbing, and skiing. Add the welcome cycle of the four seasons and you have a region where virtually every sport has its moment in the sun—or snow, as it were.

In the profiles of Western Pennsylvania's recreational activities, we've tried to avoid describing commercial establishments in the belief that you have plenty of other resources to find these. Instead, information on coordinating associations and interest groups that could be hard to track down otherwise are offered. You won't find descriptions of the region's bowling alleys, for example, but you will learn about the organizations that sanction bowling leagues and tournaments. The exception to this is in the "yoga" section, where several yoga centers are listed. They're hard to find if you don't know where to look.

One caution about phone numbers and addresses. In the case of clubs, these may be accurate only as long as the president or captain keeps the job. As a hedge against shifting organizational responsibilities, we've tried to list the venues where clubs practice and perform, so that you always can make contact by dropping by.

ARCHERY

Allegheny County Sportsmen's League
Route 56, New Kensington
(412) 882-9115
www.acslipa.org

Archery is a popular activity in Western Pennsylvania, but it's sometimes difficult to identify appropriate sites and organizations. That's because much of the activity occurs inside private shooting clubs; you'd be hard pressed to know that archery takes place at the club. Allegheny County Sportsmen's League can provide you with a directory of shooting clubs. You can use that to find archery facilities.

Chieftain Archery Club is one of the few in the area dedicated exclusively to archery. You'll need to join the club and provide your own equipment to participate. When you do go, you're welcome to bring a guest for a fee of $2.00. The club sponsors a youth program, with those age 18 and younger invited to shoot each Friday evening for the nominal fee of $2.00. Watch for the club's annual Everett Leseuer Invitational, named for the 11-time Pennsylvania champion archer.

AUTO RACING

Don Martin's Lernerville Speedway
278 North Pike Road, Sarver
(724) 353–1511
www.lernerville.com
Sprints, late models, modifieds, pure
stocks . . . Don Martin's Lernerville Speedway has all the variety you could desire in
dirt-track racing. Moreover, the track often
features its division in competition on the
same evening, creating an unusually
diverse program that's sometimes spiced
with such special events as demolition
derbies. You'll find the track in action from
April through September as weather permits. If you plan to enjoy the action from
the stands, admission is $10, with dis-
counts for kids and senior citizens. If you'd
prefer to get down and dirty on the track,
the speedway will welcome your entry as
long as your car meets safety specs.

BASEBALL

Most communities feature an organized
youth baseball program. The city of Pittsburgh goes that one better through its
B.I.G. ("Baseball Is Great") League Baseball
program, (412) 323–7226 or (412)
323–7939. B.I.G. coordinates rookie, pony,
and colt leagues that involve about 4,000
youths in organized baseball. The colt and
pony leagues play their championship
games at Three Rivers Stadium, a special
treat for young players.

B.I.G. conducts clinics in association
with the Pittsburgh Pirates and also
enables community programs to acquire
their equipment through B.I.G. and realize
the discounts the city of Pittsburgh often
enjoys on bulk purchases. B.I.G. administrators will refer you to an organized program in your neighborhood. Perhaps best
of all, if youngsters don't have opportunities to play in their neighborhood, B.I.G.
will find spots for them in its program.

Kids in the region's inner-city neighborhoods—encompassing both Pittsburgh
and its suburbs—will find additional

opportunities through Reviving Baseball in
the Inner-city (RBI), (412) 231–2300. Major
League Baseball sponsors RBI in 70 cities
in six countries. In Western Pennsylvania,
it's run by the Boys and Girls Clubs of
Western PA in cooperation with Pittsburgh's B.I.G. League Program. Funding
for the program is provided by the
Roberto Clemente Foundation, an affiliate
of the Pittsburgh Pirates.

Locally, about 300 boys and girls from
ages 13 to 18 participate—boys in baseball,
girls in fast pitch softball. An All-Star team
selected from local participants is eligible
for national post-season competition that
culminates in a World Series typically held
in a Major League Baseball stadium, a
thrill for the young players. The program
goes beyond baseball to offer career
development counseling and advice on
conflict resolution. A nice added touch: all
teams in the local program sport names
and uniforms that honor Negro league
teams, such as the Pittsburgh Crawfords
and the Homestead Grays. Youths who
would like to participate should contact
Richard Earl Harris at (412) 363–8469.

BASKETBALL

The city game is healthy in Western Pennsylvania, as men and women of all ages
compete regularly in gyms provided by
schools, churches, and other institutions.
Many such competitions aren't really
leagues, as the players "pick up" teams
each evening. The best way to find out
about these games is through word of
mouth or by checking with those schools
and churches to determine when games
are played.

For youths, many city of Pittsburgh
recreation centers sponsor regular competition—3-on-3 for the youngest kids, 5-
on-5 for teenagers. Check with your local
rec center for its schedule.

If you're in or approaching your second childhood, there's a venue for you as
well. The Southside Market House, 1200
Bingham Street, Pittsburgh, (412)

488–8404, a city of Pittsburgh recreation center, runs a gym exclusively for players at least 60 years old. Senior basketball leagues begin in August, while open play is available daily. There are also shuffleboard leagues, a walking club, and opportunities for line dancing. If you don't live in the city, you're still eligible. Call Ray Fisher at (412) 422–6402 for more information. Let the games begin!

BIKING

Bikers in Western Pennsylvania have their own signature event—the Great Ride. It occurs each summer and features competition at three distances—15 miles, 25 miles, 35 miles—all within the same race. Sponsored by the city of Pittsburgh, the event will take you up Pittsburgh's hills and along the rivers. It is a great ride, and one you can take every day, since much of the course is considered a bike route. Be advised that, except for the day of the Great Ride, you'll share much of the course with vehicular traffic.

WPW Bicycle Club
(412) 422–2234
www.wpwbikeclub.org
The premier touring organization in the region, the WPW Bicycle Club boasts more than 2,000 members who typically ride from March through November, weather permitting. The club meets monthly and publishes a monthly newspaper and maps depicting nearly 7,000 miles of bicycle routes. Join them and you'll be able to participate in a highlight ride each month as well as the annual Fall Rally in September.

You can keep up with club activities by calling the hotline—the number listed above—or by visiting its Web site. You'll enjoy riding with the club, as well as the members' offbeat humor. When we sampled the hotline, we were advised that the upcoming highlight event was "an oddball ride for unusual people—the destination depends on your whim." Incidentally, the "WPW" in the group's name stands for "Western Pennsylvania Wheelmen," the club's original moniker ditched for political correctness.

BILLIARDS

Oh so quietly, billiards has become one of the faster growing sports in the region. You'll find more than three dozen establishments that sport multiple tables, to say nothing of the countless taverns that have installed a table to satisfy the clientele. Among the year's highlights is the Greater Pittsburgh Amateur 9-ball Championships, held each year to benefit the Autism Society of Pittsburgh.

BIRDING

Audubon Society of Western Pennsylvania at Beechwood Farms Nature Reserve
614 Dorseyville Road, Fox Chapel
(412) 963–6100
www.aswp.org
Experience the sights and sounds of a night hike along a moonlit trail. Search for turtles and other creatures in a pond teeming with aquatic life. Follow the colorful tracings of butterflies in a meadow awash with wildflowers. Explore the fascinating lives of birds on a walk through a singing woodland. These and many other experiences await you at Beechwood Farms Nature Reserve, home of the Audubon Society of Western Pennsylvania.

Known as "Pittsburgh's Outdoor Classroom," Audubon at Beechwood offers most extensive, year-round environmental programs for the entire family, from young children to adults. Offerings range from Outdoor Discovery Programs, which provide thousands of school-age children each year with hands-on guided experiences of nature, to programs designed for family participation. Programs range in duration from weeklong summer nature camps for children in grades K–5 to two innovative programs for preschool children as young as 2 months old. Audubon at Beechwood also offers a monthly series of bird outings to regional sites; guided bird walks on Wednesday mornings; the annual Christmas Bird Count; and other popular events such as the Secret Gardens Tour of spectacular Fox Chapel gardens and Applejamm, one of the oldest fall festivals in the area.

Thousands of people visit Beechwood Farms all year to enjoy informal outdoor activities on its 5 miles of nature trails and 134 acres of woodlands, meadows, ponds, and wetlands. Others visit Beechwood to shop at the Audubon Nature Store, with its wide selection of bird feeders, birdseed, and nature-related items. Beechwood also features a modern education center with facilities for children's birthday parties, the new Audubon Center for the Native Plants, and a natural history reference and reading library. Beechwood's trails are open 365 days a year, dawn to dusk.

BOATING

Western Pennsylvania's waterways beckon to boaters. Whether you're sailing, canoeing, kayaking, paddling, rafting, or motoring under electrical power, you'll find waters in the region that will accommodate you. Perhaps the best place to start is with a comprehensive state map available free from the Pennsylvania Fish and Boat Commission, (717) 705-7800; www.fish.state.pa.us/. The map is free. The map depicts nearly 1,000 boating and fishing opportunities in the state and provides a guide to parking, launch ramps, and horsepower limits.

You'll also want a copy of the commission's *Boating Handbook,* 45 pages of rules and advice. Several of those regulations are particularly noteworthy. You will need to register your boat; the fee, good for two years, ranges from $10 for unpowered boats to $40 for craft more than 20 feet long. You'll need to display your boat registration number on your boat; kayaks, sculls, and sailboards are exempt from this

Each year at Christmas time, Jim Valimont of the Audubon Society of Western Pennsylvania leads a group that undertakes a regional bird count. You're welcome to join them.

requirement. The state also provides boat titling, at a cost of $15, to help deter theft. The handbook will familiarize you with state requirements for personal flotation devices and regulations regarding alcohol consumption while you're boating. The commission can provide you with brochures on each topic.

If you're a boater and an angler, you'll get a particular kick from *Pennsylvania Angler & Boater,* the commission's official magazine. It's published six times each year and offers lush color photography, how-to pieces, and commission updates. Cost is $9.00 annually.

The Parks chapter will introduce you to boating opportunities at state parks and federal recreation areas. For more specific information about any state or federal facility, contact the Pennsylvania Bureau of Parks, (717) 772-0239; the Pennsylvania Parks Information and Reservation line, (888) PA-PARKS; or the U.S. Army Corps of Engineers, (412) 395-7500.

Hosteling International/American Youth Hostels, Pittsburgh Council
Corner of Fifth and Shady Avenues
(412) 431-4910
The council organizes many exciting and challenging outdoors activities, including a broad variety of boating outings. These include frequent canoeing and kayaking adventures, some designated for experienced paddlers only. Since these outings tend to be weather dependent, the group encourages you to call (724) 443-8972 to check the day's plans with event organizers.

You can sail with the council as well. On grand summer days, you'll find the council sailing and racing on Moraine State

Fun on the Water

Pittsburgh's three rivers easily accommodate fishing, kayaking, canoeing, and boating. In partnership with various related groups, such as Sustainable Pittsburgh and the Three Rivers Rowing Association, Three Rivers Water Trail provides a good source of information for boaters, fishers, and other water thrills seekers about river safety, how to use the area's locks and dams, and historical and natural points of interest along the rivers. Call (866) 3KEEPER or visit www.friendsof theriverfront.org.

Ohiopyle State Park and the Youghiogheny River are hailed as the birthplace of white-water rafting. To arrange a white-water ride, call or visit the Web sites of these reputable tour companies:

Laurel Highlands River Tours
(800) 472-3846
www.laurelhighlands.com

Mountain Streams
(800) 723-8669
www.mtstreams.com

White Water Adventures
(800) 992-7238
www.wwaraft.com

Wilderness Voyageurs
Also offering historic float tours, showcasing the rich history of the times during the French and Indian War and the Whiskey Rebellion
(800) 272-4141
www.wilderness-voyageurs.com

Park's Lake Arthur. If you'd like to join them but don't know the ropes, take the club's introductory sailing classes and help them maintain their sailboat. You'll learn in a hurry. For more information about sailing, contact the council at (412) 431-4910 or the contact the Moraine Sailing Club at www.morainesailingclub.org/website.

Three Rivers Rowing Association
300 Waterfront Drive
(412) 231-8772
www.threeriversrowing.org
One of the city's most compelling sights is that of crews plying the Allegheny River, intermittently visible through the early morning mist. That vista is brought to you by Three Rivers Rowing Association (TRRA), a group founded in 1984 with the mission of providing broad-based rowing opportunities in the Pittsburgh area. The group is headquartered on Washington's Landing, an Allegheny River island about 2 miles north of downtown Pittsburgh. The island houses the group's 15,000-square-foot boathouse, which features large boat storage bays, exercise equipment, lockers and showers, and meeting space.

The association offers orientations, clinics, and other instructional activities to get you started. Of particular interest are the club's programs for special populations. These include programs for youths, seniors, and rowers with certain disabilities. There is also a special summer corporate rowing program. TRRA also offers a variety of sprint racing and tours for kayaks. A basic adult membership in the association costs $30 annually. Much more information is available at www .threeriversrowing.org.

Among the highlights of the rowing year is the Head of the Ohio Regatta, typically held in early fall along the Allegheny just before it merges with the Monongahela to form the Ohio. It's a prestigious event, generally drawing several thousand entries. You may not be ready to enter, but you'll love the spectacle of this one.

BOWLING

Greater Pittsburgh Ten-Pin Bowling Association
Pittsburgh Women's Bowling
Penn Plaza, Suite 206, Turtle Creek
(412) 824-4850
Bowling is such a popular pastime in Pittsburgh that you really don't need the help of an organization to get started; just visit your local lanes and ask about leagues. In fact, if you're not in a league, you may find open alleys hard to come by during peak times. That said, the Greater Pittsburgh Ten-Pin Bowling Association and Pittsburgh Women's Bowling perform important functions for local keglers.

The companion organizations, which are run from the same office, sanction leagues and tournaments with the American Bowling Congress. Since more than 15,000 men and women compete locally in sanctioned events, this is a key service. The organizations also sponsor tournaments, present awards for high scores, sponsor a junior bowling program, and publish yearbooks that feature most area lanes and leagues.

You can see a men's or a women's yearbook online at gptpba.com.

BOXING

As it is at the national level, administration of boxing activities in Western Pennsylvania is somewhat fragmented. However, this is all sorted out on the amateur level with the Golden Gloves tournament held each March. Call Gloria Sztukowski, co-director and chief of officials for the local amateur league, at (412) 298-7373. She'll give you a listing of the gyms where boxing is held in your neighborhood.

BRIDGE

A true story about bridge in Pittsburgh: A newcomer to town some years ago was invited to a veteran bridge player's house for a private game featuring some of the area's elite players. As the evening progressed, the newcomer smelled something burning. Sure enough, when she looked up, she saw orange flames shooting ever higher from a wastebasket. "There's a fire in the garbage can," she said. No one moved. No one looked up. Finally, overcoming her shyness as the newest player, she arose and stamped out the fire. No one thanked her or even noticed that she had been gone.

That incident tells you something about bridge in our area. It's not that players are unfriendly, but they are intense. A little thing like a wastebasket fire won't bother them. If you aspire to that level, you can learn bridge at the Jewish Community Center, (412) 521-8011, ext. 225, in Pittsburgh's Squirrel Hill neighborhood, which sponsors instruction at various levels. Older Adult Service and Information System (OASIS), (412) 232-9584, offers bridge classes for senior citizens; the classes usually are fully subscribed. OASIS is located on the 10th floor of Kaufmann's department store in downtown Pittsburgh.

Pittsburgh Bridge Association
(412) 683-GAME
If duplicate bridge is your game, you'll want to be in touch with the Pittsburgh Bridge Association, an affiliate of the American Contract Bridge League. Association members will make you aware of as many as 40 games throughout the region each week. The association also stages its own games and publishes a

directory including games and the names and phone numbers of 1,400 players. The directory is online at www.pittsburgh bridge.org/ClubDirectory.htm.

CAMPING

If you're an avid camper, you're likely to become mighty familiar with Pennsylvania's state park system. The Commonwealth maintains more than 7,000 campsites in 57 state parks, many of them within an easy ride of Pittsburgh. Check out the Parks chapter for an introduction to camping at Western Pennsylvania state parks, or call the Pennsylvania Parks Information and reservations line, (888) PA-PARKS, for more comprehensive information and a fee schedule.

State parks offer a variety of overnight options. These include family campsites; group cabins and tent areas; and cabins, both modern and rustic. Whichever option you select, you'll find more campsites and cabins open from early April until late October. Some sites welcome campers through December and a handful are open year-round. From Memorial Day through Labor Day, your stay will be limited to 14 consecutive days. At other times, your maximum stay is 21 consecutive days. Most sites are available on a first-come, first-served basis, although you can reserve other sites. The state prohibits alcohol and pets at its sites.

The U.S. Army Corps of Engineers maintains campsites at its recreation areas, although the number can't compare with the total offered by the state. If you lack appropriate camping gear, ask about the "Rent-A-Tent" program, which will provide you with enough equipment to host up to five friends. For information, call the Corps at (412) 395-7500.

You'll find many private campground operators who have opened businesses near state and federal facilities to capitalize on any overflow. You can get a useful list of 200 privately operated campgrounds from the Pennsylvania Campground Owners Association, (888) 660-7262. The list is not comprehensive, since some operators don't belong to the association, but it's a great place to start.

CAVING

Several local outdoors groups, while not devoted exclusively to the activity, feature caving on their roster of events. The Explorers Club of Pittsburgh, www.pittccp .org, occasionally explores caves in West Virginia. Allegheny Group, Sierra Club, (412) 351-4068; www.alleghenysc.org ventures to caves on Chestnut Ridge. If you contact Allegheny Group, they'll advise you on the degree of difficulty of each outing.

CHESS

Pittsburgh Chess Club
5604 Solway Street
(412) 421-1881
www.trfn.clpgh.org/pcc/index.html
The Pittsburgh Chess Club has been staging tournaments for more than 50 years, making it one of the older chess organizations in the country. Located in a former elementary school in the city's Squirrel Hill neighborhood, the organization stages both club tournaments and those rated by the United States Chess Federation. In addition, the club sponsors instruction and competition at local schools and has reached about 6,000 students through these efforts.

The club's nearly 200 members engage in open play on Wednesday and Saturday and in tournament play on Tuesday. Visitors always are welcome. When you drop by, make sure to check out the extensive chess library, an asset utilized by many researchers.

One of the largest neighborhood chess organizations is the Hill Carnegie Chess and Checker Club, which hosts open play at the Hill District Branch of the Carnegie Library, 419 Dinwiddie Street, Pittsburgh, (412) 281-3753. The club sponsors teams in competitive play, and its nearly 100 members enjoy the club's services free of charge. The group's name is something of a misnomer, though—there's nary a checkers player remaining in the organization.

CLIMBING

Explorers Club of Pittsburgh
www.pittecp.org
Founded in 1948, the Explorers Club of Pittsburgh is dedicated to two purposes; exploration at home and abroad, and the promotion and instruction of exploratory sciences. The club's 250 members meet monthly and offer instruction in mountaineering and basic and advanced rock climbing. If you enjoy travel, you'll find this group cheerfully peripatetic. Their outings have included rock climbing at West Virginia's Seneca Rocks and ice climbing in Colorado, Canada, and the Adirondack Mountains. They've climbed the Andes and the Himalayas, and enjoyed scuba diving in the Bahamas. Other club expeditions include caving and mountain biking. For your $20 annual membership fee, you'll receive the club's monthly newsletter.

DOG SHOWS

Western Pennsylvania Kennel Association
208 Old McBride Road, Canonsburg
(724) 746-4794
The largest kennel club in Western Pennsylvania, the Western Pennsylvania Kennel Association stages two all-breed shows each spring, most commonly at the David L. Lawrence Convention Center in downtown Pittsburgh. A portion of proceeds benefit the American Kennel Club's Canine Health Foundation and the local humane societies, so there's a great reason for patronizing the shows.

Annual association dues range from $15 to $20; membership entitles you to free admission to the association's shows as well as its newsletter. There are other kennel clubs in the region. A comprehen-

According to Explorers Club of Pittsburgh, climbing and mountaineering are distinct activities. Climbing involves scaling the face of a peak, while mountaineering means a more lateral traversing of mountains and coping with snow, ice, and crevasses.

sive listing is available from the *AKC Gazette*, 5580 Centerview Drive, Raleigh, NC 27606-3390, (919) 233-9767.

FENCING

Fencers in Western Pennsylvania are relatively small in number, but they are dedicated. With a little help from us, you'll be sure to find a salle, a studio where fencing takes place.

Fencing Institute of America
(412) 931-0235
Fencing is a movable feast at the institute, as this nonprofit organization provides fencing opportunities in a number of neighborhoods, including Squirrel Hill, Monroeville, Mt. Lebanon, the North Hills, Ligonier, and Washington. In some cases, the municipalities engage the institute to provide fencing opportunities for the public. You will be charged for group and private lessons, and open fencing is available for a fee. The institute does solicit donations to help defray costs.

The institute boasts several strengths. First, its three coaches and two apprentices are accredited by the U.S. Fencing Association. In addition, it offers instructions in all three of the sport's weapons: foil, epee, and saber. They'll provide you with all the equipment you need to get started.

Three Rivers Fencing Center
7501 Penn Avenue, Point Breeze
(412) 731-4454
www.trfn.clpgh.org/fencing
Three Rivers Fencing Center offers both group and private instruction in foil and

saber as well as open fencing on Tuesday and Thursday. The center offers full-time professional coaches, and its members compete in tournaments locally and throughout the country.

Dress in regular workout clothes when you visit, and don't worry about equipment if you're new to the sport. The center will provide your weapons, jackets, masks, and gloves. You will be responsible for fees for any lessons, and a $10 per night charge for open fencing. If you join the center and pay annual dues, open fencing is included.

FISHING

Fishing in Pennsylvania is a joy that can be utterly different each time you take to the waters. How extensive are the state's fishing opportunities? Consider that a map of state fishing and boating opportunities provided by the Pennsylvania Fish and Boat Commission depicts nearly 1,000 locations for those activities. You'll find state and federal lakes, streams, and impoundments (waters behind a dam) marked on the map, as well as a guide to parking and other facilities. Once you've studied your map, you'll be ready for more specific brochures that detail where you can find trout and warm-water species. All these publications are available from the commission, 1601 Elmerton Avenue, Harrisburg, PA 17101, (717) 705–7800.

When you contact the commission, you'll also want to acquire the state's Summary of Fishing Regulations and Laws, a must for all anglers. Some of the regulations won't surprise you. You'll learn that all anglers age 16 and older must have a license, with fees ranging from $4.00 for resident senior citizens to $35.00 for nonresidents. If you're fishing in Lake Erie or for trout or salmon, you'll need a special permit at an additional cost. You'll also learn about "special regulation" waters, including catch-and-release areas and those reserved for children and anglers with certain disabilities. Did you know that, each year, the state sponsors two "Fish-for-Free" days, when licenses are not required? You'll find this information—and much more—in the summary.

Among the commission's many publications, you'll find two others especially useful. One is the commission's official magazine, *Pennsylvania Angler & Boater*. This is a slick, four-color journal with great photography; first-person articles; tips on where they're biting; and commission updates on seasons, sizes, and regulation modifications. Cost is $9.00 annually.

The second piece is the commission's pocket guide to seasons, sizes, and creel limits. With this guide tucked into your pocket, you'll never be out of season or over the limit. For an introduction to fishing opportunities at state parks and federal recreation areas, see the Parks chapter.

FLYING DISC

Pittsburgh Flying Disc Society
153 LaBelle Street
(412) 734-0321

The Pittsburgh Flying Disc Society administers two types of activities. The first is a golf league, which plays at Schenley Park and Phillips Park in the city of Pittsburgh and Knob Hill Community Park in the North Hills. In golf, players throw discs into a basket posted on a pole about 2 feet off the ground. The courses wind through wooded areas, so it's a scenic activity as well. The society, which was formed in 1978, awards prizes at each competition. Don't worry if you're new to the sport—you'll receive a handicap that will make you the equal of veteran players.

The second activity is more demanding. It's called ultimate, a blend of football, basketball, and soccer with continuous action. The sport is coed, and you can keep up with it by phoning the ultimate hotline, (412) 521-2441. Ultimate is not a sedentary activity.

The society coordinates clinics, the Professional Disc Golf Association Tour's annual stop at Knob Hill, and Pittsburgh's participation in the World's Biggest Disc Golf Weekend, an international event that attracts 17,000 players. "Why not?" says society president Gary Dropcho. "You don't have to be Arnold Schwarzenegger, run really fast or jump really high." Sounds like our kind of sport.

FOOTBALL

In the hometown of "The Stillers," you would expect football to be a popular activity. You would be correct, but at the participant level, the game you're most likely to see differs in key areas from the one they play at Three Rivers Stadium. This variation is called "flag football," and it's played on sandlots throughout Western Pennsylvania. In this variation, players wear belts to which two "flags"—strips of cloth or plastic—are attached. A ball carrier is "tackled" when a flag is pulled off his belt.

It can be a hard-hitting game complete with certain oddities. If you've never seen the game before, this will be your first opportunity to witness unsportsmanlike conduct penalties for "shielding the flag." The trouble here is that leagues and personnel are ever shifting. Some leagues are organized by team captains, others by officials' groups. It's hard to find a central organization that stays put. One idea: check with municipal and county field permitting offices. They'll always be able to tell you which groups have fields reserved.

If your youngster wants to play, the path to participation is much easier. Just contact the Boys & Girls Clubs of Western Pennsylvania, 920 Cresswell Street, Pittsburgh, (412) 431-2203, or visit the Web site at www.bgcwpa.org. The organization runs the Dapper Dan Charities/Pittsburgh Steelers Flag Football League, which each year involves about 600 youths as players . . . and another 75 as officials, scorekeepers, timers, and statisticians. The league plays at eight city fields and includes both boys and girls—some playing together on coed teams.

When you're discussing the sports of flying disc golf or ultimate, it's incorrect to use the word "Frisbee" indiscriminately. Frisbee is a brand name; flying disc is a generic term that encompasses several manufacturers.

GYMNASTICS

The sight of elfin young girls twirling gracefully and perilously over imposing apparatus has contributed to an explosive growth of gymnastics facilities in Western Pennsylvania. The region boasts about three dozen gymnastics schools and facilities—more if you include dance schools that also offer gymnastics instruction. No coordinating or trade organization has emerged, so your best bet for information may be USA Gymnastics, (800) 345-4719, which can tell you about its affiliates in our region.

HIKING

With its far-reaching inland waterway network, vast expanses of forest, and many miles of abandoned railroad rights-of-way, Western Pennsylvania is a hiker's paradise. In fact, there are so many outstanding hiking opportunities here that you may want to familiarize yourself with local trails before you set out. You'll find a number of useful resources.

For trails in City of Pittsburgh Parks, the City of Pittsburgh Department of City Planning has produced a colorful brochure called "Pittsburgh Outdoors." You can get your free copy by contacting the department at (412) 255-2200. For information on a group of longer and more challenging trails called Heritage Trails of Southwestern Pennsylvania, contact the Southwestern Pennsylvania Heritage Preservation Commission, 105 Zee Plaza, P.O. Box 565, Holidaysburg, PA 16648-0565, (814) 696-9380. The commission also can provide you with a useful guide

Allegheny Group, Sierra Club, and Hosteling International/American Youth Hostels, Pittsburgh Council welcome volunteers to help maintain hiking trails throughout the region. So does Friends of the Riverfront, www.friendsoftheriverfront.org, which developed the 11.5-mile trail around Pittsburgh's three rivers.

to the rails-to-trails program in the state called *Pennsylvania's Rail-Trails* that details more than 700 miles of such trails. Cost is $12.95, including postage and handling.

We'd also recommend the book *Hiking Pennsylvania,* by Rhonda and George Ostertag, which features 75 hikes of varying difficulty across the Keystone State.

Allegheny Group, Sierra Club
P.O. Box 8241, Pittsburgh, PA 15217
(412) 561-0203
www.alleghenysc.org

You'll enjoy the varied outings of the Allegheny Group. The group's hikes average 8 to 9 miles along the region's most scenic trails on Laurel Ridge, Chestnut Ridge, and in such state parks as Moraine, McConnell's Mill, and Raccoon Creek. Allegheny Group rates its hikes as "easy," "intermediate," "strenuous," and "strenuous and exploratory," so you'll always know what awaits you. For the most leisurely outings, try the club's Wednesday rambles. These seldom exceed 4 miles.

The group also organizes backpacking events throughout the region and offers a Basic Backpacking Course each April. The best way to keep up with events is through the club's newsletter at an annual cost of $2.50. You can subscribe by writing to the group at 210 College Park Drive, Monroeville, PA 15146-1532.

Hosteling International/America Youth Hostels, Pittsburgh Council
830 East Warrington Avenue
(412) 431-4910

The group organizes frequent hikes and hiking/backpacking events along such

venues as the Rachel Carson Trail and the Baker Trail, which is about 50 miles north of Pittsburgh. If you don't quite have the time to allot for that, try the group's "Wednesday Rambles," which are shorter hikes that take place in the Pittsburgh vicinity. A good way to keep up with group activities is through its newsletter. You can get your copy by calling (412) 431-4910 or by going to the open Thursday night meetings held at Mellon Park.

HORSE SHOWS

Fort Armstrong Horsemen's Association
RD#6, Friendship Plaza, Kittanning
(724) 295-3294

Crooked Creek Horse Park, operated by the Fort Armstrong Horsemen's Association, is one of the Mid-Atlantic's most comprehensive equine facilities. Encompassing 113 acres, the park features stable facilities for nearly 150 horses during events only, barns, outdoor arenas, electrical hook-ups for trailers and recreational vehicles, an equine museum, and 300 miles of riding trails. You'll also find pavilions sprinkled through the park. The association sponsors quarter horse, walking horse, and Arabian shows as well as an annual 100-mile sanctioned race. You can lease the park and also utilize the adjoining Crooked Creek Lake and the federal recreation area encompassing it. For more on Crooked Creek Lake, see the Parks chapter.

The Paper Horse
HCR 67 Box OH95, Mifflin
(717) 436-8893
www.thepaperhorse.com

Fort Armstrong is one of the region's most prominent horse organizations, but dozens of others are active. To keep up with all their events, try *The Paper Horse,* a monthly magazine that will keep you current with many shows in Western Pennsylvania and throughout the Commonwealth. You can subscribe for $14 (3rd-class mail) or $30 (1st-class mail).

Pennsylvania Equine Council
P.O. Box 21, Dallas, PA 16827-0570
(888) 304-0281
www.pennsylvaniaequinecouncil.com
The council is a good place to find a
horsemen's group to suit your needs and
tastes. It publishes a directory of 30 to 40
such groups as well as a newsletter that
will update you on events as well as leg-
islative and other activities. Annual membership costs $15 with discounts for
families and those younger than age 19.

If you belong to an equine group, you
might want to take advantage of the
council's fire prevention and rescue program—they'll travel to your barn to offer
instruction.

HUNTING

Hunting in the Commonwealth is the preserve of the Pennsylvania Game Commission. The commission provides many
opportunities for hunters in Southwestern
Pennsylvania—check out the Parks chapter for an introduction to which state
parks permit hunting—but it's best to
know some of the rules before you begin.

It's easy to remember that you must
be licensed and wear fluorescent orange
safety clothing. But do you know the seasons for each species? The limit on kills for
each species? The regulations on goose
blinds, dog training, and hunting from tree
stands? If you're new to hunting in the
state, chances are you'll need some help in
becoming familiar with Pennsylvania regulations. If you contact the commission,
2001 Elmerton Avenue, Harrisburg, PA
17110-9797, (717) 787-4250, they'll send
you *A Digest of Pennsylvania Hunting &
Trapping Regulations*. You'll want to spend
some time with it—it runs 55 pages.

Once you know the rules, you're ready
to enjoy the approximately 1.4 million
acres in Southwestern Pennsylvania that
are open to public hunting. Most common
quarry are grouse, squirrel, deer, raccoon,
rabbit, turkey, and pheasant. Trappers will
find both beaver and red fox within sight

*Each year the city of Washington
in Washington County hosts The
Pony League World Series at—where
else?—Pony League Field.*

of Pittsburgh's suburbs. If you venture
east to the Chestnut, Laurel, and
Allegheny ridges, you may encounter
black bear. One of the better guides to
area game is the Pennsylvania Game
Commission's "Hunting in Southwestern
Pennsylvania." You'll find detailed acreage
and game lists for each hunting tract.

A good way to keep up with hunting
news in the state is through the official
monthly magazine of the Pennsylvania
Game Commission. It's called *Game News*,
and you can subscribe for $12 per year.

ICE HOCKEY

B. M. L. (Before Mario Lemieux), ice
hockey was an informal kids' game played
whenever the pond froze over. Today,
thanks to the influence of Mario Lemieux
and the success of the National Hockey
League's Pittsburgh Penguins, youth ice
hockey in Western Pennsylvania is a
sophisticated, complex business that has
given rise to hundreds of organizations as
well as occasional jurisdictional squab-
bling. We'll try to sort out the organizational structure for you.

The Mid-American District of USA
Hockey is the coordinating body for amateur youth hockey in Western Pennsylvania, Ohio, West Virginia, Indiana, and
Kentucky. Within its region, the district
keeps track of 280 organizations, 2,400
teams, and more than 30,000 players and
coaches. If you're looking for a hockey
organization based in your community,
the district will point you in the right
direction. You can call their hotline at
(412) 884-2922.

The South Hills Amateur Hockey
Asssocciation (SHAHA), (412) 833-8500,
unlike TAHA or the Mid-American District,

is not an administrative body. Rather, it stages playoffs for local organizations that include 7,000 kids. The league's Web site, pahockey.com, is a great source for information on local organizations and tournaments.

That's a quick guide to the structure of youth ice hockey. Here's a look at some of the most prominent organizations.

Pittsburgh Amateur Penguins Hockey Association
1400 Route 8, Glenshaw
(724) 444-3190

This program is affiliated with the Pittsburgh Penguins, a relationship that dates from 1983. The Amateur Penguins compete at the highest level of amateur hockey, in the Buffalo-based Empire West League. The program is for youths ages 8 to 20 with a serious commitment to hockey. They practice two or three times a week at BladeRunners Ice Complex in Warrendale and Harmarville, pay about $1,500 to the association, and adhere to the group's dress code.

Steel City Stars
706 Heathergate Drive, Fox Chapel
(412) 767-5049

The Stars are a junior "C" team. That means a relaxed atmosphere and very little travel. The club, which features three teams with players up to 20 years of age, practices at BladeRunners Ice Complex in Harmarville and plays college hockey squads and other junior "C" teams. The teams hold tryouts annually before the season starts, but endeavor to find a place for all who want to play. Players are responsible for fees—make sure to inquire about them.

ICE SKATING

Ice skating in the region is inextricably linked with ice hockey. Not every ice skater is a hockey player, of course, but hockey teams snap up so much ice time at commercial facilities that it's sometimes difficult for others to find ice time at con-

venient hours. Public facilities may be your best bit, and two of these merit special attention.

The Schenley Park Skating Rink, operated by the city of Pittsburgh in the Oakland neighborhood, is open year-round for ice skating and in-line skating. In addition to public sessions, the city operates leagues and pickup hockey programs for ice hockey and roller hockey and rents rink and meeting-room time. Call the rink at (412) 422-6523 for schedules and fees.

You also will find ice time for rent at the Belmont Complex, (724) 548-1067, operated by the Armstrong County Recreation Authority, where skating and hockey are two of the principal activities. For more on Schenley Park and Belmont Complex, see the Parks chapter.

Ice skating is a special treat at state parks and federal recreation areas—no hockey teams to contend with here—though you will need cooperation from the weather. The Parks chapter will introduce you to ice skating opportunities at these facilities. For more comprehensive brochures, contact the Pennsylvania Parks information and reservations line, (888) PA-PARKS.

LAWN BOWLING

Frick Park Lawn Bowling Association
427 Dorseyville Road, O'Hara
(412) 782-0848

Lawn bowling in the region is the domain of the Pittsburgh Lawn Bowling Association . . . literally. As far as we know, you won't find lawn bowling anywhere else in the state. The city of Pittsburgh provides lawn-bowling rinks at Frick Park, but the association, founded in 1938, raises funds to maintain the facility through private donations and several plant-selling fund-raisers each year.

The genteel game is played on rinks that are 120 feet long and 15 feet wide and is distinct from boccie ball, where the course is a gravel pit with sidewalls. The season generally begins in May and lasts until Labor Day, or as long as weather permits. The association engages in league play on Tuesday and Wednesday, while pickup action occurs Thursday and Friday evenings. The action is pretty much continuous on weekends. Newcomers are always welcome—in fact, veteran bowlers will provide complimentary lessons. So give it a try!

Annual membership in the club costs $150 for adults with equipment provided, and other packages are available. There's also a new youth league offering free supplies and lessons for four weeks. If you're an adult new to the sport, you can play for free in May to determine if you like it. When you join, beyond helping with plant sales, you will be required to wear traditional white dress in tournaments; "No white, no play," is a venerable club rule. Don't knock it. The sight of the bowlers in their tourney whites on the perfectly smooth green is one of the city's most appealing and relaxing tableaux.

POLO

Darlington Polo Club
6517 Mars Road, Darlington
(724) 827-2800, (330) 426-4739
www.us-polo.org/clubs/darlington.htm
In 1937, Glenn Watterson founded the Darlington Polo Club. Today, Glenn Watterson II operates the club, maintaining this unusual asset for the region. The club competes—at the Beaver County field it owns—in the Mid-States Circuit, which also includes clubs from Grand Rapids, Toronto, Lexington, Cincinnati, Virginia, Cleveland, and Columbus. You can catch the club each Friday at 8:00 P.M. from May through August. With admission at only $3.00, you can't beat the price for an evening's entertainment. It's best to call ahead if skies are threatening, because rain will force cancellation of the match.

The club welcomes new members, but you must provide your own equine partner. Oh yes. One of the current club member is a young man named Glenn

In this chapter, you'll find several different phone numbers for Allegheny Group, Sierra Club, and Hosteling International/American Youth Hostels, Pittsburgh Council. That's because we've listed the numbers of activity coordinators rather than a central office or hotline number that won't be as immediately useful.

Watterson III. Looks like the Darlington Polo Club has a secure future.

RUGBY

Western Pennsylvania is a hotbed of rugby, though the participants themselves aren't sure why. Some attribute it to the popularity of collegiate rugby in the region; as college players graduate, this theory goes, they've created clubs to extend their opportunities to play. In any case, the region boasts at least six major clubs, which always welcome new players. All the clubs profiled below feature spring and fall seasons; most practice during the week and play their matches on Saturday afternoons.

Before you begin play, talk to club members to gauge their intensity. Each of the clubs has developed a "culture," so to speak. You'll want to select the club that best fits you; you're sure to fit in somewhere. Also, if rugby is a little rugged for your tastes, but you'd like to get involved anyway, think about officiating. There's a chronic shortage of officials. You can reach the society at (412) 351-3455.

South Pittsburgh Rugby Football Club
1604 McFarland Road
(412) 734-8998
www.shoppittsburgh.net/clients/rugby/home.htm
Formed in 1978, the Hooligans, as these players are known, perform in both the Allegheny Rugby Union and the Midwest Rugby Union. Edgebrook Field in South Park serves as home field. By their own

admission the Hooligans are perhaps the most social of the area's rugby clubs. It's not that they don't take their rugby seriously. It's just that they take the postgame party just as seriously.

Pittsburgh Women's Rugby Club
40 South 22nd Street
(412) 741-7021

They're nicknamed the "Angels," but there's nothing angelic about the game these women play. They practice twice a week and play their home matches at Frick Park in the city of Pittsburgh's Regent Square neighborhood. Because there are comparatively few women's rugby clubs, the Angels schedule matches against squads from Ohio, Washington, D.C., and other distant cities, so you can expect some travel if you join. New members are most welcome.

Greensburg Area Rugby Football Club
104 North Sixth Street, Youngwood
(724) 331-2749
www.greensburgrugby.com

Their nickname is "Gorillas" and they play at Mammoth Park. Does that tell you what you need to know about this club? The club plays in the Allegheny Rugby Union and practices at Lynch Field in Greensburg. The organization welcomes new Gorillas.

Westmoreland Highlanders REC
126 Cedar Avenue
(412) 260-3644

The Highlanders' home games in the Allegheny Rugby Union, part of which is a national organization, take place in Pittsburgh. The Highlanders are a Division 3 team and a good venue for developing your game. The 160-member club is always looking for new members.

RUNNING

You can run to your heart's content in Western Pennsylvania. Many parks offer walking and jogging trails—see the Parks chapter for which parks have the most

appropriate facilities. More commonly, runners in the region practice their sport informally, tackling the region's hilly terrain with gusto. A warning is in order: If you're not used to hill running, introduce yourself to Pittsburgh's terrain gradually. You might not realize how taxing hill running can be.

Two of the premier events in the region are staged by the city of Pittsburgh. The Pittsburgh Marathon occurs annually on the first Sunday of May, and it's preceded by a festive week that features clinics, receptions, and the occasional merchandise sale. The course falls entirely within city limits, winding across the rivers and offering its share of slopes. In each neighborhood, residents turn out to cheer the runners, transforming the marathon into a 26-mile celebration. It's a serious event, however, and has been used as an Olympics qualifier. The marathon features men's, women's, and wheelchair divisions—prize money is awarded in each division—as well as shorter races incorporated within the marathon.

If you're not quite ready for the challenge of marathoning, try the Richard S. Caliguiri Great Race, a 10-kilometer event staged each September. The course begins at Frick Park in Squirrel Hill and ends at Point State Park downtown. The Great Race is extremely popular, typically drawing more than 10,000 runners, so it's a great place to socialize as well.

The Pittsburgh Marathon and the Great Race are the region's signature running events, but there are hundreds of others. The *Pittsburgh Post-Gazette* publishes a schedule of running events each Sunday and produces an annual calendar of races each March. In addition, two organizations can keep you posted on coming events.

Runner's High, 83 Cranberry Road, Grove City, (724) 458-4435, provides timing services for many of the region's races and publishes a road race directory about once every three months providing details for approximately 500 races per year in Western Pennsylvania, as well as all such race results. (S. Mark Courtney, founder and principal of Runner's High, meticulously records the names of all finishers in important races.) An annual subscription to the directory costs $10, or you can visit the organization's Web site, runhigh.com, for similar information.

A second race timing service, operated by Dave Mapes, provides a free race calendar that catalogues about 80 races per year. You can write this service at 1502 Grandview Avenue, Somerset, PA 15501, (814) 445-6213. If you enclose a self-addressed, stamped envelope with your request, Dave will send you his calendar free of charge.

SHOOTING

Allegheny County Sportsmen's League
1028 Hulton Road, Verona
(412) 882-9115
www.acslpa.org
Shooting is a popular Western Pennsylvania activity, as witnessed by the more than 40 organized sportsmen's clubs. The Allegheny County Sportsmen's League serves as their umbrella organization, publishing an annual directory of clubs and their facilities. You can contact the organization for a current directory. You'll find facilities for a broad variety of shooting, including skeet- and trap-, high-powered rifle-, and handgun-shooting, as well as a civilian marksmanship program that utilizes older military rifles. Many of the clubs host competitions and leagues, and some feature archery ranges and private lakes for fishing.

Greater Pittsburgh Trap & Skeet
920 King Road, Bulger
(724) 796-9111
www.greaterpghgunclb.com
Most area sportsmen's clubs are private. Greater Pittsburgh Trap & Skeet is one of the few exceptions, offering public facilities as well as hosting a private club. Skeet, trap, and sporting clays are the organization's most popular offerings.

You'll also enjoy rifle-, pistol-, and combat-shooting, as well as an archery range, with all facilities available daily. NSCA shoots are held once a month.

For relaxation, the clubhouse is open all weekend, plus Wednesday and Thursday evenings. Pay by the day or hour, and if you need equipment, ammunition, or ear protection, just knock on the door of proprietor Tex Freund, who lives on the premises. He'll be happy to rent you whatever you need. The guess here is that Tex goes through a lot of ear protection equipment himself.

SKIING

The hills elsewhere may be alive with the sound of music, but in Western Pennsylvania, they're alive with the sights of skiers. With its climate and topography, the region provides excellent skiing venues. You'll find plenty of opportunities for cross-country and downhill skiing, as well as a skiing community that loves its après ski (the after-ski party). We've highlighted Western Pennsylvania slopes and cross-country trails, but keep in mind that you'll find additional opportunities nearby in West Virginia, Maryland, and New York. Our region boasts a run for just about every skier, whatever your level of experience. Here's the dope on slopes.

Cross-Country Skiing

Cross-country skiing is a staple of many state parks and federal recreation areas. The Parks chapter will introduce you to local facilities that offer this activity. Keep in mind that some parks offer well-delineated trails, while at others, the skiers just go with the flow. For more detailed information on particular parks or recreation areas, contact the Pennsylvania Bureau of State Parks, (888) PA-PARKS, or the U.S. Army Corps of Engineers, (412) 395-7500.

Several local organizations organize cross-country ski outings. Allegheny

Group, Sierra Club, (724) 327-8737, hosts ski-touring treks at such locations as the Laurel Mountains and West Virginia's Canaan Valley. Often, the group doesn't determine its destination until several days before the outing, in the hope of encountering the best weather conditions. It's always best to call ahead. They'll rent you all the gear you need. Participants carpool for most outings, so you'll be expected to pony up your fair share.

Downhill Skiing

Boyce Park
675 Old Frankstown Road, Plum
(724) 733-4665
You can't beat the convenience of Boyce Park, which is operated by Allegheny County. You'll find it in the easternmost portion of the county, no more than a 30-minute drive from anywhere in the county. Boyce features beginners' and intermediate slopes with a total of nine runs, including moguls, Nastar timing runs with gates, jumps, and night skiing. The vertical drop is 180 feet, and lifts include two double chairlifts, one poma, and one T-bar. You can pay by the day or purchase a season pass. The park provides equipment rentals as well as special group rates on lift tickets.

Kids will have a grand time here with several special events, including an annual Mini-Junior Olympics for boys and girls from 5 to 12 years of age. You can learn the sport at the ski school and try cross-country skiing along the park's trails and hills using your own equipment. Snowboarders will fancy the Alpine Terrain Park and its 200-foot halfpipe. Whichever activity you choose, you'll enjoy après ski at the Four Seasons Ski Lodge. For more on Boyce Park, see the Parks chapter.

Hidden Valley Resort
One Craighead Drive, Hidden Valley
(814) 443-8000, (800) 458-0175
www.hiddenvalleyresort.com
Hidden Valley bills itself as the "Total Winter Fun" place, a handle that seems most appropriate. Spanning 88 acres, the facility boasts an uphill, per-hour capacity of more than 12,000 skiers who utilize eight lifts, including 1 quad chairlift, 2 triples, 3 doubles, and 2 handle tows, as well as 17 runs and trails. The vertical drop ranges from 340 feet to 430 feet, so you know you're in for a fun ride. You'll also enjoy more than 50 kilometers of cross-country trails.

Part of Hidden Valley Resort, the ski facility offers a 400-foot halfpipe for snowboarding, as well as snow tubing, sleigh rides, and snowshoeing. You can rent downhill and cross-country ski equipment as well as snowboarding gear. For your pleasure at Hidden Valley, you can pay by the day or purchase a season pass entitling you to unlimited skiing. There's no charge for skiers younger than age 5 or older than age 70.

You can take advantage of a variety of instructional packages. If you're worried about the kids while you're snowboarding or skiing, drop them at the resort's Mountain Kids Ski Center, which offers babysitting services and organized activities, including a variety of youth ski and snowboard programs.

When you're ready to relax, you'll have the entire resort at your fingertips. You'll find more about the amenities of Hidden Valley in the Accommodations and Golf chapters.

For a report on current ski conditions, call the Hidden Valley hotline, (800) 443-SKII.

Nemacolin Woodlands Mystic Mountain
1001 La Fayette Drive, Farmington
(724) 329-8555, (800) 422-2736
www.nemacolin.com
Mystic Mountain ski area is part of Nemacolin Woodlands Resort & Spa, which tells you right out of the chute that you're in for top-quality activities and amenities. When you leave that chute, the vertical drop is 300 feet. Mystic Mountain is equipped with one regular quad chairlift and one handlebar. You'll find a full line of rental equipment,

including cross-country skis and snow-
boards. Groups of 20 or more receive
special discounts on ski tickets and
rentals. Hours are 9:00 A.M. to 8:00 P.M.
seven days a week.

If you need some help before you
tackle the mountain, the resort offers
three group instruction sessions each day.
You can supplement that with private lessons, including an intense session that
lasts three hours. You also may take
advantage of a youth program for kids
from 7 to 10 years of age. Lunch is
included, but ski equipment is not. For
other Nemacolin features, see the Accommodations and Golf chapters.

Seven Springs Mountain Resort
RD#1, Champion
(814) 352-7777, (800) 452-2223
www.7springs.com

You've reached a certain pinnacle when
you ski at Seven Springs—the vertical
drop ranges from 360 feet to 750 feet,
while the skiable terrain measures 500
acres. Just as breathtaking are the facilities, which include 31 slopes and trails, 3
quad chairlifts, 7 triples, and 8 tows. The
lift capacity is 24,600 per hour, and the
longest run stretches for 1¼ miles. If you're
ready to tackle all this, you can rent all the
equipment you need and enjoy such
related activities as snow tubing. There
are also snowmobile tours and snowcat
rides available. If ever you need help on
the slopes, the resort maintains a 150-
member ski patrol to assist you.

The resort's Kids' Corner offers child-
care services as well as a Tiny Tots
instructional program. Seven Springs provides a variety of lodging packages,
instructional programs, and skiing packages. Of course, you're always welcome to
pay by the day. The resort is an accommodating place for après ski—make sure
you try the outdoor hot tubs! Check the
hotline, (800) 523-7777, for a report on
current ski conditions. See the Accommodations and Golf chapters for more about
Seven Springs.

SNOWMOBILING

You'll find some of the best snowmobiling
trails in the region at state parks, forests
and game lands, and federal recreation
areas. The season generally runs until about
April 1, or until the weather no longer is
conducive. Remember that on state terrain,
you'll need a valid snowmobile registration
as well as proof of liability insurance coverage. The Parks chapter will tell you which
local facilities offer snowmobiling. For more
comprehensive brochures, contact the
Pennsylvania Parks Information and Reservations line, (888) PA-PARKS; the Pennsylvania Game Commission, (717) 787-4250;
or the U.S. Army Corps of Engineers, (412)
395-7500. For a nominal fee, the Game
Commission also will provide you with
detailed maps of its lands.

McKean Snowriders Club
P.O. Box 27, McKean, PA 16426
(814) 476-7221

If you're willing to travel a bit for your
snowmobiling thrills, you'll find some like-
minded riders in Northwestern Pennsylvania. The McKean Snowriders Club belongs
to the Erie County Snowmobile Affiliation,
an alliance of five groups that plans exciting and challenging outings while undertaking useful projects, such as mapping
snowmobile trails. One of the club's
favorite rides is along a 175-mile loop in
the Allegheny National Forest. The
snowriders welcome participants from
Southwestern Pennsylvania.

SOCCER

Though it may seem like sacrilege in what
was traditionally football country, soccer
has become the sport of choice for many

---

*To check the condition of snowmobile
trails at state parks, call the state's
Snowmobile Hotline, (877) SNOMBLE.*

---

area youths. In fact, it's estimated that there are more than 55,000 registered players in the region. It would be difficult, if not impossible, to detail all the region's soccer organizations. Instead, we offer you information on the coordinating agency as well as several of the most important clubs that operate in different geographic regions.

PA West State Soccer Association
855 MacBeth Drive, Monroeville
(412) 856-8011

Through the United States Soccer Federation, PA West Soccer serves as the overall coordinator for all nonscholastic soccer in this half of the state. Its numbers are impressive, as it encompasses 124 youth clubs with 55,000 members as well as eight adult leagues and 2,000 members. For its members, the association handles registrations; scheduling; and referees, who number 2,300 strong.

Of special interest are the association's programs targeted to disadvantaged youths and those with physical and mental challenges. If you're looking for the best soccer opportunity for your particular situation, this is the best place to start. You can visit the group's Web site at www.pawest-soccer.org.

Beadling Soccer Club
P.O. Box 435, Bridgeville, PA 15017
(412) 221-3880
www.beadling.com

If you visit Beadling in Pittsburgh's South Hills, they'll be pleased to show you a photograph of the 1898 Beadling club. Needless to say, Beadling is one of the oldest soccer organizations anywhere. Today, the club administers 20 boys' and girls' teams that play in the Classic League. Beadling also boasts membership in the Continental Alliance, a group of 22 elite clubs. Players range in age from 12 to 20 and must try out for the teams. Some of the teams enter tournaments that take them as far away as France. Youths accepted for the program must provide $500 to cover the club's costs. Club members also participate in less formal adult men's leagues.

Penns Forest Football Club
P.O. Box 17337, Pittsburgh, PA 15235
(412) 371-1301

Based in Pittsburgh's eastern suburbs, the club sports 15 teams of youths ages 11 to 19. They play in a number of leagues, including the Classic League, the Premier League, and the National League, with home fields located in Harmarville and the Westmoreland County community of North Huntingdon. Players must try out for teams and are responsible for all expenses.

Pittsburgh Strikers
(724) 898-8090
www.pittsburghstrikers.com

Boys and girls between the ages of 12 and 18 are eligible to try out for the Strikers, who play at a number of fields in the North Hills. The club participates in the Classic League. Be sure to ask about costs, as the Strikers don't publish a fee schedule.

SOFTBALL

Softball—the slow-pitch variety—is a popular warm-weather activity in Western Pennsylvania, so much so that it's hard to find an open field at the height of the season. While leagues abound, the sport lacks an overall coordinating body, so that a league appropriate for your skill level may be hard to locate at once. Many teams are company based, meaning you can play only if you work there. Word of mouth may be the best way to find a league, but here are a few suggestions, whether you're searching for a team or your team is looking for a league or tournament play.

One of the neatest opportunities is with the 50 And Older Softball League, (412) 343-5438. Nearly 100 players ages 50 to 83 play twice weekly games at fields in the South Hills. Your $25 fee includes a jersey and cap. The league uses standard American Softball Association rules, with some modifications. For example, players may not slide into home plate.

If your team is looking for a highly competitive league, try the Amateur Softball League of Pennsylvania. Each year the league brings together about 85 men's and women's teams that play at fields throughout Allegheny County. The best teams travel to national tournaments, and the league also sponsors touring youth teams. You can reach them at (724) 658-7838.

The Penn Hills Sports Shop Softball League, (412) 795-3636, typically fields a league of about 30 men's teams, most based in the city of Pittsburgh's eastern suburbs. The teams are grouped by ability to assure the most enjoyable competition. One variation here: since the league is not run by a municipality, teams are expected to provide their own permitted fields.

For tournament play, you can get your season off to a running start with the Bud Lite Sports Page Softball Tournament held each April in Pittsburgh's eastern suburbs. The event usually pits about 30 teams and offers prize money to the winners. All proceeds benefit the Mario Lemieux Foundation.

SWIMMING

The city of Pittsburgh operates an extensive network of pools, with the outdoor season generally from early June through Labor Day. The network includes 31 outdoor pools as well as the Oliver Bath House on the Southside, which is open year-round. The pools are open to city residents and nonresidents alike, although city dwellers receive discounts on admissions fees. The city also offers a discount for recipients of public assistance. For schedules and fee information, contact Citiparks' pool hotline at (412) 594-4645.

You'll also find swimming opportunities at other municipal pools and at state parks and federal recreation areas. The Parks chapter will suggest some swimming venues for you. Keep in mind that some state and federal facilities offer sand beaches, others turf beaches. Some without lakes have large swimming pools. Food concessions and changing and showering facilities also vary. For comprehensive brochures, contact the Pennsylvania Parks Information and Reservations line, (888) PA-PARKS, and the U.S. Army Corps of Engineers, (412) 395-7500.

TENNIS

The tennis boom may be long over, but the sport continues to flourish here. Most of the courts constructed during the boom of the 1970s remain, and they're more available than ever before. You'll find indoor and outdoor courts aplenty at municipal parks, as well as courts at commercial facilities and private clubs.

The City of Pittsburgh's Citiparks, (412) 244-4188, offers a broad variety of tennis opportunities. If you're a beginner, you'll benefit from free group lessons provided through USA Tennis, a tennis industry program that also barnstorms Pittsburgh's neighborhoods with youth clinics. Cityparks also offers group clinics with varying fees.

You'll soon be ready for the Cityparks Adult Grand Prix Tennis League, which matches singles and doubles players of comparable skills. Some fees are involved. Finally, the Citiparks program includes clinics specially tailored to senior citizens and "munchkins" from 5 to 7 years of age. Munchkins is their word, not ours. When we're charging the net, we have great respect for anyone with a racquet—munchkin or not—on the other side.

TRIATHLON

Triathlons can be demanding. So demanding that it's sometimes hard to assemble a healthy field year after year. For that reason, you won't find many triathlons in the area; those you do discover won't be steeped in tradition and history.

Perhaps the newest of the area's triathlons is the Friends of the Riverfront Triathlon, founded in 1998 by Friends of the Riverfront to promote the development of riverfront trails and expose Pittsburgh's waterfronts to a greater audience. The event features 20 kilometers of biking and 5 kilometers of running, and, in a departure from the usual event agenda, a 5K canoeing or kayaking test along the Allegheny River in place of swimming. For information, contact Friends of the Riverfront at 33 Terminal Way, (412) 488-0212, www.friendsoftheriverfront.org.

YOGA AND MEDITATION

You'll find yoga and meditation being practiced in all kinds of venues in the Pittsburgh area: hospitals, health clubs, yoga centers, churches and synagogues, community centers, local colleges and universities, holistic health centers, and meditation rooms in private homes. There are almost as many forms of yoga and meditation being practiced as there are venues: various schools of Hatha yoga, such as Iyengar yoga, Kirpalu yoga, and Ashtanga yoga; Zen meditation; and Kundalini yoga. Because Zen meditation is associated with Zen Buddhism, some information is included in the Worship chapter. Note also that all forms of yoga represented here teach some type of meditation as well.

Several of the forms, including Kundalini yoga and gentle forms of Hatha yoga, offer special benefits and/or exercises for pregnant women. Kundalini is especially good for people trying to build strength and balance the internal systems of the body, particularly the immune and glandular systems. That includes people recovering from or coping with severe illness.

Below are contacts for some of the main groups or centers that offer yoga and meditation. Health clubs, due to their commercial nature, have not been included. We encourage you, however, to check out

clubs through the Yellow Pages. When you're looking for a yoga teacher, you'll want to find out what form she or he teaches; how the form will help you achieve the results you want; where the teacher was trained and how extensive the training was; and how many years the teacher has been practicing yoga.

Breathe Yoga Studio
East Carson Street
(412) 481-YOGA
Located on Pittsburgh's Southside, this studio is on the third floor of an old office building. The space is beautiful with hardwood floors, high ceilings, and windows that offer a view of the sky as well as the gargoyles on the building next door. It's great to stretch up during Cobra pose and catch a glimpse of those gargoyles! Courses in a variety of forms of yoga, dance, and related disciplines are offered at the center daily. When we called, classes scheduled were beginning, intermediate, and advanced Hatha yoga, Vinyasa (or "flow") yoga, Kundalini yoga, Middle Eastern dance, and Ashtanga yoga. The studio is continually adding new classes, and workshops on various topics are held there regularly. Integrative Yoga therapy and massage are also available. Drop in for a class for $12. Check out the variety of discount class cards available when you pay a lump sum from $40 to $90 and make a regular commitment to your health and well-being.

The studio shares its home with Labco Dance, a modern dance company with up-and-coming choreographers. An art gallery is on the second floor of the building the studio shares. Come, relax, get cultured! Yoga Sadhana studio is a fun and peaceful place.

Yoga Training Association
of Pittsburgh (YTAP)
(412) 421-1506
www.ytap.org
Founded by a small group of yoga teachers more than 25 years ago, YTAP's purpose "is to foster education about and

practice of the ancient science and art of yoga." Currently, YTAP membership is a mixture of yoga teachers and yoga students of varying levels. Except during summer months, YTAP holds monthly meetings during which a teacher of yoga or a related discipline presents a class. The group also brings in several nationally or regionally known yoga teachers each year and hosts an annual "Yoga Day Out" devoted to showcasing a variety of the forms of yoga and related disciplines available in the Pittsburgh area. YTAP also offers the opportunity for those practicing yoga to stay in touch with other like-minded individuals, to make new friends, and to network.

The group publishes five newsletters per year advertising the dates of some of the major yoga events in the area and offering various philosophical meanderings related to yoga and meditation. Periodically, the newsletter includes a simple directory of members; the names of teachers are marked with a "T." If you're a yoga teacher looking for a substitute for one of your classes, this list is one of the best places to start. Yearly membership in the organization is $25. We've not listed an address for YTAP, because the organization meets at a different location each month in an effort to make meetings convenient for members living in the various Pittsburgh neighborhoods.

GOLF

Golf in Western Pennsylvania is more than a sport or hobby—it's something approaching a regional passion. The relatively short season may be a handicap, but there are several compelling reasons why golf is so popular here.

Pittsburgh was for many years a leading corporate headquarters town—at one time outranked only by New York and Chicago—as well as a center for manufacturing. Golf always has been a popular getaway for corporate executives, a fondness that tended to trickle down throughout such organizations. Today, even though the region boasts a more diversified economy, that heritage of golf as the ideal vehicle for relaxation and competition remains.

A second pillar of golf's foundation in Western Pennsylvania can be summarized in two words—Arnold Palmer. One of golf's legends, Palmer was reared in Westmoreland County, created several golf courses here, and remains highly visible, staging tournaments for charity, maintaining his offices near his hometown of Latrobe, and popping up on countless television commercials. The rage for golf in Western Pennsylvania is part of Arnold Palmer's gift to the community.

The statistics are impressive. Of Pennsylvania's 705 public and private golf courses, the National Golf Foundation reports that Allegheny County and Westmoreland County rank second and third in the state, respectively, in the number of courses, with a combined total of 81 18-hole equivalents. Butler County is not far behind, ranking sixth.

Of 309 metropolitan areas in the country for which the foundation keeps records, the average golf hole per population rate is 76 holes per 100,000 people. In Pittsburgh, the rate is 101 holes per 100,000 people.

The region boasts courses to suit all tastes and talents, ranging from quick-play executive courses to storied Oakmont Country Club, site of a number of major Professional Golf Association tournaments over the years. You'll find courses carved from mountainsides, a course built atop a slag heap, even a municipal course operated by a university.

In the descriptions below, we've tried to feature most public courses in our service area, though the rate of construction and course openings makes development of a comprehensive list nearly impossible. Unless otherwise noted, costs cited include the price of electric cart rental. Keep in mind that prices change from season to season—you might find slight variations from those we've provided. We've noted where starting times are available, suggested, or required, and we've tried to describe unusual or compelling features of the courses.

Your tour through Pittsburgh's golf courses will be enjoyable, but take care. When you put "the sticks" in your car trunk permanently, because you never know when you'll get a chance to "hit a few," you'll know that the Pittsburgh golf bug has bitten you.

PUBLIC GOLF COURSES

North

Aubrey's Dubbs Dred Golf Course
P.O. Box 2053, Mercer Road, Butler (724) 287-4832
At Dubbs Dred, you'll be playing target golf, hitting over ravines and gullies to tight landing areas. It's a challenging course from stem to stern. Distance for the par-71 course ranges from 6,500 yards to 6,850 yards. Starting times are required

on weekends and holidays, but are optional during the week. Cost is $18. Dubbs Dred offers a limited-service pro shop and a small lounge.

Bostonia Country Club
Route 66, New Bethlehem
(814) 275-2553
Bostonia Country Club is located at the northernmost reaches of Armstrong County. Its relatively remote location means you can get on and off the course quickly, and without a starting time. The 9-hole, par-35 course covers 2,800 yards. The cost for nine holes during the week is $8.00, on weekends $10.00; for 18 holes during the week it's $10.00, on weekends $12.00. Annual memberships priced from $120 for students to $500 for families allow unlimited golf. You'll find a newly remodeled pro shop and a snack bar.

Buffalo Golf Course
201 Monroe Road, Sarver
(724) 353-2440
Perhaps the most challenging hole on Buffalo Golf Course is No. 15, a 438-yard par 4. there's a pond along the right side of a rising fairway, and trees reach out and hang over the green. Distance of this flat, par-71 course ranges from 6,138 yards to 6,324 yards. Weekend and holiday starting times are available. Cost is $17 weekdays and $23 on weekends, with senior citizen discounts offered during the week. You'll find a pro shop and a snack bar.

Cabin Greens Golf Course
Ford City Road, Freeport
(724) 295-3744
Cabin Greens is a pleasant, unpretentious 9-hole course that's a great place to get in a quick round after work. The par-36 course ranges from 2,462 yards to 2,907 yards. Cost is $26 for 18 holes, $18 for 9 holes, with senior citizen discounts available. Starting times are available on weekends and holidays only. Cabin Greens offers a pro shop and a snack bar.

Cherry Wood Golf Course
204 Truxall Road, Apollo
(724) 727-2546
When Carol and John Chernega designed Cherry Wood, they had golf in mind, of course, and much more. The Chernegas participate in the national Audubon Cooperative Sanctuary Program to promote native habitats and more natural environments. The course design so complements wildlife habitats that the Chernagas have recorded sightings of 50 species—including foxes, mink, wild turkeys, and vultures—on Cherry Wood. Perhaps the most important residents are such birds as woodpeckers, which feed on insects and reduce the need for pesticide application.

If you interrupt your commune with nature to golf, you'll find a 9-hole, par-35 course. Distance ranges from 1,895 yards to 3,115 yards. Starting times are not offered. Cost for a round of 9 holes is $20.00 during the week and $4.00 more on weekends. Senior citizens enjoy a special discount during the week. Amenities include a pro shop, a snack bar, and a driving range with grass tees.

Clover Hill Golf Course
2200 Reis Run Road, Franklin Park
(412) 364-2447
While this 2,300-yard, par-32 course won't test your long-driving ability over its 9 holes, it does place a premium on shot making. That's especially true at No. 7, a 173-yard par 3 where you'll hit over a lake to a two-tiered green.

Cost for a round of 9 holes is $10.00 and you can play a second 9 for $4.00. Seniors receive a daily $2.50 discount. Clover Hill offers neither starting times nor dining facilities, but you will find vending machines in the small clubhouse.

Conley Resort Inn
740 Pittsburgh Road, Route 8, Butler
(724) 586-7711, (800) 344-7303
Could it be that Coleridge was describing Conley's course when he wrote "Water,

Going Public

Golf in Western Pennsylvania can be a rich and rewarding experience . . . if you can find the dozens of public courses the region offers. You'll find several useful guides. Each spring the *Pittsburgh Post-Gazette* publishes a map that will help you locate courses, as well as a calendar of the season's charity events and competitions. The map and calendar appear as part of the newspaper, so all you have to do is buy that day's edition to get the golf extras.

The Pennsylvania Golf Course Owners (PGO) publishes an annual map of public courses in Pennsylvania as well as a discount book that, for $40, will get you coupons for two rounds for the price of one at more than 60 participating courses. Not all Pennsylvania courses are shown on the map, since some are not PGO members. But the approximately 140 that are listed will get you off to a swinging start. For a coupon book, send a check for $42.00 ($2.00 shipping and handling) to PGO, 122 Heatherlynn Court, White Oak, PA 15131. You can reach the PGO by phone at (412) 896-1955 or (800) 872-1483.

water everywhere?" Probably not, but you may feel like the Ancient Mariner when you play Conley. Both irrigation and scenic water hazards come into play on five holes. These include No. 7, a 520-yard par 5, where you must hit over water to reach the green.

Distance ranges from 6,200 to 6,515 yards, with par varying from 70 to 72. The fee is $42 on weekdays and $52 on weekends, with starting times available from Good Friday until December. You'll find a pro shop as well as a full-service restaurant called the Tavern. For more on Conley Resort Inn, see the Accommodations chapter.

Deer Run Golf Club
287 Monier Road, Gibsonia
(724) 265-4800

This semiprivate club is open to nonmembers, although members get first crack at tee times. If you don't belong, you may call two days in advance to arrange a starting time. You will enjoy the facilities, which include a pro shop, locker rooms, restaurant, bar, and banquet areas.

Distance of the par-72 course ranges from 6,345 yards to 7,018 yards. Pay special attention to No. 11, a scenic 382-yard par 4. Your second shot must carry over water to a green sheltered behind by a steep hill dotted with flowers. Cost for a round is around $60. If you're looking for accommodations nearby, check out the Sun and Cricket Bed and Breakfast in the Bed-and-Breakfast Inns chapter; it's right next to the golf course, just through the woods.

Green Valley Golf Course
647 Lowries Run Road, Ohio Township
(412) 364-9980

The fairways at Green Valley are narrow, but there are few hills and water hazards. If you can position your drive well, you'll find inviting approaches to the greens in most cases. An exception is No. 8, a lovely par 4 where the green sits atop a plateau.

The par-35, 9-hole course covers 2,661 yards. Starting times are not available. If you do hit the green on No. 8 in regulation, you can crow about it later at the snack bar. To play the 9-hole course, it costs $8.00 on weekdays and $9.00 on weekends. If you'd like to play a second round, it's $5.00 at all times. Seniors receive a discount during the week.

Hartmann's Deep Valley Golf Course
169 Hartmann Road, Harmony
(724) 452-8021
This is an easy walking 18-hole course, popular with senior citizens, with a back 9 dotted by picturesque water hazards. The par-72 course covers 6,310 yards, with no starting times necessary. For 18 holes, the cost is $14.00 during the week and $19.00 on the weekends and holidays; for 9, it's $7.50 on weekdays and $10.50 on weekends. (These prices don't include electric carts, since the course isn't difficult to walk, but carts are available for an extra charge.) Senior citizens receive discounts during the week. Take advantage of the picnic and banquet facilities, as well as the pro shop, snack bar, and the Watering Hole restaurant/lounge.

Lake Arthur Country Club
255 Isle Road, Butler
(724) 865-2765
Lake Arthur offers a great fishing hole, and the entire course was upgraded recently. The fairway on No. 18 is flanked by lakes with a small landing area between them. Even if you find the fairway, getting your par 4 on this 451-yard challenge is hardly a sure bet.

Distance for the par-69 course is 6,629 yards. Cost (without cart) is $17 on weekdays and $23 on weekends, with senior citizen discount cards available in the pro shop. Lake Arthur offers starting times every day. In addition to the pro shop, you'll find a chipping green, a bar and lounge, and banquet facilities. If you play the Lake Arthur and have time for even more fun, stop at nearby Moraine State Park.

Lake Vue North Golf Course
691 Pittsburgh Road, Butler
(724) 586-7097
Lake Vue North offers many picturesque holes that feature water hazards and elevated or hidden greens. Distance for the par-72 course ranges from 5,690 yards to 6,355 yards. Weekend starting times are available. An 18-hole round will cost $34 for two people; a 9-hole round is $22 for two people. Weekday discounts are available for senior citizens. You'll also find a limited-service pro shop, a snack bar, a lounge, and banquet facilities. If your youngster is a budding golfer, ask about Lake Vue North's junior league.

Lenape Heights Golf Course
Route 66, Ford City
(724) 763-2201
www.lenapeheightsgolf.com
Lenape Heights is a 6,245-yard, par-71 course that features a pro shop and a sandwich shop. The cost to play this 18-hole course is $30 on weekdays and $37 on weekends, with weekend starting times available.

The signature hole is No. 13, an unusual 531-yard par 5. What makes it so striking is an island, which measures about 20 yards across. If your ball somehow stays on the island, it's in play. Lenape now has meeting rooms that can accommodate from 2 to 400 guests.

North Park Golf Course
Pearce Mill Road, Allison Park
(724) 935-1967
One of two golf courses administered by Allegheny County—South Park is the other—North Park is exceptionally popular and does not offer starting times. To avoid the crowds, try to play the course during the late morning, the early afternoon, and on Fridays, when things are a bit slower. The 6,805-yard, par-72 course is an open, gently rolling affair with large greens and no water, a fun outing no matter what your level of play.

Cost for a round is $15 on weekdays and $18 on weekends. If you're age 60 or older, your age entitles you to a $5.00, 18-hole round of golf and a $3.00, 9-hole round; these prices don't include carts. North Park offers a pro shop, a putting green, a driving range, and a full-service restaurant. The course is open year-round.

For more on the amenities of North Park, see the Parks chapter.

The Western Pennsylvania Golf Association, (412) 826-2180, performs several useful services for local golfers. It publishes an annual schedule of amateur tournaments, provides a list of course ratings and slope ratings, and can help you establish your handicap.

Pittsburgh North Golf Club
3800 Bakerstown Road, Gibsonia
(724) 443-3800

Pittsburgh North offers both an 18-hole course and a 9-hole course known to habitues as "the Fox." The 18-hole course, with a 134 slope rating from the back tees, can be challenging. Distance ranges from 5,075 yards to 7,000 yards, with par at 72 or 73 depending on which tees you play. The course features several tough par-3 holes, including No. 14, a 232-yard challenge where you must hit over water and avoid a sand trap guarding the right of the green. If you miss to the left, you're likely in the water or the accompanying dam.

The Fox, a par-35 course, ranges from 2,051 yards to 2,796 yards. Weekend and holiday starting times are available. Cost for 18 holes is $16 on weekdays and $34 on weekends, while you can play the Fox for $14. The club features a pro shop, a bar, and a seasonal driving range. Pittsburgh North regularly hosts group functions of up to 150 people, including outdoor barbecues. Three PGA pros are on staff; they offer a golf school.

Rose Ridge Golf Course
4769 Route 910, Allison Park
(724) 443-5020

To give you some idea of the crowds that Rose Ridge attracts, starting times begin at dawn, and the course maintains a fleet of 90 electric carts. The par-72 course measures 6,520 yards. You'll enjoy No. 11, a 165-yard par 3 with an elevated tee and a lake guarding the green. You'll also like the sight of Deer Creek, which winds its way for nearly a mile through the course.

Cost is $27, with weekend and holiday starting times available. Rose Ridge features a driving range, a lounge, and a sandwich shop.

Saxon Golf Course
839 Ekastown Road, Sarver
(724) 353-2130

Saxon Golf Course is a duffer's dream. It offers 27 holes, with nary a water hazard or sand bunker to be found, and both the 18-hole course and the 9-hole layout are flat. Distance for the par-72 18-hole course ranges from 5,131 to 6,177 yards, while the tight little 9-hole course, a par 34, covers 2,255 yards.

Starting times are available on weekends and holidays. Cost for the 18-hole course on weekdays is $17.00, on weekends $21.00 or the 9-hole course, it's $9.50 on weekdays, $11.50 on weekends. You'll find a snack bar, a driving range, chipping areas, and a picnic shelter you can reserve for a group outing. When you get to know course operators Frank Ekas Sr. and Frank Ekas Jr. you'll be encountering a bit of local history—Ekastown Road was named for their family, early blacksmiths who helped settle the Saxonburg area.

Shamrock Public Golf Course
481 Grove City Road, Slippery Rock
(724) 794-3030

This par-35, 9-hole course is deceptive. While its layout of 2,686 yards seems inviting, there are three par 4s longer than 400 yards. You'll also encounter a challenge at No. 2, a 155-yard par 3 with a green surrounded by steep hills. Miss in any direction and you're in double-bogey territory.

Cost for a round of 9 holes is $7.00, and you can play 18 for $13.00. Carts are available at an additional cost. Starting times are not offered. You'll enjoy the chipping area, snack bar, and banquet facilities.

Stoughton Acres Golf Course
904 Sunset Drive, Butler
(724) 285-3633

No. 13 at Stoughton Acres will challenge you. It's a 524-yard par 5 that forces you to cross both water and a highway to reach the green. The par-71 course covers 6,054 yards. Reserved tee times are available on weekends. You'll find a pro shop and a snack bar. Stoughton Acres does not publish its very reasonable green fees and cart charges. We recommend that you check Stoughton Acres out, especially if you want to play a nice round without emptying your wallet.

Suncrest Golf Course
137 Brownsdale Road, Butler
(724) 586-5508

The front nine at Suncrest is flat—that will get you in shape for the hillier back nine. Distance for the par-72 layout ranges from 5,415 yards to 6,243 yards. Cost for a round is $31, with weekend starting times available. Suncrest offers senior citizen discounts during the week. Facilities include a pro shop and a snack bar.

Venango Trail Golf Club
1305 Freeport Road, Warrendale
(724) 776-4400

If you've cranked up your long game, you can let it out on Venango Trail's No. 8, a 590-yard par 5 with a lake, a creek, and a ravine all threatening you about 400 yards from the tee. A prudent player will lay up before the trouble, but if you're feeling feisty, go for the green on your second shot.

The par-72 course measures 6,200 yards. Starting times are available each day. Cost is $36. Venango Trail offers memberships for individual players, senior citizens, corporations, and families. Member benefits include unlimited golf, priority tee times, and discounts in the pro shop and restaurant.

John Sandherr, Venango's director of golf, says you'll be "treated like a king or a queen." In return for such treatment, be prepared to dress a little more royally.

Venango does not permit blue jeans or revealing clothing, and all shirts must have collars. You may wear shorts.

Woodlawn Golf Course
917 Bull Creek Road, Tarentum
(724) 224-4730

Woodlawn is an enticing par-32, 9-hole course that's not as easy as it looks, despite measuring only 2,376 yards. That's because Bull Creek, a natural phenomenon that still supports fish and other aquatic life, runs through the course, coming into play on five holes.

The cost for a round is $10 on weekdays, $11 on weekends for 9 holes; $15 on weekdays, $17 on weekends for 18 holes. Senior citizens enjoy a $1.50 discount on weekdays. Woodlawn offers a pavilion for group outings.

East

Carradam Golf Course
2151 Hahntown Road, North Huntington
(724) 863-6860

This Jim Harrison–designed course features great finishing holes as No. 9 and No. 18 sport tree-lined fairways and mounding around the greens. The par-71 course measures 5,904 yards. When you're planning your golf outing, note that reserved starting times are available on weekends and holidays only, and that Carradam entertains leagues most evenings. The cost for 18 holes is $20 on weekends; the cost for 9 is $10 on weekdays and $11 on weekends. You'll enjoy country-club-quality greens, a fully stocked pro shop, a snack bar, and a picnic pavilion.

Champion Lakes Golf Course
Route 71 North
P.O. Box 724, Ligonier, PA 15658
(724) 238-5440

Champion Lakes is located in the Laurel Mountains, and the 13th hole offers a particularly beautiful view of the mountains. The fairway on the 380-yard par-4 hole is part of a valley that splits two soaring

The National Golf Foundation estimates that about 1 million of Pennsylvania's 12 million residents play golf.

peaks, while a picturesque lake guards the green.

The fee for the 6,608-yard, par-71 course is $37 on weekdays and $42 on weekends. Reserving a tee time is imperative because of the regular schedule of tournaments. Facilities include a restaurant, a bar, a pro shop, and banquet capabilities.

Champion Lakes is the creation of former Pittsburgh Pirates Jerry Lynch and Dick Groat. Groat still resides there during the summer, and so, too, can you—for a little while, anyway. That's because Champion Lakes Bed & Breakfast adjoins the course, with all sleeping rooms named for former Pirates. For more on this bed-and-breakfast, see the Bed-and-Breakfast Inns chapter.

Cherry Creek Golf Course
1000 Spyglass Hill, Greensburg
(724) 925-8665

This par-70, 18-hole course is styled as an "executive course" because of its appealing 4,500-yard length. During the week, the cost is $10 for 9 holes and $16 for 18; on weekends, the cost is $16 for 9 holes and $24 for 18. (We haven't included the cost of carts, since you'll probably enjoy walking this course.) Senior citizen discounts are available. You'll enjoy the pro shop and snack bar, known as Duffers Deli. Cherry Creek takes pride in its smooth, well-manicured greens.

Cloverleaf Golf Club
P.O. Box 55, Delmont, PA 15626
(724) 468-4173

Cloverleaf offers three 9-hole courses; for your round of 18, you can select any two of the courses. Depending on the combination, the yardage for 18 holes ranges from 6,016 to 6,215 yards, while par ranges from 70 to 72. Your round of 18 will cost you $25, and starting times are not available. You'll find a limited-service pro shop, a

snack bar, and a tree-shaded pavilion that is popular with Cloverleaf's 30 leagues.

Donegal Highlands Golf Course
P.O. Box 130, Donegal, PA 15228
(724) 423-7888

The Laurel Highlands provide a scenic locale for Donegal Highlands, which is located at an elevation of 1,850 feet in southeastern Westmoreland County. Pro Jeff Mowrer doesn't believe the elevation will help your length, but he does commend the view on No. 15, a 487-yard par 5 that, in addition to featuring a hard dogleg right and water on both sides of the green, is flanked by Chestnut Ridge and Laurel Ridge.

The 6,153-yard, par-72 course is demanding; its slope rating is 124. Starting times are required daily. Cost for a round is $32 for cart and greens, $40 on weekends, while senior citizens can play Monday to Thursday for $25. You'll enjoy the pro shop, a two-tier driving range with grass tees, and a tavern called the Black Dog Pub.

The Golf Club at Hidden Valley
One Craighead Drive, Hidden Valley
(814) 443-1907, (800) 458-0175

Golfing at Hidden Valley Resort will get you high . . . literally. The course is situated atop a 3,000-foot summit in the Laurel Highlands, offering spectacular views of the countryside for up to 30 miles. Your ball will travel well in the rare air, and you'll find the entire experience invigorating.

The par-72 course ranges from 5,027 yards to 6,589 yards and features narrow, tree-lined fairways. You'll hit long here, but the course demands precision. The cost for 18 holes changes by season—call for fees. The resort also offers weekend golf packages.

Amenities include a pro shop, a driving range, a putting green, and Dundee's Restaurant. You may also take advantage of an instructional program that includes camp and private lessons. For more on Hidden Valley Resort, see the Accommodations and Recreation chapters.

Grand View Golf Club
1000 Clubhouse Drive, North Braddock
(412) 351-5390

If there's a golf course that says "Pittsburgh," it's Grand View. The course sits atop a converted heap of slag, a useless by-product of industrial operations. The club's owners have done a commendable job reclaiming the land, although if you're interested, you can still make out evidence of the slag at several points along the course.

A round over the 6,111-yard, par-71 course will cost you $35 on weekdays and $45 on weekends; senior citizen discounts are offered during the week. Starting times are available, and you'll enjoy a pro shop, a driving range, and a full-service restaurant. Club pro Thomas Beeler points out that from the lofty perch of Grand View, you can see as far away as downtown Pittsburgh to the west and the Laurel Mountains to the east.

Irwin Country Club
594 Simpson Road, Irwin
(724) 863-6016

You'll especially like the back nine at Irwin Country Club—that portion of the course was carved from surrounding woods and offers many scenic vistas. The par-70 course covers 5,600 yards. Cost for a round is $27 on weekdays and $30 on weekends, with starting times available on weekends and holidays. The club features a pro shop, a lunch counter, and a bar.

Linden Hall
432 Linden Hall Road, Dawson
(724) 529-7543

Golf is one of many attractive features at this resort about 37 miles from Pittsburgh. The course is scenic, offering compelling views of the Youghiogheny River, but as Linden Hall pro Ron Fronczak points out, it's also a stern test. Most holes have sand traps, and seven holes present water hazards. Yardage on the par-72 course ranges from 5,900 to 6,675.

Cost for a round is $42 on weekdays and $52 on weekends, with senior citizen discounts available. You also can purchase golf packages from the resort. Starting times begin at 6:00 A.M. In addition to the amenities of the resort, the course features a pro shop; a bar; a restaurant; and a "halfway house," a snack shack after the ninth hole. Linden Hall hosts about 50 group outings each year as well as leagues virtually every weeknight. The Accommodations chapter provides a fuller description of Linden Hall's recreation and hotel facilities.

The Madison Club
519 Yukon Road, Madison
(724) 446-4000

Bill Kossack, pro and general manager at the Madison Club, an upscale facility, challenges you to test your shot-making skills on No. 8, 181-yard par 3. You'll hit downhill along a fairway guarded by a massive stone wall. The green is protected by a lake in the rear, a steep hill on the right, and a venerable red oak tree on the left.

Distance for the par-72 course ranges from 4,905 yards to 6,847 yards. Starting times are available daily. Cost is $39 on weekdays and $48 on weekends. Amenities include a driving range, a snack bar, and a picnic pavilion that your group can reserve.

Mannito Golf Club
RD #1, P.O. Box 258
New Alexandria, PA 15670
(724) 668-8150

To master Mannito, you'll need a sharp game throughout, as the course features two tough closing holes. No. 9 is a 245-yard par 3, while No. 18 is an even longer par 3 at 254 yards. If you get home on regulation on those two tough nuts, you can consider your round a success.

Par for the 6,900-yard course is 71. Cost is $20 on Thursdays before 2:00 P.M., otherwise it's $27 a day and $31 on weekends, with senior citizen discounts available ($20 before 2:00 P.M.) on weekdays. You can reserve a starting time on weekends. Facilities include a pro shop, a restaurant, a driving range, a chipping

GOLF

area, and a picnic shelter that your group of up to 150 may book.

Manor Valley Golf Course
2095 Denmark Manor Road, Export
(724) 744-4242
If you've ever had that sinking feeling as darkness closed in and shortened your round, you'll appreciate Manor Valley. The course is one of the few in the region with lights for evening play. A number of Manor Valley leagues don't get under way until 7:00 or 8:00 P.M.

The par-72 course measures 6,327 yards. Weekend starting times are available. Cost is $29 all week, with senior citizen discounts available during the week. Manor Valley offers a pro shop, a snack bar, a bar, several chipping greens, and banquet facilities.

Maplecrest-Monroeville Golf Course
3892 Logans Ferry Road, Monroeville
(412) 372-7770
Tucked away in a wooded area far from the frenzy of Monroeville's shopping district, Maplecrest is a scenic 9-hole course where relaxation and quick play are the norm. The par-33 course covers only 2,100 yards and presents no bunkers or water hazards.

Cost is $14 on weekdays and $15 on weekends. Senior citizens enjoy daily discounts, and starting times are available. Pro Jim Daum offers private lessons as well as instruction through the municipality. Maplecrest sports a pro shop, a snack bar, and many junior leagues—this is one course that courts kids.

Meadowink Golf Course
4076 Bulltown Road, Murrysville
(724) 327-8243
To play this 6,139-yard, par-72 course, the cost is $20 on weekdays and $27 on weekends, with senior citizen discounts available during the week. (Carts aren't included in these prices, since many people prefer to walk this course.) You can reserve a starting time every day. Mead-

owink offers a pro shop and a snack bar, as well as one of the toughest par 3s around. From the elevated tee at No. 11, you'll see the green 149 yards away guarded by sand and water in front and left, a steep hillside to the right, and woods in the rear.

"You really need to hit the green," says Meadowink operations manager Joyce Miller. "If you can do it, it's a routine hole. If you don't, it's trouble. This is not a place to miss."

Mt. Odin Golf Course
Mt. Odin Park Road, Greensburg
(724) 834-2640
Operated by the city of Greensburg as part of a municipal park, Mt. Odin is an 18-hole course that features a pro shop, a snack bar, a driving range, and considerable league play. Distance ranges from 4,743 yards to 5,445 yards, with a par of 70. Cost for 9 holes during the week is $14, on weekends $16 for 18 holes, during the week, you'll pay $25 on weekends $26. Senior citizens can purchase a restricted pass ($400) or an unrestricted pass ($350) that covers greens fees for the entire season. For more on Mt. Odin, see the Parks chapter.

Murrysville Golf Club
3804 Sardis Road, Murrysville
(724) 327-0726
Murrysville Golf Club opened in 1930 with a classic Scottish design—plenty of grass bunkers but no sand. It maintains that philosophy today. The par-70 course spans 5,320 yards but features tricky winds to compensate for the moderate distance. Cost is $35, with senior citizen discounts daily. You'll find a pro shop, a snack bar, and a putting green, but no starting times.

Norvelt Golf Club
RD #5, Mt. Pleasant
(724) 423-5400
This par-72 course covers 6,387 yards. You can reserve starting times on weekends and holidays and enjoy the club's pro shop

and snack bar. Cost for a round is $24 on weekdays and $32.66 on weekends, with senior citizen discounts offered daily.

Oak Lake Golf Course
1208 Oak Lake Road, New Kensington
(724) 727-2400

The Conley family owns and operates this 5,706-yard, par-72 course, and they've created several signature holes. You'll be tempted by No. 17, a 496-yard par 5 that invites you to go for the green in two shots. First, you must contend with a double dogleg as well as a large sand trap guarding the green. The more conservative approach is to lay up, but if your round needs a pick-me-up, go for it!

Starting times are offered on weekends. Cost for a round is $36, with weekday senior citizen discounts available. Oak Lake features a pro shop, a bar/restaurant, and pavilions for group outings.

Oakmont East Course
909 Hulton Road, Oakmont
(412) 828-5335

Oakmont East is the next best thing to storied Oakmont Country Club. In fact, the country club owns this public course, a par 72 that measures 5,720 yards. Starting times are offered on weekends. Cost is $16 on weekdays and $19 on weekends, but seniors may purchase $450 memberships that cover their greens fees for a year. Oakmont East features a snack bar and a limited-service pro shop.

Note: During its major tournaments, Oakmont Country Club closes the public course and uses it as a parking lot. It may happen only once every several years, but it is a good thing to know in advance.

RidgeView Golf Course
Gravel Hill Road, Ligonier
(724) 238-7655

This 9-hole course provides a sweeping view of Chestnut Ridge in the Laurel Highlands; you'll enjoy that view for much of the 2,650 yards of this par-36 course. Cost is $8.00 for a round of 9 on week-

days and $9.50 on weekends, $13.00 on weekdays and $14.50 on weekends for a round of 18. RidgeView offers starting times, a snack bar, a lounge, an outdoor deck, and a limited-service pro shop.

Rolling Fields Golf Course
Hankey Church Road, Murrysville
(724) 335-7522

You'll be rolling along at Rolling Fields when you reach the challenging No. 13, a 375-yard par 4, with a dogleg left and a severely undulating green. Did we mention that you must hit over water to reach the green? Get home in four here and you'll have earned your par.

Cost for the 6,095-yard, par-70 course is $21, with senior citizen discounts available on weekdays. After your round, you can relax in the snack bar.

Fabled Oakmont Country Club, about 10 miles east of downtown Pittsburgh, has played host to 15 major tournaments: the PGA Championship in 1922, 1951, and 1978; the U.S. Open in 1927, 1935, 1953, 1962, 1973, 1983, and 1994; and the U.S. Women's Open in 1992. (Note: The course is not written about in this chapter because it's not open for public play.)

Schenley Park Golf Course
Forbes Avenue and Schenley Drive
(412) 622-6959

Club pro Bruce Stephen likes to say that Schenley offers the best golfing in the city of Pittsburgh. That's indisputable, since this is the only course within city limits. Part of Schenley Park, the course is owned by the city of Pittsburgh and operated through a lease agreement by a nonprofit corporation affiliated with Carnegie Mellon University.

The par-67 course measures 4,620 yards, which is considered executive length. You won't find bunkers or water hazards, but you will have a unique

Pittsburgh boasts more than 100 golf courses in and around the city. That's the largest concentration in the country.

opportunity to hit across roads protected from stray balls by fences, and you'll enjoy a beautiful view of the city skyline as you play. You'll encounter highway hazards no fewer than six times. For your troubles, you'll be rewarded at No. 5, a 122-yard par 3 that probably produces more aces than any other hole in the area. A number of nonprofit organizations stage hole-in-one contests on No. 5.

Cost for a round with a pull cart—electric carts aren't available—is $15. If you buy a special "Frequent Golfers" card, you'll get 10 rounds for $120. Schenley offers weekend and holiday starting times, a pro shop, a restaurant, putting greens, and lessons from Stephen. The course is open year-round. For more on Schenley Park, see the Parks chapter.

Seven Springs Mountain Resort
RD #1, Champion
(814) 352-7777, (800) 452-2223

The golf course at Seven Springs is very much in keeping with the resort. It's beautiful and well appointed. You'll enjoy the facilities, which include a pro shop, locker rooms, and the Tee Top Lounge. The 11th hole is particularly appealing. It's a 195-yard par 3 where the undulating green is guarded by a lake, a bunker, and a large mound. Distance for the par-71 course ranges from 4,913 yards to 6,360 yards.

Cost during the week is $58 for guests of the resort, otherwise, $68; on weekends, it's $67 for guests of the resort, otherwise, $72. Resort guests may reserve starting times two weeks in advance, while others can get their tee times two days in advance. You can get a good feel for the course by asking pro Fred Haddick for the brochure that will provide a detailed hole-by-hole description . . . including tips on how to approach each hole.

For more information on Seven Springs, see both the Accommodations chapter and the Recreation chapter.

Timber Ridge Golf Course
Mulberry Hill Road, Mt. Pleasant
(724) 547-1909

You'll enjoy your round at Timber Ridge, if you hit straight. Otherwise, you may get up close and personal with the bunkers featured on just about every hole as well as the water hazards on three holes. Distance for the par-72 course ranges from 5,277 yards to 6,340 yards. Reserved starting times are available on weekends. Cost is $28 during the week and $30 on weekends, with weekday discounts for seniors. You'll find a pro shop, a bar/restaurant, and banquet facilities for up to 200 people.

Timberlink Golf Course
Route 30 West, Ligonier
(724) 238-7310

This executive length course—a par 55 that covers 2,375 yards—is attractive of itself, and it's also one of the many features that draw visitors to Ligonier. During the week, the cost to play 9 holes is $6.00, on weekends $7.00. An 18-hole round during the week is $11, and on weekends, it's $12. Timberlink does not offer starting times, but you will enjoy the small pro shop and snack bar.

Valley Green Golf & Country Club
RD #2, Box 449F, Greensburg, PA 15601
(724) 837-6366

Club pro Larry Liprando calls Valley Green one of the region's best walking courses—it's uncharacteristically flat for a Western Pennsylvania layout. The par-72 course measures 6,450 yards. Cost for a round is $27.50 on weekdays and $31.00 on weekends, with weekend and holiday starting times available. You'll find a pro shop, a bar, and a snack bar.

Vandergrift Golf Club
Community Park Road, Vandergrift
(724) 567-7413

Vandergrift Golf Club is semiprivate—nonmembers are welcome to play, but call ahead for weekend starting times. During the week it's first-come, first served.

The 9-hole, par-36 course spans 3,136 yards. Cost for 9 holes is $12, and you can play 18, using the second set of tees, for $14. (Prices do not include carts, although they are available.) The pro shop is limited, but you'll enjoy a snack bar/grill, a driving range, and a chipping area.

Windyhill Golf Course
603 Windyhill Drive, Plum
(412) 793-7771

If you're a veteran golfer, this 9-hole course might not be your cup of tea. At 1,700 yards, however, it's a great par 30 for juniors and beginners. Cost for 9 holes with a pull cart (electric carts are not offered) is $6.00 while you can play 18 holes for $8.00. You won't need a starting time.

South

Butler's Golf Course
800 Rock Run Road, Elizabeth
(412) 751-9121

The unusual design of Butler's Golf Course includes four 9-hole courses that you can combine according to your preference, unless heavy crowds prevent that. Whichever two nines you play, the distance is 6,606 yards and the par 72. Cost is $35 on weekdays and $47 on weekends, with starting times required every day.

The course also entertains many leagues—59 during one recent season. If you're interested in joining a league, club pro Carmen Costa will match you with a group looking for players. One of the great attractions for leagues is the Rock Run Inn, the course's spacious, full-service restaurant that offers a huge and varied menu. In fact, it's a destination dining spot

in the Elizabeth area, whether you golf or not, and it offers full banquet and outing facilities.

Costa calls No. 9, a 185-yard par 3, the signature hole, with its peculiar L-shaped green. "If you miss left," Costa says, "you're in the water. If you miss short, you're in the bunker or water, if you miss right, you're in a bunker or on a hill. If it's long, it's in a flower bed." Best advice: don't miss the green.

Enjoy the driving range, putting green, par-3 practice course, and the popular shotgun outings offered at this course. Call for more information about the latter. *Note:* shotgun outings are events in which everyone playing starts at the same time on different holes—no firearms involved.

Carmichaels Golf Club
471 Harts Road, Carmichaels
(724) 966-7500

Located in Greene County, Carmichaels Golf Club technically is beyond the coverage area, but we thought it worth noting because of the scarcity of courses in the sparsely populated county in the state's southwestern corner. Distance for the par-70 course ranges from 4,584 yards to 5,393 yards. On the back nine, be prepared to contend with several ponds and many hills. Cost for a round is $27 during the week and $32 on the weekend with starting times available on weekends and holidays. The club offers a pro shop and a snack bar.

Cedarbrook Golf Course
215 Route 981, Belle Vernon
(724) 929-8300

You can select from two 18-hole courses at Cedarbrook. The par-72 Gold Course ranges in distance from 5,138 yards to 6,710 yards, while the par-71 Red Course ranges from 4,577 yards to 6,154 yards. Cost to play either is $36 on weekdays and $46 on weekends. Senior citizen discounts are available, and starting times are required. You can visit the pro shop and relax in the full-service Clubhouse Grille.

Golf course architect Dr. Michael Hurdzan designed Cedarbrook's courses, which feature large flat greens. Don't be deceived, as the courses offer some stiff challenges. No. 6 on the Gold Course is a monstrous 578-yard par 5 with ever-narrowing fairways. "I don't know if it's ever been reached in two from the back tees," says club pro Bryon Palonder.

On the Red Course, the 531-yard, par-5 No. 10 offers a split fairway divided by an uninviting thicket. The right fairway is longer, the left more dangerous. Which one does Palonder choose? "Whichever one the ball lands in," he says diplomatically.

Chippewa Golf Club
128 Chippewa Road, Bentleyville
(724) 239-4841

Architect Jim Harrison designed plenty of water hazards into Chippewa, but he spared you the heartbreak of sand. There's not a single sand bunker on the course. Distance for the par-70 layout ranges from 5,104 yards to 6,051 yards. Starting times are available each day. Cost is $28.50 on weekdays and $32.00 on weekends, with weekday discounts for senior citizens. Chippewa offers a limited-service pro shop, a snack bar, and a picnic pavilion. Soft spikes are required.

Eighty Four Golf Course
1344 Route 519, Eighty Four
(724) 746-1510

This course features one of the longest holes around. No. 4, a par 5, measures 600 yards with a dogleg right. Get out your driving clothes for this one. The par-70 course measures 5,450 yards. Starting times are not available. Cost is $29.50, with weekday discounts for senior citizens. You'll find a pro shop, a lounge, and a full-service restaurant.

Fort Cherry Golf Club
Fort Cherry Road, McDonald
(724) 926-4182

Fort Cherry has a number of scenic and challenging holes, perhaps none tougher than No. 4. The par-3, 201-yard hole features water left and right as well as bunkers guarding the green's right side. Distance for the par-70 course ranges from 5,888 yards to 6,205 yards. Starting times are available in season. Cost is $28 on weekdays and $32 on weekends, with weekday discounts for senior citizens.

In addition to the Fort Cherry Golf Club's pro shop and full-service restaurant, Fort Cherry offers impressive banquet facilities, including a large hall that can accommodate up to 600 guests; a patio bar spacious enough for 100 people; and the Green Room, a glass-enclosed hall overlooking the golf course where you can entertain up to 120 people. These facilities are quite popular for wedding receptions and other functions—you'll want to book them well in advance.

Frosty Valley Golf Course
2652 Hidden Valley Drive, Upper St. Clair
(724) 941-5003

Frosty Valley once was the course of Hidden Valley Country Club, which relocated some years ago, and this 9-hole course still resembles a country club layout in some ways. The flat course is easy to walk, but water hazards affect six of the nine holes. The par-36 course plays from 2,371 yards to 3,250 yards. The cost is $13.00 during the week and $15.00 on weekends; cart rentals start at $7.00. Reserved starting times are available on weekends and holidays.

Residents of the adjacent Friendship Village retirement community enjoy complimentary privileges at Frosty Valley. (For more on Friendship Village, see the Senior Scene chapter.) Amenities include a pro shop, Mickeys on the Green restaurant, and banquet facilities.

Holly Hill Inn & Golf Center
1110 Towervue Drive, Baldwin Borough
(412) 882-4222

Holly Hill is situated about 15 minutes from downtown Pittsburgh; if you keep your "sticks" in the trunk, this is a great place to grab a quick round after work, and you won't need a starting time. Distance for the par-33, 9-hole course ranges from 2,148 yards to 2,480 yards. A round of 9 holes will cost you $10, while you can play 18 for $18. You'll enjoy the pro shop, restaurant, and banquet facilities.

Lindenwood Golf Club
360 Galley Road, Canonsburg
(724) 745-9889

Lindenwood sports 27 new championship holes as well as a new 9-hole executive course. The golf club also features three 9-hole courses that the club configures on a daily basis to give you a different-looking 18 each time you play. Depending on the day's configuration, the distance ranges from 5,017 to 6,699 yards, with par at 71 or 72. This is a scenic course; you won't spy any homes or highways as you play, as Lindenwood is carved from bucolic woodlands.

Amenities include a pro shop, a driving range, a grill room, and banquet facilities. Nonmembers can reserve a tee time four days in advance. Cost for a round Monday through Thursday is $34; during the rest of the week and on holidays, the cost is $46.

Mt. Lebanon Golf Course
1000 Pine Avenue, Mt. Lebanon
(412) 561-9761

This 9-hole course is operated by the municipality of Mt. Lebanon. While only residents and their guests can play on weekends and holidays, nonresidents are welcome at other times. Cost is $20.50 per weekday for nonresidents and $12 per weekend day for residents. Discounts are available for juniors and seniors citizens. You'll find a pro shop and vending machines.

Distance for the par-34 course is 3,034 yards. You'll like No. 2, a 400-yard, tree-lined par 4 with its two-tier green protected by a bunker. The hole typically plays longer due to a stiff wind. If you'd like a tip or two, look up pro Matthew Kluck.

Nemacolin Woodlands Resort & Spa
1001 Lafayette Drive, Farmington
(724) 329-6111, (800) 422-2736
www.nemacolin.com

When noted golf course architect Pete Dye designed Mystic Rock at Nemacolin Woodlands, he had a lavish $19 million budget to work with. The course shows it. The par-72, 6,832-yard course utilizes Nemacolin's natural assets to create a course as beautiful as it is challenging, with a 146 slope rating. You'll find undulating greens and plenty of water and rock that connect fairways with foliage. Nemacolin hosts the Mystic Rock Charity Pro-Am, which in 1997 attracted no less a player than Tiger Woods. If you think you'd like a tip or two, in order to play your best game, look up pro Delo Mees.

Nemacolin also features a second handsome course called The Woodlands Links, a par-71, 6,643-yard adventure with thick woods, high rough, and lakes aplenty surrounding the fairways. The Links is no slouch—the slope rating is 131—but it may seem like a vacation after Mystic Rock.

Resort guests can reserve starting times two weeks in advance; others can reserve their starting times a week ahead of time. Guests can play Mystic Rock for $130, while others pay $150. For The Links, the cost is $84 for all. Whichever course you play, you'll enjoy the extensive facilities, which include a pro shop, a driving range, practice greens and sand traps, and locker rooms. If hunger strikes as you approach the 9th tee at Mystic Rock, pick up the courtesy phone and order from the restaurant just off the 9th green. After you sink that birdie putt, your lunch will be ready for you. For more on Nemacolin, see the Accommodations chapter.

Riverview Golf Course
Bunola Road, Elizabeth
(412) 384-7596

Riverview is an 18-hole layout with dual personalities. The front nine is tight, demanding precision shot making, while the back nine is more open. You'll need most of the clubs in your bag for Riverview.

Distance for the par-71 course ranges from 4,817 to 6,382 yards. You can arrange a starting time in season and take advantage of the pro shop and snack bar. Cost is $34 on weekdays and $44 on weekends, with senior citizen discounts available on weekday mornings.

Rolling Green Golf Course
Route 136E, Eighty Four
(724) 222-9671

Distance for this par-71 course ranges from 6,011 yards to 6,621 yards. Weekend and holiday tee times are available. Cost is $27 on weekdays and $29 on weekends, with senior discounts available every day. Facilities at Rolling Green include a limited-service pro shop, a snack bar, and a picnic pavilion your group can reserve for $35.

Seven Springs of Elizabeth Golf Course
357 Pineview Drive, Elizabeth
(412) 384-7730

If your ball has an unerring nose for the water, you'll enjoy Seven Springs of Elizabeth (not to be confused with the similarly named resort). There are no significant water hazards on the 18-hole, par-71 course, or the 9-hole, par-35 course, although both courses feature liberally bunkered greens. The length of the 18-hole course ranges from 5,582 to 6,503 yards. You can reserve a starting time every day, and management suggests that you do. Cost for a round is $35 during the week and $40 on weekends, with senior discounts available. The course features a pro shop, a lunch counter, and bar and banquet facilities.

South Park Golf Course
East Park Drive, Library
(412) 835-3545

South Park offers both an 18-hole course and a 9-hole course. As with North Park, the other course operated by Allegheny County, crowds can be huge. Chuck Cullison, pro at all three courses, advises that playing in the late morning or early afternoon is one way to beat the crowds. Starting times are not offered, so you may have to wait to play.

The par-72, 18-hole course covers 6,584 yards. It offers a number of tree-lined fairways with tight landing areas. Bring all your clubs, Cullison advises. The 9-hole course is a par 34 that spans 2,652 yards. South Park offers a putting green, a chipping area, a pro shop, and a full-service restaurant.

Costs for 18 holes are $15 during the week and $18 on weekends; for 9, you'll pay $10 during the week and $12 on the weekends. Carts are available for an additional fee. If you're age 60 or older, you can purchase a $60 season pass. The Parks chapter provides a more detailed look at the features of South Park.

Village Green Golf Course
4050 Henderson Avenue, Hickory
(724) 356-2282

Enjoy the first half of your outing at Village Green—the back nine is a lot hillier than the front. Distance for the par-72 course ranges from 5,625 yards to 6,480 yards. A round will cost you $20.00 during the week and $28.50 on weekends, with senior discounts offered during the week. If those hills leave you huffing and puffing, you can relax in the pro shop, the bar, or the full-service restaurant.

Willowbrook Golf Course
RD #2, Route 201, Belle Vernon
(724) 872-7272

At 3186 yards, this 9-hole, par-36 course can be deceptive. Just when you think you can take it by storm, you'll find the creek that runs through five holes. Cost for nine holes is $11.50, and you'll enjoy a reduced rate for a second round of nine. If you're older than age 62, snap up the discounted rate of $5.00 (without cart) for nine holes. Willowbrook does not offer starting times, but it does feature a small pro shop and a snack bar.

Wyndon Links Golf Club
3001 Race Street, Scottdale
(724) 887-8858

Welcome to the fun world of the Yelinek family, proprietors of Wyndon Links . . . and a lot more. The 9-hole course sports a number of unconventional touches, including a heart-shaped green on the 227-yard, par-3 No. 3—a little touch of whimsy after you've crossed a pond and avoided woods to reach the green. You'll also encounter a practice area with a cactus-shaped bunker to complement the motif of the club's Cactus Star Restaurant.

Distance for the par-36 course ranges from 2,457 yards to 3,282 yards. A round of nine holes will cost you $10 during the week and $11 on weekends, with starting times required. In addition to the restaurant, you'll enjoy a pro shop, banquet facilities for up to 220 people, and a "target driving range" that includes greens sprinkled through the landing area. Wyndon Links hosts accuracy competitions on its driving range. You can see why the course is popular with leagues—they play five nights a week in season.

Another special touch: The Yelineks are real-estate developers and have constructed a number of homes that border the 9th hole. They not only will sell you a lot, but their construction company can also build your house. Each homeowner gets a golf cart specially equipped with a headlight to tool around the grounds.

West

Black Hawk Golf Course
644 Blackhawk Road, Beaver Falls
(724) 843-5512

Black Hawk features two 18-hole, par-72 courses, ranging in distance from 6,114 yards (No. 1 and No. 2 courses) to 6,300 yards (No. 3 and No. 4 courses). Watch out for the fifth hole on No. 3 course. This 420-yard par 4 was voted by local golfers the "Toughest Hole in Beaver County."

"The fairway slopes left to right, so you never have a level lie," says Garen Steele, club pro. "You're hitting into a blind green. You can't miss on any side because of the big hills. Most people take a shorter club and look for bogies and double bogies."

Cost is $28 during the week and $34 on weekends, with senior citizen discounts offered on weekdays before 3:00 P.M. You can relax in the full-service restaurant or book the course and its pavilion for a group outing.

Bon Air Golf Course
505 McCormick Road, Coraopolis
(412) 262-2992

Bon Air is a popular course with visitors staying at hotels near Pittsburgh International Airport, which is only minutes away. The 5,800-yard, par-71 course generally plays quickly, so there's plenty of time to enjoy a round and still make your meeting or flight. Cost is $34.50, with weekend and holiday starting times available. You'll find a snack bar and limited-service pro shop.

Fox Run Public Golf Course
River Road, Beaver Falls
(724) 847-3568

If you like water, you'll love Fox Run. All of the course's par-3 holes feature water hazards. Twice each year, course personnel fish hundreds of balls from the water and place them on sale at the pro shop for a buck apiece.

The par-72 course covers 6,508 yards. Tee times beginning as early as 6:00 A.M. are offered on weekends and holidays. Cost for a round is $27 on weekdays and $32 on weekends, with senior citizen discounts available on weekdays. In addition to the pro shop, you'll enjoy the driving range and snack bar.

Grassy Lane Golf Club
470 McCaughtry Run Road, Darlington
(724) 336-5006

Watch out for the hole they call "The Chute." It's No. 4, a 363-yard par 4 with a narrow, tree-lined fairway that broadens as it approaches the green. This 9-hole, par-36 course covers 3,035 yards. Cost is

$12.00 with a $2.00 discount for your second round of 9. Senior citizen discounts are offered during the week.

Only large groups may reserve starting times. Amenities include a limited-service pro shop, a snack bar, a chipping area, and a picnic shelter your group can book.

Hawthorne Valley Golf Club
122 Daniels Drive, Midland
(724) 643-9091

This 18-hole course is popular with evening leagues. If that's when you're planning to play, you might want to call ahead to check whether it's a league night. Starting times are available on weekends.

The par-72 course measures 6,237 yards. A round of 18 will cost you $15 during the week and $17 on weekends, with carts available for an additional fee of $11. Senior citizens receive discounts during the week. Hawthorne Valley offers a pro shop and a snack bar.

Marada Golf Course
1434 Route 30, Clinton
(724) 899-2600

Only 2 miles from Pittsburgh International Airport, Marada draws quite a few players laying over at the airport. Distance for the 9-hole par-35 course ranges from 2,485 yards to 3,090 yards. Arrival and departure times are important here, but you won't need a reserved tee time. For nine holes, the cost is $11 on weekdays and $12.50 on weekends. For 18, you'll pay $17.50 during the week and $20 on weekends. These prices do not include carts. Senior citizens receive discounts during the week. Marada offers a small clubhouse and a snack bar.

Quicksilver Golf Club
2000 Quicksilver Road, Midway
(724) 796-1594

Quicksilver has hosted five events on the Senior PGA tour and three events on the Buy.com tour (formerly the Nike Tour), as well as many tristate PGA and USGA events. That will give you some idea of the quality of the course. The amenities will reinforce that idea. You'll find a pro shop, a driving range with grass tees, Murphy's Restaurant, and Murphy's Pub. The club's owner, if you hadn't guessed, is Bob Murphy.

Distance for the par-72 course ranges from 5,067 yards to 7,083 yards. One of the favorite holes of general manager Sean Parees is No. 8, a 199-yard par 3 with a green guarded on three sides by water and sand. The course is a "fair challenge for all golfers with ability," according to Parees. Cost is $65 during peak season, with reduced rates for out-of-season and twilight play. For a $2,000 annual membership, you'll receive a locker, handicap service, a charge account, and the opportunity to reserve starting times 14 days in advance. Nonmembers can reserve tee times six days ahead of time.

Oglebay Resort and Conference Center
Route 88 North, Wheeling, WV
(304) 243-4000, (800) 624-6988

If you long to play a course that tempts and challenges the pros, try the Speidel Championship Golf Course at Oglebay, longtime host of the West Virginia LPGA Classic. Designed by the legendary Robert Trent Jones Sr., Speidel is a gorgeous course with compelling views of the hillsides that surround the resort. It's those same hills, however, that create the course's challenge.

One of the toughest holes is No. 17, a 456-yard par 4 with narrow landing areas protected by a line of trees and a steep hill. The green is enormous—about 32 yards deep. The par-71 course plays from 5,515 yards to 7,000 yards, with a fee of $60—modest, considering the course's heritage.

Arnold Palmer recently designed a new par-71 course at Oglebay. You'll pay $70 to play this one.

You'll enjoy the pro shop, locker room facilities, and the Hamm clubhouse for dining.

If you're not quite comfortable with the challenge of Speidel or the Arnold Palmer course, you can enjoy the same great Oglebay vistas at the resort's Crispin Golf Course, a 5,670-yard, par-71 course. Cost for a round at Crispin is $30.

Oglebay offers a variety of golf packages that include such features as overnight accommodations, breakfast buffets, and a second round at a 50 percent discount. Call Oglebay for details, and see the Accommodations and Day Trips chapters for more information about the resort.

Ponderosa Golf Lands
2728 Route 168, Hookstown
(724) 947-4745

Just as Ben Cartwright was concerned about irrigating his Ponderosa, the owners of Ponderosa Golf Lands have lavished attention on their watering system. It's all computerized, keeping the course green throughout the season.

Distance for the par-71 course ranges from 5,525 yards to 6,283 yards. Starting times are available in season. Cost for a round is $30.25 on weekdays and $36 on weekends. Facilities include a pro shop, showers and locker rooms, and a full-service restaurant.

Rolling Acres Golf Course
350 Achortown Road, Beaver Falls
(724) 843-6736

You'll love the unusual timber-frame clubhouse at Rolling Acres. It's a popular spot for banquets, accommodating up to 300 people. In addition, you'll find a snack bar and lounge.

Rolling Acres offers three 9-hole courses, with staff determining your configuration based on the day's volume. The distance for 18 holes ranges from 5,878 yards to 6,518 yards, with par varying from 71 to 73. While the courses are mostly free of sand and water, you will find many mounds and grass bunkers. Starting times are offered each day. Cost for 18 holes is $28 during the week and $34 on weekends, with senior citizen discounts available during the week.

SPECTATOR SPORTS

In Western Pennsylvania, the term "spectator sports" is almost an oxymoron. The identification of residents with local sports teams is active, emotional, and deep. Spectators in Pittsburgh may be outside the white lines, but we participate nonetheless with our sports teams.

Some have suggested that the local love for sports is rooted in the economic and social history of Pittsburgh. Because many Pittsburgh residents labored long and hard in coal mines and steel mills to feed their families, this theory goes, they turned to sports for recreation, relaxation, and the rewards that were few and far between on the job. They found physical and psychic satisfaction both in their own play and in the success of the teams that represented them.

If that's true, it must be added that the region's emphasis on family helps broaden the affection for sports. In Pittsburgh, sports tends to be a family pursuit. If you check out youth basketball or football games in the area, in addition to the young athletes on the field, you'll most often find Mom and Dad out there, too, volunteering as yard-line markers, concession booth operators, and team chauffeurs.

For whatever reasons, we love our sports teams. The metropolitan area supports professional teams in baseball, football, and ice hockey, top-level collegiate football and basketball programs, a harness-racing track, and a radio station that features sports programming almost exclusively. In few other communities will you find baseball's home opener regarded as a civic holiday. Here, otherwise dutiful parents cheerfully falsify school excuses to allow their children to attend the game, perpetuating a generations-old tradition.

When our teams win, we dress up in the colors of the local heroes, hang signs of support from office buildings, and party hearty. When the local teams lose, we phone the talk shows to offer heartfelt advice on how the lads can improve—"Get ridda de bums!" would be one example.

The new century is an especially exciting time to be a sports fan in Pittsburgh, as both our baseball and football teams have moved into new stadiums. For 30 years, both the Pirates and Steelers played at Three Rivers Stadium, but in 2001, the franchises went their separate ways. See the sidebar in this chapter for details on the new stadiums.

Broadcast coverage of local teams deserves special mention. Some who may not appreciate Pittsburgh look at our sometimes half-empty arenas and label us a "bad sports town." What they may not fully understand it that, for reasons that sociologists someday will probe, many local residents—particularly those of a certain age—are notorious stay-at-homers who follow their teams religiously on radio and television, but who seldom make it out to the game. For them and for you, details of the broadcast schedules and personnel for each team are provided.

We've also gathered information on transportation options, points of interest about the various sporting venues, and specifics about ticket prices. A word of caution about prices: these can vary from season to season, and many of the teams offer more packages than could be detailed here. This is especially true for the teams preparing to move to greener pastures. We've noted the most popular package and provided the most current pricing information available, but you may encounter some variations.

BASEBALL

Pittsburgh Pirates
In 1889 the Pittsburgh professional baseball franchise was accused of stealing a

second baseman from the Philadelphia organization. Pirates, these rascals from Pittsburgh were called. The name stuck, and today, the Pittsburgh Pirates continue as one of the bedrock franchises of Major League Baseball.

The Bucs (short for Buccaneers), as local fans affectionately call them, have a storied past, with World Series victories in 1909, 1925, 1960, 1971, and 1979. The club has produced 13 Hall of Famers over the years, including Honus Wagner, Pie Traynor, brothers Paul and Lloyd Waner (known as "Big Poison" and "Little Poison"), Ralph Kiner, and such contemporary greats as Roberto Clemente and Willie Stargell. The Pirates were involved in what may be the most dramatic moment in baseball history—Bill Mazeroski's home run to defeat the heavily favored Yankees in the 1960 World Series.

The Bucs compete in the National League's Central Division, where their rivals are the Chicago Cubs, Milwaukee Brewers, St. Louis Cardinals, Cincinnati Reds, and Houston Astros.

The 2000 season was the Pirates' last in Three Rivers Stadium. In April 2001, the team christened PNC Park, a new "old-style" park a few blocks up the Allegheny River. PNC Park is the latest in a nationwide trend toward retro ballparks. It features natural grass (as opposed to the artificial turf at Three Rivers), an asymmetrical outfield, and a spectacular view of the Downtown skyline. The park is designed by HOK Inc. of Kansas City, the firm that designed a number of retro parks around the country, including Oriole Park at Camden Yards in Baltimore.

The new park seats 38,127 people, and includes 69 suites and two restaurants. A 21-foot wall in right field honors Pirate great Roberto Clemente. The park is bordered by General Robinson Street, Federal Street, Stadium Drive East, and the Allegheny River, and there is a pedestrian walk along the water.

For those games when you can't make it to the stadium, the Pirates maintain a heavy broadcast schedule to bring the action to you. You can catch all 162 games on radio. Flagship of the 48-station radio network is KDKA-AM in Pittsburgh, 1020 on the dial. For television, cable's Fox Sports Network typically carries a healthy schedule of games each season and is available on most local cable television systems. In addition, Pirates games sometimes are featured on national broadcasts. The popular Lanny Frattare, voice of the Pirates since 1976, is ably assisted by Greg Brown and two former Bucs pitchers, Bob Walk and Steve Blass, he of the button-down humor.

Make sure you pay particular attention to game starting times, as the Pirates vary them to accommodate school schedules and fans concerned about the possibility of chilly weather.

The Pirates offer a variety of ticket plans. Prices for individual game tickets range from $9.00 to $35.00. The club also features season tickets, multiple-game plans, and discounted packages for groups. If you really want to treat your group to a memorable night at the ballyard, reserve the Grand Slam Box, which doubles as the football press box. Your group of 50 or more will dine in style and enjoy discounted tickets.

You can purchase your tickets at the Advance Ticket Window beneath the stadium's Gate A or at a number of off-site locations. These include TicketMaster outlets located in Giant Eagle, Kaufmann's, National Record Mart and Oasis Music and Video, and Pirate Clubhouse Stores in three local shopping plazas—Monroe Mall, Ross Park Mall, Westmoreland Mall—and Galleria Mall in Johnstown. You also can make credit-card purchases over the phone by calling (412) 321–BUCS or (800) BUY–BUCS.

For most games, you'll find $4.00 parking in the lots that circle the stadium. Other options include public transportation or parking downtown and walking across the Fort Duquesne Bridge to the stadium.

One of the neatest aspects of the Pirates' operation is the club's extensive involvement in the community. The Bucs have a special unit called Pirates Partners to coordinate a far-reaching program of school appearances, youth clinics, neighborhood athletic field restorations, donations of memorabilia, ticket giveaways to disadvantaged youths and autograph appearances—including an annual event at the Pittsburgh Zoo & Aquarium.

In the off season, Pirates Partners each week showcases a player who returns to Pittsburgh for a week of community-based activities. If you're involved in a community group and would like to work with Pirates Partners, call them at (412) 323-5000. You'll find the club is Major League : . . on and off the field.

BASKETBALL

Who says you need a professional basketball team to generate fan excitement and loyalty? While Pittsburgh lacks an NBA team, it doesn't lack for basketball thrills. The city sports three institutions that compete in NCAA Division I, the best college basketball in the land. Rare is the evening during the season when you can't enjoy a major college game, either in person or in the comfort of your living room.

Actually, Pittsburgh has featured several professional franchises, none of them in the NBA. The Pittsburgh Rens—short for Renaissance—performed in the old American Basketball Association. Later, in the American Basketball League of the late 1960s—the league of the red-white-and-blue balls—the Pittsburgh Condors won the league's inaugural championship behind the swooping grace of Connie Hawkins, who used that experience as a springboard to NBA fame. In the 1990s,

Pittsburgh was the brief home of the Piranhas entry in the Continental Basketball Association.

All three franchises were short-lived; that entrepreneurs launched them here, however, gives you some sense of basketball's popularity in Western Pennsylvania. If you're new to town and wondering if quality basketball is available, have no fear. The city game is alive and well in Pittsburgh.

Duquesne University

The men's basketball program at Duquesne University has long been both an artistic and a popular success. The Dukes have been to the NCAA tournament 5 times and to the National Invitation Tournament 16 times, capturing the NIT in 1955. Its legendary alumni include Chuck Cooper, Sihugo Green, Willie Somerset, and Norm Nixon—perhaps the most recognizable name for current fans, as Nixon was one of the key players in the Magic Johnson–led Los Angeles Lakers dynasty.

The Dukes, coached by Darelle Porter, compete in the Western Division of the Atlantic 10, a conference that features such traditional basketball powerhouses as Temple, Massachusetts, George Washington, Xavier, and Dayton.

Duquesne's home court is the A.J. Palumbo Center, an attractive building that opened in 1988, seats 6,200, and retains the feeling of newness. The center is located on Duquesne's campus along Forbes Avenue, making it quite accessible, as it is only a few blocks from downtown. Parking lots are available near campus as well as around the Civic Arena a few blocks away. You can also shoot for limited on-street parking. Forbes Avenue and the parallel Fifth Avenue are part of many Port Authority of Allegheny County bus routes, so using public transportation to see the Dukes is easy.

The Palumbo Center rarely is sold out, so you can get tickets on game days, through the mail or by calling the ticket office at (412) 396-4638 (GODU). Individual tickets are priced at around $13.00

and $18.00 in advance; you can purchase $5.00 tickets at the gate. You also may purchase season tickets as a convenience, but there's no discount involved.

Duquesne's TV appearances are limited and difficult to predict from season to season. Typically, regional cable network Fox Sports Pittsburgh offers several games; check local TV listings for those. While we don't recommend staying home to catch the Dukes, if you do find yourself listening to them on WDUQ-FM (90.5 on the dial), you're in for a treat. The broadcast team of Ray Goss and Nellie King is worth not paying the price of admission. Goss, who has been broadcasting Dukes' games since 1968, can squeeze more words into a broadcast—intelligibly—than can any other announcer we've heard.

One other Duquesne note: When you're at the Palumbo Center, several times each game you'll see the crowd rise and chant as one, "Shoo Shoo, Rah Rah." It may sound like a weird new mantra, but it's really a cheer developed by Duquesne's No. 1 all-time fan, the late Maurice "Mossie" Murphy.

Robert Morris University

For much of its basketball history, Robert Morris University played at the junior college level. In 1976, however, the Colonials jumped all the way to NCAA Division I— and they did it with flair. The Colonials have reached the NCAA tournament five times since then and have been a mainstay of Division I basketball ever since.

Coached by Mark Schmidt, the Colonials play in the Northeast Conference, which also features such schools as Long Island, Monmouth, St. Francis (New York) and St. Francis (Pennsylvania). Home arena for Robert Morris is the Charles L. Sewall Center for Leadership, a facility that also serves as a business training and meeting hub. Located on the college's Moon Township campus, Sewall Center is only a few miles from Greater Pittsburgh Airport.

While seating capacity at Sewall Center is 3,056, you'll find that tickets on most occasions are readily available. With the top ticket price at about $6.00—kids get in for $2.00—and with free parking in several lots around Sewall Center, you'd be hard pressed to enjoy major college basketball more economically. Season tickets also are available, with costs ranging from $50 to $70. For ticket information, call (412) 299-2403.

When you watch Robert Morris play, you'll find that most fans are students . . . some in outlandish garb. During one recent season, some students were so involved with the game that the officials assessed the Colonials a technical foul for student misbehavior. That's the kind of excitement that will capture you when you watch the Colonials.

Catching the Colonials on the air is a bit more difficult. Their games are broadcast on WPIT-AM (730 on the dial), a station not received uniformly well throughout the region during the evening. Likable veteran Chris Shovlin handles play-by-play. WBGN-TV, a low-power television station, occasionally airs videotaped replays of Colonials games. Check your local cable television listings to see if your system carries WBGN. If you live in Beaver County, you may be able to pick up the station directly over the air.

University of Pittsburgh

The University of Pittsburgh has fielded a men's basketball team in every season since 1910, a remarkable achievement that has carried through several world wars and a variety of other dislocations. It is a proud history that includes 7 All-Americans, 13 appearances in the NCAA tournament, 7 appearances in the National Invitation Tournament. Among the highlights: the magical season of 1973-1974, when the upstart Panthers, largely a home-grown squad led by future NBA star Billy Knight, compiled a 25–4 record, losing in the NCAA tournament's Eastern Regional final to eventual champion North Carolina State.

Coach Jamie Dixon and his Panthers compete in the Big East, one of the premier basketball conferences in the nation.

If you follow the Panthers, you'll enjoy such top teams as Georgetown, Villanova, Connecticut, Syracuse, St. John's, and West Virginia—all conference members—as well as an attractive nonconference schedule. Big East teams typically contend for top national honors, and Pitt is more than competitive in the conference, with a 1987–1988 Big East title to its credit. The brand of basketball you'll see is both fast-paced and physical.

If you're a fan of college basketball, you'll want to catch the Panthers in person in their new arena, the Petersen Events Center, located on the school's upper campus. The "Pete" provides a state-of-the-art, 12,500-seat venue "that promises to be one of the finest college basketball arenas in the country."

When you can't make it to the "Pete," you can follow the Panthers on radio on WTAE-AM, 1250 on the dial, which carries the complete Panthers schedule. Bill Hillgrove and Dick Groat are the capable, veteran broadcast team—they've been at the mike together since 1978. There is no set television schedule, but local stations and cable and broadcast networks find Pittsburgh and the Big East so attractive that they combine to show about a dozen games each season. You'll see games on local broadcast station WTAE-TV, Fox Sports Network, and ESPN.

The ticket policy requires a bit of explanation. When Pittsburgh joined the Big East in 1982, interest in the team skyrocketed, and a seat at a conference game became one of the tougher tickets in town. Day-of-game tickets typically are available for nonconference opponents but may be scarce for Big East foes. Tickets for fieldhouse games are typically less expensive than games at the Mellon Arena, and games against West Virginia and Syracuse usually carry a premium. Single game tickets can usually be had for $20 or less. You can make credit-card purchases over the phone at (800) 643-PITT, and you can access the ticket hotline at (412) 648-PITT.

Season tickets are another matter.

These are available at prices ranging from $210 to $310, but you must make a contribution of at least $1,000 to the school to be eligible for season tickets.

The university maintains several parking lots on its upper campus to accommodate fans, but if the truth be told, parking on the upper campus can be a crunch. A good way to beat that crunch: park on the lower campus, which offers more on-street parking, and ride the campus shuttle bus to the Field House.

FOOTBALL

Pittsburgh Steelers

The romance between the Pittsburgh Steelers and their adoring fans is one of the enduring love affairs of sports. The team was founded in 1933 by the late Arthur J. Rooney, one of the grand old men of the National Football League and one of the game's great sportsmen. He launched the Steelers with money won at the race track, and he remained a sharp and successful handicapper until his death. Success couldn't spoil Rooney. He never moved from his house near Three Rivers Stadium, walked to work each day, gave generously to anyone in need, and "loafed," to use the expression he favored, with the friends he had grown up with.

Rooney was beloved, but the Steelers had a hard time winning until the 1970s, when the team under Coach Chuck Noll won four Super Bowls and became a dynasty. Nine Steelers from that era—including Rooney, Noll, Joe Greene, Jack Ham, Mel Blount, Terry Bradshaw, Franco Harris, Jack Ham, and Mike Webster—have been enshrined in the Pro Football Hall of Fame.

Rooney and Noll are gone, but the Steelers success continues under club President Daniel M. Rooney, Arthur Rooney's son, and Coach Bill Cowher, who led the Steelers to postseason appearances in each of his first six years at the helm, an unprecedented coaching performance. Nor has the fans' ardor flagged a bit. Every Steelers home game since mid-1972 has sold out the 58,729-seat Three Rivers Stadium. The waiting list for season tickets is 6,000 names long.

Like the Pirates, the Steelers have left Three Rivers Stadium. See this chapter's sidebar for details on the Steelers' new stadium.

Because the games are sold out well in advance, the Steelers are able to televise every contest, home or away, preseason, regular season, or postseason. During the regular season, you'll find Steelers games on KDKA-TV (the local CBS affiliate), WPGH (Fox 53), WTAR-TV (the local ABC affiliate), and ESPN, depending on the day and opponent. Since area cable television systems assign these networks different channel numbers, make sure you check local listings to determine where to catch the Steelers.

Steelers radio broadcasts on WTAE-AM (1250 on the dial), flagship of a 46-channel radio network, are a popular local institution themselves. Bill Hillgrove capably handles the play-by-play, but it is longtime color analyst Myron Cope who excites the crowd. Cope invented the "Terrible Towel"—wave it and good things happen for the Steelers—and you'll see them by the thousands at every game. It's not uncommon for fans watching a Steelers telecast to turn down the volume on their television sets so they can listen to Hillgrove and Cope on the radio. If you listen to a few of their broadcasts, you'll find yourself saying things like "Yoi!" and "Okel dokel," and wondering where on earth you could have picked up those expressions.

Since home games are always sold out, traffic and parking can be troublesome. Most Steelers fans are veterans and know the parking rope. If you do manage to come by tickets for a game, make sure you leave home early enough for the obligatory tailgate party. Before Steelers games, the parking lots around the stadium resemble a sprawling picnic grounds, with parties ranging from elaborate catered affairs to simple munchfests

A good place to see the Steelers in person is at their summer-training site—St. Vincent College in Latrobe, about 40 miles east of downtown Pittsburgh.

with center-cut jumbo. What's center-cut jumbo? It's a 'Burgh thing. You'll catch on.

University of Pittsburgh

What do Mike Ditka, Tony Dorsett, and Dan Marino have in common? They all are National Football League greats, and they all played collegiate football at the University of Pittsburgh. The Panthers long have been a major college football power, producing such standouts as Joe Schmidt, Hugh Green, Matt Cavanaugh, Bill Fralic, Bill Maas, and Craig "Ironhead" Hayward, in addition to Ditka, Dorsett, and Marino. In all, 46 Panthers have won All-America honors, ranking Pittsburgh No. 6 among all NCAA Division I-A schools.

Pittsburgh plays in the Big East conference, which means that when Coach Walt Harris and company take the field, they line up against such name opponents as Syracuse, and West Virginia, as well as tough nonconference opponents. Pittsburgh won a national championship behind Dorsett in 1976—its third unanimous national title—and has appeared in 19 bowl games.

The Panthers play at the new football stadium. For three-quarters of a century, the team played at venerable Pitt Stadium on Campus, an antiquated facility that was razed to make room for a new convocation center.

Saturday at the stadium on a glorious fall day is a memorable event, and typically an accessible one. While games with such traditional rivals as Penn State, Notre Dame, and West Virginia can sell out, tickets tend to be available for most games. Ticket prices are $25, with youth discounts offered. For "backyard brawls" against West Virginia and Penn State, ticket prices are higher. You also can purchase season tickets and multigame pack-

Stadium Stats!

Quick—name the third professional franchise to call Pittsburgh's former Three Rivers Stadium home. Steelers, Pirates, and no shame in forgetting—the hapless Maulers of the defunct United States Football League. Hardly a highlight, they went 3–15 in their only season (1984). Blame it on the team's purple and orange color scheme.

Games in the town are played in black and gold and, until its implosion February 11, 2001, on the Tartan then Astro turf at Three Rivers Stadium. For 30 years, this gargantuan yet aesthetically mundane concrete structure hosted some of Pittsburgh's most memorable sports moments, including perhaps the premier call in NFL history, Franco Harris's 1972 "Immaculate Reception."

Three Rivers also saw Roberto Clemente's 3,000th hit; the first World Series night game; four Super Bowl Championship teams; two World Series champions; and for diehard facility fans, the largest crowd ever to see a concert in Pittsburgh—nearly 66,000 for Bruce Springsteen in 1985. But that was then. It took just 19 seconds that February morning for 4,800 pounds of dynamite to put the stadium on the disabled list forever . . . and usher in Pittsburgh's next generation of hallowed sports ground: PNC Park and Heinz Field.

PNC Park: 115 Federal Street on Pittsburgh's North Shore
Tickets: (800) 289–2827; $10 to $35
The Pirates have had five residences in their 116-year history, including the newest domain, PNC Park, which opened April 9, 2001. Ironically, it seats just over 38,000, roughly 3,300 more than Forbes Field, where the "Bucs" played before Three Rivers. Named after the financial institution founded and headquartered here, the park sports an old-time feel whose design intimacy—at the highest point, fans are only 88 feet above the field—contrasts artfully with the scenic view of the city's skyline to create one majestic background for America's pastime.

Add in a riverside location, classic archways, the silkiness of a natural grass surface, an architecture that seems to naturally place it within the cityscape, and the nostalgia permeates like warm apple pie with each crack of the bat. Other features include an outfield picnic area and party pavilion, an outdoor amphitheater, an arcade with a restaurant, an interactive theater and Pirates Hall of Fame, and a 500-person party deck in left field.

In *USA Today* (March 3, 2003), Jay Ahuja, author of *Fields of Dreams: A Guide to Visiting and Enjoying All 30 Major League Ballparks* (Kensington Books), cites PNC Park as one of the top

10 places to watch a game. The charm resonates from the structure right out to the retail and restaurant rows along Federal and General Robinson Streets on the North Side, just across the bridge from the stadium. Parking is fairly plentiful around the facility, but there's added convenience in leaving the car downtown (some garages offer $3.00 game-day rates) and taking the five-minute walk across the Roberto Clemente Bridge, which closes to vehicle traffic during events. Or access the $216 million park by river walk or boat. For $6.00 round-trip, the Gateway Clipper Fleet at Station Square will shuttle you back and forth every 15 to 30 minutes starting two hours before the game and a half hour after it ends.

Heinz Field: 400 Art Rooney Avenue on Pittsburgh's North Shore
Tickets: (412) 323–1200 for the Steelers; (800) 643–PITT (7488) for the Panthers
The ketchup bowl? For the first NFL stadium named after a global food company, such a game may not be far behind. Welcome to Heinz Field, home of the NFL Pittsburgh Steelers and the University of Pittsburgh Panthers, located about a kickoff return from PNC Park. The world's condiments king, Pittsburgh's H.J. Heinz Company, is pouring out a cool $2.85 million per year for 20-year naming

rights to the facility, which features two, 35-foot-tall, 8,000-pound neon, animated ketchup bottles attached to the scoreboard. They dump their virtual contents when the home team reaches the "Red Zone" (20 yards from the end zone).

Like its baseball counterpart, Heinz Field combines two-tiered construction, real grass surface, terrific sight lines, and a horseshoe shape with the open end offering a dramatic downtown view of city highlights such as Point State Park, PPG Place, Fort Pitt Bridge, and Duquesne Incline. The stadium seats close to 65,000 people, about 6,000 more than Three Rivers, but getting a season ticket may be tougher than tackling a 300-pound lineman—the waiting list is 10 years. At Gate B, step inside the Coca-Cola Great Hall, a 4,000-square-foot area of fun, food, and football entertainment—and a celebration of Panthers and Steelers history. Savory concessions include hometown favorites such as Benkovitz Fish and the legendary Primanti Brothers, offering their sandwiches with the fries *inside*. Six interactive displays offer trivia and games and also showcase team memorabilia. Marvel at the Lombardi Trophy columns commemorating the Steelers' four Super Bowl victories. A Steelers Hall of Fame showcases memorabilia from star players.

—Michael J. Dongilli

ages. You can get your tickets by calling (800) 643–PITT and using your credit card. For the status of seats for any game, call the ticket hotline at (412) 648–PITT.

HORSE RACING

Ladbroke at the Meadows

If you've ever thrilled to the beauty of equine athletes as they thunder toward the finish line, then Ladbroke at the Meadows is the place where you'll find that thrill. Located in the Washington County town of Meadow Lands, about 25 miles from downtown Pittsburgh, Ladbroke features live harness racing—the type where the horses pull a sulky with a driver in it—five nights a week during warm-weather months, four nights a week during the winter. The races begin at 6:40 P.M. every Tuesday, Thursday, and Saturday; 4:00 P.M. Friday. If you're not currently a fan, the excitement of track announcer Roger Huston calling the action will convert you in a hurry.

When you come to enjoy the races, you'll find much to do. Ladbroke features a full-service restaurant, a sports bar, and a cafe for lighter fare. The kids will enjoy Ladbroke's pinball arcade.

But for the dedicated horseplayer, the real attraction of Ladbroke is the amazing menu of simulcast races that the track offers. The concept is simple. To enhance its own card, Ladbroke imports races from up to 25 harness and thoroughbred tracks across North America—there's even thoroughbred racing from Australia—and shows them to patrons at monitors placed throughout the facility. You can wager on any or all races at any of the tracks featured. The action typically begins just after noon and usually lasts until about midnight, seven days a week.

That's not all. Ladbroke offers that full racing menu at six wagering and dining facilities in the area. Thus, if you can't make it to the Washington County track, you can visit a Ladbroke facility in Greensburg, New Castle, Harmar, Moon, West Mifflin, or Johnstown and take advantage of the same viewing, wagering, and dining options that patrons at the track are enjoying.

Ladbroke heightens convenience even more by broadcasting its live races—as well as about 100 simulcast races from other tracks—into viewers' homes over satellite and via affiliation with local cable television companies. If your cable company features the Ladbroke Racing Network, or if you acquire the appropriate satellite signal decoder, you'll receive 12 hours of racing each day in the comfort of your home. Plus you can wager by phone by opening a Call-A-Bet account with a cash, check, or credit-card deposit. To do so, call (800) 242–RACE. Ladbroke won't let you bet more than you have in your account, although you can replenish your account at will. If you plan to participate from your home, you can pick up race programs at dozens of neighborhood newsstands and convenience stores.

Finally, the track offers aficionados a high-tech enhancement. If you visit the Web site brisnet.com, you can view real-time betting odds at racetracks across the country.

Your experience at Ladbroke can be as simple or as complicated as you like. Some will find a wagering interest—however modest—heightens the enjoyment of the races. For others, the beauty of equine and human athletes in action will be enjoyment enough. Ladbroke also offers group outings that include such features as a race named for your group and a photo of you and your guests in the winner's circle, posed with the winning horse and driver.

ICE HOCKEY

Pittsburgh Penguins

For many years, the Pittsburgh Penguins were synonymous with their superstar, Mario Lenieux, arguably the greatest National Hockey League performer of all time. When chronic back problems forced Lemieux's retirement at the end of the 1996-1997 season, he went out with a

Getting to the Game

When 55,000 people descend on Heinz Field for a Steeler game, you may be looking for a way to avoid traffic and parking hassles. Port Authority of Allegheny County may have that alternative for you.

PAT operates two special shuttle buses between downtown and the stadium for each Steelers game. The 96C services stops downtown only, while the 96X stops at downtown points and the civic Arena. Cost for the shuttles is 75 cents each way for adults, 35 cents each way for children ages 6 through 11. Kids five and younger ride free.

To reach town, try PAT's special game-day express buses, which depart from these suburban points: Heidelberg/Green Tree, Whitehall, McKeesport, North Hills, South Hills, and Monroeville. Cost ranges from $1.25 to $4.50, depending on the number of zones traversed.

If you really get into bus travel, try PAT's Jerome Bettis Bus Pass, named for the popular Steelers running back nicknamed "The Bus." Buy the pass for $10 and you'll receive free fare on each ride taken on any PAT route all day during Steelers home dates, playoff games included. For information on any of these special plans, call PAT at (412) 442-2000. For baseball and hockey games, PAT bulks up its fleet but has no special routes.

---

flourish, leading the league in scoring for the sixth time and winning First All-Star Team honors for the fifth time. Most important to Penguins fans, he led the club to two Stanley Cups in 1991 and 1992. After retirement, Mario bought the team, ensuring the future of hockey in Pittsburgh.

Yet even during the apex of Lemieux's career, the Penguins were much more than a one-man team; in their Stanley Cup seasons, they played championship-caliber hockey during Lemieux's prolonged injury-related absences. In the P.M. (Post-Mario) era, led by such stars as Jaromir Jagr, they continue to excel as one of the NHL's top clubs.

The Penguins under Coach Eddie Olczyk perform in the Northeast Division of the Eastern Conference. That means they skate against Buffalo, Montreal, Ottawa, and Boston on a regular basis. If the regular season isn't enough hockey for you, you also can catch the Penguins in training; their preseason drills are public and take place at the Iceoplex at Southpointe in Washington County.

Home ice for the Pens is the Mellon Arena, but you won't want to call it that. To local fans, it's "the Igloo." The Arena in downtown Pittsburgh seats 16,958 for hockey and features the world's largest retractable stainless-steel roof. Chances are you won't get to see the roof in action during hockey season.

One of the best features about the Igloo is its accessibility. Many Port Authority of Allegheny County bus routes end in, or depart from, downtown, making it easy to reach or leave the arena by public transportation. If you drive you'll find parking in both the arena lots and in several nearby indoor garages, but parking can get sticky when crowds are large.

Another good idea—get your tickets in advance. Tickets are accessible for many games, but fans turn out in big numbers for the best teams and for contests they consider important. The Pens offer season and partial-season plans as well as dis-counted group packages. For ticket infor-mation, call (412) 642–PENS.

If you can't make it to the Igloo, it's still easy to follow the Pens. WDVE-FM, 102.5 on the dial, carries the complete Penguins schedule. On the television side, regional cable network Fox Sports Pitts-burgh is the main provider, while local broadcast stations WB22 and WPGH/Fox 53 also air a number of games. Among them, they'll provide you with nearly every regular-season match.

You'll get quite a kick out of the broadcast teams of Mike Lange and Paul Steigerwald on television, Matt McConnell and Peter Taglianetti on radio. The veteran Lange, the lead broadcaster since 1976, is not only sharp and swift in his call, but he also has coined such trademark phrases as "Look Out, Loretta," "Scratch My Back With a Hacksaw," "Buy Sam A Drink (And Get His Dog One, Too)," and the immortal "Elvis Has Left the Building," to signal that a game is out of reach. Most of this Lange-Slang has entered the local lexicon. No less a figure than Sophie Masloff, when she was mayor of Pittsburgh and speaking at a Three Rivers Stadium rally, exhorted the crowd to "scratch her back with a hacksaw" in tribute to Lange.

The Penguins maintain a close rela-tionship with their fans through an active community involvement program. Their initiatives include school visits, scholar-ships, development of youth hockey and financial support for nonprofit organiza-tions. Perhaps the most innovative aspect of the program is the Penguins Information Booth at the arena, which nonprofit organizations can use on game days to distribute information to fans. For information about the booth, call (412) 642–1800.

DAY TRIPS AND 🚗
WEEKEND GETAWAYS

We frankly believe that there's so much to see and do in and around Pittsburgh that you'd never need to leave! But for those of you stricken with a case of wanderlust, or just itching to get out in the country, we present a number of destinations for your consideration within a half-day's drive (at most) of the city.

Whether you venture just 30 minutes from your home base, take to the highway for a leisurely drive, or even opt for the express airline service offered locally, there are plenty of fascinating escapes just hours from Pittsburgh.

Some of these lend themselves to the affordable family getaway. Others might have the word "golf" written all over them (and for more focus on that subject, turn to the Golf chapter in this book). Educational exploration is certainly prevalent in the area. So is boosting the economy of several sites in Western Pennsylvania. Finally, a few of the destinations you might consider remind us of romance—dare we say, even reminiscent of the second honeymoon you've put off. Well, now is the time to take it!

The day excursions and weekend trips presented in this chapter fall within approximately three hours of Pittsburgh. From the western communities, count on some extra time when traveling east, and vice versa. The only other caveat is to let go, relax, and enjoy yourself exploring new sights, loading your car with new wares, and sampling fine food, entertainment, and hospitality.

Bon voyage!

ERIE COUNTY

Find out why areas north are Erie-sistible. Roughly three hours from Pittsburgh, Erie County offers something for every member of the family, from amusement parks and water recreation to arts, museums, and fun shopping.

Getting There

Reach the Erie area by taking Interstate 79 north from Pittsburgh. It's a straight shot up one single highway! Once in the area, the Presque Isle Express is a 36-passenger vessel designed to taxi you across the water from Dobbins Landing to Presque Isle (which isn't really an island, but a nice park with a beach). Weather permitting, the water taxi operates seven days a week from 10:00 A.M. until 6:00 P.M. It's wheelchair and bicycle accessible, and maintains a 60-minute schedule.

For more general information about Erie County and environs, write the Erie Convention & Visitors Bureau at 208 East Bayfront Parkway, Erie, PA 16507, or call (800) 524–ERIE (3743).

Erie County Attractions

As you might have guessed from the name, Erie County borders Lake Erie, one of the five Great Lakes, and the lake is an integral piece of life here. You'll want to explore the waters of Lake Erie, and what better way to do it than at the Erie Maritime Museum, 150 East Front Street, (814) 452-2744, on the bayfront.

At the Erie Zoo & Botanical Gardens, West 38th Street, (814) 864-4091, kids can visit 300 animals exhibited indoors and out. Especially enticing are the dual-level otter exhibit, the white Bengal tiger, and the African wild-bird exhibit. Sightseeing train rides are also popular.

Summer is always fun at Waldameer Park and Water World, found at the entrance to Presque Isle State Park, (888) PA-PARKS, where you'll experience more than 75 rides, slides, and attractions. There are fun games, great gift houses, snacks, and food to help pass the time. Conneaut Lake Park, 12832 Center Street, Conneaut Lake (25 miles southwest of Erie), (814) 382-5115, also boasts rides, festivals, and family fun.

Presque Isle State Park, (814) 883-7424, has been rated by *Birder's World* magazine as one of the top birding spots in the country. In addition, you'll find approximately 13 miles of hiking trails in the park (bicycles are not permitted on the hiking trails). A good place to begin your visit is at the Stull Interpretive Center, located near Barracks Beach. Here you'll learn about the park's many resources, including its access for people with disabilities. There's no charge to enter the park.

The Presque Isle Lighthouse, in the park, was built in 1872 and first lit on July 12, 1873. The U.S. Coast Guard still maintains it with its flashing white light. Visitors aren't allowed inside the lighthouse. At Misery Bay and the Perry Monument, you'll find the temporary home of the fleet of ships commanded by Commodore Oliver Hazard Perry in the Battle of Lake Erie. Six of his nine vessels, including two brigs—the *Niagara* and the *Lawrence*—were constructed from local trees along Erie Bay. It was his victory and the War of 1812 that assured we didn't become Canadians!

The Lake Shore Railway Museum, 31 Wall Street at Robinson Street, (814)

825-2724, welcomes visitors Wednesday through Sunday from Memorial Day weekend through Labor Day weekend, in addition to Saturday and Sunday in September and October. Admission is free of charge to relive the days of the steam locomotive-powered trains that ran along Pennsylvania's picturesque Northeast countryside. Walk through a 1926 "Nightstar" sleeping car built by Pullman and see the Centralized Traffic Control board, built in 1943, showing how a single dispatcher controlled large stretches of track at one time.

A day trip for the grown-ups wouldn't be complete without a sampling of Pennsylvania wine. Stop at the Penn Shore Winery & Vineyards, 10225 East Lake Road, Route 5, (814) 725-8688, for it's one of the largest and longest established wineries in the state. Mazza Vineyards, 11815 East Lake Road, (814) 725-8695, offers wine-tasting tours daily, seven days a week, year-round.

Erie County Shopping

Are you in the mood for souvenirs? The Nature Shop, at Presque Isle State Park (see write-up above), has books, field guides, and other nature-related items for you to purchase and enjoy from your day trip. Proceeds benefit the state park.

Also, Penn Shore Wines (see above) can ship its vintage, table, and sparkling wines in Pennsylvania via United Parcel Service (UPS), if you don't want to take the bottles home with you.

Each season the Mason Farms Country Market, 839 Peninsula Drive, (814) 833-9933, brings exciting treats and experiences to store customers. Choose from a large selection of perennials, annuals, and shrubs in the spring, fresh fruit and vegetables over the summer months, pumpkins around Halloween, and country crafts for Christmas.

The Bayfront Gallery, part of the waterfront revitalization, is Erie's artists' co-op located at 17 East Dobbins Landing, (814)

455-6632. It's open seasonally for its unique blend of antique wares and local artistry.

Customary shopping at chain establishments and some local merchants is found at the Mill Creek Mall, Upper Peach Street, (814) 868-9000. Boasting a Kaufmann's, Elder-Beerman, JC Penney, Sears, and more than 200 specialty shops, it's no wonder you could spend the entire day shopping. In fact, the entire Upper Peach Street area has been peppered with more stores and restaurants (see below).

Erie County Accommodations

Featuring in-room movies, coffeemakers, an outdoor pool, laundry facilities, and airport transportation, the Holiday Inn Downtown Erie, 18 West 18th Street, (814) 456-2961, assures you'll be at the center of activity. Enjoy a free breakfast buffet with your room.

The Bel-Aire Hotel, 2800 West Eighth Street, (814) 833-1116, has an indoor, heated pool, Jacuzzi, and fitness center for its guests, as well as restaurants and room service. At Hampton Inn North, 3041 West 12th Street, (814) 835-4200, the swimming is outdoors, but you can enjoy a complimentary continental breakfast, free HBO, and airport limousines. The Hampton Inn South, 8050 Old Oliver Road, (814) 866-6800, is accessible to Interstate 90 and nearby I-79. Avalon Hotel, 16 West 10th Street, (814) 459-2220, is in the heart of downtown Erie, near the Erie Art Museum and the Erie Playhouse. And, for business travel, the Courtyard by Marriott, I-90, exit 6 (Scott Drive), boasts a full-service hotel with 110 guest rooms, an indoor pool, and several suites. Right next door is the Ambassador Banquet & Conference Center, which will accommodate up to 500 people for business and social functions. Call (814) 866-8300 for both hotels.

Families might prefer renting a cottage near Presque Isle State Park. Presque Isle Cottage Court, 320 Peninsula Drive, (814) 833-4956, offers one-, two-, or three-bedroom individual and deluxe cottages, all with kitchenettes, carpeting, private baths, and porches, and some with living rooms as well as decks. There's even a central playground for the kids.

Erie County Restaurants

Oh, the waters—and what better way to experience the wonder of Lake Erie than on a dinner cruise aboard *The Victorian Princess*. Leisurely dinner sailings are offered in Victorian style from April 1 through November 1. Cost is $29.95 per person for dinner cruises. Group and children's rates are also available. For reservations, call ahead at (814) 459-9696. Dinner (as well as sightseeing only) cruises board at Dobbins Landing.

You can sample various cuisines at area restaurants. Hibachi Japanese Steak House, 3000 West 12th Street, (814) 838-2495, features food as the name implies. As we mentioned in the shopping description, restaurants have been part of the Upper Peach Street expansion, adding chains such as Don Pablos, Max & Erma's, and the newest site for Quaker Steak & Lube (read a description in Lawrence and Mercer Counties, below). Pufferbelly Restaurant, 414 French Street, (814) 454-1557, operates out of an old Erie firehouse. Spinner McGee's Steakhouse, 4940 Peach Street, (814) 886-7746, is in an old railroad car, and features Western ambience.

Dock your boats near Dobbins Landing for dinner at Rum Runners, (814) 455-4292, or sit on the veranda at Smuggler's Wharf, (814) 459-4273. There's also the Waterfront Seafood & Steakhouse, (814) 459-0606, with seating on three decks. In addition, there are plenty of casual, family-oriented eateries, among them Applebee's, Damon's, Eat 'n Park, Perkins, and TGI Friday's at numerous locations throughout Erie County.

LAWRENCE AND MERCER COUNTIES

What you know of Lawrence and Mercer Counties may be through your children, as each fall, another mass exodus begins for families with college students attending Westminster, Grove City, and Thiel Colleges, the Penn State Shenango campus, and nearby Slippery Rock University. Perhaps you've noticed the beauty of the farm fields on your trips here, but never stopped to truly enjoy the countryside. Maybe you've visited a shop or two, but you haven't taken the time to explore the hidden treasures off the beaten path.

For more information on traipsing through Lawrence and Mercer Counties, call the Lawrence County Tourist Promotion Agency at (724) 654–8408, or the Mercer County Tourist Agency at (800) 637–2370.

Getting There

From Pittsburgh, you can reach these counties by driving north on I-79, Route 19, or Route 60, if you're starting out from Pittsburgh's west suburbs. Route 208 runs between the towns of New Wilmington and Grove City, crossing over I-79.

Mercer and Lawrence County Attractions

If you thought Tara was found only in the South, guess again. Tours of Tara—A Country Inn, nestled in the little village of Clark, outside Sharon—are popular for day-trippers. Visitors peruse the antique furniture, books, and an original jacket worn by Vivian Leigh's Scarlet O'Hara in *Gone with the Wind*. There's an antique slave cradle and many other rare finds. The custom-made glass doors in the entry hall were handcrafted and beveled by Bob Lutz & Sons of New Castle, and most definitely add to the elegance of the man-

sion (see more about Tara below in Accommodations).

If you're like most visitors, you'll want to allow time to explore the Wendell August Forge, 620 Madison Avenue, Grove City, established in 1923 in Brockway before moving in 1932 to its current location. You can't miss the signs, well placed along the major routes into town. Free tours are available, but to make sure the forge is open when you want to visit, it's best to call (724) 458-8360 or (800) 923-4438.

The forge is one of the few remaining in the country that continue to produce forged aluminum, pewter, bronze, sterling, and silver articles entirely by hand, using no production machinery. The showroom/museum houses a historical collection of artifacts and a complete line of giftware that has been commissioned by corporate executives, leading companies, even the U.S. Congress. Visitors get to see the artisans hammering and chiseling these art forms when they take the free, self-guided tour.

Mercer and Lawrence County Shopping

Adventurous shoppers seeking the best prices will track down the authentic Amish shops that make a trip north fun in itself. Visitors can ponder a selection of quilt supplies and fabrics, baby and children's shoes, and have also been known to drive to the Amish harness shops for their custom-made saddles and leather goods. If you get lost, ask the locals to head you on your way to your next stop, since many of these are tucked off on back roads in private homes, without noticeable signage to guide you. (See the Amish Close-up in this chapter.)

Market Street in New Wilmington is the center of retail activity with crafts, antiques, and gift merchandise. Don't miss the New Wilmington Collection of Artisans, 205 South Market Street, (724) 946-2310, for its vast array of handcrafted gifts and Amish furniture. The Quilting Bee, 126 South Market Street, offers quilting supplies, colorful fabrics, and classes too. For those in search of antiques, head to Nest Egg Antiques, 139 South Market Street, where you'll also find J.G. McGill's local artwork.

If you take I-79 and Route 208 to New Wilmington, you'll drive through Volant, where you can't miss The Volant Mill, a major tourist stop featuring crafts and gifts. Built in 1812, it operated as a gristmill and flour mill until 1963. Today it sits across the street from the minimall of refurbished train shops. (See the Shopping chapter for more.)

Downtown Sharon, sometimes referred to as the world's largest small town, is full of shopping. It's known for the Winner, 32 West State Street, which owners Jim and Donna Winner proclaim to be the world's largest off-price fashion store; Reyer's, City Centre, which locals say is the world's largest shoe store, claiming to stock every size; Daffin's Chocolate Kingdom, 496 East State Street, where candy making is an art; and Kraynak's, 2525 East State Street, with special Christmas and Easter displays. For more traditional types of chain stores, head to the Shenango Valley Mall located on Routes 18 and 62 in Hermitage. Anchor stores include Kaufmann's, JC Penney, and Sears.

Of course, if you want to shop until you are absolutely exhausted or spent (literally!), then head to the Prime Outlets along I-79 and Route 208. Here you'll find every type of store you could possibly imagine, and prices that sometimes can't be beat. (See the Shopping chapter for more details.)

Mercer and Lawrence County Accommodations

With so much to see, you're most likely looking for a place to rest your weary feet. Sprawling development has brought along with it a choice of popular chain motels and hotels, usually clustered off Interstates 79 and 80. But don't overlook the small and elegant, the rural and charming. Several bed-and-breakfast establishments have thrived, offering a delightful alternative for guests.

At the most elegant end of the spectrum is Tara—A Country Inn at 2844 Lake Road, Clark, (724) 962-3535 or (800) 782-2803.

A home whose refurbishing was inspired by the movie *Gone with the Wind*, Tara is a graceful 1854 antebellum home—the embodiment of the Old South. Purchased in 1984 by innkeepers Jim and Donna Winner, it's a frequent stop for travelers who want to tour the grounds and mansion, or dine in one of three restaurants.

Visiting Tara isn't just a culinary experience, or tourist stop to tour. There's a little history lesson as well as your guide tells you about the property, including the formal gardens overlooking the beautiful 450-acre Shenango Lake. No tour is complete without walking through the mansion, a virtual museum of rare and priceless antiques, works of art, and collectibles, many of which the owners purchased on trips abroad.

Each room is decorated differently—many with canopy beds, crystal lamps, marble fireplaces, and sunken whirlpools. Guests enjoy swimming in the indoor spa, sipping afternoon tea on the sunporch, or curling up with a favorite book or videotape checked out of the library.

The Winners own not only Tara, but also the Buhl Mansion in Sharon, Mercer County. An art gallery, guesthouse, and spa, this home was built in 1890, and it's listed on the National Register of Historical Homes. The grand oak staircase ascends to the second and third floors. Each suite has a gas fireplace and luxurious bath. For reservations, call (724) 962-3535 or (800) 782-2803.

In recent years, several chain hotels have established themselves, due in large

CLOSE-UP

New Wilmington's Old Order Amish

Beyond the bonnets and wide-brimmed hats, the plain white farmhouses, and the strict code of conduct, the Old Order Amish thrive in the New Wilmington area, approximately one hour north of Pittsburgh. Visitors come to browse in the craft shops, ponder a carpenter's handiwork, or merely enjoy the drive through farm pastures and life at its simplest.

While there are many retailers displaying Amish-made goods, adventurous shoppers seek out their own best buys directly from these creators of country quilts, custom-made leather saddles, and solid wood rockers, cradles, toys, or complete dining and bedroom sets. In warmer weather, you'll spot Amish women selling homemade baked goods at roadside stands.

For the Amish, their cottage industries are just that. Many make their living from the bounty of the land or the skill of their hands, using diesel power (with car batteries to start their equipment) instead of electricity and horse-drawn buggies and farm equipment rather than cars and tractors. The average family boasts 8 to 10 children, and hard work is a way of life.

part to the tourist attractions and the outlet shipping. Spend the night in West Middlesex at the Radison Hotel Sharon, off I-80, on Route 18, (724) 528-2501, and relax in the heated indoor pool. Right across the street is the Holiday Inn Express and Suites of Sharon/Hermitage, (724) 982-4600, with its golf packages and outdoor pool facility as well as the Comfort Inn Shenango Valley, Route 18 and Wilson Road, (724) 342-7200, which has an indoor heated pool, whirlpool suites, and complimentary breakfasts available.

The Howard Johnson Lodge & Restaurant, 835 Perry Highway (Route 19) in Mercer, (800) 542-7674, is just 10 minutes from the outlet shops. In Grove City itself, choose from bed-and-breakfasts such as Lynnrose, (724) 458-6425, at 114 West Main Street, or the Snow Goose Inn, (724) 458-6425, at 112 East Main Street. The Snow Goose is across the street from

Grove City College, while Lynnrose is within a short walking distance. The Ameri-Host Inn, a two-story hotel at 1924 Leesburg Road, Grove City, (724) 748-5836, boasts a pool, whirlpool, and saunas.

Within New Wilmington, charming bed-and-breakfasts abound as well. Consider the Beechwood Inn, an old Civil War home with Victorian decor, found on the road by the same name (175 Beechwood Road to be exact). When your day is complete, sit on one of three covered porches at this inn. Call Beechwood at (724) 946-2342.

Gabriels' Bed & Breakfast at 174 Waugh Avenue, (724) 946-3136, is another Victorian romantic getaway featuring featherbeds, and Behm's Bed & Breakfast nearby at 166 Waugh Avenue, (724) 946-8641, is a gem just blocks from Westminster College. Here you're treated to Nancy Behm's watercolor studio in this 1895 home.

Amish education takes place in a one-room schoolhouse where children learn reading, writing, and arithmetic. Religion is taught in the home, not in churches, as small groups gather in homes one Sunday and visit other Amish the next.

Baptism is saved for adulthood, not undertaken at birth. So vital is this passage that teenagers yearn to experience the English world, as they call it, before the commitment is made. Finding young people to hang around with is hardly a problem here, as New Wilmington is also home to Westminster College, a four-year liberal arts college related to the Presbyterian Church.

As you drive along Route 18 (north from New Castle or south from Sharon), you'll spot Amish homes and farms by the tell-tale white sheets tied back as curtains in the windows. New Wilmington's Amish are entrepreneurial in spirit, but far less so than their neighbors across the state. There are signs, but they won't knock you over.

Most establishments are open year-round except on Sundays and major holidays. Do stop in and chat, but please don't take pictures at close distances. The Amish prefer to live in the world; they just don't like to be of the world. They're a friendly, honest, and hard-working group of people!

Mercer and Lawrence County Restaurants

At Tara, guests can enjoy Ashley's for gourmet dining and Stonewall's Tavern for lighter fare, including great steaks and salads. Ashley's menu features wine selections honored by the coveted *Wine Spectator* Award of Excellence. Call for reservations at (724) 962-3535.

Quaker Steak & Lube, a popular watering hole famous for its atomic wings and unusual display of race cars and auto memorabilia, is found in the heart of downtown Sharon, 101 Chestnut Street, (724) 981-7221, as well as in Hermitage, on East State Street, (724) 983-8646. Locals call it "the Lube."

Likewise, the Iron Bridge Inn, (724) 748-3626, is popular for its good food and rustic charm. Despite the name, there's no lodging here, just a restaurant that bills itself as "foodmerchants and brewmasters." Conveniently located on Route 19 between Westminster and Grove City, it attracts tourists by day, college crowds by night. Also along Route 19 is Rachel's Roadhouse, (724) 748-3193, a sister restaurant literally just down the road, between the Iron Bridge and Route 208.

Longtime area visitors still enjoy pleasant meals at the Tavern in New Wilmington, (724) 946-2020, where the menu is read aloud, or the Penn Grove Hotel, 129 East Pine Street, Grove City, (724) 458-7400, established long before any golden arches or popular family chains dotted the landscape. At the Penn Grove Hotel, enjoy a Friday evening seafood buffet or a Sunday buffet from noon to 3:00 P.M.

LAUREL HIGHLANDS

This scenic expanse in Southwestern Pennsylvania encompasses a broad stretch of more than 100 miles throughout several counties to the south and east of Pittsburgh. With the region named in deference to the mountain laurel, you could be in the Laurel Highlands if you're in Greene, Fayette, Somerset, even Westmoreland Counties. Since this last county is a part of this book's general coverage area, I'll cover only the highlights here. Indeed exploring the Laurel Highlands for a day, or perhaps several, is a pleasant option.

The Laurel Highlands is a vast area for day-trippers, but if you need assistance, write the Laurel Highlands Visitors Bureau at 120 East Main Street, Ligonier, PA 15658, or call (724) 238-5661.

Getting There

There are several routes to take to the Laurel Highlands, depending upon where you depart and which area you'd like to visit. The Pennsylvania Turnpike is popular, with exits at Donegal, Somerset, and New Stanton. Traveling along Route 30 or U.S. Route 40 (the former National Road) in Fayette County will also take you to many of the sites described here.

Laurel Highlands Attractions

Fallingwater, in Mill Run, (724) 329-8501, was once the weekend retreat of department store owner Edgar J. Kaufmann and his wife, Liliane. Tucked away in the Laurel Highlands, architect Frank Lloyd Wright designed this outstanding example of organic architecture. Though there is much walking and many stairs to climb, the curious love to tour Fallingwater. Similarly, Kentuck Knob, located at Chalk Hill, Ohiopyle, (724) 329-1901, is another of Frank Lloyd Wright's creations, though less popular than Fallingwater. Regular tours of Fallingwater are available (see the Architecture and Attractions chapters for details). Reservations are required to guarantee admission.

Travel back to the French and Indian War at Fort Necessity National Battlefield, along U.S. 40, (724) 329-5512, in Fayette County just southeast of Uniontown. This became George Washington's "fort of necessity" because a large force of French and Indians attacked his army of 400.

Ligonier, in the far reaches of Westmoreland County, is a charming town, known for "the Diamond" town square with its old-fashioned gazebo, ice-cream parlor, and antiques and craft shops. But most historic is Fort Ligonier, named in honor of Sir John Ligonier, a British commander-in-chief. In 1946, the Fort Ligonier Association was charged with re-creating the 1758–1766 garrison, and with building a museum. Though never occupied by the enemy, this fort, and its three-day festival every October, commemorates the battle at Fort Ligonier in 1758 during the French and Indian War. Fort Ligonier Days (see Annual Events) features craftspeople, merchant sidewalk sales, entertainment, and a huge Saturday parade. Of course, there's plenty of great food to sample.

Families will love the beautiful setting of Idlewild Park, (724) 238-3666, with its theme areas, especially suited for kids who want to have fun (see Kidstuff). Another area of noted interest in the Laurel Highlands is Seven Springs (see "Skiing" in Recreation). For thrills of another kind, you won't want to miss white-water rafting on the Youghiogheny River at Ohiopyle (see Attractions). In addition, there are miles of excellent bike and walking trails throughout the highlands.

The Laurel Highlands also boasts the largest natural cave north of the Mason-Dixon line. Laurel Caverns, 5 miles west of US 40 on Caverns Road near Uniontown, offers guided and self-guided tours through this limestone catacomb cave with more than 2 miles of passages. Visitors should dress warmly, as the average temperature hovers around 52 degrees Fahrenheit year-round. For information, call (724) 438-3003.

Laurel Highlands Shopping

Outlet shopping in Somerset and Mt. Pleasant is plentiful, but you'll also find many small shops scattered around the Laurel Highlands. Major malls, specialty merchants, and factory outlets are covered in the Shopping chapter; it's best to include this reading in your research.

In Fayette County, you'll find the Uniontown Mall at 1368 West Main Street, (724) 437-9411. In Connellsville, shop at Youghiogheny Station: Glass & Gallery at 900 West Crawford Avenue, (724) 628-0332. It's the beautifully refurbished P&LE passenger station just minutes from Fallingwater, Ohiopyle, Nemacolin Woodlands, and Greensburg. The shop offers everything glass, from paperweights to perfume bottles and lamps. Of course, the tourist attractions maintain their own gift shops, which you'll want to browse for souvenirs or unique gifts, including Frank Lloyd Wright references and works at Fallingwater.

Finally, it's Christmas year-round at the Christmas Shop and Countree Cupboard along US 40 East, Chalk Hill. Call the store at (724) 439-6500.

Laurel Highlands Restaurants

In Somerset, the Oakhurst Tea Room on Route 31, (814) 443-2897, established in 1933, is famous for its smorgasbord and desserts. There's a Friday seafood buffet, and Sunday brunch among other items on the menu. Seven Springs Mountain Resort boasts five restaurants, ranging from snacks at the coffee shop to elegant dining at Helen's, (800) 452-2223.

Look for the innkeeper's menu selections at the Mountain View Inn, (724) 834-5300. Favorites include salmon Oscar, lobster Delmonico, and scallops of lamb with apple butter. Family-style meals are served

If you plan to shop in a traditional Amish establishment, do arrive well before dusk, since there are no electric lights to help you size up the merchandise.

on Sundays. There are also health-conscious menu items and early bird specials.

Vallozzi's, approximately 4 miles east of the U.S. Route 199 junction, on Route 30 East near Greensburg, features northern Italian specialties for lunch or dinner. However, it's closed on major holidays and Sundays. Call for reservations at (724) 836-7663.

Nemacolin Woodlands offers three full-service restaurants, as well as casual corners to catch a bite. At Lautrec, the menu is French and on the expensive side, with such appetizers as escargots and entrees such as chateaubriand or roast rack of lamb. The Golden Trout lunch menu is very reasonable in price, yet dinner is moderately expensive. The Caddy Shack is also a good place for lunch in a moderate price range. Take the kids to the Hungry Moose Café or P. J.'s Pizza and Ice Cream Parlor for soup, salads, sandwiches, and a children's menu at relatively inexpensive prices. (For a much more detailed listing of Nemacolin, see the Accommodations chapter.)

For more casual dining in a relaxed setting, head to the Sun Porch Restaurant along US 40 in the Hopwood Business District, east of Uniontown, (724) 439-5734. River's Edge Cafe in Confluence features both indoor and outside dining for lunch and dinner. Call for seasonal operating hours, (814) 395-5059.

Laurel Highlands Accommodations

Indeed because much of the Laurel Highlands exists in and around the Pennsylvania Turnpike and other major highways, accommodations are plentiful. Among the highlights, however, is Mountain View Inn, conveniently located between Greensburg and Latrobe in central Westmoreland County. Guest rooms are all unique, some with king-size beds, whirlpool tubs, and fireplaces. Some have the elegant formality of the 18th century, while others are early American in charm. It's the perfect venue for a romantic weekend. To book a room call (724) 834-5300.

Seven Springs Mountain Resort (see the Accommodations chapter) is certainly an option as well as the Holiday Inn, 202 Harmon Street, Somerset, (814) 445-9611, or the Hampton Inn, at 324 Laurel Crest Road, (814) 445-9161. In addition to the resort and spa setting of Fayette County's Nemacolin Woodlands, you might also be interested in the Summit Inn Mountain Resort at the Summit in Farmington, (724) 438-8594.

ALTOONA/STATE COLLEGE/ JOHNSTOWN AREA

This area an hour or two east of Pittsburgh is popular for day trips, especially for Penn State fans venturing in the fall to Nittany Lion football games. While the area is accessible for a day, why not stay the night and make it a weekend?

To obtain a visitor's map or area information, call the Allegheny Mountains Convention and Visitors Bureau at (800) 84-ALTOONA. In State College, the staff of the Central Pennsylvania Convention and Visitors Bureau is available at (800) 358-5466. For specific Johnstown infor-

For a more extensive listing of bed-and-breakfasts throughout the region, write to the Western Pennsylvania Bed & Breakfast Association at RD#2, 151 Bennett Drive, Ellwood City, PA 16117, or visit their Web site at www.western pabandb.com.

mation, contact the Greater Johnstown/ Cambria County Convention and Visitors Bureau at (800) 237-8590.

Getting There

There are several routes to take to these destinations. If you're headed to Altoona and State College from Pittsburgh, follow Route 22 east and Route 200/Interstate 99 north to Altoona and Blair County. Continue on Route 220/I-99 and make a right onto Route 322 for your destination of State College.

En route to Johnstown, follow Route 22 east and you'll find the signs for Johnstown long before Altoona and State College. You could also reach Johnstown going north on U.S. Route 219 from the Pennsylvania Turnpike.

Altoona/State College/ Johnstown Attractions

The Frost Entomological Museum, Headhouse III, (814) 863-2865, in State College has more than 500,000 insects and arthropods, all well preserved and labeled for public display. Each September, highlights at the Great Insect Fair include cockroach races, an insect zoo, and honey extracting and tasting. Also in State College, the Matson Museum of Anthropology, in the Carpenter Building, (814) 865-3853, tracks human evolution with a genetics exhibit, artifacts, needlework, and ceramics of far ranging cultures. Pennsylvania's prehistoric treasures are found here as well.

Just minutes from I-80 in Nittany Lion Country is Penn's Cave, Centre Hall, (814) 364-1664, filled with glittering stalactites and stalagmites reminiscent of national tourist attractions. You tour this all-water cavern by boat, learning the legend of Indian princess Nitanee, from whom the Penn State Nittany Lion was named.

Speaking of the Nittany Lion, Penn State's mascot since 1904, stop at the Nittany Lion Shrine near the recreation building, on campus. This landmark was created by Heinz Warneke in 1940 from a 13-ton block of Indiana limestone. During the second week of July each year, plan to browse the Central Pennsylvania Festival of the Arts.

Altoona's Horseshoe Curve, 1300 Ninth Avenue, (814) 946-0834, is a historic landmark that tells the story of how railroads were the key in coast-to-coast commerce. The challenge of carrying the Pennsylvania Railroad Mainline over the mountainous terrain was met with the construction of the Horseshoe Curve. You can board a train, say in Pittsburgh, and ride along to see this engineering marvel that was carved out of a mountainside to help trains cross the steep mountain pass. Young rail fans will enjoy the journey, and adults will appreciate the view, as well as the amenities of the visitor center, including shops and the Railroaders Memorial Museum, 1300 Ninth Avenue, (888) 425-8666, (814) 946-0834. Every member of the family will enjoy and learn something about railroad history from the interactive displays here.

Lakemont Park & The Island Waterpark, I-99, Frankstown Road exit, Altoona, (800) 434-8006, offers more than 30 rides and attractions, go-karts, miniature golf, and picnic facilities.

To learn the devastation of natural disaster, set out for the Johnstown Flood Museum, 304 Washington Street, Johnstown, (814) 539-1889, where state-of-the-art exhibits and an Academy Award-winning documentary re-create the powerful force that swept through town in May 1889. The Johnstown Flood National Memorial overlooks the ruins of the South Fork Dam, which burst that May 31. It was indeed one of the worst, if not the worst, flood in American history. The Grandview Cemetery there is the plot where 777 unidentified victims of the flood are buried in the Plot of the

Unknown. No admission is charged, and it's open daily 10:00 A.M. to 5:00 P.M.

The Johnstown Inclined Plane, found at Route 56 and Johns Street, (814) 536-1816, was built in 1891, and is one of the steepest vehicular inclines in the world. It is 996 feet long with a 71 percent grade. Witness the spectacular Johnstown view from the observation deck.

Altoona/State College/ Johnstown Shopping

In State College, head to the shops along College Avenue. In addition, if you purchase items at the Penn State Bookstore, (814) 863-0205, your purchases directly benefit Penn State scholarships. At the Creamery, 12 Borland Laboratory, University Park, (814) 865-7535, sample and take home some of Penn State's famous ice cream, mushrooms, and cheeses. At Mount Nittany Vineyards & Winery, 300 Houser Road, Centre Hall, (814) 466-6373, you can sip and purchase local wine.

There are specialty shops in Historic Hollidaysburg, (814) 695-7543. Also in the area is the Slinky Toy Outlet at James Industries, found on the Beaver Street Extension, Hollidaysburg, (814) 695-5681, home to the original Slinky toy and many other souvenirs. Take the self-guided tour of Benzel's Pretzel Bakery, 5200 Sixth Avenue, Altoona, (814) 942-5062, ending up with samples and a chance to shop in the outlet store. Boyer Candy Factory Outlet & Emporium, 821 17th Street, (814) 944-9401, contains gift baskets, tins, baking ingredients, and of course, lots of candy for those family members with a sweet tooth!

Johnstown offers shoppers the Richland Mall at 3200 Elton Road as well as the Johnstown Galleria, along US 219, with more than 100 specialty shops. In addition, there is lots of shopping along Johnstown's Scalp Avenue. Twenty minutes south, you'll find outlet shopping in Somerset (see the Shopping chapter).

Altoona/State College/Johnstown Accommodations

In State College, many opt for the Nittany Lion Inn, 200 West Park Avenue, (814) 865-8500, located near the Nittany Lion Shrine sculpture. Others head to Toftrees Resort and Conference Center, One Country Club Lane, (814) 234-8000, featuring designer guest rooms, golf villa suites, four-star golf, tennis, and swimming. The Atherton Hotel, 125 South Atherton Street, (814) 231-2100, is just a block from campus. Located downtown, and also a block away from PSU is the Days Inn Penn State, 240 South Pugh Street, (814) 238-8454, with its heated, indoor pool, sauna, tanning beds, free weights, and Nautilus equipment for guests.

If you're looking for a bed-and-breakfast establishment, the Fairmount, 234 West Fairmount Avenue, (814) 237-1101, is within walking distance of the PSU campus and downtown. Ten miles away, Reynolds Mansion, 101 West Linn Street, Bellefonte, (800) 899-3929, is Victorian with fireplaces, whirlpool tubs, private baths, and a billiards room.

The Holiday Inn, 250 Market Street, Johnstown, (814) 535-7777, is conveniently located at the intersection of Route 56 and U.S. 219. It's within walking distance of the flood museum and inclined plane, and boasts an indoor pool, hot tub, and exercise room. Just east of US 219, stay at the Comfort Inn, 455 Theatre Drive, (814) 266-3678. While the indoor heated pool is small, some rooms have microwaves, radios, and refrigerators. Special amenities include the free breakfast and newspaper.

Bed-and-breakfast establishments are also available for a quiet stay in Johnstown. One mile off of US 219, you'll find the Iron Bridge Bed & Breakfast, (814) 845-2106, with five rooms in a secluded, wooded setting. The Iron Bridge is wheelchair accessible. The Windmill Bed &

Breakfast, 145 Hostetler Road, Johnstown, (814) 269-4625, boasts a full bath with skylight, equipped kitchen, large great room, and scenic gardens.

Altoona/State College/Johnstown Restaurants

At Toftrees Resort, (814) 234-8000, there are three restaurants—the Down Under Steak House, the 19th Hole Bar and Grill, and Le Papillon—for special functions and occasions.

At the Allen Street Grill, 100 West College Avenue, (814) 231-GRILL, entrees are served in the ambience of the restaurant's historic porch overlooking downtown. Mario & Luigi's, 114 South Garner Street, (814) 237-0374, has wood-burning ovens and rotisserie in view, health-conscious menu items, and carry-out service available. There's another Mario & Luigi's located at 1272 North Atherton Street, (814) 234-4273. Whisker's Lounge and Courtyard at the Nittany Lion Inn features a pub menu (see listing above).

The Tavern Restaurant, 220 East College Avenue, (814) 238-6116, is another popular pick for American cuisine. Here, you'll find photos of Penn State and Pennsylvania on the walls.

Native to Penn State's Happy Valley is Zimm's Family Restaurant, 2541 East College Avenue, (814) 234-2447, with a children's menu, carry-out service, salad bar, and all-you-can-eat daily specials.

At the Incline Station Pub & Restaurant, 709 Edgehill Drive, Johnstown, (814) 536-7550, you can dine at the top of the world's steepest incline. At the time of printing, the Incline Station was closed for renovations until further notice. Surf 'n' Turf Inn, 100 Valley Pike, Johnstown, (814) 536-9250, specializes in steaks and fresh seafood.

Within these areas of Altoona, State College, and Johnstown, there are plenty of casual, family-oriented, and inexpensive chain restaurants as well.

CLEVELAND

Approximately two hours from Pittsburgh, a drive northwest into Ohio brings you to Cleveland. Yes, the rivalry among football fans is fierce, with the Cleveland Browns pro football team back in the league. But putting those feelings aside, there's plenty to do for families, business travelers, and anyone who wants to see a different set of scenery.

To obtain a visitor's guide to the area, or any additional information, contact the Convention and Visitor's Bureau of Greater Cleveland at (216) 621-4110 or (800) 321-1001.

Getting There

Cleveland is easily accessible from several major interstate highways. From Pittsburgh, take the Pennsylvania Turnpike west to the Ohio Turnpike and continue on Ohio 76 until you join Interstate 77 north. I-80 will also lead you to I-77.

Cleveland Attractions

The Rock and Roll Hall of Fame and Museum, 1 Key Plaza, opened in 1995, with improvements in 1998, to provide information on each of the Hall of Fame inductees. Multimedia productions combine film footage, music, interviews, animation, and still photography to tell the stories of these famous musicians. During the holidays and peak tourist periods, advance reservations are available by calling (800) 493-ROLL.

Amusement parks are popular in Cleveland, especially Cedar Point in nearby Sandusky. Power Point, the newest attraction at this park, opened in 1998. It's the tallest of its kind in the world, an amusement thriller consisting of four towers rising 240 feet, topped with connecting arches. Two of the towers blast riders up, and two will plunge them back down at 50 mph! Get wet at

Soak City, and take the little ones to Berenstain Bear Country, Kiddy Kingdom Oceana, and the petting zoo. For details and hotel packages, call (419) 627-2350.

Six Flags/Geauga Lake in Aurora is located on Ohio 43, 9 miles north of the Ohio Turnpike, at exit 13, (330) 562-8308. Take in more than 100 rides, shows, and attractions, including the terrifying Mr. Hyde's Nasty Fall and the Serial Thriller, a suspended looping roller coaster.

There are more than 300 golf courses in the area, abundant waterways, and many museums located in Cleveland, including The Cleveland Museum of Art, University Circle, (216) 421-7340, where admission is free. Football fans won't want to miss the Pro Football Hall of Fame, 2121 George Halas Drive NW, Canton, (330) 456-8207, about 45 minutes south of Cleveland. Visit the five-building complex, movie theatre, displays, museum, enshrinement halls, and the store.

True Pittsburghers would have a hard time admitting they "might" root for the Cleveland Browns, but if you're going there to cheer on the Steelers, check out the $283 million Cleveland Browns Stadium, seating 73,200 people and standing 12 stories tall.

Leisurely excursions can be had aboard the *Goodtime III*, a 1,000 passenger, triple-decker sightseeing ship on the Cuyahoga River and Lake Erie. For reservations, call (216) 861-5110. The Observation Deck, located on the 42nd floor of the Terminal Tower, offers breathtaking views of downtown Cleveland, and is open to the public Saturday and Sunday. Hours vary.

The Convention & Visitors Bureau also has a "Walk Cleveland" booklet featuring a pedestrian's guide to Cleveland architecture and public art. Call (800) 321-1004 for the self-guided booklet.

Cleveland also has lakefront parks and beaches, fishing expeditions, trolley tours, wineries, and breweries to visit. In the winter months, there's even ski resorts to try. Read on for the visitor's guide later in this section, which will help you find a weekend (or several) of fun possibilities.

Cleveland Shopping

Downtown Cleveland boasts shopping that includes the Avenue at Tower City Center, Terminal Tower, Public Square, (216) 623–4750, with upscale shopping in a historic landmark. Also, browse the Galleria at Erieview, East Ninth and St. Clair, (216) 861–4343, with its glass-enclosed stores such as Williams Sonoma, Eddie Bauer, and the Cleveland Indians Team Shop. In addition, there are unique retail arcades—the Colonial Arcade and the Euclid Arcade. Call (216) 621–0057.

Beachwood Place, 26300 Cedar Road, Beachwood, (216) 464–9460, is Cleveland's premier fashion destination with such department stores as Dillard's, Saks Fifth Avenue, and Nordstroms. Factory outlets include the Aurora Premium Outlets, 549 South Chillicothe Road, Aurora, (330) 562–2000, just minutes from Sea World and Geauga Lake, as well as the Prime Outlets at Lodi, 9911 Avon Lake Road, Burbank (330) 948–9929, 40 minutes south of Cleveland.

Also within Cleveland is a 10-block shopping district on Larchmere Boulevard, where you'll find more than 15 antiques shops and art galleries. European pastry shops and fine restaurants line this boulevard as well.

Cleveland Accommodations

In the Cleveland area, you'll choose from more than 15,000 hotel rooms. Some of these are of the elegant nature that befits the Ritz-Carlton Cleveland, 1515 West Third Street, (216) 623–1300; Renaissance Cleveland Hotel, 24 Public Square, (216) 696–5600; and Marriott Downtown at Key Center, 127 Public Square, (216) 696–9200.

A new 293-room hotel opened in downtown Cleveland in spring of 2001.

The Hyatt Regency Cleveland at the Arcade, 420 Superior Avenue, is an architectural gem featuring the refurbishment of the Arcade's 62,000 square feet of shops and restaurants. To make reservations, call (216) 575–1234.

There are several Holiday Inn locations, including Lakeside City Center, (216) 241–500, and Beachwood, (216) 831–3300, as well as some Hampton Inn locations, such as Hampton Inn Cleveland/Wickliffe, 28611 Euclid Avenue, Wickliffe, (440) 944–4030, and Hampton Inn & Suites, 6020 Jefferson Drive, Independence, (216) 520–2020.

In addition, try the Fairfield Inn Willoughby, 35110 Maplegrove Road, (440) 975–9922. There are budget and economy-minded motels that dot the landscape, including several Travel Lodge, Days Inn, and Red Roof Inn franchises. You'll find an extensive listing in the *Greater Cleveland Official Visitors Guide* by calling (800) 321–1001.

Cleveland Restaurants

Dining in Cleveland is just as abundant as places to stay. The *Nautica Queen* is a luxury cruise and dining ship featuring lake and river cruises. Docked in the Flats Nautica Entertainment Complex, the ship serves up to 400 passengers and runs from April until December. For reservations, call (216) 696–8888.

Seafood reigns supreme on the shores of this city. Hornblower's, 1151 North Marginal Road, (216) 363–1151, is a seafood house to head to, on the shore of Lake Erie. Barnacle Bill's Crab House, 14810 Detroit Avenue, Lakewood, (216) 521–2722, also serves seafood and steaks with its raw bar and beer varieties in a nautical setting. Try some more ales and lagers brewed on the premises of the award-winning local brewery, the Great Lakes Brewing Company, 2516 Market Street, (216) 771–4404, where you'll also dine on fine food.

Sans Souci Restaurant in the Renaissance Cleveland Hotel (see above) specializes in French country fare. It's among Cleveland's better and more expensive restaurants. Morton's of Chicago, Cleveland, 1600 West Second Street, (216) 621–6200, is another upscale restaurant serving great steaks, fresh seafood, and shellfish.

Those preferring Chinese can head to Lu Cuisine, 1228 Euclid Avenue, (216) 241–8488, for cuisine from the Shandong province of Northeast China. And for a family-style buffet in a nonsmoking atmosphere with Norman Rockwell decor, there are at least a half dozen Hometown Buffet locations around Cleveland. Check the long list in the visitors guide mentioned in Accommodations.

OGLEBAY, WEST VIRGINIA

Less than two hours west of Pittsburgh sits a playground, golf spot, and shopping destination, complete with lodging and food, all for your pleasure in Wheeling, West Virginia. Oglebay started as a farm, then became the elegant summer estate of Cleveland industrialist Col. Earl W. Oglebay. Later, the property was given to the city of Wheeling for use as a park and recreational site.

Seasonally, there are attractions that may become favorite traditions, such as the Winter Festival of Lights, a spectacular outdoor light show that you drive through during the holidays. Regardless of the time of year, the people of Wheeling have long known of the wonderful offerings of Oglebay. Now, you can also! For reservations or more information on any of the facilities at Oglebay, West Virginia, call (304) 243–4000.

Getting There

Follow I-79 south out of Pittsburgh until you pick up Interstate 70 west in Washington, Pennsylvania. Then, follow the signs to Wheeling and Oglebay. It's that simple!

Oglebay Attractions

The Winter Festival of Lights we mentioned above is sometimes called America's largest light display, complete with model trains and a laser light show (every hour, on the hour); admission is priced by age, per person, not by car as some winter light shows are structured.

During the warmer months, walk through Bissonnette Gardens, with a different floral display each season. These elegant gardens existed at the turn of the 20th century and have been carefully re-created to cover the hilltop region of Oglebay. From April through October, you can stroll along winding brick pathways among hanging baskets, fragrant flowers, ever-flowing water displays, and the finest of trees.

The Speidel Championship Golf Course, designed by noted golf architect Robert Trent Jones, is a perfect challenge for the serious golfer who needs a change in scenery. There's also a par-3 golf course and driving range.

At the Good Children's Zoo, bears, otters, bison, and rare red wolves are at home in this specious natural setting. Kids will especially enjoy the 3000-gallon fish tank and the barnful of friendly domestic animals. Take the 1½-mile train ride, enjoy the playground, and do allow time for the Benedum Science Theater and planetarium.

In addition, at Oglebay, there is a huge outdoor swimming pool as well as tennis at the Crispin Center. Get your exercise paddling a boat upon Schenk Lake, right on the grounds.

In the winter, if there's enough snow, the par-3 golf course becomes some mild ski slopes. Both cross-country and downhill skiers are accommodated.

Less physical fun can be had touring the beautiful, white, Mansion Museums' period rooms. Finally, to learn how glass is made, visit Oglebay's Glass Museum with its audio tour.

Oglebay Shopping

Eight distinctive shops complement Ogle-bay's full range of activities and recreation. But then, shopping is indeed recreation for some!

Start at Carriage House Glass, the most recent addition to the shopping scene, boasting the area's largest selection of West Virginia decorative glass, with items produced right before your eyes.

Christmas in the Gardens is a store located in Bissonnette Gardens with hard-to-find holiday items, available to you year-round. Next, there's the Mansion Museum Gift Shop, featuring collectibles and a line of specialty gifts. Garden Center Gift Shop has flowers, accessories, and gifts made of natural materials whereas the Palm Room boasts seasonal plants, herbs, and hanging baskets. These last few shops are also located within the gardens.

Wilson Lodge's Resort Shop features logo merchandise and resort clothing. Golfers are certainly in their element in the Speidel Pro Shop, located in the Hamm Club House on the golf course. Here, they will find golf apparel and equipment. During the off-season when the Festival of Lights operates, this store is decked out for the holidays, and offers shoppers fine gourmet foods and West Virginia wines.

Finally, you and the children will enjoy the Nature Express store at the Good Children's Zoo.

Be sure to familiarize yourself with safety procedures and the rules of the waterways at Deep Creek Lake, Maryland. Police patrol by boat and will pull you over to run safety checks and inspect for fishing licenses. You will be fined if you're caught boating recklessly or under the influence of alcohol.

Oglebay Accommodations

Wilson Lodge provides excellent overnight accommodations with modern luxuries such as an indoor pool, Jacuzzi, and fitness center. See the Accommodations chapter for further details.

For those who require additional space, Oglebay offers a choice of cottages, deluxe or standard, rented by the day, the weekend, or the week. Each has a large living area, a fully equipped kitchen, and either two, four, or six bedrooms for sleeping.

Oglebay Restaurants

Ihlenfeld Dining Room in Wilson Lodge serves American cuisine at its finest in a family-friendly setting. The menu features gourmet selections as well as entrees the kids will surely enjoy. Overlooking Schenk Lake and the surrounding countryside, the view is an added attraction each season. Winter guests will enjoy the Festival of Lights, and summer patrons can look out over the lake's 150-foot fountain with its music and colored lights.

DEEP CREEK LAKE, MARYLAND

Once called "Maryland's Best Kept Secret," Deep Creek Lake in Garrett County, Western Maryland, is now well known in many seasons.

Each October, the annual Autumn Glory Festival is reason for a drive not only to witness the spectacular foliage, but also to partake of banjo and fiddle contests, square dancing, bagpipes, bands, baseball card shows, and of course, wonderful food.

When it snows (and boy, does it snow in Garrett County!), the slopes at the Wisp Ski Resort are bustling with downhill activity. There are 22 trails, a halfpipe for snowboarders, snowmaking capability, an indoor lodge, and restaurants to warm the hearty. For more information on such winter recreation, turn to the Recreation chapter.

However fun a downhill run is in December, summer is Deep Creek's most popular season. As the largest freshwater lake in Maryland, Deep Creek boasts 65 miles of shoreline. Built in 1925 by the Youghiogheny Electric Company, the lake was purchased by the Pennsylvania Electric Company in 1942. Currently, it's owned by the state of Maryland, and plenty make this their summer playground and weekend retreat.

If you're thinking of spending any time at Deep Creek Lake, pick up a copy of the *Garrett County & Deep Creek Lake Vacation Guide,* updated annually. Write the Deep Creek Lake–Garrett County Promotion Council at 15 Visitors Center Drive, McHenry, MD 21541, or call (301) 387-4386. Pick up a guidebook at the visitor center, located along US 219, or contact the promotion council.

Getting There

From Pittsburgh, you can reach Garrett County from different routes. If you originate south or west of Pittsburgh, take I-79 through Washington (there's a stretch that becomes I-79 and I-70) and continue on I-79 through West Virginia until you pick up Interstate 68 (older maps show this as Highway 48, but the designation was changed some years ago to 68). Follow I-68 to the Maryland border, until you reach the Friendsville exit (approximately 4 miles after the border). Take Route 42 to McHenry, Maryland, the first sighting of Deep Creek Lake.

From points south and east of Pittsburgh, take Route 51 south to Uniontown, until you pick up US 40 East. Continue to US 219 at Keyser's Ridge. Follow US 219 south to McHenry, Maryland.

Deep Creek Lake Attractions

Watersports abound here at Deep Creek. Just be sure to learn the rules of the waterways before taking off in your rental boat, towing a water-skier, or cruising around on your Jet Ski. For motorboat rentals, consult the vacation guide listed at the conclusion of this section.

Since the lake is home to the *Flying Scot* 19-foot daysailer, sailboat races are a popular activity on weekends. The nautical crowd takes to the water in the yacht club. Kids and adults can learn to sail with weeklong classes conducted by the Deep Creek Sailing School, 365 Back Bay Road, Swanton, (301) 387-4497.

Swallow Falls State Park, where tall hemlocks and four waterfalls cascade along a beautiful backdrop, is a perfect place for camping, picnicking, and hiking the scenic trails.

Funland Family Fun Center, across from McHenry Plaza, US 219, (301) 387-6168, is perhaps the best local amusement besides the annual county fair each August. There's a carousel for all ages, a go-kart track for kids ages four and older, bumper cars, miniature golf, and an indoor arcade with video games.

Courses at the Wisp Resort and in Oakland keep the family golfers happy while area trails are prime for mountain bikers. If you prefer to ride horses, there are several stables for pony and horseback rides. Consult the vacation guide listed above.

Deep Creek Lake Shopping

Schoolhouse Earth, 2 miles north of Deep Creek on Route 42, (800) 223-4930, is a country shop with gifts for year-round Christmas shoppers, as well as those searching for cards, handcrafted jewelry,

lamps, country accessories, framed calligraphy, music, books, rugs, and more.
Antique reproduction furniture and custom framing are also available. For the
kids, visit the petting zoo, open daily in
the summer season and on spring and fall
weekends, weather permitting.

There's nothing like a good book to
read in the warm sunlight. Head to the
Book Mark'et & Antique Mezzanine, 111
South Second Street, Oakland, (301) 334–
8778, for books, cassettes, CDs, and a
complete children's area. Newly added
antiques make this a must-stop.

Within Mountain Village Shops, check
out The Tourist Trap, (301) 387–7900, for
souvenirs, gifts, swimsuits, music, cards,
and miscellaneous gifts. The Christmas
Chalet, (877) 387–4646, is exactly what
the name implies, with Christmas-themed
gifts and collectibles.

Arrowhead Market, along US 219 next
to Alpine Village, has expanded over the
years to be a one-stop shopping establishment for almost any provision you
need. Open 24 hours, the store stocks
baked and canned goods, fresh meats and
produce, roasted chickens, ready-made
sandwiches and beverages, as well as
newspapers and beer. Arrowhead even
has a business service center, photo
developing center, gas station, and it's
accessible by boat with its own dock. Call
(301) 387–4020 for more information on
the store's provisions and services.

Yoder's Country Market, Maryland 669,
Grantsville, (800) 321–5148, (301) 895–
5148, is not necessarily at the lake itself,
but if you are traveling US 40, or if you
plan to eat at Penn Alps, we'd be remiss if
we didn't tell you about it. Do stop for
county fare, including jams, jellies, baked
goods, and other Amish specialties.

Deep Creek Lake Accommodations

Depending upon your personal preferences, you'll find many types of accom-

modations at Deep Creek Lake. For those
families opting to rent a cottage, contact
Railey Rentals, (800) 447–3034, or A&A
Realty Rental, (800) 336–7303. If having
direct access to the waterfront is important to you, be sure to ask for it. Cabins
advertised as having "lake access" could
still mean the lake is a considerable hike
from your accommodations.

Campers will find several state parks
nearby, with Deep Creek Lake State Park,
(301) 387–4111, providing a beach, boat
launch, and camping facilities. Camping
trailers up to 29 feet in length are permitted in Maryland state parks, and there are
electric hookups. Improved campgrounds
provide centrally located washhouses, toi-
lets, lavatories, and hot-water showers.
Cabins are available, some with wheelchair
access. Make your site reservations up to
one year in advance, especially for the
busy summer months. Some parks do
permit pets.

Vacationers may also prefer motels,
hotels, or a bed-and-breakfast inn, and
there are plenty of these in the area. For a
complete listing, consult the vacation
guide. Alpine Village, (800) 745–1174, sits
right off US 219 next to Arrowhead Market.
With a private beach and outdoor pool,
the village includes some cottages and
some motel rooms. Point View Inn, (301)
387–5555, also sits along US 219, offering
lakefront access, boat docking, a private
beach, and a restaurant on the premises.

The Wisp Hotel & Conference Center is
a center of summer and winter activity. In
addition to taking to the ski slopes, golf
course, and hiking trails, you can swim a
few laps in the indoor pool. However, the
Wisp does not have a beach, and it's a walk
to the waterfront. For reservations, call
(800) 462–9477. Affiliated with the Wisp
are the Will O' The Wisp Prestige Condominiums, US 219, (301) 387–5503, with an
indoor pool, whirlpools, a sauna, fireplaces,
exercise and game rooms, a sandy beach,
boat docking, and a restaurant.

The bed-and-breakfast crowd will want
to check out the Carmel Cove Inn, Glendale Road, (301) 387–0067. This former

monastery boasts beautifully appointed rooms with fireplaces, whirlpool baths, and private decks. Guests can swim from the dock, fish from shore, or enjoy other amenities such as the great room with billiards and cable television. Lake Pointe Inn, off Marsh Hill Road, (800) 523-LAKE, is 13 feet from the water's edge and a five-minute walk from the Wisp resort. All rooms have lake and/or ski slope views. There's a private dock, too.

Deep Creek Lake Restaurants

Penn Alps Restaurant and Crafts Shop, half a mile east of Grantsville, (301) 895-5985, isn't exactly at Deep Creek, but it's en route from Pittsburgh. So plan to stop for Amish-style food, along with their soup and salad bar. Visit the artisan village next door.

Not far from McHenry is McClive's Restaurant & Lounge, (301) 387-6172, where you can dine with a spectacular view of the lake. Early bird specials begin at 5:00 P.M. and boat docking is available. In the mood for a light bite or happy hour? The Courtyard and Patio Lounge is downstairs.

Next to Arrowhead Market, Pizzeria Uno Restaurant & Bar, (301) 387-4866, features a great view of the lake if you choose deck seating in the summer. Just a few steps away is their Honi-Honi Bar, a Deep Creek watering hole for decades. Live music takes the stage on summer weekends, where families or couples often sit out on the open lawn. Both establishments are accessible by boat dock.

Across the street, Dr. Willy's Seafood Company, (301) 387-7380, is a carry-out fish market that's great for a quick bite to eat. If you prefer a more formal sit-down dinner, drive just a bit further on US 219, turning onto Glendale Bridge Road. Here you'll find the Silver Tree Ristorante, (301) 387-4040, featuring nightly specials, including Italian entrees. Right next door is the Silver Tree Inn, a much more casual lakeside seafood bar, accessible by boat as well.

Sip a cappuccino with a croissant or enjoy the country French or American cuisine at the Cornish Manor Restaurant & French Bakery, Memorial Drive, Oakland, (301) 334-6499, only 10 miles south of Deep Creek Lake. Reservations are required for lunch and dinner, and the restaurant is closed on Sunday through Tuesday.

HERSHEY

Otherwise known as Chocolate Town, U.S.A., Hershey is the sweetest place on earth. To be floating high up in the air at Hersheypark, the popular amusement park, you only need to breathe in the scent of cocoa to know where you are! The sweet smell drifts from the factory into the park.

A three- to four-hour drive east from Pittsburgh, Hershey is definitely a weekend getaway as opposed to a day trip. But if you can spare a few days, head on out to see the town Milton Hershey pretty much created for his employees. The Hershey Entertainment & Resort Co. will assist you in supplying information and/or booking your stay. Call them at (800) HERSHEY.

Getting There

Take the Pennsylvania Turnpike east about 200 miles to exit 19 (Harrisburg), then follow Route 283 North. Join Route 322 East into the town of Hershey. Amtrak runs trains daily to Harrisburg, the state capital. If you book reservations at the Hotel Hershey or Lodge (see below), you may be able to take advantage of free shuttle service (which is also available for those flying into Harrisburg International Airport, 15 minutes away).

The holiday season at Hershey begins in mid-November with a winter wonderland of horsedrawn carriage rides, carolers, Santa Claus, and of course, chocolate! Call (800) HERSHEY for details.

Hershey Attractions

Turn-of-the-century confectioner Milton Snavely Hershey didn't actually start out in chocolate. Caramels were his focus, and he did very well in business. But he made an interesting discovery along the way: it was the chocolate adhering to the caramels that children licked off and seemed to enjoy the most. Thus, Hershey sold his Lancaster Caramel Company for $1 million but shrewdly reserved the rights to sell chocolate. And sell he did, building a company town rich in benevolence, and just plain fun to visit. Hershey opened his chocolate factory in 1905.

Hersheypark, (717) 534-3900, began as a place for his employees and their families to relax. It was largely picnic grounds, built in 1907. Today, it's one of the cleanest and most exciting amusement parks in the country. Ride the Great Bear, an inverted steel looping roller coaster; the Sidewinder; the Comet; one of several water rides; or some kiddie rides. Children love to determine their ride status by measuring their height against popular candy bars, posted throughout the park.

Adjacent to Hersheypark is Zoo America, (717) 534-3860, opened as the Hershey Zoo in 1910 as a place for Mr. Hershey to showcase his wild animal collection. Now, there are more than 200 animals for everyone to see. Hours for Hersheypark vary according to the month, but the park generally opens at 10:00 A.M. ZooAmerica is open daily, year-round, from 9:00 or 10:00 A.M. to between 5:00 and 8:00 P.M. depending on the time of year, with the exception of Thanksgiving, Christmas, and New Year's Day. Call the toll-free info line, (800) HERSHEY, for more information. Admission for these two attractions falls under the one-priced admission plan, which changes most seasons. Ride height restrictions apply.

Many years ago, tours of the Hershey factory used to attract a million people each year. When the tours became too popular to manage, they were stopped and the education shifted elsewhere. Visit Chocolate World, (717) 534-4900, for a Disney-like tour of chocolate production and facts. You'll ride through the displays in automated cars, and as you exit, reach out your hand for that complimentary candy bar! Admission to Chocolate World is free. Hours vary depending upon the season so be sure to call the toll-free Hershey information line listed above.

What better way to learn about the town Mr. Hershey built (complete with chocolate kiss–shaped streetlamps on Chocolate Avenue) than by riding the Hershey Trolley? Visit Trolley Works, (717) 533-3000, right inside Chocolate World, to purchase your ticket for this fun-filled and educational ride through town. You'll learn how Milton Hershey gave so much back to the community that during the Depression he kept many townspeople employed by building a community center, a sports arena, a stadium, and the palatial Hotel Hershey (see description below). In addition, you'll learn that Milton and his wife Catharine, unable to have children of their own, founded a school for needy children, today known as the Milton Hershey School.

What began as a rose garden in 1937 became the Hershey Gardens, (719) 534-3492, a 23-acre botanical display garden that includes Butterfly House, representing more than 25 different North American plant species. It's located on Hotel Road across from the Hotel Hershey, and is open from 9:00 A.M. until 6:00 P.M. April 1 until October 31. During the summer months, the Gardens stay open on Fridays and Saturdays until 8:00 P.M. before Labor Day. Admission is charged according to age.

A short walk from Hersheypark and Chocolate World is the Hershey Museum, (717) 534-3439. It's a self-guided tour that explains how Milton Hershey overcame business failures to create his chocolate empire, and how he became the philanthropist he's remembered as today. There's a Discovery Room for young children. The museum is open from 10:00 A.M. until 5:00 P.M. Memorial Day through Labor Day, the museum stays open until 6:00 P.M. and it's closed Thanksgiving, Christmas, and New Year's Day. Admission is charged according to age.

Hershey Shopping

Most of the Hershey attractions have gift shops on the premises. One you won't want to miss is the giant candy feast-land inside Chocolate World. In fact, the ride lets you off at the entrance of the gift area. Here, you'll find some types of candies packaged differently than you're used to in stores back home, in addition to shirts, hats, mugs, ornaments, and more. The Hershey Museum and Hershey Gardens also offer gift shops, and in Hersheypark and ZooAmerica there are multiple chances to purchase souvenirs.

The Factory Stores at Hershey, (717) 520–1236, give you plenty of stores. You'll find the usual array of outlet establishments for men's and women's apparel, children's clothing, footwear, books, stationery and gifts, home furnishings and housewares, intimate apparel, leather goods and luggage, and much more. They're located at 46 Outlet Square in Hershey, just 1 block east of Hersheypark, on Hersheypark Drive. Visit Monday through Saturday, 9:30 A.M. until 9:00 P.M. and on Sundays from 11:00 A.M. until 5:00 P.M. but hours may be shorter during the winter months so do call in advance.

Hershey Accommodations

Built with European charm, the Hotel Hershey is elegant with its Mediterranean design, luxury amenities, and guest services. You'll enjoy valet parking, concierge service, 24-hour room service, baby-sitting, laundry services, indoor and outdoor pools, bike rentals and carriage rides, therapeutic massages, saunas, tennis, golf, lawn bowling, and much more. The Fountain Lobby, with hand-carved wooden balustrades, custom-painted tile, and the famous painted cloud ceiling, is a wonderful display of craftsmanship. The Hotel Hershey certainly rivals some of the finest hotels in the world.

At the Hershey Lodge and Convention Center, you'll enjoy fitness facilities, indoor and outdoor pools, miniature golf, concierge service, and valet parking as well, in addition to the many meeting and business facilities. Kids will love the free chocolate bars upon check-in too!

For reservations at either the Hershey Hotel or the Hershey Lodge and Convention Center, call the reservations and information line at (800) HERSHEY.

The Milton Motel, located at 1733 East Chocolate Avenue, (717) 533–4533, offers comfortable, more budget-conscious accommodations. Amenities include free coffee, free HBO/ESPN, a heated swimming pool, a game room, and senior discounts.

Campers will appreciate the Hershey Highmeadow Campground featuring more than 290 campsites on 55 beautiful acres of countryside. Choose from cabins, with electricity and small kitchen equipment, or sites for camping and recreational vehicle hookups. There are two outdoor swimming pools, plus a kiddie pool, playgrounds and a country store, self-service laundry, a game room, recreational facilities, and more. Contact the information line at (800) HERSHEY for further information on camping in Hershey.

Hershey Restaurants

The most exclusive restaurant at Hershey is the Circular Dining Room, built in the Hotel Hershey so that no guest would have to settle for a corner table. The cuisine is contemporary American with an extensive wine list. The dining room over-looks formal gardens and a tranquil reflect-ing pool. For more casual fare, try the Fountain Café.

Reservations are recommended at any of the Hershey restaurants, with the exception of the Cocoa Beanery coffee shops and the lounges. Call (800) HERSHEY for the Hotel Hershey and (800) HERSHEY for the Lodge and Convention Center.

At Chocolate World, visit the Chocolate Town Café for overstuffed sandwiches, salads, home-style meals, and great, chocolate-y (what else!) desserts. For more information, call (717) 533-2917.

NEIGHBORHOODS, REAL ESTATE, AND RELOCATION

At various times in its history, Pittsburgh has been defined by its rivers and bridges, by its steel mills and coal mines, by its sports teams. More than anything else, however, Pittsburgh is a city of neighborhoods, of residential communities that are both distinct and distinctive. In its relatively small space of less than 59 square miles, the city proper officially includes 90 neighborhoods. Beyond the city itself, Allegheny County spans 130 municipalities. Add the neighborhoods in the other five counties in our coverage area, and you have a region blessed with hundreds of attractive places to live.

Pittsburgh's emphasis on neighborhoods has firm roots in both topography and history. The region's riverfronts and mountains serve as natural boundaries to neighborhoods. Traveling across town in Pittsburgh can mean traversing hills and major waterways, providing some incentive to remain close to home. This was especially true during Pittsburgh's industrial heyday, when workers did not want to live too far from their mills and factories.

Perhaps even more important, Pittsburgh was settled by immigrants who tended to cluster together, taking comfort in the familiarity of people and customs from their native lands. The principal waves of immigration ended many decades ago, yet even today, the center of activity in many neighborhoods remains the local church constructed by early immigrants.

All of which provide Pittsburgh's neighborhoods with unusual solidity. Most neighborhoods in the region feature business districts—ranging from several stores to several blocks or more—to assure that residents can meet their shopping needs without leaving the neighborhood. The region also has witnessed the growth of neighborhood-based development organizations, known locally as community development corporations, which inspire neighborhood development and involve residents in their own well-being.

Most Pittsburghers live in single-family residences, although this is hardly the exclusive style. Many of the city's elegant older homes have been subdivided into apartments, and larger multi-unit buildings dot the region as well. Region-wide statistics on apartment life are not completely reliable, but a good guess is that about 30 percent of city of Pittsburgh residents live in rental properties, condominiums, or cooperative housing. Many residents spend their entire lives within their neighborhoods. Call it parochial if you will, but it's an enduring strength of Pittsburgh that contributes to the richness of residential life here.

Outside the city proper, you'll find a broad diversity of styles in residential communities. Pittsburgh has many close-in suburbs of both the affluent and working class variety. A number of nearby cities, such as Greensburg and Beaver, blend both sophistication and charm. If rural life is more your style, you can be in lush farm country by driving about 20 minutes—in just about every direction—from downtown Pittsburgh.

From riverfront to mountaintop living, from homes with spacious grounds to those with shared or "party" walls, you're pretty likely to find the style of living you prefer in Pittsburgh's attractive neighborhoods.

In describing some of Pittsburgh's neighborhoods in this chapter, we could present only a fraction of the communities where you might choose to live. We've tried to pick neighborhoods that are interesting in and of themselves and others—such as Kittanning, an Allegheny River town, or Penn Hills, an affluent suburb—that may be representative of a large number of communities.

One final word about Pittsburgh's neighborhoods. Maps may formally delineate neighborhood boundaries, but cartographers don't necessarily have the last word. Pittsburghers will heatedly defend their perceptions of their neighborhoods in utter defiance of what the maps may say. On certain corners in the city, you can talk to residents and discover that you are simultaneously in Brookfield, Garfield, Lawrenceville, Shadyside, and East Liberty. Don't fight it. Ultimately, neighborhood in Pittsburgh is more than a place. It's a state of mind, a creed, a way of life. Don't be surprised if it becomes your way of life very soon.

NEIGHBORHOODS

Downtown

Downtown life offers proximity to the city's vital center, with its primary business facilities—and many of its cultural amenities—within easy walking distance. Remember that you can traverse the entire length or breadth of Downtown in less than 30 minutes. If you're living Downtown, you're close to everywhere.

Downtown living is almost exclusively high-rise living, in such buildings as Gateway Towers near Point State Park; the Pennsylvanian, a refurbished former railroad station at Downtown's edge approaching the adjacent Strip District; and Washington Plaza, an apartment complex near the Mellon Arena. You'll find additional luxury apartments just across

the Seventh Street Bridge in a complex called Lincoln at North Shore.

A newer downtown residential style is lofts, which were late to come to Pittsburgh but are available from a small number of developers. (See the Close-up on Eve Picker later in this chapter.)

Most downtown residences bring you both convenience and views of the rivers. Downtown boasts about 3,000 residents, many of whom belong to a residents' association.

North

ASPINWALL

A scenic community just north of Pittsburgh, Aspinwall is an appealing blend of the old and new. About half its homes are sturdy brick affairs predating World War II, which sell for $46,000 or less. The town also features recently constructed dwellings that can bring as much as $150,000. Rental properties are popular in Aspinwall, as fewer than half its homes are owner-occupied.

The business district is particularly appealing. With the Allegheny River as its backdrop, the commercial section features a variety of small specialty shops with a handsome, old-fashioned decor. If you're of a mind to promenade, parasol upon your shoulder, this is the perfect setting for it.

If shopping plazas are more your metier, you'll find the Waterworks Mall conveniently placed along Route 28, which also connects Aspinwall to Pittsburgh's North Side, about 6 miles away. Other amenities include the Pittsburgh Zoo & Aquarium, which is just across the Allegheny River, and St. Margaret Memorial Hospital, which, through the mysteries of politics, is located in the city of Pittsburgh without being contiguous to any part of the city.

With a population of just under 3,000, Aspinwall has been able to preserve its considerable charm.

BUTLER

Between 1992 and 1996, Butler County saw the creation of more manufacturing jobs than any other county in Pennsylvania. That augurs well for employment in Butler County and the city of Butler, the county seat, which has continued to maintain a strong employment base since 1996. Among the leading employers are steelmaker ARMCO Inc., with a major complex just outside Butler, and the Veterans Affairs Medical Center and its sprawling hospital/residential complex.

Residential style in Butler is a mix of affordable single-family homes and rental properties. Though no official figures exist, some longtime Butler residents believe that four of every 10 Butler residents live in rental units. Renovating older homes is a popular pursuit here.

The city of just more than 15,000 residents was named for a Revolutionary War general. It's accessible from Pittsburgh, about 25 miles away, by Route 8, which also serves as a gateway to communities further to the north.

CRANBERRY

Cranberry has been perhaps the hottest growth area in Western Pennsylvania. This Butler County township was for many years a largely rural community when folks discovered that its location—at the juncture of the Pennsylvania Turnpike, Interstate 79, and Route 19—meant easy access from and to just about everywhere. That signaled the start of a growth spurt that hasn't stalled yet.

The average home price is about $175,000, and many lots include spacious grounds. About 17 percent of Cranberry residents live in rental units. Shopping is a breeze at the many malls along Route 19.

Cranberry is full of seeming contradictions. Turn away from the busy shopping plazas and you'll quickly find yourself in unspoiled terrain without sidewalks. The shape of the township's development remains a topic of considerable debate among residents. One owner of a large

unimproved site, upset with Cranberry's development rules, threatened to cut down every tree on his property if the process wasn't liberalized. He reached a compromise with elected officials, and the amazing development of Cranberry continued.

Reader's Digest rates Pittsburgh the fifth best place to raise a family, and Working Mother magazine rates the Pittsburgh region second best for working moms.

FOX CHAPEL

One statistic tells you much of what you need to know about Fox Chapel: The average home price here is more than $350,000, an extraordinary figure for the Pittsburgh area where affordable housing is the norm. Housing prices beyond $1 million are not uncommon in Fox Chapel, which neighbors Aspinwall.

As you might guess, homes here are large, frequently set back from streets atop winding drives and lush grounds. Mansions may be a word out of favor, but whether they're politically correct or not, you'll find plenty of them here. The community is so woodsy that town fathers on occasion must develop ways to cope with a deer overpopulation that threatens residents' shrubbery.

There's more to Fox Chapel than gorgeous homes. The borough maintains six parks totaling 280 acres, and it's home to the Beechwood Farms Nature Reserve and Hartwood Acres, an Allegheny County park that is a popular summertime site for theatrical and musical performances. For more on Hartwood Acres, see our Parks and Recreation chapters.

You won't find much of a commercial district, but residents can purchase just about everything they need at the Waterworks Mall and other Route 28 shopping plazas. If you're driving from Downtown,

Pittsburgh has been ranked seventh in the nation as the home of Fortune 500 headquarters. Entrepreneur magazine has also rated it the ninth best place in the country for small businesses.

you'll reach Fox Chapel in about 25 minutes. If Fox Chapel is your home, you won't mind the drive.

HARMONY

In 1804, Johann George Rapp and his religious separatist followers abandoned the German duchy of Wurttenberg and began constructing a communal town in what today is Butler County. They gave the name Harmony to the town they built along the banks of the Connoquennessing, in the hope that it would reflect their communal style. The Harmonists developed other communities in Western Pennsylvania as well.

Ultimately, the Harmonists' experiments died out, but the town they constructed retains much of its original charm. Its shopping district features an appealing variety of antiques and artisans' shops. Approximately 1,200 people live here, most in single-family dwellings but some in rental units. You'll find no highrises here.

Among Harmony's leading employers are Sippel Company, a steel fabricator, and Paragon Trade Brands, which produces diapers.

KITTANNING

The county seat of Armstrong County, Kittanning shares many qualities with its fellow Allegheny River communities, including attractive riverfront homes and vistas. Single-family homes dominate the town, although recent developments include three highrise buildings featuring housing for the elderly.

Large employers in this community of about 5,100 include Alltel Pennsylvania, a telecommunications provider, and Stan-

dard Products, a rubber company. As a county seat, Kittanning boasts its own daily newspaper and proximity to several hospitals and a branch of Indiana University of Pennsylvania.

Kittanning is about a 40-minute drive from Pittsburgh along Route 28, which becomes a highspeed highway once it leaves Pittsburgh.

MCCANDLESS

The town of McCandless is representative of Pittsburgh's burgeoning North Hills in many regards. Most residents live in single-family homes, with more than half the town's dwellings built after 1970. The average home price is just less than $138,000. Residents have access to the many malls and shops along Route 19 and McKnight Road.

What makes McCandless noteworthy, even among Pittsburgh's splendid northern suburbs, is that it sits squarely in the middle of North Park, one of the jewels of the Allegheny County park system. The park offers such activities as fishing, boating, biking, tennis, jogging trails, swimming, golf, and ice skating—read more about it in our Parks chapter. If you live in McCandless, North Park is your back yard.

MEXICAN WAR STREETS

Near as we can tell, Pittsburgh did not play a prominent role in the Mexican-American War. Nevertheless, this city of Pittsburgh Northside neighborhood features streets like Palo Alto and Monterrey named for battles and heroes of that conflict. The community was developed in the 1860s and 1870s—perhaps the freshness of the war in the minds of the developers helps account for the homage to the soldiers who fought it.

The neighborhood is one of the city's architectural showcases. Carefully restored row houses reflect a broad variety of styles, with Greek revival doorways, Gothic turrets, stained glass, and Richardsonian stonework. Many residents are longtime homeowners, while some homes here are purchased as investments. Because owners have such different purposes, prices of Mexican War Streets homes vary a good deal—from $30,000 for "fixer-uppers" to $100,000 and more for fully restored Victorians.

If you live in the Mexican War Streets, downtown is less than 2 miles away, and you'll be within walking distance of such amenities as Allegheny General Hospital, PNC Park, Heinz Field, the Carnegie Science Center, and the shopping district of East Ohio Street. Plus, when someone asks what in the heck Buena Vista Street is doing in Pittsburgh, you'll have an answer of sorts.

OBSERVATORY HILL

Not often can you find stately older homes with such features as window seats, carved wooden doors, front porches, and third-floor rental units. It's rarer still when such homes sell for an average price of $39,000. That's what you'll find, though, in Observatory Hill, a neighborhood at Pittsburgh's northern boundary.

The neighborhood draws its name from Allegheny Observatory; perhaps a more important feature for you is Riverview Park, one of the city's grandest, which features acres of open greenery and such activities as picnic shelters and hiking, biking, and riding trails. See our Parks chapter for more on Riverview Park.

Observatory Hill is home to both a public elementary school and a public high school. It's several miles from downtown Pittsburgh, although the steepness of the neighborhood's hills encourages driving to town rather than walking. No matter. If you live here, you won't want to leave too often.

TROY HILL

Whoever coined the term "neighborhood" probably was inspired by a vision of Troy Hill—or a community very like it. Troy Hill was settled by European immigrants, and today, this city of Pittsburgh neighborhood retains the look and feel of an Old World village.

From its base near the Allegheny River, Troy Hill winds up a series of steep hills to a plateau that overlooks the city and the river. Here you'll find brick and frame row homes and solid single-family houses, with not much in the way of rental units. Prices for homes—between $20,000 and $35,000—are yet another attractive old-fashioned feature.

With few entrances and exits from the neighborhood, Troy Hill has been able to retain much of its close-knit character, contributing to a low crime rate and a genuine sense of community.

East

BLOOMFIELD

While many city of Pittsburgh neighborhoods boast a strong European heritage, in Bloomfield, that heritage is alive and well in daily activities. Just east of downtown, Bloomfield was settled by Italian immigrants, many of whom passed on their homes, language, and traditions to their descendants. As a result, the bustling business district along Liberty Avenue is dotted with ristorantes and groceries. When you walk along Liberty Avenue, don't be surprised when you hear residents conversing in Italian.

Homes here typically are small but well-maintained, providing a quaint quality to the narrow streets. The average Bloomfield home sells for about $50,000.

Amenities include West Penn Hospital and Dean Field, a football field beneath the Bloomfield Bridge where the legendary Johnny Unitas got his start. Dean

---

Many local communities sport colorful names. For example, you can drive from Moon (Township) to (the Borough of) Mars in about 40 minutes.

i

The Region

Pittsburgh
www.city.pittsburgh.pa.us
The people who live and work here are connected by more than the region's famous rivers. They share a history of innovation, the work ethic to get things done, and an affordable, high quality of life. The top three major employers in Pittsburgh are the UPMC Health System, the U.S. Government, and the Commonwealth of Pennsylvania.

Allegheny County
www.county.allegheny.pa.us
In addition to Pittsburgh, the largest municipalities in Allegheny County are Bethel Park, McKeesport, and Monroeville. The U.S. Government and the Commonwealth of Pennsylvania are large employers in the county. Looking at industry alone, however, the top three are UPMC Health System, West Penn Allegheny

Health System, and the University of Pittsburgh.

Armstrong County
www.armstrongidc.org
www.armstrongcounty.org
Armstrong County is recognized as a hub of technology-based industries, carbide tool and die-making, and electro-optics innovation, including the U.S. Navy's National Center of Excellence in Electro-optics Manufacturing. The top three employers are Armstrong County Memorial Hospital; Eljer Plumbingware, Inc.; and Creekside Mushrooms.

Beaver County
www.beavercountyced.org
www.beavercountychamber.com
The largest municipalities in Beaver County are Hopewell, Ambridge, and Beaver Falls. The top three major employers are

Field was one of the first gridirons in the city to boast an artificial surface. Never mind that the laying area is only 70 yards long. Johnny U. graduated to the big time from Dean Field, and that's an inspiration for all the kids in Bloomfield.

EDGEWOOD

This community just east of the city of Pittsburgh spans less than one square mile, yet it is something approaching a living book of the region's history. A farming community until the mid-19th century, Edgewood took on an industrial character with the growth of Union Switch & Signal Company. Today, as industry has declined, Edgewood is a lovely community of just under 4,000

residents, with large, inviting homes throughout the borough but especially prominent along tree-lined Maple Street.

Edgewood boasts two shopping hubs—a string of small shops along South Braddock Avenue, and Edgewood Towne Center, a popular strip mall that draws shoppers from throughout the eastern suburbs and Pittsburgh's eastern neighborhoods. With its location along Interstate 376 (the Parkway East), Edgewood is about a 15-minute drive from both downtown Pittsburgh and the Pennsylvania Turnpike.

An oddity: If you walk a certain six-block route here, you can pass through four municipalities: Edgewood, Wilkinsburg, Swissvale, and the city of Pittsburgh.

Anchor-Hocking Corporation, Koppel Steel Corporation, and Service Link.

Butler County
www.butlercountychamber.com
Butler County capitalizes upon a strategic location and highly diverse economic and recreational base that includes Cranberry Township—one of the fastest developing communities in the eastern United States. The largest municipalities in the county are Cranberry Township, Evans City, and Butler Township. The top three major employers are A-K Steel; Butler Memorial Hospital; and TRACO, which manufactures windows.

Washington County
www.investwashingtoncounty.com
www.washcochamber.com
The largest municipalities in Washington County are Peters Township, California, and Canonsburg. While the Commonwealth of Pennsylvania and the County of Washington are major employers here, among other industries the top three are Washington Hospital, Monongahela Hospital, and Giant Eagle, Inc.

Westmoreland County
www.economicgrowthconnection.com
www.co.westmoreland.pa.us/index.shtml
The largest municipalities in the county are Hempfield, Murrysville, and North Huntingdon Township. The top three major employers are Sony Technology Center, Westmoreland Health System, and Latrobe Area Hospital, Inc.

Information courtesy of the Pittsburgh Regional Alliance

You don't win anything. It's just an interesting quirk.

GREENFIELD

Greenfield borders Squirrel Hill to the east. Homes here generally top out at $80,000 or less, so if you'd like to be within walking distance of the conveniences in Squirrel Hill at a lower price, this may be the neighborhood for you. Greenfield, too, offers many conveniences, including a senior citizens center, baseball field, and public pool, as well as shops, doctors' offices, and service businesses. A considerable percentage of Greenfield's residents are former steel mill workers. If you're interested in relocating to Greenfield, you may want to pick up a copy of the *Greenfield Grapevine,* a small monthly newspaper published by a Greenfield neighborhood organization. You can usually find a copy at the Giant Eagle on the corner of Murray Avenue and Loretta Street.

GREENSBURG

Once you spy the gleaming dome of the Westmoreland County Courthouse, you know you're in a city with character. That's Greensburg, a rather small city with an outsized appetite for culture. While Greensburg's population is just over 16,000 and the city spans only about 5 square miles, it is home to three institutions of higher learning—Seton Hill College, the University of Pittsburgh's Greensburg campus, and Westmoreland

According to Uniform Crime Reports, Pittsburgh's crime rate is the seventh lowest of 44 major U.S. cities.

County Community College—as well as the popular Westmoreland Museum of American Art; the Westmoreland Symphony Orchestra; and the Palace Theatre, a downtown hall for performing arts.

The city offers many large, gracious homes as well as a growing number of planned developments that feature single-family homes, townhouses, condominiums, and rental units. Shopping here is fun. You'll have the option of browsing downtown establishments or heading to the large malls that just about surround the city.

Greensburg is about 30 miles east of Pittsburgh along Route 30. Perhaps more important, it sits at the foothills of the Laurel Highlands and so serves as the gateway to the popular recreation areas located there. You'll be delighted by Greensburg, a city of sophistication and charm.

THE HILL DISTRICT

Live in the Hill District and you'll be part of a community steeped in history. Because of its adjacency to downtown Pittsburgh, the Hill District has been home to immigrant groups of many nationalities. Today, it boasts a primarily African-American population and is the center of African-American culture. Among the most important institutions in the neighborhood is Hill House, a multifaceted facility that sponsors social and educational programs as well as cultural events.

For many decades, the neighborhood has been the hub of the city's jazz activities, attracting multi-racial fans to such historic centers as the Granada Theater and the Crawford Grill and nurturing such international jazz stars as Pittsburgh natives Earl Hines, Erroll Garner, George Benson, Billy Eckstine, Stanley Turrentine, and Mary Lou Williams. Much of the

neighborhood's joie de vivre was burned out in rioting in the late 1960s; today, organizations such as the Hill Community Development Corporations are working to restore that inviting quality, through programs including restoration of the Granada.

The neighborhood is a blend of older housing and inviting new development such as Crawford Square, a mixture of about 500 rental and for-sale units that looks for all the world, with its grand trees and cul-de-sac drives, like a suburb plunked down in the heart of the city.

The Hill District also is a center of religion—you'll find no fewer than 40 churches in the neighborhood.

Live in the Hill District and you'll be a comfortable walk from downtown . . . and a resident of one of the city's historically important neighborhoods.

LATROBE

Welcome to Mr. Rogers' neighborhood. And Arnold Palmer's. And Rolling Rock Beer's. And the banana split's. All had their start in this community of about 9,300 in Westmoreland County, about 35 miles east of Pittsburgh.

Latrobe is rich in history. It was mentioned, although not by its current name, in a 1750 entry in the diary of Christopher Gist, the surveyor credited with being the first explorer to cross the Allegheny Mountains heading west. Today, Latrobe is an appealing blend of urban and rural life. You'll find residential styles of all varieties. About 70 percent of Latrobe residents live in single-family homes, while the market value of residences is between $30,000 and $200,000. Venture just a few minutes outside downtown Latrobe and you'll be surrounded by fertile farmland.

With its central location along Route 30, the town is important to the commerce of Westmoreland County. Among the largest employers are Latrobe Area Hospital, with a staff of more than 1,500 at its main facility, and Kennametal, a For-

County Voter Registration Centers

Allegheny County
(412) 350-4510
www.county.allegheny.pa.us

Armstrong County
(724) 543-1305
www.armstrongcounty.com

Beaver County
(724) 728-5700
www.co.beaver.pa.us

Butler County
(724) 284-5308
www.butlercountychamber.com

Washington County
(724) 228-6750
www.co.washington.pa.us

Westmoreland County
(724) 830-3150

tune 500 company that produces cutting tools. The area's industrial directory lists about 200 manufacturers, a reliable source of employment for local residents.

One of Latrobe's cultural centers is St. Vincent College, which is operated by the Benedictine monks. In addition to hosting a number of important lecture series, the college each summer serves as the training site for the Pittsburgh Steelers.

Can you say, "Go, Stillers?"

LIGONIER

When Westmoreland County residents refer to "the Diamond," they're not talking about precious stone deposits or a baseball field. Rather, they're referring to downtown Ligonier, where the shopping area—in the shape of a diamond—is one of the region's most charming. You'll find a variety of quaint shops as well as a bandstand that is the center of the town's civic activities.

Ligonier is one of the most prestigious addresses in the region; some who live elsewhere have second homes in Ligonier. Residences can be breathtaking, with woodlands stretching to the backyards and pristine streams coursing through the properties. Not all homes here are quite

that spectacular—the Ligonier Valley offers a broad mix of income levels—but it is those picture-postcard dwellings that provide Ligonier with its reputation.

Located in the Laurel Highlands, Ligonier is close to some of the region's most popular resorts as well as Idlewild Park, an amusement park with an unusual rustic flavor. See our Kidstuff chapter for a more complete description of Idlewild Park. Also an enduring attraction is Fort Ligonier, an important British redoubt in the 18th-century struggles for supremacy with the French.

"We offer a tranquil respite from the fast-paced tempo of living today," the town fathers are wont to say. Come to think of it, maybe there is a diamond in Westmoreland County after all.

OAKLAND

Oakland may be the city's most cosmopolitan neighborhood, drawing on its university-medical complex for a rich variety of residents, visitors, and amenities. The neighborhood is home to the University of Pittsburgh, Carnegie Mellon University, and Carlow College, attracting students, faculty, and visitors who contribute to the neighborhood's vitality.

The hills are alive in Southwestern Pennsylvania. In the suburbs, you'll find the North Hills, the East Hills, the South Hills, and the West Hills. In the city, the hill bill includes Squirrel Hill, Troy Hill, Observatory Hill, Polish Hill, Spring Hill, Summer Hill, New Homestead Hill, the Hill District, and Perry Hilltop.

The medical complex, including the University of Pittsburgh Medical Center, Children's Hospital, and Magee Women's Hospital, is among the most highly regarded in the world. Dr. Jonas Salk developed the polio vaccine here, and it serves as the base for Dr. Thomas Starzl, one of the world's transplant pioneers. See the Health Care chapter for more detail on Oakland's hospitals.

The style of life in Oakland covers a wide range. Beyond the transient community of students, the neighborhood boasts a solid residential base. South Oakland features streets of closely built homes that stretch all the way to I-376 (the Parkway East), where they overlook the Monongahela River. Schenley Heights features large older homes, while at Oakland's eastern end, you'll find many attractive highrises, where residents live in close proximity to hospitals, doctors' offices, and such cultural amenities as the Carnegie. The chapter about the Arts contains a complete description of the Carnegie. The average Oakland home price is about $73,000.

Though Oakland is only about 4 miles from downtown, it contains two shopping districts—student-oriented businesses along Forbes Avenue, and more upscale galleries, shops, and restaurants near The Carnegie along South Craig Street.

In a word, Oakland will energize you.

OAKMONT

If you follow the professional golf tour, you've heard of Oakmont. It's the home of Oakmont Country Club, which has hosted a number of PGS and U.S. Open tournaments through the years and is considered one of America's premier country clubs. As you travel from the Allegheny River up steep Hulton Road toward the country club, you'll see many well-appointed homes with spacious grounds.

The commercial district is a charming slice of small town Americana, featuring professional offices and artisans' shops. You won't find a mall anywhere near this business district. Oakmont also offers a popular walking nature park, a yacht club, and public golf courses near the private country club.

If you're traveling to Oakmont from downtown, it's best to stay on high-speed Route 28 on the other side of the Allegheny, then cross the Hulton Bridge to Oakmont. You can't miss the Hulton Bridge—it's lavender.

PENN HILLS

Next to Pittsburgh, Penn Hills is the largest municipality in Allegheny County, some 53,000 residents strong. The community was formerly a cluster of independent local mining enclaves brought closer together by the completion of I-376 (the Parkway East).

Penn Hills spans 20 square miles as well as a variety of residential styles. You'll find single-family homes on quiet suburban streets as well as large multiunit residential buildings. The community boasts an appealing diversity of residents representing many races, income levels, and styles.

Shopping districts here are long and linear, stretching for miles along both Rodi Road and Frankstown Road, and there are several smaller shopping clusters as well. Penn Hills is a few minutes' drive from the Pennsylvania Turnpike and about 25 minutes from downtown Pittsburgh.

SHADYSIDE

Shadyside often has been compared to Washington's Georgetown neighborhood, and there are similarities. In Shadyside, you'll find some of the city's loveliest and largest homes, including stunning Victorian mansions. You'll also find one of the trendiest and nicest shopping districts along Walnut Street, home to a variety of restaurants and upscale boutiques. Exploring Walnut Street is a treat, as you'll find many unusual and unheralded shops tucked around corners and up stairs. The neighborhood hosts an annual arts festival that packs them in on Walnut Street.

The average single-family home price is about $147,000, but you can find condominiums for under $100,000; there are also some grander homes that fetch higher prices.

The neighborhood is home to Chatham College and Shadyside Hospital, as well as a number of stately churches. Shadyside is an easy bus trip from downtown Pittsburgh, about 5 miles away.

SQUIRREL HILL

Meet one of the most attractive and diverse neighborhoods in the city of Pittsburgh. Squirrel Hill is an especially large city neighborhood with nearly 30,000 residents. You'll find a broad variety of residential styles here, including many high-rise apartment buildings and sprawling brick mansions along Beechwood Boulevard and in the section of the neighborhood informally called "North of Forbes." The average sales price of a Squirrel Hill home is about $160,000, though the upper end of the range is $500,000 and beyond. Surprisingly, it's also possible to find some homes in the $45–$60,000 range on side streets in Squirrel, especially in the area where the neighborhood borders on Greenfield.

Just as important as the attractive housing is the neighborhood's blend of residents. Squirrel Hill is an important center of Judaism, home to a dozen synagogues and temples as well as the Jewish Community Center. The defining characteristic of life here is ethnic diversity. Walk along the bustling Murray Avenue shopping district and you'll see delicatessens;

pizza parlors; a Middle Eastern bakery; and Greek, Chinese, and sushi restaurants. At the hub of the neighborhood, the corner of Murray and Forbes Avenues, the Jewish Community Center stands alongside St. Edmund's Academy, which is a Diocese of Pittsburgh elementary school, and across the street from Sixth Presbyterian Church.

The shopping district lacks a major department store as anchor but is just about self-sufficient in every other way, with businesses ranging from convenience stores to movie theaters to couturiers. And, notably, you'll be only ten minutes from the Waterfront, the new shopping and entertainment mecca, which boasts major anchor stores, such as Kaufmann's Department Store, and discount stores, such as Marshall's and Target, as well as restaurants and a huge movie theater. For recreation, Frick Park is an urban jewel, with miles of hiking and jogging trails, picnic areas, athletic fields, and, believe it or not, a birding stand. For more on Frick Park, see our Parks chapter.

Squirrel Hill is about 5 miles from downtown Pittsburgh, easily accessible from I-376 (the Parkway East). When you visit the neighborhood, check out the former school where a portion of the film *Diabolique* was shot. The movie was bad; Squirrel Hill gets four stars.

SWISSHELM PARK

Ask Pittsburgh residents about Swisshelm Park and you'll probably evoke a lot of puzzled looks. That's because Swisshelm Park, though within the City of Pittsburgh, is cut off from the rest of the city by sprawling Frick Park. In fact, if you begin from any point in Pittsburgh, you can't drive to Swisshelm Park without first leaving the city.

That isolation has enabled Swisshelm Park to develop as a tight-knit, family-oriented neighborhood of about 1,500 residents. Residential style here is largely single family, with few rental properties available. You'll find primarily suburban-

Relocating to Pittsburgh

Pittsburgh has much to offer, with numerous neighborhoods and suburbs full of character, a splendid variety of cultural and sports activities, great food and shopping, great healthcare, beautiful parks, excellent schools. That's a start on life for those considering relocating here.

Ellen Roth, Ph.D., president of Getting to the Point, a corporate relocation services company, and one of the Top 50 Women in Business according to Pennsylvania's governor, shares her expertise about considerations for moving, encouraging newcomers to put "their bases in place." That means not only will you want to find just the right place to live—easy enough to do in the diverse Pittsburgh area—but also "anchor yourself within a community." What kinds of social or networking groups are you used to being part of? Do you want to belong to a religious organization or group associated with a spiritual path? Where will you go, and what will you do for recreation? How will you meet new friends? If you have children, ditto these questions for them, and add schools. If you're moving with a spouse, what will he or she do? Does your spouse want to continue along an established career or personal path or seize the move as an opportunity to begin a new dream?

Wow! What a list! But aren't these the things that shape a life, beyond a job or college or the person you're moving here to be with? Roth, a former mental health professional, cautions people in transition to remember that moving can be traumatic. While answering all these questions for yourself may seem overwhelming, as the old Nike ad goes, "Just do it." What you will accomplish is to support yourself in making a successful transition to your new home.

The first place we suggest you begin is Xplorion (www.xplorion.org). Xplorion is a state-of-the-art showcase for Southwestern Pennsylvania that combines aerial photography, a geographic information system, and other advanced technologies into a powerful tool for quickly learning about the region's assets; attractions; and industrial, residential, and commercial sites.

If you're already visiting Pittsburgh, you can check out XplorionQuest, a virtual-flight theater that provides a tour of the region's highlights; and XplorionConnect, visitor kiosks that quickly provide access to a host of online resources for the region. Xplorion is on the street-level floor of the Regional Enterprise Building downtown, 425 Sixth Street, (412) 391-5590. The office is open Monday to Friday, 10:00 A.M. to 4:30 P.M., excluding major holidays. You can also log onto xplorion.org from your current home, where you will have access to a smaller, but still quite impressive, number of card-catalogue–like "entries" that provide links to Web sites relating to the region and its resources.

For example, when we clicked on "finding a home" in the area, numerous subject categories invited exploration: available homes and apartments, choosing a community, community governments, how-to guides for homebuyers, relocation assistance, school districts, shelters and low-income housing, and student housing. Then, under each category, at least 50 entries popped up. Downtown at Xplorion's physical location, we would have seen almost 300 resources popping up under many of the categories. How's that for efficient research time?

Likewise, Three Rivers Freenet (www.trfn.org), a Web resource directory and host for Web sites of numerous nonprofits, offers comprehensive information about the area and its opportunities. Sponsored by the Carnegie Library system, TRFN is integrated with the library's subject guide. So, you'll link not only to Web resources, but to publications the library has to offer. (If you're searching from another area, perhaps your local bookstore or library has those same publications.) We especially like TRFN's information on community organizations,

which is extensive, and it offers an excellent events calendar for the area, too.

Finally, in addition to the representative list of excellent area realtors included later in this chapter, here are a few sites and phone numbers that will prove useful in finding a house or apartment. You will find these sites and more like them indexed on xplorion.org and trfn.org. The National Association of Realtors offers the largest database of homes for sale in the world at www.realtor.com. The Web sites www.homefair.com and www.home store.com enable searches for both apartments and homes and post tips about the moving process as well. In addition, at www.aptselector.com/pittsburgh/, a free apartment listing service offered since 1959 (originally only in print, of course), you'll find an excellent selection of apartments of all sizes throughout the city. If you prefer to make calls about apartments, good places to start would be Apartments

Unlimited, Squirrel Hill (412-521-7838); Pittsburgh's Apartment Source, West View (412-939-1686); and Northside Properties (412-231-3032). At www.city.pittsburgh. pa.us, under the Community and Visitors section, you'll find excellent links to descriptions of local neighborhoods. Finally, if you're in the city for a visit, just drive around: You'll see signs indicating homes for sale and apartments for rent, and what better way to find a place than to see it in person.

*Once you're settled in, go to www.dot
.state.pa.us to find the driver's license
center nearest you. The number to call
for car registration is PennDOT, (800)
932-4600.*

style ranch homes and two-story brick
dwellings, with the typical home selling
for about $60,000.

The center of recreational and civic life
is the Sarah Jackson Black Community
Center, with a wide range of outdoor
activities offered in Frick Park. Swisshelm
Park does not offer any businesses to
speak of—a blessing or a curse, depending on your point of view. You'll find
plenty of shopping opportunities, however, in adjacent Swissvale and the nearby
Edgewood Towne Center.

For a great place to raise a family . . .
and retain some mystery about your
lifestyle . . . try the splendid isolation of
Swisshelm Park.

South

BETHEL PARK

Some key statistics will give you a good
feel for this attractive South Hills suburb
of Pittsburgh. The average home price is
better than $106,000. About 91 percent of
the community's high school graduates go
on to further education. Four of every five
homes are owner-occupied.

If you're getting the sense of a family-
oriented community of some means, welcome to Bethel Park. The community is
less than 10 miles from downtown Pittsburgh, but many residents find all the
amenities they need in local shopping
malls, such as the massive South Hills Village. While the drive to Pittsburgh is easy,
many commuters prefer to utilize park-
and-ride lots and the "T" trolley-subway
system. For more on this system, see our
Getting Here, Getting Around chapter.

Most homes in this community of
nearly 38,000 were constructed after
World War II. They tend to feature two to
four bedrooms and well-maintained lawns.
Bethel Park is adjacent to South Park, a
1,999-acre, Allegheny County-run facility
that glitters as one of the jewels of the
municipal park system. For more on South
Park, see our Parks chapter.

BROOKLINE

Brookline reflects many of the attractive
qualities of Pittsburgh's South Hills. A large
city neighborhood of nearly 15,000 people,
Brookline is less than 4 miles from Downtown, which is accessible by both bus and
the trolley-subway system known as the
"T." It's also on the doorstep of the region's
heavily populated southern suburbs.

For many years, the near-exclusive
residential style in Brookline was single
family, with solid homes well-spaced along
tree-lined streets surrounding Brookline
Boulevard. In recent years, the neighborhood has entertained development of an
apartment building, a townhouse development, and two senior citizen highrises,
diversifying residential life. Prices for
homes often range from $20,000 to
$120,000.

The neighborhood's business district,
though without major anchors, will meet
most of your shopping needs. Brookline
also boasts two community swimming
pools and Seton-LaSalle Catholic High
School.

MOUNT LEBANON

Mount Lebanon is one of Pittsburgh's
showcase communities; a home in this
South Hills suburb represents the aspira-
tions of many local residents. Most homes
in this community of more than 33,000
sell for between $150,000 and $250,000,
although you'll find plenty well beyond
that range. The typical Mount Lebanon
home is freestanding, made of brick, with
three to four bedrooms and spacious
grounds. Homes are set back from tree-

lined streets that are part of Mt. Lebanon's rich history—the community was named for two Cedars of Lebanon trees planted on Bower Hill Road, a main thoroughfare.

Mt. Lebanon's many amenities provide another foundation for the community's reputation. The upscale Galleria Mall anchors the busy business district. For recreation, the community offers 300 acres of parklands, a swimming pool, a tennis center, a nature reserve, an athletic field with artificial surface, an indoor ice skating rink, and a nine-hole golf course.

For all that, it is Mt. Lebanon's education system that is perhaps its most admired feature. Excellent public and private school networks lead to the high school, from which 92 percent of graduates go on to post-secondary education. As you might expect, residents are aware and politically active. It's a great place for a debate . . . as you stroll along quiet, shady streets.

MT. WASHINGTON

Few urban areas can offer the visual excitement that Mt. Washington provides. Located at the top of Mt. Washington (naturally), the neighborhood offers breathtaking views of the city and its rivers below. Grandview Avenue, the neighborhood's main thoroughfare, provides several observation decks and souvenir shops, as most visitors to Pittsburgh include Mt. Washington on their itinerary. If you've enjoyed those sweeping views of Pittsburgh in films and advertisements, chances are they were shot from Mt. Washington.

Because of the view, homes in Mt. Washington can be quite dear. Newer condominiums—some of them actually cut into the mountain—can fetch up to $800,000.

Once past such conversation pieces, however, you'll find a community of stable homes that sell for an average of $58,000. The grand view may be a block or two away, but you'll find an active business

district along Shiloh Street and a stable population of about 10,000.

You'll also have an opportunity to utilize one of the most unusual means of transportation—that inclined plane, sort of a trolley car that shuttles passengers up and down the mountainside. The Duquesne and Monongahela inclines are tourist attractions, but residents who work downtown also ride the inclines; they're at work in a few minutes, and they avoid parking hassles. For more on the inclines, see our Getting Here, Getting Around and Attractions chapters.

PETERS

Peters has been one of the strong growth areas in Western Pennsylvania. The township is strategically located just across the Allegheny County border in Washington County, thus able to attract residents from Pittsburgh's South Hills as well as those in Washington County and points south and west.

Transformed from a semi-developed community, Peters is now home to more than 14,000 residents who live in spacious homes with large, landscaped lots. Home prices begin at $100,000, with some larger homes selling for $500,000 or more. The average home price is about $200,000.

Most homes—92 percent—are owner-occupied, and there is scant commercial development here. With its location along Route 19, residents have access to as many shopping malls as they would ever need.

Peters residents value education, as 93 percent of the township's high school graduates continue their education.

SOUTH SIDE

Frequently, the term "neighborhood in transition" is a euphemism for a community on the downhill side. South Side is a city of Pittsburgh neighborhood that has been in transition, and the result is one of the most lively neighborhoods you'll find.

CLOSE-UP

Eve Picker

Eve Picker's ambitions for downtown Pittsburgh and surrounding areas have manifested. Back in 2000 the architect-turned-city planner-turned-developer had just taken on the task of introducing residential lofts in the heart of the city. Three years later, No Wall Productions, (412) 456–0829, www.nowall.com, offers nine buildings with both commercial and residential loft space available.

When No Wall began, artists' lofts in the city were nothing new, but previous developers who had tried to create residential lofts had been frustrated by the prevailing architecture of downtown. Pittsburgh's older structures, jewels though they be, are architectural Olive Oyls, tall and skinny, not conducive to the development of living space with workable dimensions. Conversion of such buildings to marketable living quarters is laborious and risky, so fraught with uncertainties—so it seemed until Eve Picker came along—that financial institutions were reluctant to underwrite downtown loft developments.

Picker, a native of Sydney, Australia, with a master's degree in urban design from Columbia University, proved to have just the right mix of experience and determination for the job. Her training as an architect familiarized her with the design principles that helped her envision residential lofts—and convinced her that she didn't want to remain an architect.

"I'm not sure it was architecture so much as it was me," she says. "I'm an entrepreneurial type. I want to work on big projects that affect public spaces, yet at a large firm, I'd be sort of at the bottom of the ladder, not really knowing I contributed.

"I'm impatient and need a lot of things happening at the same time. In development, you're involved and responsible every step of the way. As an architect, you can't do that. You're only responsible for a little piece of it."

She served a stint with the City of Pittsburgh Department of Planning, a position that enabled her to become familiar with virtually every foot of usable space in downtown Pittsburgh, and worked with a dozen residential developments.

When she found an abandoned former paper products warehouse in downtown's Firstside district along the Monongahela River, she knew she had the right property for the first lofts. Financing remained the final piece of the puzzle. Picker surmounted that by signing on National City Bank as both her financier and equity partner, remaining somewhat "edgy" about the bold risk she was taking.

The neighborhood, a long, linear community that stretches for about 30 blocks along the Monongahela River, for many years was characterized by older multi-story homes with party walls. Many residents worked at LTV's South Side Steel Mill, which would become a casualty of Big Steel's decline. The business district

After about 18 months of work, the building, renamed 429 Firstside Lofts, was ready. The eight-story structure features commercial space on the ground floor, then one loft on each of the remaining stories. The lofts are marvelous blends of original elements and practical new touches. Picker retained much of the building's original steel, including a number of discolored imperfections. Powder rooms just off the elevators feature the building's original brick walls on one side. To preserve as much living space as possible in the 1,850-square-foot lofts, Picker wall-mounted appliances in the kitchen, as well as the washers and dryers tucked unobtrusively into the principal bathroom. There are no doors from the elevator to the lofts. Step off the elevator, and you're in your space.

Perhaps the neatest touch is the rooftop deck, where residents can gather to relax, dine, and enjoy the river traffic along the Mon below. To Picker's relief and delight, buyers quickly snapped up six of the seven lofts, priced between $155,000 and $195,000. Picker bought the seventh herself and plans to rent it out until what she playfully calls her two "teenage appendages" are on their own and she and her husband need less space.

These days, eight "fresh and charming" condominiums, called Osterling Flats, are for sale in Brighton Heights, indicating No Wall Productions' venture outside the borders of downtown. The development, named after Frederick J. Osterling, the prominent Pittsburgh architect who designed the original structures, offers "a 'hipness' factor that you might find in some of Pittsburgh's trendier areas," according to No Wall's Web site. In addition, Brighton Heights is close to the cultural attractions of the city, with easy access to nearby conveniences of the suburbs. Pricing ranges from $125,900 to $135,900, with special financing in the form of a deferred second mortgage of up to $41,250 for income-qualified applicants. We love Pittsburgh! These are prime spaces. Where else are you going to find this kind of opportunity?

Revealing her aesthetic as developer, Picker asserts, "Every building is different. They speak to me and tell me what they want to be."

Picker also has seven other loft spaces offering gorgeous, rentable units, priced between $1,100 and $1,950 monthly, in keeping with Pittsburgh's reasonable market. These buildings can be found in the Cultural District downtown, the Penn Avenue Arts District on the edge of the Strip, and in the Strip District itself. New loft office spaces on Oakland's Craig Street are priced at $16 per square foot, plus utilities. Eve Picker has started a successful housing and commercial trend.

along East Carson Street was community serving but sedate.

In the 1980s, young professionals discovered the South Side as a way to beat downtown rents and began renovating older structures for their offices. Trendy taverns, restaurants, galleries, and retail shops sprang up to serve this new younger crowd. South Side Local Development Company initiated a project, with the Urban Redevelopment Authority of Pittsburgh, to create 300 units of riverfront housing. URA also is working to renovate the abandoned LTV site.

All this development has served to create a vibrant neighborhood, as renowned for its nightlife as it is for its family life. The price range for South Side homes is broad, reflecting the varying styles. While the average price is about $47,000, you can acquire an older, party-wall-type home for as little as $20,000. On the other hand, newer or renovated homes sometimes bring $200,000 or more in this up-and-coming neighborhood.

UPPER ST. CLAIR

When you see the initials "USC" in Western Pennsylvania, don't mistake the acronym for reference to the University of Southern California or the University of South Carolina. In these parts, USC means Upper St. Clair, an affluent community at the southwestern edge of Allegheny County near the Washington County border.

Why is USC so recognizable? Perhaps it's because of the quality of the township's homes. Prices begin at about $100,000 and rise to $250,000 or more for spacious homes with well-manicured grounds. Most of the homes were built after World War II, and most—93 percent—are owner-occupied. You will find some modern apartment complexes, but large family-style homes remain the rule.

Perhaps USC is so prominent for its emphasis on education. An astonishing 98 percent of its high school graduates pursue post-secondary education, a figure that may be unequaled in the region.

Shoppers have access to a clutch of malls along Route 19, the highway that connects Allegheny and Washington Counties, and Upper St. Clair is only a few minutes' drive from I-79. The township is about a 20-minute commute from downtown Pittsburgh.

WASHINGTON

For years, Pittsburgh area residents have referred to this city 25 miles southwest of Pittsburgh as "Little Washington." While that may seem a logical way to distinguish it from that city inside the Beltway, you can understand why residents of Pennsylvania's Washington could be a little miffed. This is a city with a colorful history and a strong modern identity.

Washington was the center of the Whiskey Rebellion, an 18th-century challenge to the federal government's taxing authority, as well as an important stop on the National Road and the Underground Railroad. Today the city is home to Washington & Jefferson College, where the Olin Fine Arts Center stages many cultural events, and 45 place of worship.

Washington is strategically positioned at the junction of two interstate highways—I-70 and I-79—providing easy access to West Virginia and Ohio. Once a center for manufacturing, Washington now relies on the service and professional sectors for employment opportunities.

West

BANKSVILLE

Just west of downtown is a neighborhood that combines many elements of city of Pittsburgh life. Banksville offers stately older homes as well as newer dwellings that seem more suburban, with sweeping, manicured lawns and colorful flower beds. While such homes are popular with families, the neighborhood is also home to Crane Village and Hiland Hills, two of Pittsburgh's largest garden apartment complexes, which typically cater to more transient residents. Homes in Banksville generally sell for between $60,000 and $90,000.

The heart of the shopping district is Banksville Road, a strip of shopping plazas that can satisfy most of your shop-

CLOSE-UP

Relocation Services

If moving seems just too overwhelming, you may be able to obtain some professional assistance from one of Pittsburgh's two corporate relocation services, Getting to the Point (www.getting-to-the-point.com, 412-362-3363) or Presenting Pittsburgh (www.presentingpittsburgh.com, 412-481-5100, and 877-408-5100). Traditionally, relocation services companies work exclusively with employers, such as corporations, hospitals, and academic institutions, and the employer foots the bill. Employees and individuals negotiating their contracts can bargain to have relocation services included in the package. In addition, Presenting Pittsburgh, owned by business partners Megan Misgalla and Christine Probert, offers services to individuals as well employers. Misgalla explains that she offers packets of detailed information about the Pittsburgh region ($35 and $65) for individuals, as well as customized tours and "settling in" assistance.

Both Getting to the Point and Presenting Pittsburgh offer services that include complete touring and orientation; help finding temporary rental housing, if necessary; assistance with the home-buying process and finding community services; assistance with making connections within schools, such as with teachers and coaches; and assistance with settling in and "finding a place" within one's community, such as through volunteerism. Moreover, Getting to the Point offers a career assistance program for "trailing" spouses and "Getting to the Point for Women," a program geared toward helping women newcomers meet other prominent women in the area.

Perhaps Ellen Roth, Ph.D., of Getting to the Point epitomizes the raison d'etre for relocation companies when she says, "We take care of people. Our goal is for people moving to the area to experience a smooth transition and a confident start."

---

ping needs. Banksville Road also functions as the main thoroughfare. Inbound, it takes you to the Parkway West and downtown; outbound, it leads on to the heavily populated South Hills. Banksville is a taste of the suburbs within the city.

BEAVER

"Imagine a rolling English landscape, with the softest of blue skies, dotted at three-mile intervals with quiet little villages, or aggressive little manufacturing towns." That's how Rudyard Kipling described the Beaver Valley in a letter to a friend. Today,

the community of Beaver, the county seat of Beaver County about 30 miles southwest of Pittsburgh, retains much of the charm that so enamored Kipling.

With little or no industry in the town itself, Beaver offers broad, shaded streets, lush parks, and views of the nearby Beaver and Ohio Rivers. Most residents live in single-family homes and enjoy such amenities as the Gazebo in the heart of town, which features live entertainment during warm weather months.

Stability is the watchword in this community of about 5,500. The town's

Based on a survey of apartment locator Web sites, it appears you may get better deals on rent if you approach local sources, such as rental agencies and building managers, directly.

churches represent nine different denominations. Residents show such pride in their community—and such concern for their neighbors—that the police department and parent-teacher organizations sponsor an annual bicycle registration to discourage theft.

BEAVER FALLS

Among the notables who have called Beaver Falls home is one Joe Willie Namath, one of the National Football League's legendary quarterbacks and party goers. Sometimes it's hard to imagine Broadway Joe in this quiet, friendly town of about 10,500 located west of Pittsburgh along the Beaver River in Beaver County.

A center of social activities in Beaver Falls is 37th Street Park, where folks gather on park benches and kids enjoy the annual Easter egg hunt around the gazebo. The largest local employers include Republic Steel; Armstrong World Industries, a manufacturer of ceiling tiles; and Geneva College, situated in a popular residential area called College Hill.

Residential style is eclectic, with single-family homes, duplexes, rental properties, and highrise multiunit buildings all available.

CANONSBURG

Is it possible that one small Southwestern Pennsylvania town produced both Perry Como and Bobby Vinton? Indeed it is, and that town is Canonsburg, off I-79 in Washington County, about 15 miles southwest of Pittsburgh. The community has changed a bit since the days when Mr. C. was crooning for the patrons of his barber shop. Single-family homes still honeycomb the hillsides between I-79 and Pennsylvania

Route 19, but the town also has seen a number of planned communities.

Most prominent among these is Southpointe, a complex that features industrial, office, residential, and recreational uses. You can admire Southpointe's townhomes and golf course from I-79; if you drive in for a closer look or inquire about residential opportunities, you won't be the first passerby to do so.

Many of the town's 9,500 residents work at local businesses, including Pennsylvania Transformer Technology, Sarris Candies, and the antiques shops that dot the main thoroughfare. One of the real attractions of Canonsburg is that location along I-79, about 35 minutes from the West Virginia and Ohio borders.

MOON

Moon traces its history to 1788, when it was among Allegheny County's initial group of townships. The origin of its name remains something of a mystery, though some say it derives from the crescent-shaped bend in the Ohio River, which forms Moon's northern border.

In contemporary times, Moon has experienced significant residential and commercial growth, thanks in part to the expansion of Pittsburgh International Airport a few miles away. To meet the needs associated with the airport, Moon offers a variety of recently constructed housing, including both single-family dwellings and luxury multiunit buildings.

The township of about 25,000 residents is home to Allegheny County's Settler's Park as well as the township-operated Robin Hill Park, site of many recreational and cultural activities, and five golf courses. With its location near Interstate 279 (the Parkway West), Moon is within easy reach of both the airport and downtown Pittsburgh.

SEWICKLEY

Once a summer retreat area for Pittsburgh's wealthiest families, Sewickley today is a charming residential community, one of a chain of such towns along the Ohio River in Allegheny County. In Sewickley and neighboring Sewickley Heights, you'll find some of the largest and most expensive homes in the region, but you'll also find lovely and more afford-able housing as well.

The commercial district features a vil-lage atmosphere and quaint boutiques, art galleries, antiques shops, and restaurants. Sewickley's approximately 4,000 residents take great pride in the breadth and quality of the public services the community pro-vides, including careful oversight of reno-vations to historic older homes.

Sewickley offers five recreational com-plexes. If you live in Sewickley, you'll be well-positioned for convenient travel. It's about 10 minutes from Pittsburgh Interna-tional Airport, 20 minutes from downtown Pittsburgh, and right on the doorstep of Beaver County.

WESTWOOD

Westwood has such an underdeveloped look to it that many Pittsburgh residents might not be aware there's a neighbor-hood here. This city of Pittsburgh neigh-borhood about 3 miles from Downtown has a rural flavor to it, with wooded areas and yards that sometimes resemble pas-toral fields. One Westwood homeowner with just such a flat, grassy yard leases the field for company picnics.

Homes in Westwood—from grand old Victorians to two-story neocolonials—typi-cally sell for about $52,000 and often include undeveloped acreage. The com-munity recreational complex offers a swimming pool and tennis courts, and res-idents enjoy easy access to the shopping malls along I-279.

Westwood offers an old-fashioned sense of neighborhood; residents stage block parties and watch their kids play soccer in the streets. Westwood isn't exactly a neighborhood that time forgot, but it is a throwback.

REAL ESTATE

Pittsburgh residents tend to stay put. Nevertheless, you'll find thousands of homes on the market at any given time, with activity peaking in the spring. The region's housing stock is a blend of older homes, many of them beautifully reno-vated, and recently constructed dwellings. Thus, the price range for homes in the area is quite broad, beginning as low as around $20,000 for some "handyman's specials" and soaring to $1 million or more at the high end.

Because neighborhoods in the region are numerous and diverse, you might find it helpful to work with a real estate agency to identify some options for you. The real estate sector here is large, active, and sophisticated. Their marketing thrusts include the traditional, such as printed materials, as well as the innovative, includ-ing television programs and comprehen-sive Web sites.

We've profiled a number of agencies to help point you in the right direction. The list is by no means exhaustive, but our profiles will introduce you to the largest agencies in the area as well as number of neighborhood specialists. Happy hunting!

Realtors

Albert Anthony Real Estate
528 East Eighth Street, Munhall
(412) 461-5209

Albert Anthony and his wife Judie handle the sale of homes in the East End and the South Hills. They also offer residential property management and commercial appraisals. While the median price range of homes they sell is $79,900 to $129,000, some homes—like large, stately places of residence in Squirrel Hill—may bring as much as $400,000. The Anthonys also are happy to sell marketable homes in their area in lower price ranges. Their son has recently joined them in their business, and

the Anthonys have added rental properties to their selections as well.

The Anthonys' office is only about a
mile from their own homes, and they
know the areas they represent personally.
They'll be sure to give you personal service, too.

Barnes and Associates Real Estate
102 Lexington Avenue, Aspinwall
(412) 781-3171

Barnes and Associates concentrates on
homes in Fox Chapel and surrounding
communities. They average about 50 sales
per year, significant volume with such a
small geographic concentration, so you
know the agency is highly regarded in the
community. The homes they handle range
in price from about $50,000 to $250,000
and more, and each deal gets the personal
attention of proprietor Maryanne Barnes.

If doing most of the work to sell your
own home (and avoiding paying commis-
sions) appeals to you, check out Maryanne
Barnes' brainchild, Real Estate Express.
For very modest fees, Maryanne will provide you with everything you need to sell
your own home and you'll have her and
her associate's expertise at your fingertips.
The best news is that this service could
save you anywhere from $6,400 to
$44,000, depending on the selling price
of your home.

Century 21
6 Sylvan Way, Parsippany, New Jersey
(800) 221-5737
www.century21.com

One of the largest agencies in the region,
Century 21 boasts 26 offices in Southwestern Pennsylvania, each independently
owned and operated.

The company offers an innovative program called Century 21 Communities, an
America Online site that provides access
to information about 700 neighborhoods
across North America. Enter a ZIP code
and you can find what a community's
residents like to drive, read, and watch
on television.

Coldwell Banker Real Estate
9576 Perry Highway, McCandless
(412) 366-1600

With 14 offices and 800 agents in
Southwestern Pennsylvania, Coldwell
Banker tries to make buying and selling
homes as convenient as possible for its
clients. Dedicated divisions handle mortgages, relocations, and title services, while
the company deploys a special unit for
homes priced at $350,000 and above.

The company adheres to a 22-point
guarantee for sellers and buyers. Among
the company's service guarantees: If they
don't convey a decision about your loan
application the same day it's filed, they'll
pay you $250; if they don't meet the
scheduled closing date, they'll reduce
your interest rate by $1/8$ percent. (Certain
restrictions apply; call for details.)

Coldwell Banker publishes *The Real
Estate News & Buyers Guide,* featuring
pictures and descriptions of every home
in its inventory. It runs as an insert in a
number of local newspapers, or you can
subscribe for free by calling the agency.

Dunn Real Estate Services
512 Foreland Street
(412) 322-2000

Here's a small agency with four agents
that specializes in city of Pittsburgh properties, with particular emphasis on 15
Northside neighborhoods that produce 85
percent of the company's business. You'll
find an exhaustive knowledge of those 15
neighborhoods at Dunn, as well as familiarity with special financing programs—
an important plus for first-time buyers.
Because it's so well-known on its turf, the
agency can reach special audiences, such
as employees of Northside companies,
that mass advertising might miss.

Equity Real Estate
2029 Murray Avenue
(412) 422-9200

Equity is a mid-size agency specializing
in the city's eastern neighborhoods. The
company has 40 agents with thorough

knowledge of their territory. If you visit Equity, you'll find its ownership and senior management right there on the premises, every day. The agency maintains contacts with a wide variety of lenders to ensure that buyers have access to the best financing packages.

Harris Realty
2214 Murray Avenue
(412) 521-7050

If you're looking for a home in Pittsburgh's eastern neighborhoods, the folks at Harris are your prospective neighbors. Its three full-time and eight part-time agents are residents of such eastern neighborhoods as Squirrel Hill, Shadyside, Greenfield, and Point Breeze. They know your turf and can help you negotiate it, whether you're in the market for an estate or a fixer-upper. When you phone Harris, your call will be taken by a real, live person, 24 hours a day.

Howard Hanna Real Estate Services
119 Gamma Drive, O'Hara
(412) 967-9000
www.howardhanna.com

For more than 40 years, Howard Hanna Real Estate Services has been one of Western Pennsylvania's most prominent agencies. It's the largest, family-owned, full-service real estate company in the Pennsylvania, Ohio, and West Virginia tri-state area. It operates 58 offices with approximately 1,100 full-time sales associates. Among the services Howard Hanna provides are appraisals, financing, and relocation and closing services.

With the breadth of the agency's coverage come a number of valuable customer services. These include a "money back guarantee" for the buyer of your home; an advanced equity loan program, which allows the purchaser of your home to borrow against equity from Howard Hanna Real Estate to meet current mortgage payments; and an apartment trade-in program, so that if your home is

purchased by an apartment dweller, Howard Hanna Real Estate will assume the renter's lease.

The agency also employs marketing techniques with a technology twist, such as producing the weekly *Real Estate Digest/Showcase of Homes* each Sunday morning on KDKA-TV, and featuring the agency's entire list of homes on its Web site.

Lavelle Real Estate
2909 Central Avenue
(412) 621-2992

Many companies claim to be family businesses; Lavelle Real Estate walks the walk. Robert R. Lavelle received his broker's license in 1951 and still runs the business. His son and wife are Lavelle Real Estate brokers, while his daughter-in-law serves as office manager, coordinating the activities of five agents.

It's no coincidence that the agency is located in the Hill District, the hub of Pittsburgh's African-American community. "As a minority-owned institution," Robert Lavelle says, "we're trying to help black people own homes. We want to motivate people, to let them see a black business with the accoutrements of success." This is an agency with experience—and a mission.

Northwood Realty Co./
Better Homes and Gardens
4100 Route 8, Allison Park
(412) 487-3200, (800) 245-6172
(relocation)

Northwood is a full-service firm that operates throughout Southwestern Pennsylvania, with 32 offices and 700 agents. Just as significant, its Better Homes and Gardens affiliation provides it with the opportunity for national and international referrals. If you're planning to move almost anywhere, chances are Northwood has an affiliate there.

The agency has a number of special programs to serve customers. It offers a 30-minute television show each Sunday at 11:30 A.M. on WPXI-TV to showcase all

"For Sale by Owner"

With more than 350 real estate agencies listed in the phone book, it's sometimes difficult to know where to begin when you're in the housing market. Many Realtors in the region participate in a cooperative organization known as West Penn Multi List; when you deal with these companies, they'll have a comprehensive list of homes available, rather than the listings of one agency only.

If you'd prefer to get a feel for the market yourself, you can pick up a free copy of *Homes Guide By Realtors,* a twice-monthly publication of the Realtors Association of Metropolitan Pittsburgh (RAMP) that provides a comprehensive list of homes for sale and is available free at many area supermarkets.

Also available at supermarkets are reprints of the Sunday real estate section of the *Tribune-Review,* a Pittsburgh daily newspaper. The section includes both comprehensive listings and feature stories. You also will find the section at the *Trib*'s Web site, www.tribune-review.com.

While you're at the grocery store picking up all this material, check out a newer publication called *Homes for Sale by Owner.* The twist here is that the own-ers represented in this bi-weekly publication are marketing their homes without agents. You can buy a photo ad for two weeks for as little as $49. For more information, contact the company at (412) 920-1589.

If selling a home all by yourself seems a little daunting, check out the "Real Estate Express" service offered by Barnes and Associates Real Estate (see their write-up for more). For some good guidelines on selecting a home, apartment, or builder, try these referral agencies: RAMP (412) 261-5200; Apartment Association of Metropolitan Pittsburgh, (412) 231-8111; and Builders Association of Metropolitan Pittsburgh (412) 231-8111. RAMP also will provide a free directory of Realtors, as well as a spiffier, more informative version priced at $100. While these trade organizations will not recommend specific companies, they will offer good advice on how to evaluate agencies and contractors. You also can try the Real Estate Hotline of the *Pittsburgh Post-Gazette*'s PG Link. If you call (412) 261-1234, you can get round-the-clock general information on closing costs, warranties, negotiations, and market appraisals.

homes on its current list. To learn the status of any home, you can call (412) 492-1100 around the clock, punch in the home's five-digit code, and hear a tape of an agent describing the unit and its status.

Finally, Northwood maintains an "Elegant Homes" division to market homes priced at $300,000 and above.

Prudential Preferred Realty
9401 McKnight Road
(412) 367-8028, (412) 261-4800
(relocation)
www.prudentialpreferred.com
Though owned and operated locally, Prudential Preferred is a franchise of Prudential nationally, providing it with strong

relocation services. With in-house capabilities for mortgages, insurance, and settlement services, Prudential Preferred can provide something approaching one-stop shopping for buyers.

Prudential Preferred operates 23 offices with more than 600 sales associates, giving it broad reach throughout Southwestern Pennsylvania. If you purchase a home through Prudential Preferred, the agency will buy your former residence, at a mutually agreeable price, if they can't move it within six months. If you're thinking of real estate as a career, try Prudential Preferred's in-house instructional program, which will prepare you for the appropriate state exams.

Karen L. Smith & Associates
26 South 27th Street
(412) 488-0100

The South Side is one of Pittsburgh's hottest neighborhoods, offering a compelling mix of restored older homes and new construction along the Monongahela River. Karen L. Smith & Associates specializes in South Side properties as well as other city of Pittsburgh neighborhoods. When proprietor Karen Smith offers advice about South Side housing, she speaks from experience, having acquired a renovated building in the neighborhood for her own home. The company employs four full-time agents.

CHILD CARE

ew services are as important to families as quality, reliable child care. As the frequency of dual wage earners within families has increased, the quest for child-care services has become a key determinant in the availability of both parents to continue working, to meet their economic goals, and to provide a supportive and loving environment for their children. Fortunately, the news on this front in Southwestern Pennsylvania is good. There is help as you embark on the search for reliable, safe, and educational care for your children.

For many local residents, child care goes by the decidedly unscientific names of Grandma and Grandpa. Family roots run deep in this region, with extended families often residing together or in the same neighborhood. For parents living in extended families, the need for professional child care may not be compelling. Yet that same emphasis on families and family values has helped inspire a broad network of professional child-care sources for those parents who live outside extended families.

Parents here have many choices. Not only will you find licensed day-care centers, but you'll also discover family-run child care in private homes. Hiring independent babysitters, signing up with a Mother's Day Out program, or enlisting the services of an au pair also may work well for your set of circumstances. In addition, there are agencies that can assist you if your child becomes ill and you're unable to take off work to be the primary caregiver.

With the exception of unique child-care arrangements, this chapter will not list, describe, or recommend individual day-care establishments. The purpose is to guide your decision making, explore the standards for what most experts regard as quality care, introduce community resources, and present alternatives. This chapter does contain a list of support groups and organizations that help both parents and other caregivers provide for healthy, happy nurturing.

UNDERSTANDING QUALITY CHILD CARE

The Pennsylvania Commission for Women has produced a handy Day Care Checklist to guide parents in choosing quality child care. This two-sided, blue checklist describes the characteristics you should look for in caregivers and staff, signs of safe facilities, health and safety factors, program components, and other indicators of good care. It suggests questions to ask potential providers, such as "May I drop in any time?" and "Is there a parents' group or program?" To get your checklist, write the commission at P.O. Box 1326, Harrisburg, PA 17105, or call (717) 787-8128.

In Pennsylvania, the state Department of Public Welfare is the agency that regulates day-care facilities in the following categories:

- Day Care Centers—state-licensed facilities providing care for seven or more children
- Group Day Care Homes—state-licensed facilities providing care for no more than 12 children
- Family Day Care Homes—state-certified family residences that have one caregiver for four, five, or six children unrelated to the caregiver
- Nursery Schools—part-time pre-school facilities licensed by the Pennsylvania Department of Education

For more information about day-care facilities in the Commonwealth, call one of the state's regional toll-free hotlines. In Southwestern Pennsylvania, that number is (800) 222-2149. Parents also may use this line, staffed by the Pennsylvania Department of Public Welfare, to investigate complaints, obtain day-care regulations, or ask other questions.

Additionally, Metlife Consumer Education Center has produced a useful pamphlet called "Choosing Childcare." While the booklet does not offer referrals for our region, it does an excellent job of explaining the differences in types of child care and presents points to cover when you inspect facilities and interview potential caregivers. For your free pamphlet, call (800) METLIFE.

REFERRAL SERVICES

Child Care Partnerships
305 Wood Street
(412) 261-CARE

A program of the YWCA of Greater Pittsburgh, Child Care Partnerships (CCP) is committed to improving the quality of child care, providing referral services to parents at every economic level, providing subsidies to eligible parents, and enhancing the child-care system within the region.

If you're a parent searching for child care, CCP's referral specialists will provide information on regulated (licensed or registered) child-care providers as reported by the Department of Public Welfare. Parents ultimately are responsible for screening and monitoring their child-care providers, but CCP has valuable information to guide parents to the best choices.

CCP also provides consultation and information to businesses interested in helping their employees balance work and family life. Employers contract with CCP for resource and referral services as well as work-site seminars, workshops, and other speaking engagements related to job and life issues.

Finally, Child Care Partnerships houses a Resource Room at its downtown location where child-care providers can borrow training materials, videos, books, and other tools. Training programs for

providers—scheduled in the evenings and on Saturdays—also are available.

Childcare Choices
1030 Eighth Avenue, Beaver Falls
(800) 322-8504

Childcare Choices offers information to parents about the location, costs, and eligibility requirements of day-care programs in Beaver County. The office maintains a directory of available programs that offer both private and subsidized child care.

National Association for the Education of Young Children (NAEYC)
1509 16th Street, NW, Washington, D.C. 20036
(800) 424-2460

Write or call this nonprofit, professional organization to receive a free list of accredited programs in the Pittsburgh area. Day-care facilities that are accredited by this national group have met a stringent set of guidelines that promote the well-being of children. Child-care programs participate in the NAEYC assessment program on a voluntary basis.

The Early Childhood Initiative
1 Smithfield Street
(412) 456-6793

A public-private partnership, the Early Childhood Initiative is designed to help low-income children up to five years of age become successful, productive adults by enrolling them in high-quality early care and education service. The Initiative is a United Way agency.

EF Au Pair
One Education Street, Cambridge, Massachusetts 02142
(800) 333-6056

EF Au Pair provides carefully screened young men and women, ages 18 to 26, who will join a family and care for the children during a yearlong cultural exchange program. As live-in companions, au pairs work up to 45 hours per week—no more

When you call Child Care Partnerships, (412) 261-CARE, you'll receive a checklist titled "Choosing Quality Childcare" that can help you make the best choices.

than 10 hours on any day—providing child care in exchange for room, board, and a valuable cultural experience.

SPECIAL CARE

The Get Well Room
327 Craft Avenue
(412) 641-1267

Located in the city's Oakland medical complex, The Get Well Room is a separate area of the Children's Center of Pittsburgh, comfortably equipped to care for children from 6 months through 12 years of age with mild respiratory or gastrointestinal illnesses. It's affiliated with Magee-Womens Hospital.

Supervised by a pediatric nurse, the staff provides a warm, caring atmosphere for children who cannot attend their regular child-care programs due to illness. The nurse decides how many children can be accepted on any given day.

Children may participate if they have mild fevers (103 degrees or less) or bronchitis, croup, asthma, diarrhea, occasional vomiting, or pain or fever from vaccinations. Children suffering from chicken pox, respiratory distress, continuous vomiting or diarrhea, and those with fevers higher than 103 degrees are not appropriate candidates for the Get Well Room.

If the service of the Get Well Room might help you, you'll need to complete a registration form and have your child's physician complete a health appraisal. Both forms must be on file at the Children's Center before your child can use the Get Well Room. The registration fee is $15 per family.

In addition, fees for services are due when those services are rendered. Some businesses offer their employees assis-

tance in paying for this form of child care. All medications should be brought in their original, labeled containers. The Get Well Room is open from 7:00 A.M. to 5:30 P.M. Monday through Friday.

The Therapeutic Parents'
and Children's Center
330 Boulevard of the Allies
(412) 562-9440

The Therapeutic Parent's and Children's Center, a program of Family Resources, is a therapeutic preschool for children suffering developmental and emotional delays as a result of abuse or neglect. This service intervenes early in children's lives to help keep them on track developmentally and to aid their families in meeting their special needs. Call Family Resources for more information if you feel this type of care is appropriate for your child. Other services of Family Resources are described under Support Organizations, below.

PART-DAY AND AFTER-SCHOOL PROGRAMS

In many communities in the region, you'll find part-time programs to help you meet your child-care needs. Churches and synagogues offer Mother's Day Out programs for infants to kindergarten-age children. After registering your child, you can arrange a schedule that gives you several hours of child care at nominal charges, similar in most cases to what you would pay a babysitter. To find such respite when you need it, contact churches and synagogues in your community.

In addition, many school districts can direct parents to after-school programs. Check with your school district's administrative office to determine if it offers such a program (see the Education chapter for school district contact information).

Organizations such as the YMCA or YWCA offer after-school or latch-key programs, while some churches also provide midweek programs for children and youths. Since the Greater Pittsburgh community is so vast, the range of services offered varies considerably. Each YMCA or YWCA, for instance, reflects the social and economic needs of the individual community. Thus, there could be subsidized child care available in some neighborhoods, and latch-key programs in others.

Regardless of the type of program you consider, do ask a few basic questions, including:

- Are these programs for children of a particular age? Or are various ages combined within the same program?
- What kinds of activities are offered?
- Who supervises the children?
- Are the surroundings safe?
- Is there a fee to be involved, or is membership or residency required (in the case of the YWCA, a church, or a school district)?
- Does the program operate during summers, holidays or snow days, or solely on school days?

Armed with these questions, you should turn to your local telephone directory or yellow pages to begin your search for the care that's appropriate for your child.

SUPPORT ORGANIZATIONS

Alliance for Infants and Toddlers, Inc.
Hough Building, 2801 Custer Avenue
(412) 885-6000

The Alliance provides developmental screening and tracking for children from birth to 3 years of age throughout Allegheny County. Your child may participate if there is parental concern or a history of medical, environmental, or biological factors such as prematurity or a stay in a neonatal intensive care unit. To be eligible for Infant/Toddler Early Intervention Services, children must be diagnosed with physical or mental conditions that place them at high risk for developmental delays. Services of the Alliance are free and confidential. Call

them to arrange an assessment to determine eligibility.

ARC-Allegheny
711 Bingham Street
(412) 995-5000

The mission of ARC-Allegheny is to protect the rights of, and promote opportunities for, those with mental retardation and developmental disabilities, and to do so within a family context. The organization's diverse services include early intervention, assessments and therapy for infants and toddlers, family support networks, respite and sitter care, specially designed homes to meet the needs of older adults, employment initiatives, and recreational, vacation, and summer camp opportunities.

You'll find more on ARC-Allegheny in the Health Care chapter. While ARC-Allegheny serves Allegheny County, you'll also find ARC organizations in four other counties within the primary service area. These are:

- ARC-Beaver County, (724) 775-1602 or (800) 272-0567
- ARC-Butler County, (724) 282-1500
- ARC-Washington County, (724) 222-6960
- ARC-Westmoreland County, (724) 837-8159

Allegheny Intermediate Unit
475 East Waterfront Drive, Homestead
(412) 394-5700

The Allegheny Intermediate Unit (AIU) is the largest of Pennsylvania's 29 intermediate units, which provide curriculum-enhancement services to school districts. Working with school districts throughout Allegheny County, this nonprofit regional education agency administers such

For a listing of the Top 25 largest day care providers in the region, consult the **Book of Lists** *published annually by* **The Pittsburgh Business Times.** *It's available in most libraries, with a new version published each year.*

initiatives as Head Start, Project DART, and programs for gifted students.

Each school district in Pennsylvania is served by an intermediate unit. See the Education chapter for a description of intermediate units in our region.

---

i

To find a Parents Anonymous group in your county, call the state resource office of Parents Anonymous at (800) 448-4906.

**Big Brothers and Big Sisters
of Greater Pittsburgh
5989 Penn Circle South
(412) 363-6100**

This agency matches caring adults with at-risk children from single-parent households in Allegheny and Washington Counties. These one-to-one mentoring relationships help children thrive. Volunteers are welcome, but the selection process is rather rigorous, including a thorough interview, background checks and clearances, and training.

You'll find a similar organization in each county in the primary service area. You can reach them at these numbers:

- Big Brothers Big Sisters of Armstrong County, (724) 763-4181
- Big Brothers Big Sisters of Beaver County, (724) 728-4300
- Big Brothers Big Sisters of Butler County, (724) 287-4733
- Big Brothers Big Sisters of Westmore-land County, (724) 837-6198
- Big Brothers Big Sisters of Greater Pitts-burgh, Washington County Office, (724) 228-9191

**Family Communications, Inc.
4802 Fifth Avenue
(412) 687-2990**

The Mister Rogers' Neighborhood Child-care Partnership is a joint effort of Family Communications, public television sta-

tions, and others committed to the education and welfare of children. The partnership offers training and support materials for child-care providers as well as a quarterly newsletter.

Another project, *The Mister Rogers Plan & Play Book,* extends the popular television program to the child-care setting, with more than 400 richly illustrated pages of easy-to-do activities. For more about Mister Rogers and his pioneering work with children, see the Kidstuff chapter.

**Family Resources
141 South Highland Avenue
(412) 363-1702**

Family Resources is the largest child-abuse treatment and prevention agency in Allegheny County. It works to strengthen families and neighborhoods by providing training for professionals as well as crisis intervention for families where abuse has occurred. Licensed as an outpatient mental health facility and provider of enhanced mental health services, family resources is a United Way member agency.

The services offered by Family Resources are diverse. They include parent support services such as Parents Anonymous groups, nurturing courses, The Therapeutic Parents' and Children's Center described above, and a 260-acre Family Retreat Center in Warrendale that is available year-round to community organizations, social and religious groups, schools, and businesses. Family resources can help connect parents with primary health care, substance abuse treatment, housing services, and job placement and recreational programs.

In addition, the agency operates the WARMLINE, a telephone service offering parenting information, referrals, and support. You can ask nonmedical questions regarding such topics as discipline, postpartum depression, children's bedwetting, and general parental stress. The WARM-LINE is staffed by trained volunteers. It's free and confidential. You can reach it at (412) 641-4546, (800) 641-4546 if you're outside Allegheny County.

**Familylinks Parent
& Child Guidance Center
2644 Banksville Road
(412) 343-7166**

This nonprofit organization provides a
diversity of mental health, mental retardation, educational outreach, testing, and
consultation services for children and families, as well as outpatient clinical treatment and a therapeutic preschool for
children ages 3 to 5 with severe social and
emotional delays.

One of the center's most heavily utilized programs is called Families In Transition. It offers education for parents and
others dealing with separation, divorce,
remarriage, and family alcoholism.

The center also maintains the Parent-
line, (412) 343-7166, a telephone service
for parents and other primary caregivers
who wish to discuss their concerns with a
professional. There is no charge for Par-
entline, and callers may remain anonymous if they wish. The line operates five
days a week, Monday through Friday, from
9:00 A.M. to 5:00 P.M.

**Parental Stress Center
5877 Commerce Street
(412) 381-4800**

The mission of the Parental Stress Center
is to prevent child abuse and neglect
through education, counseling, and support services. Its Critical Differences Program provides intensive in-home assistance
to families under severe stress due to economic, health, social, or environmental
pressures.

The center also offers parenting workshops, teen groups, support groups, and
other family-related education and training services; center personnel will help
you schedule these for weekdays, weekends, and evenings in locations throughout Allegheny County. In addition, the
agency's Fathers' Resource Center helps
fathers maintain an active role in their
children's lives. Services include weekly
support groups for dads, anger management programs, and mentoring opportuni-

ties. For more information on this program, call (412) 381-4800.

Parental Stress Center is a United Way
member agency. For more on the center,
see the Health Care chapter.

**Parents Anonymous
2001 North Front Street, Building 1,
Suite 210, Harrisburg
(800) 448-4906**

If you feel occasional anger and frustration
associated with the challenges and pressures of raising children, Parents Anonymous support groups can help you
develop coping and management strategies. When you contact the Parents
Anonymous state resource office in Harrisburg at the number listed above, they'll put
you in touch with support groups in your
area. Parents Anonymous is run by various
organizations throughout the state.

You also may contact Family Resources,
(412) 363-1702, if you're in Allegheny
County, or Parent-wise Inc. for Parents
Anonymous of Westmoreland County,
(800) 544-0227. In Beaver County, Family
Enrichment runs the program; call (724)
774-0522. Family First is the host agency
in Butler County at (724) 284-4894.

**Ronald McDonald House
500-512 Shady Avenue
(412) 362-3400**

Opened in 1979, Ronald McDonald House
is a home away from home for families
who must travel hundreds, even thousands
of miles from their own communities for
medical treatment for their children.
Located near Children's Hospital, the
house is designed to encourage interaction
between guests and to help them cope
during a trying period.

**Safe Sitter
5670 Caito Drive, Suite 172
Indianapolis, Indiana
(800) 255-4089**

Founded in 1980 by Indianapolis pediatri-
cian Patricia A. Keener, M.D., Safe Sitter is
a babysitter training program designed to

CHILD CARE

Children's Hospital of Pittsburgh provides dozens of educational classes for parents, many of them free. Call the Community Education line at (412) 692–7105 for class schedules and parenting information.

reach young persons ages 11 to 13 before they begin actively babysitting. In one-day or two-day courses, usually offered at local hospitals, Safe Sitter teaches youths what to expect when dealing with children, how to avoid difficult situations, and how to solve problems if they occur. Students learn such techniques as rescue breathing and accident management, and they're also grounded in the business aspects of babysitting.

The program helps young baby-sitting entrepreneurs, of course, but it also is a boon to parents, providing them with a pool of well-trained baby-sitters. Safe Sitter includes more than 550 participating hospitals and teaching sites—including

those local hospitals listed below—in the United States and abroad. In fact, St. Clair Hospital in Pittsburgh's South Hills served as the pilot site for the rollout of Safe Sitter's one-day instructional program.

While participating hospitals cannot recommend particular sitters, they can verify that a potential caregiver you might be considering has successfully completed a Safe Sitter course of study. Local participants include:

- Allegheny Valley Hospital, (877) 284–2000
- Canonsburg Hospital, (724) 745–6100
- Brownsville Hospital, (724) 785–1876
- Children's Hospital of Pittsburgh, (412) 692–7105
- Latrobe Area Hospital, (724) 537–1755
- Mercy Hospital of Pittsburgh, (412) 232–8111
- St. Clair Hospital, (412) 344–6600 ext. 1027
- UPMC Health Center, (412) 422–9802
- The Washington Hospital, (724) 223–3840

EDUCATION

The diversity of local government in Southwestern Pennsylvania extends to the area of education. It's an arena that's always important, usually colorful, and sometimes frustrating. Sheer numbers tell a large part of the story here. Of the 501 school districts in the Commonwealth of Pennsylvania, 100 of them serve this guide's six-county principal coverage area. Since many aspects of public education are left to the discretion of local school districts, standardization in any area is rare.

Local residents care deeply about their schools and the quality of education those schools are providing. Media have responded to that keen interest by expanding their coverage of schools and school districts. With at least 100 board meetings to cover every month, to say nothing about day-to-day and ongoing issues, local media must devote a great deal of attention to schools. This, in turn, creates additional interest, which generates even broader coverage. It's a cycle that assures thorough coverage of—and ever-widening interest in—the educational scene.

Rather than provide you with profiles of 100 school districts, which would be numbing and counterproductive, a somewhat different approach is taken in this chapter. We've tried to explore the most important issues—most notably school choice and standards—and to provide some insight into how local school districts are dealing with these issues. This treatment is by no means exhaustive; it seems unlikely that any could be.

We've rounded out our look at the education scene with some background on diocesan schools and profiles of other private schools, or independent schools, as they sometimes prefer to be known. You'll find that when it comes to education in Southwestern Pennsylvania, you may have more options than you ever imagined.

PUBLIC SCHOOLS
Organization

Public education in Pennsylvania is provided by 501 school districts; our six-county coverage area boasts 100 of those school districts, making education here diverse and colorful. Many districts have been formed through consolidation, so that most districts encompass several municipalities or more, though this is not universally the case. Some districts have taken their names from the communities they serve. Carlynton School District in Pittsburgh's western suburbs, for example, spans the municipalities of Carnegie, Rosslyn Farms, and Crafton. On the other hand, on the heels of some mergers, district administrators couldn't find names that incorporated all their communities, so they threw up their hands and went in other directions. When schools in Dormont, Castle Shannon, and Green Tree merged into a single district, they opted for the name Keystone Oaks, a pleasant-sounding appellation with no syllabic echoes of any of the participating communities.

School districts are governed by nine-member elected boards that in turn name superintendents to lead district administration. The Pittsburgh School District, including the city of Pittsburgh and the borough of Mt. Oliver (a municipality surrounded by the city), is the region's largest, serving more than 40,000 students in 12 high schools, 19 middle schools, 57 elementary schools, five special-use schools, and one adult education school.

Outside of Pittsburgh, the largest district in the region is the sprawling North Allegheny School District, which includes 12 schools and more than 8,300 students. The smallest district in our region is Beaver County's Midland Borough School District, with 365 students and one school. In one of those regional quirks you'll come to love, Midland Borough high-school students actually attend East Liverpool High School across the border in Ohio, because there aren't enough students to support a local high school.

Most districts have separate buildings for elementary, middle, and high schools, but you will find a number of junior-senior high schools. Several of the smallest districts teach all their students, irrespective of grade level, in the same building.

Grade Levels and Nomenclature

As most facets of education in Southwestern Pennsylvania, grade levels and nomenclature are far from standard. Districts tend to group their students into three broad grade levels, but you'll find a great deal of variation in how the levels are defined and what they're called. A common structure is kindergarten through grade 5 for elementary school, grades 6 through 8 for middle school, and grades 9 through 12 for high school. A few school districts divide grades 9 through 12 into intermediate and senior high schools, while a few eliminate the middle level entirely. All school districts offer kindergarten and some have pre-school programs.

This may not be the most vital aspect of education in our region, but if you're used to a structure that includes middle schools, for example, you might want to seek out a district that offers such schools.

Standards

Academic standards are a matter of state policy—and an issue that generates more discussion locally than any education-related issue other than school choice.

In fact, the Pennsylvania Legislature regularly considers revamping statewide standards.

Currently, the state wants its students to achieve competence and understanding in the following areas: communications; mathematics; science and technology; environment and ecology; citizenship; arts and humanities; career education and work; wellness and fitness; and home economics, which the state describes as "principles of money management, consumer behavior, and child health." This translates into a variety of required courses at the high-school level. These include:

- Language arts, integrating reading, composition, listening, speech, literature, and grammar;
- Mathematics, including problem-solving, algebra, and geometry;
- Science, including at least one laboratory science featuring hands-on experiments;
- Social studies, including Pennsylvania, U.S., and world history, as well as civics, economics, geography, and multicultural studies;
- Environmental education;
- The arts, including art, music, dance, and theater;
- Microcomputers and software;
- Information skills;
- Wellness and fitness, incorporating physical education, aerobic fitness, and alcohol, chemical and tobacco abuse instruction.

If you were graduated from a Pennsylvania high school, you may be saying, "Gee, I never had all those courses." You probably did, but not as distinct classes. The state gives school districts the option of folding instruction in these areas into other, related courses.

School districts must offer vocational-technical education, AIDs prevention courses, at least two languages other than English, and an English program geared to students for whom English is not the "dominant language."

Curriculum

In a refrain you'll hear repeated throughout this chapter, curriculum is largely a district prerogative. Since all school districts must assure that their students meet state standards, the academic core at each curriculum is fairly standard. From there, it's a wide-open affair. Electives vary widely. Driver's education, for example, is among the most popular electives but not universally offered. If you're considering locating in a local school district, one question you'll want to ask will be about electives offered.

Curriculum Enrichment

Enhancing and enriching the classroom experience is an area where Pennsylvania school districts shine. Some years ago, the state realized that teachers and administrators would be too burdened with day-to-day matters to give much consideration to curriculum innovations, so they developed 29 new groups reaching every county of the state and charged them with the mission of innovation. The organizations, known as intermediate units, function in specific geographic areas. Our region boasts seven IUs: IU1, serving Washington, Greene, and Fayette Counties; IU2, for Pittsburgh and Mt. Oliver; IU3, the state's largest, covering Allegheny County, except Pittsburgh and Mt. Oliver; IU4, including Butler, Lawrence, and Mercer Counties; IU7, for Westmoreland County; IU27, covering the Beaver Valley; and IU28, serving Armstrong and Indiana Counties.

The impact of the IUs is varied and broad. Their services range from the Head Start program for preschoolers to programs for gifted students. They work with the Governor's Schools of Excellence, six residential summer programs held on college campuses. In Allegheny County, the IU has worked with four schools to establish a distance learning network; at the

With more than 40,000 students enrolled, Pittsburgh city schools actually have the lowest dropout rate of any urban school system in the nation—only 15.7 percent.

same time, the Allegheny Intermediate Unit provides educational services to adjudicated students, such as those at the Shuman Center, the county's principal juvenile detention center. IU1, which works largely with rural school districts, has linked 45 schools in a fiber optic network that provides teleconferencing capability; IU1 also is implementing a mobile computer program that will use vans to deliver computer and internet capability to schools.

The work of the IUs is challenging and exciting—the Allegheny Intermediate Unit applies 1,500 full- and part-time employees to the task. They're an essential element in Pennsylvania's education system. If there were no IUs, we'd have to invent them.

Textbooks

Since textbook selection is a school district prerogative, the region has no standard textbooks. Rather, there are many. While textbook selection has been a flashpoint in some parts of the country, it's generally been less than incendiary here. The only way you can get involved is to work with your school district.

Teachers

All public school teachers in the Commonwealth must be certified by the Pennsylvania Department of Education, which maintains different requirements for different teaching levels. Pennsylvania has reciprocal certification agreements with a number of other states, so if you're a teacher relocating to the Keystone State, you'll still have to apply for your certification, but you may not have to worry about any further requirements.

Hiring policies are pretty much the domain of school districts. A few, such as the Pittsburgh School District, impose residency requirements, but most do not. Virtually all public school teachers in our six-county coverage area are represented by unions—the two most prominent are the Pennsylvania State Education Association, an affiliate of the National Education Association, and the Pennsylvania Federation of Teachers, an affiliate of the American Federation of Teachers.

One of the practical implications of the broad teacher unionization in Southwestern Pennsylvania is that as contracts expire, negotiations between unions and their school districts become quite public—and sometimes passionate. With 100 school district–teacher union contracts in the region, bargaining is pretty much a constant. Counting down the days to a potential strike or lockout is something of an annual rite of summer here. Fortunately, delays in the start of the school year are averted most of the time.

Special and Gifted Education

While all states require programs for students judged exceptional—often called special education—Pennsylvania is among the minority of states that also requires educational programs for those deemed gifted. The rules for both sets of programs are fairly similar. In each case, the designation "exceptional" or "gifted" is determined through a process called a multidisciplinary review, which may be requested by the school or a parent. In all cases, the schools prefer to consider parents part of the evaluation team and seek parental consent for, and participation in, the review. Where parental consent is withheld, the district may seek a court order for a review, but this is rare.

If the review panel determines that a student needs special programs, these may be provided through the district and specially assembled Individualized Educational Teams, or the students may be referred to one of 11 special services schools in our region, including the Western Pennsylvania School for the Blind and the Western Pennsylvania School for the Deaf. In a related program, preschoolers under the age of five may be eligible for a school-district's early intervention services following an evaluation; parents may request the evaluation.

That gives you some background on the rules, but it doesn't begin to describe the variety of programs for exceptional and gifted students. The state provides overall supervision but expects school districts to develop and fund their own programs. The Pittsburgh School District operates three centers that offer specially designed instruction for exceptional children; other districts offer their services on-site. Similarly, in the area of gifted education, the Pittsburgh School District maintains special centers that elementary- and middle-school students attend one day per week; high-school students, on the other hand, typically receive their special programs on-site.

While there's no charge to parents for special or gifted education programs, there's no end to the variations in the ways area school districts provide these programs. If you're considering locating here, this is clearly an area you'll want to explore.

Alternative Education

Many districts provide alternative programming for suspended students and others who need support due to behavioral and academic difficulties. These may be site-based programs or schools dedicated to alternative education. The Pittsburgh School District, to cite one important example, offers both types of programming. Its alternative elementary-school programs are site-based, while middle-school and high-school students may be assigned to dedicated buildings. If you have the opportunity to choose your school district, you may want to inquire about its alternative education programs.

School Choice

This has been perhaps the hottest topic in the impassioned debates about education in Southwestern Pennsylvania, usually triggered by the busing plans that several districts employ to achieve racial balance in their schools. Groups rally round the "busing" and "neighborhood schools" flags with vigor and conviction. The issue, however, may be more symbolic than an actual concern, since even the few districts that bus students tend to keep it to a minimum. Thus, the number of students affected by busing is relatively few.

A more far-reaching component of the school choice debate involves the possibility of public financial support for parents who opt to send their children to private schools. Advocates have proposed publicly supported tuition vouchers for students who attend private schools. While this proposal has failed to carry the Pennsylvania Legislature, look for this debate to continue.

For many students and their families, the debate about choice is theoretical, as students in most cases are required to attend the schools designated by the districts in which they reside. There are several opportunities for choice.

Under state law, students may opt to attend public schools outside their district, provided they pay tuition to the schools they attend. Tuition rates are established by the state, based on the cost of education in each district; among Allegheny County school districts, annual tuition rates range from approximately $5,000 to $11,000. You will find a catch here, however. No school district is required to accept students from other districts. So even if you're willing to pay

the price for sending your child outside your district, you need the cooperation of the other school district.

Yet another element of choice is provided by the Pittsburgh School District through its "magnet schools" program. Magnets are elementary and secondary schools that focus on particular areas of study. Since one of the goals of the magnet program is to achieve racial balance through voluntary choice, 50 percent of slots at each magnet are reserved for African-American students, 50 percent for students of other races. Some magnet options are sequential, beginning in kindergarten and continuing through middle school and high school. Some give preference to younger siblings of those enrolled in magnet programs, or to students who reside in particular neighborhoods.

At the high-school level, the district offers magnets in international studies, creative and performing arts, pre-engineering, computer science, and teaching. Law and public service, junior ROTC, public safety, high technology, and vocational-technical training, as well as one called a "Traditional Academy" in a highly structured and disciplined setting. Other magnets are available at the elementary and middle school levels.

Magnets are open to students throughout the city, so long as racial balances are preserved; when there are more applicants than a school can accommodate, slots are awarded by lottery.

Charter Schools

The sentiment for school choice has inspired a new type of educational option in the region–charter schools. In June 1997, Pennsylvania became the 27th state to enact legislation authorizing charter schools, which may be defined as independent public schools that are designed by individuals or groups to fulfill a specific educational mission. Each charter school must be approved and funded by the local school district in which the charter

For more on the Pittsburgh public schools, see the district's home page, www.pps.k12.pa.us/. If home schooling is more your bailiwick, check out www.pahome schoolers.com/.

school is located. Any students can opt to attend charter schools in their districts, and no tuition charges are permitted.

In early 1998, school boards reviewed and approved a number of proposed charter schools. As a result, the first charter schools in Southwestern Pennsylvania opened their doors in September 1998. Among these were Manchester Academic Charter School, Urban League of Pittsburgh Charter School, and the Thurgood Marshall Academy. Recently, a new charter school, the Career Connections Charter School, was opened, accommodating ninth graders only in 2000, with plans to add other grades. While the missions of charter schools differ, most plan longer school days and school years than found in traditional schools.

If a charter school sounds like an option you'd like to consider, you'll find several sources of information about them. Locally, Duquesne University has established the Charter Schools Project, (412) 396-4492, which tracks charter-school information and has staged conferences about the subject. The U.S. Department of Education Office of Educational Research and Improvement has undertaken a four-year study of charter schools in America and published a first-year report. It's available at several Web sites: www.uscharter schools.org and www.ed.gov/pubs/charter.

Transportation

The groundswell of support for school choice is manifest in the area of transportation as well. Under state law, school districts may provide transportation for their students, or they can elect not to. A number opt out of transportation, forcing students to find their own way to school. Why would they impose this requirement on their students? It might be because state law also mandates that districts providing transportation for their students must provide the same type of transportation for nonpublic school students within their districts. Moreover, students can attend nonpublic schools up to 10 miles beyond a district's borders and still be eligible for free district-provided transportation.

Some public school districts have contested this requirement; the Pittsburgh School District filed and lost court action against the requirement, pointing out that transportation for nonpublic students—by bus, van, and cab—accounts for about 28 percent of its annual transportation budget.

The purpose of the policy, of course, is to make it easier and less expensive for parents to choose private schools for their children. Whether or not you agree with the policy of public financing for certain aspects of private schools, there's no doubt that the state's transportation program has made private schools more accessible to more families.

Homeschooling

The increase in homeschooling throughout the Commonwealth is one final ramification of the thrust for school choice. Since 1986, parents, guardians, and legal custodians have been authorized to teach their children at home. In 1988–1989, the statewide total of children so taught was 2,152; by 1996–1997, the total had grown to 17,861. In our six-county service area, 99 of 100 school districts reported at least one student being taught at home. The only exception: Clairton City School District in southern Allegheny County.

Those teaching their children at home must file an annual home education affidavit with their school districts. This notarized document must specify the name of the home education supervisor, an outline by subject area of proposed educational objectives, and evidence of each child's immunization and access to health services. The affidavit also must specify any curriculum materials—including textbooks—to be borrowed from the school district.

In many cases, school districts welcome home-taught children to the fold, opening their extracurricular activities to such students. In other districts, home-taught children will feel like beggars at the feast, with districts grudgingly agreeing to their participation in school activities. If you plan to teach your children at home but want them to enjoy some of the socialization benefits of group schooling, the best approach may be to discuss your plans with district and school administration. At the very least, you'll get a good idea where you stand.

Athletics

Interscholastic athletics in Pennsylvania is largely the domain of the Pennsylvania Interscholastic Athletic Agency (PIAA)—its administrative unit in our region is the Western Pennsylvania Interscholastic Athletic League (WPIAL). PIAA rules and regulations govern interscholastic sports for 1,300 schools in the Commonwealth—including 130 private schools—and 225,000 students. The PIAA operates and organizes championships in 11 boys' sports and 10 girls' sports.

The roster of interscholastic sports offered varies from district to district, but among the most popular are baseball, basketball, cross country, football, soccer, swimming and diving, tennis, and track and field for boys, and basketball, cross country, field hockey, soccer, softball, swimming and diving, tennis, track and field, and volleyball for girls. You'll also find interscholastic programs in bowling, golf, ice hockey, lacrosse, and rifle. Most districts also maintain active intramural programs.

To assure fair and fun competition, the PIAA classifies its member high schools by enrollment, with categories ranging from Class A for the smallest schools to Class AAAA—Quad A, as it's known—for the largest schools. Classifications may vary from sport to sport. For example, a high school with 175 boys in grades 9 through 12 would play in Class A in baseball but in Class AA in basketball. The PIAA modifies its classification guidelines as enrollment fluctuations dictate. For the most current classification, playoff schedule, and other PIAA news, check out the agency's Web site, www.piaa.org.

Keep in mind that if your children want to participate in interscholastic sports, they must maintain certain academic standards. Generally, the WPIAL requires a 1.5 grade point average for sports participation. School districts, however, have the option to impose more stringent standards. The city of Pittsburgh has done that, requiring a 2.0 grade point average of its student-athletes.

Parent Involvement

The fragmentation of government in Southwestern Pennsylvania may be lamentable in some areas, but the great number and diversity of schools and school districts in the region provide unusually rich opportunities for parent involvement in their youngsters' education. Parent-teacher organizations are a traditional model for parent involvement, but there are others that afford a more hands-on approach. Consider the Pittsburgh School District as an example. In the city, each school has a Parent School Community Council that works with administrators on such operational areas as curriculum and other academic programs. In all, these councils involve about 1,400 people in the administrative process.

With 100 school districts in the region, voters must elect 900 school board

members. You may never have considered
public service as an elected official, but
Southwestern Pennsylvania provides you
with that chance. Many school board members have little prior political experience;
they became involved because they wanted
to help their children as the youngsters
progressed through the system.

If you do consider a run for a school
board seat, remember that this is full-
fledged politics. The parties nominate
their candidates in primary elections, with
the winners determined in general elections. While some seats are uncontested,
other elections are intense, involving
media coverage and debate that may be
less than genteel. Electoral politics is not
for all tastes, but if you can endure the
rough and tumble nature of elections, a
school board seat may await you.

DIOCESAN SCHOOLS

Diocesan schools are a powerful and
important force in our region. If you considered the Catholic schools of the Diocese of Pittsburgh a school district, they
would constitute the fourth largest school
district in the Commonwealth. The Diocese of Pittsburgh and the Diocese of

Greensburg include all six counties in this
guide's principal coverage area. Together,
they operate 154 schools—including 13
high schools—that serve more than
40,000 students.

Each diocese is divided into administrative units known as deaneries that
include elementary and secondary
schools, or elementary schools only. The
two deaneries in Washington County, for
example, offer elementary schools only, so
graduates of those schools will have to
travel a bit to continue their education at
a diocesan secondary school. Teachers at
most—but not all—diocesan high schools
are represented by the Federation of
Pittsburgh Diocesan Teachers.

The emphasis on academics at diocesan schools is tangible. Diocese of Pittsburgh secondary schools send 96 percent
of their graduates on for further education, an impressive statistic. The high
schools typically offer extensive honors
and advanced-placement programs as
well as innovative college-in-high school
programs that inspire and prepare students for higher education.

Diocesan schools are private, so state
mandates for gifted and special education
don't apply to them in the same ways as
they do to public schools. However, public
school districts include students of diocesan schools in some of their programs for
exceptional children. In two of its high
schools, the Diocese of Pittsburgh also
offers a noncollege-directed curriculum
for developmentally challenged students,
who take most courses in a resource room
but share some regular courses with the
general student body.

The range of extracurricular activities
available to students is broad, including
clubs for drama, instrumental and vocal
music, and forensics, as well as school
newspapers and yearbooks. In athletics,
the schools participate with public schools
in the Western Pennsylvania Interscholastic Athletic League in such activities as
baseball, basketball, bowling, crew, cross
country, field hockey, football, golf, ice
hockey, lacrosse, soccer, softball, swim-

ming, tennis, track, volleyball, and wrestling. Note that some schools offer a number of these sports as club or intra-mural activities, rather than as inter-scholastic sports, and that some diocesan high schools impose more stringent grade requirements than does the WPIAL.

Since diocesan schools are private, they maintain both admissions standards and tuition charges. While admission is generally open, the schools will review placement tests, academic records, and personal interviews. Many schools offer financial-aid programs, with need assess-ment performed by an independent out-side agency, as well as work-study programs. In the Diocese of Pittsburgh, all students are eligible for support from the Bishop's Education Fund, which offers need-based grants.

The schools welcome parental involve-ment through such vehicles as school, parent advisory, and development boards, and activity booster organizations—these are particularly supportive of athletic and musical activities. If diocesan schools sound like an option you'd like to explore, you can contact the Diocese of Pittsburgh Education Secretariat at (412) 456-3100 or visit the Web site for the Diocese of Greensburg, www.catholicghg.org, for information on schools. These sources may also be able to refer you to Catholic education contacts in other districts.

OTHER PRIVATE SCHOOLS

If you're shopping for a private school, you'll find a rich variety in Southwestern Pennsyl-vania. The region boasts a wide assortment of college-prep schools, religion-focused schools, and those targeted to students with special needs. Presented are profiles of schools that offer high-school education—private grade schools would be too numer-ous to cover effectively—but where such schools offer primary education as well, we've noted that. (Our one exception is the Waldorf School, which we felt was too note-worthy not to mention.) Unless otherwise

noted, the schools charge tuition and are coeducational.

Keep in mind that private schools are just that—private. They operate largely outside the purview of the State Depart-ment of Education and so are free to establish their own guidelines and policies in most areas of operation. If you're researching private schools, ask as many questions as you can, as their programs and policies vary widely.

North

Bethel Christian Academy
2438 California Avenue
(412) 321-6333

Bethel Christian Academy, located on Pittsburgh's North Side, offers kinder-garten, elementary, and high-school pro-grams that employ Accelerated Christian Education, an individualized learning pro-gram that enables students to learn at their own pace. Each classroom is equipped with a computer, and high-school students have the opportunity for more extensive classwork on computers. The Pittsburgh–Mt. Oliver Intermediate Unit provides remedial services where needed to Bethel Christian students.

Students compete with other Christian schools in such sports as soccer, volley-ball, and basketball. They also bring their own lunches, because Bethel Christian does not provide them. You can opt to pay tuition in 10 monthly installments. Bethel Christian is a day school.

Shadyside Academy
423 Fox Chapel Road, Fox Chapel
(412) 968-3182

Founded in 1883, Shadyside is the region's largest private school, with its junior, middle, and senior schools. The senior school (high school) offers a five-day boarding program, an attractive and unusual asset; 500 students are enrolled in the senior school alone. The campuses span 172 acres, 25 buildings, and 10 athletic fields. (If you're interested in the junior school, it's located in the East End of the City of Pittsburgh in a neighborhood called Park Place.)

Shadyside's emphasis on college preparation is strong; typically 100 percent of graduates attend four-year colleges or universities. Distinguished alumni include Pulitzer Prize-winning author and historian David McCullough and former astronaut Jay Apt, who once served as director of Pittsburgh's Carnegie Museum of Natural History. The school boasts a student-teacher ratio of 9:1. Shadyside provides financial aid—most of it need-based—to more than 15 percent of its students.

Students participate in more than 50 clubs and are invited to become involved in the school's operations through membership on committees for curriculum, admissions, discipline, and independent study. For hands-on environmental study, Shadyside's Maine Coast Semester affords students the chance to live on a working farm for half a school year. Shadyside's varsity athletic teams compete in the Western Pennsylvania Interscholastic Athletic League as well as head-to-head with other independent schools

If you're thinking about applying to the senior school, Shadyside requires both an interview and a campus tour.

**Vincentian Academy—
Duquesne University
Peebles and McKnight Roads
(412) 364-1616
www.vaduq.org**
Vincentian Academy's relationship with Duquesne University is a strong attraction. The academy is linked to Duquesne's computer network, bringing its students access to that resource. Vincentian also is part of Duquesne's Campus Ministries Program to assist in its commitment to values and public service. Perhaps most importantly, Vincentian graduates who enroll at Duquesne University are eligible for both automatic admission and 25 percent tuition scholarships. The academy

emphasizes that it expects and encourages its students to enroll at prestigious colleges and universities across the country rather than at Duquesne exclusively. Still, having that admission in the bank can be quite a comfort.

Located in Pittsburgh's North Hills, Vincentian is a day school that participates in the International Baccalaureate, an academic program offered by more than 700 schools worldwide. The IB program strives for a balanced education that facilitates geographic and cultural mobility and promotes international understanding through shared academic experiences. The curriculum includes studies in language, individuals and societies, experimental sciences, mathematics, and a range of electives. One specific advantage of an IB Diploma: a number of college and universities grant up to a year's academic credit for students who earn it.

The student-teacher ratio is an appealing 7:1. Vincentian offers financial aid but describes the program as "limited." Students participate in 12 sports and more than two dozen additional extracurricular activities. If someone in your family is interested in Vincentian, take advantage of the school's "shadowing" program, which invites prospective students to spend a day with current students.

East

**The Ellis School
6425 Fifth Avenue
(412) 661-5992
www.theellisschool.org**
Founded in 1916, Ellis is an independent school for girls in kindergarten through 12th grade. Its seven-acre campus lies in Pittsburgh's Shadyside neighborhood, just a quick bus trip from all the amenities of Oakland's university complex. Some statistics about Ellis will tell you much about the school. Its student-teacher ratio is 8:1, while its student-computer ratio is 4:1. Of the seniors among the 460 students, each typi-

cally is enrolled in at least one advanced-placement course.

The academic program at Ellis blends required courses with a diverse menu of electives. All ninth graders, for example, study the Concepts of Physics, which kicks off a three-year science sequence that also includes chemistry and biology. Ninth graders also write at least 10 papers for English class and a research paper in the social sciences. On the other hand, more than 90 percent of students opt for electives in the fine arts. In addition to their class work, students provide volunteer service for more than 60 organizations.

Ellis administers tests to all applicants for admission. These usually are scheduled in December and January, but the school will make special arrangements to accommodate your schedule. More than 15 percent of Ellis students receive financial aid.

Heritage Christian School
200 Elicker Road, Plum
(412) 795-3311

A member of the American Association of Christian Schools, Heritage Christian School offers kindergarten through 12th grade education based on the philosophy that the school is an extension of the Christian home. Textbooks are Bible-based, and the school itself operates from the Bible Baptist Church in the eastern suburb of Plum.

The school bases its calendar and certain graduation requirements on the state's public school guidelines, but it also features a number of variations. Admissions, which are based on an interview, academic performance, and placement testing, always are granted on a probationary basis, giving the school an opportunity to determine how students handle the traditional structure of Heritage Christian, which maintains a dress code and other conduct guidelines more stringent than public schools. Conveniently, the school offers an after-school ride program for those students whose parents are unable to pick them up when the school day ends.

Parents may opt to pay tuition for their children in 10 monthly installments.

The Kiski School
1888 Brett Lane, Saltsburg
(724) 639-3586
www.kiski.org

In 1878, ambitious developers constructed a rambling Victorian hotel on the cliffs above the Kiskiminetas River in the Westmoreland County town of Saltsburg to serve pilgrims who flocked to the area for the alleged curative powers of its mineral springs. The "Magic Waters" soon dried up, leaving the hotel for purchase and conversion to the Kiskiminetas School for Boys at Saltsburg. It flourishes still on that site, but today, it's known more simply as the Kiski School.

It's a 350-acre, residential, college preparatory school for 250 boys from grades 9 through 12. The academic schedule is demanding and Kiski doesn't apologize for it, claiming that a rigorous approach "is designed to allow a boy to enter a college equal to his ability and to succeed once he is there." Average class size is 10. Homework averages one hour per class meeting, and just to be sure underclassmen are completing that homework, Kiski conducts a two-hour supervised study period each evening. The school requires three years of language study and a Life Skills course, which

---

Information on private schools can be hard to come by because the schools are, well, private. For a comprehensive listing, try the Pennsylvania Education Directory. *This annual also lists every public school, by district and county, in the Commonwealth, as well as proprietary and trade schools. You can get yours from Applied Arts Publishers, Box 479, Lebanon, PA 17042-0479, (717) 272-9442. Cost is $14.00 plus tax, with a $2.00 discount for educators, school districts, and libraries.*

---

includes instruction in computer literacy, health and wellness, and speech.

Kiski is serious about athletics as well. If you don't plan to participate in an interscholastic sport in each of the three athletic seasons, you may arrange an "alternate physical development activity" with the permission of the athletic director or headmaster. You'll find other extracurricular activities—including 30 special interest activities—that aren't quite so mandatory, as well as a summer program of classes and sports.

Among Kiski's most distinguished alumni is Bob Mathias, the first man to win the Olympic decathlon twice (1948 and 1952). An equally impressive achievement: Kiski's headmaster, John A. "Jack" Pidgeon, has served in that position continuously since 1957. "If I had only one rule for the boys," the headmaster writes, "I think it would be 'Behave like gentlemen,' which implies a rather complete code of conduct."

The Pennsylvania Association of Independent Schools, 37 East Germantown Pike, Suite 302, Plymouth Meeting, (610) 567-2960, can help you find a private school. They won't make a specific recommendation, but they can tell you which accredited schools are located near you.

The Oakland School
362 McKee Place
(412) 621-7878

If you're looking for individualized education for your children, you'll find it at the Oakland School, where the average class size is six. To maintain that class size, this day school limits its total enrollment to 60 students. The school is coeducational and situated in the heart of Oakland's university-medical complex, from which it draws both energy and resources.

The academic program includes studies in communications, mathematics, arts, humanities, science, social studies, and computer education, as well as programs in up to six foreign languages, depending upon student interest: Latin, French, Spanish, German, Japanese, and Russian. Students may participate in a wide variety of extracurricular activities and are required to perform community service. A work-study program provides students with academic credit for field experience, while a mentor program pairs students with staff advisors. The Oakland School describes its financial aid opportunities as "limited."

Trinity Christian School
299 Ridge Avenue, Forest Hills
(412) 242-8886

Since 1953, Trinity Christian School has been "educating students for a lifetime of learning and service to God," as the school describes its mission. The program is based on the Reformed tradition, but these days the school welcomes all denominations. Its 370 students in kindergarten through high school represent nearly 100 churches. More than 90 percent of Trinity Christian graduates seek higher education. The school enhances its curriculum with honors programs in physics, calculus, and advanced mathematics. Facilities include computer and photography labs, as well as an art room and soccer and softball fields.

The Waldorf School
201 South Winebiddle
(412) 441-5792
www.waldorfpittsburgh.org

Waldorf education was started in the early 1900s by a philosopher/scientist named Rudolf Steiner. The Waldorf School provides a classical education, with a firm grounding in language arts, math, history, and science. The school's distinction is the way children are encouraged to learn—through arts, music, and movement—and the emphasis that's placed throughout the different grades on children's self-awareness, self-trust, and confidence.

In the three-day nursery program and the five-day kindergarten program (there are half- and full-day options for each), the focus is on imaginative play as the most important objective, with lots of artistic activities, singing, and movement games. As children are developmentally ready for learning academic subjects in larger blocks of time, for each subject, they create their own textbooks, using their neatly handwritten, original compositions and accompanying illustrations. Writing and reading are incorporated into all their subjects, in fact, and math is taught in a way that is imaginative, fun, and relevant for the students.

In addition, starting in first grade, children take two languages (Spanish and Russian), watercolor painting, beeswax modeling, and a handwork class, where they learn to knit, crochet, and do cross stitch. They also learn to play the flute. Starting in third grade, there are stringed instrument, games, and music classes.

Attesting to the effectiveness of Waldorf education, as students graduate from the school and continue their studies elsewhere, they are confident among their peers and test higher in most subjects than other children. The school is currently beginning to expand from its nursery through grade five program to include students in grades through eighth.

The Winchester Thurston School
555 Morewood Avenue
(412) 578-7500

Winchester Thurston boasts two campuses—a campus in Pittsburgh's Shadyside neighborhood for students from kindergarten readiness through grade 12, and a campus in the northern suburb of Allison Park for students in kindergarten through grade 5. In all, the school serves about 600 students with an attractive student-teacher ratio of 9:1, affording each student a great deal of individualized attention.

The school has undergone changes in recent years. From its founding in 1887 through 1991, Winchester Thurston admitted girls only. Beginning in 1991, boys were phased in, so that the school is now fully coeducational. All receive strong prepara-

tion for college, as evidenced by the class of 2003. Of graduates that year, 98 percent went on to four-year colleges or universities, while the balance chose two-year colleges or vocational schools.

Areas of study include English, social studies, modern and classical languages, science, mathematics, health and physical education, computers, and visual and performing arts. Winchester Thurston encourages students to enhance their classroom instruction by taking advantage of the many cultural amenities of the nearby Oakland university-medical complex, and through participation in extracurricular activities. In addition to athletics, these include more than 30 clubs and activities that focus on interests as diverse as rocketry; poetry; math; world affairs; and the student newspaper, yearbook, and literary magazine. Students also may take advantage of opportunities for international travel, study, and exchanges.

Admission requirements include academic testing, which typically is scheduled in January and February. Financial aid takes the form of need-based grants.

Yeshiva Schools of Pittsburgh
2100 Wightman Street
(412) 422-7315
www.yeshivaschools.org/site/

The goal of Yeshiva Schools, located in Pittsburgh's Squirrel Hill neighborhood, is to offer a traditional Jewish education that combines an emphasis on moral values and a comprehensive secular education. Classes range from Tiny Tots through high school,

If you want to get involved with education policy for the region, try the Education Policy and Issue Center and the Commission of Workplace Excellence, (412) 281-2000. The groups are a collaborative effort of business, civic, education, and philanthropic leaders dedicated to developing public policy strategies for education and workforce development.

with boys and girls in separate classes and buildings once they reach high school. Total enrollment is 425.

For high-school students, the secular curriculum focuses on the development of analytical and communication skills, while the Jewish Studies curriculum includes coursework in Jewish Law and History, Jewish Philosophy, and Bible and Prophets with Commentaries. Students participate in a wide range of community projects, including a weekly hospital visitation program.

Yeshiva is such a magnet for Jewish youths that about 5 percent of its students come from out of town and board with local friends of the Yeshiva. In 2000, Yeshiva Schools of Pittsburgh was awarded the prestigious Blue Ribbon Award of Excellence from the U.S. Department of Education.

West

Sewickley Academy
315 Academy Avenue, Sewickley
(412) 741-2230
www.sewickley.org
The facilities at Sewickley Academy are outstanding. Over its 21 acres about 12

miles northwest of downtown Pittsburgh, this day school boasts two libraries; six science labs; three computer labs; four athletic fields; two gyms; studios for music, dance, and art; a 635-seat auditorium; an art gallery; three playgrounds; and two tennis courts. That's enough to make a college jealous.

The academy offers an early childhood program as well as lower, middle, and senior schools; total enrollment is around 800 students, with an overall student-teacher ratio of 8:1. In the senior school, the academy supplements its core curriculum with a variety of electives and study abroad options. These include programs in Paris, Munich, and Sydney. On the domestic front, students can opt for a Maine Coast Semester, which focuses on environmental studies.

The academy requires community service and gives seniors the option of undertaking a two-week field project to learn about career opportunities. Prospective students are evaluated on the basis of previous school records, teacher recommendations, an entrance examination, and an interview. Sewickley Academy provides financial aid to about 20 percent of its students.

HIGHER EDUCATION

It would be hard to imagine a richer selection of educational options than those offered by the colleges and universities of Southwestern Pennsylvania. In the six-county coverage area, there are no fewer than 31 degree-granting institutions with a compelling diversity of academic programs, campus settings, and social and extracurricular opportunities.

You'll find private institutions, institutions owned by the state, and those that are somewhere in between; colleges with large enrollments spread over multiple campuses and colleges with fewer than 1,000 students; schools that focus on the liberal arts and those that emphasize technical disciplines; colleges that pulsate with the rhythm of urban Pittsburgh and those set in idyllic locales. Strong in their diversity, colleges and universities are a powerful force in the region.

Most of these institutions have proud histories that span many decades if not centuries. That's not to say, however, that higher education is static. In fact, few sectors have been more dynamic in recent years. As the market for traditional-age students has become more competitive, colleges and universities have changed accordingly. For many years the region had four institutions that admitted one gender only; three of those now are coed. Our liberal arts colleges have implemented career-related thrusts, and our technical institutes have introduced core curricula in the liberal arts.

A common denominator has been the expansion of services for nontraditional students. What this means for you is an unprecedented range of continuing education courses—both for credit and leisure learning—that the institutions often will deliver to your worksite or neighborhood.

It's an exciting scene, one you'll want to explore. Profiled here are the local institutions that offer associate, baccalaureate, or graduate degrees, capturing the highlights of their academic and continuing-education programs, campus life, and opportunities for social and education enrichment. *Peterson's Guide to College in the Middle Atlantic States* is a source for some of the information. Where institutions maintain multiple campuses, we've profiled each campus separately, in case you're targeting schools in specific geographic areas.

DOWNTOWN

Duquesne University
600 Forbes Avenue
(412) 396-6000

Duquesne University opened its doors in 1878 as the Pittsburgh Catholic College of the Holy Ghost, with an enrollment of 40 students. To say that the university has grown would be an understatement. Today, Duquesne boasts a student enrollment of more than 9,400, and it's one of the most important educational institutions in the region. Its 43-acre campus sits on "The Bluff," a hill overlooking both downtown Pittsburgh and the Monongahela River. The excitement of Downtown is only a few blocks away, but in the seclusion of the Bluff, Duquesne is very nearly a self-contained community.

Within the university, nine schools of study offer baccalaureate, master's, and doctorate degree programs, many developed as partnerships with local corporations and philanthropists. These include the Bayer School of Natural and Environmental Sciences, developed with the support of the Bayer Corporation, and the A. J. Palumbo School of Business Administration. The Mylan School of Pharmacy features a six-year doctor of pharmacy program, while the Rangos School of Health Sciences offers programs in physi-

In today's competitive market, local universities will go to great lengths to accommodate students. How far will they go? In 1997, Duquesne University staged a special commencement for one graduate, an Orthodox Jewish student who could not participate in the general commencement because it fell on the Jewish Sabbath.

cal and occupational therapy, physician assistant, and perfusion technology. You'll also find schools of law, education, music, and nursing. The university offers a variety of study-abroad programs through affiliations with institutions in Spain, Colombia, France, and Belgium. In addition, Duquesne confers many graduate degrees (both master's and doctorate) in a multitude of disciplines. More than 78 percent of students receive some form of financial aid.

Continuing education plays an important role at Duquesne. The university's Saturday College program leads to a bachelor's degree in professional studies and a master's degree in leadership and liberal studies. The university customizes leadership and liberal studies training programs for on-site delivery to local corporations, and it participates in the educational consortium that provides programs at the Harrisburg Dixon Center in the state capital.

About 57 percent of the undergraduate students live on campus, where they enjoy computer access in every dorm room. In fact, Duquesne was named one of the nation's 100 "most wired" colleges and universities by *Yahoo! Internet Life* for two consecutive years. Student activities take on a strong communications flavor, as students participate in the campus newspaper, *The Duke,* and two radio stations. WDSR is a campus-only station, while WDUQ-FM is a National Public Radio affiliate that broadcasts a full schedule of public affairs, jazz, and sports programming to the entire community.

Speaking of sports, Duquesne's varsity basketball teams participate in the NCAA Division I Atlantic 10 Conference, while its men's football program is a member of NCAA Division I-AA. For a more detailed look at Duquesne basketball, see the Spectator Sports chapter.

Duquesne is a Catholic university—its former name is Duquesne University of the Holy Ghost. When you study here, you'll find an emphasis on values. Duquesne has stressed that emphasis in a variety of advertising campaigns, perhaps an unusual pitch for a university in a highly competitive market. Duquesne's continued growth demonstrates how well that competitive market has responded.

Point Park College
201 Wood Street
(412) 391–4100
www.ppc.edu

If you're looking for a college in the heart of downtown Pittsburgh, look no further. Despite its name, Point Park College is not located exactly in Point State Park. It is, however, squarely in the center of Pittsburgh's business district, which provides it with energy and excitement.

The college offers its 2,300 full- and part-time students more than 50 academic programs leading to associate and baccalaureate degrees. Point Park is especially known for its programs in performing arts and communications, represented by majors in children's theater, dance, film and video production, journalism and communications, and theater arts. In addition, Point Park awards the master of arts in journalism and communications as well as the master of business administration. Classes at Point Park average 15 to 20 students.

The college's facilities also have the distinctive flavor of communications and performing arts. You'll find seven dance studios, a color television studio, a newsroom, a desktop publishing laboratory, and a radio station. Performing-arts students gain practical experience at the landmark Pittsburgh Playhouse of Point

Park College, located in Pittsburgh's Oakland neighborhood, about 3 miles from the college. The Playhouse, which the college has owned and run since 1968, typically hosts 15 productions each year.

If your schedule won't allow you to attend weekday classes, consider Point Park's "Saturday Fast" program, where you can earn your baccalaureate degree in business or applied corporate communications after two years of Saturday-only classes. The college offers the Saturday Fast program at its downtown campus, at Beaver County Community College, and at a satellite site in Cranberry, Butler County.

About 40 percent of the full-time students reside on campus in a 21-story dormitory that once was a hotel. Point Park sponsors six varsity sports and competes in the Keystone-Empire Collegiate Conference of the National Association of Intercollegiate Athletics. Extracurricular activities include ad, television, environmental, health, and ski clubs, and the *Cavalcade* literary magazine. About 90 percent of Point Park students receive some form of financial aid.

Robert Morris University
Pittsburgh Center
600 Fifth Avenue
(412) 227-6857

While we've profiled the main, Moon Township campus of Robert Morris University in the "West" section of this chapter, we'd be remiss if we didn't note RMU's Pittsburgh Center in downtown Pittsburgh. At its Pittsburgh Center, RMU provides an appealing roster of continuing-education programs, including programs for professional and career development; professional designation and certification; prelicensing and relicensing; certificates; supervisory and leadership development; and professional skills-building.

The center is only 2 blocks from Grant Street, the hub of Pittsburgh's political activity, and a quick walk from such major employment centers as USX Tower, One Oxford Center, and One Mellon Bank Center. Most courses are offered in the evening, and the college will customize courses for delivery at worksites.

NORTH

Butler County Community College
College Drive, Butler
(724) 287-8711

Chartered in 1966, BCCC was the region's first community college. It serves more than 3,000 enrolled students and a total of 14,000 people who take advantage of the college's many educational opportunities. BCCC awards three degrees—associate of arts, associate of science, and associate of applied science—but its reach extends far beyond degree programs.

The college offers for-credit courses at three community sites: Cranberry Community College Center in Butler County, Lawrence County Area Vocational Technical School in New Castle, and Lenape Area Vocational Technical School in Ford City, Armstrong County. In addition, BCCC provides an extensive schedule of leisure-learn courses in such areas as occupational advancement, public safety, literacy, and computers. Its Business and Industry Training Institute works with local business on training and productivity programs, while its Center for Economic Education provides workshops and instructional materials for elementary and secondary economics teachers.

The sprawling, 13-building campus is set on 323 acres of rolling hills with venerable oak trees. Among those buildings are the computer learning center, where students may access terminals, and the student union. The field house features a basketball court that converts to tennis courts, volleyball courts, a batting cage, racquetball courts, and weight-lifting apparatus, while outdoor facilities include golfing areas and jogging and walking trails—many available for community use.

BCCC maintains an open admissions policy—all high-school graduates and those with diploma equivalents are granted admission. Tuition is three-tiered. The tuition for Butler County residents is half that for residents of other Pennsylvania counties, which in turn is two-thirds of the charge for out-of-state residents. The college offers a diverse financial-aid program.

Community College of Allegheny County
800 Allegheny Avenue
(412) 323-2323
www.ccac.edu

The reach of the Community College of Allegheny County is hard to overestimate. It's the largest community college in Pennsylvania, with more than 25,000 enrolled students. Among the reasons for CCAC's popularity are its open admission policy and a tuition schedule that favors local residents. Tuition for Allegheny County residents is half that of tuition for residents of other Pennsylvania counties, and one-third of the charge for out-of-state residents. Roughly 40 percent of students receive financial aid.

It's more than attractive tuition that draws students to CCAC, as the college offers more than 200 academic programs leading to the associate of arts, the associate of science, and the associate of applied sciences degrees. In addition, students in CCAC's elementary education program can earn baccalaureate degrees from Indiana University of Pennsylvania while studying at CCAC. The average age of CCAC students is nearly 30, indicating that many are returning to studies after an extended absence.

While the college's academic programs defy easy summary, many are part of the following broad departments: arts and humanities; information sciences; business and accounting; mathematics and science; allied health programs; nursing; social sciences; and engineering technologies. Through the information sciences program, students earn degrees and certificates in office technology and court reporting. Students in allied health programs may specialize in nuclear medicine, radiation therapy, or diagnostic medical sonography, while nursing students can participate in cooperative education programs with more than 200 area health-care agencies.

In a word, CCAC is accessible. It maintains four area campuses, in addition to its North Side administrative offices, for the convenience of students—you'll find profiles of these in the "North," "East," and "South" sections of this chapter. The average class size is 20, and students have access to more than 1,500 microcomputers linked across the campuses by local area network. The campuses together boast more than 1 million square feet of classroom space and more than 200,000 volumes in their libraries. CCAC offers child-care centers at each campus as well as intramural and varsity sports.

While the sports lineup varies from campus to campus, the teams participate in three conferences: the Western Pennsylvania Collegiate Conference, the Pennsylvania Collegiate Athletic Association, and the National Junior College Athletic Association. About the only thing you won't find at any of the sites is on-campus housing.

Among the most impressive and attractive aspects of CCAC is its broad program of continuing education. In addition to programs at its four campuses, the college maintains eight off-campus continuing education centers—in Bethel Park, Braddock, Downtown, Homewood-Brushton, McKeesport, Neville Island, Robinson, and Turtle Creek—where more than 62,000 people participate in continuing-education and community service programs. Even more impressive, CCAC delivers continuing-education programs—many of them customized corporate training programs—to more than 400 off-campus sites.

Community College of Allegheny County—Allegheny Campus
808 Ridge Avenue
(412) 237-2525

Located on the North Side near CCAC's administrative offices, the Allegheny Campus is the largest of the college's four campuses, with more than 8,600 students. The campus is a blend of stately older buildings that trace their roots to the early-19th century and modern structures built in the 1970s. The 52,000-square-foot student services center features a theater-auditorium, classrooms, and a cafeteria.

The convenient locations mean you can walk from campus to Downtown or such North Side attractions as PNC Park and the National Aviary. Make sure you take a walking tour of the mansions near the campus. One was the home of industrialist Harry Thaw, who gained notoriety by gunning down architect Stanford White in a famous 19th-century love triangle.

Community College of Allegheny County—North Campus
8701 Perry Highway
(412) 366-7000

The North Campus of CCAC serves students in Pittsburgh's northern and western suburbs. The campus serves more than 6,500 students in a 153,000-square-foot building. That's a far cry from the campus' more humble origins—a trailer in the parking lot in what was then North Hills Passavant Hospital.

Grove City College
100 Campus Drive, Grove City
(724) 458-2000

Grove City College is dedicated to being "a Christian college of liberal arts and sciences," a mission infused in all aspects of study and life at this Butler County college. Though affiliated with the Presbyterian Church, the college is not narrowly denominational but expects attention to matters of faith from its students. Each student must attend a minimum of 16 chapel services per semester. If you need any other indications of Grove City's commitment to its vision, consider this: The college eschews all state and federal aid, the better to maintain its independent vision.

Grove City awards the bachelor of arts, the bachelor of science, the bachelor of music, the bachelor of science in electrical engineering, and the bachelor of sci-

ence in mechanical engineering degrees. The engineering programs are distinctive, offering dual emphases in science and technology and liberal arts. Core courses stress cultural literacy and communications skills, while non-engineering majors must study a language. Coursework is demanding but fulfilling, as about 80 percent of entering freshmen graduate from Grove City.

The lovely campus spans more than 150 acres and 27 buildings just a few minutes from Interstate 79, making it accessible from Pittsburgh some 60 miles to the south. Of the 2,300 students, more than 90 percent reside on campus. The Technological Learning Center includes 121 microcomputers and three big-screen projection systems. Grove City enhances those facilities by providing each freshman with a notebook-size computer and a color printer. For extracurricular activities, the college sponsors more than 100 organizations and special interest groups; for relaxation, students enjoy events at the J. Howard Few Fine Arts Center and bowling, handball, and racquetball at the student union. Grove City features an extensive intramural sports program and fields 18 intercollegiate teams for men and women.

Grove City is relatively affordable for a private school. Since the college maintains a sizable endowment, tuition is usually lower than similar schools. About 50 percent of freshmen receive financial aid. Admission to Grove City is quite competitive, which may be due to its popularity, price, and fine reputation. If you or a family member is thinking of applying, the college strongly recommends an interview with its staff. While visiting, check out the Prime Outlets (see Shopping) and the nearby towns (see Day Trips and Weekend Getaways).

Indiana University of Pennsylvania
1011 South Drive, Indiana
(724) 357-2100
www.iup.edu

Located about 50 miles northeast of Pittsburgh, Indiana is known as the "Christmas

> *Most colleges and universities offer a full range of noncredit courses—sometimes tuition-free for senior citizens—so you can enjoy your favorite hobby or interest in a classroom near you.*

Tree Capital of the World" and the hometown of actor Jimmy Stewart. If it's not as prominent for Indiana University of Pennsylvania, it should be. Founded in 1875 as Indiana Normal School, a small teacher-training institution, IUP has evolved into a major university with 13,000 students representing nearly every state and 60 countries. It's the largest university in the State System of Higher Education (which does not include Penn State University).

Academic offerings include more than 100 undergraduate majors with a variety of internship and study-abroad programs. At the graduate level, IUP offers more than 40 master's programs and eight doctoral programs. Extensive as those offerings are, the university further enhances them through a variety of creative partnerships. Through a joint initiative with the Western Pennsylvania Hospital in Pittsburgh, IUP provides a program of study in respiratory care that has achieved a 100 percent employment rate for its graduates. In cooperation with Allegheny General Hospital and MCP-Hanemann School of Medicine of Allegheny University of the Health Sciences, IUP offers a pre-professional program for students planning to serve as general practice physicians in the Pittsburgh area.

You'll find academic support services at IUP quite convenient and useful. Campus buildings are connected via a private fiberoptic link, which provides resident students with in-room Internet access and other computer capabilities. The university's Robert E. Cook Honors College is more than a mere designation, as members live together in the same residence hall and form a community.

IUP features a large resident student community—about 4,500 strong—and about 120 student organizations including a newspaper and radio and television stations. The school sponsors an intramural sports program as well as 17 varsity sports, participating in the NCAA Division II Pennsylvania State Athletic Conference. Students living on campus enjoy IUP's unusual in-room video service. Rather than contract with the local cable television provider, IUP developed its own television programming service that blends the customary satellite-delivered fare with more education-oriented programming, such as foreign language channels.

IUP is a bit outside our principal coverage area, but as you can see, it's worthy of inclusion. IUP also runs the Monroeville Graduate and Professional Center in eastern Allegheny County. At the center, IP offers master's programs in adult and community education, business administration, criminology, elementary education, and industrial and labor relations.

La Roche College
9000 Babcock Boulevard
(412) 536-1048

The Sisters of Divine Providence founded La Roche College in Pittsburgh's North Hills in 1963, when the northern suburbs began the great growth spurt that continues to this day. As a result this private, Catholic, liberal arts institution offers a beautiful suburban campus to a growing population base while still providing access to the business and social attractions of Pittsburgh. It's been a formula for success at La Roche.

La Roche awards the bachelor of arts, bachelor of science, and master of science in human resources degrees, as well as bachelor's and master's degrees in nursing. The college's 1,500 students select majors from 35 disciplines covering the humanities, including elementary education, language and literature, international studies, and sociology; the arts, including dance, professional writing, graphic design, and interior design; business, including accounting, finance, and international management; and science, including computer science, biology, chemistry, medical technology, and psychobiology. Students in virtually every major have the opportunity for internships—many with top Pittsburgh employers.

Residence life is one of the neatest aspects of the La Roche experience. The college's 350 resident students live in apartment-style suites that feature two or three bedrooms. Typically four to six students live in each suite. The Keer Fitness and Sports Center includes a gymnasium, an elevated track, a dance and karate studio, a weight room, and racquetball courts. Other activities include a student newspaper, a drama club, and men's and women's varsity and intramural sports. La Roche belongs to the NCAA Division III Allegheny Mountain Collegiate Conference.

One of the most interesting and satisfying opportunities for students is participation in the La Roche Challenge program, through which honor students teach pupils at 14 participating Catholic elementary schools. The younger students visit the La Roche campus for 20 classes each year, including instruction in such areas as computer graphics, desktop publishing, ballet, and Native American history. It's a great way to serve the community and get valuable practical experience in return.

Slippery Rock University
Old Main, Slippery Rock
(724) 738-9000

Founded as a teacher-education institution, Slippery Rock has grown into a multipurpose university with roughly 7,800 students and more than 60 degree programs in the four colleges and other departments and graduate studies. The university is in Butler County, about 75 minutes from Pittsburgh along I-79. It's one of 14 institutions in the State System of Higher Education.

If you study biology or geology at Slippery Rock, you'll have the opportunity to travel to the Marine Science Consortium at Wallops Island, Virginia. The consortium is a nonprofit corporation

dedicated to research and instruction in the marine sciences, and Slippery Rock is a member of the consortium.

The university also offers a broad continuing-education program that features credit courses, workshops, and seminars. It offers classes at a satellite site in Cranberry, Butler County, and at the St. Francis Hospital School of Nursing in New Castle, Lawrence County. The community also takes advantage of Slippery Rock's conference facilities, which include banquet halls that can accommodate up to 1,000 people in overnight facilities.

One of the most compelling aspects of the university is its campus, spread over more than 600 acres and dotted with woods, streams, and ponds. Moreover, it's near the McKeever Environmental Learning Center, a state-operated facility that provides general environmental education and instruction in environmental education for student-teachers. The college also boasts 11 residence halls, 9 auditoriums, 12 athletic fields, and tennis courts. If that's not enough, head to Morrow Field House, where you'll find a gymnasium, a swimming pool, handball courts, a dance studio, and a running track.

About 35 percent of students live on campus, and about 80 percent receive financial aid. Slippery Rock sponsors 22 varsity sports and competes in the NCAA Division II. Students take advantage of the setting and the facilities through such organizations as skiing and hiking clubs and the campus television and radio stations.

Westminster College
South Market Street, New Wilmington
(724) 946-8761, (800) 942-8033

This Lawrence County liberal arts college is slightly north of our principal coverage area, but you ought to know about it—if only for its convenient location, excellent reputation, and nearby tourist attractions. It's about 60 miles from Pittsburgh, primarily via I-79, and only about 85 miles southeast of Cleveland, making it accessible from both major urban centers.

Westminster, however, is decidedly not urban. Its 300-acre campus in the rolling hills of Western Pennsylvania offers tranquility that you'll appreciate. Affiliated with the Presbyterian Church, Westminster was founded in 1852 and was among the first colleges to offer equal admissions to women seeking baccalaureate degrees. Today, the college offers 39 academic majors—with internships available in each one—and 6 preprofessional programs. Among the most interesting majors is Sacred Music, a joint program with Duquesne University through which students take classes on both campuses. Class size typically is smaller than you'll find in many colleges and universities.

Virtually all of Westminster's 1,500 students live on campus, where they take advantage of a broad computer network that provides them with Internet access and other functions from their dorm rooms. One of the most important volunteer activities on campus is service with Habitat for Humanity, which involves about 300 Westminister students in its programs of constructing homes for families in need. If you're looking for a less arduous leisure activity, try some stargazing at the observatory in the Hoyt Science Resource Center. Westminster sponsors an intramural sports program and 16 varsity sports at the NCAA Division II level. There's a proud tradition of sports excellence here. The football team has achieved 6 national titles and 11 undefeated seasons. When the football team left the National Association of Intercollegiate Athletics in 1997, it left as the all-time leader in wins.

While Westminster is a college affiliated with the Presbyterian Church, it's known among students and graduates as being less strict in the areas of dorm room inter-visitation and chapel attendance.

New Wilmington and the surrounding areas of Volant, Sharon, and Grove City (with the Prime Outlets) surely make this an attractive destination to visit while transporting kids to and from college, or merely checking out the campus. (See the Day Trips and Weekend Getaways and Shopping chapters.)

EAST

Carlow College
3333 Fifth Avenue
(412) 578-6000, (800) 333-CARLOW
www.carlow.edu

Carlow College was founded in 1929 by the Sisters of Mercy to help women realize their potential. While Carlow today admits men without actively recruiting them, it remains a Catholic, liberal arts college primarily for women. It's set on a hillside overlooking Pittsburgh's Oakland neighborhood; as you stroll through the quadrangle, you get a satisfying sense of community while knowing that the amenities of Oakland's university-medical complex are just down the hill below.

Carlow confers three baccalaureate degrees—bachelor of arts, bachelor of science, and bachelor of science in nursing—as well as three master's degrees. Undergraduates select from 34 majors. While these are rich in humanities programs including creative writing, English, philosophy, history, social work, and sociology, they also feature such business programs as accounting, business management, and medical marketing, and such science-based programs as chemistry and four biology tracks.

Carlow offers pre-professional programs in dentistry, medicine, optometry, osteopathy, pharmacy, physical therapy, podiatry, law and veterinary medicine. Whatever your major, Carlow requires study in a core curriculum that represents the humanities, natural sciences, and social sciences, as well as such interesting courses as public speaking and women's studies.

Students participate in more than 20 organizations—when they're not too busy enjoying the many social and cultural opportunities of Oakland. While Carlow offers only one residence hall, students

Staying in State

If you're a Pennsylvania resident or thinking of relocating to the Commonwealth, you'll want to become familiar with the State System of Higher Education, the administrative agency for 14 universities in Pennsylvania. Profiled are the three member universities in our coverage area—California, Indiana, and Slippery Rock. You'll find the other 11 in Bloomsburg, Cheyney, Clarion, East Stroudsburg, Edinboro, Kutztown, Lock Haven, Mansfield, Millersville, Shippensburg, and West Chester.

It's a large system encompassing more than 94,000 students. One of the most important features of the system is the attractive tuition for state residents—generally, several thousand dollars lower than what out-of-state students and their families pay. It's no accident that 92 percent of system students are Pennsylvania residents.

are guaranteed housing. The college sponsors five varsity sports, offers crew as a club sport, and provides a fitness center, swimming pool, and gymnasium. Approximately 92 percent of full-time students receive financial assistance.

One of Carlow's most appealing strengths is its extensive continuing-education programs. In addition to maintaining satellite sites in Beaver, Cranberry and Greensburg, the college offers the Carlow Weekend College and the Carlow Accelerated Program. Both enable working students to develop class schedules that accommodate their professional schedules while working toward degrees. Through Carlow Hill College, a continuing-education program targeted to the primarily African-American residents of Pittsburgh's Hill District neighborhood, students develop leadership skills and enhanced career possibilities.

Carnegie Mellon University
5000 Forbes Avenue
(412) 268-2000
www.cmu.ed
Few degrees are as prestigious as those from Carnegie Mellon, a private university of about 7,500 students with a dual focus

on education and research. It was founded in 1900 by industrialist and philanthropist Andrew Carnegie, whose vision was a vocational training school for the children of the city's working class. It was renamed Carnegie Institute of Technology in 1912 and merged with the Mellon Institute in 1967.

An important component of Oakland's university-medical complex, Carnegie Mellon includes four undergraduate colleges (in technology, fine arts, humanities and social sciences, and science) and three graduate schools—the Graduate School of Industrial Administration, the School of Computer Science, and the H. John Heinz III School of Public Policy and Management.

The university is perhaps most prominent for its leadership in the arts and technology, an unusual combination but one

The latest **U.S. News and World Report's** *rankings for the best colleges and universities in the United States place both* **Carnegie Mellon and Duquesne in the top 25.** *The rankings are based on academic reputation, faculty resources, student selectivity, retention, graduation rate, financial resources, and alumni giving.*

The intersection of the campuses of Carnegie Mellon University and the University of Pittsburgh is one of the most engaging spots in the city. Along the informal border, you'll find Carnegie Library of Pittsburgh, the Hillman Library, the Frick Fine Arts Building, Phipps Conservatory and Botanical Gardens, and Flagstaff Hill, a great site for lounging and people-watching. Look very carefully and you'll also pick out a brick wall that is the last surviving portion of Forbes Field, former home of the Pittsburgh Pirates.

that works well at Carnegie Mellon. The university introduced its undergraduate drama degree in 1917; since then, a number of young men and women who later would gain fame as actors, directors, and set and costume designers learned their art and craft at CMU. Among actors who have studied at the university are George Peppard, Holly Hunter, Ted Danson, and Jack Klugman.

In technology, Carnegie Mellon operates the National Robotics Engineering Consortium. Located in Pittsburgh's Lawrenceville neighborhood along the Allegheny River, the consortium develops robots to explore volcanoes and other hazardous environments, and vehicles that can be driven without human operators on board. The work of Carnegie Mellon students and faculty in such fields as computer science, software development, and robotics has resulted in the creation of more than 70 "spinoff" companies.

Carnegie Mellon's strength in technology has important implications for the university's students. About 85 percent of students use computing in their educational activities. Through the university's computing network—called "Andrew" after benefactors Andrew Carnegie and Andrew Mellon—all students have access to personal computing workstations.

The campus spans 103 acres and 66 buildings. Student activities vary from

special interest clubs and a newspaper and a radio station to fraternities and sororities. The university sponsors 17 varsity athletic teams—the men's football team participates in the University Athletic Association of NCAA Division III. Fitness and recreation facilities include tennis courts, gymnasiums, racquetball courts, swimming pools, and weight/fitness rooms. In an innovative arrangement, the university, through an affiliated corporation, operates the city of Pittsburgh's Schenley Golf Course, which is adjacent to campus. (For more on the course, see the Golf chapter.) About 75 percent of undergraduate students reside on campus, and about 65 percent receive some form of financial aid.

Chatham College
Woodland Road
(412) 365-1100
www.chatham.edu

When you're enjoying the freshness and beauty of Chatham's 32-acre wooded campus, surrounded by the converted mansions that serve as the college's residence halls, you'll probably forget that Fifth Avenue, one of the city's busiest thoroughfares, is only a hillside away. That sense of splendid isolation within the bustling city is part of Chatham's charm.

Chatham is the last of the region's exclusively single-gender institutions of higher learning (men are admitted to graduate programs only)—it's been preparing women for personal and professional success since 1869. Its more than 40 baccalaureate degree programs feature small, seminar-style classes and a variety of hands-on learning experiences, including two guaranteed internships in a field related to your major as well as a mentoring relationship with a leading professional woman.

Chatham also offers master's level programs in physical therapy, occupational therapy, physician assistant studies, teaching, management, and counseling psychology. Chatham graduates receive preferred entry into these programs. Collaborative programs provide a bridge to medical school, engineering, and an environmental and occupational health master's program.

Providing broad and challenging experiences is one of Chatham's key goals, one the college achieves through several innovative programs. One is a senior tutorial, a yearlong independent research project on a topic of each student's choosing. Another is Chatham Abroad, an exciting opportunity for travel through which each student experiences a three-week trip with faculty and classmates to countries such as Egypt, France, Spain, England, Belize, Ireland, Morocco, and Italy. Chatham's Global Focus Program provides international events and activities, with a different area of the world highlighted each year.

Of Chatham's roughly 900 students, about 45 percent reside on campus or in college-owned apartments on Fifth Avenue. More than 92 percent of students receive some form of financial aid. A fiberoptic network connects everyone on campus and provides each student with Internet access. Chatham sponsors more than 40 student organizations, NCAA Division III teams in six sports, and a variety of club and recreational sports. One of Chatham's most distinguished graduates is Rachel Carson, founder of the modern environmental movement. In her honor, Chatham maintains the Rachel Carson Institute, an advocate for the environment that also produces environmental awareness programs for high school students.

Community College of Allegheny County—Boyce Campus
595 Beatty Road, Monroeville
(412) 371-8651, (724) 327-1327
Nearly 6,000 students are enrolled in academic programs at Boyce Campus; sometimes it's hard to imagine how they concentrate on their studies. The campus serving Pittsburgh's eastern suburbs is adjacent to Allegheny County's Boyce Park, which offers the closest downhill skiing slopes to Pittsburgh. For students who can manage to stay off the slopes—we're only

kidding here, as Boyce Campus students are as dedicated as any other students— the campus provides a multipurpose center that includes a gymnasium, a theater, and classrooms. If by some chance you are interested in Boyce Park, you'll find a profile in the Parks chapter.

Electronic Institutes
4634 Browns Hill Road
(412) 521-8686, (800) 721-8686
Electronic Institutes prepares students for employment in fields related to engineering, with programs of study leading to the associate in specialized technology degree in electrical technology or electronic and computer technology. As befitting such a focused program, the academic schedule is fairly rigorous, with classes in session about 48 weeks of the year. Instructors take attendance each day, further emphasizing the seriousness of the mission here.

Electronic Institutes sits on Browns Hill Road, a steep hill overlooking the Monongahela River that connects Pittsburgh to the Homestead High Level Bridge and the suburb of Homestead just across the river. While classrooms and laboratories offer a wide variety of electronics equipment for hands-on training, the institution does not offer residences, so students must find their own housing. Electronic Institutes provides assistance in that search, as well as placement services whenever graduates require them. Electronic Institutes offers a number of financial-aid programs.

Penn State McKeesport
University Drive, McKeesport
(412) 675-9000
A regional campus of the Pennsylvania State University, Penn State McKeesport offers the first two years of more than 160 baccalaureate degree programs. Those are far from the only academic options here, as students also pursue associate degrees in five programs and master's degrees in adult education and counselor education. Students in the business administration and liberal arts associate degree programs

have the opportunity to attend weekend and evening classes to better accommodate their schedules.

Founded in 1948, the college is about 10 miles southeast of Pittsburgh. Of the nearly 1,000 students, about 200 reside on campus. For those who commute, Penn State McKeesport maintains plenty of free parking, an important perk. Students participate in such activities as theater production and the campus radio station. Through community outreach services such as the Penn State Educational Partnership Program and the Educational Opportunity Program, student tutors assist middle-school and high-school pupils in after-school study programs, a nice way of blending education and community service.

The student-faculty ratio is 16:1, while the student-computer ratio is 8:1, helping assure that students get the attention and support they need. Students participate in an intramural sports program as well as two varsity sports—men's basketball and women's volleyball. The teams compete in the Western Pennsylvania Collegiate Conference and the Penn State Commonwealth Campus Athletic Conference. About 80 percent of students receive some form of financial aid.

Penn State New Kensington
3550 Seventh Street Road
Upper Burrell
(724) 334-5466
Like the Penn State campuses in McKeesport and Beaver, Penn State New Kensington is part of the Pennsylvania State Commonwealth College and draws on its considerable resources. Students at the 72-acre Penn State New Kensington, founded in 1958 and located in Westmoreland County about 20 miles from Pittsburgh, can complete the first two years of almost any of Penn State's 160 baccalaureate degree programs. Seventy-two percent of Penn State New Kensington students are enrolled in such programs.

There are, however, other options, including four-year programs in nursing

and electromechanical engineering technology that can be completed on-site. In addition, the college offers associate degree programs in business administration, allied health, engineering technology, liberal arts, and sciences. Class size is comfortable—the student-faculty ratio is 18:1. When they're not studying, students relax at the gymnasium, racquetball courts, and fitness center, or broaden their experience through the Outdoor Adventure Club, the Multicultural Club, and such community projects as homebuilding with Habitat for Humanity.

Penn State New Kensington offers an intramural sports program as well as two varsity teams—men's basketball and women's volleyball—that compete in the Western Pennsylvania Collegiate Conference and the Penn State Commonwealth Athletic Conference. You won't find on-campus housing; many students rent apartments in a building adjacent to campus. About 80 percent of students receive some form of financial aid.

Pittsburgh Institute of Aeronautics
5 Allegheny County Airport, West Mifflin
(412) 462-9011, (800) 444-1440
Pittsburgh Institute of Aeronautics was founded in 1927 by Glen Curtiss and Orville Wright—yes, that Orville Wright—so you know the history of the institute is solid. You may not be flying solo over Kitty Hawk, but you will have the chance to study for an associate degree in specialized technology in one of two programs. The Aviation Maintenance Technician Program leads to a test for the airframe and powerplant license. The Avionics Technician (AVT) program will prepare you for the FCC General Radiotelephone license.

You can complete the programs in 21 months, making them especially attractive. For the first six weeks, you'll study such basics as English, algebra, and physics. After that, it's all hands-on work with airplanes, jets, and helicopters, as well as work in the shop and the lab. You can begin your classes at one of four

Financial Aid for College

If you're considering college in the Commonwealth, it will be worth your while to become familiar with the Pennsylvania Higher Education Assistance Agency, the state's most important source of financial aid for college and university students. PHEAA offers more than financial aid alone, valuable though its dollars may be. Its Early Awareness Program, for example, introduces middle-school students and their families to the benefits of early planning for higher education.

You can reach PHEAA in a number of ways. For information, the best number is (800) 692-7392. You can write PHEAA at 1200 North Seventh Street, Harrisburg, PA 17102-1444, or visit their Web site, www.pheaa.org.

times during the year. Graduates interested in pursuing baccalaureate degrees can receive advanced standing credits at any of the 12 colleges and universities with which PIA maintains cooperative agreements. Two of those cooperating institutions are in Pittsburgh: Community College of Allegheny County and Point Park College.

PIA does not offer its 225 students housing or financial aid, though it gladly accepts grants, scholarships and private funding you receive from other sources. PIA claims an outstanding placement record, indicating that its graduates typically receive from four to six job offers. Prepare for takeoff!

Pittsburgh Institute of Mortuary Science
5808 Baum Boulevard
(412) 362-8500

This is the region's only degree-granting institution for mortuary science, so it has a comparatively large enrollment—about 150 students. The institute welcomes about 50 new students each January, May, and September; the trimester approach means that most students can find a convenient time to launch their studies.

Located in Pittsburgh's Shadyside neighborhood, the institute awards the associate in specialized business degree, which usually leads to a career in funeral service management, and the associate in specialized technology degree, which focuses more on the technical aspects of mortuary science. In addition, the institute maintains cooperative programs with four colleges and universities—Point Park College, California University of Pennsylvania, Thiel College, and Gannon University—that enable its graduates to earn bachelor of science degrees at the campuses of the cooperating institutions.

In addition to the technological aspects of mortuary science, students learn about the human and historical components of the business through such courses as world religions, ethics, gerontology, communication skills, and the psychology of grief and counseling. The institute offers financial assistance but no on-campus housing.

Pittsburgh Theological Seminary
616 North Highland Avenue
(412) 441-3304

The seminary was founded in 1794 in a log cabin with six students and one teacher. For more than 200 years, it has pursued the same vision: nurturing men and women in their faith, while preparing them for pastoral ministry and Christian lay leadership. The seminary is affiliated with the Presbyterian Church, but its community is ecumenical, with more than 20 denominations represented in the student body.

Located in Pittsburgh's East Liberty neighborhood and boasting 13 acres of green grounds, the seminary confers the master of divinity, master of arts, master of sacred theology, and doctor of ministry degrees. Joint degree programs with local colleges and universities allow students to earn a master of divinity degree from the seminary and a master's degree in law, social work, public health, business, or sacred music from the collaborating institution. Similarly a Ph.D. program from the University of Pittsburgh is available to seminary students. The seminary offers an evening program that enables master of divinity students to complete their work in six years.

Students can take advantage of a number of continuing-education programs as well as the Metro-Urban Institute, which provides field education experiences. The seminary provides both dorm rooms and unfurnished apartments (pets aren't permitted in either) as well as child-care services during regularly scheduled daytime class hours. The student association arranges recreation and athletic events, utilizing the seminary's tennis courts. Students also have limited access to the gym and swimming pool at Peabody High School, just across North Highland Avenue, and they enjoy a weekly volleyball game at a local church. Financial aid is available.

The purposes of the seminary clearly are serious, but you'll also appreciate the zest for life here as embodied in the warning signs along campus drives. The signs say THOU SHALT NOT PARK HERE.

Reformed Presbyterian Theological Seminary
7418 Penn Avenue
(412) 731-8690

If you drive along Penn Avenue in Pittsburgh's Point Breeze neighborhood, you might mistake this campus and its attractive grounds for the estate of a wealthy industrialist. It may look that way, but

there's serious work going on here, as the seminary's primary purpose is to train ministers of the gospel for church leadership. The student body is small, numbering about 100 students, yet those students represent more than 20 denominations.

The seminary was founded in 1810 and boasts a colorful history. In its early days, the Synod of the Reformed Presbyterian Church elected a professor of theology; whenever he moved to a different congregation, his students moved with him. Thus, the seminary had five different locations between 1810 and 1856.

Today, the seminary awards the master of divinity degree with emphasis in biblical studies, systematic theology, church history, and pastoral theology. The institution stresses the importance of local churches, offering practica in different areas of ministry and requiring a local church recommendation for admission to seminary.

Technology plays an important role in scholarship at the seminary. A climatized rare book room houses more than 1,000 volumes, while computer terminals feature Hebrew and Greek characters for display and study of ancient texts.

Saint Vincent College
300 Fraser Purchase Road, Latrobe
(724) 532-6600

Saint Vincent is a Catholic, Benedictine liberal arts college in Westmoreland County, about 35 miles east of Pittsburgh. About 25 percent of the faculty are Benedictine Monks, infusing the campus with a zest for life and learning. At Saint Vincent, you'll find plenty of opportunity for both.

The college offers baccalaureate degrees in more than 50 disciplines, spanning a wide range of humanities, business, and science programs. You'll find a number of appealing concentrations in the arts, business administration, and family and consumer sciences tracks, as well as preparatory programs in law, medicine, dental medicine, engineering, health professions, chiropractic, optometry, podiatry, theology, and veterinary medicine. Through cooperative programs with Seton

Hill College and Duquesne University, Saint Vincent students may pursue additional programs, including occupational therapy, pharmacy, and physical therapy, leading to graduate degrees at Duquesne. The college offers study abroad through its relationship with Fu Jen Catholic University of Taiwan.

Of Saint Vincent's 1,200 students, about 875 reside on the 400-acre campus. The campus features a number of neat structures. These include the central commons building, which offers an amphitheater, a planetarium, and a robotics lab, and the Instructional Technology Resource Center, where students go online. You can participate in the campus radio and television stations, provide community service through the Campus Ministry Program, or participate in six men's varsity sports or five women's varsity sports. The college competes in the National Association of Intercollegiate Athletics. Saint Vincent provides financial assistance to more than 90 percent of the students who apply for it.

You'll come to appreciate the college's productive relationship with Seton Hill College, which is less than 10 miles west along Route 30. For most of their respective histories, when Saint Vincent admitted only men and Seton Hill only women, the two institutions developed a "brother-sister" relationship that featured cross registration for courses and joint social functions. Today, both schools are coeducational, but their productive relationship remains. A free shuttle bus operates between the two campuses.

Seton Hill University
Seton Hill Drive, Greensburg
(724) 834-2200, (800) 826-6234

The word "community" is used rather loosely these days, but when you visit Seton Hill University, you'll know at once that you've arrived at a community. Founded in 1918 by the Sisters of Charity, Seton Hill is a Catholic liberal arts college with a lovely 200-acre campus high atop a Greensburg hill, about 35 miles east of

Pittsburgh. For most of its years a women's college, Seton Hill now is fully coeducational with a faculty that features members of the Sisters of Charity and lay persons. The campus includes both retirement quarters and a cemetery for the sisters—both of them not far from tennis courts and an exercise course for the college's roughly 1,100 students. The campus is dotted with intriguing pipe sculptures produced by Josefa Filkosky, a member of the Art Department faculty. You won't find many colleges with a stronger commitment to a mission and a community.

Undergrads choose from more than 40 areas of study, including physician assistant, biology, psychology, education, management, and visual and performing arts. Class size typically is comfortable, with a student-faculty ratio of 13:1. Honors programs, independent study, and seminar work are available to students, and study in most majors includes internships. At the graduate level, Seton Hill awards the master of arts degree in elementary education, special education, and art therapy. In addition, the college offers an innovative program in which students may earn a bachelor of arts degree, certification in elementary education, and a master's in elementary education in five years—all for the price of a bachelor's degree.

Seton Hill's Accelerated Saturday Degree Program is designed for students who wish to pursue degrees while continuing to work full time. Through the program, students can obtain their degrees in management, accounting, general studies, or human services within the traditional four years while taking classes on Saturdays only.

Students participate in the campus newspaper and literary magazine as well as intramural and varsity sports. Seton Hill sponsors varsity teams in basketball, cross country, equestrian, soccer, softball, tennis, and volleyball. For leisure, you'll find a gymnasium, a swimming pool, volleyball and badminton courts, softball and soccer fields, and a fitness trail that winds through

Financial aid at area colleges and universities can take a number of forms—scholarships, grants, loans, part-time employment, or a combination of these tools.

the surrounding hills. The college also provides van transportation for trips to local and Pittsburgh shopping districts, while students plan regular excursions to New York City and Washington, D.C.

Seton Hill awards merit-based scholarships in theater, art, music, biology, chemistry, and mathematics. Through the Seton Hill College Presidential Scholarship Program, students who graduate in the top 30 percent of their high-school class are eligible for awards up to $6,320 annually. When you're checking out the facilities, make sure you stop in Reeves Memorial Library to enjoy the unusual sculpture of a student, head down on the table, weary or asleep from studying.

As befitting a college where community is so important, Seton Hill provides important services to the broader community. These include plays staged by the theater department in Reeves Theatre, exhibitions of student art in Harlan Gallery, and the Lynch Lecture Series, which brings nationally prominent speakers and performers to campus. The college is home to the National Catholic Center for Holocaust Education as well as the National Education Center for Women in Business, which serves as a nationwide clearinghouse for information and research on women's business ownership, while offering consulting services and classes in entrepreneurship.

University of Pittsburgh
Fifth Avenue at Bigelow Boulevard
(412) 624-4141
www.pitt.edu
The importance of the University of Pittsburgh would be hard to overestimate. It serves approximately 32,000 undergraduate and graduate students. If you don't find that figure impressive, consider it another way; roughly 5.5 percent of all students enrolled in institutions of higher learning in Pennsylvania are enrolled in the University of Pittsburgh.

The school was founded in 1787 as the Pittsburgh Academy, and it has remained close to the community it serves. Its signature building, the 42-story Cathedral of Learning, was financed in the 1920s largely through the contributions of area residents, who "bought" bricks for a nickel apiece. The university has produced 180,000 graduates—many are among the region's business, professional, and civic leaders.

When you're speaking about the university, it's important to discuss both education and research, as Pitt is a leader in each. In education, the university offers 367 distinct degree programs as well as other dual, joint, and cooperative degree programs. It offers graduate programs in arts and sciences, business, dental medicine, education, engineering, health and rehabilitation sciences, information sciences, law, medicine, nursing, pharmacy, public and international affairs, public health, and social work. The College of General Studies offers undergraduate programs on a part-time basis for students with full-time jobs or other commitments, while the Honors College provides attractive seminar-style classes for high-achieving students. The university maintains regional campuses in Bradford, Greensburg, Johnstown, and Titusville.

In the area of research, Pitt is a member of the prestigious Association of American Universities, a consortium of the 62 leading research universities in North America. Its faculty has pioneered the way in such discoveries as silver-sheathed superconducting wire and development of a method to decontaminate chemical weapons. Among the university's most prominent research centers are the University Center for International Studies, the Center for Biotechnology and Bioengineering at the Pittsburgh Technology Center, the University Center for Social and Urban Research, the Thomas E. Starzl

Transplantation Institute, and the University of Pittsburgh Cancer Institute. In addition, Pitt's six schools of the health sciences work closely with UPMC Health System, the region's largest network of hospitals, clinics, and research centers. For more on UPMC Health System, see the Health Care chapter.

You won't want for academic support here, as Pitt's libraries house approximately 4 million volumes and subscribe to about 25,000 journals and periodicals. All dormitories are equipped with personal computing facilities, and you'll have access to portable laptop computers at Hillman Library, the university's principal library.

The split-level campus dominates the Oakland neighborhood, spanning 90 buildings and 132 acres. On the lower level, on and around Fifth and Forbes Avenues, you'll find the Cathedral of Learning and its Nationality Rooms, 24 authentically designed rooms depicting the ethnic art and culture of their respective lands. For more on the Nationality Rooms, see the Attractions chapter. Nearby, you'll see a trio of buildings both historic and functional. The Center for American Music is housed at the Stephen Foster Memorial, a tribute to the great Pittsburgh-born composer. Heinz Memorial Chapel, an interfaith chapel built in the French Gothic style, features magnificent stained glass windows that soar skyward and is a popular venue for weddings; better make your reservation before you pop the question, as the waiting list typically is lengthy. The William Pitt Union, the center of student life, opened in 1898 as the grand Hotel Schenley, a favorite stopping place for visiting dignitaries and actors.

On the upper campus, you'll find such amenities as the brand-new sports arena—Petersen Events Center—the university's principal gymnasium, swimming pool, and other student and community athletic facilities, and the residences of campus fraternities and sororities.

Student life is as varied as you would expect. While many students are commuters, about 5,000 live on campus, and many others rent apartments off campus. Tuition for state residents is about half that for out-of-staters. About 70 percent of undergraduates receive financial aid. The university sponsors more than 400 student organizations, including a campus radio station and the *Pitt News,* a newspaper published five times each week. You'll want to scan the newspaper for coupons good at Oakland businesses and ads for sales and housing availabilities.

The university sponsors a full range of intramural sports and 19 varsity sports for men and women, who compete in the Big East Conference. For more on varsity football and basketball at Pitt, see the Spectator Sports chapter.

This is a vital urban campus, where social and cultural opportunities abound. Rare is the day when you can't find at least several appealing lectures or performances on campus. On the other hand, if you'd prefer to spend your noon hour sunning on the Cathedral lawn, that's part of the Pitt charm, too. And if you want to take classes in the Cathedral of Learning but not for degree status, investigate one of the many sources through Pitts' Informal Program (a noncredit division), with classes in everything from how to become a writer to learning more about Pittsburgh's history and architecture.

University of Pittsburgh at Greensburg
1150 Mount Pleasant Road, Greensburg
(724) 837-7040

This 205-acre regional campus of the University of Pittsburgh was built on the former private estate of Commander Charles McKenna Lynch. It's only 3 miles from downtown Pittsburgh, but it will give you an appealing sense of satisfaction and community. The university serves 1,500 students through 17 four-year programs leading to baccalaureate degrees and a number of pre-professional programs completed at the university's main campus in Pittsburgh.

Majors include accounting, administration of justice, anthropology, biological sciences, environmental science, informa-

Hollywood producers Steven Bochco and Bud Yorkin studied at Carnegie Mellon University. Bochco studied drama, but Yorkin was an engineering student.

tion science, management, and political science, and you also may design your own major. All students must complete general core requirements that include courses in communications, mathematics, and critical reasoning, as well as five courses each in humanities, social science, and natural sciences. If you can't attend class every day for personal or professional reasons, try the University External Studies Program. You'll attend three on-campus workshops per term and complete the balance of your studying at home.

About 45 percent of full-time students live on campus, where they enjoy the McKenna Computer Center; Chambers Hall, which features a gymnasium, a running track, and racquetball courts; and Millstein Library, which provides access to the Internet as well as the University of Pittsburgh Digital Library. A member of the NCAA Division III Allegheny Mountain Collegiate Conference, the university sponsors seven varsity sports as well as intramural sports. The financial aid program is extensive and varied, with all awards based on need.

Westmoreland County Community College
400 Armburst Road, Youngwood
(724) 925–4000
One of the most appealing aspects of WCCC is its reach. In addition to the main campus about 6 miles south of Greensburg and 35 miles east of Pittsburgh, the college maintains Westmoreland County campuses in Belle Vernon, Latrobe, New Kensington, and Penn Township, to accommodate its 5,770 full- and part-time students. In addition, WCCC uses distance learning technology to teach certain courses simultaneously at several or all campuses, minimizing students' travel

requirements, and it offers telecourses for students who can't make it to campus.

Academic programs prepare students for careers or transfer to baccalaureate degree programs at four-year institutions. The college awards the associate in arts degree and the associate in applied science degree, with nearly 50 majors available. Principal programs include accounting, allied health, business, computer information systems, engineering science and industrial technology, horticulture, hospitality management, human services, liberal arts, and science, media technology, and office administration. Study in certain specialties within those departments leads to a certificate or diploma.

The main campus in Youngwood spans 80 acres and four buildings. Students have access to more than 500 computers with Internet access. For relaxation, the college provides a gymnasium, racquetball courts, a health fitness center, and an indoor track. Area employees take advantage of the classrooms, laboratories, and offices in the Business and Industry Center at the Youngwood campus.

If you're a Westmoreland County resident, you'll like the tuition schedule—you'll pay half what nonresidents pay. WCCC offers a variety of financial aid programs, including many scholarships endowed by local businesses and foundations.

SOUTH

California University of Pennsylvania
250 University Avenue, California
(724) 938–4000
Nestled in a bend of the Monongahela River about 30 miles from Pittsburgh, California University is an important member of the State System of Higher Education and one of the key institutions of Washington County. The university awards associate, baccalaureate, and master's degrees in more than 100 academic programs offered through the College of Education and Human Services, the College of Liberal Arts, the Eberly College of Science

and Technology and the School of Graduate Studies and Research. Continuing-education students will find a rich selection of courses in the Lifelong Learning program and at the university's satellite site at Southpointe Technology Park in Canonsburg.

California serves nearly 5,800 students on its 80-acre campus, which includes six residence halls that house 1,500 students. One of the most inviting features on campus is the 104-acre Roadman Park, which includes athletic fields and courts, running facilities, and a stadium. You won't have to worry about academic support here, as the university boasts more than 1,800 computers—more than one-third of them available to students for e-mail and Internet access and other functions. The student-faculty ratio is 21:1.

Students participate in more than 130 organizations, including the *California Times* newspaper, the *Flipside* magazine, a radio station, and a television station. The university sponsors a program of intramural sports and 13 varsity sports, participating in the NCAA Division II Pennsylvania State Athletic Conference. In 1996–1997, the women's softball team captured the NCAA Division II national championship. If you're a Trekkie, you'll get a kick out of the athletic team's nickname—the Vulcans. More than 75 percent of students receive some form of financial aid.

Community College of Allegheny County—South Campus
1750 Clairton Road, West Mifflin
(412) 469-1100
ww.ccac.edu

The South Campus of CCAC serves Pittsburgh's southern suburbs on a 200-acre site near Century III Mall. Its six-story principal building features a learning assistance center, a community library, a theater, a student dining area, and classrooms. In addition, the campus boasts a learning resource center that offers computer labs and an allied health/nursing complex, and a gymnasium-fitness center. Nearly 6,600 students are enrolled.

Washington and Jefferson College
60 South Lincoln Street, Washington
(724) 223-6078

"Two great presidents . . . one great college" is a tag line W&J frequently uses as a quick introduction to the institution. As you learn a little about W&J, you'll probably agree. It was founded in 1781, making it the oldest college west of the Allegheny Mountains, and has maintained its focus on liberal arts and small classes for more than 200 years. With a student-faculty ratio of 12:1, W&J offers its 1,117 students plenty of individualized attention in its classes.

The college offers baccalaureate degrees in a broad variety of majors. The humanities—including programs in art, art education, education, French, German, Spanish, history, sociology, and political science—are well represented. You also can major in business-focused disciplines such as business administration and entrepreneurial studies and science-based areas including biology (the most popular major), biochemistry, chemistry, environmental science, and neuroscience. The college offers preparatory programs in law, medicine, dental medicine, optometry, physical therapy, podiatry, and veterinary medicine. Through exchange programs, W&J students may study abroad at the University of London and the College of Higher Studies in Colombia.

One of the highlights of the academic calendar is the break between terms, which W&J has formalized as "January Intersession," when students are encouraged to broaden their experiences. Many do just that. During one Intersession, students traveled to such destinations as Egypt, Greece, East Africa, and Australia for study trips led by W&J faculty. Other

---

Washington and Jefferson College is the *smallest school ever to play in the Rose Bowl. In the 1922 "Granddaddy of Them All," W&J played the University of California to a scoreless tie, using only 11 players in the process.*

---

students contributed to the 4,200 hours of community service that the college's faculty, staff, and students log annually.

The 43-acre campus is located in the city of Washington, an easy 25-mile drive south from Pittsburgh along I-79. Ohio and West Virginia are about 30 minutes from the W&J campus via interstate highways. About 82 percent of students live on campus. The Student Resource Center and a related teaching lab offer 70 computers for student access. About 70 percent of students receive some sort of financial aid.

W&J belongs to the Presidents' Athletic Conference and the NCAA Division III, sponsoring 11 men's and 9 women's varsity sports as well as a diverse intramural sports program. If you spend time on campus, you'll also get to know the Olin Fine Arts Center, which includes both an art gallery and a hall for performing arts.

Waynesburg College
51 West College Street, Waynesburg
(724) 627-8191, (800) 225-7393
www.waynesburg.edu
While Waynesburg College is southwest of our principal coverage area, it's an important institution in our region that you should know about. Moreover, it's just off I-79 in Greene County, about 50 miles from Pittsburgh, so accessibility is no problem.

This private college, founded in 1849, is affiliated with the Presbyterian Church and serves more than 1,200 students on a campus just 2 blocks from the Waynesburg business district. Degrees offered include master of business administration (offering a criminal justice track), bachelor of arts, bachelor of science, bachelor of science in business administration, bachelor of science in nursing, associate in business administration, and associate in general studies. Within those degree programs are several innovative initiatives.

Waynesburg offers a program in marine biology that features an academic year at Florida Institute of Technology in Melbourne, Florida. The college cooper-

ates with several university schools of engineering to provide joint programs in chemical, electrical, and mechanical engineering, among other engineering-related disciplines, and offers similar joint programs in medical technology.

Community service is important here—the college requires 30 hours of such service from each student—and includes such activities as building homes with Habitat for Humanity and teaching computer skills aboard the college's mobile technology van. As further service to the community, Waynesburg maintains a center for education and technology to provide training and programming for local businesses as well as an adult continuing-education center in Pittsburgh's South Hills.

If you're studying communications, you'll enjoy the extracurricular opportunities at Waynesburg. They include a campus radio station, television studio, newspaper, yearbook, and poetry magazine. The college is a member of the NCAA Division III and competes in seven men's and seven women's varsity sports.

More than 80 percent of Waynesburg students receive financial aid in a typical year.

WEST

Community College of Beaver County
Campus Drive, Monaca
(724) 775-8561
When CCBC moved from its temporary headquarters in 1971, the college's leadership was looking for a location that would be convenient for most Beaver County residents. They found it here, within 4 miles of the geographic center of the county. The distance from the 75-acre campus to the most remote point in the county is 17 miles, meaning that no Beaver County resident has more than a 30-minute drive to get here.

The college offers 39 programs of study leading to associate degrees. These include programs in allied health, nursing, and aviation sciences. The Aviation Sciences Center features a functioning air traffic control tower at Beaver County Airport, operated by students and college faculty who are professionals in the field. The program is so progressive that the Federal Aeronautics Administration has established an Aviation Education Resource Center on-site and has an agreement with CCBC for direct hire of the college's air traffic control graduates.

The college's open admissions policy works particularly well for older students returning to classes after some time away; the average student age here is 26. You'll find three levels of tuition, with Beaver County residents offered the lowest tuition, followed by tuition for residents of other Pennsylvania counties and then for out-of-state residents. CCBC provides support to students with families through the Campus Child Care Center. The Library Resource Center offers multimedia retrieval capability among its research tools. All of the college's roughly 1,150 full-time students are commuters, as there are no on-campus housing facilities.

CCBC offers varsity athletics in baseball, basketball, golf, softball, tennis and volleyball, participating in the National Junior College Athletic Association. The campus also is home to the Beaver County Hall of Fame, where such sports legends as Joe Namath, Mike Ditka, and Tony Dorsett—all reared in Beaver County—are enshrined.

Geneva College
3200 College Avenue, Beaver Falls
(724) 846-5100, (800) 847-8255
www.geneva.edu

Set on 55 scenic acres overlooking the Beaver River, Geneva College is an institution with a mission: to educate students through biblically based programs anchored by the historic evangelical and reformed Christian faith. It's a mission that informs all of Geneva's programs.

Degrees offered by the college include bachelor of arts; bachelor of science in education, business administration, and

engineering; and associate in business administration, engineering, and biblical studies. Geneva also provides pre-professional programs in cardiovascular technology, criminal justice, medical technology, and nursing.

While the college's mission is rooted in Christianity, that doesn't mean Geneva subordinates vocational preparation. A number of the college's most innovative programs include strong practical components. It offers a dual-degree program in aviation/business administration, in cooperation with the Community College of Beaver County, that leads to an associate degree in aerospace management, air traffic control, or professional piloting, as well as appropriate Federal Aviation Administration licenses and certification. Biology majors studying for a B.S. may spend one of their four years at Virginia's Fairfax Hospital. For study in other medical disciplines, Geneva maintains affiliations with the University Hospitals of Cleveland, St. Joseph's Hospital in Lancaster, and St. Vincent Health Center in Erie.

Students in all programs have broad access to the tools of technology. To cite one example, Northwood Hall, site of business and psychology classes, offers more than 100 computers for student use. The college estimates that more than 90 percent of its students receive some form of financial aid. One of the more innovative methods of helping students is an honor scholarship presented—regardless of need—to each student in an academic program who meets certain academic standards.

The student center is the heart of campus life for the more than 1,750 Geneva students, more than half of whom are commuters. Activities include a student newspaper, cable television and FM radio stations, a yearbook, a literary magazine, a marching band, and an a cappella choir. Geneva participates in a variety of intramural and varsity sports, the latter as a member of the National Association of Intercollegiate Athletics.

Penn State Beaver
110 University Drive, Monaca
(724) 773-3500

One of 12 campuses that form Penn State Commonwealth College, Penn State Beaver is a 100-acre campus set in the heart of Beaver County, about 30 miles northwest of Pittsburgh and 15 miles from Pittsburgh International Airport. For its 825 students, the college offers the first two years of more than 180 Penn State baccalaureate degree programs. In addition, the college offers four associate degree programs—liberal arts, science, electrical engineering technology, and hotel, restaurant, and institutional management. In one component of the hotel, restaurant, and institutions management program, students operate a dinner cafe one day a week as part of a field practicum. Penn State Beaver also offers professional certificate programs and graduate-level courses for teachers, with evening class schedules available for these programs.

Student life is full and varied, especially for those residing in the college's two residence halls. Among the most popular student activities is participation in the Masquers, which has brought live theatre to preschool and elementary school children since 1969. Students also participate in five intercollegiate sports, a variety of intramural sports, and the campus radio station, WBVR.

As the Masquers demonstrate, Penn State Beaver strives to be a force in the community, providing students with the opportunity to network and form useful contacts. Since 1976, the Broadhead Cultural Center on campus has staged free or low-cost concerts and theatrical productions in the 700-seat, open-air J.P. Giusti Amphitheater. The campus sponsors an annual celebration of the birthday of the Rev. Martin Luther King Jr. with a program and a guest speaker.

The college's adult literacy program provides educationally disadvantaged adults with tutoring in reading, math, civic literacy, family support, and English as a foreign language, while its partnership with the Aliquipa School District enriches the lives of disadvantaged youths and their families by providing academic and life skills support.

Robert Morris University
881 Narrows Run Road, Moon
(412) 262-8206, (800) 762-0097

Robert Morris University is named for one of the key financiers of the Revolutionary War; most campus buildings bear the names of America's early heroes and patriots. The pleasant campus is spread over 230 sloping acres about 5 miles from Pittsburgh International Airport. It's a convenient location for visitors.

Once you start to talk about academics at RMU, you'll leave the 18th century pretty quickly, as this private university means business—literally. RMU focuses on business education at the undergraduate, graduate, and continuing education levels. Its productive relationships with many local businesses help graduates find jobs and advance in their careers. More than 18,000 RMU alumni live and work in the region. The university's Sewall Center for Leadership, a meeting, convocation, and athletic center, is a popular site for corporate training programs.

You can pick from more than 30 majors leading to the bachelor of arts, bachelor of science, and bachelor of science in business administration degrees. Among the undergraduate majors you won't find at many institutions are sport management, tourism management, and aviation management. The university awards associate degrees in business administration and computer and information systems; in a joint program with Allegheny General Hospital and Pittsburgh's Ohio Valley General Hospital, students may earn an associate in science degree from the college and a certificate in radiologic technology from one of the hospitals. At the graduate level, RMU offers 14 programs of study leading to the master of science, master of science in business administration, and master of business administration degrees. For stu-

Checking Out Your School

For help coordinating your visit to check out colleges in Pittsburgh, view www.thecollegecity.com, which offers great travel tips and bona-fide deals, as well as information about schools and careers here. The site is associated with Campus Visit magazine, based in Wellesley, Massachusetts. Visit www.campusvisit.com.

---

dents with busy professional schedules, the college offers the One-Day-A-Week Program, which enables students to take the bulk of their classes on Saturdays. The program is available at both the Moon campus and the Pittsburgh Center.

For years, businesses have lamented the poor communications skills of their employees. RMU has come to the rescue with an innovative Communications Skills Core program for all students in bachelor's degree programs. The communications requirement includes five courses in the first several years of study and four courses during the upperclass years. The courses focus on five key areas: communication principles; skills and strategies; written, oral, and nonverbal language; collaborative, interpersonal and intercultural skills; support technologies; and affective behaviors.

RMU's 5,000 full-time and part-time students enjoy access to the Academic Media Center, which features photography and audio production facilities as well as a crackerjack television production studio, one of the finest campus studios you'll find. TV production here is no academic exercise, as RMU students program a channel for the local cable television operator, which provides in-room cable services to the college's 900 resident students. RMU competes in the NCAA Division I Northeast Conference in all its varsity sports but football, which is a Division II program. (For a more detailed look at RMU basketball, see the Spectator Sports chapter.) The university offers an extensive intramural sports program. More

than 80 percent of RMU students receive financial aid.

RMU offers extensive continuing education programs through its Pittsburgh Center in downtown Pittsburgh. For a profile of the Pittsburgh Center, see the Downtown section of this chapter.

Trinity Episcopal School for Ministry
311 Eleventh Street, Ambridge
(724) 266–3838, (800) 874–8754
"Serving Jesus Christ within the Episcopal Church, while welcoming committed Christians from all traditions." That's how Trinity Episcopal School for Ministry describes its mission, which it pursues in a variety of ways. Located in Beaver County, Trinity is a graduate school for religious study offering the doctor of ministry, master of divinity, master of divinity/master of arts in professional psychology, master of arts in religion, and master of arts in mission and evangelism degrees.

Trinity is set on a city block in the heart of Ambridge, symbolizing its role in the community. The school emphasizes field education opportunities, which include preaching, leading small groups, service as hospital chaplains, and work with missions for the homeless. Through the Trinity Episcopal Extension Ministries program, students may earn up to 24 credits prior to enrollment through home study supplemented by some time on campus. TEEM also is available to students in seven other cities.

While the school advises students to expect a demanding academic schedule, it provides plenty of support, including weekly meetings with advisee groups comprised of both professionals and students and two quiet days each term, when students get a break from their studies to reflect and worship. Married couples are welcome here—consistent with the school's belief that husbands and wives should minister as partners—but school-provided housing is limited.

When you're here, check out the mural that covers the entire back wall of the library building. Painted by students, it blends biblical themes and representations of local settings.

Proprietary Schools

In addition to degree-granting institutions, Southwestern Pennsylvania offers a large and eclectic group of for-profit trade schools, many of which award certificates in specialized trades. Business schools and beauty academies probably are the largest groups, but you'll also find schools for massage, pet grooming, gunsmithing, floral arrangement and care, truck driving and diesel technology, lethal weapons training . . . well, you get the idea.

These schools are so numerous—easily more than 100 in our principal coverage area—that they defy easy summary or description. To my knowledge, no one has tried. For a statewide list of private licensed/registered schools, a good resource is the Pennsylvania Education Directory, an annual published by Applied Arts Publishers, Box 479, Lebanon, PA 17042-0479, (717) 272-9442. Cost is $14.00 plus tax, with a $2.00 discount for educators, libraries, and school districts. You'll get names, phone numbers, and addresses, but no descriptions.

HEALTH CARE Ⓗ

Southwestern Pennsylvania has many attractions, yet its health-care sector may be one of its most abiding strengths. The region is a center for medical treatment and research, bringing local residents high-quality health care and the promise that they will be the beneficiaries of cutting-edge developments. In addition, the region's reputation as a leader in health care serves as a magnet for medical professionals, who in turn contribute to the strength of the sector, creating a cycle of growth.

The center of the region's health-care sector is Oakland's medical complex, which derives much of its energy and personnel from the University of Pittsburgh Medical Center (UPMC). Community medicine is well represented in the region, too, both by independent hospitals throughout our six-county coverage area and by providers affiliated with Pittsburgh-based health systems.

One could chart the history of health care here through its pioneers and milestones, such as Dr. Jonas Salk's development of his polio vaccine; Dr. Thomas Starzl's trailblazing work in organ transplantation; even in the development of the Mr. Yuk poison prevention program, an initiative that has saved an inestimable number of lives. Most recently, holistic medical alternatives have begun to be offered along with allopathic medicine at several UPMC hospitals, West Penn Allegheny Health System, and at doctors' offices throughout the area. You'll also find holistic practitioners, such as licensed acupuncturists and qualified practitioners of herbology and homeopathy, practicing in offices of their own. Just as Salk and Stazl were pioneers in saving lives, the holistic practitioners in the area are pioneers in saving the *quality* of lives.

No history of Pittsburgh health care would be complete without mentioning the contributions of Pittsburgh's workers and labor unions. When Pittsburgh was the industrial heart of America, it was laborers, unions, and their companies that advanced the notion of employer-provided health insurance. There may be no single person to credit for this, but it's an important contribution nonetheless.

In our look at the region's health-care system, you'll find profiles of holistic health practices, hospitals, rehabilitation centers, and health insurance providers. We've also provided descriptions of organizations that can serve as valuable resources—and sources of referrals—for you. Finally, we've presented descriptions of some special services providers. You might not need them now, but it's sure comforting to know they're here.

WELLNESS

Unless you're experiencing a life-threatening emergency, you can call one of the referral sources listed in the Resources section to find the name of a physician, or confidently visit one of the practitioners listed below. In some cases, both acute and chronic, working with a holistic practitioner can heal your illness; in almost all others, you can improve your quality of life.

While the modalities holistic practitioners use vary widely, one thing you'll find in common among these trained professionals is that they all ask you questions about you and your life, not just questions about your symptoms of illness. They do this because they take into account the gestalt of who you are when they're treating you—that's the nature of the "holistic" approach. In addition, most holistic practitioners strive to create a comfortable and nurturing healing environment.

Some of the most commonly used holistic modalities are acupuncture, chiropractic, massage, homeopathy, and herbology. Acupuncture—which involves the insertion of needles about the thickness of a strand of hair into particular, superficial points on the body—is useful in treating a range of symptoms, as well as the root causes of illness, including pain, headaches, hormonal imbalances, systemic weakness related to various diseases, addictions, and acute and chronic viral illnesses. In chiropractic, the spine is manipulated, with the goal of relieving pain and freeing the body's energy for health and well-being. While there are many types of massage, most are pleasant, pain-relieving, and relaxing; discuss your goals with the massage practitioner you contact to make sure the type of massage she or he does will help you achieve what you desire.

Homeopathy and herbology, often confused by new holistic health patients, are distinct sciences. Used widely in European countries, homeopathy works on the principle of "like produces like" and uses remedies containing only the "energy imprint" of the physical substances from which they were produced. These remedies address physical, mental, and emotional symptoms and can be used to bring the body back to balance during either acute or chronic illness—or simply to strengthen an individual's constitution. Herbology uses either Western or Chinese herbs in single or combination form to effect changes in the same way that pharmaceutical drugs do. Some traditional drugs are even made from herbs. For instance, the heart medication digitalis is made from foxglove, a plant originally found in the wild. In any case, many of the holistic modalities you may try have been used successfully for thousands of years—

that's longer than any clinical trial we know of.

The list below is by no means exhaustive. Out of the many practitioners in the area, we've selected the people we or our trusted friends personally know are top-notch. If you're looking for a type of practitioner we haven't described here, call the Nuin Center at (412) 661–6108 or pick up a copy of *Point of Light* magazine at one of Pittsburgh's health-food stores.

The Nuin Center is a Highland Park professional building and group-meeting location center once part of the Mellon estate. The majority of the tenants are healing-arts practitioners, as the intention of the center's founders was to create a space supportive of the healing arts. *Point of Light* is a free, quarterly magazine that covers healing arts and "New Age" happenings from a popular perspective. Many reputable practitioners advertise in the magazine.

Downtown

The Midwife Center for Birth and Women's Health
2825 Penn Avenue
(412) 321–6880
www.midwifecenter.org
Since 1982 the certified nurse-midwives at the Midwife Center for Birth and Women's Health have provided personalized health care to thousands of women and have assisted in the delivery of over two thousand babies. It is the only freestanding, licensed birth center option in Northwestern Pennsylvania, and there is also the option of hospital birth facilitated by the center's physician.

The Midwife Center, located in the Strip District, strives to increase the health of women and their families by providing excellent woman-focused healthcare services and family-oriented birthing services. Many people think that midwives only help women have babies, but midwives also provide well-woman gynecological care and family planning to women during all stages of life, from puberty through to menopause. Services include pregnancy care and delivery; complete history and physical exams; pelvic exams and pap tests; referrals for mammography; natural family planning and fertility awareness; contraceptives; pre-conceptual counseling and testing; sexually transmitted disease screening and treatment; wellness promotion; menopausal care, including hormone replacement therapy or alternatives; and educational programs. All of the care is viewed within the context of reproductive and sexual health as part of normal life processes, and providers do not intervene without evidence of a problem, including during childbirth and menopause.

When care is called for, the midwives take the time to listen and talk with their clients about things that affect them, their family, work, and personal issues. The waiting area and exam rooms are cheerful and warm and are decorated in ways more typical of someone's living room than a "clinical environment." Reflecting the midwives' philosophy, it feels cozy and safe here.

During appointments the midwives take into account each woman's physical, emotional, and spiritual needs. The midwives believe that a woman should be in control of her own health care, including her birth experience. They are particularly knowledgeable and gentle in dealing with issues related to past sexual trauma, and overall the language they use and the way they interact with patients supports a positive sense of well-being, even during pelvic exams!

The Midwife Center is a private, non-profit practice, supported in part by grants; patient fees; United Way Contributors Choice; and tax-deductible contributions from businesses, foundations, and individuals. They accept most insurance plans and are a member organization of Family Health Council, Inc. Through their "With Woman Fridays" program, they provide free and sliding-scale-fee health care to underinsured and uninsured women and their children.

North

Acu-Care: The Acupuncture Center of Pittsburgh
7500 Brooktree Road, Suite G102, Wexford
(724) 452-9334, (724) 933-4646
Sharon Tillotson-Gallagher, R.ac. implements the Japanese style of acupuncture in her practice. As compared to traditional Chinese acupuncture, this style often uses fewer needles inserted even more superficially than in the Chinese style. While Sharon treats people of all ages and genders, she says her average patient is a woman aged 20 to 80 who has a relatively healthy lifestyle and diet and is seeking either preventative care or care that will help her maximize her health. Sharon describes her specialties as preventative care and women's health issues; although she has treated severely ill patients, this is not her focus. Representative conditions that she has treated successfully are amenorrhea and dysmenorrhea, PMS, infertility, recurring headaches, allergies, arthritis, sports-related injuries, and addiction to cigarettes. It takes about 20 minutes to reach her office from downtown Pittsburgh.

The Integrated Medicine Program at Allegheny General Hospital
320 East North Avenue
(412) 359-8951
www.wpahs.com
Located on Pittsburgh's Northside, the Integrated Medicine Program at Allegheny General Hospital was designated fourth in its class by *Natural Health Magazine* in 2001. The program's mission is dedicated to blending the science of allopathic medicine with the wisdom of natural healing practices to enhance the health and well-being of its patients, helping them learn to tap into their own self-healing capacity.

The Proper Medicine: Community Drug Makes Filling Prescriptions an Exact Science

The sign that hangs beneath the pharmacy window at Community Drug reads: ASK YOUR PHYSICIAN IF COMPOUNDING IS RIGHT FOR YOU.

Eleven steps below in the basement of the Greenfield pharmacy is a brightly lit, 450-square-foot compounding lab. Here, a handful of trained workers prepare specialized medications to help everybody from a two-week-old infant with seizures to a constipated cat.

"We are here to solve problems," said David Hairhoger, president of Community Drug Inc. and Community Drug Compounding Center. Both entities are licensed separately with the Pennsylvania Board of Pharmacy. Hairhoger bought Community Drug from the son of its original owner in 1980 and opened the compounding lab in 1996 because "we want to do the right thing," he said.

That right thing involves preparing medications to help solve challenging problems for patients and their pets, Hairhoger said. He explained that many medicines are available in limited strengths only and compounding pharmacists can custom-make prescriptions.

"I market to physicians, dentists, podiatrists, pediatricians, veterinarians, physical therapists, and other pharmacies," said Hairhoger. He spends about 15 to 20 hours a week in marketing and making office visits on behalf of Community Drug Compounding.

"When I call on physicians, I stress that we're here to solve medication problems," Hairhoger said. He added that he typically receives favorable feedback from physicians. "The one thing they say is that, 'I've never seen a pharmacist stop by and talk to me,'" Hairhoger reported.

And every physician can find the need for a compounding pharmacist, according to Hairhoger. "Even if it's as simple as customized doses," he said.

The Integrated Medicine Program offers "Mind/Body Medicine," such as biofeedback, yoga and meditation, breathwork, and prayer and nondenominational spiritual support; Traditional Chinese medicine, including acupuncture, Chinese herbology, and nutrition and lifestyle counseling; body and energy work, such as therapeutic massage, reflexology, and Reiki; the "R& R Program (Relaxation and Recovery)" that prepares patients for surgery and helps them recover afterwards; the "Lifestyle Program," which combines customized medical and lifestyle changes for health management; and, perhaps most notably, the "Functional Bowel Program," one of only three programs in the country that offers a multidisciplinary approach to bowel disorders. Also quite notably, many of these therapies are available to inpatients as well as outpatients.

The Integrated Medicine Program was co-founded by Paul Lebovitz, M.D., and

Dr. Wynne Browne, an obstetrician/gynecologist who retired from conventional medicine last year after seventeen years, said she began working with compounding pharmacies about four years ago because she—and her patients—weren't happy with conventional hormone prescriptions.

"I wasn't satisfied with conventional hormone prescriptions because the 'one-dose-fits-all' just doesn't work," said Dr. Browne, who now practices alternative medicine and has offices in Highland Park and White Oak. "Women are all very different."

She said that compounding pharmacies are helping to bring back relationships among physicians, patients, and pharmacists. "It's the relationship we've heard about from years ago. We've re-created that," said Dr. Browne.

Dr. Browne holds informational seminars with Susan Merenstein, a pharmacist at Community Drug Compounding, to educate women on natural alternatives to conventional hormone replacement therapies that can be used during menopause. Merenstein said this area is expected to grow for the compounding center. "It's easy to count and put some pills in a bottle, but it's a whole different ball game when interfacing [with patients] like this," said Merenstein.

All told, the Community Drug Compounding Center works with at least 100 different physicians, filling on average 30 to 35 compounded prescriptions daily. Upstairs, the traditional pharmacy fills about 200 prescriptions a day.

"It takes time," said Hairhoger of compounding. Turnaround on compounded prescriptions usually takes about two days. While Hairhoger declined to reveal sales figures, he said the compounding pharmacy is operating in the black.

By Lynne Glover, Reprinted with permission from the *Pittsburgh Business Times*

Kathleen Krebs, R.N. Lebovitz, who was nominated for the *Pittsburgh Business Times*' 2002 Healthcare Hero award, is a board-certified gastroenterologist and the program's medical director. He also leads the Functional Bowel team. Krebs, clinical director, was designated in 2002 by the *Pittsburgh Post-Gazette* as one of a "dozen making a difference in health care in Pittsburgh." She assesses patients' needs and their state of health and assists them in employing mind/body medicine techniques. Other staff include nationally board-certified acupuncturist Don Thompson, L.Ac., and Dr. Jorge Vazquez, who is board-certified in both internal medicine and nutrition.

In addition, the Integrated Medicine Program operates a volunteer component that trains mature adults in Reiki, Healing Touch, and hand massage, so they can offer these therapies free of charge to the inpatient and outpatient population. The program also serves as clinical site for the

Community College of Allegheny County's massage therapy program.

East

Acupuncture Energetics
Wellspring Valley Center
183 Donegal Lake Access Road
Stahlstown
(724) 593-6237

Acupuncture Energetics forms the cornerstone of the Wellspring Valley Center, which was founded by Christine Simmons, R.ac. Christine holds a master's degree in acupuncture and Chinese medicine from the Traditional Acupuncture Institute in Columbia, Maryland. To assist her clients in achieving greater health, along with acupuncture, Christine often uses Chinese and Western herbs, Jin shin acupressure process, polarity therapy, movement therapy, and the Feldenkrais and Alexander techniques. One of Christine's specialties is helping clients access and recognize their emotions, with the goal of transforming emotional blocks that contribute to reduced mental and physical health. She treats clients of all ages with both acute and chronic illnesses, as well as those who are seeking preventative medical treatment, and describes the purpose of her work as being "to help people help themselves as they travel their personal journey to wholeness and self-knowledge."

You may reach Christine via e-mail at wellspringvalley@LHTCH.net. Although it will take you at least 45 minutes to travel from Pittsburgh to see Christine, it's worth it. She's an experienced and talented prac-

If you're interested in keeping up with regional health-care trends, try a subscription to Hospital News, (412) 395-1775, priced at $28 annually. While this monthly tabloid is targeted to medical professionals, many of its features are of interest—and comprehensible—to the rest of us.

titioner, and you'll enjoy the lush country setting across from Donegal Lake, where Christine lives and works.

Alan Berman, D.C.
4354 Murray Avenue
(412) 422-7005

Alan is a graduate of the Sherman College of Chiropractic and uses various techniques in his adjustments, including diversified and cervical specific. He has been in practice in the same location for 20 years, and he accepts a wide range of insurances. Massage, various forms of physical therapy, and consultations with nutritional counselors are also available through his office.

Wynne Browne, M.D.
The Nuin Center, 5655 Bryant Street
(412) 521-2236

Wynne Browne is a board-certified OB-GYN and a licensed acupuncturist, as well as a practitioner of "energy medicine." She retired from "conventional medicine" after 17 years and now offers a nontraditional practice with numerous areas of specialty. Her office environment today offers comfortable chairs, soft music, and is decorated with objects reflecting her Native American heritage.

Dr. Browne says she's "never really believed that people have to suffer," and she "holds the space" for her patients to experience "physical, mental, emotional, and spiritual healing." She views a major part of her role as a doctor as being able to "help people take responsibility for their health and health care." Her philosophy that "medical care is a process that happens with a patient, not to them" goes hand in hand with that.

Dr. Browne is well known in the Pittsburgh area for her work with natural hormone replacement therapy for women and men (men, she explains, go through an "andropause"). She provides traditional acupuncture sessions, and in particular, has seen this modality be effective for many patients with fertility issues.

She also offers energy work sessions using Flow Alignment and Connection and Cellular Expansion, and often combines Flow Alignment and Connection with acupuncture. She has seen dramatic shifts within patients experiencing both severe physical and mental illnesses while they committed themselves to the Cellular Expansion modality, and she's especially excited about this pioneering form of energy practice, which works on the somatic level.

Her other areas of specialty include nutrition and weight management; anger management; and medical hypnosis, in which her training is quite extensive. Dr. Browne received her medical training at the University of Pittsburgh Medical School and did her residency at Magee-Womens Hospital.

Julie Ann Caryl, D.C. and Pamela Huston, D.C.
2020 Ardmore Boulevard, Forest Hills
(412) 273-3600

Julie and Pam are graduates of the Palmer College of Chiropractic and are certified in applied kinesiology and the Nambudripad Allergy Elimination Technique (NAET). Applied kinesiology is a system that evaluates structural, chemical, and mental aspects. It employs muscle testing and other standard methods of diagnosis. Nutrition, chiropractic adjustments, acupressure, exercise, and education are used therapeutically to help restore wellness.

In addition to the standard applications of chiropractic, Julie and Pam help clients with problems with environmental sensitivities, allergies, and myriad acute and chronic health problems. NAET is one of the means they use to do this. NAET diagnosis and treatment of allergies integrates methods from the disciplines of kinesiology, chiropractic acupressure, and nutritional science. It's likely your insurance will reimburse you for treatment with the doctors, who offer comprehensive 30-minute and 1-hour sessions.

The doctors are members of the Pennsylvania Chiropractic Association, the Human Ecology Action League, The Center for Science in the Public Interest, and the Physicians Committee for Responsible Medicine. You'll start feeling more relaxed as soon as you sit down next to the burbling meditation fountain in their waiting room and have a cup of tea.

The Center for Pain Treatment
1312 East Carson Street
(412) 431-9180

A chiropractor, Kathleen C. Clarkin, and four board-certified trigger-point myotherapists—Tassos Spanos, Mark Spanos, Nancy Shapiro, and Richard Finn—comprise the Center for Pain Treatment. In addition to their certification, all the myotherapists have personally studied with Dr. Janet Travell, the originator of trigger-point myotherapy and White House physician to Presidents Kennedy and Johnson.

To understand how trigger-point myotherapy works, it's useful to know that a trigger point is a self-sustaining irritable spot on a muscle. This irritable spot gradually causes the affected muscle to become tighter and shorter, limiting the function and motion of the muscle and causing weakness and/or pain. Most of the time, the trigger point, which is at the site of a trauma to a muscle, refers pain to another area of the body, just like a hole in a roof may cause a leak in a distant area of the ceiling. Using various massagelike techniques, a trigger-point myotherapist stretches the muscle, unwinding the trigger point and thus easing the patient's pain.

Trigger-point myotherapy is useful in treating a wide variety of pain syndromes, including carpal tunnel, TMJ, migraines, sciatic, tendonitis, arthritis, and both fibromyalgia and myofascial pain syndrome (which is often misdiagnosed as fibromyalgia). The therapy is also useful in improving the performance of athletes and musicians, and in cases where muscle weakness or distortion, rather than pain, is present. (Cases like the latter might include people recovering from strokes, for instance.) There's a good chance your insurance carrier will reimburse you for your sessions, as long as treatment is supervised by the chiropractor on staff.

Donna Davis, R.N.
7424 Washington Avenue, Swissvale
(412) 271-7050

Donna implements a wide variety of massage techniques in her practice. She does traditional Swedish massage, Paul St. John Neuromuscular Therapy, the Ingram method of foot reflexology, therapeutic touch, and the Upledger form of cranial sacral therapy.

Although the state of Pennsylvania does not require massage therapists to be certified, Donna has successfully completed the national certification test for massage. She's a member of the American Massage Therapy Association as well as the International Association of Healthcare Practitioners. We find her to be a particularly compassionate practitioner.

Joyce Gelles, D.C.
Murry Ridge Professional Center
5290 Logans Ferry Road, Suite B
(724) 325-4554

Joyce began her practice in 1980, shortly after she graduated from Palmer College of Chiropractic. She offers gentle chiropractic treatment for all ages, implementing multiple low-force techniques, Sacro Cranial, acupressure, myofascial release, micromanipulation, neuro-emotional technique, and Nambudripad Allergy Elimination technique. She accepts insurances, but is not part of any HMO groups.

Pittsburgh School of Massage Therapy
10989 Frankstown Road (Penn Hills)
(800) 860-1114
www.pghschmass.com

When the Pittsburgh School of Massage Therapy opened its doors in 1986, the school was the first in Western Pennsylvania to offer professional massage therapy training, and today it remains the only school devoted exclusively to massage and related subjects in Southwestern Pennsylvania. The school continues to train profes-sionals, provide professional continuing education courses, and offer weekend introductory courses, such as "Massage for Friends and Family" that are popular among community members at large.

The school offers a "massage therapist locator" service to individuals who call the school looking for referrals. A receptionist can search a database during the call or send a directory of graduates who've agreed to be listed. Qualified graduates of the school have offices throughout Pittsburgh and the surrounding area. All have core training in Swedish and sports massage, and some practitioners go on to do advanced or specialized training in such techniques as neuromuscular work, trigger-point myotherapy, myofascial release, shiatsu, pregnancy massage, and reflexology, among others.

At the school, there's also a professional clinic, where it's possible to make appointments with a professional who is either a graduate of the school or an instructor there. Visitors to the school will also find a retail store on site, stocked with massage and bodywork supplies, aromatherapy and spa items, and books and videos related to wellness and massage.

Squirrel Hill Family Wellness Center
5801 Beacon Street, Squirrel Hill
(412) 422-LIFE

Franne Berez, M.D., N.D. founded the Squirrel Hill Family Wellness Center in 1988. She is a board-certified family practitioner with a special interest in holistic medicine for women and children, although she treats patients of all ages and genders. Complete evaluation includes a standard Western medical interview, lab evaluation, hospital testing with referral to appropriate medical specialists if needed, and psycho-social evaluation. These conventional medical practices are combined with time-honored methods of naturopathic, homeopathic, and traditional Chinese diagnosis; in fact, most patients coming to see Franne seek her expertise in homeopathy.

And don't worry if doctors' offices usually set your teeth on edge. You won't even see the exam room until the last few minutes of your interview with the doctor, and forget the paper gown. You'll tell Franne about what ails you while you sit in a rocking chair in her casually decorated office. You might even still be sipping the last bit of that tea you made for yourself in the waiting room.

Franne shares space with several practitioners at the center who work closely with her. Mary Magan, L.Ac., who is a nationally certified acupuncturist and herbalist, takes an approach to her patient interviews that's similar to Franne's. Treatments with Mary, whom we find exceptionally gentle, often include acupuncture, herbology, homeopathy, nutritional counseling, massage, or electrical therapy.

Other Squirrel Hill Family Wellness practitioners include Denise Happe, who is a board-certified doctor of naturopathy; Beverly Spin, who is a certified nurse practitioner with specialties in therapeutic touch, EMDR (a psychotherapeutic technique often used in healing trauma issues), yoga, interactive guided imagery, and co-active coaching; and Rachel Walton, who is a women's health nurse practitioner offering care for women and teens that draws on conventional and natural modalities, with an emphasis on self-care.

Two organizations are also now associated with the center: Developmental Delay Resources and Key Stone Reiki. The first provides the most current information available about causes, interventions, and preventions for ADHD, learning disabilities, and autism, and the second offers hands-on energy healing techniques from the Usui System of Reiki Healing.

UPMC Shadyside, The Center for Complementary Medicine
5230 Centre Avenue
(412) 623-2121
www.complementarymedicine.upmc.com
Interestingly enough, when it originally opened its doors in the early-19th century, Shadyside was an independent, homeopathic hospital. While that ceased to be its identity a long time ago, Shadyside was one of the first hospitals in the country to offer such programs as medical hypnosis, pain management utilizing therapeutic touch and biofeedback, and therapeutic touch for inpatients. When national demand pushed doctors and hospitals to consider how complementary medicine could interface with conventional, allopathic medicine, the hospital was a natural site for innovation.

UPMC Shadyside's Center for Complementary Medicine was chosen by *New Age* magazine as one of the top six complementary medicine centers in the country. The center's mission is to work in cooperation with physicians treating patients with all kinds of health conditions and to individually tailor programs for patients that suit not only their presenting conditions, but that also take into consideration what suits their personality types and spiritual and emotional needs

The center offers acupuncture, traditional Chinese medicine, botanical medicine, biofeedback, polarity therapy, chiropractic manipulative therapy, naturopathic counseling, EMDR, medical hypnosis relaxation therapy and guided imagery, body-centered psychotherapy, reflexology, shiatsu, therapeutic massage and touch, and comprehensive holistic evaluations by physicians.

Whole Health Resources
2015 Murray Avenue, Squirrel Hill
(412) 421-7760
www.wholehealthresources.com
Whole Health Resources is synonymous with the work of Deborah Barr, who founded this center for holistic counseling in 1985. Deborah—who has many years of training in meditation, yoga, whole-foods nutrition, and spiritual development—provides counseling sessions relating to holistic health, macrobiotics and other forms of nutrition, natural weight loss, and attitudinal healing. She frequently gives personal development workshops and provides corporate and personal wellness coaching and teleseminars. She also offers shiatsu massage, foot reflexology, acu-

pressure facial massage, and whole-foods cooking instruction. Deborah's clients, each of whom participate in a wellness program they've designed with her, regularly report improvements in their health, such as stable blood sugar levels, better sleep quality, and more balanced energy. We find Deborah's positive attitude rubs off—a nice bonus.

Classes in tai chi, yoga, aromatherapy, and other forms of personal and professional development are held at Whole Health Resources on a regular basis. One-on-one yoga therapy sessions are available by appointment.

HOSPITALS

Southwestern Pennsylvania is justifiably renowned for its leadership in medical research and treatment, and its many teaching, community, general, and specialized hospitals form the core of the health sector. In recent years, however, the region's medical group has experienced considerable volatility, as hospitals have in some cases merged to form networks and absorb physicians' practice groups, restructured to create for-profit arms in other cases, and downsized in still other cases. The result has been a new look for the health sector here; while many of the players remain the same, the names and services may have changed.

The two largest networks are UPMC Health Center, which encompasses 20 hospitals and a number of other units, and the West Penn Allegheny System, which includes 6 hospitals, a hospice, and a nursing center. Smaller networks include Pittsburgh Mercy Health System and Heritage Valley Health System.

In the description of area hospitals, we've noted where facilities are part of a network. Where a network or system operates multiple hospital, we've listed each hospital in its proper geographic section, while noting its affiliation with the network. If a network or system provides services apart from its hospitals, we've

described those under the system or network header. Keep in mind that the sector continues to be volatile, experiencing at least several consolidations each year.

Downtown

Mercy Hospital of Pittsburgh
1400 Locust Street
(412) 232-8111

The flagship of Pittsburgh Mercy Health System, this tertiary and teaching hospital is located in uptown Pittsburgh near Duquesne University. The 500-bed facility groups its special services into five "Centers for Excellence": Mercy Heart Institute, Mercy Cancer Institute, Mercy Women's Health Center, Mercy Children's Medical Center, and Mercy Trauma and Burn Centers.

Mercy Heart Institute cares for approximately 10,000 patients annually, while the Mercy Cancer Institute was the region's first to offer radiation therapy in the 1950s. Mercy offers Pittsburgh's only Level 1 Regional Resource Trauma Center and Burn Center, which features a trauma team available around the clock.

Key components of the Mercy Children's Medical Center include units for neonatal intensive care, 24-hour pediatric emergencies and pediatric trauma intensive care, and ambulatory and short-stay pediatric care, as well as a newborn nursery. The Children's Medical Center also offers a program that meets the changing medical needs of women and children as they advance through life.

Mercy's community outreach includes the Parish Nurse and Health Ministries Program, which places nurses in inner-city parishes in the Diocese of Pittsburgh, a pediatric clinic at the downtown Salvation Army, and Operation Safety Net, which meets the medical needs of Pittsburgh's homeless. Through Operation Safety Net, a collaborative effort with a number of human services organizations, teams of health-care providers travel the streets of

Pittsburgh to meet the homeless on their turf and render medical care.

Pittsburgh Mercy Health System
1400 Locust Street
(412) 232-8111

Mercy Health System boasts one of the richest traditions in the region's health-care sector, tracing its roots to the 1847 founding of its predecessor hospital by seven Sisters of Mercy from Carlow, Ireland. System executives describe the organization as a "Catholic system of health care." In addition to Mercy Hospital of Pittsburgh and Mercy Providence Hospital, both described in this section, the system includes a 150-bed skilled-nursing facility, a 26-bed personal care residence, and a network of primary care physicians.

The system also operates Mercy Behavioral Health, a network of commnity-based mental health, mental retardation, drug and alcohol services, and an outpatient physical rehabilitation facility in partnership with St. Clair Health System.

North

West Penn Allegheny Health System
Armstrong County Memorial Hospital
One Nolte Drive, Kittanning
(724) 543-8500

As a community hospital, Armstrong County Memorial emphasizes outreach and education programs, featuring classes on 10 different topics including breast-feeding, CPR, baby-sitters emergency care, osteoporosis education, and a safe-driving course for seniors. The hospital operates primary care centers in the communities of Elderton, Leechburg, and Sarver, and will provide you with physician referrals if you call (724) 543-8473.

At its main campus, the 215-bed hospital offers magnetic resonance imaging, psychiatric care, home health services, the Richard G. Laube Cancer Center, physical and occupational therapy, and programs in rehabilitation therapy and aquatic therapy. You'll find programs in cardiac reha-

bilitation, organ and tissue donation, sentinel node biopsy, Stereo TacTic, breast biopsy, bracytherapy (prostate seeding program), and pre- and post-natal care, as well as a sleep disorders lab and a wound care clinic. You can get your annual flu shots at Armstrong County Memorial and attend the annual health fair that the hospital sponsors.

Have a disability? Need a special parking placard or plate? Contact the Pennsylvania Department of Transportation, toll free, at (800) 932-4600.

Butler Health System—Butler
Memorial Hospital
911 East Brady Street, Butler
(724) 283-6666

Butler Health System describes itself as a community-based system of health-care services that provides multiple facets of health care, including prevention, treatment, and expanded outpatient services. What that means for you is a variety of useful and timely programs and services. The system centers around Butler Memorial Hospital, a 308-bed facility with more than a century of experience. An acute care hospital, Butler Memorial offers inpatient and outpatient services, as well as skilled-nursing beds.

Among the services the hospital offers are a heart center, including open-heart surgery; a center for sleep disorders; a women's health center; a round-the-clock emergency department; CAT scanning and magnetic resonance imaging; and pain management programs. The hospital also offers prenatal care and delivery services, post-partum care, pediatric assessment, and home visits. Its birthing suites allow for labor, delivery, and recovery—all in the same room. The hospital also sponsors the Butler Regional Recovery Program for drug and alcohol abuse treatment, with community centers in Butler, Cranberry, and Natrona Heights.

Butler Health System provides outpatient lab and X-ray services at several community locations, including the Butler Mall and locations in the East Brady, Slippery Rock, Zelienople, and Saxonburg communities. As part of its education program, the hospital offers classes in babysitting, diabetes care, personal stress management, and smoking cessation.

Mercy Providence Hospital
1004 Arch Street
(412) 323-5600

Mercy Providence Hospital, part of Pittsburgh Mercy Health System, is a 144-bed community hospital on Pittsburgh's North Side. Its surgical facilities include five suites and a specially designed urology room. Surgical specialties include total joint replacement and cataract surgery. Two-thirds of all procedures are completed on an outpatient basis.

Most of the hospital's outpatient services are centralized in the Arthur J. Rooney Diagnostic and Treatment Center, which provides diagnostic imaging and cardiology services and houses a 24-hour emergency department and a 24-hour psychiatric evaluation and referral center.

UPMC Passavant, Cranberry
One St. Francis Way, Cranberry
(724) 772-5300

UPMC Passavant, Cranberry is only a half-mile from Interstate 79, providing easy access for residents of Butler and Beaver Counties and the North Hills of Allegheny County. It offers round-the-clock emergency care, enhanced by an on-site helicopter to transport critically ill patients, as well as other state-of-the-art care.

The University of Pittsburgh Medical Center includes 40 buildings in a "superblock" in Oakland bounded by Fifth Avenue and DeSoto, Terrace, and Darragh Streets. It's one of the world's most concentrated medical complexes.

Suburban General Hospital
110 South Jackson Avenue, Bellevue
(412) 734-6000

Part of the West Penn Allegheny Health System, Suburban General provides important services to residents of the Pittsburgh suburbs known as the North Boroughs. The 195-bed community hospital offers care in more than 30 medical surgical services, outpatient services, critical care, physical rehabilitation, kidney dialysis, cosmetic surgery, and occupational medicine. In addition, the hospital features an emergency department and a physical rehabilitation unit.

Suburban General provides a free health education club for those older than 55 years of age. It's called the Senior Advantage Club, and it holds monthly health education programs and provides free flu shots, blood pressure readings, and a variety of health screenings. The hospital also sponsors a wide range of health education programs and support groups.

UPMC Passavant
9100 Babcock Boulevard
(412) 367-6700

Located 12 miles north of Pittsburgh, UPMC Passavant is a 260-bed facility serving northern Allegheny County and southwestern Butler County. Founded in 1849, Passavant offers medical specialties in cancer and cardiac care, emergency medicine, obstetrics and gynecology, and orthopedics. The hospital features a chest pain center; subacute care units; surgical services; physical and occupational therapy departments; and centers for sleep, pain management, and speech, voice, and swallowing disorders.

UPMC St. Margaret
815 Freeport Road
(412) 784-4000

UPMC St. Margaret provides 250 acute care beds and has more than 500 physicians on staff offering medical specialties in arthritis, rehabilitation, orthopedics, family practice, gerontology, and occupational health. The hospital was founded in

1898, merged with UPMC in 1997, and serves as a valuable resource for more than 200,000 residents of Pittsburgh's northern and eastern suburbs. St. Margaret reaches into the community through such programs as paramedic response teams to assist local volunteer units, athletic training services for schools, and a variety of health screening programs.

One quirk about the hospital's location: While it's surrounded by suburban municipalities, it is part of the city of Pittsburgh.

VA Medical Center
325 New Castle Road, Butler
(724) 287-4781, (800) 362-8262

Approximately 35 miles north of Pittsburgh, this U.S. Department of Veterans Affairs center provides a wide range of primary medical services, including outpatient care, preventive services, and acute hospitalization. Special programs include geriatric/extended care, physical rehabilitation, substance abuse treatment, and mental health care. The center offers home-based primary care, a program for homeless veterans, and an outpatient facility in the Butler County community of West Middlesex. While affiliated with the VA Pittsburgh Healthcare System, the Butler facility is administered separately.

VA Pittsburgh Healthcare System
1010 Delafield Road, Aspinwall
(412) 688-6000

7180 Highland Drive
(412) 365-4900, (800) 647-6220

University Drive
(412) 688-6000, (800) 309-8398

While the U.S. Department of Veterans Affairs VA Pittsburgh Healthcare System operates three facilities in the Pittsburgh area, we'll address them as a single unit, since that's the way system administrators regard it. Together, the three divisions comprise a major medical/surgical tertiary care facility with programs in orthopedics, same-day surgery, rehabilitation, radiation

therapy, mental health, and substance abuse. The system features a liver transplant center, a regional cardiac surgery center, and an oncology network center. For your initial contact with the system, try the Aspinwall Division at the number listed above.

East

Life Care
225 Penn Avenue, Wilkinsburg
(412) 247-2424

This 155-bed facility, part of the Allegheny University Hospitals system, is located just across the city of Pittsburgh border and specializes in extended acute care, a specialized treatment program targeted to acutely ill patients who face a prolonged hospital stay due to complex medical problems. The emphasis is on intensive nursing attention and frequent physician care as part of a multidisciplinary approach. The hospital estimates that it can provides such care for 60 to 75 percent of the cost of a traditional hospital stay.

The program includes a high-observation unit as well as a therapeutic apartment used by patients prior to discharge to help them adjust to life at home. AUH Forbes Metropolitan also offers a skilled-nursing unit, inpatient rehabilitation services, and geriatric psychiatry.

Forbes Regional Hospital
2570 Haymaker Road, Monroeville
(412) 858-2000

This 347-bed hospital serves Pittsburgh's eastern suburbs with a broad variety of specialties. These include obstetrics and gynecology; pediatrics; mental health; oncology; emergency medicine; and cardiology and diagnostic imaging, including magnetic resonance imaging and cardiac catheterization. The hospital's campus also includes the Forbes Family Health Center and the InterCommunity Cancer Center, which provides outpatient radiation therapy and chemotherapy as part of the hospital's cancer care services.

The facility's extensive obstetrics services include classes in Lamaze, prenatal care, breastfeeding, infant/child CPR, and understanding puberty and sibling relationships. At the Forbes LifeStyle Center, you'll find programs in wellness, weight loss, diabetes management, and cardiac rehabilitation.

Children's Hospital of Pittsburgh
3705 Fifth Avenue
(412) 692-5325

Children's Hospital has a legendary history. Dr. Jonas Salk developed and introduced his polio vaccine here. Children's personnel developed the "Mr. Yuk" poison prevention campaign in 1971—a program still saving lives today. More recently, Children's developed one of the world's largest pediatric transplantation centers in association with the University of Pittsburgh and Dr. Thomas Starzl.

Part of Oakland's Medical Complex, Children's is the only freestanding hospital in the region dedicated solely to the care of infants, children, and young adults. This 235-bed facility and its approximately 600 physicians pursue a three-part mission that encompasses patient care, biomedical research, and education. Children's offers services in cardiology, cardiothoracic surgery, diabetes, hematology/oncology, neurosurgery, organ and tissue transplantation, orthopedics, otolaryngology, and pediatric surgery. The hospital maintains centers for pediatric trauma and pediatric emergency care, treating more than 150 children each day in these units.

With its $12 million annual research budget, Children's focuses on such conditions as juvenile diabetes and the causes and treatment of otitis media (inner ear disease) in infants and children. Special service include a child abuse investigation unit, summer campaign programs that focus on quality of life after transplantation and heart disease, and community education classes in positive parenting and injury prevention.

The hospital functions as a regional referral center, serving roughly 5.5 million children in the tristate area. It also operates three regional facilities: Children's South in Bethel Park, Children's North in Sewickley, and Children's East in Monroeville. The regional facilities offer a wide variety of outpatient services as well as same-day surgical services. For directions to any of the Children's facilities, call the Direction Hot Line, (412) 692-8088.

Citizens General Hospital
651 Fourth Avenue, New Kensington
(724) 337-5000

Since 1912, Citizens General has been serving residents of the Allegheny and Kiski Valleys. Its medical staff numbers nearly 200 physicians operating in more than 35 specialties. Among the hospital's most important services are a Radiology Department that assists in the early detection of breast cancer, a Heart Station with advanced diagnostic capabilities, and a Rehabilitation Services Department that offers a far-reaching sports medicine program. In addition, Citizens offers a senior behavioral health center geared specifically toward seniors experiencing mental illness

The Citizens General Health Place program offers screenings and seminars, including sessions on diabetes management, relaxation and massage techniques, urinary incontinence, hypertension, breast cancer awareness, and insurance counseling. The hospital provides rehabilitation at a community-based site in Plum.

Latrobe Area Hospital
121 West Second Avenue, Latrobe
(724) 537-1000

Latrobe Area Hospital is a 260-bed community teaching hospital that serves primarily Westmoreland County. The facility provides an array of basic and specialized health-care services, including general medical and surgical services, round-the-clock emergency care, gynecology and obstetrics, pediatrics, coronary and intensive care, and home health care. The hospital also offers cardiovascular diagnostic and rehabilitation care as well as a wide range of outpatient services, including arthritis care and physical, occupational, and speech therapy. The hospital's cancer program features a radiation oncology center.

In keeping with its community-serving mission, Latrobe Area Hospital sponsors a variety of education and wellness programs as well as seven satellite centers. The satellites—located in Blairsville, Hannastown, Latrobe, Ligonier, Mt. Pleasant, Norvelt, Saltsburg, and Greensburg—offer diagnostic, mental health, and home health services. Not all satellite centers offer all services.

Magee-Womens Hospital
300 Halket Street
(412) 641-1000
www.magee.edu

Since the opening of Magee-Womens Hospital in 1911, women have been at the center of the institution's mission: providing excellence and innovation in clinical care, education, research, and the health of women and infants. The hospital's impact on the region has been, and continues to be, far reaching. Rare is the Pittsburgh-area family that hasn't selected Magee for a birth or some aspect of neonatal care.

The hospital calls its philosophy "Womancare," and a review of Magee's services leaves no doubt that the name is appropriate. Highlights of Magee's services include the latest in infertility treatment; a maternal-fetal medicine program for high-risk mothers and infants; a comprehensive array of educational programs to prepare parents and siblings; and an obstetrics program that boasts the region's newest labor, delivery, and recovery suites, plus private post-partum rooms in a totally family-centered environment.

Magee is a nationally designated Center of Excellence in Women's Health and one of the top recipients for National Institutes of Health funding for women's and infants' health research. In addition, Magee believes in empowering women with education and resources to give them the confidence they need to take an active role in their health-care decisions.

Testifying to Magee's excellence in this area, the Magee/University of Pittsburgh Cancer Institute Breast Program was rated as one of the top 10 breast programs in the country by *SELF* magazine and encompasses the most up-to-date, research-driven care for the prevention and treatment of breast cancer. Magee also makes itself a part of the Greater Pittsburgh Community. Five Womancare Centers located throughout Allegheny County act as sites for Magee's educational programs and offer mammography, ultrasound, bone density screenings, specialty physician services, and ob/gyn practices. In addition, Magee has seven Neighborhood Health Centers that provide prenatal and primary care to patients.

UPMC Braddock
400 Holland Avenue, Braddock
(412) 636-5000

This 217-bed hospital serves the Turtle Creek and Mon Valleys with 225 respected community-based physicians. Medical specialties include chemical dependency/detoxification, emergency medicine, orthopedics, coronary and medical/surgical intensive care, and same-day surgery. The hospital features three units dedicated to the needs of patients coping with mental illness, as well as a 30-bed progressive care center that functions as a long-term care facility.

UPMC Health System
3811 O'Hara Street
(412) 647-2345

UPMC Health System, affiliated with the University of Pittsburgh Schools of the Health Sciences, strives to be an integrated system for health care in Western Pennsylvania, offering a full range of health-care services. At its Oakland campus, UPMC operates UPMC Presbyterian, UPMC Montefiore, Eye and Ear Hospital, Western Psychiatric Institute and Clinic, and the University of Pittsburgh Cancer Institute. In all, these hospitals provide 1,221 beds and form the core of Oakland's medical complex.

Two of UPMC's hospitals—UPMC Presbyterian and UPMC Shadyside—are tertiary care facilities, and there are nine community hospitals: UPMC Beaver Valley, UPMC Braddock, UPMC Passavant, UPMC South Side, UPMC St. Margaret, UPMC McKeesport, UPMC Bedford Memorial, UPMC Horizon, and Lee Regional. All those within our six-county coverage area are profiled in this Hospitals section.

At the hospitals on UPMC's Oakland campus, medical specialties include cardiology, human genetics, sports medicine and orthopedics, geriatrics, occupational and environmental medicine, AIDS treatment and immunology, trauma and emergency medicine, ophthalmology and otolaryngology, neurosurgery, cardiothoracic surgery, psychiatry (including inpatient care), and critical care medicine. The complex also includes the renowned Thomas E. Starzl Transplantation Institute, named for Pittsburgh's pioneering organ transplant surgeon.

UPMC's Physician Division manages practices encompassing more than 3,000 primary care physicians and physician specialists, while its Insurance Division offers managed care products. Through this Diversified Service Division, UPMC provides rehabilitation and in-home services, a mail-order pharmacy, durable medical services, technology transfer ventures, international health care initiatives, and retirement living options.

UPMC Shadyside
5230 Centre Avenue
(412) 623-2121

This 486-bed hospital in Pittsburgh's Shadyside neighborhood traces its roots to 1866 and merged with UPMC Health System in 1997. Its specialty areas include primary care, cardiology, cardiovascular surgery, oncology, women's health services, neuroscience, orthopedics, geriatric services, endocrinology, gastroenterology, sinus surgery, diagnostic imaging, rehabilitation, and obstetrics and gynecology services. The medical staff includes more than 600 primary care physicians and specialists.

Getting back to its roots as a homeopathic hospital, Shadyside opened the Center for Complementary Medicine several years ago. For more information on the center and the modalities it offers, refer to the Wellness section in this chapter.

The Western Pennsylvania Hospital
4800 Friendship Avenue
(412) 578-5000

One of the flagship hospitals of the Western Penn Allegheny Health System, West Penn is a 512-bed tertiary care medical center, founded in 1848 and set in Pittsburgh's Bloomfield neighborhood. Services provided by the 900-member medical staff include sophisticated treatments for cancer, cardiovascular disease, high-risk pregnancies, and diabetes, as well as an innovative, aggressive approach to burn care. The hospital's bone marrow transplantation program is one of the top 20 in the nation, and its burn trauma center was the first in the region to successfully pass the rigorous verification procedures of the American Burn Association and the American College of Surgeons Committee on Trauma. West Penn also has a breast diagnostic imaging center, an infant apnea center, and an outpatient rehabilitation center.

In addition, the hospital was one of the first in the region to have a dedicated patient-focused care unit, and in July 1995, the hospital opened the nine-story Patient Care Tower, specially designed around the patient-focused care concept.

Westmoreland Health System
532 West Pittsburgh Street, Greensburg
(724) 832-4000

In addition to operating Westmoreland Regional Hospital, Westmoreland Health System provides a number of additional services for Westmoreland County residents. These include The SurgiCenter at Ligonier, specializing in outpatient ophthalmic plastic laser surgery as well as pain management, and MedCare Equipment Co., which offers medical supplies for purchase or rent. Other system units are Westmoreland Regional Hospital

Foundation and CareGivers of Southwestern Pennsylvania which offers homemaker, live-in, and home health aide services.

Westmoreland Regional Hospital
532 West Pittsburgh Street, Greensburg
(724) 832–4000

A 356-bed hospital, Westmoreland Regional is the flagship of Westmoreland Health System. It offers a Community Comprehensive Cancer Care Center—which features surgery, chemotherapy, radiation therapy, free screenings, and a patient transportation program—and the Heartcenter, which include a cardiac catheterization laboratory and open heart surgery.

The Westmoreland for Women program offers a wide range of gynecological service and classes for pregnant women and those considering pregnancy. These include sessions in personal birthing plans, lactation, infant/child CPR, and sibling and grandparent education. As part of its obstetrics program, the hospital provides labor delivery/recovery suites. Other services include rehabilitation, diabetes treatment, home health care and hospice, and a sleep disorders center.

South

Canonsburg General Hospital
100 Medical Boulevard, North Strabane
(724) 745–6100

If you're scheduled for surgery at this Washington County facility, you have the option of enrolling in the hospital's Custom Care Program, an initiative that prepares patients for surgery and rehabilitation through education and one-on-one relationships with staff. Nurses will visit your home to explain the surgery process and help you fill out the necessary paperwork, and you'll also get a visit from a physical therapist, who will discuss medication and rehabilitation and possibly conduct a home safety evaluation.

The 120-bed hospital, part of the West Penn Allegheny Health System, features a subacute; skilled-care unit (for patients no longer in need of acute care but not quite ready to return home), an emergency department, rehabilitation and laboratory services, medical imaging, and a mammography center.

Canonsburg General offers a number of innovative community programs. Project Healthy Children, an early detection and prevention initiative, offers health fairs, baby-sitting training, and shadowing/mentoring programs. Lifeline provides nearly 200 chronically ill senior citizens with the ability to communicate from their homes directly with the hospital's emergency department. Through the Watchful Shepherd program, children at risk for abuse—those referred to the hospital by county authorities or court order—are equipped with push-button devices that activate alarm signals to the hospital's emergency department. Nurses answering the alarms speak directly to the children to assess the situation and can dispatch police to the home.

Jefferson Hospital
Coal Valley Road, Jefferson
(412) 469–5000

The largest component of the Jefferson Hospital is a 392-bed facility that boasts a medical staff of more than 400 physicians in 37 specialties. Jefferson offers a wide variety of emergency, inpatient, diagnostic, rehabilitative, and therapeutic services. Among its special initiatives are an occupational medicine program, a sleep lab, drug and alcohol detoxification, speech pathology, and a sports medicine program. One of the most consumer friendly aspects of the hospital is its spacious parking lot, which features nominal rates and security guards.

St. Clair Hospital
1000 Bower Hill Road, Mt. Lebanon
(412) 561–4900

St. Clair Hospital is a 308-bed, general acute care community hospital that principally serves 13 communities in the South Hills. Medical services include family prac-

Brad Magill: Answering the Emergency Call for Emergency Communications

Western Pennsylvania has a proud medical history. It was here that Dr. Jonas Salk developed and implemented his polio vaccine, here that Dr. Thomas Starzl performed his pioneering work in transplant surgery. When it came to emergency communications, however, Allegheny County was until recently the sick man of Southwestern Pennsylvania.

Put most simply, the problem was a multiplicity of unintegrated systems across the county's 130 municipalities. The county's checkerboard of municipal fiefdoms can be quite charming, creating distinctive communities with their own attractions and flavor. In emergency communications, that lack of coordination was anachronistic and dangerous—anachronistic because every county adjacent to Allegheny County already boasted a fully functioning 911 communications system, dangerous because residents had many emergency numbers to remember and dispatchers often couldn't tell which calls emanated from their service areas. As recently as the start of 1998, the local white pages listed more than 150 emergency numbers—including ambulance, police, and fire departments—across Allegheny County.

Enter J. Brad Magill, who had operated Butler County's 911 system for 17 years. Magill, deputy chief of the Division of Emergency Services, was charged by the county with creating a unified 911 system out of the crazy quilt of existing mechanisms.

Magill got some sense of the difficulty of the task at early planning meetings, when he was lobbied by numerous municipal representatives to designate their towns as 911 centers.

"They wanted 41 centers," Magill recalls, "And I was able to get it down to six. People told me I did a helluva job. Now, as I look back on it, I'm disappointed I didn't push for one center."

Five of the centers are known by their regional locations—Eastern Regional, Mon Valley, South Hills, Southwest Regional, and Northwest Regional. The sixth center, serving many of the county's northern communities, is called NEWCOM, a bizarre quirk that resulted when a temporary name jotted down on preliminary paperwork somehow stuck. The city of

tice, obstetrics/gynecology, pediatrics, psychiatry, surgery, anesthesiology, emergency medicine, medical imaging, and laboratory functions. The hospital operates a fertility center and a heart center that offers patients the convenience of

testing, treatment, recover, and rehabilitation, all at the same hospital.

St. Clair reaches out to the community through a variety of educational and support programs, many at no cost. These include Feminine Focus, the Cancer Sup-

Pittsburgh constitutes an unofficial seventh center, though the city is a full participant in the system.

Even then, Magill's work wasn't done, as the county was sued by 16 municipalities who stubbornly resisted the consolidation. Once those obstacles were surmounted, Magill was ready to purchase and install the equipment to complete the coordinated system. The equipment provides dispatchers with the name and address of each caller, facilitating speedy response, although Magill says dispatchers still question callers to glean as much useful information as they can.

Magill is quick to point out that the system is not foolproof. If you call 911 from an Allegheny County institution with multiple phones and addresses, for example, the system can relay only the institution's principal address, a problem with calls from, say, college campuses. Cell phone calls represent an ongoing frustration for all 911 systems, as current technology cannot convey the address of call origination.

"Cellular phones drive us crazy," Magill says. "The first question we ask when someone on a cell phone calls about an accident is, 'Where are you?' The answer is 'I don't know,' or 'I'm on the Parkway or Route 8.' The second question we ask is 'Are there any injuries?' The answer usually is, 'I don't know, I didn't stop.'"

"If you're on a cell phone and you don't know where you are and you haven't stopped, keep on going. Someone else [with better information] will call us."

Addresses on the border between two communities—whether within Allegheny County or adjacent to it—still will be troublesome, although Magill expects much more active dispatcher collaboration in the new system. Moreover, since address changes must be manually entered, the system will be no stronger than the companion mechanism that captures and enters address changes.

"We have almost 1 million phone addresses, and 8,000 of them change every day," Magill laments. "Businesses open and close, people move in and out. That means that every day, there are 8,000 opportunities to mess up the database. I believe there are 10,000 errors in our database and probably another 5 percent we don't know about."

Technological advances will help all regional 911 systems overcome those problems. In any case, the flaws seem minor in light of the achievement. Thanks to Magill, all you'll have to do if you're in trouble in Allegheny County is dial 911.

port Group, Maternity Education, and Changes and Choices for Older Adults and Their Caregivers. You can get a complete guide to the hospital's community programs through its Public Relations Department (412) 344–6600, extension 1025.

**Monongahela Valley Hospital
County Club Road, Monongahela
(724) 258-1000**
Mon Valley Hospital was formed in 1972 through the merger of Charleroi-Monessen Hospital and Memorial Hospital in Monon-

Among its many medical firsts, Pittsburgh was the site of the first hospital-based helicopter in the Northeast—Life Flight.

gahela, both of which traced their roots to the turn of the century. Thus, this facility has an outstanding track record of service to Mon Valley residents.

The 277-bed facility boasts a 180-member medical staff representing more than 40 specialties. Among the services offered are obstetrics/gynecology, psychiatric, critical and cardiac care, rehabilitation, emergency medicine, occupational health, and drug and addictive disease treatment. Mon Valley provides comprehensives oncology services, including a regional Cancer Treatment Center, and it features a Same Day Surgery Center. The campus also includes an education conference center complex.

Uniontown Hospital
500 West Berkeley Street, Uniontown
(724) 430-5000

Since opening its doors in 1903, Uniontown Hospital has been the primary health-care provider for Fayette County. In the late 1980s the hospital underwent a major expansion, adding a four-story ancillary service wing. Today this 195-bed community hospital employs more than 150 staff physicians, who practice more than 30 medical specialties. Services offered include cardiac care, a comprehensive cancer program, diagnosis and treatment of gastrointestinal disorders, rehabilitation, same-day surgery, a comprehensive obstetrical program, and a variety of home-care services.

UPMC South Side
2000 Mary Street
(412) 488-5550

Part of the UPMC Network since 1996, this hospital was founded in 1889 and today boasts 216 beds and a variety of medical specialties. These include acute medical/surgical services; rehabilitation; physical,

occupational, and speech therapy; geriatric services; emergency and occupational medicine; and subacute care. The facility on Pittsburgh's South Side also offers an inpatient psychiatric unit, a cardiac catheterization laboratory, a sleep laboratory, and a peripheral vascular lab.

The Washington Hospital
155 Wilson Avenue, Washington
(724) 225-7000

The Washington Hospital and its School of Nursing have provided valuable services to Washington and Greene County residents since 1897. The 258-bed facility, the largest employer in Washington County, offers cardiac care, obstetrics and women's services, occupational medicine and rehabilitation, home health and hospice services, emergency care, mental health treatment, sleep disorder care, and a wellness center.

In addition, you'll find a children's therapy center, a cancer care center, and a reentry program that helps patients return to everyday living. Washington Hospital operates 20 satellite facilities in the region.

West

The Medical Center, Beaver
1000 Dutch Ridge Road, Beaver
(724) 728-7000

Part of Heritage Valley Health System, The Medical Center is a 358-bed facility that traces its roots to 1894. The hospital offers emergency treatment and maternity and child-care services, as well as cancer and cardiology treatment, including open heart surgery. Other services include home care, occupational medicine, plastic and reconstructive surgery, psychiatry, rehabilitation, and rheumatology care.

Pittsburgh's Ohio Valley
General Hospital
Heckel Road, Kennedy
(412) 777-6161

This 103-bed hospital was founded in 1906 as McKees Rocks General Hospital, so its record of service to the community spans nearly a century. Ohio Valley's services include emergency and primary care, specialty medicine, cancer care, cardiology, cardiac rehabilitation, critical care, general and specialty surgery, respiratory therapy, rehabilitation, obstetrics and gynecology, home care, lithotripsy, and such diagnostic services as magnetic resonance imaging and SPECT imaging.

The hospital also offers a number of special services, including the Wound Care Center, for treatment of chronic, nonhealing wounds; the Cataract & Eye Surgery Center; the Sleep Evaluation Center; and a health and wellness program for those age 50 and older. Ohio Valley operates a school of nursing, which offers a 22-month diploma program with 36 credits from Carlow College, and a school of radiology, leading to a certificate and an associate degree from Robert Morris College.

To fulfill its mission of service to the community, Ohio Valley maintains a speakers' bureau and community education programs.

Sewickley Valley Hospital
720 Blackburn Road, Sewickley
(412) 741-6600

Sewickley Valley Hospital, a component of Heritage Valley Health System, offers 191 beds and a variety of services that include cardiology, diagnostic radiology, orthopedic surgery, rehabilitation, peripheral vascular surgery, ophthalmology, oncology, psychiatry, and transitional care.

UPMC Beaver Valley
2500 Hospital Drive, Aliquippa
(724) 857-1212

UPMC Beaver Valley feature 83 beds and numerous medical specialties including home health and hospice care, skilled nursing, emergency medicine, psychiatry, cardiac catheterization, and occupational medicine. It offers cancer treatment in conjunction with the University of Pittsburgh Cancer Institute and maintains a cardiopulmonary physiology lab for diagnosis for heart and lung disease.

REHABILITATION CENTERS

While a number of area hospitals offer rehabilitation services, Southwestern Pennsylvania also boasts facilities that focus on rehabilitation. The organizations described below span the full range of services, including physical rehabilitation and rehabilitation from alcohol, drug, and chemical dependency.

Eagle Physical Therapy
201 Smith Drive, Suite B, Cranberry
(724) 772-4700

Eagle provides a full range of outpatient physical rehabilitation services at 12 area offices north and west of Pittsburgh, including Allison Park, Moon, Robinson, Murrysville, Westview, Bridgeville, and Wexford in Allegheny County; Butler, Mars, and Zelienople in Butler County; Baden in Beaver County; and Uniontown in Fayette County. Treatment covers such conditions as athletic joint and spinal injuries, hand therapy, arthritis, pediatric rehabilitation, osteoporosis, TMJ, headaches, foot and ankle sprains, women's health, and neurological disorders. Eagle also offers occupational and speech-language therapy.

You'll need a doctor's prescription before utilizing any of the services of this for-profit company. Insurance plans typically cover—in full or in part—many of Eagle's services.

Gateway Rehabilitation Center
Moffett Run Road, Center Township
(412) 766-8700

A nonprofit agency, Gateway offers both inpatient and outpatient chemical dependency treatment programs—for adults and adolescents—at nine Southwestern Pennsylvania locations: Ambridge, Beaver Falls, Center Township, Cranberry, Fox Chapel, Greensburg, Green Tree, Monroeville, and Peters. Gateway provides specialized programs for women, youths and young adults, residents of public-housing communities, and referrals from the Pennsylvania Department of Corrections. Gateway has opened a dual disorders treatment program at its Center Township facility for adults with concurrent chemical dependency and mental health problems.

Gateway offers comprehensive community and school-based prevention services through its VISION Prevention Program. The center also provides employee assistance program services, training, and professional conferences.

A special touch: When clients have achieved six months' sobriety, they're invited to participate as Gateway volunteers.

---

i

More heart-assist devices have been transplanted in Pittsburgh than any other place in the United States.

UPMC Rehabilitation Hospital
1405 Shady Avenue
(412) 420-2345

This 85-bed facility in Pittsburgh's Squirrel Hill neighborhood helps area residents with brain injuries, spinal cord injury and disease, stroke, and orthopedic injuries recover, live with their conditions, and work toward independence. The hospital offers acute inpatient and outpatient services. Individual patient treatment programs include behavioral medicine; nutrition services; occupational, physical, and speech-language therapy; and vocational/community reentry services. The hospital also offers an arthritis swim program open to both outpatients and members of the community at large.

The Watson Institute
301 Camp Meeting Road, Sewickley
(412) 741-1800

The Watson Institute provide comprehensive special education programs for children ages 3 to 12 who have developmental disabilities, including autism (the Watson Institute's specialty), cerebral palsy, muscular dystrophy, neurological impairments, and pervasive developmental disorders.

HEALTH MAINTENANCE ORGANIZATIONS

HMOs have become a vital aspect of daily life. Many Southwestern Pennsylvanians—whether self-employed or employed by firms large or small—now have the option to receive medical insurance from HMOs. They've become so important, if not downright omnipresent, that a local non-profit organization, the Pittsburgh Business Group on Health, has begun publishing regular statistical reports on certain aspects of HMOs. Those reports are described in the "Resources & Referrals" section below. In the following section, We'll introduce you to the primary players. The category "commercial enrollees" includes enrollees not receiving Medicare or Medicaid assistance.

Keystone Health Plan West
120 Fifth Avenue
(412) 544-7000

Keystone Health Plan West is operated by Highmark Blue Cross Blue Shield, the region's largest health insurer. The plan operates in 29 counties and has 2.5 million members in Western Pennsylvania alone.

HealthAmerica Pennsylvania
11 Stanwix Street, Suite 2300
(412) 553-7300, (800) 735-4404
www.healthamerica.cvty.com

HealthAmerica and HealthAssurance, headquartered in Pittsburgh and Harrisburg, Pennsylvania, provide managed-health-care products and services including HMO, POS, PPO, and Medicare + Choice to 6,300 employers and more than 500,000 members in Pennsylvania and Ohio. In 1999 HealthAmerica was ranked by *Newsweek* magazine as the best health plan in Pennsylvania, and the best in the nation for women's and child and adolescent care. In 2003, HealthAmerica earned Excellent Accreditation by the NCQA (National Committee for Quality Assurance).

Med Plus Three Rivers Health Plans
300 Oxford Drive, Monroeville
(800) 400-4003
Nearly 100 hospitals and close to 5,000 doctors participate in the company's programs, which serve Medicaid and CHIP program recipients only. (CHIP is a health plan for uninsured children and youth ages 18 and younger.)

UPMC Health Plan
112 Washington Place
(800) 644-1046
Owned by UPMC Health System, UPMC Health Plan serves nearly 350,000 members. In our principal coverage area, the plan features dozens of participating hospitals and over 6,000 participating doctors. One notable feature of UPMC Health Plan is that if your doctor orders something, you've got it. There are no administrators policing doctor's decisions in this plan.

UPMC For *You*
One Chatham Center
112 Washington Place
(800) 286-4242
This program, which operates in 10 counties, serves many of Pennsylvania's Medicaid recipients.

Aetna US HealthCare
5313 Campbell's Run Road, Robinson
(412) 788-0500, (800) 233-3105
A total of 52 hospitals, 1500 primary care physicians, and 2,600 physician specialists in the region participate in Aetna US HealthCare plans. The plan boasts 120,000 commercial enrollees and 30,000 Medicare enrollees in the Western Pennsylvania region.

RESOURCES & REFERRALS

Western Pennsylvania presents a rich variety of health-care opportunities—so rich, in fact, that determining the best opportunity for you and your family can be challenging. A number of organizations are dedicated to helping you navigate the health-care system. Consider these organizations valuable resources for referrals and pertinent information.

Allegheny County Medical Society
713 Ridge Avenue
(412) 321-5030
When you're looking for a physician, the Allegheny County Medical Society can provide you with information that will help in your selection. The society will not make specific recommendations, of course, but it will provide information on office location; hospital privileges; specialties and subspecialties; and board certification and education, including undergraduate, medical school, and residency credentials.

There's no charge for the information, but the service has limitations. You can request information for up to three physicians per call. The society does not provide information on specific procedures performed or disciplinary actions. Finally, while the society includes more than 3,000 member physicians, it has no information to offer you about nonmember physicians.

Consumer Health Coalition
650 Smithfield Street
(412) 456-1877
The coalition focuses on educating the public about children's health and managed-care issues—and on important policy changes in these areas. The group holds information meetings, distributes a free quarterly newsletter, and works with policy makers to convey public input. When you call them, they'll be happy to provide information and referrals.

Contact HelpLine
P.O. Box 111294, Pittsburgh, PA 15238
(412) 578-2450, (412) 255-1155
Imagine a friend you could call round the clock, seven days a week, for advice on any medical or emotional problem that was troubling you. You don't have to imagine it, because you have just that friend in HelpLine. Operating with Contact Pittsburgh, HelpLine is an information and

referral center staffed all day, every day, by phone counselors who will listen as you describe your situation, then refer you to community resources.

HelpLine is affiliated with a number of selfhelp and support networks. While their service area generally is Allegheny County, they won't let you down if you call them from another county. If they can't offer immediate assistance, they'll refer you to a sister information and referral center that operates with a nationwide scope.

HelpLine also publishes "Where To Turn," a directory of health and human services in Allegheny County, a guide that first appeared in 1908. While HelpLine's phone counseling and referrals are free of charge, there is a cost for the directory. HelpLine is a partnership of Contact Pittsburgh and United Way of Allegheny County.

The Hospital Council of Western Pennsylvania
500 Commonwealth Drive, Warrendale
(724) 776-6400

The council includes most of the hospitals in Western Pennsylvania, and most of its services are targeted to member hospitals. Nevertheless, council staff are knowledgeable about most health-care providers, services, and institutions in the region, and they'll be happy to point you in the right direction when you call. They will not, however, recommend specific physicians or providers.

Pittsburgh Business Group on Health
507 Virginia Avenue, Ambridge
(724) 251-0230

The Pittsburgh Business Group on Health (PBGH) is a nonprofit organization promoting the delivery of quality, cost-effective, value-based health care in Southwestern Pennsylvania. Members include large and mid-sized employers who combined provide health-care benefits to more than 400,000 employees, retirees, and dependents in the region.

While many PBGH services are targeted to its members, the organization performs several important functions of considerable interest and value to consumers. Perhaps the most significant of these is an annual report called Western Pennsylvania HMO Performance Scorecard that provides information about local HMOs in many key categories. For example, the Scorecard will tell you the percentage of participants in each HMO who benefited from such services as mammography screening, pap smears, prenatal care, immunizations, retinal screening, and a number of other procedures. This information can help you determine which HMO might work best for you. There is a charge of the Scorecard. You can get yours by contacting PBGH at the address or phone number above.

Rx Council of Western Pennsylvania
1709 Boulevard of the Allies
(412) 471-9570

The council offers a valuable and unusual service by providing emergency prescription assistance to low-income Allegheny County residents. A nonprofit organization, the council focuses on those in danger of falling through the cracks—people who can't afford to pay for their prescriptions but are not eligible for assistance from other programs.

The council offers two companion programs. First, it issues emergency vouchers to cover the cost of a monthly supply of a prescribed medication. Prescriptions can be filled at any pharmacy, which may enhance the benefits by offering its medications at a discount. Through the second program, the council helps its clients apply to the pharmaceutical industry's indigent programs, which provide a complimentary six-month supply of prescribed medicines. The council also acts as an advocate for admission of eligible clients into programs that could provide more comprehensive health-care coverage.

The council maintains income eligibility guidelines for its programs.

Special Kids Network
5320 North Pioneer Road, Gibsonia
(800) 986-4550

If you have a child with a chronic or disabling health condition, Special Kids Network can help you find the services you need. A service of the Pennsylvania Department of Health, it's a statewide network with six regional office throughout the Commonwealth. Trained telephone counselors will provide referrals from a statewide database grouped into six broad categories: education/training, health-care products/services, recreation/leisure, social service/counseling, support/advocacy, and therapy. The database includes more than 5,300 agencies.

SPECIAL SERVICES

With its active and multifaceted health-care field, Southwestern Pennsylvania is blessed with a broad variety of special services providers. For example, you'll find support groups for most ailments and many hospital-based community outreach programs. While it would be impossible to profile all of the region's special services providers, described below are some that stand out because of the broad applicability of their services.

The Alliance for Infants & Toddlers
Hough Building, 2801 Custer Avenue
(412) 885-6000

Do you have questions about the way your child plays, learns, moves, or talks? The Alliance for Infants & Toddlers coordinates early intervention services for the children from birth to their third birthday. The various early intervention supports and services are designed to build and enhance the natural learning that occurs in a child's life. Services include developmental screening and assessment, family support, and resources coordination. All services are provided in the home, day-care, or other community setting identified by the family. Services are provided at no cost to the family.

Forbes Hospice
6655 Frankstown Avenue
(412) 665-3301

Forbes Hospice opened in 1979 as the first of its kind in the state, offering both inpatient and home-care services. The hospice provides for the physical, emotional, and spiritual needs of patients with terminal illnesses and their families. Through its eight-bed unit, an extensive homecare program, and bereavement counseling services, the hospice supports death with dignity, removing the stigma and isolation that often accompanies a terminal illness. Forbes Hospice has been a model for both its innovative care protocols and for reimbursement reform.

ARC-Allegheny
711 Bingham Street
(412) 995-5000

The mission of ARC–Allegheny is to promote opportunities for, and protect the rights of, people with retardation and developmental disabilities. In ARC's Children's Division, 600 infants and toddlers each year receive assessment and therapy through early intervention. The agency's Senior Project includes three homes specially designed for older adults.

Other programs include Parent to Parent, which links families whose children may have similar circumstances or needs; integrated camping and recreational opportunities for children and adults; ESPRIT, which offers families raising at-risk children instruction in housekeeping skills; medical appointment scheduling; toy selection; and Time-Out, which provides respite care for families. ARC's Parc-Way Supported Employment program employs 238 workers at four facilities and has placed more than 100 adults with retardation on the payrolls of local businesses.

Burger King Cancer Caring Center
4117 Liberty Avenue
(412) 622-1212
trfn.clpgh.org/cancercaring
The center is a nonprofit organization dedicated to helping people diagnosed with cancer—as well as their families and friends—cope with the emotional impact of the disease. This is not a medical treatment facility; its services help those undergoing treatment cope with the emotional impact of cancer.

Services—all free of charge—include a telephone helpline; professional guidance from social workers; and support groups targeted to children, young adults, women with breast cancer, families of those with cancer, and survivors of those claimed by the disease. The center provides a newsletter, a resource library and community resource referrals, as well as workshops in nutrition, exercise, music therapy, and journaling. The center is funded by Southwestern Pennsylvania Burger King franchisees and their corporate partners, Heinz USA and Coca-Cola Foundation.

Child's Way
5425 Baum Boulevard
(412) 365-6065
A joint program of the Children's Home of Pittsburgh and The Rehabilitation Institute, Child's Way is an outpatient day facility that supports the prescribed care needs of medically complex children. When children are here, they enjoy socialization and interaction with other youngsters while receiving care from pediatric nurses, therapists, development specialists, and caregivers. In addition, Child's Way pioneered the first pediatric extended-care center in Pennsylvania.

The two sponsoring organizations founded Child's Way after watching families struggle to meet the needs of medically fragile children. In such situations, one parent often is forced to sacrifice employment to care for their child, aggravating the financial strain. One of the goals of Child's Way is to enable parents to return to work or school, knowing that their children are well cared for at Child's Way.

Donated Dental Services
907 West Street
(412) 243-4866
DDS provides complimentary dental service to people who are disabled, elderly, or what the program calls "medically compromised." That includes those who have a permanent disability and can neither afford dental care nor receive it through other programs. Services also may be provided for those who are Medicaid eligible but with dental needs not covered by any current provider. The condition must be severe enough to prohibit or significantly limit gainful employment. Due to the overwhelming need, no one may receive program services more than once.

DDS is a program of the Foundation of Dentistry for the Handicapped, with funding from the Mellon Foundation and support from the Pennsylvania Dental Association and Eastern Area Adult Services. More than 350 Western Pennsylvania dentists, as well as many specialists and laboratories, contribute their services to DDS.

Family House and The Inn
at Montefiore Hospital
242 McKee Place
(412) 578-5811

514 North Neville Street
(412) 578-3640

5245 Centre Avenue
(412) 802-8200, (412) 647-8777
While Pittsburgh was growing as a medical center—and particularly prominent for its treatment of children—it became apparent that something was lacking in services offered. Families who journeyed to town for medical care for their relations often could not locate affordable lodgings that also were convenient to Oakland's medical complex. Family House was one of several local organizations that stepped into that breach.

Family House maintains the three facilities listed above for minor and adult patients and their families who travel to Pittsburgh for evaluation or treatment of serious illnesses. Patients and their families may stay at the Inn or at either Family House location—they're both within walking distance of Oakland's medical center, but UPMC also provides courtesy shuttle service.

The facilities feature both single and double rooms as well as suites for four to six people. All rooms have private telephone lines. You'll find communal kitchens, private bathrooms, television lounges, and laundry facilities. Guests at Family House residences are responsible for fees, but these are well below the market rate for commercial lodgings.

HealthPlace
120 Fifth Avenue Place
(412) 544-7391

If you've ever imagined a shopping mall where every service or product you could buy was designed to improve your health, then you've imagined HealthPlace. A division of Highmark Blue Cross Blue Shield, HealthPlace shapes the idea of prevention into a bright, fun environment, with a variety of stations that provide many benefits. You'll find a site for cholesterol, blood pressure, and skin cancer screening; a site for lifestyle change programs; and stations that offer referrals, counseling, and information.

Physicians often prescribe HealthPlace so patients can learn more about their conditions and diagnoses. HealthPlace also sponsors programs in smoking cessation, relaxation, CPR, yoga, and tai chi, among other topics. In addition to the center in downtown Pittsburgh, you'll find HealthPlace at 11 other locations in Western Pennsylvania.

HomeHelp
903 West Street, Second Floor
(412) 247-4000

This is a nonprofit agency that provides home care throughout Allegheny County and the surrounding areas. It's sponsored by a multidenominational group that includes Baptist Homes of Western Pennsylvania, the Jewish Association on Aging, and Presbyterian SeniorCare. The agency offers skilled-nursing care, rehabilitation, and medical-social services, all of which generally are covered by health insurance programs. Other services include household chores, live-in companion, and sleepover services, all of which are on a self-pay basis.

Jewish Association on Aging
200 JHF Drive
(412) 420-4000

Among the many valuable services provided by the association is the Sivitz Jewish hospice, which is staffed by professionals and volunteers who are specially trained to understand Jewish values and traditions. Other services include adult day services; kosher meals for delivery to homebound adults; and personal care, assisted-living, and nursing/rehabilitation centers.

John J. Kane Regional Centers
955 Rivermont Drive
(412) 422-6800

100 Ninth Street, McKeesport
(412) 675-8600

110 McIntyre Road, Ross
(412) 369-2000

300 Kane Boulevard, Scott
(412) 429-3000

The Kane Regional Centers are skilled-nursing facilities offering 360 beds per facility. While the region boasts other providers of skilled nursing services, the Kanes have a distinguished and unusual history. Formerly operated by Allegheny County as a broad health-care provider for the indigent elderly, the Kanes were turned over to a private operator in the 1990s and have broadened their mission.

They offer a variety of rehabilitation services including physical, occupational, and speech therapy, as well as dietary services for those with special needs.

Physicians and other medical specialists are brought to the centers to care for patients' needs.

The Kane environment offers large activity rooms, intimate sitting areas, outdoor barbecue courts, acres of landscaped grounds, nonsectarian chapels, and onsite barber-beauty shops. Accepted methods of payment include medical assistance, medical assistance pending, third-party insurance, private payment, and contracts with HMOs on a case-by-case basis. Evening and weekend admissions are common to help families manage their busy schedules.

William and Mildred Orr
Compassionate Care Center
6023 Harvard Street
(412) 362-3550

With hospitals discharging patients more quickly than ever, elderly patients and those at risk of homelessness can be placed in a precarious position upon their discharge, sometimes lacking residences and caregivers to help them through their recuperation. The Orr Compassionate Care Center has stepped into that breach by providing post-hospitalization respite care for the elderly, the frail, and the homeless.

The 14-bed facility in Pittsburgh's East Liberty neighborhood is a Christian ministry that not only provides three meals a day, laundry service, case management, and pastoral care to residents, but it also helps them work toward self-sufficiency for their eventual release from the center. Physicians, social workers, and clergy typically refer prospective residents to the center. Because the facility is not a medical center, residents must provide and administer their own medication, make arrangements for any nursing care or therapy, and provide detailed information about their medical histories. Most stays at the center range from a few days to three weeks.

Parental Stress Center
5877 Commerce Street
(412) 361-4800

Parental Stress Center provides solution-focused family education, counseling, and support in southwestern Pennsylvania and beyond. Locally, intensive in-home service is combined with neighborhood-based parenting education and support to provide the necessary assistance to families. The agency operates seven days a week.

Specific populations are served, including both families, foster and adoptive families, grandparents and other care givers, noncustodial parents (especially fathers), and teens. Special programs include Family Unification Services, Community Visitation Network, Critical Differences (support, information, referral), Father's Resource Center, Parenting Education, Training and Support, and Grandparents as Parents.

No family is denied service due to difficulty with payment. Private donations cover these costs. Also, anyone may make a referral, and self-referral is acceptable as well.

If you're interested in furthering the work of this nonprofit agency, they'll welcome you as a volunteer.

The Pittsburgh Poison Center at
Children's Hospital of Pittsburgh
3705 Fifth Avenue
(412) 692-5325, (800) 222-1222

If you have kids, chances are you're pretty familiar with Mr. Yuk, that nasty-looking green-faced guy whose face you've slapped on dozens of potentially dangerous household products. Mr. Yuk—and the accompanying Poison Prevention Program—were developed there in 1971 and now constitute the largest poison prevention program in the nation, spanning 22 states and the United Kingdom.

Beyond its prevention program, the center is staffed by registered nurses—available round the clock—who also are clinical toxicologists and certified specialists in poison information. When you need advice about a substance or treatment, call the hotline at (412) 681–6669. They'll tap a database that provides instant access to treatment protocols on thousands of chemicals, medicines, plants, and everyday household products. The center is funded by government monies and private contributions.

Pittsburgh Specialty Hospital
215 South Negley Avenue
(412) 661–0814

Located in Pittsburgh's East End, Pittsburgh Specialty Hospital (formerly the Podiatry Hospital) has expanded its services to now include podiatry, pain management, and plastic and reconstructive surgery. For the past 26 years, Pittsburgh Specialty Hospital has provided comprehensive foot and ankle care. Of its services, 90 percent are performed on an outpatient basis in a well-staffed, comfortable environment. Within the hospital, the outpatient department provides quality nonsurgical evaluation and treatment of ankle and foot problems.

The Pain Management program offers a multidisciplinary approach to the evaluation and treatment of chronic neck and back pain, fibromyalgia, reflex sympathetic dystrophy, and migraines. Patients are evaluated by a board certified anesthesiologist, chiropractor, and physical therapist working as a team to provide the maximum pain relief and return to a normal lifestyle.

To maximize your comfort, the hospital invites you to spend the night before and after any scheduled surgery as its guest, at no charge to you.

Ronald McDonald House Charities of Pittsburgh
500 Shady Avenue
(412) 362–3400

Ronald McDonald House Charities of Pittsburgh meets the lodging needs of people traveling to Pittsburgh for medical treatment of family members. This organization, however, specializes in the needs of parents, and it achieves this goal through three important services.

First, the organization developed and maintains the Ronald McDonald House of Pittsburgh, a short-term facility for the families of children being treated in the city. The facility offers each resident family a room of their own, a kitchen, laundry facilities, and toys for their children. The group living arrangements help families interact and cope.

In 1994, the Ronald McDonald House expanded its services by opening a second house to provide long-term housing. Finally, the organization established a grants program that awards funds to other nonprofit groups. The organization is funded by individual and corporate donations, as well as fund-raisers. Guests at the organization's house pay a small fee, but the organization pledges to help all, regardless of anyone's ability to pay.

Transitional Infant Care Hospital
5618 Kentucky Avenue
(412) 441–4884

Operated by the Children's Home of Pittsburgh, Transitional Infant (TIC) Hospital is a pioneer in providing medical and nursing care for infants who have progressed from natal intensive care units but may not be ready for home just yet. TIC patients, all of whom must be medically stable, typically are premature infants, at-risk babies with congenital anomalies, and babies under the care of hospices. Your physicians may refer you to TIC, but you're also welcome to contact the hospital yourself.

Families benefit from TIC's care by developing hands-on ability to deal with complicated treatment regimens, by learning to recognize potential problems at their earliest stages. In addition, TIC will work with you to create a care schedule that is feasible for you to manage. The hospital develops a care team for each infant that includes a physician, a primary care nurse, a medical social worker, and an infant development specialist. TIC offers transitional ventilator services and an infant massage program; they're happy to teach parents massage techniques.

If you or your physician is considering TIC, they ask that you take a pre-admission tour. You'll find softly playing music, a nursery, nesting rooms where families can care for their infants privately, a rocking chair beside each crib, cameras so that you may take pictures of your child, and handmade baby quilts in each room—a gift from TIC's volunteers when you're ready to take your baby home.

MEDIA

As we've indicated in other chapters, Pittsburgh is a city of divergent cultures, many different interests, and great loyalty. Thus, it's no surprise that the media serving its populace is just as varied in its commitment to disseminating news, information, and entertainment.

Pittsburgh used to be a two-newspaper town, with the *Pittsburgh Post-Gazette* and the *Pittsburgh Press* both publishing from Downtown offices. Following a lengthy strike in the early 1990s by non-reporting staff of both papers, the *Press* fell by the wayside, leaving the city with only the *Pittsburgh Post-Gazette*. But others saw the void and quickly filled it. So when you read the following listings you'll see that, once again, Pittsburgh is a two-paper place.

Because we're so neighborhood oriented, you'll find a plethora of weekly community newspapers, most of which publish on Wednesdays. And rest assured, we're wired. Many of the newspaper, radio, and television listings offer Web sites where you can find out plenty of information on-line.

As of this writing, Greater Pittsburgh ranks 21st in terms of national television market size, as measured by Nielsen. Arbitron puts our radio market ranking at 23rd nationwide. Regarding radio, there are so many choices on the dial that I don't give individual write-ups to the stations, but have provided a thorough list to guide your listening choices. Note that if you're a fan of National Public Radio, you can tune into WDUQ, a radio station broadcast from Duquesne University at 90.5 on the FM dial.

Also worth mentioning is that we have local affiliate television stations for all major networks, not to mention the first public educational station in the nation (WQED). You may be surprised to learn that a young Fred Rogers left a promising career at NBC in New York City to pioneer educational television in Pittsburgh at WQED.

Of course, with pride and achievement comes controversy. For many years, Pittsburgh enjoyed two public, educational TV stations, with WQED and its sister station WQEX. While they were under the same umbrella organization, they broadcast mostly different material. But when financial woes caught up with the stations, WQED sought to unload the smaller, struggling entity. In fact, in November 1997, it no longer broadcast separate material but merely simulcast on WQEX whatever was on WQED airwaves.

Things looked promising when the FCC approved the elimination of WQEX and the transfer of its educational license and Channel 16 dial position to Christian broadcaster WPCB. Paxton Communications was to buy Channel 40 (WPCB), and that money would have been split between WQED and Cornerstone Television, which operated WPCB. The sale would have allowed WQED to pay down substantial debts.

Somehow former presidential candidate Senator John McCain got involved, urging the FCC to make a faster decision. A group called Save Pittsburgh Public Television waged a campaign against the proposed sale, and by the looks of the editorial pages, many residents had strong opinions also, calling some of the maneuvers strong-arming without any interest in the public good.

The three-way deal fell through in January 2000 when Cornerstone Television abruptly pulled out of the license-swapping agreement with WQED and Paxton Communications. Its reason was simple—the FCC had restrictions and a drastically different idea of what constituted educational programming. The religious broadcasting network would have had to alter its programming and mission. This sent all groups back to the drawing board.

Now that you have some background, we believe you'll enjoy perusing the list, and most likely, you'll find a media outlet to bring you the news, commentary, listings, or entertainment you need to fill your disposable time. We'll start with a rundown of metro and community daily newspapers. Next, we'll turn our attention to magazines and specialty publications in our region, followed by television and radio outlets. For sure, you won't be without information!

METROPOLITAN NEWSPAPERS

Pittsburgh Post-Gazette
34 Boulevard of the Allies
(412) 263-1100
www.post-gazette.com

William and John Block serve as the publishers of this daily newspaper, founded in 1786. A decade ago, Pittsburgh was a two-newspaper town with the *Pittsburgh Post-Gazette* published in the morning and the *Pittsburgh Press* published every afternoon. As odd as it may sound, both papers were housed in the same building and shared some combined services and support staffs under a joint operating agreement. Editorial functions, however, were always kept on separate floors, and indeed the two papers were competitors.

In May 1992, a strike by nonreporting staff effectively halted operations for both papers. The *Pittsburgh Post-Gazette* introduced a town crier who stood on particular Downtown street corners to essentially shout the news to passersby. A fax service was also popular for those who simply needed their daily fix of headlines and top stories in print.

The strike lasted eight months, and culminated in the disbanding of the *Pittsburgh Press,* which was a Scripps-Howard paper. The *Pittsburgh Post-Gazette* bought the *Press,* and incorporated numerous reporters and support person-

nel into its staff. Today, the paper is considered by many to be more liberal in its editorial views than its main rival, the *Tribune-Review.* Well-known syndicated columnists as well as a few local favorites are found within the pages of the *Pittsburgh Post-Gazette,* sometimes known by its initials "the PG" for short.

Readers will come to look for particular sections they may deem their favorites each week, such as Health on Tuesday or Homes on Saturday. Each Monday, read the financial advice of Jane Bryant Quinn, and Tuesday through Saturday the personal finance column of Bill Flanagan, who doubles as the money editor at KDKA-TV. If you want to know who was "seen" around town, read Monday's magazine section. Other *Post-Gazette* columnists include Tony Norman, Bryan O'Neill, and Sally Kalson for general commentary, and others covering television, radio, and restaurant beats. The *Post-Gazette* on Sunday features the "Parade" magazine supplement.

Tribune-Review
503 Martindale Street, Third Floor
(412) 320-7914
www.pittaburghlive.com

This daily paper, once known more commonly as the Greensburg *Tribune-Review,* gained great ground during the newspaper strike in 1992. With both Pittsburgh dailies out of commission, Richard Mellon Scaife, conservative owner of the paper, began publishing more Pittsburgh news that year. The new paper was known as the *Pittsburgh Tribune-Review,* and it continued after the strike ended. Thus, if you hear someone speak of "the Trib," you'll know they mean the *Tribune-Review* and some of the history associated with this paper. Scaife bought several smaller newspapers in 1997, incorporating them into his publishing umbrella. Among them were the *North Hills News Record,* the *Valley News Dispatch,* and the *Leader Times* in Kittanning.

Founded in 1889, the *Tribune-Review* is known to have a more conservative slant than the more liberal *Post-Gazette*. The address given above is for Pittsburgh operations, yet a sizable staff exists at Cabin Hill Drive in Greensburg. You can reach that office at (724) 834-1151.

Each Friday, the *Trib* publishes "the Ticket," filled with the weekend entertainment offerings. It's in every paper, but you can sometimes find the supplement by itself at stores and movie theaters, free of charge. On Sundays, you'll read the supplements, "USA Weekend," "Focus," and "Access: America's Guide to the Internet." Syndicated national columnists in the *Trib* include Martha Stewart and Cherie Bennett. Ed Blank writes about entertainment, and Jack Markowitz, the retired business editor, keeps an eye on the business scene. Other local columns are written by Dimitry Vassilaraos, Lynne Glover, Eric Heyl, and Mike Seate, and you can find them on the paper's Web site as well. And if you're a fan of love in the afternoon, keep tabs on plot movement with the "Soap Scene" column.

OTHER DAILY NEWSPAPERS

Beaver County Times
400 Fair Avenue, Beaver
(412) 761-7441
www.timesonline.com
A daily paper serving all areas in Beaver County and the western suburbs of Allegheny County, the *Beaver County Times* was founded in 1946, making it a younger paper than many of its peers. F. Wallace Gordon publishes the newspaper.

Butler Eagle
114 West Diamond Street
(724) 282-8000
www.butlereagle.com
As a daily newspaper founded in 1869, this newspaper serves Butler County readers, including the areas of Cranberry Township

and Slippery Rock. Vernon Wise Jr. is the current publisher.

Latrobe Bulletin
1211 Ligonier Street, Latrobe
(724) 537-3351
Published Monday through Saturday, this newspaper was founded in 1873 to serve eastern Westmoreland County communities. Thomas Whiteman serves as publisher.

Observer-Reporter
122 South Main Street, Washington
(724) 222-2200
www.observer-reporter.com
Founded in 1808, this daily paper serves the communities surrounding the city of Washington, including Canonsburg, Waynesburg, Peters Township, Monessen, McMurray, and parts of Greene County. John and William Northrop are the current publishers.

The Daily News
409 Walnut Street, McKeesport
(412) 664-9161
www.dailynewsmckeesport.com
Published Monday through Saturday, this paper is also known as the *McKeesport Daily News*. It primarily covers this town as well as the surrounding communities of Clairton, Duquesne, Homestead, Munhall, West Mifflin, and White Oak. Patricia Mansfield Miles serves as the publisher. The paper was founded in 1884.

Valley News Dispatch
210 Fourth Avenue, Tarentum
(724) 224-4321
www.triblive.com
Founded in 1891, this daily newspaper serves the areas of Armstrong County as well as parts of Butler and Westmoreland Counties. Richard Mellon Scaife, publisher of the *Tribune-Review,* purchased the paper in 1997 along with several other newspapers in outlying communities.

ALTERNATIVE WEEKLY/ MONTHLY NEWSPAPERS

City Paper
650 Smithfield Street
(412) 316–3342
www.pghcitypaper.com
Billed as a locally owned news and
entertainment weekly, the *City Paper* is
managed by Steel City Media and was
founded by Brad Witherell. Since its
start in 1991, it has covered a wide range
of off-beat news from local vocals to
the current buzz on the street, newly
released movies, the arts scene, dining,
and nightlife. Each issue features an
indepth cover story. While you can
subscribe to the paper for a fee, why
bother? It's given away, free of charge,
at many locations and outdoor boxes,
especially at music and bookstores as
well as some movie theaters.

New Pittsburgh Courier
315 East Carson Street
(412) 481-8302
Founded in 1910, this newspaper is
published twice weekly for the African-
American community with relevant
issues and prominent Pittsburghers.
Rod Doss serves as the current editor
and publisher. The paper's editorial
offices are on the city's South Side.

Pittsburgh's Out
Out Publishing Co. Inc.
1000 Ross Avenue
(412) 243-3350
www.outpub.com
One of the oldest gay publications in the
country, *Out* began in 1973 as a single-
page newsletter produced by Gay Alternatives Pittsburgh. As it grew, it tried various
formats until 1980, when it slipped into its
current garb as a monthly tabloid serving
the GLBT (gay, lesbian, bisexual, transgendered) community in Allegheny and surrounding counties, eastern Ohio, and West
Virginia. Its current publishers, Tony
Molnar-Strejcek and Ed Molnar-Strejcek,

purchased the company in November 1994
and have added color, more pages, and
more advertising.

Out offers the GLBT community a
wide range of information not readily
available in any other single source: local
and national news, health information,
commentary, arts and entertainment features and reviews, a complete guide to
the month's local events ("Out and About"
and "Nightlife" sections), announcements
and a "What's Happening" calendar of
events and local resources.

A few years ago, *Out* became a
national star when it began to be promi-
nently featured on Showtime's *Queer As
Folk* as an important source of news—
which many consider the only realistic
detail in the fictionalized Pittsburgh.

Planet Q
P.O. Box 81246, PA 15217
(412) 784-0440
www.planetq.com
Planet Q grew out of the 1990s activism
of Billy Hileman, its founder/publisher/
editor. One of the national co-chairs of the
1993 March on Washington for GLBT
rights and a spokesperson for Cry Out!
Act-UP, Pittsburgh, Hileman is an openly
gay schoolteacher who uses the paper to
take local as well as national leaders to
task when they ignore or discriminate
against the GLBT community.

Published twice a year, the tabloid contains news and reviews of books, music,
movies, and local theater productions.

MAJOR WEEKLY NEWSPAPERS

Gateway Publications
610 Beatty Road, Monroeville
(412) 856-7400
www.ghplus.com
Several community newspapers are published by Gateway Publications and come
out on Wednesdays. The company is
headquarters in Monroeville, but there are

local offices for many of the papers outside the eastern suburbs.

Gateway Publications include the *Bridgeville Area News, Coraopolis Record, Cranberry Journal, Moon Record, Murrysville Star, North Journal* (covering Pine, Richland, Marshall, Franklin Park, and Bradford Woods communities), *Norwin Star, Oakmont Verona Advance Leader, Penn Hills Progress, Plum Advance Leader, Sewickly Herald, Signal Item* (covering Carnegie, Collier, Crafton, Green Tree, Heidelberg, Ingram, Rosslyn Farms, Scott Township, and Pennsbury Village), *South Hills Record, Times Express* (covering Monroeville and Pitcairn), and *Woodland Progress* (covering Wilkins Township, Churchill, Forest Hills, Turtle Creek, Chalfant, Wilkinsburg, Edgewood, and Swissvale).

Pittsburgh Business Times
2313 East Carson Street
(412) 481-6397
www.amcity.com/pittsburgh
Published weekly for the business community, the *Pittsburgh Business Times* covers regional issues of interest to executives and industry leaders as well as Pittsburgh business headlines. The paper often profiles business trends and prominent people, and it offers a diet of popular columnists. The publisher is Alan Robertson with offices on the city's South Side. The paper is affiliated with American City Business Journals Inc. The *Business Times*, as it's frequently referred to, also publishes the *Employment Paper*, distributed through the mail, at libraries and various other locations with information for job seekers.

Suburban Gazette
421 Locust Street, McKees Rocks
(412) 331-2645
Founded in 1892, this community newspaper covers the areas of Robinson and Kennedy Townships and nearby Ingram—all of which make up the Montour School District. Virginia Schramm is the current publisher of this paper that comes out in tabloid format on Wednesdays.

The Jewish Chronicle
5600 Baum Boulevard
(412) 687-1000
www.pittchron.com
Published on Thursdays by the Pittsburgh Jewish Publication and Education Foundation, this weekly paper is printed in tabloid form. Founded in 1962, it provides local, national, and global news of Jewish interest.

The Mount Pleasant Journal
23 South Church Street, Mount Pleasant
(724) 547-5722
This weekly newspaper covers the Westmoreland County community of Mount Pleasant and surrounding neighborhoods. The paper was founded in 1873, and its current publisher is Joseph Soforic.

The Pittsburgh Catholic
135 First Avenue
(412) 471-1252
Founded in 1844, this paper relates news of importance to the Catholic community. Thus, Bishop Donald Wuerl serves as the current publisher for the Diocese of Pittsburgh. Parishioners usually obtain a copy of the paper at church each Sunday so the paper is published at the end of each week.

MAGAZINES

Monroeville Matters
2700 Monroeville Boulevard
Monroeville
(412) 856-1000
This glossy magazine is published three times a year by the Municipality of Monroeville, and it includes full-length and short features of local interest, as well as the Recreation and Parks activities guide for each season. The magazine is mailed free of charge to local residents and businesses.

Pittsburgh Magazine
4802 Fifth Avenue
(412) 622-1360
www.wqed.org
Pittsburgh Magazine is a division of WQED Pittsburgh, home to the city's pub-

lic television and radio stations. Those who become members of WQED during pledge drives or mail solicitations automatically receive a subscription to *Pittsburgh Magazine*. This monthly magazine features all things Pittsburgh including dining listings and a schedule of upcoming programming on both WQED-TV and WQED-FM. Look for the magazine to name its Pittsburgher of the Year each December. Past recipients have included Fred Rogers and Mario Lemieux. Each summer the magazine published its annual City Guide edition. *Pittsburgh Magazine* is distributed by mail and is also available for sale on newsstands.

Pittsburgh Parent
P.O. Box 374, Bakerstown, PA 15007
(724) 443-1891
www.pittsburghparent.com
If you're a parent or soon will be one, this is the resource for you. In fact, since *Pittsburgh Parent* is distributed free of charge to more than 500 locations in Allegheny, Beaver, Butler, and Westmoreland Counties, teachers and many other professionals read it as well. Each issue features an in-depth cover story, while the rest of the editorial comes largely from wire services or public relations material. Look for the annual "Around & About Pittsburgh Guide," and each issue be sure to peruse the calendar of events and fun activities for families.

Pittsburgh Prospects
4802 Fifth Avenue
(412) 622-1360
www.wqed.org
Pittsburgh Prospects is a magazine of regional development in Southwestern Pennsylvania, spotlighting companies that make up the area's new economy. The magazine's mission is to address what needs to be done to further economic expansion and growth in the Pittsburgh area. It's distributed by subscription and newsstand sales. *Pittsburgh Prospects* is published approximately six times a year through a partnership between the Pittsburgh Regional Alliance and *Pittsburgh Magazine,* a division of WQED Pittsburgh.

Whirl Magazine
1731 Grandview Avenue
(412) 431-7888
Look out *Vogue,* you've got a rival in Pittsburgh. Actually, *Whirl*'s focus is the social scene here, but you'll see plenty of fashion in the photos on every page and in *Whirl*'s advertisements, which, the publisher, Jack Tumpson, says are so eye-catching its consumers read them like the rest of the magazine. *Whirl*'s mission is to present successful Pittsburgh, and it does that very well. It's readership, by the way, is the highest per capita income population in the region. *Whirl* is available by subscription and on newsracks with other fine magazines.

TELEVISION STATIONS

Fox Sports Pittsburgh
Two Allegheny Center
(412) 322-9500
The channel you receive Fox Sports broadcasts on will vary according to the cable or satellite system you use, but for all things sports-related, you'll want to tune in here.

KDKA-TV
One Gateway Center
(412) 392-2200
www.kdka.com
Airing on Channel 2, KDKA-TV is the Pittsburgh CBS affiliate with offices and studios in downtown Pittsburgh. With newscasts in the morning, at noon, at 5:00 and 6:00 P.M. and wrapping up the

day with the 11 o'clock news, KDKA's coverage is comprehensive in all areas, including sports, weather, and consumer and investigative reporting.

The station plays up its "Hometown Advantage," stemming from the fact that many reporters and anchors hailed from Pittsburgh. Locally produced programs include the *Lynn Hayes-Freeland Show,* focusing on African-American issues each Sunday morning, and Bill Flanagan's *Sunday Business Page.* Community initiatives have included raising funds for Pittsburgh's Children's Hospital and the KD Turkey Fund each Thanksgiving.

WTAE-TV
400 Ardmore Boulevard
(412) 242–4300
www.thepittsburghchannel.com

This television station is the local ABC affiliate, with offices and studios just off the Parkway East in Wilkinsburg. "DeNardo Weather" is short for the forecasts brought to viewers by WTAE's chief meteorologist Joe DeNardo. Two hours of local news each morning leads into *Good Morning America.* WTAE-TV also offers noon, 5, and 6 o'clock broadcasts and a wrapup of the day's events at 11:00 P.M. It offers a full range of quality reporting on consumer and investigative issues, as well as sports.

For many years, the station has been involved with a program called Project Bundle-Up, which provides coats and warm clothing for needy families. The station hosts and auction to raise funds. In addition, WTAE-TV has been aligned with the Race for the Cure, a charity run-walk to raise awareness and funds for breast cancer research. The station has been the media partner for this event since its inception in 1993.

WPXI-TV & PCNC
11 Television Hill
(412) 237–1100
www.realpittsburgh.com/partners/wpxi/

This NBC affiliate has its offices and studios high atop a hill on the city's North Side. Known for its reports aboard Chopper 11, this station also gives you Carnegie Science weather, for there is a weather station set up in the Carnegie Science Center, also on the North Side. On Channel 11, watch for health tips and the medical beat covered by Dr. Mike Rosen, a medical doctor now on the station's reporting staff.

Channel 11 also works closely with its cable channel, PCNC (the Pittsburgh Cable News Channel). WPXI-TV news is rebroadcast on PCNC throughout the day, but also look for original television talk shows on the cable channel each morning.

WQED-TV
4802 Fifth Avenue
(412) 622–1300
www.wqed.org

WQED-TV is Pittsburgh's affiliate for the public broadcasting system (PBS). It airs locally on Channel 13 (though this will vary on each cable system).

The best-known program produced here at WQED is undoubtedly *Mister Rogers' Neighborhood,* seen around the country. On Q made its debut as a televised magazine show five nights each week at 7:30 P.M. beginning in January 2000. The half-hour program covers area business, politics, and current happenings with guests and special reporters appearing alongside the hosts.

WPCB-TV
One Signal Hill Drive, Wall
(412) 824–3930

Founded by the late Rev. R. Russell Bixler in the 1970s, WPCB-TV is a Christian-based broadcasting station owned by Bixler's company, Cornerstone Television. This station and Bixler's mission survived during a time period when many televangelists fell to scandals. Yet Bixler and his wife built the station into a small network with four broadcast facilities—WPCB in Wall, WKBS in Altoona, and low-powered stations in Hermitage and Brookville, as well as a 24-hour satellite channel, and 163 affiliate stations.

**WPGH-TV and WCWB-TV
750 Ivory Avenue
(412) 931–5300**
These smaller stations operate together. WPGH-TV is a Fox affiliate that also produces 10 o'clock local news each evening on Channel 53 (that number, of course, varies according to your cable system). On Sunday mornings, there's also *Focus On Pittsburgh,* a locally produced program.

WCWB-TV airs on Channel 22, and it's the Warner Brothers affiliate owned by Pittsburgher Eddie Edwards (who formerly had the call letters WPTT-TV). "WB," as it's known for short, produces *Eddie's Digest, Inside/Outside Pittsburgh,* and scouting programs that are locally produced.

**UPN
100 First Avenue, Suite 300
(412) 552–1900**
Only a local sales and marketing office exists here for UPN. Channel 19 airs UPN programming as well as syndicated shows such as *Jenny Jones* and *Divorce Court.*

RADIO STATIONS

There are numerous radio stations throughout our six-county coverage area. Here, we present the major stations with a brief description of the programming each offer:

NEWS & TALK

KDKA 1020 AM, www.kdkaradio.com
KQV 1410 AM, www.kqv.com
WPTT 1360 AM, www.1360wptt.com
WEAE ESPN 1250 AM,
   www.wtaeradio.com
WJJJ 104.7 FM

ROCK

KISS 91.6 FM, www.kissfm961.com
WDVE 102.5 FM, www.dve.com
WXDX 105.9 FM, www.wxdx.com
WRRK 97 FM, www.rrk.com
WAMO 106.7 FM/860 AM,
   www.wamo.com

CONTEMPORARY/SOFT ROCK

WBZZ 93.7 FM, www.b94fm.com
WSHH 99.7 FM, www.wshh.com
WLTJ 92.9 FM, www.wltj.com

OLDIES

WWSW 94.5 FM/970 AM,
   www.3wsradio.com
WJPA 95.3 FM/1450 AM, www.wjpa.com

COUNTRY

WDSY 107.9 FM, www.y108.com

CLASSICAL

WQED 89.3 FM, www.wqed.org/fm

JAZZ

WDUQ 90.5 FM

CHRISTIAN

WORD 101.5 FM, www.wordfm.com
WPIT 730 AM
WWNL 1080 AM
WPGR 1510 AM
WGBN 1150 AM

MUSIC/NEWS/SPORTS/TALK

WISR 680 AM, www.wisr680.com

SENIOR SCENE

I f you're looking for a town with a vital senior citizens community, with diverse programs and services for older residents, wonderful and meaningful volunteer opportunities, and government and nonprofit organizations that understand the needs of seniors, then you've come to the right place in Pittsburgh. You may not consider Pittsburgh an ideal retirement community just yet, but we'll give you plenty of reasons to change your mind.

The fact is that family and neighborhoods are so important to most local residents that many not only live and work their entire careers here, but they also choose to retire close to their roots. Statistics tell a key part of the story. For example, of the more than 1.2 million people in Allegheny County, better than 21 percent are age 60 or older, giving Allegheny the second highest percentage of seniors among America's counties.

With seniors comprising such an important part of the population, both the private and public sectors are attuned to their contributions and particular needs and concerns. You'll find a wide variety of senior recreational centers, residential communities, support organizations—even opportunities to use your experience and expertise to contribute to the region's businesses. The senior scene is vigorous in Pittsburgh.

Government in Pittsburgh, at both the municipal and county level, is active in sponsorship of programs tailored to seniors. Some government-offered services may be restricted to residents of the offering municipality or county. Even where such services are open to all, you're probably more likely to take advantage of opportunities close to your home.

Therefore, to help you best utilize Senior Scene, material has been organized in two ways. The first section is a county-by-county look at programs, services, and opportunities for seniors; in this section, the city of Pittsburgh is grouped with Allegheny County, as the two entities share administrative responsibility for many services.

Following that, the second section features unrestricted services and opportunities, as well as those where some travel might be expected.

Have fun exploring Pittsburgh's Senior Scene. You'll find it a rewarding journey.

Pittsburgh & Allegheny County

The extensive services and programs for seniors in Pittsburgh and Allegheny County are coordinated by two agencies: Allegheny County Department of Aging, (412) 350–5460, and the City of Pittsburgh Department of Parks, (412) 422–6570, popularly known as SeniorInterests.

Nineteen other agencies, including nonprofit groups and church-related organizations, assist in the administration of programs in the city and county, with services distributed geographically to every community in the county. Want to know the location of the senior center nearest you, or the most active support group in your neighborhood? The best way is to call the county's Department of Aging for its annual directory of services. It's free of charge, and it will give you all the information you need to make those first phone calls.

Seventy-seven senior centers are located throughout Allegheny County, including some twenty-three centers within the city of Pittsburgh. The centers offer hot meals each weekday—most of them once per day—as well as recreation and socialization opportunities. And don't expect that recreation to be sedentary only. In addition to such standards as bingo, cards, and movies, the centers offer dancing, exercise, crafts, and classes in languages, music, and art appreciation. Up for something a little wilder? The South Side center in Pittsburgh offers basketball—on a regulation court—as one of its senior activities.

Transportation opportunities in Pittsburgh and Allegheny County are far reaching. Older Persons Transportation (OPT) will deliver you to medical appointments, grocery shopping, and senior centers, weekdays from 6:00 A.M. to 6:00 P.M. Service is door to door, and the cost is nominal.

Even broader is the service provided by Access, a shared-ride service that will take you anywhere in the county. Call Access at (412) 562-5353 to set up an account with them; about two weeks thereafter, Access will put you in touch with your local carrier, which is likely to be a local taxi service. Access operates from 6:00 A.M. through midnight, seven days a week, with advance reservations required. You'll pay for your rides with tickets purchased form Access, but if you're age 65 or older, you'll pay only 15 percent of the regular charge.

Armstrong County

In Armstrong County, adjacent to Allegheny County about 25 miles north of Pittsburgh, the Armstrong County Agency on Aging is the principal provider of services and programs for seniors. To qualify for some services, you must be formally assessed by the agency. Give them a call, toll free, at (800) 368-1066, or (724) 548-3290, if you don't mind paying for the call. They'll help

you determine which services fit your needs.

The county operates 11 seniors centers in all its major population points—Apollo, Brady's Bend, Dayton, Elderton, Ford City, Freeport, Kittanning, Leechburg, Parker, Rural Valley, and Worthington. General hours are from 9:00 A.M. to 2:00 P.M. Monday through Friday, with hot meals served at noon. Reservations for lunch must be made one day in advance. If you're unable to cook for yourself, the county will deliver meals to you, once your eligibility for the program has been certified.

In addition to providing opportunities to socialize, the centers offer valuable services, including blood pressure and general health checks under the supervision of registered nurses. For fun, try the craft outlets located at the Ford City and Kittanning centers.

And if you'd like to visit more than one center, don't worry about transportation. The centers provide complimentary rides between all facilities for center programs and activities.

From time to time, we all encounter household chores that we just can't handle. The county is ready to help with those chores, as well as light housekeeping, errands, and laundry. If you have legal questions, the county also will provide legal counseling and representation in such areas as wills and power of attorney.

Beaver County

The Beaver County Office on Aging, (724) 728-7707, provides services and programs for senior citizens in Beaver County, a picturesque 20-minute drive from Pittsburgh along the Ohio River through attractive riverfront communities. The office operates five senior centers, in Aliquippa, Baden, Beaver Falls, Midland, and Monaca. The centers serve hot lunches and welcome spouses to join in. To participate, make your meal reservations one week in advance. Once approved by a caseworker,

Independendently Monroeville

The Monroeville Senior Citizens' Center, 6000 Gateway Campus Boulevard, Monroeville, (412) 856-7825, is a particularly active hub for adults 50+. Regular activities at the center include aerobics, yoga, shuffleboard, computer classes, numerous types of card games, woodcarving, Brazilian embroidery, quilting, crocheting, creative scrapbooking, and bingo. Anyone 50 or older, from any geographical area, may participate in the center's activities, attend the informative lecture series held by ThirdAge Forum, or attend the two special meals held monthly. In addition Monroeville and Pitcairn residents may join one of the four membership clubs, which regularly feature meetings, programs of interest, luncheons, dinners, and trips and tours. The center is especially notable in that it's not part of Allegheny County's network of senior centers. Funding for the Monroeville Senior Citizen's Center, built in 1980 for its present purpose, is generated by participants' fundraising efforts, state grants, and the Municipality of Monroeville. Two annual fundraisers of special interest are the center's flea market and the large golf tournament, both of which, of course, may be attended by people of any age.

you also may order home-delivered meals Monday through Friday and take advantage of county-provided assistance with household chores.

If you're age 65 or older, transportation is a snap in Beaver County, as you may ride Beaver County Transit Authority buses free from 9:00 A.M. to 3:30 P.M. If you're more than a quarter-mile from public transportation, you may arrange door-to-door, shared-ride transportation with Demand and Response Transit (DART) buses.

The county also sponsors varied activities for seniors; many of these are important but others are just plain fun. To make sure seniors are aware of all appropriate events, the county produces an insert in the monthly Beaver County Senior News newsletter called *Kenn-Age News* featuring articles of interest to seniors, as well as a weekly radio show, *Spotlight on Senior Citizens,* which airs Sundays on WBVP-AM, 1230 on the dial.

For fun, join other seniors at the Beaver Valley Mall the second Wednesday of every month. Beginning at 10:00 A.M., "Day at the Mall" features refreshments, prizes, entertainment, blood pressure screening, and store discounts.

And if gardening is your thing, you'll love the county's "Mini Gardens" program, operated in conjunction with the Pennsylvania State University, which reserved gardening lots for senior citizens each spring.

Butler County

If you're a senior citizen in Butler County, about 25 miles north of Pittsburgh, you'll have every opportunity to tune in to county happenings. The Butler County Area Agency on Aging, (724) 282-3008, provides a number of useful communications vehicles to ensure that you're aware of local happenings.

The *Senior Voice* radio show airs every Sunday at 7:10 A.M. on WISR-AM, 680 on the dial, while subscribers of Armstrong Cable can catch *Seniors Today* on Channel

The list of residence options in this chapter is by no means exhaustive. Get on the Web and check out www.senior housing.net. This site, a link of www .rent.net, allows you to search for retirement community listings in any geographic area within the United States, with regional and city searches as options. A search for "Pittsburgh and surrounding communities" yielded 213 listings when we tried it. The site also lists great explanations of the terms used to describe senior residence options.

10 for a look at events and timely features. The agency also produces and distributes a monthly newsletter called *Senior Express*.

The agency maintains 10 senior centers—in Bruin, the city of Butler, Chicora, Cranberry, Evans City, Mars, Mt. Chestnut, Saxonburg, Slippery Rock, and Zelienople—which serve hot meals daily. Don't forget to make your meal reservations at least one day in advance.

The agency also offers home delivery of meals to those who qualify, as well as a referral service for caretaking and home chores. Perhaps the most comprehensive of agency services is transportation, provided by the Butler Area & Rural Transit (724) 282-6060. Known locally as B.A.R.T., the shared-ride service will transport those age 60 and older from their homes to senior centers, medical appointments, shopping malls, and grocery stores. You can ride anywhere in the county at no charge.

Washington County

The hub for senior services and programs in Washington County, which lies about 20 miles southwest of Pittsburgh, is Aging Services of Washington, Greene, and Fayette Counties, (724) 228-6856. The agency has more than three decades' experience in helping seniors and serves

more than 5,000 residents each month.

You can choose from nine Senior Community Centers that feature recreation, socialization, and educational programs. Each center provides a free hot lunch each weekday and will deliver meals Monday through Friday for those unable to cook for themselves. The centers are located in Avella, Bentleyville, Burgettstown, Canonsburg, Claysville, McDonald, and Vestaburg, with two centers in the city of Washington.

Seniors in need of home support services, including laundry, shopping, and cleaning, will find agency workers ready and willing to help.

Westmoreland County

The Westmoreland County Area Agency on Aging, (800) 442-8000 or (724) 830-4444, likes to describe life as an orienteering event, in which contestants navigate unfamiliar terrain using a map and a compass. The agency thinks of itself as the compass, helping senior citizens reach their destination.

The nerve center for the agency's services to senior citizens is the network of senior centers it operates. A total of 13 such centers dot this county to the east of Pittsburgh. They're located in Avonmore, East Vandergrift, Greensburg, Herminie, Jeannette, Latrobe, Laughlintown, Laurel Valley, Monnessen, New Alexandria, New Kensington, New Florence, and West Newton.

As do senior centers throughout the Pittsburgh area, Westmoreland's centers offer hot meals as well as the opportunity for home delivery of those meals. Centers in Westmoreland also emphasize health and wellness through a variety of neat and unusual classes, exercise, tai chi, and aqua aerobics among them.

For transportation to key activities, you'll find two types of subsidized services available. If you're age 60 or older, you're eligible to use Priority Transportation, funded through the county, for rides

Because You Drive Safely...

Here's a great way to save money on your auto insurance. If you're age 55 or older, have a Pennsylvania driver's license, and take a driver refresher course, your insurance company must offer you a discount of 5 percent or more for three years. Three organizations in the state offer refresher courses:

AARP
(717) 238-2277, (888) 227-7669

AAA Western Pennsylvania–West Virginia
(412) 365-7211

National Safety Council
(412) 856-5400

to medical appointments, senior centers, senior center-based shopping, adult day care, and the county's vision center only. You'll receive a 95 percent discount on the cost of your taxi or van trip. If you're age 60 or older, you'll receive the same discount and be able to travel to many more destinations in your area, using a shared-ride service funded through the state. You may also ride Westmoreland county buses for free. Now you're all set for life's orienteering!

SERVICES & OPPORTUNITIES

Publications

With senior citizens comprising such an important force in Pittsburgh, it could be difficult to keep up with all the services, programs, and opportunities available. Fortunately, the private and public sectors have teamed to produce a number of publications to help you identify just the right opportunities for you.

Particularly useful is *Pittsburgh Senior News,* (412) 367-2522, a tabloid that can keep you current with activities because of its monthly publication schedule. The newspaper blends information about activities and services with cultural and entertainment news, as well as feature

stories by and about senior citizens. Pay close attention to the advertisements, which often bring news of discounts and bargains for seniors.

The newspaper also offers up-to-date information about current activity schedules for local chapters of the American Association of Retired Persons (AARP)—a valuable tool, as Pittsburgh offers more than 100 AARP chapters. Subscription rate for the publication is $15, but seniors may get it for $12. You can pick it up for free at scores of distribution points, many of them located at newspaper honor boxes.

The *Resource Guide for Older Adults and Their Families* takes a somewhat different, but equally effective, approach. This publication comes out every two years and focuses on well-detailed listings of services and programs. The guide cannot deal with current events, of course, but it provides a broad look at opportunities for seniors that are unlikely to change.

Categories covered include community outreach and referral services; crisis, mental health, and caregiver services; Medicare, Medicaid, and medical insurance; medical and health-care services; and housing options. The outreach section, in particular, is as good as any you're likely to find, offering both familiar and more obscure service providers.

The guide is published under the auspices of Older Adult Service and Infor-

The State of Pennsylvania offers "ombudsman" services to answer your questions and provide information about your rights as a consumer. To reach the ombudsman's office, call (717) 783-7247, or contact any county area agency on aging. Also, see the Web site www.aging.state.pa.us.

mation System (OASIS), a public-private partnership headquartered in Kaufmann's department store in downtown Pittsburgh. You can order your free copy from OASIS, (412) 232-9583, or (800) 921-9443.

A second helpful publication is the *Senior Citizens Guide to Pittsburgh,* which is produced by Spindle Publications headquartered in suburban Pittsburgh. As an annual, this guide, too, is limited in the current information it can convey. Instead, the publication focuses on interesting travel features and "how-to" pieces, as well as service directories.

Two of the best directories offered are the listing of senior citizens centers and the guide to volunteer organizations. If one of your goals is to remain active in the community, you'll find plenty of opportunities in this publication. The publication, begun in 1987, is available free at any of the area agencies on aging described in this chapter. You also may contact Spindle Publishing, (412) 531-9742; they'll be happy to mail you one copy for free, but if you require multiple copies you're responsible for postage.

Volunteer Programs

Volunteerism is alive and well in Pittsburgh, at least in part because of the leadership of senior citizens. Seniors provide valuable assistance to both nonprofit and for-profit organizations, which are happy to rely on the experience and expertise that would otherwise be hard to acquire. When seniors volunteer, they—

and the organizations they assist—are sharper for it.

One of the most fertile and rewarding volunteer opportunities is helping fellow senior citizens in need. Preserve, the Volunteer Support Network for Seniors, (412) 456-6887, offers just such opportunities by pairing volunteers with seniors who might benefit from a friendly phone call. New Heritage Volunteer Program, (412) 464-1300, offers similar opportunities; its senior volunteers often serve meals at senior centers.

Reach Out Pittsburgh, (412) 422-6402, goes one step beyond by dispatching teams of volunteers out into the neighborhoods to inform seniors about the rich variety of services available to them. Many of the volunteers are seniors, who can speak first hand about their experiences. Volunteers hit the streets twice a year.

More comprehensive still are the check-in services offered by Interfaith Volunteer Caregivers of Southwestern Pennsylvania, (412) 687-6712. Volunteers call on seniors in need and help out with shopping, transportation, and completion of Social Security and Medicare forms. Interfaith Volunteer Caregivers also offer errand, "friendly visiting," and "telephone reassurance" services.

Hospice Preferred Choice, (412) 271-2273, works with home-care patients. Volunteers provide companionship as well as respite for caregivers.

Perhaps working with children would give you the most satisfaction. If so, try the Foster Grandparents Program, (412) 263-3163, which operates in Allegheny, Beaver, Butler, and Washington Counties. Through the program, low-income volunteers age 60 and older spend 20 hours each week with disabled or special-needs children. You'll receive a tax-exempt stipend—and immeasurable satisfaction—for your efforts.

At the University of Pittsburgh, in the Generations Together program, (412) 648-7150, senior volunteers mentor and tutor youths. A special Generations Together feature matches seniors who have been professional artists with kids eager to learn artistic skills. A similar program in Westmoreland County, also called Generations Together, (800) 442-8000, utilizes senior volunteers to counsel abused and neglected children. There's an added benefit—volunteers are paid at minimum wage rates for their valuable efforts.

If using your experience to help consumers is your primary concern, try the Better Business Bureau of Southwestern Pennsylvania at (412) 456-2700 and ask for the volunteer coordinator. BBB is well known for helping consumers answer questions about, and resolve complaints against, local businesses. Senior volunteers perform many of these key functions. You'll play an important role in telephone answering, complaint handling, mediation and arbitration, data entry, and public speaking. Check out the BBB's Web site, www.pittsburgh.bbb.org, to learn more about these opportunities.

For broader volunteer opportunities, several agencies will do the job. Since 1972, the Southwestern Pennsylvania Chapter of the American Red Cross has sponsored the Retired and Senior Volunteer Program of Allegheny County (RSVP), (412) 263-3179, a program that matches volunteers with such nonprofit organizations as arts and cultural groups, hospitals and schools, and consumer agencies.

The program is large and diverse. More than 1,000 volunteers participate in at least 117 organizations, contributing meaningful volunteer service and enriching their own lives as well. RSVP also hosts an annual awards dinner to recognize outstanding volunteers. If you're age 55 or older, respond to RSVP. It may kickstart you on a new career.

Pittsburgh Cares, (412) 471-2114, offers a similar broad range of opportunities for its 1,450 volunteers, which continue to increase in number. The agency schedules more than two dozen monthly events, ranging from delivering holiday meals to the homebound to craftmaking with mentally challenged people. Pittsburgh Cares works with more than 80 community service agencies, an indication of how deeply the roots of volunteerism grow in Pittsburgh. Yet another Pittsburgh trademark; the agency encourages families to volunteer together. Check out this organization on the Web at www.pittsburgh cares.org

RETIREMENT COMMUNITIES

We're living longer, we're enjoying our mature years more, and we're looking for more residential options that are tailored for our needs and desires. In Pittsburgh, with its sizable population of seniors, you'll find just those options in an appealing variety of retirement communities.

The number of such communities has mushroomed in Pittsburgh in recent years, although not quite as fast as the number of people who want to live in them. This has resulted in waiting lists at a number of the most popular communities. We haven't noted which communities have waiting lists, since that's so changeable, but it is something you should be aware of as you check out these listings.

Nevertheless, such a rich variety is available today that you'll want to carefully consider your preferences before making a selection. Do you prefer communities away from the city center, tucked into the rolling hills of Western Pennsylvania? Or would you be most happy in an urban setting, close to all the city's opportunities? You'll find both types in Pittsburgh and environs.

You'll also want to carefully consider the services, amenities, and pricing options. At some communities, residents pay a monthly rental fee. In other communities, you can own your home by making a sizable up-front payment, which in some cases is partially refundable when the unit is turned over. Condominiums also can be an option.

CLOSE-UP

Miles to Go

When Horace Miles retired from his multi-faceted career, he expected to enjoy a leisurely retirement. Some retirement. Today, Miles is a very active member of the Pittsburgh chapter of the Service Corps of Retired Executives (SCORE), a volunteer agency that mentors young companies across the entire business spectrum. The Pittsburgh chapter of SCORE, formed in 1964, was among the nation's first. Its membership numbers 60 strong, all of them retired and all on the prowl for young companies they can counsel in such key areas as personnel, financing, marketing, and other operational challenges. SCORE is sponsored by the Small Business Administration, which propelled Miles into his leadership role.

"The former district director of SBA suggested that I consider this as a way to keep my skills up," Miles recalls. "I found it appealing because to me, the most interesting thing is doing something new, learning something new, I'm working harder now than I ever did."

Miles' varied career helped prepare him for his "retirement," providing him with diverse expertise in all facets of management and business development. With undergraduate degrees in math and physics, he entered the computer field in the late 1950s. In the infant computer industry, Miles' expertise was in demand. He worked for a bank and later founded an international consulting company that coordinated computer services for clients in Canada, Italy, and France.

"The thing that always interested me is business," Miles says. "It's the toughest thing you'll ever do, and it's becoming more of a challenge. But in a sense, business problems are business problems are business problems. It's formulaic in that sense. From that standpoint, when you work with young companies, you can find out what's needed. They can feed back, and you find out where the cracks are."

The companies that Miles has mentored reflect the breadth of his career:

- A pet-sitting business that was expanding and considering new hires. Miles' advice: Use contractors rather than full-time employees, to avoid the expense of benefits packages and the like.
- A plasma physicist in the business of producing robots for semiconductor manufacturing. "He had some technical problems in making his product, but what he really needed was an inventory system, and to make sure he was ordering his parts in an economical manner."

Make sure that you inquire about the common or community fee, which typically is assessed monthly. Services and amenities that come with such fees can vary widely. These can range from the most basic, such as meals and laundry, to the most lavish, such as use of a nearby golf course.

If you're selecting a retirement community, probably the best initial advice

- A singer-songwriter who wanted to reach a broader, more lucrative market: "I don't feel qualified to comment on whether his songs are good or bad, but I do have some friends who have listened to his work and essentially blessed it. My role is to see how he might market his work while retaining control over it."

Success stories are not uncommon for SCORE. Perhaps its most amazing rags-to-riches tale is that of Riverside Design Group, a producer of high-design giftware, including private-label products for corporate clients. Aided by a SCORE counseling team, Riverside Design streamlined its planned product lines and now sells to more than 400 museums, giftware retailers, restaurants, and catalogues.

Miles does not commit all his hard-earned leisure time to SCORE. In his idle moments he produces videos with musical themes, tinkers with magic, fences, and serves on the boards of two non-profit organizations. But even his recreational activities benefit SCORE. In the workshop staged for all potential SCORE clients, for example, Miles works in several of his magic tricks.

While the organization includes women and minority volunteers, one of the chapter's goals for the future is to further diversify its membership. Because there are comparatively few minorities who are both retired and former executives, this one may take more than sleight of hand.

If you're looking for a way to contribute your years of expertise to young businesses, call SCORE at (412) 395–6560, or visit them at their headquarters in the Federal Building, 1000 Liberty Avenue, in downtown Pittsburgh, or at their McKeesport or Beaver outreach centers. If you volunteer with SCORE, you'll get your transportation costs reimbursed . . . and a large measure of satisfaction.

"Business is a blood sport," Horace Miles says, "It's difficult to create and sustain a business. The satisfaction in this work is helping a company grow and seeing it progress over a number of years. The frustration is that a lot of companies we see either don't have the wherewithal or they don't really understand what needs to be done. So you don't see them again.

"It doesn't mean they aren't good entrepreneurs, it's just that 'this' isn't a good idea. If you save people from going down that road, that's satisfying, too."

His broad experience has given him firm ideas about what separates successful businesses from mere wannabes.

anyone can give you is this: take your time. Do your homework. Make a day out of visiting a prospective new home, taking the tour that each will gladly offer you, and asking a lot of questions to make sure the community fits your needs. Your patient research will result in the best match for you.

North

LAS/Crown Pointe
100 New Haven Lane, Butler
(800) 641-7788

LAS/Crown Pointe is located on a former dairy farm about 25 miles north of Pittsburgh. You won't find any bovine types around now, of course, but the former use of the site gives you some idea of the placid setting.

At LAS/Crown Pointe, you have three different options for living arrangements. If you prefer to buy your residence, your purchase price will be a little over $100,000. If renting is more your style, your payments will range from around $400 to a little over $2,000 per month. And you also can opt for a leasing contract.

You'll enjoy restaurant-style dining, fitness and wellness programs, a full schedule of recreational and social activities, and the opportunity for a continuum of care if needed.

The homes are attractively designed, featuring two or three bedrooms, cathedral ceilings, and air-conditioning. LAS/Crown Pointe is royally appointed, indeed. The complex is operated by Lutheran Affiliated Services, which also operates LAS/Crown Pointe retirement communities in Zelienople (described below) and Greensburg.

LAS/Passavant Retirement Community
401 South Main Street, Zelienople
(724) 452-5400, (800) 641-7788

The second of the three Pittsburgh retirement communities operated by Lutheran Affiliated Services, this community is set in a rustic locale about 35 miles north of Pittsburgh.

Living options include cottages and apartments, with monthly fees ranging from a little over $1,000 to a little over $2,000. You'll get quite a bit for your monthly fee, including utilities, cable TV service, social services, and two meals per day. For an additional fee, you can take advantage of laundry service and visits to doctors and the beauty and barber shops.

One of the most appealing opportunities at all three LAS communities is the emphasis on leisure learning. At Zelienople, classes range from horseback riding to safe driving, while activities include such fun events as hayrides, bonfires, softball, and line dancing.

And if you're an angler, here's one just for you: The community sponsors regular fishing outings at nearby Moraine State Park. You might just want to cast your lot right here.

Sherwood Oaks
100 Norman Drive, Mars
(724) 776-8100, (800) 642-2217

Yes, it really is located in Mars. And Sherwood Oaks does resemble a heavenly body. Set on 84 pastoral acres 23 miles north of downtown Pittsburgh, Sherwood Oaks boasts its own lake, with the shore dotted by the townhomes that comprise the community. Choose from eight different floor plans for your town home.

Sherwood Oaks involves committing a one-time entrance fee around the price of a nice home, in addition to monthly service fees. Make sure to ask about the three refund options for your entrance fee—you may be able to get a substantial percentage back.

You'll want to take advantage of the indoor pool and hot tub; boating and fishing on the lake; the woodworking shop; the hairstyling salon; and the croquet, boccie, shuffle-board, horseshoe, badminton, and putting facilities. For a good read, check a book out of the community library. For your medical needs, a health-care center is available on-site, and the community is affiliated with the nearby North Hills Passavant Health Corporation. Assisted-living services and skilled-nursing care are available where needed.

Sherwood Oaks is near two major highways—the Pennsylvania Turnpike and Interstate 79—so visitors have easy access. When they come, put them up at the community's guest lodge.

East

Canterbury Place
310 Fisk Street
(412) 622-9000

Been an urban type all your life and can't bear to leave the throb and throngs of the city? Then Canterbury Place may be your place. The facility offers a continuum of care, including independent living, assisted living, personal care, nursing care, and Alzheimer's care, all contained within a stately brick building about 2 miles from downtown—and even closer to the medical center complex in Oakland. In fact, Canterbury Place is affiliated with the University of Pittsburgh Medical Center, providing access to first-rate medical care. Living options include semiprivate, studio, and one- and two-bedroom apartments.

The staff plans meals and activities far in advance, so you'll always have a good idea of coming attractions. While you'll be close to all of Pittsburgh's entertainment spots, the events calendar at Canterbury Place might persuade you to stay at home. Featured are cocktail hours, concerts, bingo, video biographies, and films.

And if you want to invite friends to join in, feel free. You can use the Chalfant Room, an on-site private dining room, free of charge.

Clover Commons
600 Cloverview Circle, Plum
(412) 793-2333

If you prefer a variety of homes from which to choose, Clover Commons may be the community for you. Designed by builder Myles Sampson, the site about 15 miles east of downtown Pittsburgh along Route 286 offers dozens of floor plans, with homes built to your specs starting at $69,000. In addition to accessibility from Route 376 (get into the habit of calling it "the Parkway East"), Clover Commons is within hailing distance of the Pennsylvania Turnpike.

Sampson and his associates built this community with active and enjoyable lifestyles in mind. Thus, you'll find a

heated swimming pool; cabana; a pool table; and shuffleboard, horseshoe, and boccie facilities.

You can ride the community minibus, bike and walk with friends . . . in fact, you'll enjoy all the advantages of neighborhood living, because Clover Commons and its handsome homes are a neighborhood.

When you visit Clover Commons, make sure you take a few minutes to inspect its two sister retirement communities—Cloverleaf Estates in Delmont and the Village of Clover Ridge in Murrysville. They're a few minutes' drive from Clover Commons and offer substantially the same living and recreational options.

Longwood at Oakmont
500 Route 909, Verona
(412) 826-5800

How popular is Longwood at Oakmont? Consider that residents have come from 13 states to retire there. Pretty impressive for a region where people tend to stay put. Longwood is located just a chip shot from Oakmont Country Club, the site of many major Professional Golf Association tour events. That may account in part for Longwood's popularity, but there are many other attractions.

You'll have plenty of residence options at Longwood, beginning with a studio apartment and reaching all the way to an elegant three-bedroom country home.

Entrance fees, which are 90 percent refundable, range from $94,265 to $275,170, while the monthly maintenance fee goes from $2,022 to $2,986. Add $968 to the monthly fee for a second occupant.

Longwood calls itself a continuing retirement care community, meaning that should the need arise, you can take advantage of unlimited nursing-care days at the on-site health center at no additional cost.

The range of services is breathtaking. Airport transportation, newspaper, grocery, and pharmacy delivery, guest accommodations—all are available to residents at no extra cost. The clubhouse

Statewide Senior Discount

With more than 2.4 million of its citizens age 60 or over, the Commonwealth of Pennsylvania has a significant stake in the well-being of senior citizens. The state reaches out to seniors in a variety of ways—by providing funding for 52 area agencies on aging across the Commonwealth; by dedicating proceeds from the Pennsylvania Lottery exclusively to programs for seniors; and by operating a number of major programs on a statewide basis. In all, the state funds or administers more than 50 programs or benefits for seniors.

Among the most far-reaching programs are Pharmaceutical Assistant Contract for the Elderly (PACE), which helps to pay for prescribed medicines, and rent and property tax rebates, which can amount to as much as $500 per year. Both programs are targeted to those age 65 and older who meet income eligibility guidelines.

To enroll in PACE or for rent and property tax rebates, pick up your application at any area agency on aging, pharmacy, senior community center, or legislator's office, or contact the Pennsylvania Department of Aging in Harrisburg. The toll-free number for PACE is (800) 225-7223.

offers swimming and a Jacuzzi, and you'll also enjoy movies, lectures, musical programs, and food festivals, to name just a few of the regular activities.

And if you're looking to join the Senior Tour, where better to go?

South

Asbury Heights
700 Bower Hill Road, Mt. Lebanon
(877) 865-9877

The variety of living options is one of the most important features of Asbury Heights, which is operated by United Methodist Services for the Aging. The community offers townhomes and a multitude of styles of apartments, suites, and residential rooms, all set on a 27-acre campus only minutes from downtown Pittsburgh.

With that diversity of residential options, you'll want to spend some time reviewing the pricing plans. Asbury Heights will be happy to provide them.

The pleasant campus is ideal for outdoor activities, including walking, gardening, shuffleboard, horseshoes, and putting. For shopping and personal services, try the on-site skylight mall, with banking and postal facilities, a beauty parlor and barber shop, and an ice-cream parlor, and country store.

One of Asbury Heights' most unusual features is its elevation. Located at one of the highest points in Allegheny County, the community offers commanding views of Western Pennsylvania's rolling hills. At Asbury Heights, you'll be on top of the world.

Asbury Heights includes facilities for assisted living; nursing care; and a dedicated facility for Alzheimer's care, which is decorated beautifully. In addition to on-site doctors, the community provides regular visits from a dentist, a podiatrist, and an ophthalmologist. Moreover, a social worker is assigned to each resident of the community, just to check on each person's well-being.

Fair Oaks of Pittsburgh
2200 West Liberty Avenue
(412) 344-9915

Want the best of urban and suburban retirement? Try Fair Oaks of Pittsburgh. The community is situated on 15 hilly acres in Pittsburgh's South Hills, isolated enough to provide privacy, but only a mile from all the attractions and opportunities of downtown Pittsburgh.

Fair Oaks features 80 efficiency and apartment units that offer independent living as well as assisted living and personal care, assuring a continuum of care. Two entrance plans are available: the management plan, which offers you the option of making a small down payment ($3,000) and then paying a monthly rental fee; and the endowment plan, which requires a large down payment up front, but offers a low monthly payment.

You can shop at the Fair Oaks Country Store or pamper yourself at the on-site beauty shop. You won't have to worry much about how to spend your time, as the Fair Oaks staff plans its recreational activities well in advance, providing a monthly activities calendar. A calendar we sampled featured a trip to a local restaurant, a current events lecture, sessions of bingo and Scrabble, and on-site concerts by a clarinetist, an orchestra, and a barbershop quartet. The Fair Oaks folks will have you singing "Sweet Adeline" in no time.

Friendship Village
1290 Boyce Road, Upper St. Clair
(724) 941-3100
www.friendshipvillagepa.com

For a retirement community with a track record, try the friendly folks at Friendship Village. The community is operated by Life Care Services Corporation, a nonprofit company with more than 30 years' experience operating 100-plus retirement communities. Those communities serve more

than 20,000 residents across the country, so the extended Life Care community is a large one, indeed.

Set on 70 acres in the lovely suburb of Upper St. Clair, about 15 miles south of Pittsburgh, Friendship Village offers one-, two-, and three-bedroom apartments, which residents appoint with their own furnishings. The village offers 14 different apartment styles as well as private carriage homes. Entrance fees start at $65,200—90 percent of it refundable. Monthly service fees range from $1,188 to $3,026. Additional fees apply for a second person.

If golf is your game, you'll become more than familiar with the nine-hole Frosty Valley Golf Course next door to Friendship Village; rounds are complimentary for residents. Amenities include laundry, housekeeping and maintenance service, and a village store and bank, while recreational facilities are an exercise room, a woodworking shop, a library, studios for crafts and the arts, and landscaped walking paths. You can putter about your own garden or relax with friends in the pub.

Friendship Village guarantees lifetime nursing care, should the need arise, at its on-site Health Center. Sounds to us like a friendly village.

Residence at Country Meadows
3570 Washington Pike, Bridgeville
(412) 257-4581

When George M. Leader was governor of Pennsylvania in the late 1950s, he appointed the first commissioner on aging and inspired other legislation designed to improve conditions for seniors. This was more than a passing political fancy for Leader. Today, his family operates the Residence at Country Meadows, one of eight such retirement communities in Pennsylvania developed and operated by the Leader family.

At the community only a few miles from downtown Pittsburgh, residents enjoy a variety of accommodations and care options, including, respectively, apartments, efficiencies, and rooms, and

Stay in Contact

Questions about programs and services for seniors? Often, the best places to look for answers are the area agencies on aging, which administer state programs and supplement them with local initiatives. You'll find them at these numbers:

Allegheny County Department on Aging
(412) 350-5460, (800) 344-4319

SeniorInterests
(412) 422-6570

Armstrong County Agency on Aging
(800) 368-1066

Beaver County Office on Aging
(724) 728-7707

Butler County Area Agency on Aging
(888) 367-2434

Aging Services of Washington County
(800) 342-8980

Westmoreland County Area
Agency on Aging
(724) 830-4444

Other frequently called numbers include:

Eldercare Locator
(800) 677-1116

Elderlink
(412) 422-0400

South Hills Health System Senior Services
(412) 469-7099

Contact Helpline
(412) 578-2450

independent living, assisted living, and nursing care arrangements. Monthly rentals start at $1,526.

The residence has developed a "Total Wellness Program" that includes exercise classes as well as social opportunities. Through its continuum of care philosophy, the complex also offers assisted living, a nursing and rehabilitation center, and an Alzheimer's residence.

Three cheers for the Gov.!

Vanadium Woods Village
50 Vanadium Road, Bridgeville
(412) 221-2900
Vanadium Woods offers the best of city and suburban life. It's nestled in a secluded tree-lined development, yet it's only minutes from the large shopping malls of Pittsburgh's South Hills. The community is part of a growing network of retirement communities being developed by the Retirement Villages of St. Margaret.

The recently built, three-story Vanadium Woods is reminiscent of a grand hotel, offering a beautiful atrium and many attractive lounges, plus a library, chapel, barber shop, activity centers, and many other amenities. Two of residents' favorite activities are on-site performances and trips to the Pittsburgh Symphony. Apartment rentals range from $1,361 to $2,156 (add $410 for double occupancy), and include just about everything you could think of: common fee, three meals per day, repairs and maintenance, cable TV, housekeeping, transportation, educational and wellness classes—even light bulbs and toilet paper.

It's all part of what the folks at Vanadium Woods call "management from the heart," a philosophy that extends to such niceties as published weekly menus and van schedules. Community managers say they like to provide "pampered retirement lifestyle" for their residents. Hey, don't feel guilty about it. You deserve it.

WORSHIP

Immigrants who settled in Southwestern Pennsylvania for the purpose of prosperity brought with them riches of another kind—adherence to their spiritual past. As a result, our region is as diverse in its religious make-up as it is in its ethnicity.

Many of the churches and synagogues in which Pittsburghers worship tell their stories better than any words could. For instance, the stained-glass windows inside St. John the Baptist, a Ukrainian Catholic church on the South Side, chronicle immigrant life, including the life of the church. The Strip District's St. Patrick-St. Stanislaus Parish, more commonly referred to as Old St. Patrick's, was founded by Irish immigrants in 1808. Here, you'll find a set of 28 marble stairs, a replica of the holy stairs that Jesus had to climb to reach the court of Pontius Pilate. To comply with local custom, you may ascend these stairs only on your knees.

Perhaps the most spectacular religious building in Pittsburgh is Rodef Shalom synagogue, the fountainhead of Reformed Judaism in Western Pennsylvania and one of only five synagogues in the nation designated as a national landmark. The building, 4905 Fifth Avenue, Oakland (www.rodefshalom.org) was designed by Henry Hornbostel, the same architect Andrew Carnegie commissioned to produce blueprints for Carnegie Mellon University (then Carnegie Tech). The building's exterior was modeled after the Church of Hagia Sophia, now a mosque, in Istanbul, Turkey. Built of bricks made from local clay, Rodef Shalom is also notable for its double dome ceiling 90 feet in diameter. The breathtaking "Eye of God" stained glass window on top of the dome, made by the famous Willet Studio, dramatically filters light down into the large sanctuary. Outside, a one-third acre biblical botanical garden displays more than 150 plant varieties, each with a biblical name or reference. The garden setting is reminiscent of ancient Israel, with a stream representing the River Jordan flowing through it. The garden is open from June 1 through September 15, Sunday through Thursday 10:00 A.M. to 2:00 P.M., Wednesday 7:00 to 9:00 P.M., and Saturday noon to 1:00 P.M. Admission is free, and tours of both the garden and temple can be arranged by calling (412) 621–6566.

Family heritage is largely responsible for the strength and continuity of religion in Greater Pittsburgh. Because many extended families remain in the region, it's not uncommon for them to remain in their religious institutions of origin as well. Some congregations boast three or four generations of Pittsburgh families in their membership, a sturdy and natural conveyor belt for traditions and beliefs. Whether it's making peirogies (potato dumplings) in the church kitchen, teaching children the art of pysanky (hand-painted Easter eggs), or simply preserving historic houses of worship, such cherished rituals make churches, synagogues, and other congregations pivotal players in their respective communities.

Most smaller communities have newspapers that may list worship services as well as social and educational events sponsored by local houses of worship. Sampling these opportunities is a great way to get to know people, and ultimately, find a religious home.

Christian Associates of Southwest Pennsylvania, (412) 688–9070 offers information about churches and denominations in nine regional counties. The

If you're looking for listings of worship opportunities, check out the Saturday editions of the daily newspapers, or your own community weekly paper.

nonprofit organization encompasses 24 Christian faith traditions.

Likewise, the United Jewish Federation of Pittsburgh (412-681-8000, www.ujf.net) is a wonderful resource for locating a synagogue in the area, where many branches of Judaism flourish. The site also posts community news and an extensive list of resources related to living a Jewish lifestyle.

STRENGTH IN DIVERSITY

Of the many religions represented in Southwestern Pennsylvania, Catholicism has the most adherents. Second in number are the Presbyterian denominations. In fact, there are more Presbyterian churches here than anywhere else in the country, perhaps due to the influence of the Scotch-Irish immigrants who brought their religious fervor with them. Lutherans, Methodists, Episcopalians, Baptists, Charismatics, and Unitarians also thrive here, as do Christian and Missionary Alliance, Church of the Brethren, United Church of Christ, Assembly of God, and Greek and Russian Orthodox congregations.

Pittsburgh's Squirrel Hill neighborhood is the hub of the Jewish community, and the hub of the hub is the Jewish Community Center; (412) 521-8010. Several major

branches of Judaism are well-represented within Pittsburgh. In addition to the Reformed congregation at Rodef Shalom, you will find a strong Orthodox congregation at Poale Zedeck in Squirrel Hill (412-421-9786); two conservative congregations, also in Squirrel Hill, Beth Shalom (412-421-2288) and Tree of Life (412-521-6788); and Dor Hadash, a Reconstructionist congregation (412-422- 5158), which varies its meeting place. You'll also find synagogues throughout the suburbs and outlying counties.

African Methodist Episcopal churches dot the Hill District, the heart of the region's African-American community, as well as suburban communities just beyond the city. While they make up a small percentage of the religious population on this side of the state, the Amish also are represented in Western Pennsylvania, particularly in Lawrence and Mercer Counties somewhat north of our principal coverage area. (See our Day Trips and Weekend Getaways chapter for more information on the Amish.)

In Pittsburgh's eastern suburbs of Monroeville and Penn Hills, many more congregations make their home. There are followers of the Baha'i, Hindu, Sikh, Zen, and Islamic traditions. Indeed, the SV Temple, just off Interstate 376 (the Parkway East) in Penn Hills, is said to be the first authentic Hindu structure in America. The Muslim Community Center of Greater Pittsburgh, in Monroeville, offers both a mosque and a social hall. The center conducts services five times daily and offers special services during holy periods. All are welcome at the center, as it maintains no membership as such.

The region also boasts a healthy number of independent congregations and churches that attract residents and visitors with their unique missions and spiritual focus. The Western Pennsylvania division of the Salvation Army, to name only one, is comprised of many corps where worshippers can participate.

Finally, you may be seeking a setting for that once-in-a-lifetime service, such as a wedding. For these events, nondenominational churches are available, including Heinz Chapel on the University of Pittsburgh campus, as well as the Old Stone Church in Monroeville (maintained by the Monroeville Historical Society). Contact campus personnel—or municipal officials where appropriate—to determine how you may use historic or prominent churches for your special event.

WHERE TWO OR THREE ARE GATHERED . . .

As diverse as worship is here, it's reassuring to note that organized religious bodies regularly collaborate on worthy causes. Examples of this include interfaith efforts to combat racism, religious institutions joining together to raise funds for the hungry, and multidenominational support for the erection of domestic violence shelters.

Interfaith consortiums, such as the Monroeville Interfaith Ministerium, bring religious leaders together to promote unity and work for the good of the community. Congregations within such groups wholeheartedly support each others' efforts. While one organization might sponsor a food pantry, another might provide a clothing ministry; religious leaders routinely encourage their members to support the efforts of other congregations.

UNIQUE MINISTRIES

If you look through any local newspaper's worship listings, you'll discover services that are taped for radio broadcast or televised for home-bound viewers. Some of these services are signed for the hearing-impaired. Cornerstone Television, incorporated in the 1970s as a nonprofit organization, is a television ministry that provides religious and inspirational programming throughout much of Pennsylvania. From its headquarters midway between Greensburg and Pittsburgh, its signal reaches such distant points as

Pittsburgh has a large Buddhist community, representing both Tibetan and Zen lineages and also numerous temples representing Indian religions, in Monroeville. There is a resident priest at the Zen Center of Pittsburgh, Sewickley (412-741-1262, www.prairiewindzen.org/zcp/). The center, situated on six secluded acres, offers daily meditation classes and services at its beautiful Deep Spring Temple. The focal point for Tibetan practice is the Three Rivers Dharma Center (www.threeriversdharma.org/).

Altoona and Jefferson, Perry, Lawrence, and Mercer Counties. To enhance Cornerstone's programming, volunteers staff telephone prayer lines as a form of outreach. You'll find more about Cornerstone in our Media chapter.

Another unusual ministry is that of Fred Rogers, highly acclaimed host of public television's *Mister Rogers' Neighborhood,* which was produced in Pittsburgh at WQED-TV and broadcast nationally. Although Rogers passed away in 2003, his ministry continues through archives of his program over the years. Some may find it surprising to learn that he was an ordained Presbyterian pastor. Indeed, Mr. Rogers attended the Pittsburgh Theological Seminary, took graduate courses in child development at the University of Pittsburgh, and worked with Pittsburgh's Arsenal Family and Children's Center. When he was ordained in 1963, he was given the special charge of ministering to children through television. He accomplished it by creating a sanctuary of truth and honesty where his young viewers are accepted just as they are—a founding principle of many faiths. (See our Kidstuff chapter for a profile of Fred Rogers and his work with children.)

You'll find yet another unique ministry in the most unlikely of places—the suburban shopping mall. Among so many secu-

Numerous opportunities exist for GLBT-friendly worship in the Pittsburgh area. There's the Metropolitan Community Church, which holds services at the Friends Meeting House in Oakland (412-683-2994) as well as other organizations that are affiliated with mainstream religious organizations. For example, Dignity serves GLBT Catholics and their friends and families (412-362-4334) and Beth Tikvah addresses the spiritual and social needs of its growing Jewish Community (412-362-7025, www.bethtikvah.org).

lar storefronts, it may seem strange to find the Monroeville Mall Ministry, but this volunteer-staffed "talk shop" has been a permanent part of the mall since the complex was built in the early 1970s.

Much of this group's ministry involves simply listening, even about mundane matters such as finding the right store. For all that, a surprising number of shoppers stop by to confide their worries, their personal or family problems, and their need for assistance. Volunteers are equipped with referral information but do not proselytize. Their mission is to maintain a presence and to help their fellow Pittsburghers in need.

VALUES AND SPIRITUALITY

To describe the region's stately churches, diversity of faiths and unusual ministries, useful through that may be, does not quite get to the heart of religion in Southwestern Pennsylvania. Just as the immigrants who settled here built houses of worship to resemble those they had left behind, they also constructed a system of values based on those of the Old World. Those values remain as the foundation of modern Pittsburgh.

The strength of religious beliefs in Southwestern Pennsylvania infuses our region with spirituality that is an important component of our personal and professional lives. Religion and commerce here are intertwined. Clergy have served as elected officials, labor leaders, chiefs of important civic organizations. Their impact goes well beyond their immediate roles, as our clergy often serves as directors for nonprofit organizations and public corporations, bringing a set of values and a spiritual outlook to the world of commerce and public service.

Of the degree-granting institutions and hospitals that we profile in our Health Care and Higher Education chapters, many are administered by, or affiliated with, religious orders. The Catholic Diocese of Pittsburgh operates an elementary and secondary school network that, were it a public school district, would be the fourth largest in the state. Is it any wonder, then, that our hospitals play a key role in providing services to the homeless and other populations in need?

Usually, the interrelationship of religion and commerce works to the benefit of each. Some years ago during the death throes of Big Steel, when bitter disputes between labor and management were common and costly, the warring sides in one impasse were encouraged to meet over breakfast and prayers. The results were so successful for the relationship that prayer breakfasts became commonplace.

Community spirit is something you'll find not only among the religious institutions here, but among many different kinds of organizations and groups of people. Volunteerism is popular here, and networking among business people is usually done with a spirit of openness and trust. You'll also find many a good neighbor in the 'Burgh. Overall, you might say, Pittsburgh is a city with a good soul.

INDEX

ABOUT THE AUTHORS

JENN PHILLIPS

Jenn Phillips is a writer, editor, and con-
sultant who works internationally from
her office in Pittsburgh. She regularly
works in the areas of magazine writing
and editing, branding and marketing,
grant writing, and editing for books and
journals, offering a particular specialty in
medical and wellness topics. She has
recently begun expanding her business,
Writing Well Communications, to include
corporate training in writing and editing.

She holds a bachelor's degree in
professional and creative writing from
Carnegie Mellon University. She's now
completing a master of fine arts degree
in creative writing at the University of
Pittsburgh, where she formerly taught
as an adjunct faculty member.

She loves Pittsburgh.

LORIANN HOFF OBERLIN

Loriann Hoff Oberlin was born and raised
in Pittsburgh. She is the author of several
other books, including *Surviving Separation & Divorce: A Women's Guide to Making It Through the First Year* and The

Angry Child, written with Timothy F. Murphy, Ph.D. Loriann has also written *Writing for Money* and *Working at Home
While the Kids Are There, Too.* Loriann
has been a guest on numerous talk
shows and news programs, including
the *CNN Morning News*, and she has
spoken at writers' conferences throughout the country.

EVAN M. PATTAK

Evan M. Pattak, a Pittsburgh native, is a
writer, editor, publicist, and teacher,
among other pursuits. His magazine writing has won Golden Quill and Women in
Communications Matrix Awards and was
anthologized in *Our Roots Grow Deeper
Than We Know*, a collection featuring
Pennsylvania writers. He began his career
as a reporter for the Associated Press
after graduating from the University of
Pittsburgh.

He is an official scorer for Major
League Baseball's National League and
serves as part-time host and handicapper for the Ladbroke Racing Network.